The Bloomsbury Companion to Religion and Film

Other volumes in the series of Bloomsbury Companions:

Hindu Studies, edited by Jessica Frazier, foreword by Gavin Flood
Islamic Studies, edited by Clinton Bennett

Forthcoming in Religious Studies:

Jewish Studies, edited by Dean Phillip Bell
New Religious Movements, edited by George D. Chryssides and
  Benjamin E. Zeller

The Bloomsbury Companion to Religion and Film

Edited by

William L. Blizek

B L O O M S B U R Y
LONDON · NEW DELHI · NEW YORK · SYDNEY

Bloomsbury Academic
An imprint of Bloomsbury Publishing Plc

50 Bedford Square
London
WC1B 3DP
UK

175 Fifth Avenue
New York
NY 10010
USA

www.bloomsbury.com

First published in 2009 by Continuum

British Library Cataloguing-in-Publication Data
A catalogue record for this book is available from the British Library.

ISBN: HB: 9780826499912
PB: 9781441107961
ePub: 9781441138781
PDF: 9781441150912

Library of Congress Cataloging-in-Publication Data
The Bloomsbury companion to religion and film / edited by William L. Blizek.
p. cm. – (Bloomsbury companions)
Originally published: The Continuum companion to religion and film.
London ; New York: Continuum, c2009.
Includes bibliographical references and index.
ISBN 978-1-4411-0796-1 (pbk.) – ISBN 978-1-4411-3878-1 (epub) –
ISBN 978-0-8264-9991-2 – ISBN 978-1-4411-5091-2 (ebook) 1. Religious films–
History and criticism. 2. Motion pictures–Religious aspects.
3. Religion in motion pictures. I. Blizek, William L. II. Continuum
companion to religion and film.
PN1995.9.R4C66 2013
791.43'682–dc23
2012037245

Typeset by Newgen Imaging Systems Pvt Ltd, Chennai, India
Printed and bound in Great Britain

Contents

Contents

Acknowledgments

When I was approached by Continuum Books about a Companion to Religion and Film I was asked, as a founding editor of the *Journal of Religion & Film*, for advice about whether such a volume might be useful and what it might include. Over the period of several months Rebecca Vaughn-Williams and I carried on an exchange of ideas that was particularly stimulating and in the end I made some recommendations regarding what I thought ought to be included in this kind of resource volume. Although Rebecca is no longer with Continuum Books, I want to thank her for that ongoing, interesting discussion about religion and film. It was a discussion that was worth having, independent of any subsequent publication. I also want to thank Tom Crick and Kirsty Schaper from Continuum Books who took over the project without missing a beat. Their assistance and encouragement were necessary to the completion of the volume.

After I had made my suggestions, the board accepted the proposal that Rebecca brought before them and after the acceptance of her proposal I was asked if I would be interested in now editing the volume. I agreed, but editing any volume means finding the right authors. I needed scholars who were able to express themselves clearly to an audience that included not only other scholars but also people who although not scholars were very interested in religion and film. I also needed scholars who could meet the deadlines we had, since in an edition of this sort everyone is dependent upon everyone else. As one might expect, the very best people were also very busy with many other projects, so I was very fortunate to be able to secure the contributions of such distinguished authors. Since each author received only a modest honorarium, each essay is essentially a labour of love and I want thank profusely each author for his or her contribution. I must say that many of the essays in this volume turned out to be quite different from what I would have anticipated. I also must say that this volume is a much more interesting account of religion and film than it would have been if everyone had merely written what I had expected.

I am very fortunate to work at the University of Nebraska at Omaha (Omaha, NE), which publishes the *Journal of Religion & Film*. This meant that I had access to the editorial board of the *Journal* and others who are especially interested in and well-versed in the study of religion and film. Michele Desmarais, Julien Fielding, Christian Haunton, Guy Matalon, Rubina Ramji, Paul Williams and Birud Sindhav provided a unique pool of talent that made this volume possible in the form that I wanted it to be. Part of that pool of talent includes Kathryn Cox Schwartz, the managing editor of the *Journal of Religion & Film*. Kathy made the preparation of the manuscript particularly easy because she brings to the table both her skill as a formatter and her skill as an editor. Kathy deserves a special thank you for her contribution to the book and her contribution to my sanity.

I want to express my appreciation to the University of Nebraska at Omaha for funding my faculty development leave in the spring of 2008. The daily life of an academic has become so filled with bureaucratic business that extended periods of concentration are virtually impossible in the normal semester. Without the faculty development leave, this book would still be a work in progress, competing with the various administrative tasks that have become so prominent in academic life.

Most importantly, I want to thank my wife, Monica, for her continued support. As every author or editor knows, completing a book requires an intense focus that excludes for large segments of time those who are close to you. Projects like this, especially toward the end, also test your sanity. Thanks to Monica for keeping in touch with me throughout the process and for helping me maintain some modicum of normalcy in my life.

Melanie J. Wright (1970–2011)

I want to take this opportunity to remember Melanie Wright and her many contributions to the study of religion, especially the study of religion and film and the study of Jewish-Christian relations. Melanie lost her battle against cancer in January 2011, at far too early an age. In addition to Melanie's contribution to this volume, she also authored *Religion and Film: An Introduction* (2007), a book that by chance I happened to referee for the publisher and recommend for publication. Melanie also was interested in Judaism and Jewish-Christian relations. She published *Understanding Judaism* in 2003, wrote more than 50 entries for the *Dictionary of Jewish-Christian Relations* (2005), and completed most of her book, *Studying Judaism: The Critical Issues*, before her death. It was published posthumously in 2012. Melanie also procured an MA in the Study of Jewish-Christian Relations, awarded by Anglia Ruskin University, and a Master of Studies in the Study of Jewish-Christian Relations, awarded by the University of Cambridge. Melanie received her doctorate from Oxford University (Christ Church) and most recently taught at The Open University. Hers was a gentle voice, a voice of compassion, and one that we will all miss.

Introduction

This volume assumes that some questions about religion and film have now been settled. First, film is a legitimate object of academic study. It is legitimate either as an art form or as a part of popular culture. This legitimacy has paved the way for the study of religion and film. Forty years ago people were not sure that movies could make a contribution to our understanding of religion or that religion could make a contribution to our understanding of film. Today there is wide agreement that relationships between religion and film are a fruitful source of academic study.

Second, everyone now agrees that movies have a unique power to influence how people think and feel. I believe that the power of film comes in part from the power of the visual (over the written word or sound). There is a phrase to the effect that one picture is worth a thousand words. If 1 picture is that powerful, it is not difficult to imagine how powerful 24 pictures per second might be. Given the power of film to influence culture, sometimes in positive ways and sometimes in negative ways, we ought to be paying close attention to film and its impact on individuals and on the culture at large. Mel Gibson's *The Passion of the Christ* is an excellent example of a movie that had a significant impact on the lives of individuals. Many people reported 'giving their hearts to Jesus' as a result of seeing the movie. Rubina Ramji's Chapter 16 in this volume shows how Muslims are stereotyped in popular American film and how this stereotypic image is damaging to relations between American Muslims and other American citizens. The very power of film makes it something to which we should be paying close attention, including its relationship to religion.

Third, movies now permeate culture. In the early days of film, people had to go to the local theatre to see a movie. With the advent of television, people could see a movie on television's night at the movies without ever leaving home. The addition of cable channels, especially the all movie cable channels, meant that people could not only see movies in their home on Thursday or Sunday evenings, but they could now see movies whenever they wished and they could see all kinds of movies that had not been available on network television. Add to this the movie rental business, including having movies sent to your home by mail, and we have almost unlimited access to movies. Movies are now even available on your home computer – see *5 Minuti*.[1] Given their power or influence and their wide accessibility, movies are an appropriate subject of academic study, including movies that are related in one way or another to religion.

Part I

The essays in this volume are designed to be academic in nature. That is, they do not presuppose a particular religious perspective, nor are they intended to promote any particular religious theology or practice. Apart from this common basis, interest in religion and film covers a multitude of sins. There is not yet much agreement regarding a single methodology for the study of religion and film. Part I, then, provides several accounts of different interests in religion and film, from story telling to theology, from cultural studies to world cinema, from religion and women to ethics. The chapters of Part I discuss the various considerations of religion and film that have been undertaken by religious studies scholars to date. Essentially these chapters cover the field of religion and film as it has been practiced over the past thirty or so years. Over the next twenty years these various interests might change, but my guess is that many of the present interests will remain the same. The one change that I would like to see come about is the expansion of religion and film from primarily a study of Christianity and Western movies to a study of the religions of the world through films from around the world. A start in this direction can be found in *Discovering World Religions at 24 Frames Per Second* by Julien R. Fielding[2] and in *Representing Religion in World Cinema: Filmmaking, Mythmaking, Culture Making* edited by S. Brent Plate.[3]

Part II

The chapters in Part II focus on movies related to particular religious traditions. Since so many of the movies considered in religion and film scholarship to date have been related in one way or another to Christianity the question was how to cover this very broad topic. The easiest group of films to identify as Christian movies is the Jesus movie genre. Jesus movies, however, have their own set of issues and problems and it seemed to me that this genre is more like a religious theme than a specific religion. For that reason, I put Adele Reinhartz essay on Jesus movies (Chapter 19) in Part III (religious themes) rather than Part II (individual religious traditions). The second group of films easily identified as Christian movies are those related to Roman Catholicism. Because of the sheer volume of Catholic movies, these movies get an entire chapter of their own (Chapter 12). Other movies related to Christianity seemed to be about particular themes, such as redemption or salvation (Chapter 22) or the end of days (Chapter 27). These movies are discussed, then, in the chapters that deal with religious themes. Some Bible movies are also Christian movies, but not all of them are, so some Christian movies will be discussed in Richard Walsh's Chapter 20 on Bible movies. Given that Christian movies come in so many different sizes and shapes, the question was whether there was anything that could be said about Christian movies that would parallel what would be said about Hindu movies (Chapter 14) or Buddhist movies (Chapter 13) or movies about indigenous religions (Chapter 17). Here I asked Terry Lindvall to suggest such an essay and he very creatively proposed an essay on the history of Christian movie making (Chapter 11).

Chapters on Buddhist, Hindu and Muslim movies were easy to include under the heading of particular religious traditions. As the influence of Hollywood diminishes, as it surely will, and the influence of world cinema (see Brent Plate's Chapter 8) increases, more movies will be made that deal with Buddhism, Hinduism and Islam. Not only will more movies related to these religions be made, but more of these movies will be seen around the world. Although religion and film has focused primarily on Christianity to date, the future of religion and film likely will broaden its focus to include at least the major religions of the world.

A chapter on Jewish movies did not seem to be in the same category as chapters on other religions. There are not as many movies on Judaism per se as there are movies on other religions, but the issue of Jewish identity in film has a long history. Allison Smith took this approach in Chapter 15, focusing mostly upon American movies. In the next ten or twenty years, the growing Israeli film industry will produce a plethora of films that will add an Israeli perspective to Judaism and Jewish identity in film.

Something similar applies to indigenous religions. In the case of indigenous religions, there are many movies that portray indigenous peoples, but usually indigenous people are portrayed as the enemy of the white man or as people in need of salvation, salvation that only the white man and his culture can bring them. The American western movie is an excellent example of a genre that portrays indigenous peoples, but does not show them as spiritual or religious peoples. Julien Fielding focuses upon movies that give us some access to indigenous religion. As we correct the history of the American west and as indigenous people in general gain more recognition and respect around the world, we more likely will see an increase in movies that take indigenous religion seriously. The Native Forum and World Cinema sections of the Sundance Film Festival already have made significant contributions to our understanding of indigenous religions.

In Chapter 18, Wendy Wright has captured not only the distinction between the religious and the spiritual, but she has provided a historical account of the spiritual that culminates in a list of virtues that includes beauty, faith, compassion, justice, love, wonder, yearnings and being present, among others. When the category of religion includes the spiritual, religion and film explodes exponentially. Movies that are related to any of the many virtues or that are included in the category of the spiritual now count as movies to be considered under the rubric of religion and film. One of the reasons there is so much interest in religion and film, and not only among religion and film scholars, is that there is so much interest in the kinds of maxims, virtues or wisdom sayings that make up the spiritual.

Part III

Part III of this volume includes essays devoted to particular religious themes that have been found interesting by religion and film scholars. Jesus movies, Bible movies and Holocaust films seem to be rather special categories that deserve individual attention. There are many films that have redemption as a theme and an equal number that include saviour figures. The image of God on the silver screen was one of the very first areas of interest in religion and film.[4] Karma and evil are two on-going religious themes in film, including popular Hollywood movies such as *Groundhog Day* and *Se7en*. The devil or Satan makes an appearance in several films, including *Little Nicky* and *The Devil's Advocate*. One of the most popular topics of contemporary film has been the end of days. In many of these films, what brings about the end of the world is not God, but rather some natural phenomenon like an asteroid or a tsunami, or some product of human misdeeds, like global warming or a nuclear holocaust. The afterlife also makes its appearance in film, but most movies that concern the afterlife are less concerned with the nature of the afterlife than they are with the ways in which we live our present lives.

There are several topics related to religion and film in which scholars have expressed significant interest that have been excluded from this volume. One is an interest in audience response. That is, people are interested in interviewing movie audiences to see how they respond to movies. What do those audiences tell us about movies that we might not otherwise have considered to be important? This seems to me to be more about social science or communication theory than about religion and film, so I have not included an essay on this area of interest. Melanie Wright's essay on religion, film, and cultural studies (Chapter 9), however, touches on this topic. Rubina Ramji's essay in Chapter 16 includes a discussion of the stereotyping of Muslims in film and Allison Smith's Chapter 15 considers Jewish identity in film, including the effects of such identity on our culture. Alyda Faber's essay in Chapter 4 on religion, ethics and film does take up the issue of how we learn ethics. She argues that we learn ethics from film in a visceral as well as an intellectual way. Other chapters that touch on audience response are Greg Watkins essay on film theory (Chapter 7); Clive Marsh's essay on theology (Chapter 5) and Christian Haunton's essay in Chapter 24 on images of God.

There has been some talk about how going to movies is similar to going to church. The idea is that we enter a sacred space and carry out particular rituals in the theatre as well as the sanctuary. So far I have not found enough similarities to pursue this topic. The comparison might work as far as it goes, but it does not seem to me to go far enough to make an investigation fruitful.

Finally, this volume does not take up, television, video games and material seen on the computer – what might be called generally visual culture. Clearly, movies can be seen on television and they can be played on the computer, but the connection between religion and television programs, video games, and computer material seems to me to be enough different from our understanding of film that it deserves its own consideration. There also is enough material to deal with under the heading of religion and film that adding other visual culture material will only confuse the study of religion and film. As scholars pursue all of visual culture, they may find some principles that will help us better understand religion and film, but at the moment the larger study of visual culture seems beyond the scope of religion and film.

The purpose of this volume is to assist the reader in understanding the newly developing field of religion and film. When someone becomes interested in evil in film, for example, he or she can turn to Bryan Stone's essay on evil in Chapter 29 and find out what has been said about evil in film and what films one might consult to discover something about evil. As another example, when someone hears comments about the next Jesus movie, he or she can consult Adele Reinhartz's essay on Jesus movies for a history of the genre. What kinds of movies have been made about Jesus and what do these movies tell us about the next Jesus movie? Some of the chapters are designed to introduce the reader to a wider range of films than those with which the reader might be familiar. And, some of the essays might introduce the reader to topics the reader had not considered as part of the discussion of religion and film. This volume should give the reader the background necessary for further exploring the study of religion and film.

William L. Blizek
Omaha, Nebraska

The Future of Religion and Film

Although there has been a virtual explosion of interest in religion and film over the past twenty years or so, the academic study of religion and film is just in its infancy. This volume provides a reasonable picture of the present landscape of work in religion and film. But there may be other ways to view the present landscape that also are interesting and helpful and the present landscape may shift significantly over the next twenty years. It is possible that the problems, questions or theories that are of particular importance to us at this point in the history of the study of religion and film will not be the problems, questions or theories that are of interest to future generations. In the following paragraphs I would like to make some suggestions about future research in religion and film.

The Analysis of Individual Movies

One of the most popular activities for people interested in religion and film is to watch a particular film and to find religion, in one form or another, in that film. We might call this the analysis of particular films and because of its popularity we can expect that people will continue to view and interpret particular films. Since many films are released each year, the number of films available for analysis from the perspective of religion offers many opportunities for this kind of research. There are also a good number of movies that have been released in the past that have not received much attention from religion and film scholars and these movies also provide a fertile field for the analysis of particular films.

Religion and World Cinema

The reason for including Brent Plate's essay on religion and world cinema in this volume is to indicate how many places around the world are now producing a significant number of films, places other than Hollywood and countries other than the United States of America. Given the increase in film production in countries and regions around the world, each of these production sites will provide additional films for analysis from the perspective of religion and film. Many of these centres of film production will create movies, the analysis of which will not be from a Christian perspective. World cinema provides a significant opportunity for religion and film to expand into a consideration of the religions of the world. The earliest analysis of film focused upon American and European films and upon Christianity in relation to those films. The expansion of world cinema creates an opportunity for religion and film scholars to consider many of the other religions of the world.

India is probably the best example of a country that is now producing more and more movies. Indeed, India now produces more films per year than Hollywood, the city that used to be the largest movie producer in the world. Indian movies, both serious dramas and popular films, will be infused for the most part with elements of Hinduism – its rituals, myths, stories, theology, ethics and so on – and to a lesser degree with elements of Islam. Many of these films will be important to research in religion and film.

What is true of India also will be true of Israel and Iran, Japan and Korea, Africa and Latin America, and, of course, China. How long it takes for the film industry of China to become a significant player in world cinema is an open question, but that China will become a significant player on the world stage is a certainty. And this will open up an entirely new realm of investigation for religion and film scholars.

One of the continued directions of research will be the investigation of individual films from countries around the world, but there also may be kinds of movies produced elsewhere and collections of movies that call for analysis and investigation. My colleague, Guy Matalon, has begun to teach a course on Judaism through Israeli film. This is an example of using a genre of film – Israeli movies – rather than an individual film to explore Judaism. The study of world cinema, then, suggests that we can compare the films made in a particular location with films made in other locations on particular religions or religious themes. It also might be that some centres of film production focus upon, for example, documentary film rather than narrative film. Such a centre would then raise issues of authenticity and propaganda in film. Hollywood has been accused of its own bias in the presentation of different cultures in film. Now the new centres of film production will need to be monitored for the possibility of introducing new biases.

Using Movies, Using Religion

In this volume I have suggested that two of the most prevalent approaches to the study of religion and film are using movies to critique religion and using religion to interpret film. I think that most of the work done in religion and film falls under one or the other of these two headings, but I did include Melanie Wright's essay on religion and film as cultural studies so that readers would be able to see an alternative to my own understanding of the field.

Wright's essay, as well as the work of Margaret Miles (*Seeing and Believing*) offer an alternative way of understanding religion and film study. Since religion and film is seen as a study of culture, the process of film production and audience responses become a part of the discussion of religion and film. Both of these areas of investigation offer many opportunities for further research. Mel Gibson's *The Passion of the Christ* is an excellent example of both how the production of the movie affects our understanding or interpretation of the film and how the audience responses influence the analysis of the film. The expansion of religion and film into the investigation of production and audience response also attracts to the field scholars from communication and media studies, and film studies, in addition to religious studies scholars.

Within the context of cultural studies, there seem to be some religions that are so deeply imbedded in culture that it is difficult to distinguish what is religious and what is merely cultural. Native religions and Hinduism seem to be of this kind. Other religions seem to be more easily separated from culture. Or, maybe it is a disservice to any religion to separate it from the culture in which it is found. Maybe that separation gives an over simplified perspective of religion. This seems to me to be one of the areas where scholars, whether religious studies scholars or scholars from other disciplines (anthropology or sociology, for example), have much to contribute to our understanding of religion and film.

Ethics and Film

The connection between religion, film and ethics has a long history focused mostly upon censorship. That is, religions have made a significant effort to control the content of movies, especially where that content might influence the behaviour of those who view the films. But, Alyda Faber has offered a quite different direction for research into religion, ethics and film. I believe that the connection between film or stories and how these influence moral belief and action is where future discussion will take place. Some of this discussion will not be necessarily about religion, but it will concern ethics and that will be applicable to the ethics of various religions. While these connections have been identified, it seems clear to me that there is much work yet to be done exploring how ethics are influenced by stories and by film – what might be called visceral ethics.

There is probably a different issue in relation to stories. That is, we live our lives as stories. We are in some very important sense 'the stories of our lives'. This means that stories reach us in a way that lectures or sermons do not. When it comes to the interconnections between religion, film and ethics, I believe that Faber's chapter is only the tip of the iceberg. What Faber offers is the beginning of a conceptual framework that allows us to understand religion, film and ethics in a new and quite different way. There may be more to this conceptual framework and there surely is much more to the application of new ideas to this area of religion and film.

Religion and Film Theory

Greg Watkins and I have been discussing the issue of religion and film theory for many years. This is an area that has been largely ignored until now and I am delighted to be able to include Greg's essay. In his essay Greg discusses several ways in which film theory can play a role in our understanding of religion and film. The question for future scholars will be in what other ways are film theory related to religion and film?

Some consideration should be given to film as an art form and the representation of the sacred. Is film a medium that can present the sacred? If religions do not want the sacred represented in film, what can the film maker do? In addition to the sacred, questions about the nature of film also apply to presenting images of God on film and probably to presenting images of Jesus as well. The question would be: if this is the nature of film, how can we best represent Jesus or God or the sacred in the movies? The question does not presuppose only one answer regarding the nature of film. So we might ask: if film is (fill in the blank here), then how do we use film to represent various aspects of religion.

Some of this discussion will have to do with film production. That is, film makers will have to apply film theory, rather than simply using the story that they want to tell, in order for them to use film to accomplish the goals they have in mind regarding religion. The issue of film theory also will apply to questions of audience response. That is, if I want to have a particular audience response to my film, how can I use the medium to achieve that response?

There are many areas to be explored regarding the relationship between film theory and religion and film. Some of these areas may be of special interest to religion and film scholars, but others may well be of interest to media studies scholars, communication scholars and those interested in cultural studies. And, all of these connections turn out to be different depending upon how we understand the nature of film.

Religions and Film

For the chapters in this volume on particular religions and film, each author adopted an approach that would give the reader a way of understanding the connection between a particular religion and its appearance in films of various kinds. But, in each case there are other approaches that might be used as well. Some scholars might be interested in discovering other approaches to understanding movies and particular religions. Some scholars might apply methods already in use in relation to some religion to a different religion, one to which those methods have not been applied.

Peter Malone, for example, provides an account of the Catholic Church that goes beyond its institutional framework. Following Avery Dulles (*Models of the Church*), Malone discusses the Church as mystical communion, sacrament, herald, servant and a community of disciples. He then explores how movies deal with these descriptions of the Church, thereby providing a much more complete understanding of the connections between the Church and film. Something similar might be done in relation to other religions – the possibilities here are almost unlimited. And, the new models for considering religions will broaden our understanding of religion and film.

Religion and History

In the section on religions and film there are chapters on Buddhism, Islam, Hinduism and so on. It would be natural, then, to have a chapter on Christian movies. But, the category of Christian movies is very large and includes at least two categories worthy of chapters themselves – Jesus movies and movies about Roman Catholicism. There also were categories of Bible movies and such topics as salvation and redemption. This meant that I gave Terry Lindvall the unenviable task of writing about what was left over from the other chapters that dealt in one way or another with Christianity and film. Terry chose to take a historical approach, giving a history of the production of Christian films. This suggests another path for scholars – considering the history of films related to particular religions. The historical approach to particular religions and film is not only fruitful in its own right, but it also allows us to see how collections of films, rather than merely individual films, have an impact on our understanding of religion as well as religion and film.

Indigenous Religions

One of the interesting questions that arose in writing about indigenous religions is the question of what counts as an indigenous religion. Usually or popularly indigenous religions are seen as those of the indigenous tribes or nations of North America and South America. Occasionally indigenous religions include the tribal religions of Australia or New Zealand. But why would the tribal religions of Africa not count as indigenous religions? Or, why would the people of Tibet not be considered to be practising an indigenous religion? There may be reasonable answers to these questions, but they do seem to be questions that should be asked by religion and film scholars who are interested in indigenous religions. Questions of religion and its relation to culture also are appropriate in the context of indigenous religions.

Spirituality and Religion

The connections between religion and spirituality raise some of the most interesting questions in relation to religion and film. If we include all of those topics from spirituality under the heading of religion, do we not make it so that virtually every film is a film related to religion? Can we not find some spiritual element in almost every film? Does this not blur the line between religion and film and other ways of understanding film?

But virtues such as justice or courage or love do seem to have a close connection to religion and many of the spiritual topics also have roots in religion. So, how will we deal with these virtues and topics? How are these topics and virtues related to secular culture? When will a topic count as religious? Will it have to be connected to a particular religion? And, how will we distinguish between what a film has to say about a particular religion and what it may say about religion in general? Can movies comment on religion in general or do they have to specify particular religions?

All of these and many more are questions to be investigated in relation to religion and spirituality. Wendy Wright's chapter identifies some ways in which people have tried to answer these questions, but there are many other possible answers waiting to be explored. And the introduction of film into the equation gives all of these questions an additional twist.

Redemption and Salvation

Originally we were going to include one chapter on redemption and another chapter on salvation – in addition to the chapter on saviour figures in film. But the question arose as to how to draw the distinction between salvation and redemption. It is not that a distinction cannot be drawn. It can be drawn and probably in a variety of ways. But, the issue became how such a distinction would play itself out in film. And, how good is film for drawing such a distinction? It may be that this returns us to the issues of film theory, but there does seem to be a question of what film can do or, at least, what film can do well, and what film is not suited to do. This may be seen as a larger question about the relationship between film and theology. How good is film at presenting theological ideas? Or, is film better suited to presenting theology in a different form? And, we can ask here about the role of theology in different religions of the world. What will different roles for theology mean to religion and film?

Filming God and the Afterlife

In Christian Haunton's chapters on imaging God in the movies and filming the afterlife, he gives a general overview of how God appears in film, what the afterlife looks like in those films that use the afterlife as a part of their stories. Here we have an interesting set of connecting issues, some filmic and some religious. Religions may have something to say about how God should be shown in film – or not shown. Do filmmakers need to be sensitive to how God is used in film? Can films be used to challenge conventional images of God? If religions provide a way of understanding God, how can filmmakers bring that understanding to the screen? What film techniques can be used to bring new images of God to the screen? How can filmmakers contribute to the religious understanding of God? Many of these questions raise an interesting issue of how religion is connected to filmmaking. This may be part of the question of film production.

It is interesting that so many of the movies that include some elements of the afterlife are movies that are commenting not on the afterlife but rather on how we live this life – the life before death. What does this fact tell us about religion and film? And what can films do to say something meaningful about life after death? One would expect that with all of the special effects available we would now be seeing the afterlife in film in quite new and different ways. But, we are not and what does this mean about life after death? Again, this looks like an area where a dialogue between filmmakers and religions has much to offer and for religion and film scholars this is an area that calls for further exploration.

Mormonism, Taoism, Sikhism, Confucianism and the Bahai Faith

The religions mentioned here are religions that have so far not received much attention in the world of films. Surely the Mormon Church has received more attention than Confucianism, but overall these are religions that have not yet been the focus of religion and film scholars. But, as the world grows smaller and more interdependent, these and other religions will become a part of the discussion of religion and a part of our communities. Even where religions are not very popular and many people do not feel a need to understand them or to give them serious consideration, the people of particular religions often feel that telling their story or stories and doing so on film is an important component of their own religious or spiritual lives. This is often true for indigenous religions where the story is told by indigenous filmmakers. Movies give people a voice and even if others are not listening, it is important for people to speak, to tell the stories that are important to them. Here we encounter issues of religion and identity and the importance of stories to religion and identity.

If we are the stories we tell, then film is one of the ways in which we can tell our stories. Here there is much work to be done – telling the stories of religions that are less prevalent in our own culture. Or, in understanding the stories being told in other cultures, stories about who we are and in what we believe.

Dialogue

A number of religion and film scholars have identified religion and film as a dialogue between movies and the believer. In my own account of methodology, I suggest that movies have something to say about religion or religions – they can provide a critique of religion, whether positive or negative. We should be listening to what movies have to say about religion or about our own religion. There may be much to learn from movies. At the same time we can draw on religion and religious ideas to give new meaning to films. But the idea of dialogue seems to me to be something quite different from 'using movies' or 'using religion'.

The idea of dialogue suggested by some scholars is one in which movies (or popular culture in general) have something to contribute to our understanding of our own religion and how we practice that religion. We make a mistake when we ignore movies and listen only to theologians or academics. Movies and popular culture can give us insight into how others understand our religion, how we might better practise our religion, how we might better explain our religion to others and so on. This is what I would ordinarily call the religious study of movies. We watch and consider movies and discuss them with others in an effort to be better practitioners of our faith.

This idea of dialogue may help us to distinguish between the academic study of religion and film and the religious study of movies. How can such a distinction be drawn? How are these two activities different? Answering this kind of question might be much easier if it were not for the fact that some of the very best discussion of movies and religion takes place in the religious, rather than academic, context. Sorting out this variety of questions provides a significant opportunity for further research.

The Study of Religion and Film

One of the great joys over the past fifteen years or so has been participating in a new discipline. Instead of finding some arcane issue to which I can make some small contribution, studying religion and film has been an opportunity to talk about not only interesting movies, but to try to figure out how the process will work – at least, how it will work in a way that is satisfying. Many of the paths I have started down have come to a dead end, but I get to turn around and go back to the starting point and try a different path to see where it leads. This has been a very enjoyable undertaking and it is possible only when a field is still 'wide open'. Much work has been done in religion and film over the past fifteen years, but so far we have scratched only the surface. So many questions remain to be answered; so many suggestions deserve to be considered. So many paths are open. The future of religion and film may look very different from its present arrangement. It will be most interesting to see how the field changes and evolves over the next twenty years.

Part I

The Study of Religion and Film

Religion and the Movies

William L. Blizek

There are different kinds of movies in which religion and film scholars may be interested, from Hollywood blockbusters to foreign films, from documentaries to shorts. Religion and religious themes can be found in different kinds of movies and this fact is one reason for the wide interest in religion and film studies. The following chapter provides some categories of films that include religion or religious themes.

1. The first category is the feature length narrative film. Feature length films run approximately from one and one half to two and one half hours, although some may run longer. This distinguishes them from short films that usually run less than one hour. Narrative films are those that tell a story that is open to interpretation. This distinguishes them from documentary films which purport to provide factual information about the world outside of the film itself. Feature length narrative films are the movies with which most people are familiar, the movies showing at the local Cineplex.

A. Within the category of feature length narrative film, however, there are subcategories that can be identified, one of which is the Hollywood block-buster.[1] The Hollywood blockbuster is a movie, usually made by a Hollywood studio, that makes a great deal of money compared to the average film. A recent example would be *The Matrix* (1999) and its sequels, *The Matrix Reloaded* (15 May 2003) and *Matrix Revolutions* (5 November 2003). *The Matrix* might be considered a secular movie in which religious symbolism or content is discovered. *The Passion of the Christ* (2004), however, is an example of a blockbuster film that would be considered a religious film. An earlier example of a Hollywood blockbuster might be the Oscar winning *One Flew Over the Cuckoo's Nest* (1975). Finding religion in these very popular movies has increased significantly the popularity of religion and film studies.

The Matrix is the story of Thomas Anderson, a young man who discovers that there are in fact two worlds, a false world in which most people live and a real world in which the truth is to be found. Anderson is given the name, 'Neo', often interpreted as 'The One'. He is seen as the Christ on the basis of his name and since he plays the role of a saviour of others. *The Matrix* is often interpreted as a story of orthodox Christianity – Neo comes to the world of the Matrix from another world and offers salvation to those who will follow him at considerable risk to himself.[2] But the story also can be seen as representing Gnostic, rather than orthodox, Christianity. For Gnostic Christianity, there is one supreme God, but also a malformed deity who breathes the divine spark into human beings. The malformed deity in *The Matrix* is represented by Artificial Intelligence (AI) – the creator of the matrix – and the redeemer is represented by Neo. *The Matrix* is a very popular movie in which people have found both orthodox and Gnostic Christian ideas.

There may be more to *The Matrix* from a religious perspective, however. Some people have found important elements of Buddhism in *The Matrix*. For Buddhists, human beings are trapped in a cycle of birth, death and rebirth, a cycle from which one can escape only through enlightenment. Enlightenment is the discovery of another plane of existence without desire and suffering. In *The Matrix*, there are two planes of existence. One is the world in which human beings are trapped and in which they suffer – the matrix. The other plane of existence, discovered by Neo, is the real world, a world that is similar to the Buddhist state of enlightenment and in which people no longer suffer. Neo reaches the stage of enlightenment and then returns to the matrix to help others recognize their condition.[3]

In addition to Christian and Buddhist themes in *The Matrix*, Julien Fielding finds elements of Hinduism in *The Matrix*. Neo may have more in common, she claims, with the Hindu god, Vishnu, than with either Jesus or Buddha. In *The Matrix Reloaded*, Neo participates in sexual activity with Trinity, something that cannot be accounted for by the chaste Jesus or Buddha. Neo has a partner in Trinity, something that neither Jesus nor Buddha had, but something that Vishnu does have in his wife, Lakshmi. Trinity is a strong and powerful woman and Hinduism is populated by strong and powerful female deities. Hinduism, then, provides an alternative to Christianity and Buddhism for understanding *The Matrix* and *The Matrix Reloaded*.[4]

Another blockbuster, *One Flew Over the Cuckoo's Nest*, is the story of a petty criminal, R. P. McMurphy, who is sent from prison to a mental institution for evaluation. While in the mental institution, McMurphy changes the lives of the other inmates. He shows them how they might live outside of the institution without fear by challenging the authority of the institution represented by the evil Nurse Ratched. In freeing the other inmates, however, McMurphy has to pay a price. He is betrayed by Billy Bibbit, one of the inmates he has helped the most. He then is crucified symbolically by means of a frontal lobotomy. He is resurrected, again symbolically, as the Big Chief escapes the asylum and 'takes McMurphy with him'. A movie that seems to be the story of a criminal treated badly by the mental health system turns out to be the story of Jesus.[5]

The very significant interest in the study of religion and film is, at least in part, a result of people finding religion in popular films. Finding religion in popular movies is something that many people enjoy. It simply is fun to discover that a popular movie that seems to have nothing to do with religion may include elements that can be given a religious interpretation. Some other movies that were very popular and that can be given religious interpretations include *Superman* (1978); *Apocalypse Now* (1979); *Star Wars* (1977) and its sequels/prequels; *Platoon* (1986) and *Amadeus* (1984).

The movies identified above are movies that usually would be identified as secular, non-religious movies. But there are some blockbuster hits that would count as religious films. These are feature length narrative films, some of which are based on Biblical stories. Mel Gibson's *The Passion of the Christ* is probably the most famous of these movies. *The Passion of the Christ* became one of the largest grossing films of all time. It is for the most part a retelling of the passion story on the big screen. Some of the controversy that surrounded the movie was similar to the controversy that surrounds other dramatic presentations of the passion, primarily the portrayal of Jews as Christ killers. But also the movie was promoted as the most accurate recounting of the Gospels ever and it soon was discovered that parts of the movie are not to be found in any of the Gospels.

Another famous religious blockbuster is Cecil B. DeMille's *The Ten Commandments*. This tells the story of Moses leading his people out of the land of Egypt and into the Promised Land. It was a large-scale spectacle movie of the sort for which DeMille became famous. The first version was released in 1923 and it was one of the most successful movies of the silent era. DeMille remade the movie and released the second version in 1956. This is the version with which most people are familiar. It stars Charlton Heston as Moses and continues to be shown on various television stations on an annual basis. Other religious blockbusters include *King of Kings* (1927), *The Sign of the Cross* (1932) and *Sampson and Delilah* (1949), all by Cecil B. DeMille; as well as *Going My Way* (1944); *The Bells of St. Mary's* (1945); *Ben-Hur* (1959); *Spartacus* (1960); *The Exorcist* (1973) and *The Da Vinci Code* (2006).

B. Other feature length narrative films are those that never had the box office success of a blockbuster. Some of these non-blockbusters are very good films and many of them are of special interest to religion and film scholars. They vary greatly in topic or approach to religion. *The Mission* (1986), *Romero* (1989) and *Priest* (1994) all provide a critique of the Catholic Church. Movies in which Buddhism plays a significant role include *Why Has Bodhi-Dharma Left for the East* (1989), *Little Buddha* (1993) and *Seven Years in Tibet* (1997). *Devi* (1960), *Kanchana Sita* (1976) and *Lajja* (2001) are movies that focus upon India and Hinduism, as are the movies of the Deepa Mehta's Elements Trilogy, *Fire* (1996), *Earth* (1998) and *Water* (2005). Movies related to Judaism and Jewish identity include *The Jazz Singer* (1927), *Gentleman's Agreement* (1948), *Liberty Heights* (1999) and *Trembling Before G-d* (2001). Movies related to Islam include

My Beautiful Laundrette (1985), *My Son the Fanatic* (1997) and *Towelhead* (2008). Movies related to indigenous religions include Chris Eyre's *Smoke Signals* (1998), *Edge of America* (2003) and *Imprint* (2007), as well as Kevin Costner's *Dances With Wolves* (1990) and Mel Gibson's *Apocalypto* (2006). Movies that relate to spirituality rather than religion itself include *Ulee's Gold* (1997), *Good Will Hunting* (1997) and *Billy Elliot* (2000). Jesus movies include *The Gospel of John* (2003), *The Last Temptation of Christ* (1988), *Jesus of Montreal* (1989) and *The Life of Brian* (1979). Holocaust movies include *Europa Europa* (1990), *The Grey Zone* (2001), *Punch Me in the Stomach* (1997) and, of course, *Schindler's List* (1993).

Movies with redemption as a theme include *The Fisher King* (1991), *The Shawshank Redemption* (1994) and *Never Die Alone* (2004). The afterlife appears in such movies as *Meet Joe Black* (1998) and its predecessor, *Death Takes a Holiday* (1934); *What Dreams May Come* (1998) and *After Life* (1998). Images of God in the movies can be found in *The Seventh Seal* (1957); *All That Jazz* (1979); *Oh God!* (1977) and *Dogma* (1999). Saviour figures can be found in such movies as *Pale Rider* (1985), *Donnie Darko* (2001) and *Iron Man* (2008). Karma plays a role in *Groundhog Day* (1993), *Twister* (1996) and *Devdas* (2002). The end of days is the focus of such movies as *The Rapture* (1991), *Armageddon* (1998) and *An Inconvenient Truth* (2006). The Devil or Satan makes an appearance on screen in such films as *Bedazzled* (1967 and 2000), *The Devil's Advocate* (1997) and *The Ninth Gate* (1999). Evil plays a central role in such movies as *Se7en* (1996), *The Killing Fields* (1984), *Crash* (2004) and *Dirty Pretty Things* (2002).[6]

C. Many foreign films are also considered feature length narrative films. There are a number of European films that have become popular in religion and film. One such film is *The Gospel According to St. Matthew*, by Italian director, Pier Paolo Pasolini, which was released in 1964. Since Pasolini was an atheist and a Marxist, the movie is often interpreted as a Marxist allegory in which the story of Jesus is used to provide a Marxist understanding of the world. Pasolini, however, found spiritual elements in the story that come to the screen in a unique way. 'The Gospel According to Saint Matthew' in the Bible, with some exceptions, is followed relatively closely, but this means that where there is no dialogue in 'The Gospel', there is no dialogue in the movie and the significance of these scenes must be inferred from the images on the screen. This gives the movie an interesting cinematic quality and offers the opportunity for spiritual reflection rather than theological analysis. *The Gospel According to St. Matthew* is frequently compared to other Jesus movies.[7]

Another European film that has caused some stir in the field of religion and film is Danish director Lars Von Trier's *Breaking the Waves* (1996). This is the story of Bess McNeill, a young simple childlike woman living in a repressive and deeply religious community in the North of Scotland. Bess meets and marries a Danish oil-rigger, Jan, to whom she is devoted. The community openly disapproves of her relationship with Jan, an outsider to the community. When Bess finds it difficult to live without Jan, who must spend most of his time at sea on the oil rig, she prays for his return. When Jan does return, however, he has been injured in an accident on the rig. Bess blames herself. When Jan finds that he can no longer engage in sexual activity, for both physical and emotional reasons, he asks Bess to engage in sex with other men and report her activities to him, thereby providing him with some sexual satisfaction. Bess is loathe to do so, but eventually comes to see such sexual activity as the will of God and as a way of healing Jan. She is shunned, of course, by the community. Toward the end of the story, Bess is killed by sailors for whom she performs the sex acts requested by Jan. In an odd twist, at the end of the movie, Jan has been healed and as Bess is buried the bells of the church that have been silent for years begin to ring.[8]

One other example is another Danish film, Gabriel Axel's *Babette's Feast* (1987). Babette comes to a small village on the western coast of Jutland looking for work. She is taken in by two sisters, who are part of a small and dwindling religious community started by their father. Babette does the cooking, cleaning and shopping for the sisters and seems to have some impact on the small religious community, bringing some joy into an otherwise rather desolate existence. Finally, the sisters decide to have a special celebration on the 100th anniversary of their father's birth and Babette asks if she can prepare the meal for the celebration. Since Babette has won a French lottery she imports all of the elements of the dinner, from plates and glasses to items on the menu, as well as the wine. Much of the movie shows the preparation for the dinner – sometimes identified as the 'last supper' – and the serving of the meal. In the end, the religious community is transformed. Old wrongs are forgiven, love is rekindled and a kind of redemption takes place during the dinner.[9]

For additional European movies related to religion, see *The Seventh Seal* (Swedish, 1957); *Proces de Jeanne d'Arc* (French, 1962); *Bend It Like Beckham* (British, 2002); *The Passion of Joan of Arc* (Danish, 1928); *Dancer in the Dark* (Danish, 2000); *Amen* (Greek, 2002); *The Ninth Day* (German, 2004); *A Man For All Seasons* (British, 1966); *The Magdalene Sisters* (Irish, 2002); *My Son the Fanatic* (British, 1997); *Le Grand Voyage* (French, 2004) and *Diary of a Country Priest* (French, 1951).

There also are films from around the world that have a connection to religion. An Israeli film directed by Amos Gitai, *Kadosh* (1999), is the story of two sisters, Rivka and Milka, living in a patriarchal, ultra-orthodox community in Jerusalem. Rivka is clearly in love with her husband, Meir, and he is clearly in love with Rivka, but they are unable to have children. Meir's father, the Rabbi, orders Meir to divorce his wife because he thinks she cannot bear him children. For Meir, his religion, represented by his father, takes precedence and Meir very unwillingly leaves Rivka to seek a relationship with another woman. Rivka is heartbroken and, although she remains a part of the ultra-orthodox community, she dies as a result of her broken heart. Milka has fallen in love with Yakov, but Yakov is seen by the community as too secular to be a good husband. A marriage is arranged, then, with Yossef, an abusive husband with few feelings for his wife. In the end, Milka is seen leaving the community, most likely on a quest to find Yakov and to marry the man she loves. The issue of the movie is how theological principles and religious practices can affect the lives of individuals, sometimes in the most harmful ways. Another example of a non-European foreign film that is of interest to religion and film is *Central Station* (1998), a Brazilian film directed by Walter Salles. This is the story of a nine-year-old boy, Josué, whose mother is killed in front of Rio de Janeiro's Central Station. Left homeless, with nowhere to go, Josué is reluctantly befriended by Dora, a cynical woman who makes a living by writing letters for illiterate people. Josué's mother was at the Station to have Dora write another letter to her husband, Josué's father, who abandoned the family. Dora finally takes Josué on a journey to Brazil's remote Northeast in search of his father. Along the way, Josué is saved by Dora – saved not only from having no place to live, but also from having no family. As well, Dora finds redemption in the act of saving Josué.[10]

After Life (1998) is a Japanese movie by director Hirokazu Kore-eda. In this movie, the newly dead are brought to a kind of holding area before they are allowed to move on. In the holding area, they are asked to select one memory of their own lives that they would like to take with them into the next life; that is, a memory they will keep forever. The newly dead are assisted in this process by celestial workers or guides who help in the selection process and who then help the newly dead to recreate the memory. That recreation is filmed, making this movie an interesting commentary on film in addition to a movie about life and death. When the newly dead have filmed the recreation of their memory, they are then allowed to pass on to the next life. In an interesting twist, the celestial guides are themselves recently dead, but they are the ones who have been unable so far to select their own single memory. Kore-eda has said that the movie is more about life than death, since it makes one think about one's own life. But, then, it might be said that death is always about life.[11]

For additional non-European foreign films related to religion and film, see *Jesus of Montreal* (Canadian, 1989); *The Last Wave* (Australian, 1977); *The Other Conquest* (Mexican, 1998); *Crimen del padre Amaro* (Mexican, 2002); *Black Robe* (Australian, 1991); *Andrei Rublev* (Russian, 1969); *Night Watch* (Russian, 2004); *Day Watch* (Russian, 2006); *I, The Worst of All* (Argentinian, 1990); *James' Journey to Jerusalem* (Israeli, 2003); *The Band's Visit* (Israeli, 2007); *Divine Intervention* (Palestinian, 2002); *Eve and the Fire Horse* (Canadian, 2005) and *Paradise Now* (Palestinian, 2005).

2. Another kind of movie that religion and film scholars find interesting is the documentary. Documentaries purport to 'present factual information about the world outside the film',[12] that is, they present themselves as providing a picture of the world as it actually is. One of the most basic and damaging criticisms we can make of a documentary film is to say or to show that the film is not trustworthy, that it does not portray the world in an accurate fashion. This does not mean, however, that documentaries are entirely neutral with regard to the world they portray. Documentaries can 'take a stand, state an opinion, advocate a solution to a problem'.[13] The director has to select what of the world will be shown from among the various possibilities and when the documentary is edited, the director/editor has to select from what has been filmed those parts that will make up the story.

Unsettled (2006) is the story of young Israelis, in the summer of 2005, who were either living in Gaza and were to be removed as part of the Israeli plan to withdraw from Gaza or were soldiers about to remove, with force if necessary, their fellow Israeli citizens from their homes. Since some of the participants resist being moved and other participants must remove people from their homes and since all are Israeli citizens, the movie clearly raises the question of what it means to be Israeli and what it means to be a Jew. If you are a good Jew, would you willingly leave the land you consider yours, leaving it to non-Jews? If you are a good Jew, would you force other Jews to leave the land that they consider theirs? Yours? What is the relationship between the State of Israel and the Jewish people? All of these questions are raised about religion and politics, and about the special politics of Israel. Another documentary on the same topic is *5 Days* (2005).

For The Bible Tells Me So (2007) is a movie about the Bible and homosexuality. The film documents the stories of five American, Christian families with gay or lesbian children, including those of former House Majority Leader Richard Gephardt, and Episcopal Bishop Gene Robinson. Drawing on such theologians as Bishop Desmond Tutu, Harvard's Peter Gnomes, the Reverend Jimmy Creech and Rabbi Steve Greenberg, the movie argues that those who interpret the Bible literally and use the Bible to stigmatize the gay community are hypocritical because they do not follow all of the Bible's admonitions, only those that speak against homosexuality. This is referred to as 'cherry picking'; taking from the Bible the admonitions you find acceptable and ignoring those admonitions that you do not find acceptable. The question of the film is: What does the Bible tell us about homosexuality? And the answer that the movie gives us is that homosexuals can be a part of the Christian community and that love is more important in how we live our lives than selected passages from the Bible. Two additional documentaries related to religion and homosexuality are *Trembling Before G-d* (2001, orthodox Judaism) and *A Jihad for Love* (2007, Islam).

Shake Hands With the Devil (2007) is the story of Romeo Dallaire, the Canadian Lt. General sent to Rawanda as the commander of the UN mission. While Dallaire seeks to keep the peace, the President of Rawanda is killed in a plane crash and in a period of 100 days approximately 800,000 Rawandans are massacred. In spite of having too few troops and being ordered not to intervene, Dallaire makes every effort to save as many Rawandans as possible. The experience took its toll on Dallaire and it was nearly ten years before Dallaire could return to Rawanda. The movie follows him on his return visit to Rawanda. Dallaire believes that with even a few thousand more troops the massacre could have been prevented, so he sees the massacre as partly the failure of the United Nations to provide those troops. But, he also sees the massacre as a failure of humanity. The title of the movie comes from Dallaire's meeting with the leaders of the massacre. It was the cold look in their eyes that indicated to Dallaire that he was 'shaking hands with the devil' and in the presence of utter evil. Dallaire is a character (played by Nick Nolte) in a feature length narrative film about the massacre, *Hotel Rawanda* (2004). A similar documentary about the genocide in Darfur is *The Devil Came on Horseback* (2007).

The Protocols of Zion (2005) documents a wide range of responses to the book entitled *The Protocols of the Elders of Zion*. First published in 1903 in Russia, the book purports to show a Jewish conspiracy to dominate the world. Although thoroughly discredited as a fraud and a hoax, the book continues to sell well. After 11 September 2001, there was a rise in anti-Semitism in the United States and Marc Levin's film makes an effort to show how that anti-Semitism follows in part from the continuing conspiracy theory found in the book. One of the most astonishing claims made by people interviewed in the film is that Jews were warned to stay home on 11 September 2001, suggesting that Israel or Jews around the world were responsible for the attack on the World Trade Center. Levin's movie is not only an argument against anti-Semitism, but it is also an argument against falling prey to conspiracy theories of any kind. In contrast to the demonizing of others based on discredited conspiracy theories, Levin interviews a widow of a Jew killed in the attack on the World Trade Center who says that we should make the purpose of our lives to leave the world a better place for our having lived.

Some other recent documentaries that are of interest to religion and film scholars include *Children of God: Lost and Found* (2007); *Jesus Camp* (2006); *The Education of Shelby Knox* (2005); *Dinner with the President: A Nation's Journey* (2007); *Be Like Others* (2008); *Order of Myths* (2008); *Recycle* (2008); *Slingshot Hip Hop* (2008); *God Grew Tired of Us* (2006); *Kz* (2006); *Iraq in Fragments* (2006); *Trudell* (2005); *Obsession: Radical Islam's War Against the West* (2006) and *Refusenik* (2008).

3. One category of films that is often overlooked when considering films

related to religion and film is the short film – less than one hour long. A number of documentary films are also short films. Some short films are very good and they would be of interest if people knew about them, but since short films do not show in theatres often, they are regularly ignored. Some short films are now showing up on the Internet.

A very powerful film that is only seven minutes in length is David Napier's *The Art of Farewell* (Australian, 2001). An elderly gentleman enters a tattoo parlour. He is largely ignored and one of the patrons makes fun of him. The tattoo artist tells the elderly gentleman that he is very busy, but the gentleman waits until closing time, when the artist can no longer ignore him. The gentleman wants a tattoo. The artist is sceptical and when he discovers that he must go to the gentleman's home to etch the tattoo he rejects the request. He is persuaded, however, by a large sum of money that the man offers him.

When the artist arrives at the gentleman's home, we notice that the gentleman is now wearing a yarmulke and we know that he is Jewish. The gentleman leads the artist into the parlour where he discovers the gentleman's recently deceased wife lying in a casket. Spooked by being in the company of the dead, the artist starts to leave, but the gentleman implores the artist to hear him out. The gentleman wants the artist to remove the concentration camp number from his deceased wife's arm so that she will not be reminded of the horror of the Holocaust in the future, whatever that future might be. The artist seems to understand this gesture and he removes the tattoo. He is now very anxious to leave, finding this situation rather unsettling, but the gentleman asks him for one more thing. The gentleman wants the artist to tattoo his wife's number on his own arm next to his own number. The artist balks, saying he thought the gentleman wanted to forget. The gentleman tells the artist that he wants his wife not to remember, but that he himself never wants to forget her. So, the artist agrees. As we see the artist leaving the gentleman's home, he pauses at the front door and leaves the wad of money that he had been given on the table. In the final scene, we see the artist back at his studio leafing through his book of tattoos. When he turns the page and sees a swastika, he takes the swastika out of the book and throws it in the wastebasket. The gentleman has said a very special symbolic farewell to his wife through the art of the tattoo artist and the artist has become a different person in the experience – he never again will apply a tattoo of a swastika.

Another short film is *Smudge* (2005), by Canadian Métis filmmaker, Gail Maurice. *Smudge* chronicles the efforts of First Nations women who have moved to the city where they seek to continue participating in various Native rituals. The city turns out to be inhospitable to Native rituals, such as smudging. So the women must find ways to continue their traditions in the midst of urban life. They find ingenious ways continue the practices of their Native

27

culture and religion. They use a city park for smudging, hoping that no one will tell them that they cannot start a fire in the park. They smudge in their cars to avoid setting off fire alarms indoors. At the end of the movie, a group of First Nations women gather on a roof top to share a ceremony dedicated to the moon. In this way they can continue the Native ceremonies without becoming the object of curiosity or scorn.

The film *5 Minuti* (2006) is the story of a suicidal woman about to leap to her death from a bridge over the canals of Milano, Italy. She is approached by a man claiming to be Jesus. He asks for just five minutes of her time to chat. They order coffee and carry on a profound conversation. Jesus tells the woman many things about herself that only Jesus would know. He carries with him a picture of the woman that he shows to her. He tells her that he has been watching her all along. She asks Jesus if what they say about the crucifixion is true. Jesus describes what it was like, not only the physical pain, but the humiliation as well. When the five minutes are up, Jesus gets up on the bridge railing where he first encountered the woman. He offers to jump (die) for her, so that she can return to being the happy woman she used to be. He tells her that it will work, that he has done it before. She needs only to have faith. Finally, her faith restored, she reaches out to Jesus and tells him that he has already done enough and that he does not have to jump in her place. They hug and then Jesus walks away. While the woman ponders what has happened, the waitress from the cafe brings her the cup of coffee she had ordered.

For additional short films, see *The Tribe* (2006); *Gesture Down* (2006); *I Just Wanted to Be Somebody* (2007); *Fighting Cholitas* (2006); *Conversion* (2006); *Linguists* (2007); *West Bank Story* (2005); *Hot House* (2007); *Moccasin Flats* (2002); *Admirational* ((2003) and *Chasing Buddha* (2000).

2 Using Religion to Interpret Movies

William L. Blizek

What everyone wants to know is: How is religion portrayed in film, how does religion appear on the silver screen? There are different motives, of course, for asking this question. Some viewers want to protect a particular image of their religion or an image of religion in general. The original Motion Picture Production Code, for example, says that 'No film or episode may throw ridicule on any religious faith'.[1] It also says that 'Ministers of religion in their character as ministers of religion should not be used as comic characters or villains'.[2]

Other viewers turn to film in order to better understand religion or to discover some criticism of religion. Martin Scorsese's *The Last Temptation of Christ*, for example, provides an interpretation of Christianity that takes the humanity of Jesus seriously. As another example, Daniel Karslake's *For The Bible Tells Me So* criticizes some fundamentalist evangelical Christians for stigmatizing the gay and lesbian community on the basis of selecting particular verses from the Bible as justification and ignoring other verses. Yet other viewers watch films to learn something about spirituality or myths associated with religion, or redemption, or karma and so on.[3]

One other interest is finding religion in movies that are not overtly religious, movies that might be called secular. Two of the best examples of such movies are the Wachowski brothers' film, *The Matrix*, and Milos Foreman's Academy Award winning *One Flew Over the Cuckoo's Nest*.[4] *The Matrix* is the story of Thomas Anderson who discovers that human beings are used as the source of energy by Artificial Intelligence. Human beings are unaware that they are being used by AI. Their minds are clouded, so to speak, by the Matrix. It is Thomas Anderson's task to show human beings that they are being used and deceived by AI so that human beings can be saved from the clutches of Artificial Intelligence. *The Matrix* is a science fiction/action movie. It is a movie about men versus machines, although the machines in this case are computers. There is a battle going on in the movie between the good guys (human beings) and the bad guys (Artificial Intelligence) and the battle includes plenty of slow motion fighting and 'shootem up'. *The Matrix* has enough violence in it to appeal to the 18–24-year-old male, the audience that has made *The Matrix* such a success. The 18–24-year-old male goes to be entertained by the movie, especially its special effects, its violence, and its clear moral distinction between the good guys and the bad guys. This is an audience that goes home from seeing *The Matrix* happy in the knowledge that the good guys win.

Religion and film scholars, however, have found religion in this science fiction/action movie. Anderson is given the name Neo and Neo is identified as 'the One', a Jesus or saviour figure. The movie can be seen as representing orthodox Christianity, since it tells the Jesus story, or it can be seen as representing Gnostic Christianity, because Artificial Intelligence appears to be like the malformed deity that gives life to human beings in the Gnostic tradition. But the movie also can be seen as representing Buddhism. The two separate worlds, the one recognized by human beings and the other hidden from them by the Matrix, have been associated with the realms of suffering and enlightenment in the Buddhist tradition.[5]

One Flew Over the Cuckoo's Nest is the story of a petty criminal, R. P. McMurphy, who has been sent to prison for statutory rape. While in prison, McMurphy fails to follow the rules or to perform the tasks assigned to him, so the prison sends him to an asylum for psychological evaluation. In the asylum, McMurphy encounters the mental health establishment and finds that it does little to help the patients live outside of the institution. Indeed, the goal of the institution seems to be to control the patients, rather than to help them live more normal lives. The greatest evil of the system is that the damage it does to individual inmates is done in the name of helping them. Since McMurphy is not insane, his behaviour exposes the sinister motives of the institution and the failures of the American mental health system in general.

Although a movie about the mental health system and how people should be treated, many religious studies scholars have found religion in *One Flew Over the Cuckoo's Nest*. They see R. P. McMurphy as a Christ figure who sacrifices his own life to save the inmates of the asylum from the oppression of the institution. McMurphy is betrayed by one of the inmates and he is given a frontal lobotomy to control his behaviour after he attacks the dishonest and manipulative Nurse Ratched.[6] When the big Chief smothers McMurphy, he tells McMurphy that he would not leave Big Mac in the asylum to be used as an example to the other inmates. As Chief Bromden escapes from the asylum he takes the spirit of McMurphy with him, providing McMurphy with a kind of resurrection. When McMurphy is seen as a Christ figure, the movie takes on a whole new meaning. It is no longer a movie about the system of mental health, but it becomes a movie about how Jesus expects us to love others and how important freedom is in living well.

Finding religion in secular movies may be seen as uncovering hidden meanings in film, meanings that can be detected, as John Lyden puts it, only by scholars who are trained in abstruse methods of analysis.[7] There is some truth to this view. That is, one may have to know a good deal about any particular religion in order to apply that religion to a secular film.[8] If viewers know nothing about karma, they will not find *Groundhog Day* to be an example of karma. If viewers know little or nothing about Jesus, they will not find Jesus in such movies as *One Flew Over the Cuckoo's Nest* or *Cool Hand Luke*. If viewers are unfamiliar with Buddhism, they are not likely to understand that the worlds of illusion and enlightenment in *The Matrix* have a parallel in Buddhism.

This means that it may be easier for scholars of Buddhism to find Buddhist elements in movies than it is for the ordinary person. It might be easier for Christian scholars to find a parallel to the story of Jesus in non-religious films than for practicing Hindus. Or it might be more likely that a Jewish scholar would find interesting world views in film than someone who pays little attention to the idea of world views at all.

But, one does not have to be a religious studies scholar to see that R. P. McMurphy is betrayed and killed and that he then rises from the dead in *One Flew Over the Cuckoo's Nest*. One does not have to be a religious studies scholar to recognize that there is a world of enlightenment and a world of illusion operating in *The Matrix*. One does not have to be a religious studies scholar trained in abstruse methods of analysis to recognize that Erin Brockovich is a David figure, slaying Pacific Gas & Electric Company (Goliath).

Much of religion in films is quite accessible to an audience larger than the community of highly trained academic scholars. Finding religion in movies, especially movies that seem to have nothing to do with religion is fun. It is interesting, enjoyable, maybe even challenging, and it attracts many people to the study of religion and film, people who are not scholars but who enjoy movies and know something about religion.

Amadeus

The story of Cain and Abel (Genesis 4) is the story of two brothers, one a sheep herder and the other a farmer. Both of the brothers bring an offering to the Lord. Abel brings the 'firstlings of his flock and of the fat thereof', and Cain brings 'the fruit of the ground'. But, 'the Lord had respect unto Abel and to his offering: But unto Cain and to his offering he had not respect', and here we have a puzzle. Why does the Lord favour one brother over the other? The *Bible* does not provide an answer. How is Cain to feel about being slighted? How is he to feel toward his brother, the favoured one? Here we are introduced to what has become known as sibling rivalry – a kind of rivalry that is within the family and is related to the favour of the parents. Sibling rivalry has an intensity that other rivalries do not have, because the stakes are so high – the favour of one's parent or parents. The intensity of this rivalry is indicated by what comes next. '. . . and it came to pass, when they were in the field, that Cain rose up against Abel his brother, and slew him'. One may be envious of one's neighbour, but this does not lead to the killing of the neighbour. But when one is envious of a sibling, that envy can be so strong as to cause one to 'slay' his sibling.

In 'Mozart & Salieri, Cain & Abel', Gregory Allen Robbins applies the story of Cain and Abel to the story of Mozart & Salieri, as told in Milos Forman's movie, *Amadeus* (1984), based on the play by Peter Shaffer.[9] It should be noted that in reality Mozart and Salieri were not enemies and Salieri did not kill Mozart. The mythology surrounding Mozart and Salieri seems to come from a poem by Alexander Pushkin, written about 40 years after Mozart's death. Shaffer and Forman take the myth that Mozart and Salieri are mortal enemies as the starting point of their story because it is more dramatic than the historical relationship between Mozart and Salieri. The conflict between the two composer/musicians in the myth provides an opportunity for raising a variety of questions about life that would not be raised from the historical story. So, it is the myth that makes the movie and it is to the fictional story that Robbins applies the story of Cain and Abel.

If we take the story of Mozart and Salieri, as presented in the movie, *Amadeus*, to be the story of Cain and Abel, then the movie raises for us, although in a rather different setting, the issues raised in Genesis 4. What are the issues of Genesis 4? Drawing on R. J. Quinones, Robbins identifies several issues. One is the essential division between human beings, a division or separateness that cannot be overcome.[10] This division is made evident in Genesis when the Lord favours Abel and his offering over Cain. In the movie, this division is made evident by the favour or lack thereof shown to the two musicians by Austrian society. The division between people becomes a tragic division when it becomes clear that the preference for one over the other is arbitrary. There is no explanation in Genesis for the Lord's favouring Abel, just as there is no explanation in the movie for the preference of one musician over the other. Living in an arbitrary world is one of the things that make life difficult.

Another issue is that of envy. One response to not being the preferred one is envy. People often behave badly as a result of their envy – sometimes harming others and sometimes harming themselves. In both Genesis and *Amadeus*, the jealous one harms the other. But, there may be more to this idea of envy when what we are envious of is the preference of the ultimate father, the Lord. There seems to be something fundamentally more important about winning the favour of a parent than there is about winning the favour of others. There is something more important to our very being in the favour of a parent. If we are all children of God, then how important is winning God's favour, God the

Father.[11] In Genesis, Cain and Abel seek the favour of God. In *Amadeus*, Salieri is portrayed as someone who has been 'possessed by one driving desire: to serve God through music'.[12] This gives Salieri's envy a stronger foundation that it would have if the envy were only about being seen by others as a better composer.

There are other features shared by the stories of Cain and Abel, and Mozart and Salieri, but Robbins puts an emphasis on the idea. The stories call for self-confrontation.[13] We must ask ourselves how we feel about difference. How do we feel about the arbitrariness of preference? How much of role does envy play in our lives? Would our rivalry lead us to violence? The story of Mozart and Salieri, interpreted as the story of Cain and Abel, does not offer us clear answers to a set of questions. Rather, the story raises a wide range of questions that are at the very core of our being.

Love Actually

Love Actually (2003) is a delightful comedy, set largely in London, that explores the relationships between a variety of couples, including the Prime Minister of England and a commoner, an over-the-hill rock star and his manager, a secretary and her boss, a recent widower and his son, a young woman and her brother, a writer and his house keeper, a couple of actor stand-ins, among others. It takes place in the weeks before Christmas and one running gag is the competition between the over-the-hill rock star and a respectable group of musicians for the number one song of the Christmas season. *Love Actually* is one of those feel good movies where almost every couple comes together at the end of the movie.

While the movie easily can be dismissed as feel good holiday fare, when religion is brought to bear on the film, *Love Actually* turns out to be a significant film about the nature of love. If one applies the Christian concept of 'agape' to the film, we see that some of the couples exhibit agape, while other couples exhibit other forms of love. In this case the movie exhibits a kind of love important to Christianity and its alternatives. But one also might see love as one of those virtues that makes up our spirituality without any special connection to a particular religion. In this case *Love Actually* can be seen as an exploration of various kinds of love and the ways in which we find love.

There are two couples that serve as especially good examples of love. The first is a man and a woman who work as stand-ins for movie stars. The couple act as though they were the actors in a film that is being made so that lighting and sets can be completely prepared for the actual filming that will occur later. The humour of this couple comes from the fact that the real actors will be filmed as engaged in various forms of sexual activity. So the stand-in couple is required to simulate that sexual activity. For each of the stand-ins this is simply a job, and they interact pretty much as co-workers might be expected to act. They talk about the traffic and weather and other ordinary topics. The humour, of course, is that these ordinary conversations take place while the couple is naked and simulating sexual activity. The ordinary conversations, however, lead to a genuine affection for each other and in the end the stand-ins become a real couple. What makes this couple particularly interesting is the contrast between what they do for a living, which represents sexual desire, lust, and romance, and the relationship which they develop. The real love they come to have for one another stands in stark contrast to the job they must perform as part of their employment. Whether the bonds they finally form represent Christian love (agape) or whether they represent a healthy relationship as one kind of love, the relationship they develop stands clearly apart from the kinds of activities which they simulate as part of their job.

A second example of agape is the over-the-hill rock star and his manager. For most of their careers together they have not paid much attention to the kind of relationship they have. The rock star is busy being a rock star, while the manager is busy being a manager. They do love each other, but neither of them recognizes that fact. When the rock star's Christmas song becomes the number one hit of the season, he is invited to a huge party on Christmas Eve at the home of the ultimate rock star, Elton John. He goes to the party, but before it is over, he leaves and shows up on his manager's doorstep. The rock star says that Christmas is a time for being with those you love and that he has just discovered that the one person he most loves is his manager. This is not a romantic or sexual relationship; it is the love of one friend for another. That the rock star discovers and acknowledges his love for his manager on Christmas, clearly indicates that this is the kind of love that Christians are to have for one another. If we do not apply Christianity to the movie, however, the rock star and his manager still exemplify a kind of love that is important to us as human beings.

However one describes or defines the Christian concept of love (agape), it can be found in many of the relationships in *Love Actually*. And, the Christian concept of love stands in marked contrast to other kinds of love to be found in the film, or at least other kinds of human relationships that are identified with love. The advantage of applying the Christian concept of love to the movie is that it gives the movie a new meaning, since we now see the kind of love expressed by various characters in the film as the kind of love that Christians should seek in their own relationships. The disadvantage is that only two kinds of love are identified in the movie – Christian love and its alternatives. But the movie also can be interpreted in terms of spirituality, rather than Christian love, and the movie can be interpreted as exemplifying a variety of loving relationships.

Superman

Superman is one of several famous comic book superheroes. He is, as everyone knows, more powerful than a locomotive, faster than a speeding bullet and is able to leap tall buildings in a single bound. Most of the time, Superman is disguised as Clark Kent, a reporter for the *Daily Planet* in the city of Metropolis. But, when trouble comes, Clark Kent must shed his suit, glasses and hat for the famous blue tights and red cape of his alter ego, Superman. Whatever the trouble may be, with Superman on the job, you can be sure that the problem will be solved, lives will be saved and the bad guys will be defeated, at least until the next episode.

In the movies, *Superman: The Movie* (1978) and *Superman II* (1981), the story of Superman, as Anton Karl Kozlovic has pointed out, has some remarkable parallels to the story of Jesus.[14] Superman (the infant Kal-El) is sent to earth from Krypton by his father, Jor-El. Kal-El is Jor-El's only son – both have a curl in the middle of their foreheads. Kal-El arrives on earth as a naked infant, much as Jesus arrived in the manger in Bethlehem.[15] Jor-El, of course, sends his son to earth to escape the destruction of the planet Krypton – the planet is indeed destroyed shortly after Kal-El is sent to earth – and God does not send his son, Jesus, to earth to escape destruction, but the parallels remain and are sufficient to make them interesting to religion and film.

Superman also performs miracles, as does Jesus. This indicates both that Superman is not of this world and that the miracles are a sign that Superman is who he says he is. Jesus is not of this world and he too is the special person that he claims to be. The first miracle in the movie is when the infant Kal-El lifts the truck of his earthly father so that the flat tire can be changed. The second miracle comes when the teenage Clark Kent kicks a football out of sight and then out runs a train. This is followed by the adult Clark Kent catching the bullet to save Lois Lane. And from that point on being faster than a speeding bullet, able to leap tall buildings in a single bound, and so on are the descriptions that identify Superman as a miracle worker. The miracles of Kal-El/Clark Kent are not the same miracles as those performed by Jesus, but they do not have to be exactly the same miracles in order to show that both are miracle workers and that this is a significant part of their identity.

Jesus begins his messianic mission at the age of 30, after having gained wisdom and stature. Similarly, Superman begins his mission to battle evil and save Earth from its own foolishness at the age of 30. And, both Jesus and Superman can be interpreted as having as their missions the salvation of the world. Such salvation may take different forms, but the salvation mission serves as further evidence of the parallel between Jesus and Superman.

Kozlovic identifies many other parallels between Jesus and Superman. Some of those parallels are more exact and persuasive than others, but there are enough of these parallels to allow the viewer to give the Superman movies a Christian/religious interpretation. When we recognize the parallels, Superman is no longer just a comic book superhero. Superman becomes a version of Jesus and what we learn from Superman and his actions may indicate what it means to be a follower of Jesus.

Platoon

Platoon (1986) is the first of Oliver Stone's Vietnam War trilogy. The other parts of the trilogy include *Born on the Fourth of July* (1989) and *Heaven and Earth* (1993). Stone's movies, showing the horrors of war and its aftermath as they do, can be seen as political statements about the Vietnam War.

Chris Taylor drops out of college to join the army. He joins Bravo Company, somewhere near the Cambodian border with Vietnam. The story of *Platoon* follows Chris through various missions he is assigned. The fighting, however, serves as a backdrop to the story of Taylor's unit itself. The unit is divided between those with a conscience, led by Sergeant Elias, and those without a conscience, led by Staff Sergeant Barnes. Elias represents those who follow the rules of war, while Barnes represents those who kill wantonly. At one point in the film Barnes' side seems to win when Barnes shoots Elias and leaves him for dead. In the end, however, it is Chris Taylor who shoots and kills Barnes.

It is the story of the platoon that Avent Childress Beck identifies as the Christian story of mankind, from the creation to the end of days.[16] What seems like a film about the horrors of war or one of a number of anti-war movies, now becomes a larger story, the story of mankind from the Christian perspective. That Beck applies the Christian story to the movie, however, is not merely an interesting exercise, but is in fact suggested by Oliver Stone himself. 'Indeed, Stone clearly indicates his reliance on the Bible, both in the film itself and in its published screenplay. We should not be surprised: Stone has said that for him the war was a "religious" experience'.[17]

The movie begins with Chris Taylor exiting the rear of his transport plane. He enters a world of swirling dust. Everything is in a state of confusion, chaos. Soldiers are moving all around him, but Chris does not understand what is happening, and the audience feels a sense of unease. As the film moves forward, however, things become settled. It becomes clear that there are two sides in the war, not the war the soldiers have been sent to fight, but the war within the platoon. One side is represented by Sergeant Elias and Chris Taylor. Beck claims that Elias represents both Christ and Elijah. When Elias is killed his side becomes represented by Chris Taylor who represents 'Christ-as-Christ', thereby connecting the story of the Hebrew Bible with the New Testament.[18] Elias and Taylor believe that some things are clearly right and some things are clearly wrong. Barnes believes that in war anything goes.

What might be wrong in some other context is no longer clearly wrong when the context is war. It is, then, between these two sides that the real war is fought, the battle between good and evil.

At one point in the film, Chris Taylor is wounded and is sent to the hospital. But he returns to the camp where one of his comrades asks: 'Whatcha doing in the underworld, Taylor?' Another comrade responds: 'This ain't Taylor. Taylor been shot. This man is Chris, he been resurrected'.[19] From this point on the battle is engaged between Chris (Christ) and Barnes (the Beast). In the end, Chris kills Barnes and goodness and righteousness prevail. 'So in Revelation, the word of God defeats the beast and the beast's army in the battle at Armageddon'.[20] The story that began in the unformed chaos, now ends with the victory of God over evil.[21]

The Mexican

The Mexican (2001) is the story of Jerry Welbach who is indebted to a local mobster, Arnold Margolese. To finally pay off his debt, Jerry is sent by Margolese to Mexico where he is to retrieve and return to Margolese a famous antique pistol, known as The Mexican. The Mexican was made for the son of a nobleman. The gunsmith hopes that the son will be pleased by the finely crafted weapon and possibly by his daughter as well. The nobleman's son is given the first opportunity to fire the weapon, but it does not fire. At this moment he notices that the gunsmith's daughter has eyes for the gunsmith's assistant, so he throws down The Mexican and aims his own pistol at the gunsmith's assistant. The gunsmith's daughter picks up The Mexican and aims it at the nobleman's son to protect the man she loves. But the assistant talks her into putting the pistol down. At that moment the nobleman's son shoots and kills the assistant. The gunsmith's daughter then points the gun and threatens to shoot herself. The nobleman's son laughs at this because he knows that the pistol will not fire. Miraculously, The Mexican fires, and the gunsmith's daughter kills herself, joining her one true love in death. Since The Mexican did not play the role that the gunsmith anticipated, indeed it killed his daughter, The Mexican is considered to be cursed. The curse follows Jerry as he travels to Mexico to retrieve the pistol, creating all kinds of comedic situations. But this movie, a romantic comedy/road movie, can be seen as presenting a particular view of how God is related to human events.

In *Esther and the Mexican*, Guy Matalon sees an example of one way of describing God's relationship to human history.[22] In the Hebrew Bible, Matalon claims, there are two rather different views on how God is related to human history. On one view, God has complete control of all events. God is in control of human thoughts and emotions. He intervenes directly in human history and God's intervention is revealed to all. God does not on this view interfere with the free will of human beings, but He is in control of everything else.

In The Book of Esther, however, the revealed direct intervention in human affairs by God is missing. King Ahasuerus has removed Vashti as queen for disobedience. All of the beautiful women in the Kingdom are brought before the King so that he can select a new Queen. The King finds Esther, a Jew, to his liking and he makes her his new queen. At the same time the King elevates Haman to the highest position in the court. Upon leaving the gates of the palace, however, Haman finds that Mordechai, Esther's cousin, will not bow down to him and so Haman devises a plan to punish all of the Jews in the Kingdom. It is up to Esther to save her people from the punishment planned by Haman. Throughout the story, God is clearly at work, He is in control. But, God is not mentioned, nor is his intervention revealed. The story of Esther seems to proceed without God, even though the events of the story could not be merely the acts of human beings.

In *The Mexican*, we see a similar process at work. Jerry knows that things are happening for a reason and that they are not just a matter of chance or coincidence. But he does not understand how things are related or how they are going to work out. God's intervention is not revealed in *The Mexican* any more than it is revealed in The Book of Esther. But, God is in control and is making things happen as they should happen. In the end, Jerry Welbach finds redemption – he delivers The Mexican and thereby pays his debt to Margolese. In the end, Esther brings about redemption for her people. Haman does not get to punish the Jews of the Kingdom. In both cases, redemption is the result of God's intervention in human affairs, but in both cases the redemption that comes at the end of the story seems to come from someone other than God, either Jerry Welbach or Queen Esther. God's intervention in human affairs remains concealed. The Mexican, a romantic comedy/road movie, can be given a religious interpretation by applying the story of Esther. This romantic comedy turns out to be an excellent example of how God works in mysterious ways.[23]

What the examples above show is that religion, in various forms, can be used to interpret any variety of movies, even movies that do not at first glance seem to have anything to do with religion. Indeed, the applications of religion to film seem to be limited only by the scope of our imagination. It may be that a religious interpretation of a film does not jump out at the viewer while watching the film, but when a religious interpretation of a film is offered, there should be a significant connection between the interpretation and the film. Finding religious interpretations of films is one of those activities that is fun, sometimes surprising, and often challenging. Finding religious interpretations of film is one of the activities that attracts many to the study of religion and film.

3 Using Movies to Critique Religion

William L. Blizek

If religion can give new meaning to movies, can the opposite also be true? That is, can movies give meaning to religion? The answer is that many movies seem to provide a critique of religion. Mel Gibson's *The Passion of the Christ* (2004), for example, emphasizes the role of Jesus' suffering and death in the Christian story, rather than the ethics or resurrection of Jesus. Film-goers are asked to consider what the humanity of Jesus really means to our understanding of Christian theology in Martin Scorsese's *The Last Temptation of Christ* (1988). *Agnes of God* (1985) explores the issue of science and faith and concludes that science cannot give us a complete understanding of the world in which we live. *Kadosh* (1990) shows the mistreatment of women as a result of some religious doctrines and practices. And, *The Mission* (1986) criticizes the Roman Catholic Church for becoming corrupt.

A critique of religion may be either positive or negative. A critique can criticize religion or religious practices for the harm they do to human beings or for the false view of the world that they present. *Kadosh*, for example, criticizes some forms of Orthodox Judaism for their unfair treatment of women and the harmful consequences that follow. The movie shows one of the women central to the story leaving the orthodox community and the other woman dying of a broken heart because she is not able to be with her beloved husband. *Leap of Faith* (1992) criticizes those who use religion to bilk people out of their money. The main characters are scam artists touring the country looking for easy marks. *The Mission* shows how the Catholic Church abandoned the Guarani Indians of South America in an effort to maintain political power in Spain. In the end the Indians are slaughtered by the Portuguese, having been abandoned by the very church that had come to save them.

But a critique also can provide an interpretation of religion that helps us understand religion or see religion from a different perspective. Robert Duvall's *The Apostle* (1997), for example, exposes the viewer to the power of the evangelical sermon and its impact on the lives of those who are born again. *Why Has Bodhi-Dharma Left for the East* (1989) gives its audience the opportunity to experience living in the present moment. *The Last Temptation of*

Christ brings to our attention the powerful sacrifice that Jesus makes by overcoming the last temptation, the temptation he faced as man.

Some of the most interesting movies, of course, have both something positive to say about religion as well as providing appropriate criticism. One of the best examples of such a movie is Duvall's *The Apostle*. For Duvall, a particular kind of evangelical church with which he was familiar from his travels in the South had been badly portrayed in film. Duvall thought that two movies in particular, *Elmer Gantry* (1960) and *Leap of Faith*, presented a distorted picture of evangelical Christianity. Duvall thought that there was much more to this version of evangelical Christianity and that the portrayal of the preacher as a fake or a fraud was unfair to evangelical Christianity in general. So he set out to give his audience a feel for 'the power of the evangelical sermon. Duvall was convinced that the evangelical sermon could have significant benefits for those in the pews. This kind of sermon could lift people's spirits and change their lives for the better. The Apostle E. F. is portrayed as someone who misuses his position as minister of the gospel but is transformed into someone for whom the lives of his congregates are more important than the glory of the minister. As the Apostle E. F. finds his own redemption he moves from sinner to humble saint.[1]

But Duvall was not interested in giving only one side of the story, as he thought other movies had done. In the beginning we learn that Sonny, who later adopts the name, The Apostle E. F., is a womanizer and prone to violence and threats of violence. Much of his ministry is about ego, as we learn when others take over Sonny's church. Duvall believed that a preacher could do a significant amount of good for others and yet be flawed himself – troubled souls can still do good things – and this is how Duvall portrayed the Apostle E. F. *The Apostle* shows that a particular kind of evangelical Christianity can be practiced for the good that results and not merely for the purpose of taking advantage of those seeking salvation. At the same time, the movie shows that individuals who practice this evangelical Christianity are not above reproach, but ordinary people facing the same struggles and temptations as everyone else. This gives the movie both a critical voice and an opportunity for viewers to better understand the impact of evangelical Christianity on the lives of those who practise it.

It should be noted that when movies criticize religion or even give the appearance of criticizing religion there often follows a significant controversy. Religion offers some kind of defence against the criticism or religion attacks the movie in response to the criticism, thereby generating the controversy. Consider, for example, *The Da Vinci Code* (2006), *The Last Temptation of Christ*, *Priest* (1994), *The Passion of the Christ*, *Dogma* (1999), or *The Love Guru* (2008). All of these movies created a public controversy about how religion was portrayed on screen. The controversies generated by a film's criticism of

religion have attracted much attention to religion and film and they hav
one of the primary reasons for the growing interest in the study of relig.
and film over the past 30 years.

Religion does have a serious interest in how it is portrayed on screen. First,
movies play a significant role in culture because they are much more accessible to a wide audience today than previously. Not only do people go to the
Cineplex to see movies, but movies are shown on television and it is now easy
to rent movies or even to purchase them. Second, for many people their only
exposure to a particular religion will be through the portrayal of that religion
on the silver screen. This means that if religion wants its public image to be of
a particular kind, then it has to control how it is portrayed in film or at least
defend itself against its portrayal on screen. Third, if a picture is worth a
thousand words, then it is not difficult to imagine how powerful the many
moving images of film will be. By now everyone agrees that movies have a
more significant influence on public opinion than other media – television
may be an exception. The power of film gives it a greater influence on public
thinking than other art forms and this gives film a special significance for
religion.

A movie's criticism of religion may be, of course, fair, honest and crucial to
the understanding of religion. But criticism also can be unfair, dishonest and a
political attack on religion. When criticism goes 'too far', we can see the criticism as merely propaganda designed to persuade the viewer to hold a
negative attitude toward religion. The line between legitimate criticism and
propaganda often may be difficult to draw and whether criticism is seen as
fair or unfair may depend upon whether you take the perspective of the critic
or the believer. That criticism can go 'too far', however, is an issue that will
arise in any consideration of movies that criticize religion. Something similar
can be said of the interpretation of religion. That is, an interpretation can go
'too far'. When movies are seen as offering an interpretation of religion, but
offer us only the positive side of religion, they may be seen as being propaganda. There is no reason to believe that interpretation cannot be exaggerated
or dishonest any more than there is reason to believe that all movie criticisms
of religion are fair. Again, the line between the interpretation of religion and
the promotion of religion (propaganda) may be difficult to draw and whether
a movie is seen as offering an explanation of religion or as propaganda for
religion may depend upon whether you begin with a favourable or negative
attitude toward religion.

It also should be noted that movies can critique religion in general, such as
Agnes of God or *Contact* (1997). Both of these movies concern the relationship
between faith and science without reference to a particular religion. *Agnes of
God* (1985) is the story of a nun, but it could just as well have been done using
some other religious context. *Contact* is a story about faith and science and

refers to no specific religion, so it can be seen as a film about religion in general. Movies, however, also can critique particular religions. *Priest*, for example, is a critique of Roman Catholicism; *The Apostle* is a critique of a particular kind of evangelical Christianity; and *Latter Days* (2003) is a criticism of the Mormon Church.

Movies also can provide a critique of religious ideas or themes with or without reference to particular religions. *Se7en* (1995), is an observation on the nature of evil. *Groundhog Day* (1993) gives us an example of karma. *Oh God* (1977) provides an image of God and *One Flew Over the Cuckoo's Nest* (1975) is one of many movies that exhibit a saviour figure. *Deep Impact* (1998) is a movie about the end of days and *Meet Joe Black* (1998) and *What Dreams May Come* (1998) concern life after death. *The Shawshank Redemption* (1994) is a film about redemption, as is *Never Die Alone* (2004).[2]

Finally, the kind of movie that provides a critique of religion in general or a particular religion can be either narrative or documentary, but the movie usually has religion as a major part of the film. *The Apostle* is a story about a preacher who loses his church and family, but finds himself. *Going My Way* (1944) is the story of two priests who try to save a parish church, each in his own way. *Kadosh* is set in Jerusalem's Mea Sherim quarter, where the women work, keep house, and have children so the men can study the Torah and the Talmud. *Priest* has two priests as the main characters and is set in a working class parish. *The Tribe* (2006) and *Jesus Camp* (2006) are both documentaries about particular religions.

Some movies, however, do not have religion as the focus of the film, yet they address in one way or another some religious theme. *Never Die Alone* is the story of a drug lord who returns to his old neighbourhood, setting off a turf war, but it is also a story about redemption. *The Sixth Sense* (1999) is a story about a young boy who 'sees dead people', but it also concerns moving on to the next world. *Groundhog Day* is a romantic comedy that provides an interpretation of karma and *All That Jazz* (1979) provides us with an image of God – Jessica Lange in a white veil. *Armageddon* (1998) is the story of how human beings deal with an asteroid that is about to hit the earth, but it also reflects on the end of days. Francis Ford Coppola's Vietnam War movie, *Apocalypse Now* (1979), is a movie about evil and *Contact*, a story about the search for extraterrestrial intelligence, raises issues of faith versus science as well as making some suggestions about the after life.

Usually people are interested in what an entire movie tells us about religion – does the movie as a whole criticize or interpret religion? On some occasions, however, only part of a movie offers a critique of religion. *The Godfather* (1972), for example, is a movie about the Corleone mob family, but at the end of the movie Michael Corleone is shown at the baptism of his child and scenes of the baptism are interspersed with scenes of the brutal killings that Michael has ordered. The contrast between the religious ceremony and the ruthless killings shows that religion can be practiced hypocritically. There is a similar scene in *Looking for Mr. Goodbar* (1977). Theresa's cruel father treats her unfairly because of his own shame, yet he is shown watching football in his Notre Dame jacket. He is shown as a kind of 'football Christian', for whom the rest of Christianity is unimportant. Again, the hypocrisy is obvious, but only as a small part of the entire film.[3]

Most of the movies noted above are feature length narrative films, and while much of the original interest in religion and film focused upon this kind of film, documentaries and short films also can provide a critique of religion and scholars have taken to investigating these films as a part of religion and film. *Jesus Camp* is a documentary account of a children's camp where kids are trained to be Christian warriors. The film is critical of treating children as though they were the front line in a battle against the other – primarily Islam. A critic of the *Jesus Camp* comments in the film that the practices we see in the movie border on child abuse. In the same year, *Obsession: Radical Islam's War Against the West* shows a similar treatment of children by Muslims. It is equally appalled by the treatment of children in the name of religion and suggests that religion, of whatever kind, has no business using children as warriors against the other.

Two other recent documentaries provide a critique of religion. One is *Be Like Others* (2008). This film explores the lives of Iranians who are changing their sex by surgical means and the role that religion (Islam) plays in this practice in a country where homosexuality is still a crime and punishable by death. The film deals with the usual issues related to sexual identity, but it also considers religious practice as it affects changing one's sex. Before his death, the Ayatollah Ruhollah Khomeini issued a fatwa that made sex change permissible. Since the fatwa cannot be disputed as a matter of Islamic theology the religion of Iran sanctions the changing of one's sex. *Be Like Others* is not so much a criticism of Islam as an explanation of its practices and the impact those practices have on Iran's transgendered population.

The second documentary is *Dinner with the President: A Nation's Journey* (2007). The directors of *Dinner with the President* find themselves literally in the home of Pakistani President, Pervez Musharraf, having a conversation over dinner with the President about the nature of democracy in an Islamic country. Although himself unelected,[4] Musharraf sees himself as a promoter of democracy in Pakistan. Musharraf, however, thinks that it is difficult to produce democracy in a nation where many people would prefer to live in an Islamic theocracy. The task of creating democracy is complicated by radical Muslims whose opposition to democracy is expressed through violence.

From the discussion above it should be clear that movies can give meaning to religion. It also should be clear that how this happens is complicated by whether the critique is positive or negative, whether the criticism or interpretation is accurate and honest or unfair. And, a critique of religion can be delivered through a feature length narrative film or through documentaries and short films.

For a more detailed analysis of a film that interprets religion, consider Antonia Bird's *Priest*. The movie provoked quite a controversy when it was released. Some of that controversy was the result of explicit sexuality, especially explicit homosexual behaviour, but some of the controversy also was likely the product of the movie's criticism of the Roman Catholic Church. There are at least four serious criticisms of the Catholic Church in this film. First, there is the criticism that the Church has great wealth and that it does not do enough for the poor. When we first meet Father Matthew, he is sitting in the office of the Bishop. As he looks around the office he sees, and we see, the trappings of wealth. In contrast, Father Matthew works in a poor parish, one that is always short of money. The contrast shows the Church as hypocritical. The Church is to serve the poor and disenfranchised, yet it accumulates wealth that is not used to serve the poor.

The second criticism concerns the vow of celibacy. Father Matthew lives with Maria, the Parish housekeeper. Father Greg, the young priest newly assigned to the parish, is appalled that Father Matthew has a mistress and is not keeping his vow of celibacy. Father Greg, however, is gay and finds himself taking a lover of his own even though he is torn between his desire for a sexual relationship and the keeping of his vow. In an exchange between the two priests, Father Matthew argues that celibacy was important to the Church because when a priest died the Church inherited whatever wealth he had. Father Matthew also argues that a celibate priesthood has little understanding of human sexuality and therefore cannot give advice to parishioners about their own sexual behaviour. The point of these conversations is that while celibacy may have been important to the Church at one time, it is no longer important to the Church and may even have harmful consequences for parishioners.

The third criticism has to do with the sanctity of the confessional. Father Greg learns in confession that one of the young girls in the parish, Lisa, is being sexually molested by her father, but Father Greg cannot report the abuse without Lisa's permission and Lisa refuses to give him permission. Father Greg expresses his pain at not being able to help Lisa in a rant directed at an icon of Jesus on the cross. It is not only a question of how God can allow this to happen to Lisa, but also a question of why the rules of the Church prevent Father Greg from protecting Lisa.

The fourth criticism is directed at parishioners who refuse to take communion from a homosexual priest because homosexuality is 'an abomination'. At the end of the film, after Father Greg has been arrested for indecent behaviour and exposed as gay, Father Matthew urges Father Greg to join him in giving communion. About half of the congregation walks out of the church. No one takes communion from Father Greg. And, one of the parishioners begins to shout Bible verses that he believes condemn homosexuality. In response, Father Greg asks for forgiveness and states that only those who are without sin should cast stones. The conflict here is between condemning the sin and forgiving the sinner. The criticism in the film is of those who cannot forgive the sinner.

If one takes these criticisms seriously, as the movie clearly expects the viewer to do, it is easy to see why the Church and many lay Catholics as well would find the movie offensive. What makes this movie especially interesting, however, is that it does not merely offer criticism of the Church. With regard to the vow of celibacy, Father Greg argues that what sets the priest apart from others is taking and keeping the vows he does, including the vow of celibacy. Keeping one's vows gives the priest the credibility needed to serve the theological and ethical needs of the parishioners. In the end, Father Greg is committed to keeping the vow of celibacy and this suggests that importance of the vow itself.

With regard to the sanctity of the confessional, it turns out that because Father Greg is angry about not being able to help Lisa, he ends a parish meeting early. Lisa's mother, as a result, goes home early and discovers her husband engaged in sexual activity with Lisa. Scenes of Father Greg shouting his pain at the statue of Jesus on the cross are interspersed, then, with scenes of Lisa's mother returning home, discovering her husband's evil behaviour, and throwing him out of the house, thereby protecting Lisa from further abuse. One might interpret this not as an expression of Father Greg's impotence, but rather as the intervention of God on behalf of his child, Lisa. If one adopts this interpretation of the situation, then the rules of the Church are not to be discarded. When the rules do not work, God intervenes in human affairs to protect his children. Rather than a criticism of religion, the movie actually offers an explanation of how we might expect God to protect us.

Finally, with regard to the issue of homosexuality, the fact that many in the congregation leave the church rather than take communion from Father Greg speaks to the condemnation of the sin. This is in quite clear contrast to the issue of forgiveness. At just the moment when Father Greg is left standing alone, Lisa comes to the front of the church to take communion from him. This is a remarkably powerful moment in the film and it demonstrates the importance of forgiveness, for both the forgiven and the forgiver. The healing power of forgiveness is given precedence over the issue of homosexuality. At this moment the volume of the music increases and we hear the words to 'You'll Never Walk Alone'.[5] It would not be inappropriate to say that in the crooked smile of the molested child, opening her mouth to take communion from the priest who had not been able to protect her, we see the face of God.[6] The priest offers an explanation of the healing power of forgiveness and the mysterious way in which God works in the world.

In the end, *Priest* is an excellent example of a movie that provides a critique of religion. The movie offers both criticism of religion and an interpretation of religion. The criticism seems to be directed at the institutional Church, while the interpretation pertains to something distinct from the institution, something that might be identified as the spirit of Christianity.

Before turning to other examples of movies that critique religion, there are several movies over the years that follow the pattern of *Priest*. That is, these movies seem to be critical of the institutional church and yet sympathetic to the spirit of Christianity or what might be called the community of believers. One such movie is *The Mission* (1986). The first part of the movie shows Rodrigo Mendoza, a slave hunter, turning away from his chosen profession and becoming a Christian. With the help of Father Gabriel, Mendoza becomes a priest and joins Father Gabriel in establishing a mission for converting the native Indians in the heart of the jungles of South America. In the 1750 Treaty of Madrid, however, Spain cedes part of South America to the Portuguese, including the land occupied by the mission of Father Gabriel and Rodrigo Mendoza. The Portuguese are slavers and they will now capture the Indians and use them or sell them as slaves, so Father Gabriel and Mendoza try to protect the mission and the Indians from the Portuguese. Mendoza takes up arms and fights the Portuguese. Father Gabriel asks God to protect them as he continues to carry the cross and minister to the Indians. Both Mendoza and Father Gabriel are killed by the Portuguese soldiers and the Indians they were trying to save are either killed or taken away to become slaves. The killing of the priests and Indians and the enslavement of the Indians that survive the slaughter is the result of a desire on the part of the institutional church to protect its political power in Spain. The movie asks and clearly answers the question: What is the 'mission' of the church?

Another example of a movie criticizing the institutional Church but interpreting Christianity in terms of serving the poor and ministering to those without influence is *Romero* (1989). Oscar Romero represents both the official Church and the community of believers. At the outset of the film, Romero, a Salvadoran priest, carries out his work in the traditional fashion, following the rules and obeying those in authority. Because Romero behaves according to the dictates of the official church, he is selected to be the next archbishop of El Salvador. As archbishop, however, Romero sees another side of his country. He is supposed to be part of the country's elite, joining in power with the military dictatorship of the country. What he discovers is that the military dictatorship is brutal in its repression of the insurgents, those who are fighting to overthrow the dictatorship and return the country to the people. Oscar

Romero's conscience does not allow him to collaborate with the dictatorship and he speaks out against the atrocities committed by the government against its own people. Romero abandons his role as leader of the Church, the official church that collaborates with the dictatorship, and adopts the role of spokesperson for the people. In the end Archbishop Romero is assassinated by the government. Romero criticizes the institutional church for collaborating with an evil government and the 'true church' is interpreted as the congregation of those who do the Lord's work.

Perhaps surprisingly, *Going My Way* is the final example of a film critical of the official church. *Going My Way* may be known best for the singing of Bing Crosby and its happy ending, but it parallels in many ways the movies described above. The official, institutional church[7] is represented by Father Fitzgibbon, the senior priest of the parish. Father Fitzgibbon dresses in a traditional frock, chastises the parishioners for sinning, provides the usual rituals, fails to keep up the physical building, and seems helpless as the parish diminishes in size and influence. Along comes Father O'Malley, a younger priest who has been sent to save the parish. O'Malley represents the spirit rather than the form of the Church. O'Malley dresses casually, enjoys sports and starts a choir for the kids in the neighbourhood to keep them out of trouble. O'Malley encourages the parishioners to behave in a moral fashion, rather than merely chastising them for their sins and he is able to rescue the parish from its financial difficulties by 'selling' his song, 'Would You Like to Swing on a Star'.[8] Since Father Fitzgibbon's behaviour seems mostly to fail and Father O'Malley's behaviour seems to succeed, the message of the movie seems to be that the formal church is not as important as the spirit of God working in the lives of the parishioners and the priests themselves.

The examples above that relate to the Roman Catholic Church are included because they offer a criticism of the Church. They also provide an interpretation of religion that separates the organization or institution from religion itself. The following two examples differ in that they are primarily an effort to help the viewer understand particular religions. These examples are interpretive or positive, rather than critical, but they are examples of movies providing a critique of religion.

The first example is *Tender Mercies* (1983). Mac Sledge is an alcoholic over-the-hill country music star, who turns his life around after experiencing the love of a widow, Rosa Lee. As the relationship between Mac and Rosa develops, the famous country singer finds something in this simple woman that he had never experienced before, real love.

Throughout the movie we see that Rosa practices a rather traditional protestant religion. She goes to church regularly, sings in the choir, has her son baptized, and so on. Mac adopts these religious practices, but they seem to be, for both Rosa and Mac, more of a social practice than the centre of their lives. But there is a centre and that is Rosa's unconditional love for Mac.

The drama of the story comes when Mac's famous ex-wife performs a concert in a neighbouring town. Mac goes to see her and he is reminded of what the fame and money offer. It is a serious temptation. The viewer can see, however, that what Mac has in his relationship with Rosa, though not glamorous, is so much more than he had when he was rich and famous. *Tender Mercies* shows how the power of love, rather than formal religion, can bring one to experience the best that life has to offer.

The second example is that of Bae Yong-kyun's *Why Has Bodhi-Dharma Left for the East?* This movie might be called an interpretation or explanation of Buddhism – clearly the movie enables the viewer to experience Buddhism.[9] The movie has a running time of 2 hours and 25 minutes, but it includes almost no dialogue. This is really a story told in pictures and in some important sense it is not really a story at all. Rather it is an opportunity for the viewer to experience the ordinary world in a way that is similar to how a Buddhist might experience the world.

Another way to describe the movie is to say that while it gives the viewer the opportunity to experience the ordinary world from a Buddhist perspective it also can generate an experience that is quite the opposite. Watching a movie without dialogue, without the usual plot, with only natural sounds, makes the viewer uncomfortable. Since there is nothing in the movie to capture the viewer's attention, nothing to keep the viewer riveted, the viewer begins to think about other things, things that are either past or future. The viewer's inability to stay in the present moment gives the viewer at least an experience that is recognizable as the opposite of the Buddhist perspective.

Most of the examples above are movies that critique some form of Christianity or that critique the Roman Catholic Church. Given that most films, with a significant distribution, have been made in Europe and North America it is easy to see why the 'religion' of 'religion and film' would be Christianity. The future, however, is likely to be quite different. More movies today are produced in India than are produced in Hollywood. More countries are developing a 'film industry' than ever before.[10] As the world grows smaller and it becomes more important for us to understand our global neighbours, film will be one of the ways in which we expand our understanding of the world around us. Therefore, it will be even more important for us to understand the religions of the world and film will be one of the most important ways of expanding our understanding of the world's religions.

Religion, Ethics and Film

Alyda Faber

In the last decade, ethical enquiry has opened up a dynamic new area within the field of religion and film studies.[1] Prior to this, ethical engagement with film was often limited to religious rating systems which assessed whether or not a film might be morally corrupting for its audiences. The first two parts of this essay consider two strands of religious ethical film criticism referring to the earlier approach as the *censorship/rating model* and the more recent one as the *ideological criticism model*. Both models focus on ethical judgment as the cultivation of a critical ethical subjectivity, specifically in relation to film, as formative for social and political life.[2] But whereas proponents of the earlier model sought to reform the movie industry into a more religiously palatable product, the later model is characterized by a critical engagement with a much wider range of films. In order to amplify the issues at stake, the third part of the essay interprets the 'visual ethics'[3] of Michael Haneke's 2004 film *Caché* in conversation with the ethical religious subjectivity proposed by Rowan Williams in *Lost Icons*.

The Censorship/Rating Model

The earliest strategy for religious ethical engagement with film, the censorship/rating model, assessed Hollywood films for their potential to corrupt the moral values of audiences. A Catholic priest, Father Daniel Lord, developed a movie code which was adopted by the film industry in 1930, and enforced from 1934 through the Production Code Association (PCA) until it was replaced by the Motion Picture Association of America's rating system in the mid-1960s. The extension to film of First Amendment protections of freedom of speech in the post-World War II years had already begun the erosion of the influence of the PCA.[4] Lord's code, with its white racial bias, prohibited films from 'glorifying criminals, gangsters, adulterers, and prostitutes ... banned nudity, excessive violence, white slavery, illegal drugs, miscegenation, lustful kissing, suggestive postures, and profanity' while insisting that films should promote 'the institutions of family and home, defend the fairness of government, and present religious institutions with reverence'.[5] The PCA was formed in response to the Catholic Legion of

Decency campaign begun in 1933, which claimed to be limited to advocating that churchgoers boycott films deemed offensive by Catholic authorities, but which resulted in 30 years of film censorship in Hollywood.

The Catholic Legion of Decency campaign rated films as morally unobjectionable (A), as morally offensive in part (B), or in their entirety (C, later O). As the 1933 membership pledge for the Legion indicates, the influence of films was deemed to be political as well as personal: 'I unite with all who protest against [vile and unwholesome moving pictures] as a grave menace to youth, to home life, to country and to religion . . . I condemn absolutely those salacious motion pictures which, with other degrading agencies, are corrupting public morals and promoting a sex mania in our land'. In a revised 1934 statement, a member pledges 'to form a right conscience about pictures that are dangerous to my moral life'.[6] The judgment that specific film content is corrupting assumes that film reception is uncomplicated, the effects on moral behaviour and values easily ascertained, and therefore that censorship is easily justified – an assumption which the current voluminous scholarship on film spectatorship would certainly disclaim. Gregory Black contends that the years of Hollywood censorship curtailed an important public venue for ethical debate by restricting open interpretation in film of the 'morals and manners, the economics and politics, and the social and ethical issues facing American society . . . The industry chose instead to interpret all social and political themes through the restrictive lens of the code' and did so out of a profit motive.[7]

Robert K. Johnson evaluates the limitations of censorship/rating type models for ethical engagement with film, at the very least, as impractical because of wide access to films on DVD.[8] He also contends that rating systems limit ethical judgment to the presence or absence of sex, violence or coarse language in a film, rather than taking into account a director's artistically expressed attitudes to the behaviour represented. Finally, he notes that these ethical judgments are relative, and vary widely based on particular historical contexts and geographical locations. For example, Europeans and Canadians tend to be more accepting of explicit sexual content in film while opposing graphic violence, while Americans tend to make the opposite judgments with regard to sex and violence in films.[9]

Ideological Criticism Model

The religious ethical criticism of the last decade has worked within, and elaborated various facets of, an ideological criticism model. If the censorship/rating model attempts to exclude from public 'consumption' images and narratives deemed to be morally corrupting, assuming that the effects of certain films can be readily ascertained, what are the aims of the ideological criticism model? In his essay, 'Ideology and film culture', Héctor Rodríguez argues that ideology critique, as it is practiced in film criticism, functions as ethical analysis. In his view, 'ideology critique is a species of moral persuasion, mainly concerned with the normative evaluation of certain ways of thinking, feeling, and acting that have a bearing on our social institutions'.[10] This ethical approach interprets what he calls 'moral pictures', which expose certain patterns of social and political commitment as morally questionable because of their implication in practices of domination and exclusion. The focus on moral pictures, in his view, while not rejecting rule-based morality, which predominates in the censorship model, complicates ethics as the cultivation of discernment, perception and responsiveness, and also less conscious processes of character formation. Rodríguez's point that ideological criticism functions as an ethical approach within film studies is valid for religious film criticism as well. Religious and theological ideological film criticism can be characterized as a *critical ethical subjectivity*: religion is used as a social critical tool – with race, class and gender analysis – to construct desirable ethical subjectivities.

Margaret R. Miles' *Seeing and Believing* was the first book length study to elaborate a religious ethical approach to film.[11] Miles contends that the filmgoer must become critical spectators of Hollywood films because they propose answers to the ancient ethical question: how should life be lived? She finds that with few exceptions, Hollywood films promote impoverished values for relational life in contrast to values solicited through practices of religious devotion. Nevertheless, she advocates engagement with these films, using categories of analysis such as race, class, gender and sexual orientation to develop her functionalist definition of religion as normative conversation about interpersonal, social and political relationships. In her view, films can foster individual and social 'critical subjectivity' through analysis of 'how [America's] reiterated representations relate to its social and institutional arrangements, its public concerns and interests, and its fears and longings'.[12]

A response to Miles' book and other works, S. Brent Plate's essay, 'Religion/literature/film: Toward a religious visuality of film', has significantly influenced the recent ethical turn in religion and film studies. Plate contends that a religious visuality of film, in order to 'see differently', must engage the distinctive visual and aural techniques of film, aspects of embodiment in film spectatorship, and independent and world cinema. Plate develops the ethical implications of his proposals with reference to the film theorist Kaja Silverman who develops ethical subjectivity extensively 'in the field of vision' as 'an active gift of love'.

Silverman's work introduces into the conversation about religion, ethics and film a theorization of subjectivity in visual terms, aligning closely embodiment and spectatorship, and she offers a richer account of identification beyond that of the rating system. Her work is also suggestive for ways film may contribute to an understanding of the significance of a religious love ethic in contemporary society and culture. Theorizing the visual at the centre of the process of subject formation through a critical engagement with Lacanian psychoanalysis, Silverman distinguishes two kinds of identification in response to images. 'Idiopathic identification' refers to an enduring narcissistic tendency to make the other the same as the self, a homogenizing tendency she sees at work in most Hollywood films. 'Heteropathic identification', the activity of love as 'productive looking', opens the possibility of seeing with empathic attention the socially despised body of the other (the poor, the sick, the racially vilified). Silverman's ethical subject is not a liberal free chooser, but implicated in a network of dominant representations and social relations that only form partially conscious habits and sensations. For this reason, interventions are required to disturb them – in her view images have the power to solicit the unconscious and conscious at once, to address subjectivity as individual and always already social and political. Silverman analyses a number of alternative films to argue that the aural and visual filmmaking techniques of these films solicit from the viewer a possible 'heteropathic identification', an active love as 'productive looking'.[13]

A number of theologians and religion scholars develop Silverman's views of seeing as an embodied ethical act in various positive disciplines of 'visual ethics', interpreting a range of films from Hollywood to alternative, but without the extensive elaboration of ethical subjectivity that she offers. Ulrike Vollmer, for example, challenges the pessimistic accounts of seeing as domination offered by philosophy, psychoanalysis and feminist film studies in her account of a positive discipline of seeing as loving, a model grounded in feminist theology, Martin Buber's relational theology and her readings of films with women artist characters and women directors.[14] Gerald Loughlin contends that film in conversation with theology can be expressive of an alternative ethic of 'dispossessive desire', though never as fully as the church guided by the gospel narratives that mandate such a desire.[15] Using a practical ethics approach, Johnson proposes that films can promote an ethical citizenship because their stories provoke affective engagement, and help us to develop a 'common moral vocabulary' for public conversations about ethical issues like immigration, euthanasia, violence and war.[16] In a co-authored essay, Miles and Plate argue that a critical practice of film viewing may disturb socially learned habits of seeing, and help cultivate 'hospitable vision' wherein films function as 'a sort of training ground, a place to be confronted by visual otherness, and to practice our response'[17] for the world 'off-screen'. The work of Kent Brintnall and others critically interprets filmic representations of otherness – extremes of violence and affliction – with reference to gender analysis, film studies and Christian theology.[18]

As noted here, the ideology criticism model advocates various social ethical mandates of visual ethics. The earlier censorship/rating model also had an interest in forming a person of conscience, albeit in terms of a rule-based morality. Silverman's work helpfully establishes some important directives for future work in the area of religious ideological criticism, which functions as ethical criticism. In the rest of the essay, one of these directives, re-imaging ethical subjectivity in visual terms (already evident in religious ethical film criticism), is explored by placing the work of a Christian theologian, Rowan Williams, in conversation with Michael Haneke's film *Caché*. Williams complicates the primary moral agent in the Christian and secular ethical traditions, the person of conscience or the Kantian sovereign subject. He offers, as Iris Murdoch articulates it, a 'darker, less fully conscious, less steadily rational image'[19] of the ethical subject, a subjectivity that Haneke's filmic techniques also both represent and solicit.

Ethical Subjectivity as Self-questioning

Williams develops a religious ethical subjectivity by engaging religion, psychoanalysis, art and politics.[20] He is both pessimistic and hopeful in his vigilant attention to the damaged and damaging effects of socio-political human relations – where consumer models dominate thought and practice – along with the expectation of grace, the possibility, sometimes realized, of transformation. The hope for transformation lies not in some general vision of social change, but in the cultivation of self-questioning on the part of individuals. For Williams, the formation of ethical and political self-consciousness is also the beginning of authentic religious practice, the place where 'the soul happens'. Religious ethical subjectivity 'begins in the attempt to attend to the moment of self-questioning – to refuse to cover over, evade or explain the pain and shock of whatever brings the self into question, to hold on to the difficulty before the almost inevitable descent into pathos and personal drama begins'.[21] According to Williams, the self is always negotiable, a work-in-progress, vulnerable to risk and criticism. In order for the self to be capable of *active responsiveness* rather than *reactive panic* under duress, she or he requires regular experience of 'planned frustration' through ascetic practices, which may include psychoanalysis, or engagement with fictions (perhaps films) that stay with difficulty, that avoid easy resolutions.[22] It is a self for whom friction and incompleteness is the norm.

The incompleteness of the always emerging ethical subjectivity that Williams evokes has to do with a porousness to others and otherness that cannot be arrested or controlled. Choices may have unforeseen and unintended deleterious consequences in the lives of others, something that can be actively acknowledged, but not undone through remorse. Remorse is a religious disposition that Williams finds is being lost given the predominance of models of choice based on consumer practices: choice imagined as utterly free in the sense of never limiting personal options or those of others, never causing harm to others. Religious ethical subjectivity, on the other hand, involves understanding the self as implicated not only in tangible relations, but also with an Other who can never be known or made present, to whom Muslims, Jews and Christians relate in worship as a non-competitive loving Other. The world will never be recreated in the image of this Other, as Williams explains with reference to icons, but it does mean a distinctly religious awareness of a life experienced as 'a life lived beyond . . . what I choose or understand',[23] with resources for transformation beyond choosing or understanding. The active side of these solicitations of otherness – both somatic and the realization of limits of understanding and articulation – is the possibility that Williams calls 'regard beyond desire', a relaxed seeing of the other without reference to a personal need or desire (similar to Silverman's 'heteropathic identity'), a possibility sometimes realized within social relations dominated by competitiveness and incitements to panic and aggression.

Consistent with his religious ethical subjectivity, Williams envisions a more-than-liberal politics, a conversational model as a middle way between individual rights and communitarian ethics. Within this model, he defines oppression as those occasions when conversation becomes impossible, where people no longer find each other difficult to understand. Like the ethical subject ever constituted through friction and incompleteness, active (rather than reactive) political engagement requires an acknowledgment of 'conflicts of interest and desire, the unavoidability of loss, the obstinacy of others . . . We "learn" each other, we cope with each other, in the trials and errors, the contests and treaties of speech; which takes time, and doesn't quickly or necessarily lead to communion'.[24]

The 'Visual Ethics' of Michael Haneke's *Caché*

Michael Haneke is Austria's most celebrated film director, known for his provocative techniques for implicating spectators in the ethical dilemmas represented in his films. His work consistently examines ethical questions about the use of media, representations of violence, and the impoverishment of communication in North Atlantic societies. In treating these themes, Haneke's films have been described in ways that resonate with Williams' religious ethical subjectivity. For example, his film *Code Unknown* (2000) is described in a *Cineaste* interview as an 'exploration of the end of communication, and that failure's relationship to racism and economic/social injustice',[25] a comment that is apt for *Caché* as well. In an ethical interpretation of Haneke's

films, Maximilian Le Cain contends that Haneke's originality lies in provoking the spectator to imagine possibilities other than the social problems
diagnosed and attacked in his films: 'most of his films propose a method of
reversal to the negative state of things that they outline, solutions that
are often as difficult and profound as they are apparently invisible on the
surface of the narrative'.[26] 'Solutions' may be too strong a term for what
Haneke evokes in his films – he insists upon leaving the spectator with
questions rather than answers in order to solicit the active ethical attention of
the spectator.[27]

The ethical solicitation of *Caché* comes from the tension Haneke creates
between an ethical attention constituted through his own filmic technique,
and the limited imagination and empathy of his main character, Georges.
This tension has the potential to provoke in the spectator the kind of
self-questioning and responsiveness that, for Williams, expresses ethical
subjectivity. In emphasizing Haneke's technique, I follow Berys Gaut's
method for an ethical analysis of art.[28] Gaut contends that the key object
of ethical assessment of art works is the attitude the artist takes toward
characters, whether good or bad, or what he calls the 'manifest artist', accessible through the aesthetic techniques of the art form, and not limited to what
an artist's intentions may have been. In this approach, the understanding
of the spectator is speculative, in contrast with current empirical or ethnographic studies of spectators.

Caché begins with a static shot of a house in a Parisian side street, held
for about 3 minutes, with very little activity in the street. This is revealed to
be a video tape when it is rewound, and a couple, Anne and Georges Laurent,
discuss who might have made a surveillance-type tape of their house.
As more tapes are left, along with child-like drawings of a face with blood
pouring from the mouth, and a bloodied rooster, the couple's sense of panic
grows. Although the film does not resolve the mystery of who sent the tapes,
certain clues in them lead Georges to Majid, the son of Algerian farm
labourers who had worked for Georges' parents. Majid's parents disappeared
after a demonstration organized by the FLN in Paris on 17 October 1961 that
resulted in a violent crackdown by police, leaving several hundred people
dead, and bodies floating in the Seine; an event erased from French public
memory until some 40 years later. Georges too is faced with a reckoning
since his lies about Majid led his parents to decide against adopting the boy,
sending him instead to an orphanage. This event clearly impacted Majid's
economic circumstances, but Georges refuses to acknowledge any responsibility for the consequences of his actions as a child. And when Georges' son
Pierrot disappears for a night,[29] Georges implicates Majid and his son, who
are taken in for questioning by police and imprisoned overnight. Tension
between Georges and Majid escalates to the point where Majid commits

suicide in front of Georges, followed soon after by an aggressive exchange between Georges and Majid's son.

How does Haneke create tension between his film technique and the disposition of the main character, Georges? And how does this tension solicit ethical attention as self-questioning in relation to others and the world, at the heart of ethical subjectivity for Williams, and arguably, for Haneke as well? Throughout the film, a contrast is created between Georges' quick reactive panic and the repetition of slow static wide angled shots. The film begins with a surveillance-type shot of the Laurent's house and street, a shot repeated throughout the film. Georges' memory of Majid being taken away to the orphanage is filmed in a similar single perspective long shot, as well as a shot of the steps of Pierrot's school, with the latter image repeated as the film's conclusion. For Haneke, the simple montage is intended to slow down habits of seeing developed in television viewing which accelerates images and objectifies life and people into consumed and consumers. Cinematic images which minimize montage solicit the spectator to a greater responsibility for contemplating a visual image, taking time to understand what is seen, both intellectually and emotionally.[30] Yet within the film, Georges views the tapes with the lingering shots of his house with growing panic and aggression that leads him to escalate the violence he perpetrated as a child against Majid in his renewed acquaintance with him. He repeatedly refuses any self-questioning, any remorse, any responsibility, even when he is sent a tape of his aggressive interaction with Majid in his apartment. The film does not resolve the tension between slow images and Georges' quick reactiveness; it is precisely this irresolution that creates opportunities for the spectator to imagine a different kind of social relation.

A different social relation, or 'a method of reversal to the negative state of things' (Le Cain) is suggested in another filmic technique, the shift between videotaped images, narrative, and images that Georges imagines, dreams or remembers. This technique creates an effect described by film critics as undermining 'a viewer's sense of omnipotence', provoking uncertainty, because you are never sure what you are looking at. It is also possible to interpret this technique as Haneke's solicitation of the ethical subjectivity described by Williams, an ethics both within and beyond choice, will and consent; the realization that lives are implicated in those of others in ways that are not under anyone's control. The visual uncertainty of the film is contrasted by Georges' arrogant, dogged certainty that he did not harm Majid in any way, an attitude that culminates with attacks on Majid based on unfounded accusations, that he is sick, twisted and perverted for sending the tapes to his house. Haneke complicates Georges' professed certitude, however, with images that suggest at least a somatic responsiveness on his part – horrifying mental and dream images of Majid as a child, spewing blood and later, decapitating a rooster and threatening Georges with an axe.

The depth of the failure of communication between Majid and Georges is evident in images wherein Georges sees himself as the victim of someone he has harmed. The violence of this failure of communication does not relax into any easy assignment of victim/perpetrator roles, however. Whereas Georges' aggression has been overt throughout the film, Majid's suicide, a covert act of aggression as self-destruction, is also an act of violence as suffering that arises from a terrible implication with another person with whom more conciliatory forms of communication have been bankrupted. With Georges watching, wondering why he was called to Majid's apartment, Majid tells him, 'I wanted you to be present', and slits his throat, sending a gush of blood up the wall as he collapses. In this scene, the spectator, and Georges as witness to Majid's suicide, is confronted with what Haneke refers to as a receptivity solicited by 'a poetic of image and sound emerging uniquely from a direct encounter with human pain and the desire for something, some place, that cannot be had'.[31] For both Majid and Georges, what cannot be had is the end of the contest for the role of victim, which requires that the other take the role of perpetrator, a constant immanent threat. An important topic that requires further development is how racism functions within this dynamic of failed communication.

The social problems Haneke diagnoses in *Caché* are rooted in themes treated consistently in his work, *Entfremdung* (self-estrangement) and *emotionale Vergletscherung* (emotional glaciation).[32] The sparely furnished interior of the Laurent home underscores these themes, particularly the living room which is virtually identical to the set of Georges' television broadcast, suggesting a lack of private self, or introspection, that may also be associated with a failure to imagine the reality of an other person. Even the more private space of the Laurent's bedroom, seen for the first time after Georges witnesses Majid's suicide, is barely furnished and filmed in cool blue tones. Here he admits to his wife the lies he told that led to Majid being sent away, but he still refuses to imagine how his understandable desire to rid his home of a rival child had impacted Majid's life, accusing him of pathological behaviour: 'he's twisted – to slit his throat for that [the lies]'. After a subsequent aggressive confrontation with Majid's son at work, in the final sequence of the film, Georges calls his wife to say that he is going to bed early, and assures her that nothing is wrong. The film ends with two static shots, George's memory of the day Majid is taken away in a long shot of a barnyard, and students on the steps at Pierrot's school. The latter shot amplifies the ambiguity of Georges' response to the barnyard scene; in it, Majid's son and Pierrot talk to each other in the foreground, but not all viewers notice them. They may be accomplices; Majid's son may be threatening the younger boy, as Georges accused Majid of doing; it is impossible to know.

Haneke leaves the spectator with questions, provoking a kind of responsiveness which may become 'receptive generosity' (Romand Coles), but that Georges refuses (and the spectator may refuse as well). Haneke gives prolonged attention to the refusal of remorse, in spite of the frequency with which the word 'sorry' is spoken by Georges (but never to Majid). Also, as suggested by the events of 17 October 1961, the catalyst of the event in Georges' and Majid's lives, this story in its elliptical telling is not about ethical subjectivity restricted to the interpersonal, but also always as social and political. The refusal of remorse is held in tension with Haneke's repetition of static images and simplified montage, his patient attention to Georges' and Majid's failure of responsiveness and imagination, which provides an opening for the spectator to understand the violence of such a failure, and possibly to imagine responding differently.

Conclusion

The visual techniques and the narrative solicitations of *Caché* in conversation with Rowan Williams' religious subjectivity express a visual ethics concerned with critical ethical subjectivity, important for religious ethical analysis of film both in the ideological criticism model and in the censorship/rating model. The rapidly emerging field of ethics, religion and film has some aspects, however, that are yet to be fully engaged. As this all too brief interpretation of Haneke's film is intended to demonstrate, more work is needed to adequately theorize subjectivity through a visual ethic, and the politics of such an ethic. This implies the necessity of continued work on films' formal structures, techniques and particular ethics of seeing, as well as further theorization of issues related to film spectatorship, such as emotional and embodied responses to film. In order to do this well, theologians and religion scholars need to continue to engage film theory as 'a full, legitimate and independent conversation partner – a form of "worldly wisdom" which must be interwoven with the faith tradition'.[33] Work also needs to continue on the possibilities for a religious love ethic interpreted through film. The debate whether to engage Hollywood films or world cinema and independent films has turned a corner with the affirmation that both alternative and mainstream films ought to be critically engaged. Further ethnographic research on film reception would help counter the assumption of the early censorship/rating model that causal effects of film are easily determined, and that censorship can be easily justified. Finally, religious ethical approaches to film would benefit from perspectives on ethics and film from within Jewish, Muslim and Buddhist ethical traditions.[34]

5 Theology and Film

Clive Marsh

What is Theology?

Theology is about God. It is a discipline of thinking and acting which seeks to speak about, and make some sort of sense of, a reality within which, it is being claimed, human persons live, move and have their being. Theology is therefore also about human beings because human beings would be less inclined to undertake God-talk if it did not affect them. Even though theologians do their best to do theology in a disinterested way, so that it is God that is the focus and not simply human concerns, human issues remain tangled up in the task. This means that theology is a dangerous discipline. It can mean that human beings purport to talk about God, when they are only talking about themselves, and no one might know anyway. But if it is true that reality is greater than human beings and than human perceptions of reality, then something like theology has to be attempted, despite its dangers.

God may or may not 'exist' as a reality independent of human thought. But even if God only 'exists' in human thought, in human imagination, then theology has a job to do. For at the very least, God-language becomes the linguistic receptacle in which human beings store their deepest convictions about, and furthest hopes and aspirations for, themselves and the world in which they live. Such convictions are encapsulated within myths, stories and narratives of many kinds. These are passed on by individuals and communities standing within identifiable traditions, and are in turn enacted within rituals and practices so that they are memorable, 'owned' and prove usable in daily life. That is how religions work. Religions therefore function, and will continue to do so, whether or not the God-question can finally be answered.

The question of God's existence remains hugely significant. Realists (who support the existence of God as a reality distinct from the human mind) and non-realists (who deem that God is a necessary linguistic construction) both differ from atheists in considering that theology is an important human discipline. In fact, most people who say they believe in God are realists. Non-realism tends in practice to be a position taken up by relatively few religious believers. But analysis of the function of theology in religion and society, and of the way in which theology is done, does not depend upon a conclusive answer to the question of God's existence. There are many ways in which contemporary societies engage in God-talk. And the subject-matter of theology is being addressed in many ways, explicit and implicit. This chapter therefore looks at how films and the practice of film-watching are contributing to the doing of theology. How are films and viewers engaging in God-talk, or exploring what it means to be a human being 'in the light of eternity'?

Theology as a Public Discipline

Theology relates to three publics: academy, religious community and society. Increasingly, the study of religion and film is happening explicitly in a multi-disciplinary way in the academy. The existence of this book, and many others like it, bears witness to this. The primary locus of interaction between theology and film is, however, in the broader public sphere. It is in cinemas and living rooms, film theatres, bars and restaurants where the content of theology is being disclosed and discussed. The moment viewers begin to reflect on what a film did to and for them, then the conversation which transpires, whether internal to a person or actually spoken out, may become theological subject-matter. This occurs explicitly, of course, if God is named. Theological exploration of different kinds occurs quite naturally in response to viewings of *King of Kings* (1961), *Star Wars* (1977), *The Last Temptation of Christ* (1988), *The Shawshank Redemption* (1994) or *Bruce Almighty* (2003). It may be less explicit in response to *Cries and Whispers* (1972), *Fitzcarraldo* (1982), *The Truman Show* (1998) or *Finding Nemo* (2003). In the latter cases, it could be claimed that film promotes philosophical discussion, perhaps, though not necessarily theological. This is true up to a point. And yet, because theology is both about God and human beings, and their relationship, whenever the different topics which feature on theology's agenda are broached,[1] theology is interested.

The academic study of theology and film thus entails study not only of what is of an explicitly theological nature *in* film, be that explicitly religious or not. Its broadest brief is the study of how theology's subject-matter is being handled in public in the interaction between films and their viewers. It therefore entails scrutiny both of what is explicit and implicit in films, and what viewers, religious or not, are currently doing with material of a theological nature which they glean from, see in, or bring to a film. It is in the thick of such complex interactions – located within the study of 'media reception' or 'reception of the arts' – that theology in public is currently being done.

What, though, of the role of religious communities? Given that there is no such thing as 'religion in general', only specific religions, and the concept of religion (as a type or form of human culture), who is going to give *content* to any theology? The more detailed exploration of this question follows in the next section. Here it must simply be noted that religious communities (traditions, congregations) clearly carry a normative, authoritative role in some way with respect to the content of a religion's theology. It is true that it is rarely possible to point to a single version of a theology operative in any religious tradition. Despite the concept of orthodoxy ('right teaching') and the existence of scriptures and catechisms, religious people in practice believe a wide variety of things. That said, while it is true that people are free to believe anything they wish, it is not true that people can do this and inevitably retain allegiance to a particular religious tradition. It matters, in principle at least, what one believes in order to be able to call oneself a Jew, a Hindu or a Christian.

With respect to theology and film, it may thus far have appeared possible to conclude that it does not matter what one believes. Prior to this mention of specific religious communities it could have been argued that theological interaction with film is largely about what films *generally* offer about topics of interest to theology, or what viewers believe on those topics (before, during and after their film-watching), whatever their religious or philosophical stance. Without acknowledging the importance of this third public for theology, this would be case. 'Theology and film' could remain the academic study of what films are doing to people in public which is of theological resonance. But this will not do. For such an approach plays down why theological views exist at all (they are carried by religious communities, which seek to contribute to the fruitful shaping of human community and purpose). And it fails to respect the practical, concrete and deeply significant role which, despite their detractors and critics, religious communities play in human societies.

'Theology and film' is thus the study of the interplay between theology's three publics in so far as film contributes to how theology is working in contemporary societies. It examines what films and film-watching are doing to and for people, religious and not, with respect to theology's subject-matter. But it does so with a keen concern for how contemporary exploration of theology's subject-matter, including by religious communities themselves, occurs as a result of this interaction. Theological exploration of film's current social and ideological functions, then, occurs in the space between a general 'religiosity' or 'spirituality' and the specificity of a particular religious tradition's theology. It is interested in *what*, for example, is believed about a human being, or about redemption, or about hope, and *why*, and not merely concerned to log the fact *that* something of a vague or specific theological nature is being believed.

Trajectories in Theology and Film

The history of theology and film enquiry over the past four decades has, however, thrown up a number of ways of understanding the relationship. Each is instructive for contemporary reflection, even if not all would be sympathetic to the framework I have just proposed. I suggest that four trajectories be identified.

The first trajectory to be noted is the most dominant and obvious in theology and film discussion. Here film is seen to become part of theology's resource-material in providing, in the form of moving pictures, the content of a theological outlook. Rather than read books, learn catechisms or listen to sermons, then, people catch hold of theology through their film watching. In the memorable opening words of Neil Hurley's seminal 1970 text *Theology through Film*, 'Movies are for the masses what theology is for an elite',[2] In 1970s America, much more than now, Hurley deemed it possible to distil from people's film-watching a 'cinematic theology' discernible in and through films. Central to his argument was a major emphasis upon 'religious transcendence' which Hurley presupposed as 'a constant of man [sic], society, and culture. Transcendence is not a static quality in man but the dynamic piston in man's movement toward truth . . .'[3]

Hurley's approach was thus to seek a universal theology. He acknowledged his Christian starting point, sought to resist imperialism and to fend off a charge of mere 'eclecticism'.[4] He was right to note the huge, and growing, importance of the visual image in Western culture, especially as promoted again through the technological advances of cinema and television. He was not, however, able to see that the theological challenge of religious pluralism itself challenged the way he appealed to transcendence in his work. Transcendence remains essential – as reality and concept – in theological exploration. But appeals to a transcendental theology are less easy to make than seemed possible in Hurley's time. The transcendental theology which was sought assumed too uniform a 'world of film' and too easy a process of distillation of a film's content from film to viewer.

Many others in ensuing decades in effect followed Hurley's approach, even if they did not use his work directly. Steve Nolan calls such an approach the location of 'cinematic analogue' and identifies James Wall's and John R. May's work as similar to Hurley. It should also be said, however, that beyond the academy, in churches across the Western world, 'cinematic analogues' are sought from films by those keen to press theological points, and not always in ways which do justice to the films concerned, or the intelligence of their viewers.

Transcendence is prominent in a second type of 'theology through film'. In Paul Schrader's work – both as film and as reflection on the film-making and film-watching experience – films become a medium through which divine reality is mediated directly in a way which cannot be achieved as easily or effectively by words. Schrader is thus concerned to identify where and how what he calls a 'transcendental style' in film is evident, and explores how this style is prominent in the work of Ozu, Bresson and Dreyer.[5] Once more, in the appeal to transcendence, an assumption is made about the universality of the theology being sought beyond the specifics of religions. Schrader says that transcendental style has a 'spiritual universality'.[6]

Whatever one makes of the claims Schrader makes for the three film-makers studied, or of the theological position he espouses, his stance is clear, and has a strong doctrine of divine revelation at its core: 'Human works ... cannot *inform* one about the Transcendent, they can only be *expressive* of the Transcendent',[7] God (or 'the Holy') remains, in other words, 'wholly Other' but can be revealed in film to the viewer. God reveals Godself in particular forms of aesthetic encounter.

Unlike Hurley, then, Schrader makes much more of film as itself the medium of revelation. Film *is* theology, and therefore the participation in the theological task is an aesthetic undertaking. Theology is not now just what happens *after* watching a film, when a film's content is processed cognitively within an identifiably religious framework. And what happens during viewing is not mere encounter with a story. Nor is the focus on affective response, which, as we shall see, becomes a focal point when attention turns to the role of audience reception. For Schrader, attention has to be paid to the artistic structure of film in order fully to grasp the aesthetic experience enjoyed. The aesthetic experience and appreciation are then both intrinsic to what it means to do theology with film.

Aesthetic appreciation is also prominent in a more recent form of 'cinematic theology', that of Gerard Loughlin. Critical of much of the work undertaken in theology and film for its underplaying of film-critical insight, Loughlin seeks to show how the form and function of particular types of film work *as* theology. Less generalized than Schrader – for Loughlin is not explicitly appealing to a transcendental set of categories discernible in film through which a theology emerges – he nevertheless wishes to switch the focus from mere attention to story or plot, or from what an already-religious viewer brings to a film, to the elements intrinsic to film as an art form. Loughlin wants to show how a 'cinematic theology' must do justice to film's aesthetic power. It is through this aesthetic power also that film can destabilize accepted social norms.

Despite the sophistication of Loughlin's approach, however, it has to be asked whether the content of the theology with which Loughlin works is truly dependent on the cinematic experience. Though laudably shifting the attention away from narrative alone to aesthetic impact, theology is for

Loughlin, more so than Schrader, ultimately *illustrated* by film, or at most *evoked* in the viewer, rather than generated by it. Cinematic theology is, for Loughlin, a 'becoming-other' rather than a dialogue between theology and film.[8] Loughlin's point, then, is to highlight a theology which challenges much of the status quo, and to note how this theology is evident in particular films.

Common to both of these first two trajectories is the significance of directorial intention (in the case of Loughlin, Roeg and Jarman). The approach via cinematic analogues rests on being able to identify what films 'mean' in terms of what their directors basically intended. Similarly, attending to a film's impact on the basis of its aesthetic construction depends on appreciating a director's art. There remains the question in all such approaches whether it is therefore the director's 'theology' we are dealing with here, whether or not that was explicit in his or her mind. If, however, particular directors were to declare themselves disinterested in theology, does that then negate theological readings of their work? Significantly, particularly in the case of the second trajectory, the more that attention is paid to film *as film*, the more the balance has already started to shift from what a director intended to what a viewer makes of a film.

This brings us to a third trajectory: film as a dialogue-partner for theology. On this understanding, theology exists as the product of religious communities and is constantly undergoing development. Even if this development is very slow – religious communities are conservative institutions in so far as they are reluctant to change core beliefs and values which have proved their worth over time – it is real, for people do not believe now what people believed in the fourth century CE, even if similar words may be used. Development in theological thinking and belief occurs in response to external stimuli. It must be recognized that the notion of 'external' is itself problematic. Churches, synagogues, mosques and temples are all located in the same world. Their members may or may not seek to detach themselves from the world around them as they fashion a religious life. But even if they do, they remain part of the world. So what is 'external' and what is 'internal' always remains part of a complex culture, or set of cultures in constant interaction.

Not surprisingly, then, religions react and respond to the societies and cultures in which they find themselves, and thus to the various philosophies and value systems explicit and implicit within them. Theologies therefore develop in part in reaction to the arts and media which cultures contain. The way that theology works, however, happens at many levels. What individual believers may do with film can be markedly different from what a religious tradition, via its authoritative teachers, may explicitly do, if anything, in response to film. This distinction is a feature of this third trajectory. If theology uses film as in any sense a dialogue-partner, and if the development of religious people's belief and theology differs from how orthodoxy is handled within a tradition (as it will, for a tradition is never simply the sum of what individual believers actually believe), then it will need to be shown *how* film actually functions as a dialogue-partner in any substantive fashion. This is only spelling out what discussions about 'theology and culture' entail. And estimation of what counts as 'art' (and thus usually regarded more worthy of attention) and as 'popular culture' (and thus less so) becomes part of the discussion.

How, then, does film function as a dialogue-partner for theology? The first thing to note is that this third trajectory can actually include the first two. Without absorbing also the detail of the first two trajectories, it is possible for films *as* story, and *as* aesthetic experience, to function as a dialogue-partner for theology. The important difference is that the balance has shifted from the director or the film to the space *between* the film and the viewer. A viewer's (and a tradition's) theology has the potential to be questioned or sharpened by a film or range of films. It may be considered that theology calls the shot too much here. But in principle at least, the content of a theology is being addressed by what a film contains or how it functions. This can happen in a variety of ways.

The notion of 'film as dialogue-partner' needs, however, to be pushed further. Margaret Miles has long acknowledged the cultural significance of films.[9] She recognizes how films contribute to people's self-understanding as they negotiate their identity within a complex configuration of cultural influences. 'The purpose of paying serious attention to film is twofold. On the one hand, the ability to analyze filmic representations develops an individual's critical subjectivity. On the other hand, films reveal how a society represents itself to itself'.[10] She is ultimately not wholly positive about their influence, though wants to oppose complete pessimism about films' role in society. Her work does, however, carry a sharp critical edge. Films can help people become clear about the social context, and the complexity of that context, within which theology is undertaken. Film is, then, a dialogue-partner of sorts, if in a rather weak sense.

A stronger sense of dialogue is found in the work of a range of other writers in theology and film. Biblical scholars Robert Jewett and Larry Kreitzer have both developed ways of understanding a positive, contributive role for film in theological discussion. Jewett speaks of an 'interpretative arch' existing between the past and the present. 'One end of the arch rests in the ancient world and the other in a contemporary cultural situation reflected in a particular film'.[11] The point is not, though, simply to identify the link. Resisting the charge that we are dealing simply with cinematic analogues of already-held biblical/religious ideas, Jewett is claiming an interplay between the two worlds. Attention to film thus informs contemporary theology through reflection on biblical texts. Similarly, Kreitzer speaks of

65

'reversing the hermeneutical flow' as he draws films alongside biblical material in order not to simply illuminate their (already-known) meaning, but to seek further depths of meaning through the questions and challenges which insights from films pose.[12] The art of interpretation is in seeing the links in the first place and then playing with the results of the juxtaposition.

Neither scholar sees the content of theology as residing solely and wholly in the Bible. As theologically-interested Christian biblical scholars, they inevitably attach great significance to the biblical text in their theology. But their biblical emphasis does make the nature of the dialogue different from interpreters beginning from a contemporary theological question or formulation with which films are 'in conversation'. The question has to be asked how in their methodologies contemporary theology is able to enter into a conversation in which the explicitly theological source (Bible) is a past text.

A further, searching, question to their approach has been posed by William Romanowski and Jennifer L. Vander Heide.[13] They argue, also in critical dialogue with Robert K. Johnston, that the premise that one can somehow bracket out one's commitments in order to 'take a film on its own terms' is misguided. They note that the whole 'dialogue' approach to theology and film makes too many unwarranted assumptions about the capacity, or wisdom, of viewers' temporarily suspending pre-existing beliefs and values. Viewers do not, in other words, switch off the cognitive worlds within which they live in order to watch a film. On the contrary, they need them in order to be able to understand anything. The dialogical approach is thus in danger of devaluing the theological worlds out of which religious viewers come.

Romanowski and Vander Heide are surely right in their critique. The emphasis on 'taking a film on its own terms', has, however, been necessary in theology and film debate simply so that the theological side of the dialogue is not *over*emphasized. Where theology may ultimately be the primary interest,[14] this can all too easily occur. Working with a notion of film as dialogue-partner means listening to what a film is saying, while also respecting how it works and what it does to and for a viewer. A film may be religious, of course. 'Taking it on its own terms' then means clarifying what it is saying about its religious theme. Many more films are not explicitly religious and yet invite theological reflection on them, because they are about human being, hope, redemption, community or whatever. The Jewett–Kreitzer–Johnston approach is simply designed to ensure that a film 'speaks' in whatever way it can speak, so that, when a theological conversation is then conducted/overheard, once a legitimate juxtaposition of film and theological theme occurs, each can have its full say.

Theological reflection on film thus understood merely highlights the complexity of theology as a discipline. Theology works with themes, contemporary formulations of those themes (authoritative and exploratory), authoritative texts (including scriptures), life experience (as carried by believers who go and watch films) and all manner of cultural resources (art and popular culture, including film). The notion of film as dialogue-partner for theology thus highlights this way of working. The 1997 collection of essays *Explorations in Theology and Film*[15] sought to acknowledge all of this. More than a decade later the untidiness of Part Two of that volume, in which different methodologies were at work, and a neat 'systematic' series of essays of theological themes did not materialize, can now be seen as a virtue. A systematic theology of film is simply not possible. But a systematic theology, worked out in dialogue with all sorts of films, whose challenges to film both sharpen and develop theology's content, and demands that there are loose ends, might be. Gerard Loughlin has spoken of the danger of 'ventriloquism' here and his point is well-made. Talk of dialogue veils the fact that the films do not 'speak for themselves' in such dialogue, as the theological interpreters are always providing both voices.[16] True though this is, it is but a challenge to theologians to work with integrity. The 'real dialogues' which Loughlin hopes for are perhaps harder to record than Loughlin acknowledges.

A final trajectory in theology and film debate is that produced by attention to audience reception, through recognition that film-watching often happens in a religion-like way. John Lyden brought this especially to the fore in *Film as Religion*.[17] What, though, is the significance of this work, and the related work of Marsh[18] for *theology* and film? Similar to the way that Schrader and Loughlin's work shifts attention from films as director's stories towards films as aesthetic products, so Lyden's and Marsh's work moves the debate away from the use of film only for themes to the way that films work on audiences. Here, though, especially in the work of Marsh, the emphasis is on the *affective* dimension of film-watching.[19] The more that attention is paid to how films work affectively, the more film-watching is seen to be religion-like. Theology, then, has to take account of this. In the same way that theology, while a cognitive, rational discipline, has to work out what it does with worship and all other forms of religious *practice*, so also theological reflection on film has to take account of the multiple dimensions of the *experience* of film-watching. Theology is felt as well as thought. Were this not so it could not be an existential discipline. But it is not simply a distillation in cognitive form of a series of feelings. One no more analyses simply what happens when one feels fear, joy, sadness in watching a film, and then calls it theology, than itemizes a list of feelings drawn from participation in an act of religious worship. But to neglect all such features (in the cinema and the church, synagogue, temple or mosque) in the articulation of a doctrine of hope, redemption or creation, would be to sell theology short. As Miles rightly notes: 'A tradition that has persisted since the West was founded as a cultural and intellectual entity rejects empathic emotion as a method for learning and insight'.[20] Part of theology's task today, in interacting with film, is to oppose such neglect.

All of this does not, though, yet tell us how theology can both take account of the affective in doing its cognitive work, or how it can attend to what is actually happening for contemporary film-viewers. Theological exploration of film cannot make do with what viewers, religious or otherwise, are doing with religious film, with what religious viewers are doing with films, or with what critics, theologians or anyone else *think* that viewers are doing with film. As audience reception work is making clear, more empirical data are needed here.[21] Suffice it to say that while theology and film will always have to wrestle with the temptation to focus on what the already religious bring to film, so that what is seen in film or enjoyed as part of the film-watching experience is merely 'confirmed' by the analysis, there is yet more to be explored.

More demanding, both for theologians and anti-theological cultural critics alike, however, is the recognition that as with many other forms of art and popular culture, films are functioning as a meaning-making medium across many different societies throughout the world. The content of the theology, indeed theologies, being worked with in the midst of such interaction is difficult to grasp because of technological advances, and accelerating individualism, especially throughout the West. How, for example, can any church keep a check on what its believers actually believe when whatever beliefs and ideas they hold are being stimulated daily by a diverse package of media influence?[22] Orthodoxy was slippery anyway. It is even more slithery now.

But theology, Truth and truths will always remain close friends and refuse to accept that, while all is indeed relative, relativism is all that there is. What people are doing with film, then, is still searching for something which might once have carried the label 'truth', even while the main espoused purpose for being in the cinema is to be 'entertained'.[23] Deep in the midst of the practice of consuming the arts and popular culture, meaning is still being found and made. It will be ever so.

Prospects for Theology and Film

Where does this leave theology and film today? It is important to stress that the four trajectories just identified are not to be seen as a sliding scale of gradual development. They all still do, and should, exist simultaneously. But each of the four has particular emphases – the first two on the film and what/who lies behind it, and third and fourth on what is done in front of a film by those who view it. Each needs the others so that all of the dimensions of film-watching are addressed.[24] Each needs to critique the other.

But if there is one theme that needs highlighting in the present, then it is the role of the imagination. Robert Pope has brought this to the fore recently.[25] We need not be speaking here specifically of the religious imagination, for the importance of the function of the imagination in the reception of film is clear in film studies and the philosophy of film.[26] Pope leans, in my view, too much towards a position which (ab)uses film through presupposing a rather isolated cultivation of the religious imagination, which is then 'applied' to the film-watching practice. Thus, despite many helpful insights in his work, he remains much too close, without realizing it, to the first trajectory, without gleaning much from the other three. That said, Pope's efforts to do justice to how films work do mean that his study stands as a challenge to theology to do more than it often has with the imagination. There is more to Pope's critique of theology's overdependence on text, and on film as text, than even his own study suggests. In the same way that media entertainment proves to be a site of 'imaginative possibility, without which we would be unable to try new models, new roles, new theories, new combinations of behaviour',[27] so theology's attention to film invites creative, imaginative use of all that films actually achieve on the part of viewers.

The fact that already-religious viewers are no different from a-, non- or anti-religious viewers in so far as films work on people's bodies, emotions and minds simultaneously emphasizes the public character of theology.[28] Exploration of who/what God is happens in public. And all of the topics in which theology is interested, as was seen as the start of this article, happens in public as well as within religious communities. Religious communities participate in the public debate, while doing their best to maintain a consistent position on what/who they believe God to be. The question whether the imaginative work which is undertaken, when watching film and undertaking theological enquiry is 'mere imagination' lies well beyond the scope of this article. But it *is* imaginative work nevertheless. It is not different in kind from what any human being does. The deeper, more searching, question is how and why such imaginative theological enquiry might need to be explicit for human beings to be fully human. If the exploration of film could end up addressing that question, in public, and with the involvement of all the academic disciplines needed for such fully inter-disciplinary investigation to occur, then it would prove not just to be an academic exercise, or a matter of interests to a few enthusiasts. It might even prove existentially, socially and politically valuable.

6 Movies: The Retelling of Religious Stories

William L. Blizek and Julien R. Fielding

Stories are an important part of every culture. They allow us to pass on ideas and values to future generations. They influence us in a way that the lecture and sermon do not. When parents read bedtime stories to their children or when we listen to a story told around the campfire, we also make a significant connection with other human beings. And, maybe most importantly, stories are just plain fun, even when they scare us or make us cry. Many of us, and not only children, like to listen to stories and often to the same story over and over again.

If stories are an important part of culture, then movies also will be an important part of culture because movies are the telling of stories. Indeed, we often say of a favourite director that he or she is a great story teller and sometimes when we criticize a film we do so because the story does not hang together.[1] When we take seriously the idea that movies are stories, then one important connection between religion and film will be the connection between movies and the telling of religious stories. Milos Forman's *One Flew Over the Cuckoo's Nest* (1975) and Stuart Rosenberg's *Cool Hand Luke* (1967) can be seen as retelling the Jesus story.[2] Milos Forman's *Amadeus* (1984) can be interpreted as the story of Cain and Abel and movies like Mimi Leder's *Deep Impact* (1998) or Terry Gilliam's *Twelve Monkeys* (1995) or Roland Emmerich's *Independence Day* (1996) can be seen as retelling the story of 'the end of days'.[3] Robert Zemeckis' *Cast Away* (2000) parallels the story of the Buddha and William Wyler's *Roman Holiday* (1953) roughly follows the story of Krishna and Radha.

The importance of movies for telling religious stories, however, takes on new significance when we see movies as offering more than just particular religious stories. In one of the earliest texts on religion and film, *Screening the Sacred*, Joel Martin and Conrad E. Ostwalt, Jr., argue that religions include theology, ideology and mythology.[4] If we take seriously the idea that religions offer myths we can expand on the idea of movies telling particular religious stories. That is, movies can make available to those who view them some of the myths of religion. We might take this idea even further and claim that religious stories can become religious myths and then that religious myths can become myths that transcend particular religions and become part of the culture as a whole. That movies make transcending myths available in our culture gives the connection between religion and film an even greater reach. When we widen the scope of retelling religious stories to the telling of transcendent myths, the realm of religion and film grows considerably larger. A great many more movies become the subject of religion than we would ordinarily think of as connected to religion when we include the transcendent myth.

Consider one of the most well-known stories of the Judeo-Christian tradition, the story of David and Goliath. (I Samuel, Chapter 17) The Bible story goes like this:

> (4) And there went out a champion out of the camp of the Philistines, named Goliath, of Gath, whose height *was* six cubits and a span.
> (5) And *he had* a helmet of brass upon his head, and he *was* armed with a coat of mail; and the weight of the coat *was* five thousand shekels of brass.
> (6) And he *had* greaves of brass upon his legs, and a target of brass between his shoulders.
> (7) And the staff of his spear *was* like a weaver's beam; and his spear's head *weighed* six hundred shekels of iron: and one bearing a shield went before him.
> (8) And he stood and cried unto the armies of Israel, and said unto them, Why are ye come out to set *your* battle in array? *am* not I a Philistine, and ye servants to Saul? choose you a man for you, and let him come down to me.
> (9) If he be able to fight with me, and to kill me, then will we be your servants: but if I prevail against him, and kill him, then shall ye be our servants, and serve us.
> (48) And it came to pass, when the Philistine arose, and came and drew nigh to meet David, that David hasted, and ran toward the army to meet the Philistine.
> (49) And David put his hand in his bag, and took thence a stone, and slang *it*, and smote the Philistine in his forehead, that the stone sunk into his forehead; and he fell upon his face to the earth.[5]

The story of David and Goliath is one of the most popular stories from the Bible and we might expect that it would be retold on film in a variety of ways. Some of the details of the story do not seem to be important for the retelling, such as the fact that Goliath's spear head 'weighed six hundred shekels of iron'; what does seem to be important is the fact that Goliath was large and well protected, and that David had no weapon but his slingshot. Despite the odds, David prevails. Here is a religious story about the history of the

Israelites and the Philistines that becomes a religious myth about the courage of a young man who protects his people from the enemy. When the myth transcends its religious origin, it becomes the story of the little guy who defeats the much larger bully, and it is this triumph that people of all faiths can find attractive. When the literal story of David and Goliath becomes a myth that transcends its religious origins, we have a popular story that can be told over and over again and told on film.

One movie that tells a variation on the David and Goliath story is David Anspaugh's *Hoosiers* (1986), which is based on the true story of how, in 1954, a small town basketball team overcame insurmountable odds to win the Indiana State Basketball Championship. Representing David in Hoosiers is Coach Norman Dale, a man with a chequered past and no reputation for success. His obstacles include the high school faculty, undisciplined players, second guessing parents and a former player turned alcoholic who helps the coach lead this small-town team to victory against the most powerful schools in the state. The obstacles facing the team in *Hoosiers* are as colossus as Goliath and as seemingly impenetrable as his armour. The coach has no weapons, except perhaps his former player. In the end, David defeats Goliath.[6]

Another movie that retells the story of David and Goliath is Steven Soderbergh's *Erin Brockovich* (2000), which is based on the true story of Erin Brockovich's fight against Pacific Gas & Electric. Erin Brockovich is an unemployed single mother who takes on a multi-billion dollar utility company for polluting the city's water supply. One would be hard-pressed to find someone who has less power than an unemployed single mother, and you cannot get much bigger or more powerful than a multi-billion dollar energy company. When Erin is unable to win a lawsuit for damages she suffered in an automobile accident, she talks her attorney, Ed Masry, into giving her a job as a legal assistant to help cover her expenses. As she carries out her new duties, she discovers that Pacific Gas & Electric is trying to buy up land on which the company has been illegally dumping hexavalent chromium, a carcinogenic compound. Erin convinces her boss to bring a class action suit (is this David's slingshot?) against Pacific Gas & Electric. In the end the utility company is required to pay damages to those who have been harmed by the company's illegal behaviour – 'and he fell upon his face to the earth'. Against all odds, Erin Brockovich prevails against the big bad bully, Pacific Gas & Electric.

When we look at other movies that show a little guy overcoming great odds to defeat a giant of an enemy, we move away from what can be construed as the story of David and Goliath toward the general myth. The general myth requires much less detail than the retelling of a specific religious story. Here we might include John G Avildsen's *Rocky* (1976), which is the story of a small-time boxer who gets a million-to-one shot at becoming a champion.

Actually, Rocky Balboa does not become the champ until *Rocky II* (1979), which is directed by Sylvester Stallone. While the obstacles that Rocky has to overcome may have more to do with Rocky than his opponent, he is challenged by his opponent Apollo Creed in very much the same way as David is challenged by Goliath. By now the movie, *Rocky*, has become a franchise. The latest in this series of films is the 2006 *Rocky Balboa*, directed again by Stallone. Whatever happens in the individual movies, Rocky has become a legend, an American icon, a symbol, and a myth in his own right. Whatever he is doing in particular films, the character Rocky represents the little guy doing battle with larger, more powerful forces in the world.

In Steven Zaillian's *A Civil Action* (1998) we see a successful lawyer, Jan Schlichtmann, who stands up for families whose children have died of leukaemia as a result of toxic waste being dumped into the water supply by a company that produces leather. Proving that the leather company is responsible for the deaths of the children almost bankrupts Jan's law firm, but he persists and finally wins the suit against the company. Since Schlichtmann is a very successful lawyer prior to representing the parents, it may be difficult to think of him as a David figure. It can be argued, however, that after he has spent all of his money on the case that he has become a little guy or it might be argued that he is the slingshot and that the families of the children represent David. These details, however, seem less important in interpreting the movie than the fact that some little guy prevails against the big and powerful enemy.

Similarly, in David Lynch's *The Straight Story* (1999) the little guy overcomes great obstacles to achieve his goal – reconciling with his ailing brother. The problems that Alvin Straight faces as he rides his lawn mower from Iowa to Wisconsin may be seen as the big bad enemy in this movie. This is quite different than other David and Goliath movies, but since we have moved from the specifics of the David and Goliath story to the larger myth of the little guy overcoming great odds to be successful in his quest, *The Straight Story* can be considered another retelling of this transcendent myth.

A few additional examples of the David and Goliath story include *The Insider* (1999), a research chemist risks everything when he takes on Big Tobacco; *Michael Clayton* (2007), an in-house 'fixer' who helps to bring down a corrupt agrochemicals company; and the most recent *Flash of Genius* (2008), which is based on the true story of Robert Kearns, a Detroit professor who invented the intermittent windshield wiper in the 1960s. After the Ford Motor Company stole his invention, Kearns spent 30 years fighting them in the courts.

What the examples above show is that many movies can be seen as the retelling of the David and Goliath story, and that many more movies can be seen as the retelling of the larger myth that emerges from the story of David and Goliath. The connection between religion and film grows exponentially when movies are seen as the retelling of religious stories, religious myths and then as myths that transcend particular religions. The connection between religious story and transcendent myth, and the use of movies to express the transcendent myth is one reason for the great popularity of the study of religion and film.

Another biblical story that we find retold in film is that of Job, the blameless and upright man, who, the Bible tells us, 'feared God, and eschewed evil' (Job 1:1).[7] A wealthy man, Job is also blessed with seven sons and three daughters, many servants and plenty of livestock. Despite the fact that he is a 'model' human, God allows Satan to test him, by essentially taking away and destroying everything he has. When Job persists 'in his integrity', Satan ratchets up the attacks by inflicting Job with 'sore boils on Job from the sole of his foot to his crown' (Job 2:7). Despite his intense suffering, Job rejects his wife's suggestion to 'curse God, and die' (2:9). Job does, however, have questions about his ill-treatment, and he calls upon God to appear before him.

'I will say to God, Do not condemn me; show me wherefore you contendest this with me. *Is it* good unto thee that thou shouldest oppress, that thou shouldest despise the work of thine hands and shine upon the counsel of the wicked?' (10:2–3)

God appears to Job; however, he fails to apologize for his actions. Instead he reveals a complex world in which the universe is an 'unfolding process in which light and dark, gentle and savage, good and evil are intrinsic components'.[8] After all of his trials and tribulations, Job is rewarded by God. 'And the LORD turned the captivity of Job, when he prayed for his friends: also the LORD gave Job twice as much as he had before' (42:10). As scholar David J. A. Clines explains, 'The book of Job is the most consistently theological work in the *Hebrew Bible*, being nothing but an extended discussion of one theological issue, the question of suffering'.[9] Not only does it deal with the very real question of suffering – why do we suffer – but it also demonstrates how we should react in the face of suffering.

To find a cinematic equivalent of Job, we can turn to any number of Holocaust films, in which we encounter 'innocent' men and women who are thrust into a nightmarish world for no rational reason. Like Job, they are 'tested' by a Satan – represented by sadistic Nazi guards – and despite losing everything, including family members, friends, their homes and more, they persevere, never giving up hope or their humanity.[10] In Roman Polanski's *The Pianist* (2002), which is based on Wladyslaw Szpilman's memoirs, the protagonist, a successful Jewish pianist, lives with his family in 1930s and 1940s Warsaw in Poland. Over time, the Nazis impose stricter and more repressive measures on the Polish Jews, from relocating them to a Warsaw ghetto to sending them to concentration camps. Because of his fame, and perhaps by sheer luck, Szpilman always finds someone who offers him a helping hand, thus allowing him to escape the fate of his family and friends. This does not mean that suffering eludes him. Quite the contrary, at one point, the skeletal man is severely malnourished and suffering from jaundice. The man who was supposed to watch over him and bring him food saw the pianist as nothing more than an opportunity to amass a small fortune.

Szpilman endures many horrors but, perhaps ironically, he is spared by a sympathetic Nazi who brings him food and even offers the world-weary man his coat.[11] 'During the confrontation . . . a dumbfounded Szpilman asks why the former had saved him. The officer takes no credit for himself, somewhat cautiously proffering instead that God has meant for him to survive. The answer jars not only with the status of its proclaimer but also with all the atrocities witnessed in the film'.[12] In this moment, we see the absurdity of Szpilman's situation. As A. O. Scott of the New York Times writes Szpilman has come to resemble 'one of Samuel Beckett's gaunt existential clowns, shambling through a barren, bombed-out landscape clutching a jar of pickles. He is like a walking punchline to a cosmic jest of unfathomable cruelty'.[13] At the film's conclusion, Szpilman has resumed his life, playing piano. Before an audience in Warsaw, he performs Chopin.

Although *The Pianist* is not an exact retelling of the Job story, we can find certain shared elements. For example, like Job, Szpilman is a sympathetic, blessed man who loses everything, including his family, his home and his possessions. Szpilman, too, undergoes mental and physical suffering, and yet we can find no reason for his suffering. 'God', in the form of director Roman Polanski, remains silent on this issue. And like Job, after his ordeal, Szpilman has his fortunes restored. He performs once again before adoring crowds. The stories differ on one significant point – unlike Job, Szpilman is much more resigned to his fate. 'He is neither an especially heroic nor an entirely sympathetic fellow, and by the end he has been reduced to a nearly animal condition – sick, haggard and terrified'.[14] He is not the defiant man, asking God to respond to issues of injustice.

A 'Holocaust film' but of a different variety, Volker Schlondorff's *Der Neunte Tag* or *The Ninth Day* (2004) focuses not on the suffering of a Jew but on the suffering of a Catholic priest. Loosely based on Father Jean Bernard's memoir, *Pfarrenblock 25487*, the film centres on Henri Kremer, a dissident Catholic priest who is interred at Dachau with several other priests. That is until a Gestapo officer arranges for him a nine-day furlough. While he is 'free', Kremer is instructed to try and persuade the staunchly anti-Nazi bishop of Luxembourg to capitulate to Nazi occupation. If he is successful, Kremer is told, he will be released. As the film progresses, Kremer's physical suffering gives way to emotional suffering. He is told that should he try to escape, his comrades in Dachau will be killed. His pregnant sister and her husband are also threatened. This 'man of God' faces excruciatingly difficult ethical questions, but rather than save himself, in the end Father Kremer refuses to capitulate. He returns to the camp, bringing with him a sausage, which he shares with his fellow 'inmates'. Like Job, Father Kremer is a moral, upstanding man of God who is made to suffer for no rational reason. Kremer, too, has his 'Satan' in the guise of Gestapo Untersturmfuhrer Gebhardt, a young and ruthless lapsed seminarian who is driven by his quest for power. But what is interesting when comparing the stories is that God 'tests' Job by taking everything away; and Father Kremer is 'tested' by being tempted by the promise of getting everything back. Although we never see it, we are told that the man on whom Father Kremer is based survived his ordeal and 'in 1945 he wrote the book upon which this film is based'.

The Pursuit of Happyness (2006), which is based on a true story, contains a Job-like figure in Chris Gardner, an intelligent, hard-working medical equipment salesman who decides that the best way to build a better life for his family is to take a six-month long, unpaid internship. The odds are stacked against him, though. Because he has had little luck selling his bone density scanners, on which he spent his life savings, he owes several months rent, back taxes and many parking tickets. Fed up with their poverty-afflicted life, his wife leaves him. His situation only worsens from here: he is evicted, and he ends up living in a hotel. After he is evicted again, he and his son go from living in a public restroom to a homeless shelter. Despite the odds stacked against him he perseveres, telling his son 'don't ever let anyone tell you that you can't do something – even me'. Although *The Pursuit of Happyness* is not quite as obvious as a retelling of the story of Job, the film shows a suffering protagonist who never loses 'faith'.[15] Because of his persistence, he, like Job, is rewarded. Gardiner is hired as a stockbroker at Dean Witter, and, as we read at the end of the film, he went on to found the investment firm Gardner Rich. Almost twenty years later, in 2006, he sold a minority stake in his brokerage firm in a multi-million dollar deal.

Once again, as the match between religious story and movie becomes less precise, the story moves from specific story to more general story or myth and when the match becomes even less precise the religious myth can become a cross cultural/religious myth that is available to everyone. The specific story of Job becomes the general story of an innocent man and how he deals with suffering, a topic in which people of differing religions take interest.

Looking to the Bible once again, we find another story that seems to translate well to cinema – that of Moses, which one finds recounted in books Exodus through Deuteronomy. Moses was born during a time of persecution. 'The Egyptians became ruthless in imposing tasks on the Israelites and made their lives bitter with hard service . . .' (Exodus 1:13–14). Fearing the Israelites, the kings of Egypt told the Hebrew midwives to kill every male baby (1:16). Moses, of course, did not suffer this fate. His mother placed him into a papyrus basket and sent it down the Nile (2:3). The daughter of Pharaoh, who was bathing, saw the basket, asked her maid to bring it to her, took pity on the crying child, and took him as her son (2:5–10). As an adult, Moses is called upon by God to lead his people out of bondage (3:1–12), which he accomplishes thanks to a series of signs and plagues (7:14–12:50). Once Moses and his people depart, they are pursued by Pharaoh. Moses escapes harm by parting the Red Sea (14:21–25). Commanded by God, Moses then causes the waters to return, thereby drowning Pharaoh's army (14:28).

The next stage of the story finds our hero and his people wandering in the wilderness. While they wait below, Moses communicates with God on Mount Sinai, where he receives a series of laws, most notably The Ten Commandments (Exodus 20).

Although these story details are important to the biblical story, they are frequently absent when the myth becomes cinematic. What we find instead are Moses figures; heroes who lead, often reluctantly, their people out of bondage to a promised land, or at least offer them the hope of a promised land. Just a few examples of a Moses figure include Morpheus in *The Matrix* (1999), Spartacus in the film of the same name (1960), Maximus in *Gladiator* (2000), William Wallace in *Braveheart* (1995), Benjamin Martin in *The Patriot* (2000) and, if one can make a leap, the Rev. Frank Scott in *The Poseidon Adventure* (1972).

In *The Matrix*, Morpheus explains that human beings are no longer free, but are born and grown in pod-filled fields for the sole purpose of providing energy for machines. In the story of Moses, the Israelites, too, are slaves, providing 'hard service in mortar and brick and in every kind of field labor' (Exodus 1:14). In *The Matrix*, humans are complacent in this condition, because they are blissfully unaware of the truth that everything they see and experience is a false reality. As Morpheus says, everyone is 'born into bondage. Into a prison that you cannot taste or see or touch. A prison for your mind'. Morpheus must find the One, a messiah of sorts who will free humanity from bondage and lead them to the last free city on Earth, to Zion. In this capacity, Morpheus is a Moses-like figure.

Spartacus, Maximus, William Wallace and Benjamin Martin have similar stories. All are living under a repressive regime – Spartacus and Maximus, who are both slaves, live under a decadent and morally bankrupt Rome; Wallace and Martin live under a corrupt and 'sadistic' Britain – and all four men lead a group of oppressed peoples to 'freedom' or at least take them on the path to freedom. In *The Poseidon Adventure*, a passenger ship is hit by a tidal wave that flips it over. The Rev. Frank Scott leads a small group of people through a variety of obstacles to safety.

What is particularly interesting about these Moses-like figures is that they could also be labelled as Christ-like figures or saviour figures, as all of these characters lead followers out of harm or bondage in much the same way we think of Jesus or a saviour doing the same.[16] What might make them more Christ-like is the fact that most of the aforementioned protagonists die so that others may live; they are self-sacrificing. For instance, at the end of *The Poseidon Adventure*, the Rev. Frank Scott engages in a dialogue with God, asking him, while he is hanging onto a steam valve: 'What more do you want of us? We've come all this way, no thanks to you. We did it on our own, no help from you. We did ask you to fight for us but damn it, don't fight against us. Leave us alone. How many more sacrifices? How much more blood? How many more lives? . . . You want another life? Then take me'. After offering some words of encouragement to those he has lead through the ship, he falls into the flaming water below him. Stories about self-sacrificing saviours are ubiquitous in Hollywood, demonstrating that another set of biblical myths have taken root on film.[17]

It is true that the stories about David and Goliath, Job and Moses are frequently reinterpreted for film, but if we look at the horror genre – and often science fiction – we might say that the most popularly mined section of the Bible is the Book of Revelation, which 'concludes' the New Testament. More often than not, these apocalyptic films draw upon imagery that includes the seven seals that when broken bring war, famine and plague upon human-kind (4:1–11:19); the collapse of great cities (17:1–18:24); the rise of a 'beast' that is the personification of lust and cruelty and which threatens humanity (12:1–16:21); and the arrival of a saviour figure who will vanquish 'evil' and usher in a new age (19–20). In these films, the beast might literally be a person, as it is in *The Omen* franchise,[18] or it can be technology, often a 'super computer' as it is in *Demon Seed* (1977),[19] *The Terminator* (1984),[20] *Saturn 3* (1980),[21] *The Matrix* and the *Resident Evil* quadrilogy.[22] The saviour in these films can be either male or female; however, it is increasingly common to see a female as saviour.[23] This, of course, differs from the biblical story. As it has been said, many horror films take their cue from the Book of Revelation and reveal to the audience an apocalyptic or post-apocalyptic world that is beset by plagues, lawlessness, misery, inhumanity, chaos and usually a battle between the forces of good and evil. A small sample of apocalyptic or post-apocalyptic films includes *Children of Men* (2006),[24] *I Am Legend* (2007),[25] *The Seventh Sign* (1988),[26] *The Reaping* (2007),[27] *Doomsday* (2008),[28] and *Blindness* (2008).[29]

Western films draw mainly upon Western myths, usually ones that come from the Bible. Although rare, popular stories from Eastern traditions can be found in Western cinemas. For example, *The Legend of Bagger Vance* (2000) is a story about how a mysterious caddie named Bagger Vance helps a washed-up golfer named Rannulph Junuh to find his authentic swing. Those familiar with the Hindu classic *The Bhagavad-Gītā* will recognize Rannulph Junuh as Arjuna and Bagger Vance as Krishna, who is referred to in the tradition as Bhagavan (the divine one). In both tales, a 'divine' being dispenses important lessons about life and through his guidance gets the protagonist back on track. In 1989, British director Peter Brook made *The Mahabharata*, one of the longest epic poems in the world and a great source of Hindu mythology and philosophy, accessible to Western audiences. Starring an international cast, his adaptation runs more than five-hour long. Another Hindu classic, *The Rāmāyana*, has been retold, although not always accurately, in *A Little Princess* (1995), which itself is based on a novel by Frances Hodgson Burnett.[30]

Written during the Ming Dynasty in China, *The Journey to the West* is a popular epic story found throughout East Asia, where it has been retold in just about every format, from animated series to opera. In this tale, a Buddhist monk is joined by three companions – the Monkey King, Pigsy and Sandy – as they journey from China to India to collect Buddhist sutras. Although most adaptations of this story come from Asia, *The Lost Empire* (2001) and *The Forbidden Kingdom* (2008) prove the exception. The former was made for TV and focuses on an American journalist who has three days to locate an ancient manuscript otherwise the planet will be annihilated. He is joined in his quest by the Goddess of Mercy and the Monkey King. The latter was written by John Fusco and centres on a kung fu-obsessed American teen who, after a fight, wakes up in ancient China where he meets up with a variation of these three strangers. Their quest is to return a magical staff to the Monkey King, who was imprisoned in stone by the evil Jade Warlord. Both are only loosely based on the sixteenth-century classic.

It might be interesting to ask whether particular religious studies come first or whether the cross-religious myth comes first. Do particular religious stories transform into broader cultural myths, or are particular religious stories written as examples of the cross religious myths? Which comes first, the chicken or the egg?

The answer to this question may have significant implications for how we understand religion. But, whichever comes first and then leads to the other, it remains true that people enjoy stories and that movies are often the telling of a good story. It also remains true that the move from specific religious story to general cultural or cross-religious myth increases significantly the number of films considered of interest to religion and film.

7 Religion, Film and Film Theory

Gregory Watkins

Introduction to Film Theory

Film theory is nearly as old as the medium itself. The development of motion pictures at the turn of the twentieth century entailed a kind of necessary self-consciousness about the nature, limits and possibilities of the film medium. J. Dudley Andrew's book, *The Major Film Theories: An Introduction*, has become a standard work in the field for getting a global view of the history and terrain of film theory. Andrew's approach is to look at specific theories in light of four categories which are themselves good organizing principles for any kind of foundational thinking about the film medium: 1 – 'raw material', includes questions about the physical and mechanical nature of the medium itself, about what is seen to be fundamental to the nature of moving images; 2 – 'methods and techniques', looks at anything related to the creative process which 'shapes or treats the raw material, including technological, artistic, and economic developments'; 3 – 'forms and shapes of film', considers the possibilities of the film medium, including questions of adaptation, genre and audience expectation and 4 – 'purpose and value' of cinema, considers the larger questions of cinema's place in culture, society and meaning-making generally. His book is also organized around the now classic distinction between what Andrew calls formative theory and realist or photographic theory, with formative theory constituting the historical first wave of film theory. These two schools of theory are divided by the answer they give to the question of how best to conceive of the essential nature of recording and displaying photographic images in time, especially in the relationship between the object being created (film) and the object being recorded (reality).[1]

Formative theory – Film theorists in the formative tradition were concerned to give film the status of art, arguing that the motion picture camera was more than just a recording device and that the significance of the motion pictures it produced went well beyond the significance of the events it recorded. The general approach to such theory was to draw comparisons to other major art forms[2] while at the same time trying to cast cinema as more than just a bastard child of art forms like theatre and literature. Of course, as film got started, the very novelty of the medium was precisely in capturing reality in time, of recording events in the real world. But as the body of works of cinema grew, it became easier to establish that motion pictures constituted a *transformation* of reality. The cause, nature and effect of this transformation were at the heart of the formalist point of view, for both theorists of film and for filmmakers. By the 1930s, this battle for cinema-as-art was well in hand, theoretically and popularly. Major theorists in this tradition include Hugo Munsterberg,[3] Rudolf Arnheim,[4] Sergei Eisenstein[5] and Béla Balázs.[6]

Realist theory – Although present throughout the development of the formative tradition before coming fully into its own, realist film theory wanted to champion film precisely in its power as a recording device, in being able to show life as life is, whether that be a specifically social reality or some more metaphysical notion of reality as such. As with the formative tradition, developments in realist theory were in part a response to the growing predominance of fiction film, of movies made for their entertainment value. The great power of cinema, these theorists and filmmakers argued, is to show the nature of the reality. In this way, film can be seen as either 1) powerfully capable of documenting the realities being recorded or, more mysteriously, 2) as being uniquely capable of showing us the true nature of the reality around us. Those representing the first category are largely filmmakers in the documentary tradition, while the two major theorists of the realism of the second kind are André Bazin[7] and Siegfried Kracauer.[8]

Beyond the classical binary – In addition to formative and realist theory, Andrew makes mention of certain 'occasional' theorists of film,[9] and he closes his book with a section on contemporary French film theory, with careful looks at Jean Mitry, Christian Metz, and Amédée Ayfre and Henri Agel. The development of French film theory was grounded in a long tradition of a culture of film clubs as well as an early institutionalization of film study in the university. French film theory was also significantly affected by, and developed in, the Journal *Cahiers du Cinéma*,[10] which published articles by intellectuals, filmmakers and other artists. It was in the annals of *Cahiers* that auteur theory developed, a theory that argued for the primacy of the personal vision of the film artist in understanding particular works of film. The development of French film theory also needs to be understood in concert with general developments in philosophy and cultural theory in the same period, namely semiotics, structuralism and phenomenology.

Of course, work on film theory need not be tied so directly to 'essentialist' concerns about the fundamental nature of the film medium. The fact that cinema became the overwhelmingly dominant art form of the twentieth century meant that cultural theories of any variety would eventually take cinema as an express object of study. The organization of a more recent series of volumes on film theory, *Film Theory: Critical Concepts in Media and Cultural Studies*,[11] gives a good indication of the great range of primary subjects in the field of film theory: essence and specificity; language; technologies; authorship; genre; narrative; audiences and spectatorship; personal identities and representation; cultural identities; colonialism and post colonialism; realism and the real; modernism and postmodernism; economics and globalization.

Religion, film and film theory – The vast majority of work on film and religion has made very little use of significant works in film theory proper. This is largely because work on film and religion has 1) tended to focus on what has come to be known as the theological approach,[12] or 2) sees film as an important vehicle for cultural values broadly construed, and therefore of interest to theorists of religion generally.[13] While many other disciplinary approaches have made a great deal of progress integrating with film theory,[14] it largely remains to be seen if the study of religion entails potentially distinctive, or even unique, contributions to the understanding of film theory generally. This is not to say, of course, that works of religious criticism with respect to film have not been sophisticated with respect to the theoretical tools that are put to work in the analysis. Rather, it is precisely that film is often too readily made the object of that particular theoretical or theological point of view without careful consideration of the distinctive nature of the medium. Bringing film theory more solidly into work on religion and film might very well require reversing the direction of analysis by bringing theories about the core nature of film into conversation with various theologies and with the religious criticism of film. There are notable exceptions to this general state of affairs. Three examples of exceptions are Paul Schrader, Francisca Cho and Greg Watkins. A fourth example might be found in the connections between a recent work on film theory, *Reality Transformed: Film as Meaning and Technique*,[15] and the concerns of religion and film work generally. The first exception is a book-length treatment of religion and film by filmmaker and film critic Paul Schrader. *The Transcendental Style in Film*[16] makes an argument for seeing the films of Carl Dreyer, Yasujiro Ozu and Robert Bresson as vehicles for a distinctly cinematic encounter with what Schrader calls 'the transcendent' by way of a shared (and therefore transcultural) style of filmmaking and storytelling. Working with a substantive definition of religion, by way of Rudolf Otto's *The Idea of the Holy*, Schrader argues that the proper function of transcendental art is to express the Holy itself *rather than* express or illustrate Holy feelings.[17] The transcendental style in film achieves this purpose by way of the specific ontology of the film medium. The transcendental style, then, is able to develop cross-culturally because of both the universal desire to express the transcendent[18] and the universal nature of the ontology of film. The film critic's role in this case is to identify the style even though what wants to be expressed is ineffable and invisible.[19] Schrader argues that this transcendental style has three stages. First, it establishes a sense of the 'everyday' – the dull, banal commonplaces of everyday existence:

> In Ozu, the stylization is near complete. Every shot is from the same height, every composition static, every conversation monotone, every expression bland, every cut forthright and predictable. No action is intended as a comment on another, no event leads inexorably to the next. The highpoints of conventional drama, the beginning and the end, are neglected.[20]

This quality of 'everydayness' could be a style in itself,[21] but in the case of the transcendental style, the everyday is 'a prelude to the moment of redemption'.[22] The second stage is called 'disparity', which Schrader describes as 'an actual or potential disunity between man and his environment which culminates in a "decisive action" ' and as 'an outburst of spiritual emotion totally inexplicable within the everyday'.[23] Schrader connects 'disparity' and 'decisive action' to the transcendent in this way:

> The decisive action is the final disparity in an environment which had been becoming more and more disparate. It demands commitment. If a viewer accepts that scene – if he finds it credible and meaningful – he accepts a good deal more. He accepts a philosophical construct which permits total disparity – deep, illogical, suprahuman feeling within a cold, unfeeling environment. In effect, he accepts a construct such as this: there exists a deep ground of compassion and awareness which man and nature can touch intermittently. This, of course, is the Transcendent.[24]

Schrader calls the final stage of this style 'stasis' – 'a frozen view of life which does not resolve the disparity but transcends it'.[25] And the important point about stasis is that it is achieved formally: 'The everyday and disparity are experiential, but stasis is formalistic; it incorporates those emotions into a larger form'.[26] These three great auteurs of cinema (Dreyer, Ozu and Bresson), Schrader argues, make use of distinctive features of the ontology of film to achieve this religious end.

A second important example of this kind of work is that of Francisca Cho. In her article 'Imagining Nothing and Imaging Otherness in Buddhist Film', Cho highlights the unique power of cinema by first challenging the logocentrism of most Western analysis. Indeed, the privileging of text (as word) might be one way of explaining the relative theoretical blindness to film as a distinctive medium in most religion and film work. Certainly most of the good work on religion and film thinks carefully about how film communicates meaning visually, but it is still a logocentric emphasis on meaning, on the worded message of a film, that gets submitted to religious criticism. In her article, Cho proposes what she calls 'a non-ideological, cultic way of viewing film'[27] a way of viewing film integrally tied to the religious subject of the film she analyses – namely, the Chan Buddhism at the centre of Bae Yong-kyun's *Why Has Bodhi-Dharma Left for the East?* (1989). Without rehearsing the argument here, one can get a sense of Cho's thesis in her contrast between ideological modes of film analysis and what she calls the cultic mode of signification. She writes:

> I interpret *Bodhi* as cultic art in which ideological content is subservient to its significance as ritual function. Although rituals usually have ideological content, their 'meaning' is defined more relevantly as an event. The religious significance of these events, since we must attempt to verbalize it in some way, is that they create or manifest a momentous form of 'presence'.[28]

What is particularly exciting in this argument is the way in which film as a medium is given a religious valence at the level of the nature of the medium itself; Bae's Chan Buddhist perspective has allowed viewers to see something about the medium itself that they might not have otherwise seen.[29]

The third example of representative work, 'Seeing and being seen: Distinctively filmic and religious elements in film',[30] uses Stanley Cavell's phenomenological analysis of the film medium as a springboard for appreciation of the religious dimensions of Lars von Trier's *Breaking the Waves* (1996) and Andrey Tarkovsky's *The Sacrifice* (1986). To put it very briefly, Cavell argues[31] that it is part of the ontological nature of modern cinema to give us the experience of being able to see what is not present, a 'world viewed', and yet remain unseen. For Cavell, this ontological fact of cinema lends it its incredible power in modern life precisely because it naturalizes the equally modern experience of feeling disconnected from the world around us. As Cavell puts it:

> It is as though the world's projection [in a movie] explains our forms of unknowness and of our inability to know. The explanation is not so much that the world is passing us by, as that we are displaced from our natural habitation within it, placed at a distance from it. The screen overcomes our fixed distance; it makes displacement appear as our natural condition.[32]

The article tries to show how von Trier and Tarkovsky play with this ontologically unique feature of film precisely to achieve religious ends:

> Von Trier achieves this transformation by the simple technique of the actor looking into the camera. With Andrey Tarkovsky, the particular

combination of the shape of the narrative and the nature of the film medium makes possible its religious potency.[33]

Finally, consider the significance for religion and film work of a relatively recent work on film theory, Irving Singer's *Reality Transformed: Film as Meaning and Technique*. Singer is a professor of philosophy MIT and does not write expressly about religion and film. However, I want to argue that his basic theory of film is potentially valuable for those of us doing work on religion and film in four ways: 1) to a degree, Singer's account of film theory helps explain why work on religion and film tends to avoid film theory as such; 2) he articulates a useful, basic theory of the function and value of cinema by way of a focus on 'transformation' and 'harmonization', concepts which are particularly useful for thinking about the religious dimension of film and 3) the limitations of Singer's theory with respect to religion in particular – in light of the fact that Singer is a humanist and a materialist – suggest a direction for thinking about further theoretical work with respect to religion and cinema.

1) So why is there such little focus on film theory in religion and film work? Singer's own project is to carve out a safe place for humanistic inquiry in the otherwise tangled forest of film theory. To this end, he acknowledges that there is a kind of daunting, technical specialization in the world of film theory that makes it difficult to tackle for most people's purposes. As even my own brief summary of film theory above shows, Singer points out that film theory tends to be jargon-ridden and can be more obfuscating than clarifying. Singer's further claim, however, is that being more sophisticated about film theory does not require tackling head-on the grand theories of film.[34] Singer's central principle is the following: that the goal of art is to harmonize and 'enhance life' through the communication of meaning and that a balanced approach to the two main camps of film theory – the formalists and the realists – can help all focus on that central goal of art. What is striking about this account in relationship to religion and film work is the suggestion that the very absence of theory-specific work points to a pre-existing bias to approach film in the way Singer advocates: namely, with a focus on meaning-making and transformation. If this is correct then Singer's work serves as a way both to conceptualize and to clarify that basic strategy of religion and film analysis. As Singer himself puts it: 'I have wanted to articulate a philosophic perspective that some may find unneeded but others can use to stimulate their own critical ideas about presuppositions that have already become habitual and even encrusted in the profession'.[35]

2) So what is Singer's theory of film? Singer states his basic thesis in the preface:

I believe all art, and cinematic art in particular, is best understood as life-enhancement, and that when we study it for its human import or philosophic scope, as well as for its use of specialized technology, we find that the meanings and techniques in each work are internally related to one another. The meanings in films emanate from the cinematic devices that comprise the diversified nature of the medium. But that itself exists only as a way of expressing and exploring problems that matter to human beings, problems they care about and have to face throughout their lives. Investigation of these problems, both cognitive and affective, is the province of humanistic philosophy and literary studies in general.[36]

In order to do this, Singer needs to clear the theoretical ground of the otherwise embattled dichotomy between formalist and realist. As he puts it:

I mingle elements of both approaches in my idea that film is not inherently a re-presenting or recording of reality but rather a pictorial and usually narrative transformation of it. In developing this suggestion, and above all in my treatment of the movies I analyze, I emphasize that reality as portrayed in film is always a product of formalist techniques and creative innovations that enable some filmmakers to express what he or she considers real in the apparent world.[37]

Singer brings the two theoretical approaches together by way of his focus on transformation, arguing that film becomes an art form by *transforming* what is real instead of merely reproducing or recording it. As Singer puts it: 'to formulate a theory that can use elements of both realism and formalism, we must recognize that cinematic transformations arise from human and organic aptitudes that have a constitutive, not just causal, role in the making of movies'.[38] Even more pointedly, Singer describes what we need to explain about film as a medium[39] in this way: 'To the extent that film has a "language" of its own, it systematically transforms realities internal or external to ourselves, and does so in order to purvey novel perspectives upon those realities'.[40]

The bulk of the work of Singer's book is to explain this theoretical position with reference to three more specific issues related to art and meaning-making: appearance and reality; the visual and the literary; and issues of communication and alienation. He does this by way of analysing three specific films: Woody Allen's *The Purple Rose of Cairo* (1985), Luchino Visconti's adaptation of Thomas Mann's *Death in Venice* (1971) and Jean Renoir's *Rules of the Game* (1939). But it is Singer's early example of Renoir's *The Grand Illusion* (1937) that gives a clear and quick sense of Singer's approach. He starts with the claim that the movie is about the desire to achieve oneness through friendship and love. He then convincingly argues that the medium of film cannot simply duplicate those things; it cannot *duplicate* social, material or spiritual realities. As Singer says:

> The originals can be represented, but only through transformations that adapt them to the needs and circumstances of cinematic art. However great its likeness to some object, no image can have the kind of being that this actuality retains as just the unique and transient entity that it is. Film reproduces reality by recreating it, by transforming it through the visual and auditory technologies designed for that purpose.[41]

In other words, Singer argues, you need both realist and formalist approaches:

> In films we view the world and its reality, but only through the transformations that could not occur without the formalist techniques a filmmaker introduces to convey the thoughts, the feelings, and the overall attitudes expressed in his or her conception.[42]

Ultimately, Singer wants to hold a middle ground on several fronts, which explains his emphasis on *harmonization* throughout his argument. He wants to convince us to see film – when it is working at its best – as the harmonization of formalist and realist understandings of cinema; as the harmonization of spirit and matter in art in general; and as the harmonization of the specific features of appearance and reality, of the visual and the literary, and of communication and alienation. Remarkably, I think the lack of film theory work in religion and film is precisely because we tend to presume this middle ground as viewers and critics. Indeed, Singer argues that these are our natural modes of viewing film in the first place, and, in turn, it is the reason why certain grand theories of cinema can become so quickly misguided.

   3) The third and final point with respect to Singer, however, is to suggest some shortcomings of this theoretical middle ground as it relates to religion and film in particular. If Singer puts 'life-enhancement' at the centre of his understanding of both art in general and film in particular, do we need, then, to take particular care in describing what 'life-enhancement' might mean from the perspective of religion? Does religion fit easily into Singer's model, or do the specific concerns of religious thinking entail a distinct formulation of the theoretical questions – as with, for example, the issue of transcendence? Paul Schrader's analysis of the transcendental style, for example, fits Singer's general model of the interrelationship of both the formal and the real, but Schrader's emphasis on 'the experience of the transcendent' seems to take the issue outside of Singer's more humanistic and materialist sensibilities in a way that suggests a re-evaluation of what constitutes both the formal and the real in Singer's model. Furthermore, Singer's emphasis on

'transformation' – certainly a central concept in religious studies – is in a similar position. Would Singer be just as comfortable with the word 'conversion' for example – and if conversion is something more than, and ultimately different from, transformation as Singer understands it, how does that affect his theoretical model and, in turn, our ultimate understanding of cinema from the perspective of religious studies and religious world views?

The goal of this essay has been the exploration of film theory with the hope that, as more is understood about film theory, the titular question 'what do we need to know about film to understand religion and film' will ultimately move toward understanding what thinking from a religious perspective can teach us about things distinctively cinematic and then toward what the distinctive nature of cinema can teach us about religious thought and customs.

8 Religion and World Cinema

S. Brent Plate

In 1992, the US cultural critic Fredric Jameson published a book on cinema and titled it *The Geopolitical Aesthetic*. Part of his (neo-) Marxist concern was to demonstrate the ways film has become a dominant medium across the world, and how that medium is controlled by market forces, chiefly operating out of the United States and other industrialized nations, especially European. In the same vein, Ella Shohat and Robert Stam argue in their critical 1994 work, *Unthinking Eurocentrism: Multiculturalism and the Media*, how

> The contemporary media shape identity; indeed, many argue that they now exist close to the very core of identity production. In a transnational world typified by the global circulation of images and sounds, goods and people, media spectatorship impacts complexly on national identity and communal belonging. By facilitating an engagement with distant peoples, the media 'deterritorialize' the process of imagining communities. And while the media can destroy community and fashion solitude by turning spectators into atomized consumers or self-entertaining monads, they can also fashion community and alternative affiliations.[1]

There is much to be said about these cultural critiques, and not all of it will be covered here, yet their premises serve as the backdrop to the present chapter. First, that film has had a global impact is a truism, but there is a continuing need to work out the ways that very medium is used by people in the process of constructing, and sometimes denigrating, identity. For the purposes of this chapter, religious identity is translated from Jameson's 'geopolitical aesthetic' into a '*georeligious* aesthetic'. Second, Shohat and Stam are noted upfront as ways to 'unthink' the eurocentrism that unfortunately continues to reside in religion and film studies by highlighting the myriad ways religion and cinema are bound up with each other around the world.

In this chapter, a variety of religious experiences found throughout world cinema are highlighted, specifically in the ways in which religious identity is presented and represented. Along with this, Shohat and Stam's last phrase of the quote is key: that media 'can also fashion community and alternative affiliations'. In this light, this chapter will showcase alternative visions to those of Western-style filmmaking. After a global gambol through cinemas of the world, the chapter ends with a short section that points out how Christianity, and specifically the life of Jesus, is represented in various global cinemas, noting how the visions of Christianity are likewise altered when presented from non-Western audio-visual sources.

Religion in Cinemas Around the World

Some of the early proponents of religion and film studies[2] demonstrated a global, if eclectic, view of where we can find religion in world cinema, though that was basically relegated to films produced in the G8 nations. While these early analyses tended to offer good, strong illuminations about how religion might be revealed within more allegorical and subdued films, and were especially spurred by Paul Tillich's rephrasing of religion in terms of 'ultimate concern', these studies did not go beyond films created in the industrialized world. A number of scholars in recent years have begun to focus on religion in nations whose films have been often unknown in the West. These scholars are attuned to the role of religion in film and have provided more in-depth arguments than can be provided here. The reader is referred to the bibliography for further readings. Much of the general overview in the following draws on these studies, as it simultaneously highlights aspects of the georeligious aesthetic that have yet to be thought through.

Obviously, an all-inclusive list of religion in films and among filmmakers would be impossible to ascertain and include in a single chapter. My aim is to pinpoint several of the more fertile regions and nations around the world that are producing films with strong attention to religious traditions. There will be many films and regions missing from this list, which simply means there is much more work to be done in the academic study of religion and film.

East and Southeast Asia

Japan

The work of Akira Kurosawa and Yasujiro Ozu in Japan has been well trod, and deservedly so, as they have produced some of the greatest films in the history of cinema. From Kurosawa's earlier *Rashomon* (1950), *Ikiru* (1952) and *Seven Samurai* (1954) to *Ran* (1985) and *Dreams* (1990), the frailty and ineptitude of humanity, often in relation to the overpowering forces of nature, are worked through, just as characters seem to search for some meaning in and through their physical experiences. Ozu's later work is often considered 'more Japanese' than his contemporary Kurosawa, especially since Kurosawa drew on Western filmmaking techniques as well as Western stories. For example, *Ran* was an adaptation of *King Lear*. Two themes throughout Ozu's oeuvre are a focus on family relations (for example, *An Inn in Tokyo*, 1935; *The Brothers and Sisters of the Toda Family*, 1941; etc.) and the passing of seasons (for example, *Late Spring*, 1949; *Early Spring*, 1956; *Early Autumn*, 1961), each with perennial religious implications. But it was his later work, beginning around 1950, that his style shifted to a sparse, reduced work, what Paul Schrader would later discuss as exemplifying the 'transcendental style'. Schrader defines this style for the way it 'seeks to maximize the mystery of existence. . . . Transcendental style, like the mass, transforms experiences into a repeatable ritual which can be repeatedly transcended'.[3]

One of the greatest living filmmakers to arise in Japan in the wake of Kurosawa and Ozu is Hirokazu Kore-eda. Films such as *Maborosi* (1995) and *Nobody Knows* (2004) penetrate many of same small-scale happenings in people's familial lives that Ozu sought to portray, leaving the viewer to grapple with loss, abandonment and a search for hope.[4] Meanwhile, Kore-eda's *After Life* (1998) deals with religious questions in a much more direct way as the story is set in a kind of limbo. The recently deceased gather in a schoolhouse and are offered one week to reconstruct a single memory from their life, and then they will spend eternity living that memory out.

Comment on contemporary film in Japan cannot neglect the huge industry of *anime*. The theme of apocalypse tends to be a constant in many of these films, as well as strange and profound linkages between the organic and mechanical, the human and the machine. The list here would be immense, but a couple films of interest are Hideaki Anno's two *Neon Genesis Evangelion* films (1997), and Katsuhiro Otomo's *Akira* (1988). Hayao Miyazaki arguably holds the title as the greatest *anime* director, and his *Princess Mononoke* (1997), *Spirited Away* (2001) and *Howl's Moving Castle* (2004) have all found their way into a generally popular Western theatres. Like many US-produced animation films, Miyazaki's storylines often follow a hero mythological structure, sprinkled with many references to Shinto deities.[5]

Korea

In recent years, Korea has emerged on the global scene with big-budget, skilfully honed films. Among this newer wave of films has been what some refer to as the 'Buddhist theme' film, especially those created by Bae Yong-gyun, Im Kwon-Taek, Chang Sonu and Ki-Duk Kim.[6] Such films are not only religiously significant because they refer to Buddhist themes, but also because they evoke something of a Buddhist way of viewing films. The films themselves evoke what Francisca Cho, has called a 'cultic mode' of viewing, whereby 'ideological content is subservient to its significance as ritual function', as the religious significance creates 'a momentous form of "presence" '.[7] Bae's *Why Has the Bodhi-Dharma Left for the East?* (1989), Im's *Sopyonje* (1993) and *Come Come Come Upward* (1989), Chang's *Passage to Buddha* (1993) and Ki-Duk's

Spring, Summer, Autumn, Winter . . . and Spring (2003) all are examples of films that point to such presence, and offer alternative forms of seeing to those from Western environments.

China

The section on Chinese film offered here is barebones, despite the enormous film production of the world's most populous country. As with all other nations, this is due to the relations between politics, religion and filmmaking. With the changing political situation in China, the formerly atheistic stance of the central government has shifted. Nonetheless, the linkage between the vibrant, creative and even subversive potentials of 'art' and 'religion' has been severed, and many contemporary artists and filmmakers do not see religion in a progressive light in a way other artists from other parts of the world might.

The New Cinema Movement in China has made a huge impact on the international film scene in the last two decades, occasionally incorporating Taoist and Confucian elements. Zhang Yimou's earlier films have tended to stand in opposition to the Chinese central government, as well as traditional familial structures, such as in *Ju Dou* (1990). Meanwhile, Taoist issues arise in director Chen Kaige's *King of the Children* (1987). And one Chinese diasporic film worth noting is the Chinese-Canadian filmmaker Julia Kwan's debut feature, *Eve and the Fire Horse* (2005), in which the young 'Eve' struggles in her hybrid home in British Columbia, working between Confucian, Christian, Buddhist and other values.

Australasia

In Australia, Peter Weir has emerged as one of the most prominent film-makers on the continent, and around the world. Yet his early works like *Picnic at Hanging Rock* (1975) offer a somewhat different perspective, leading an Australian scholar to suggest that Weir's work contributes to the creation of a cinematic 'mystical gaze'.[8] Other Australian films interested in religious subjects include Nicholas Parsons's *Dead Heart* (1996) and the Christian-Aboriginal conflicts in Tracey Moffatt's *Nice Coloured Girls* (1987). From another standpoint, David MacDougall's ethnographic work within Aboriginal culture, such as *Transfer of Power* (1986), offer intriguing examinations of cultural differences, and MacDougall has been prolifically thinking through the issues of visual representation in his films and writings.[9]

Notable New Zealand films with religious interests include the works of Jane Campion: *An Angel at My Table* (1990), *The Piano* (1993) and *Holy Smoke!* (1999). Cross-cultural conflicts between Maoris, whites and others get taken up in Lee Tamahori's *Once Were Warriors* (1994) and Gregor Nicholas's *Broken English* (1996). This is to say nothing of the *Lord of Rings* trilogy taken on by former horror-film director Peter Jackson.

Indonesia

Cinema is constantly bound by politics, whether filmmakers are 'political' or not. The case of Indonesia is an instructive one in this regard, since politics, religion and an oppressive regime can make for difficult film history, and many early films have been 'lost'. As the world's most populous Muslim country the films produced there naturally take on issues of Islamic life, often mixing, merging and otherwise commingling with other traditions, notably communism and the older Hindu and Buddhist influences on the archipelago. Significantly, taken from a broad perspective, the practices and beliefs of 'Islam' are not outlined or simply worked through[10] but instead understand how political, economic, and, more importantly, everyday life occurs among people who are Muslim.

Historically, we can point toward the pioneering film director Usmar Ismail, and especially his establishment of the Perfini production company that enabled many future Indonesian filmmakers to take up pertinent local and global issues. The director D. Djayakusuma, working with Perfini in the 1950s, made films dealing with traditional cultures and conflicts that arise when confronted with other traditions. His *Tiger from Tjampa* (1953) is infused with a mixture of Islamic philosophy and traditional rituals of self-defence (*silat*). Into the 1970s, new filmmakers emerged with new foci, especially in light of living within the 'New Order' as dictated by Suharto, and the massive censorship laws that followed. The Soviet-trained filmmaker Sjuman Djaya made *Atheis* (1974) which dealt with the problems in reconciling Islam and an atheistic Marxism. Musicals, which tended to be syntheses of a variety of musical and filmic genres (Indian, Arabic and Indonesian) emerged in the 1970s and 80s, and included multiple mythological references. The actor and writer Rhoma Irama was censored for years because the Islamic understandings he provided were not in adherence with those of the state. And ultimately, another genre of filmmaking emerged in the 1980s and 90s, based on the pre-Islamic Hindu and Buddhist mythologies that have continued to exert their influence on the arts making practices of Indonesia.

South and Southwest Asia

India

Cinema based in India ('Bollywood' – Hindi films and others), because of its enormity and because mythological themes are so intertwined in Indian cultures, is almost impossible to classify. Indian film history is steeped in stories from ancient sacred texts and/or stories of Hindu saints (often classified as 'mythologicals' and 'devotionals', respectively), and today's *masala* films often incorporate many of these narratives, weaving them into song and dance routines, domestic drama and action-adventure sequences.[11]

The father of Indian film industry, D. G. Phalke, has described his experience of watching Western Christian mythological films in the 1910s and being inspired to begin screening the Hindu pantheon; to make Indian myths, in India, in reaction to the European cinema. The first feature film ever made in India was Phalke's *Raja Harischandra* (1913), based on a story from the *Ramayana* about the eponymous ancient king.[12] He went on to make several other films about the Hindu deities, including *Sri Krishna Janma* (1918).

Since that time, prominent devotionals and mythologicals have emerged. One of the most important and still cherished devotionals is *Sant Tukaram* (1936) based on the life of the seventeenth-century poet-saint. In the realm of mythologicals, worth noting is *Jai Santoshi Maa* (1975) a film that catapulted the little known titular goddess into a popular sensation throughout Northern India in the late 1970s.[13] More recently Arjun Sajnani's *Agni Varsha* (2002) offers a retelling of the Mahabharata. In distinction to such films, Westerners have tended to know of Indian film through Satyajit Ray, who won the Academy Award Lifetime Achievement Award in 1992. While Ray tended to portray scenes of everyday life (especially in the 'Apu Trilogy'), he also presented his own 'religious film', *Devi* (1960) which offers an antidote to and critique of the religious fervour and devotion of *Sant Tukaram* or *Jai Santoshi Ma*.

There are also politically-charged films in which Muslims and Hindus come into conflict with each other, especially at the end of the colonial period. This is dealt with in Kamal Haasan's *Hey Ram* (2000), Khalid Mohamed's *Fiza* (2000) and Deepa Mehta's *Earth* (1998). Films that take up Hindu–Muslim conflicts in the wake of the destruction of the Babri Mosque in Ayodhya in 1992, include Saeed Akhtar Mirza's *Naseem* (1995).

Iran

Iran is one of the most interesting and productive sites for film production in the world today, particularly stemming from the 'New Iranian Cinema' movement of the 1970s and moving into post-Revolutionary Iran. Faced with heavy censorship since the 1979 Revolution, Iranian filmmakers have continued to produce some of the most critically acclaimed films in the world, often utilizing allegorical means as ways to hide deeper messages about religion, politics and sexuality. There are a number of ways to read these highly allegorical films that point toward a Persian-Islamic worldview, and while 'Islam' may not always be present, the films are peopled with Muslims and it is crucial, as always, not to confuse an essentialist term like 'Islam' for the people who actually practice it. With the rejection of many Western films and themes, as well as poor quality dubbed 'Farsi Films', filmmakers have returned to their own cultural roots, drawing upon the rich Persian traditions of poetry, passion plays, architecture, music and storytelling.[14]

These films present the minutiae and the mundane through a variety of filmically poetic means. The mosque is a shimmering presence in the background while teenagers play in the street. Children search for lost shoes (Majid Majidi, *Children of Heaven*, 1997) or for mislaid money intended to buy a large goldfish (Jafar Panahi, *The White Balloon*, 1995). Siblings argue. Parents chide their offspring. Wives assert their independence within the constraints of violent marriage and a patriarchal society (Tahmineh Milani, *Two Women*, 1999). Women confront domestic violence or simply acquiesce to living in a masculine world (Jafar Panahi, *The Circle*, 2000). A good number of recent Iranian films concentrate upon the difficulties faced by a central protagonist trying to cope with urban or village life in a rapidly changing world or simply trying to survive in the midst of difficult circumstances. In Majid Majidi's last film, *The Willow Tree* (2005) a middle-aged blind man struggles after recovering his sight. Of course, some Iranian filmmakers concentrate upon idiosyncratic tales. For example, another movie is based on the true story of a man who is put on trial for impersonating a favourite film director in Abbas Kiarostami's *Close Up* (1990), and Kiarostami particularly continues the struggle to find hope in the midst of despair.[15] As with Kiarostami, studies of this new wave of Iranian cinema have tended to highlight the work of directors such as Majid Majidi, Mohsen Makhmalbaf and his daughter Samira Makhmalbaf. Makhmalbaf's films (for example, *From Evil to God* (1984), *Once Upon a Time, Cinema* (1992) and *Kandehar* (2001)) reflect his own vision for 'art', in distinction to 'religion' and 'politics' – though Makhmalbaf's films undoubtedly touch on all three. He describes his own movement from wanting to save others, then his country, and ultimately himself. Like many directors in Iran, the goal is to produce understated cinematic tales which highlight, subvert and criticize social injustices. There is little religious preaching or moralizing to be found here. This is often a neo-realistic, slowed down form of cinema, where stories matter and characters develop.[16]

E. Africa

North Africa

Egypt is billed as the 'Hollywood of the Arab World', and has garnered the attention of international film audiences. The best known and most critically acclaimed Egyptian director is Youssef Chahine. Films like his earlier *Saladin* (1963) and later *Destiny* (1997; focusing on the twelfth-century Andalusian philosopher Averroes) deal with the possibilities of religious tolerance, but also point out the real threats to interreligious coexistence. Other Egyptian standouts dealing with religious-political conflicts, especially with the rise of fundamentalism include the works of Atef Hetata (*Violin* [1990; short film] and *Closed Doors* [1999]).

Elsewhere in North Africa, attention should be paid to the Moroccan film-maker Ismaël Ferroukhi, whose *Le Grand Voyage* (2004) offers a stunning take on the *Hajj* to Mecca. In Tunisia, Nouri Bouzid has emerged as a prominent director and films like *Bezness* (1992) and *Clay Dolls* (2003) offer conflicting values between religious ethics, sexuality, economics and culture clashes.

Sub-Saharan Africa

Dubbed 'Nollywood', Nigeria has seen a substantial rise in film production in recent years, though here we must include in the definition of 'film' low-budget films made on video. In Nigeria (and Ghana and other parts of West Africa), there has been a boom in film production through new cheap video technologies producing 'videofilms' that have a mass appeal, many of which are produced by Pentecostal religious groups. It is difficult to point to any specific films from this production orientation, especially as they are not widely available in the Anglo-American world, and nothing has generally emerged as a 'classic'.[17] Also in Nigeria, Saddiq Balewa's *This Land is Ours* (1991) deals with conflicts that arise when modern-colonial forces confront the indigenous traditions, and when the major world religions of Islam and Christianity face off in local areas.

Perhaps the best-known and most prolific filmmaker in Africa is Ousmane Sembene from Senegal, whose many films include *Guelwaar* (1992), which offers a critique of interreligious conflicts, and *Moolaadé* (2004), which functions to criticize the practices of female genital circumcision. Sembene is clear that indigenously-created media will continue to be a strong force to help many of the problems in Africa today.[18] Like Sembene, director Med Hondo of Mauritania self-consciously makes films that offer an alternative aesthetic to that of Western filmmaking; one example is *Sarraounia* (1986) about a warrior-queen who leads her people in the challenges posed by the colonizing French. Finally, worth noting also are Drissa Toure's *Haramuya* (1995) and Dani Kouyate's *Keita: Heritage of the Griot* (1994), both from Burkina Faso, and Amadou Thior's *Almodou* (2000) from Senegal, all of which deal with cultural/political/religious conflicts.

F. Latin America

Argentina

As elsewhere in Latin America, Argentina's film production has been affected by changes in government as colonial forces, struggles within a post-colonial environment, coups, dictators and democracy have succeeded one another. Part and parcel to these political changes has been the role of the Roman Catholic Church in its involvements with, and often critiques of, the governing forces.

The works of filmmakers such as Eliseo Subiela have continually interrogated religious notions and ideas in creative ways. From *Man Facing Southeast* (1986) to *Don't Die Without Telling Me Where You're Going* (1995) to *The Adventures of God* (2000), Subiela remains intrigued by religious views of the world, but offers the related possibility that the religious person might, in fact, be insane. If religious satire was his simple aim, Subiela would not continue to return to the topic of religion, nor continue to present the topics in such ambiguous ways. By utilizing a 'fantastic' style, Subiela's take on religion offers critical overviews and possibilities.

Yet, it is not only a struggle with and without Catholicism that has made cinema in Argentina of interest to religious studies, for cities like Buenos Aires, Córdoba, and elsewhere, contain an active Jewish presence. Jewish life in South America, and South American film, is particularly interesting, since it breaks up the perceived stereotype of Judaism as a Middle Eastern manifestation, and of Latin America as a Roman Catholic manifestation. Important Argentine films with strong Jewish references include Daniel Burman's *Family Law* (2006), and Eduardo Mignogna's *Autumn Sun* (1996), the latter containing many explicit dimensions to the depth of Judaism as it exists in Buenos Aires.

Brazil

In spite of the predominance of Roman Catholicism throughout Central and South America and the Caribbean, many filmmakers attend to the nature and function of 'syncretic' religious traditions such as Candomblé. The Afro-Brazilian practice can be seen in one of the masters of Brazilian 'Cinema Novo', Nelson Pereira dos Santos, whose many films include *Jubiabá* (1987), which deals with interracial, interclass issues with a strong dose of Afro-Brazilian religious practice. Also in a Cinema Novo style is the work of the prominent, award-winning director Carlos Diegues who has made a few films with religious interests. Of note are his recent *Orfeu* (2000), a modern retelling of the myth of Orpheus and Euridice via the stylistics of Cinema Novo, and *God is Brazilian* (2003), a humorous though slight attempt to see the master of the universe in utterly human terms.

From another perspective, Tania Cypriano's documentary *Odo ya! Life with Aids* (1997) portrays the importance of Candomblé in education about AIDS, and her short, *Ex-Voto* (1990) is a devotional expression to the patron saint of Brazil, Our Lady of Aparecida, who is credited as saving the director from death by fire when she was young.

In recent years, Walter Salles has emerged on the international film scene, mixing political environments with religious belief. His *Central Station* (1998) can be seen as a type of pilgrimage, in search of a lost father, but also for its possibilities (and impossibilities) to find salvation. The acclaimed *Motorcycle*

Diaries (2004) continues Salles' interest in pilgrimage, mixing it with a road movie. Meanwhile, *Behind the Sun* (2001) continues on the theme of identity in the midst of ancestral traditions.

Cuba

Cuba's historical relation to religious films is of course marked by drastic political changes as well. From the US-supported Bautista government, to the Communist overthrow in 1959, to the more contemporary 'special period' (after the fall of Cuba's most significant trading partner, the Soviet Union), Cuba has continued to produce films that are politically engaged, including confrontations with religion. Especially since the 1959 Revolution, Cuba has been a fertile site for film production as the Communist government has strongly supported the arts. And while some censorship has been enacted, the range of socio-political critique is astounding.

Until his death in 1996, Tomás Gutiérrez Alea was one of the world's most revered Cuban filmmakers, and his films often took up the theme of religion, especially in relation to political realities. From *The Last Supper* (1976), an allegorical piece that relates the New Testament story to slavery in the nineteenth century, to *Guantamamera* (1994), which correlates political systems with the religious beliefs of Santería, Gutiérrez Alea investigated human existence in all its political and religious interactions.[19]

Santería practices also show up, for example, in Gloria Rolando's *Oggun* (1991) and Humberto Solas's *Honey for Oshun* (2001).

Mexico

Films from Mexico run the gamut from devotional praise to wholesale critique of religion, particularly Roman Catholicism, and the country has provided a home base for a variety of émigré filmmakers critical of religion, including the Soviet Sergei Eisenstein (*Que Viva Mexico!* [1932]) and the Spaniard Luis Buñuel (*Nazarin* [1959]). Following in that vein, more recent films such as Carlos Carrera's *The Crime of Father Amaro* (2002) and Nicolas Echevarria's historical work *Cabeza de Vaca* (2001) portray a Christianity that is well-worth critiquing.

Supernatural forces are confronted in the horror genre through Guillermo del Toro's Mexican/Spanish productions such as *The Devil's Backbone* (2001) and the Academy Award winning, *Pan's Labyrinth* (2006), offering strange mythical worlds that intersect with the known world. And Alejandro González Iñárritu's films (especially *21 Grams* [2003] and *Babel* [2006]) demonstrate strong religious interconnections between people who are seemingly disconnected.

From another angle, the story of Adam and Eve has been taken up at least twice in Mexican films, from the devout 1956 Alberto Gout film *Adam and Eve* to the modern day reinterpretation in Iván Avila Dueñas's *Adán y Eva (todavia)* (2004).

Conclusion: Conflict and Christianity Outside Hollywood

To conclude, it should be clear that many films around the world touch on religious themes through their presentation of conflicts. Religious traditions often incur conflict when they come into contact with various opposing forces. There are the obvious conflicts between religious traditions: Christian vs. Muslim, Muslim vs. Hindu, Jewish vs. Christian, Indigenous tradition vs. large-scale 'world religions', etc. There are also conflicts that arise when older religious values are challenged by the social, political, economic and religious realities of modern life, especially seen in the midst of a post-colonial environment. There is conflict when, due to modern life and the aftereffects of colonialism, religious people from differing traditions are placed side by side and forced to get along (or not). And conflict arises when individual gender, sexual and ethnic identities meet social-religious identities.

One other 'conflict' could be said to occur among the global presence of 'Jesus films'. US films such as Martin Scorsese's *The Last Temptation of Christ* or Mel Gibson's *The Passion of the Christ* have revived ancient conflicts over the incarnational nature of Jesus. Yet, one other conflict of Christ figures could be imagined, and that would be to contrast a 'United States Jesus Christ' with filmic figures portrayed in other parts of the world. Parallel to the negotiations that global filmmakers must constantly make in relation to industrial film productions, made by industrialized nations, is a negotiation with Christianity as presented in and through the cinemas of industrialized nations. As a way to rethink this, this chapter concludes by pointing out several films that portray Jesus as a central figure: films made in Argentina, Iran, India and South Africa. While English-speaking scholars have tripped over each other in an attempt to talk about 'Jesus in film', they seem to keep stumbling in part because they do not get out of the films created in the G8 nations. Thus, in the conclusion here I briefly highlight a few 'Jesus films' made in other countries, suggesting there is room for further comparison here.

The Argentinian Eliseo Subiela made *Man Facing Southeast*, a film with obvious Christic references, but which simultaneously questions the sanity of the 'savior' (a film that was blatantly plagiarized by the novelist Gene Brewer and made into the film *K-PAX* in the United States). The 'man' is somewhere between a messiah, a lunatic or an extra-terrestrial, and the film does not tie up any of the loose ends. In Iran, the journalist and filmmaker Nader Talebzadeh recently created *The Messiah* (2007), a story of Jesus told from an Islamic perspective. Here, Jesus is a strong and revered prophet who teaches and performs miracles, but is not crucified and is not the 'Son of God'. In South India, villagers gather in front of an outdoor screen to watch the life of Jesus in the Telugu production, *Karunamayudu* (1978) now seen by over 100 million viewers. A devout Christian-production, the film nonetheless incorporates a South Indian cast, and the film styles resemble those of Hindu devotionals more than the Western-style Jesus films. Finally, in South Africa, Mark Dornford-May has made *Son of Man* (2006), the story of Jesus but set in present-day South Africa. The message of Jesus is thus shifted to a specific political reality and offers an alternative view of the messianic nature of Jesus.

9 Religion, Film and Cultural Studies

Melanie J. Wright

Introduction

This essay proposes cultural studies as a discursive space within which investigation of the relationships between religion and film may be conducted. After briefly exploring a perennial question – 'what is cultural studies?' – it considers what a cultural studies informed approach to religion and film might entail and elucidate.

Generally speaking, the practice of cultural studies has tried to embody a spirit of openness and partnership. In Britain, its roots lie in adult education, a milieu characterized by 'dialogic democratic practice' and 'resistance to academic compartmentalizing of knowledge':[1] Stuart Hall, Richard Hoggart,[2] E. P. Thompson and Raymond Williams are among those whose ideas were forged in the classrooms of university extra-mural departments and the Workers' Educational Association. Its consolidation as a discipline is associated with two institutions distinguished by the prominence they give, or gave, to collaboration in research and teaching, the University of Birmingham's Centre for Contemporary Cultural Studies (CCCS)[3] and the Open University.[4] Accordingly, while this essay is essentially an argument, I seek to engage and not to silence other positions, including those articulated by my fellow contributors.

A good deal of today's writing on religion and film shares two characteristics – an overt or implicit nervousness about its legitimacy as an academic practice, and a lack of sustained debate on questions of theory and method. Of course, scholars of religion and film – and the cognate, but distinct, fields of theology and film, and bible and film – *do* have their own ways of working, but these are rarely the subjects of extended critical discourse. To take one recent example from a British theologian, Clive Marsh closes on a familiarly apologetic note.[5] Yet this sustained, impassioned justification for theological engagement with popular culture sits alongside a conceptualization of method as a fairly straightforward set of working practices;[6] the activities of reading and watching, 'contemporary meaning-making',[7] are recognized as complex but nevertheless remain largely un-problematized. Marsh's interest in 'actual student responses' places him within a wider trend that regards viewer experience, rather than the film 'text', as decisive for the religious moment in the cinema.[8] Yet he omits to debate his methodology and the theoretical commitments implied by its adoption.

I have suggested elsewhere that these two hallmarks of religion and film writing are linked.[9] The paucity of critical discourse on theory and method in religion and film lends credibility to the position of those who regard the study of mass cultural forms as ancillary to the main work of religious studies, leaving it vulnerable to institutional retrenchment in an age when none of us escapes the pressures of the market. But other things are at stake here, aside from the strategic institutionalization of the field. If religion and film practice is not seriously discussed, it will continue largely untested and underdeveloped, putting the brakes on the maturation of its capacity to help us, as Peter Williams neatly put it, to 'see more, and reflect more upon that seeing'.[10] Against this view, one might note that for some practitioners, the foray into film is largely, or partly, motivated by the exigencies of the classroom. Course creation and publication activity is predicated on the perception that today's students cannot be assumed to be religiously literate, or to share a common spiritual or ethnic heritage, but are *au fait* with popular cultural forms like film and television.[11] Might a turn to matters methodological and theoretical not mitigate against attempts to ensure the accessibility of theology and religious studies for twenty-first century learners? On the contrary, where approaches remain implicit or taken-for-granted, this runs counter to the democratizing impulses inherent in many-a rationale for religion and film work. Open, critical debate about the current state of play is a necessary part of the task of encouraging and empowering our students to become their own authorities in the field.[12]

The Study of Religions and Cultural Studies: Agendas and Approaches

The terrain of cultural studies, onto which much of film studies has been shifting in the past twenty or so years offers one set of discursive spaces in which the development of religion and film work may take place.[13] But what is cultural studies?

Chronologically minded accounts often begin in the 1950s with the work of three earlier-mentioned figures – Williams, Hoggart and Thompson. They then move on to cultural studies' institutional establishment, exemplified by the 1964 founding of the CCCS where, from 1969, scholarship took a neo-Marxist turn under Hall. Finally, attention is typically given to the de-centering of Marxism and the economy in favour of questions of gender, ethnicity and sexuality at the end of the twentieth century.[14] There is an inevitable arbitrariness to such histories. One might just as easily begin with Matthew Arnold and the Leavisites.[15] With an eye to cultural studies' approaches to film, an alternative departure point might be found in the work of continental European linguists and philosophers like Ferdinand de Saussure and Michel Foucault, whose semiotic and discursive approaches to representation remain influential. The story of the emergence of cultural studies is one of polygenesis not monogenesis, and this diversity continues to play out in its contemporary practice.

As described by Williams, scholars variously understand 'culture' to refer *either* to a way of life (of a particular group, or period, or of humanity as a whole) *or* to specific intellectual and artistic activities and artefacts (culture as art, music, literature, etc.).[16] However, we can speak of cultural studies 'if not as a *unity* then at least as a *whole*'[17] within which a plurality of approaches engenders not confusion but analytical strength. Acknowledging the lack of a uniform definition of 'culture', Williams argues, 'the complex of senses indicates a complex argument about the relations between general human development and a particular way of life, and between both and the works and practices of art and intelligence'.[18] Within this 'whole' we can note some common emphases that are particularly relevant to religion and film:

1. Cultural Studies is *interested in the practices and objects of everyday life, and the uses and meanings which people attribute to them.* It seeks to analyse the ways in which individual and shared meanings and identities are produced and circulated.
2. Cultural Studies *emphasizes occasionality*; it attends to the precise moment or context in which a phenomenon manifests itself. Historically, practitioners of cultural studies have been particularly interested in the ways in which the cultural landscape is impacted by relations of power and politics, broadly understood.

While cultural studies possesses a discrete disciplinary identity, it is also possible to identify a whole set of disciplines and fields that have, consciously or otherwise, taken something of a 'cultural turn' in the past twenty or so years.[19] The study of religions is one such field. Callum Brown's intervention in the secularization debate draws on cultural theory for its concept of discursive Christianity.[20] Colleen McDannell's study of popular piety in North America spawned interest in the ways that 'people learn the discourses and habits of their religious community through the material dimension' and the communication, sustenance and modification of traditions and commitments through such processes of interaction, 'through doing, seeing, and touching'.[21] In biblical studies, Justin Meggitt's work on the first Christians advocates a Thompsonian rescuing of the lives of the non-elites from the 'enormous condescension of posterity'.[22] Influenced by Raymond Williams and cultural anthropologist Clifford Geertz, Malory Nye's recent textbook argues that the study of religions should be re-conceptualized and renamed as 'religion and culture'.[23] To study Christianity, Nye says:

> one can of course study the Bible, high Christian art, and great thinking, but that does not tell us everything about the traditions of Christianity. For many centuries Christian people have been practising their religions in other ways, through producing less 'great' works of art, music, and literature, which could also be studied as forms of Christian culture.[24]

Nye's statement illustrates how the concerns of cultural studies map on to those of religious studies. First, the turn to culture is associated with a democratizing definition of religion. It seeks to address non-elite expressions as well as elite ones. Second, it entails a broadening of the traditional activities of religious studies, to encompass the study not just of sacred texts but also of material culture, things made and used by people. Although Western intellectual culture remains dominated by the written word, a growing body of work concerns itself with religion as a human practice. John Cort writes:

> Jainism, as with any religious tradition, is in part a vast historical enterprise of trying to find, realize, and express the values and meanings of human life. The study of texts alone is insufficient for an adequate understanding of that enterprise. To the extent that human life is by its very nature embodied, physical, and material, the study of religions therefore must involve itself with the study of the material expressions of religion.[25]

In other words, the turn to culture signals both new agendas and new approaches in the study of religions – challenges to which the study of religion and film has scarcely responded.

Religion, Film and Cultural Studies

What might religion and film studies look like if conducted in this way? What would it tell us? In *Seeing and Believing*, Margaret Miles rejects both the outright hostility to religious images and the perception of the film theatre as a site of moral danger that she reports to have been features of her 'fundamentalist' upbringing. Instead, she advocates a cultural studies methodology, helpfully articulated as a list of questions in the book's appendix.[26] For Miles, film is 'one voice in a complex social conversation, occurring in a particular historical moment'; scholarship's attention needs to shift 'from the film as a text to the social, political, and cultural matrix in which the film was produced and distributed'. Alongside production and distribution, Miles comments on reception: 'most filmgoers,' she suggests, 'consciously or unconsciously, will see and discuss the film they watch in relation to the common quandaries of the moment'.[27]

Miles' book is a significant starting-point, but in terms of religion, film and cultural studies it is just that, a starting-point. Most obviously, the *theological* character of the project distances it from the practice of religious studies and cultural studies. Films are, for Miles, important circulators of values. Her chosen examples include *The Last Temptation of Christ* (Martin Scorsese, 1998), *The Mission* (Roland Joffé, 1986), *The Handmaid's Tale* (Voker Schlöndorff, 1990) and *Daughters of the Dust* (Julie Dash, 1991). Her approach is to characterize each one as demonstrating one or more social problems – in Miles' phraseology, 'intimate and private confrontations of values' – and proposing a resolution.[28] So far so good. The ultimate goal, however, is not to analyse the processes by which the films circulate meaning, but to judge their treatment of values against a particular set of *norms*:

> Films should help all Americans imagine differences that are not erased or transcended, differences of race, sexual orientation, class and gender that contribute to each person's particularity, rather than positing as different anyone who diverges from a dominant norm . . . a society in which people are at risk of fatal infection through sexual exchanges needs to see images in which safe sex is sexy. A society in which people are disastrously inept at maintaining committed love relationships needs a media that does not continually polarize men's and women's erotics, and that pictures diverse erotics. . . . If any of these desiderata are actually to be met . . . funding for films needs to be diversified so that Hollywood studios no longer control all of the films that are adequately funded, advertised . . . and distributed.[29]

Despite her eschewal both of parental 'fundamentalism' and of the views of 'some of my academic friends' who castigate popular films for their 'invidious superficiality' and 'highly questionable values'[30] Miles' stance is, then, highly moralizing. In effect, she presents us with a narrative in which the spiritual and physical well-being of everyday Americans is imperilled by Hollywood vice. Practitioners of religious studies increasingly acknowledge that absolute objectivity is unattainable and that critical distance entails not a striving for some impossible scientific neutrality, but a rather more dialogical engagement between the student and the studied.[31] For its part, cultural studies has long owned that 'every project . . . is, more or less explicitly, a working out of experience and value in the world, the search for a personal point of view and a contribution, however modest, to wider ethics and politics',[32] but there is a significant dissonance between this *reflexivity*, in which the researcher's own acknowledged, scrutinized commitments are themselves risked in the course of inquiry, and the *confessionalism* more generally associated with theological study.

Setting aside epistemological questions, there are other areas in which Miles' work invites review and development. For example, whilst film reception, especially fan activity, has been a popular subject of cultural studies investigation,[33] she does comparatively little to flesh out her opening claims about spectatorship. Most of the discussion of reception is principally concerned with press reviews, that is, the interventions of professional respondents. Miles' approach also runs counter to major *foci* in contemporary cultural studies and to her plea for 'differences that are not erased or transcended' when she opts to ignore the strategies via which 'sexual and racial minorities' engage Hollywood films.[34]

What is needed is more consistent engagement with cultural studies that among other things, entails a recognition that cultural studies is more deeply implicated in the current practice of film studies than Miles allows. This will strengthen the possibility of offering an account of films as cultural products with specific histories of production, distribution and exhibition, and facilitate a more extensive dialogue with film theory, particularly in relation to aesthetics and reception. What is at stake is the ability to shift from the more straightforward extension of the subject matter of religion and film, or the *ad hoc* borrowing of tools and concepts from another discipline, to a truly interdisciplinary approach characterized by depth and rigour, which might be understood respectively as: competence in pertinent knowledges and approaches to the subject matter; and an ability to develop processes that integrate theory and knowledge from the disciplines being brought together.[35] Such a project is necessarily never complete, and to do it justice is clearly beyond the scope of a single essay. Yet, as a sometime teacher of Judaism, I am mindful not only of Cary's fear that 'of all the intellectual movements that have swept the humanities . . . in the last twenty years, none will be taken up so shallowly, so opportunistically, so unreflectively, and so ahistorically as cultural studies',[36] but also of the Mishnaic admonishment: 'It is not your part to finish the task, yet you are not free to desist from it.'[37] In the remaining pages, I sketch some of the ways in which cultural studies differentiates particular moments in the cultural process, as a means of suggesting the methods, practices and questions that might result from the drawing together of religion, film and cultural studies. I then apply these to *The Passion of the Christ* in the form of a brief case study.

The Circuit of Culture

As already noted, cultural studies is interested in practices and objects, and in the uses people make of them – the individual and collective meanings (including religious ones) that are circulated in the production and reception of artefacts (including film). Drawing on the two-fold definition of culture, it holds in tension the general or 'contextual' and the specific or 'textual'. One popular approach to conceptualizing the complexities of the cultural process is to speak in terms of a 'circuit' of distinct but articulated themes, impulses or 'moments' that taken as a whole enable us to chart the entire 'biography' of a particular artefact, be that the Sony Walkman,[38] the Mini-Metro car,[39] or *The Passion of the Christ.*

'The circuit of culture' diagram reproduced here identifies five moments, on to which we can map different aspects of the relationships between religion and film.[40] These are:

1. Consumption: including spectatorship, the processes by which viewers understand/interpret/make meaning with – or 'against' – a film;
2. Identity: how we see others and ourselves (including religious identity);

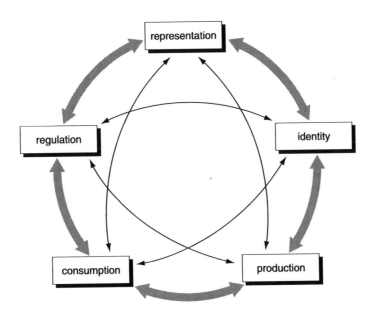

Figure 1: The circuit of culture.

Source: du Gay et al. (1997), with the kind permission of Sage, in association with The Open University.

3. Production: film production, its artistic, technical and industrial aspects *and* their associated meanings (consider, for example, the implications of referring to a film as an 'art-house', 'Bollywood' or 'Hollywood' production);

4. Regulation: including the formal processes of film classification and censorship, and informal 'policing' in the shape of newspaper film reviews or the pronouncements of religious leaders and organizations; and,

5. Representation: the film 'text' and more specifically, the ways in which it uses sound and image in order to construct stories and statements about the world in which viewers can share because they are familiar, or can in some way be made sense of. We might also include here an interest in the ways in which a film itself is represented, for example in advertising.

It will be apparent that if we regard each of these themes as necessary for an appreciation of the religion and film circuit, older forms of film criticism such as auteurism, which might simplistically be described as privileging the moment of production, and reception studies, which emphasizes consumption and/or identity, are not to be rejected. However, any totalizing claims made on their part are overturned. They are necessary, but not sufficient for an account of what, following Hall, might be termed the 'giving and taking of meaning' in the cinema.[41] Returning to the passage from Miles, this infers the character of films from their conditions of production: note the closing remarks about 'Hollywood'. But from a cultural studies perspective, while genre conventions and industrial pressures are real, so are the interpretations of audiences who enjoy – or reject – Hollywood cinema.[42] Similarly, while Miles positions films as bearers of meanings that operate on viewers, the relationships between production, consumption, regulation and so on are better understood not as linear or sequential but as interdependent, with each moment always implicated in the others (indicated diagrammatically by the profusion of arrows). No moment in the cultural circuit is determinative for the others.

The Passion of the Christ

The Passion of the Christ, directed by Mel Gibson and initially released in 2004, provides a ready case study to demonstrate the idea of the cultural circuit. Five years after its release, it is widely referenced in conversations, courses and publications on religion and film. These include a plethora of edited volumes and special issues of *The Journal of Religion and Film, The Journal of Religion and Society* and *Shofar: An Interdisciplnary Journal of Jewish Studies.* It therefore requires comparatively little narrative description on this occasion. The film's ubiquitousness in turn signals another factor that makes it appropriate for this essay's purposes: *The Passion* is a strong example of a film that carries a 'rich accumulation of meanings'.[43] Unusual among features with religious subject-matters, *The Passion of the Christ* was a piece of event-cinema. At times, debate as to the merits of choosing or refusing to see it obscured what was on the screen itself. As Goodacre wryly observes, some scholars have published their views on *The Passion* without actually having seen the film.[44] By turns castigated for its alleged anti-semitism (a charge fuelled in 2004 by Mel Gibson's refusal to criticize his father Hutton Gibson's claims that the Holocaust was exaggerated, and more recently by the director's own anti-semitic outburst during his 2006 arrest on suspicion of driving when intoxicated) and lauded by many church groups as an unprecedented opportunity for outreach and meditation, the film came to signify something of a conservative Christian wish to overcome historical criticism's perceived inroads into gospel faith and post-war liberal censuring of the conviction to preach the good news to the nations, and to establish a more secure role for Christian values in North American civic life. Describing the film's significance as a marker of particular forms of contemporary Christian identity, *The Economist* even suggested that 'The 2004 [US Presidential] election could well turn into a choice between Michael Moore's *Fahrenheit 9/11* and Mel Gibson's *The Passion of the Christ*'.[45]

The promotional campaign surrounding the film was unusual, with only modest television advertising surrounding its release and none in support of its Academy Awards campaign. Instead, on either side of the Atlantic large numbers of academics from the fields of biblical studies, Jewish studies and interfaith relations were invited to advance screenings alongside church leaders, film industry professionals and other potential opinion formers. Many churches made advance group bookings to see the film on its commercial release. In the press, the film and some of its most distinctive aspects, particularly the focus on the suffering of Jesus, rather than on his life and ministry as a teacher and healer, and the decision to use Aramaic and Latin dialogue in a film aimed at a mass audience, were represented as the fulfilment of a pious and long-harboured dream on Gibson's part. Much was made of the director's visit to the Vatican, and Pope John Paul II's reported declaration about the film: 'It is as it was.' Yet *The Passion* was also the subject of the largest concerted negative campaign in recent memory. Basing their comments on a leaked copy of the script, an *ad hoc* scholars' group condemned the film for its violence and its violation of Catholic guidelines on the presentation of Jews and Judaism in passion plays.[46] Protesters, a few of whom dressed as concentration camp prisoners, appeared outside cinemas when the film opened in the United States. Already, this sketch underscores the interpenetration and interdependency of the various moments in the cultural circuit. Promotional portraits of Gibson as a faithful, dedicated Christian who defied the system (resisted the regulatory efforts of academics and interfaith professionals, and the conventional wisdom about the kind of Jesus film that 'sells') drew together the aspects of production, identity, regulation and representation – all with the ultimate aim of establishing a connection between the film and potential consumers.

Further questions present themselves as part of the effort to investigate fully *The Passion's* biography. Turning to the traditional focus of religion and film work, the film text itself, we might examine not just the narrative (the importance of which I do not dispute) but also its strategies of representation. These include the use of subtitled Aramaic and Latin dialogue, which implies a particular kind of viewing activity; the deployment of visual techniques derived from both high art and the horror-film genre; and an active participation in theologies of the image and the relic (the exchange of the look between Jesus and his followers, and the recognition and veneration of relics are hallmarks of the film). There are also questions to explore about the process by which the film text was created, the transition from concept to film. Important for understanding both this and the public, including scholarly, perception of *The Passion* as 'Mel Gibson's film' are not just the technical-artistic factors but also the political and economic ones. Despite representations of him as an embattled, marginalized figure doggedly pursuing a dream of faith, Mel Gibson was, and remains, a powerful player in the New Hollywood context. He founded Icon, the company behind *The Passion*, and has been involved in production, direction and other aspects of film development since the late 1990s, when he became actor-producer of *Payback*, whose first director was dismissed after disagreeing with the star.[47] Of course, even such important professionals operate within the frameworks of technical possibilities and regulations, which at once provide them with opportunities and constraints. In 2004, *The Passion* was the highest-grossing R-rated film of all time in the United States. A year later, the film was re-cut in an attempt to secure a PG-13 certificate – a fairly typical marketing strategy which, like the release of the film on DVD (in 2004 and again in a new 'Definitive Edition' in 2007) seeks to generate additional revenue from completist fans and acquire a new audience of younger viewers and adults who had been deterred by the strong violence of the earlier version. However, the Motion Picture Association of America deemed the film still too violent for some pre-teens. Gibson released it anyway, as *The Passion Recut* (2005), but found that most cinema chains would not carry an un-rated film, and the project was commercially unsuccessful.

Returning, finally, to the moment of consumption and its roles in the circulation of meanings around *The Passion*, what did audiences make of the film? Gibson's traditionalist Catholicism is well known. The movement seeks a restoration of pre-Vatican II teachings and rites and, more unusually, regards the papacy as having been vacant since Pius XII's death in 1958. But the film was consumed by Christians of many different denominations including mainstream Catholics and Protestants, among them many conservative evangelicals who would normally dismiss the Catholic church as non-Christian. How did these groups respond? Was there something compelling about *The Passion*'s Jesus – a strong heroic figure who endures extreme suffering but ultimately emerges triumphant – that transcended the difficulties they might have been expected to have with Gibson's visual theology, which incorporates many details from Catholic traditions such as the Stations of the Cross and the Sorrowful Mysteries of the Rosary?[48] Or, was the representation of the film in public and private discourses decisive – did attendance at the cinema function for some viewers as a kind of Christian identity-marker? Still other possible questions arise. For some viewers, the film led to a new or renewed faith in Christianity. For many Christians, seeing and talking about the film was part of their observance of Lent and/or Easter. The film was released on Ash Wednesday 2004, and many American and British churches incorporated publicity stills from the film into their advertisements for Easter services. (Indeed, as I finalize this essay in the north of England in spring 2009, I have noticed that several churches are once more using images from the film's publicity materials to promote their Easter services.) In such cases, the film became temporarily, or permanently, and intimately connected with their personal faith-identity. For yet others, viewing the actual film was only one aspect of their consumption of *The Passion*. They also bought the DVD, soundtrack CD, books, or other licensed merchandise, including souvenir nails modelled on those used in the crucifixion scenes and sold as pendants – 'a unique and powerful way to express and share your faith' – with Isaiah 53.3 inscribed on the reverse. In themselves, these nails demonstrate the interconnectedness of production, representation, identity and consumption. Conversely, we might also consider the negative consumption or conscious rejection of the film by other groups, among them some Jews, Muslims and others, and the creation and reception of related popular cultural forms like the *South Park* episode, 'The Passion of the Jew'.

In order to understand *The Passion* phenomenon, then, we find ourselves exploring, sometimes in turn, sometimes simultaneously, each of the different moments in the cultural circuit. To investigate the different moments more fully, a wide range of analytical and ethnographical skills would be needed. As Alasuutari has suggested, approaches in cultural studies may be aptly described as *bricolage*.[49] The methods and practices selected are a pragmatic, strategic assemblage, subject to development and review in the context of particular inquiries. Lest this sound too daunting, I must emphasize that this does not mean that adopting a cultural studies approach to religion and film requires the capacity to 'do everything'. No-one will possess the skills or the inclination to research adequately every moment in the circuit. However, an awareness of other moments and lines of questioning should impact our studies and the representation of their findings.[50]

The fact that *The Passion* is a film *and* also a commodity, that the cinema is art-form *and* industry, has a bearing on both the film itself and on the ways we, including those of us who are practitioners of religion and film, respond to it. Cultural studies offers one way of recognizing and grappling with such complexities. Following a cultural studies approach, we can more rigorously address the place of film in the circulation of religious meanings by becoming sensitive to the different moments in the circuit of culture, or, to re-phrase the point, by thinking in terms of a need to triangulate meanings between film texts, contexts and audiences.[51] Yet even as it illuminates new aspects of the religion-film nexus, the reflexive stance of cultural studies also cautions us that even our best insights remain partial in both senses of the word.

10 Women, Religion and Film

Irena S. M. Makarushka

> Woman is the term, at once familiar and alien, known and unknown. . . .
> Linda Zerilli[1]

Introduction

Religion and film contend with the idea and position of woman in culture.[2] Insofar as culture is not static but continuously changing, the idea of woman, as a reflection of shifting cultural values, is a work in progress. Tracing how the idea of woman is reflected in the different modes and modalities of expression particular to religion and film and how they intersect is the focus of this chapter.[3] A discussion of the interpretative framework and the approach to the study of religion that informs this chapter is followed by an analysis of representative films that reflect, challenge and/or sustain the pervasive attitudes and values with regard to the idea of woman.

Feminist and other post-modern theories[4] shape the approach this chapter takes not only to how cultural values are constructed, but also how they inform and are transformed by social practices such as religion and film-making. Although the focus is on gender, issues of race, class and sexuality deepen and further problematize how woman signifies.[5] Like every other human endeavour that strives to elucidate experience, feminism represents a multiplicity of richly textured and diverse ways of theorizing and putting into practice the idea that women matter.[6] Feminist scholarship remains pertinent because it continues to make significant contributions to the study and understanding of religion and film.[7] There always have been women who in their own time and in their own ways challenged what is now called patriarchy and who served as role models.[8] The philosophical perspective that informs this chapter is indebted to feminist scholarship for its critical reading of religion and film as cultural artifacts that visually mediate the meaning of woman.

The word religion conjures myriad images and feelings that are markedly different for those who profess a particular faith and those who do not. Most organized religions assume that theirs is uniquely suited to answer the fundamental human questions about the meaning of life under the conditions of finitude: where did I come from, where am I going and how do I get there. Questions about the origin, purpose and end of life, in the aggregate, represent the human quest for meaning. Religion, with or without a denominational faith-claim, is the very essence of human self-understanding. Post-modern interpretations of religion locate its significance in the creative process engaged in making life meaningful. These alternative interpretations challenge the traditional paradigm that equates religion with denomin-ationalism and equates belief with adherence to specific laws, rituals and practices.[9] As a meaning-making process, religion embraces all human experiences that contend with finitude and find value in the very act of creation.

When religion is understood as a creative engagement with life, it becomes a liberatory practice that places a high value on the most basic human instinct, the desire to create. Making order out of chaos, making meaning out of mean-inglessness, humankind has for millennia left its traces. Availing itself of myriad symbols, film-making, like other forms of art-making, is an expression of the human desire to create meaning, and consequently, functions as religion in culture. Having liberated religion from denominational constraints and patriarchal privilege, post-modern – including feminist – readings of film are limited only by the human imagination. The task of the interpreter-creator is to be a thoughtful critical reader of symbols and signifiers. With regard to signifying woman, religion and film have in common the practice of narrating women's place in culture.

Political theorist Linda Zerilli offers a compelling theoretical framework for analysing how woman signifies in culture.[10] Moving beyond more traditional feminist theorists who, responding to patriarchal either/or categories, see woman as a symbol of chaos and disorder and place woman outside of the margins of cultural normativity, Zerilli argues that 'woman is neither outside the margins nor at the margins of the political; instead, she constitutes and unsettles those margins. A frontier figure that is neither wholly inside nor wholly outside political space, woman is elusive, sometimes reassuring, yet also quite dangerous. She signifies both culture and chaos – one can never be sure which. In the ambiguity lies her symbolic power for the political theorist and the possibility of feminist criticism'.[11]

Following Zerilli, this chapter acknowledges that either/or – either Eve or Mary – is too limiting to adequately represent the complex nature of women's experience and looks toward ambiguity as a potent symbol of the in-between, the *metaxu* – the sacred space that woman inhabits.[12] Insofar as both religion and film wield the power of word and image, they function as signifying and political practices. How they narrate and visualize woman has significant cultural implications that are readily accessible in visual texts that not only challenge the reductive view of women characterized by limiting dichotomies such as either Tiamat or Ishtar, Kali or Parvati, Medusa or Athena, Eve or Mary, but also celebrate the mystery embedded in possibility of both/and.

Directors such as Pedro Almodóvar, Jane Campion, Mira Nair, Claire Denis, Agnieszka Holland, Penny Marshall, Nancy Savoca,[13] Julie Dash, Deepa Mehta, Sally Potter, Marleen Gorris, Krzysztof Kieślowski, as well as others who came before and after them, liberated the idea woman from either/or signifiers, challenged cultural expectations and expanded the possibility of meaning-making. Their films chronicle women's lives across a range of historical and cultural experiences. What these directors have in common is their commitment to re-imagine critique and even parody the roles ascribed to women. Collectively, they offer a dizzying array of visual alternatives to the good girl/bad girl image of woman. Perhaps with the exception of Campion's *The Piano* (1993), many if not most of their films fall into the art house film category. This chapter focuses on the work of only a few of these directors and suggests that the images of woman reflected in their films are, to some degree, representative of the others. Beginning with films that challenge traditional values, the chapter then turns to films of directors such as Jason Reitman, Adrienne Shelly, Jonathan Dayton, Valerie Faris, Todd Fields and others who reflect today's diverse post-feminist and, in some cases, more conservative worldviews.

Women on the Verge [14]

In his critically acclaimed *Women on the Verge of a Nervous Breakdown* (1988), Almodóvar creates the character of Pepa Marcos, an actor who specializes in doing voice-overs for foreign films. As the film opens, Pepa is confronted with the fact that her lover, Ivan, is taking off on a trip, in all likelihood with another woman. The film traces Pepa's zany forty-eight-hour pursuit of Ivan with whom she wants to share the news that she is pregnant. As the narrative unfolds, Pepa finds herself in the midst of several wildly improbable situations that involve Ivan's mentally ill ex-wife, his son and the son's fiancée, her best friend who recently befriended Shiite terrorists intent on blowing up a plane, a mambo-loving taxi driver, animals running around her penthouse, a burning bed, gazpacho spiked with sleeping pills, several memorable keystone cops moments and general mayhem.

What is remarkable about this film is that Almodóvar creates female characters who are too complex to fit into simplistic categories. Out of synch in Almodóvar's Catholic Spain, Pepa is a life force that does not conform to any traditional notion of the place of women in culture. Not married, she is pregnant. The highlight of her unconventional forays into the domestic arts is the addition of a massive dose of sleeping pills to Ivan's favourite soup. Angry enough to spike his soup, when she finds out that terrorists plan to blow up Ivan's flight, she relents and tries to save his life. When Ivan is finally ready to speak with her, Pepa refuses.

Pepa's work as a voice-over actor is a metaphor for her life between two competing worlds of experience; she inhabits the space in-between chaos and culture. By dubbing voices, she mediates the meaning of films. Her role is that of intermediary, intercessor, go-between. Her life mimics her work insofar as she tries to convey the meaning of who she is, and what matters most to her. Before she can make herself understood to others, she must first interpret herself to herself. In the struggle to find Ivan, she finds her own voice and a new desire: motherhood, but on her own terms.

In films like *The Flower of My Secret* (1995), *All About My Mother* (1999) and *Volver* (2006), Almodóvar continues his exploration of the lives of women caught between two worlds. Leo, the writer in *The Flower of My Secret*, has achieved fame and fortune by writing wildly popular happy-ever-after women's fiction. As her personal life starts to unravel, however, she wants to write about lives much like her own where happy endings are not inevitable. Neither her husband, sister, mother, publisher, nor even her best friend is interested in knowing who she is beyond culturally defined images of traditional wife, sympathetic sister, dutiful daughter and glamorous celebrity. Leo decides to create a new identity by changing her name, and her life. She is hired by a newspaper and assigned to review her own book. Liberated from her past, she finds herself unsettling the margins that had previously provided stability and status. In the act of recreating herself, and thereby of engaging the world from a different position of power, she reclaims her own desire.

In *All About My Mother*, motherhood and gender are fluid rather than static experiences. Manuela, grieving the death of her son, goes in search of his father, who, it turns out, is Lola, a transvestite prostitute unaware he has a son. In Almodóvar's world, women, including those who choose to become women, who go through the crucible of grief, who shed the outer skins of their old identities, can hope to re-emerge with a renewed sense of self-knowledge and a capacity for forgiveness. He dedicates the film to those who live between two worlds: 'To all actresses who have played actresses. To all women who act. To men who act and become women. To all people who want to be mothers. To my mother.'

In *Volver*, the mother/daughter theme that appears as a subtext in many of Almodóvar's films becomes the focus. Irene, the mother of two daughters, Raimunda and Sole, is believed to have died along with her husband in a fire. However, Irene has not died; rather, she set the fire in order to kill her husband and his lover. In a mirror image of her mother's life, Raimunda finds her own husband trying to rape her teenage daughter, Paula, who believes the man to be her father. Almodóvar infuses the process of the mother and daughter trying to get rid of the body with vaudevillian hilarity. In the midst of it all, Raimunda discovers that her own mother is indeed alive. She had spent the intervening years living between two worlds as a *fantasma*, a ghost, in her invalid sister's house and taking care of her. Reunited with her daughters and Paula, her granddaughter, Irene discloses to them that Raimunda's daughter, Paula, is also her sister. Her father had raped her and she gave birth to Paula. As is typical in Almodóvar's world, the proverbial sins of the fathers are avenged by generations of women who create their own justice and redefine their desires.

Almodóvar's women, regardless of how ditzy they may be or how zany and complicated their lives and relationships, share the experience of living in the in-between space – between chaos and culture – and of taking responsibility for their own lives. Ownership and agency are hallmarks of Almodóvar's Pepa, Leo and Irene who unsettle the margin demarcating the traditional assumptions about women. Motherhood, for example, is never an ideal state but a vexed reality. Women balance precariously on the razor-thin edge between sanity and insanity, life and death. Outcomes are inevitably unpredictable in Almodóvar's universe, but the promise of a life recreated by desire is always a possibility.

The tension between empowerment and disempowerment that looms large over the lives of the women in Almodóvar's films is central to the lives of the women who inhabit Jane Campion's films. Campion inserts women into the spaces between sanity and insanity, cultural norms and desire, domesticity and creativity, visibility and invisibility. Whereas Almodóvar leavens the seriousness of his themes with a powerful dose of humour, Campion unleashes the fullness of patriarchal power on her heroines. Women suffer at the hands of abusive fathers, violent husbands and feckless lovers. An undercurrent of unutterable violence menaces women in films such as *Sweetie* (1989), *Angel at My Table* (1990), *The Piano* (1993) and *The Portrait of a Lady* (1996). However well-mannered, civilized or cultured most men appear, beneath the veneer is a sense of privilege that justifies violent sexualized power. Campion's women struggle to claim their own voices, to speak their own truths as they find themselves on the verge of being overwhelmed by male expectations. Defined by and confined within worlds not of their own making, they resist patriarchal power and through resistance find their own – regardless of the cost or the ambiguity of the outcomes.

In *Sweetie*, perhaps her darkest and least forgiving depiction of women's lives, Campion explores how women who grow up in dysfunctional families negotiate the space between sanity and insanity, life and death. She relies heavily on visual clues to suggest the aetiology of mental illness. Although the thin ascetic Kay is visually very different from Sweetie, her overweight drama-queen sister, they share a family history of incest. Incest is implied when as Sweetie is giving her father a bath, she drops the soap and dips her hands in the water between his thighs; and incest is intimated when Kay lies in bed, staring wordlessly at the ceiling and clutching the sheets under her chin. While Kay becomes merely neurotic, Sweetie becomes psychotic. Neither Kay's obsessive behaviours nor Sweetie's emotional breakdowns are directly addressed. Rather, they are visualized in Kay's obsession with miniature horses and Sweetie's sexual exhibitionism.

Ultimately, Sweetie loses her tenuous hold on reality. When her parents return from a trip, they find her in a state of rage. Feeling abandoned, particularly by her father, Sweetie climbs into 'The Princess Castle', the tree house that her father built for her. With her naked body painted black, screaming obscenities, Sweetie plunges to her death. Campion, an anthropologist interested in uncovering patterns in human behaviours, allows the images – the bones – to speak for themselves. Unlike Almodóvar's women who find themselves and their desires amidst the madness, Campion's Sweetie succumbs to it. Kay, a dabbler in a variety of religious practices, is left to sort out whether Sweetie's death was a choice or an accident and whether she herself is fated to live or die.

Campion's exploration of insanity, identity and independence continues in *Angel at My Table*, a film based on the three-volume autobiography of Janet Frame, a highly regarded New Zealand writer. The film faithfully chronicles Janet Frame's journey from an impoverished and abusive childhood in rural New Zealand of the 1930s through to her later years as a very successful and highly acclaimed writer. Central to the narrative are Frame's experiences at a teacher's college, her early efforts to become a writer and the eight years she spends in a mental institution when she is misdiagnosed with schizophrenia and narrowly escapes a lobotomy. Campion invests every frame of the film with empathy shaped by a deep and abiding conviction that, like Frame, women can and do find their voice, usually at great cost to themselves, and their rightful place, even if the place is not in the home.

In *Angel at My Table*, Campion creates a visually intimate world of interiors that mimics Frame's tendency toward introspection as well as her complex inner life. Preoccupied in this film with the tension between seeing oneself through the desires of others and finding one's own desire and creativity, Campion re-imagines this theme in *The Piano*, which takes place in New Zealand in the nineteenth century. In *The Piano*, Ada embodies the tension between culture/chaos. The fierce, turbulent, unpredictable Pacific and the hot, humid, entangled jungle mirror the turmoil of Ada's inner life that is masked by her muteness and prim Victorian dress. Campion is intrigued by the question of who owns women's desire. In Ada, she creates a character that ultimately chooses life and the fullness of her desire, but not before her intended husband chops off her finger. Typical of Campion's preference for intimation, the origins of Ada's muteness, the identity of her daughter's father and the reason her own father sends her off from Scotland as a mail-order bride for a European settler in New Zealand are shrouded in mystery. Why the piano became the voice through which Ada chose to communicate is equally unknown, as are the reasons for her compulsive playing that distracts her from attending to her own daughter, Flora.

Ada's muteness as well as her piano playing signifies differently to different people. For Flora, her mother's muteness is the space in-between two worlds – inner and outer, silence and sound, love and betrayal. Flora, the go-between, interprets her mother to the worded world. Ada's intended husband, Alistair, and his family determine that her muteness, as well as her passion for the piano, is a form of madness that marks her as the outsider, as "the other" who must be contained and made to conform. However, Baines, the European settler who goes native embracing the Maori ways, falls in love with Ada and with her passion for the piano. Accepting Ada's muteness, he communicates through gestures rather than words. Inviting Ada to teach him to play, Baines chooses to learn her language of desire. Their highly sexualized wordless exchanges contrast sharply with Alistair's, his mother's and his sisters' incessant prattle and further alienates them from Ada.

Choosing silence, Ada challenges and subverts to the law of the father. The world in which the Word invests the world with meaning is transformed by Ada's passion for music and desire to remain authentic to her will. When she is pulled into the depths of the Pacific by the weight of her piano, Ada ultimately chooses life, but no longer the life of silence. In Baines, she satisfies her desire for a life of mutuality and the acceptance of her otherness. The ending of *The Piano* flirts with the B-movie 'lives happily ever after' paradigm, and, given Campion's feminist credentials, can be read as an ironic twist on the Cinderella story. Baines, with his Maori markings and Scottish plaid clothing, is as much a signifier of the collusion of chaos and culture as is Ada with her nascent speech and new life as a piano teacher. In place of the glass slipper, Ada sports a silver fingertip which Baines wrought for her.[15]

Happily Ever After

Campion's films, as well as those of directors who share her determination to question how woman signifies and how women experience themselves and their desires, are in sharp contrast to some post-9/11 films. In the post-9/11 world, many American films reflect a degree of fatigue with political correctness, a renewed quest for happy endings and a return to family values, albeit within a twenty-first century framework. If Almodóvar and Campion explored motherhood as a vexed and conflicted site of cultural expectations and women's desires, films such as Reitman's *Juno* (2007), Morrrison's *Junebug* (2005), and Shelley's *Waitress* (2007) reflect a cultural shift to the right. These films posit the choice between independence and interdependence, individual freedom and community values as alternative realities for women to inhabit. Flirting with a more dichotomous worldview, these films not only represent a range of possible options as women sort out their desires and create meaningful lives, but, consequently, mirror cultural complexities that resist a return to simple either/or choices.

Nostalgia for the absolute may have contributed as much to the success of Reitman's *Juno* as the charming leading actor and a whimsical musical score. The film promotes values and assumptions about women's desires that align more closely with those expressed in such 1950s television comedies as *Father Knows Best* (1954) than in the films of Almodóvar and Campion. For all of Juno's brashness, smart-mouthed repartees and rejection of what passes for normative teenage girl culture, she is quite conventional in her effort to be a good girl and to do the right thing as she searches for unconditional love. Pregnant at sixteen, Juno considers an abortion, but she rejects the idea after a visit to the local clinic. Whereas Alexander Payne's *Citizen Ruth* (1996) is a parody of pro- and anti-abortion politics that took both sides to task for being exploitative, Reitman's politics seems less nuanced. His portrayal of the unprofessional staff at the seedy clinic, Juno's sense of superiority and her disdain for the group of racially diverse women she sees at the clinic suggests a tilt to the right. However noble is Juno's desire to give her baby to a woman who believes she was born to be a mother, it nevertheless reflects her naïve belief in B-movie endings – the baby will 'live happily-ever-after' with her new mother. Ultimately, Juno finds comfort in the belief that her father loves her unconditionally and in his promise that someday she will find a man who will also love her unconditionally and with whom she will have another baby.

Morrison's *Junebug* is more complex than *Juno* because it grapples more directly with the question of what women want and how they come to terms with their desires. In *Juno*, Vanessa, the well-educated and affluent woman who adopts Juno's baby, desires nothing more than to be a mother, even a single mother given the fact that her husband abandons her in the middle of Juno's pregnancy. For Morrison's Madeleine, however, a sophisticated woman who owns an outsider art gallery in Chicago, nothing could be further from her mind than pregnancy, until she meets her sister-in-law Ashley when she accompanies her new husband, George, on a visit to his parents in a small town in North Carolina. By juxtaposing two radically different cultures and value systems, Morrison explores the nexus of family values, the challenge of going home again and the fatuity of believing in promises of a happy-ever-after ending. While Madeleine sees her new Bible-quoting conservative in-laws as an alien species, they see her as exotic, mysterious and untrustworthy – quintessentially 'other'.

Morrison carefully crafts two competing worlds in which woman signifies in very different ways. With a kind of naïve certainty and deep self-knowledge, Ashley, the pregnant sister-in-law, sees beyond the either/or paradigm and does not judge Madeleine as the 'other'. Ashley knows who she is and what is right for her and her own self-understanding allows her to be more expansive in her views. Madeleine, as the outsider, observes Ashley's final stages of pregnancy, and her efforts to deal with a variety of family problems, including the behaviours of her immature husband who is not prepared to be a father. Although she is not herself interested in motherhood, Madeleine learns from Ashley that to be a mother and to nurture others does not guarantee happiness, but is a laudable way to live one's life.

Motherhood is the main attraction in Shelley's *Waitress*, a film that resembles a traditional fairy tale with an ending that has all the trappings of a 'happily ever after' B-movie. Like Patient Griselda, Jenna is rewarded for her hard work, sunny outlook on life and caring nature with a new baby, a diner of her own and her independence from both abusive husband and caring (married) lover. Like Ashley, Jenna has the self-knowledge to affirm her belief that she has chosen well.

Afterthoughts

Representing the enigma that is woman has always been and will always be a challenge for film-makers. What women desire, how they create meaningful lives, and how they experience themselves as women are questions that will challenge the next globally-focused and highly technological decades. Presumably, religion as a creative human endeavour focused on making meaning out of meaninglessness will continue to intrigue future generations. Therefore, there is little doubt that the predicament of women will remain a source of women's desire to transcend the limitations of an either/or world.

The breakdown of traditional notions of film-making at the beginning of the twenty-first century is a direct result of the creative spaces made available through the internet on U-Tube, as well as through cable channel networks such as HBO, AMC and Showtime. These channels have produced critically acclaimed films and series that have raised the question of what women want and desire in compelling and challenging ways. The expansion of film-making venues should serve women well by providing them with new opportunities to shape the agenda in an ever more complex cultural and social arena. However, there has been a scarcity of women directors in this new creative arena, although many of the female characters have mirrored cultural changes.

The films and series produced on HBO, for example, have demonstrated a willingness to explore cultural assumptions from a keener, and at times perhaps even riskier, perspective. If the universally acclaimed HBO series *Sopranos* invited a critical exploration of family values, it also raised the question about the role of women who traditionally served as the family's moral compass but choose the good life rather then a virtuous one. Similarly, AMC's *Mad Men* portrays the United States in 1960 replete with sexism, racism, homophobia and anti-Semitism. With the Nixon–Kennedy election as background noise, *Mad Men* stands on the cusp between the old and new world orders, in part because it evokes the ambiguities, hopes and desires of women. The series serves as a reminder of the power of word and image to tell us where women have been and what they can hope to become. With its exquisitely detailed portrayal of women's desires, HBO's *Sex and the City* broke new ground as it reframed the feminist mantra: the personal is political.

Part II

Religions and Film

11 Christian Movies

Terry Lindvall

In 1911, in New Britain, Connecticut, a congregational minister, the Reverend Herbert Jump leaped at the opportunity to challenge Christians to discover the innovative potential of the motion picture. The publication of his pamphlet, *The Religious Possibilities of the Motion Picture*, extolled the virtues of this new means of communication, evangelism and religious instruction, marking the venture of Christians into the production, distribution and exhibition of films. However, it would be a spotty trajectory, moving from a vigorous vision into an ambivalent acceptance to outright rejection and then a renewed interest in adapting all the available means of visual persuasion for the work of the Church.

Jump called for religious artists and leaders to imagine the possibilities of not simply telling congregations their message, but of showing it in dramatic parables. A cottage industry of religious filmmaking by various Christian individuals and groups would seek to preach, evangelize, teach and promote missions through the visual arts. These Christian films are defined as moving pictures produced by Christians with some explicit Christian purpose of promoting the faith or provoking questions of ultimate concern.

The Silent Stage

Before World War I, many clergy and educators recognized this peculiar opportunity in the making and exhibiting of non-theatrical moving pictures. Radically different from products of sheer entertainment, these films could be used to convey messages and move congregations.[1] Testimonies were abundantly disseminated in the trade press about the place and purposes of moving pictures used in churches.[2]

After the war, projection equipment used by the military went on public sale and was purchased by non-profit institutions like churches and religious schools.[3] Film exhibitions slowly began to flourish and actually provided the vigorous impetus that would give rise to a viable non-theatrical movement. While many religious groups supported the vision, they committed inadequate funding to sustain it. Nevertheless, a prominent trend began with small independent producers such as James Shields (*The Stream of Life*) contributing significant product for distribution and exhibition.

The year 1919 proved to be a momentous year for the emergence of a Christian film industry. In Chicago, the Society for Visual Education was underwritten in large part by public utilities magnate Harley Clarke. Through its official trade journal, *The Educational Screen*, it propagated an infectious vision that attracted progressive educators and clergy. Simultaneously, Eastman Kodak offered the Presbyterian Church 2000 projectors so that they might learn to exhibit their own films. In the summer of 1919, Methodists held their Centenary in Columbus, Ohio, and converted hundreds of ministers into 'visual exhibitionists'. Visited by such film luminaries as Paramount's Adolph Zukor and home-grown Methodist D. W. Griffith, Methodists took the new tools back to their churches.

The year also saw the organizational schemes of businessmen who sought to recruit competent and knowledgeable professionals to help coordinate a production of their own visual materials. Within this development were included the Christian Herald Film Bureau, the University Film Foundation of Harvard, the remarkable venture of Eastman Teaching films and Yale University's pedestrian *Chronicles of America*. In particular, the *Christian Herald* exploited the pages of its popular religious periodical to puff and promote a fledgling industry.

Exhibition proved easier than either production (although Eastman Kodak's introduction of 16 mm filmmaking in 1923 opened up new avenues for amateur filmmaking) or distribution, as churches readily adapted by projecting images on screens or white walls. Free motion pictures were furnished to children who had attended church the previous Sunday. For Pastor Adam chambers of Harlem Baptist Church, motion pictures provided the best 'bait' to attract young people.[4]

By 1926 the *Literary Digest* opined that 'The Motion Picture either can be made of assistance to the Church, as a vehicle for religious, educational and diversionary propaganda, or it may be left as an opposing weapon for satanic mischief'.[5] However, after the Hollywood scandals of the early 1920s, the invention of radio as a more affordable mass medium for preaching, and the innovation of talking pictures making film production too expensive for churches, significant Christian filmmaking hibernated for over a decade.

By the end of the silent era, movies had been abandoned to 'satanic mischief'.[6] However, one woman, Mary Beattie Brady, Director of the Harmon Foundation, envisioned the 1930s as a New Era for the church and moving pictures. Since denominations had largely retreated from motion picture production on grounds of the cost of sound pictures, the Harmon Foundation championed the use of film among Protestants. For Brady, the usefulness of film to the religious field had become axiomatic, although it had proved a dismal and disheartening failure due to inadequate equipment and lack of suitable products. Denominational visual education boards, the use of moving picture in missions, academic courses, journal columns and foci on Religious Education through visual means evinced a persuasive case for optimism.[7]

Sharing this progressive vision, Reverend R. Hellbeck announced that Protestants no longer needed to consider film to be 'The Cannon That Shoots Twenty-Four Times a Minute'. The superannuated notion of film as the devil's camera was, according to Hellbeck, inherently misleading and mischievous, in that it assumed that the moving picture was an instrument of evil taking us to hell and back in a basket of filth and pornography. Essentially, Hellbeck claimed, the medium remained rather neutral in its use.[8]

Non-sectarian religious production for churches and schools appeared auspicious; however, Depression economic pressures squeezed them out of competition. Nevertheless, six categories or genres emerged: biblical, missionary, historical, biographical, pedagogical and inspirational films,[9] all of which were intended to fulfill the Harmon Foundation's motto to 'support not supplant the sermon'.[10] These general categories remained stable in Christian filmmaking throughout for the next fifty years.

Preaching the Word

Within these six genres, the biblical film remained the staple with the longest history. Bible stories remained popular since the Passion Plays of 1898. Replacing them was Cecil B. DeMille's classic *King of Kings* (1927), a Hollywood product commandeered by the Christian film industry. Financed by New York philanthropist Jeremiah Milbank's Cinema Corporation of America, the blockbuster film illustrated familiar Bible stories, incorporated numerous hymns in its presentation and washed away fears of films. Its impact proved monumental, even evoking viewer responses as many testified that they saw the face of H. B. Warner (DeMille's actor playing Jesus) whenever they prayed.[11]

The 1930s gave birth to an international movement of missions films, with Baptists, Presbyterians, Methodists and others traversing the globe to capture the stories and needs of exotic lands and people. The films not only sought to raise awareness of the spiritual and medical needs of other people, but to raise funding for missionary endeavours.

Reverend James Kempe Friedrich dreamed of translating the stories of Daniel, David and Goliath and Jesus onto the silver screen to proclaim biblical messages.[12] Convinced that film was 'the most potent thing that man has yet created for getting ideas across', he defined his calling:[13]

What they see impresses people more than what they merely hear . . . there are hundreds of thousands of little feet toddling over the thresholds of the theatres of America . . . Too many of our boys and girls are growing up with no knowledge of the Bible. If I can rouse in them an interest to read the Bible, then, thank God, I shall have done something worthwhile.[14]

An independent producer, Friedrich invested his inheritance in a project entitled *The Great Commandment*.[15] A remarkable providence brought thousands of excess 16 mm projectors from the Army in the aftermath of World War II. Friedrich aggressively created his own market by providing churches with these projectors to watch his films.[16] His Cathedral Films' crowning glory began in 1945 with the pre-production of a12-part black and white series of short episodes of the *Life of St. Paul* immediately followed by a colour series of the *Living Christ*.[17]

Friedrich's reputation for quality Christian filmmaking opened doors for numerous joint ventures with other denominations. The Christian Reformed Church commissioned Cathedral's John Coyle to direct *The Test* (1947) in which a pastor helps a councilman vote against a pro-gambling ordinance after showing him, not surprisingly, through an optical zoom onto the screen, clips of Cathedral's *No Greater Power*, about the life of the miniature moneyman, Zaccheus.

Paralleling Friedrich, a film equipment exporter and Roman Catholic entrepreneur from Venezuela, Carlos Octavia Baptista, 'received a revelation' in 1939 about using film to teach object lessons to Sunday school children. His *Story of a Fountain Pen* allegorized redemption in a parable of a pen from a pawn shop.[18] His production and distribution company, the Scriptures Visualized Institute (SVI), founded in 1942, claimed to inaugurate the nation's first 'talking head' sermon series by placing many of the country's leading preachers and musicians on film such as Harry Ironside, Oswald J. Smith and George Beverly Shea.[19]

In 1944, Baptista and employee Max Kerr designed a portable projector, weighing only 25 pounds, calling it the 'Miracle Projector', not because of its weight, but because they guaranteed that the projector would continue to work flawlessly until the return of the Lord.[20] Baptista's straightforward and often very crude evangelistic messages represented little more than sermons on celluloid. Baptista's successor would become filmmaker Ken Anderson, whose leader tape at the start of his films announced, 'Ken Anderson Films, where the message is always first'.

A third venture originating immediately after the war focused upon the tension between science and religion. The grand auteur of Creation films, before the Disney wild life classics, Dr. Irwin Moon, experimented with illustrated sermons, incorporating electronic, photographic, stroboscopic and sonic devices, Moon sought to demonstrate the complementary kinship of the Christian faith and true science. His naturalist photography informed with a theological agenda overwhelmed audiences in the breathtaking colour and slow motion techniques of his raw documentary material, showing the handiwork of God through the marvels of the universe. Moon was approached by a Harvey Marks and the Moody Bible Institute to put 'this material on film so even the smallest churches around the nation could benefit from it'. Within a few years later, *God of Creation*, was produced, fulfilling the mission of MIS to communicate the 'first century gospel with twentieth century illustrations', using time-lapse photography to reveal God's 'hidden miracles' within the natural order.[21] Over eighteen *Sermons from Science* films were produced over the next three decades ranging from Cine award-winning *City of the Bees* (1957) to *Energy in a Twilight World* (1980).[22]

Building the Market

In an effort to release films to various religious groups, Harvey Marks had organized the Visual Aid Centre in 1945, which gave rise to a national network of film libraries catering to churches and schools. Its most urgent need was product. Envisioning a clear communication of the Gospel through film, Ken Anderson organized Gospel Films in 1949. Rather than selling films directly to churches, Gospel established a rental network. Consistent monthly cash flow from rentals would prove beneficial for further investment. In September 1974, others joined Executive Secretary Harvey Marks in coordinating the distribution of Christian films through the Christian Film Distributors Association (CFDA).

Targeting a high school market, Gospel films set up a division called Youth Films. To head up the programme the Board hired a young and aggressive Youth for Christ club leader from Indianapolis, the colourful Billy Zeoli. Billy instituted a new appeal for youth films and broadened the base of the company to reach more teenagers and college students.[23] In 1958, Zeoli secured the rights for a biography of the popular teen-recording artist who converted to Christianity after a near-fatal car accident. *The Tony Fontane Story* (1963) became Gospel's most ambitious project to date, spurring them to employ a professional Hollywood crew and director Jan Sadlo.[24] However, this new direction of Gospel Films into dramatic testimony films veered away from unequivocally direct evangelistic films, creating strains among the leadership. Anderson wished to make conservative and mission oriented films while Zeoli aggressively pursued teenage and youth oriented films.

The quiet power struggle erupted in 1959, when Anderson desired to become president of Gospel. However, in 1965, Zeoli, known as the 'godfather of Christian films', became the president of the company, apparently through internal political manoeuvring.[25] By that time, Gospel was by far the largest Christian film production and distribution centre in the world and they built a state-of-the-art film studio on their lot in Michigan.

Zeoli developed the organization into a formidable distribution centre, hiring such creative independent personalities as Mel White and John Schmidt. Anderson sought to make more explicitly sectarian films and in 1960 departed Gospel to form the Ken Anderson Company, producing such films as the didactic *Pilgrim's Progress* (1977), fulfilling the company's motto where 'the message is always first'. Two of the most impressive projects were Anderson's hagiographic studies of *Hudson Taylor* (1981) and *Fanny Crosby* (1984).

Several notable successes appeared with the new leadership of Gospel Films. The Christian film industry's first self-effacing satire was based on Christian author Joseph Bayly's popular short story, *The Gospel Blimp* (1967). Irwin (Shorty) Yeaworth Jr. directed this sly comedy about misguided evangelism conducted from a zeppelin, hauling Bible verse banners, broadcasting Christian music from above, and dropping gospel 'firebomb' tracts on the unsuspecting victims of Middletown. The International Gospel Blimps Incorporated was itself a clever satire on Gospel Films.

Gospel picked up controversial filmmaker Rolf Forsberg's remarkable adaptation of Don Richardson's *Peace Child* in 1972. Shot in Papau, New Guinea, Forsberg's film captured how the sacrificial myth embedded in foreign cultures could serve as a metaphoric bridge for communicating the death of Christ.

In 1976, Gospel released Franky Schaeffer's phenomenally successful set of films, *How Should We Then Live?*, a series which would redefine and transform the film business.[26] By visually tracing a Gibbonesque rise and decline of Western culture from ancient Rome to the new modern elite, Franky and his father, reformed evangelical apologist Francis Schaeffer, sought to excavate the past as a judgement on the present. As a documentary filmmaker, Franky explored the wilderness of visual polemics, producing one of the most notable series for engaging the cultural wars before it had become a bandwagon.[27] In 1979, Franky and his father produced a second series in conjunction with Surgeon General Dr. C. Everett Koop, *Whatever Happened to the Human Race?*, in an effort to spark a cultural and political engagement with the world on topics such as abortion.[28] The inaugural success of the Schaeffers's films was one to open floodgates of other serial films, such as James Dobson's *Focus on the Family*. Critic Mark H. Senter III argued that Christian filmmakers learned the profitable lesson that 'serials make money ... [they] can create repeat audiences, multiply ministries, and frequently increase revenues'.[29]

The instructional film, also known as the 'talking-heads', promoted a particular personality to provide teaching or inspiration. Rather inexpensive to produce, they capitalized on a speaker's popularity, expertise and charisma. Most dealt with fashionable topics and/or controversial issues. Apologetics such as Josh McDowell's *Evidence for Faith* (1984) became fashionable instructional series.

However, the champion of instructional series was the widely rented (over 60,000 times in its first decade), *Focus on the Family* (1979), Dr. James Dobson's presentation of his popular psychology Christian teachings on family issues. For a production cost of about $30,000, Dobson's seven-part series established a norm of biblical instruction regarding raising children and communicating with one's spouse.

Gospel Films recruited the brightest young filmmakers, Heinz Fussle, Mel White, John Schmidt and Johnson/Nyquist, as part of the newly expanded Gospel family. From 1980 to 1986, of the 64 new productions released by the company, only two were even co-produced by Gospel and there were 29 independents producing films for Gospel, Rick Garside, Eric Jacobsen and Mike Evans led the list for successful productions.

Filmmaker Mel White directed the hilarious and engaging Charlie Churchman series, a fresh revival of the silent film comedian in religious settings. This comedy series served as light appetizers for his meaty and provocative Twenty-third Psalm series. White would match phrases from the psalm with actual crises of suffering or faith. *In the Presence of Mine Enemies*, the dramatic story of POW prisoner Howard Rutledge launched the anthology. *Though I Walk Through the Valley* traced the courageous struggle of a Christian college professor, Tony Brouwer, with terminal cancer, editing together interviews with him and his family through the ordeal, being one of the 'first films in history to document the last year in the life of a dying man and his family'. *He Leadeth Me* opted for a buoyant, inspiring documentary on the triumphant life of blind composer/singer Ken Medema.

Incorporating humour, and parodying the popular Hollywood products, John Schmidt delivered several snappy, suburban presentations of poignant and humorous stories of church hypocrisy and Christian evangelism: *Super Christian* (1980), *The Greatest Story Never Told* (1983) and *Kevin Can Wait* (1983) topped the list of his bright, glossy, entertaining films. Spoofing the Hollywood style, Schmidt wryly addressed issues of hypocrisy, evangelism and prejudice in the evangelical community.

The parody style of old movies and television shows also caught on with Dave Christiano's *The Daylight Zone* (1986), introduced with 'Meet Carl Smith, a 35-year-old school teacher on his way home to Johnson City, Texas . . . before he reaches Johnson city, he'll make one brief stop in *The Daylight Zone*'.

In 1988 and 1989, Gospel Films acquired Thomas Nelson Communication film distribution, Fred Carpenter's Mars Hill Productions, Son Pictures and Chuck Warren's Life Productions.[30] The stigma of making religious movies stuck to many of these talented directors. After twelve years of Christian filmmaking, Fred Carpenter was asked when he was going to make 'real movies'. Carpenter explained that his task was to facilitate legitimate relationships, 'taking the whole message of Christ into the whole of creation, but not at the expense of the highest quality' to the glory of God.[31]

When Sam Hersh founded Family Films in 1946, he was not thinking of producing 'Christian films' but, rather, of producing films for the whole family. Allegedly, 'Hersh was not a Christian when he founded the company, he was an opportunist. But he became a Christian and began to produce films with a strong Christian message'.[32] Family Films' first three films, *A Boy and His Prayer, Yesterday, Today, And Forever* and *Unto Thyself Be True*, were completed in 1949 at the Occidental and Hal Roach Studios.[33] Family Films focused upon mundane social crises facing church members, with family problems addressed in *Unto Thyself Be True* and alcoholism underlying *Yesterday, Today and Forever*.[34] A typical Family Film would be *In His Name* in which a boy throws a baseball through the stained-glass window of a church, shattering the face of Christ. His act of sending an anonymous note with eight cents as a down payment propels the Pastor to establish a recreational centre for children, a playground, clubroom, library and other community projects. Such an act inspires the young vandal who decides to enter the ministry.

Touted as 'the granddaddy of evangelical filmmakers', WorldWide Pictures (WWP) officially formed in 1952 as the Billy Graham Evangelistic Film Ministry, incorporating Dick Ross's production company, Great Commission Films.[35] In 1950, Ross had filmed a Graham crusade in Portland and suggested inserting footage into a dramatic feature film. The first film, *Mr. Texas* (1951), shot during the Ft. Worth Crusade, featured Red Harper in the leading role and premiered in the prestigious Hollywood Bowl.[36]

Setting up headquarters in Burbank, California, WWP turned out numerous features, including groundbreaking popular success of *The Restless Ones* (1965) with Kim Darby, followed by *For Pete's Sake* (1968 with Teri Garr), *Time to Run* (1973 with Oscar winning Charles Rosher as Director of Photography), *The Hiding Place* (1975), *Joni* (1980) and *The Prodigal* (1983). During two decades of quality productions of religious filmmaking, World-Wide set up its own distribution system in Minneapolis, Minnesota.[37] They produced what Ken Engstrom called the 'Billy Graham signature series, pure and simple and evangelistic, true to the Gospel'.[38] These films would usually insert the protagonist struggling through a personal crisis into a Billy Graham crusade where he or she would come to Christ. In a 1966 article in *Christianity Today*, statistical record claimed over 120,000 conversions from the films.[39]

WWP's 'Message Motion Picture', *The Restless Ones*, was released in the secular theatrical market, followed by the successful films, *The Hiding Place*

(1975) and *Joni* (1980).[40] Both were directed by James Collier, convinced that true-life stories were the most effective means for communicating faith.[41] With Hollywood producer Ken Wales, Collier returned to direct the quintessential Billy Graham conversion/journey picture, *The Prodigal*. The contemporary version of Christ's parable of the wayward son expands to the overlapping tales of three desultory pilgrims, son, brother and now the father's own wife. Each gropes for meaning along his or her own road trip. Again, sin is less than credible. The issue defined by Harry Cheney was that Christian filmmakers 'violate a cardinal rule of good drama – that character, not ideology, dictates plot and action'.[42]

The film, however, sparked a spirited defence of Christian filmmaking by the two executives. Collier and Wales reflected on the challenges of the Christian film.[43] A recurring objection against WorldWide was the ubiquitous nature of Billy Graham and the explicitly and unapologetically evangelistic tenor of the films. Yet these films were intended and designed to serve audiences as 'a catalyst in their spiritual journey'.[44]

According to Wales, a second issue haunting Christian filmmakers revolved around the question of making evil explicit or implicit. For Wales, the latter option allowed audiences to bring to the film 'all their imagination, their biases, their prejudices . . . and forced the director to be creative and imaginative and to come up with some way to say what was happening [especially sexually]'. Collier felt daring in that in *The Prodigal* he was able to 'imply that people have sexual lives', although he stopped short of provoking the voyeurism of most Hollywood films. He felt pigeon-holed by Hollywood that joked that 'any script that came into a major studio that had "God" in it and didn't have "damn" behind it was immediately sent to WorldWide'.[45]

In 1972, Gateway Pictures launched the story of New York City evangelist, David Wilkerson's *The Cross and the Switchblade*, starring Pat Boone. Ken Curtis, who formed Gateway Films with initial investors, recognized the neglect and ignorance of many to church history, Curtis envisioned a series of films depicting the work of God throughout history. In 1979, Curtis hit upon the strategy of acquiring films from independent producers and secured the rights to several British biopic productions beginning with the BBC's *John Hus*, Tony Tew's *John Wycliffe* (1983) and *God's Outlaw* (1988) about William Tyndale. Out of Gateway's interest in historical films emerged *Christian History* magazine.

Year 1985 marked Gateway's crowing achievement with Gateway's co-production of director Norman Stone's poignant version of *Shadowlands*. The inspirational and remarkably literate film portrayed British author C. S. Lewis and his marriage late in life, winning numerous international awards, an Emmy and two British Academy Awards.

Benchmarks and New Passions

In 1945, the Protestant Film Commission was organized to produce high-quality non-theatrical movies with a religious message and to guide Hollywood studios towards making more moral films.[46] The PFC produced its first 40-minute feature, Sammy Lee's slick *Beyond Our Own*, promoting worldwide evangelism. The PFC designated that the film was to be shown only in churches, not in theatres.[47] For the *New York Herald Tribune*, it established a milestone in the history of the religious motivated film. Setting up their own distribution company, the Religious Film Association, the PFC rallied denominations to get on board.[48]

Several highly touted PFC programmes included *My Name is Han*, shot in China, and Paul Heard's *Kenji Comes Home*, nominated for Best Documentary Feature at the 1949 Academy Awards.[49] As several denominations such as the Methodists and Episcopalians worked with the PFC, others like the Baptist separated to develop their own production houses. Broadman films served Baptists as they turned out films, televisions series and even a very lively animated series called JOT.[50]

Several other key independent films mark the landscape of the Christian film industry. In 1954, the Lutherans released their hagiographic feature on *Martin Luther*. The apotheosis of Lutheran filmmaking climaxed in 1953 with another story of the obstreperous monk who interfered with the steady flow of ecclesiastical revenues and the collecting of indulgences. In collaboration with Lutheran Church Productions, Louis de Rochemont Associates took on the historical narrative of Martin Luther, a story of a wild boar invading the vineyards of the Roman Catholic Church.[51]

Touted as the 'most seen film in the world', Campus Crusade's *Jesus* film project appeared in 1979 and was immediately translated into scores of languages. Beginning in 1945, Campus Crusade president Bill Bright had envisioned the creation of a biblically accurate biography of Jesus in 1945, which thirty years later was realized and translated into more than 610 languages. The film garnered praise from evangelical Christian leaders as Rick Warren (*The Purpose Driven Life*) who called it the 'most effective evangelistic tool ever invented'.[52] The Radio and Film Commission of the Methodist church evolved into TRAFCO, and, in 1952, under the eye of Dr. Fred Eastman, developed a film on *John Wesley*.[53]

The most infamous Christian film erupted into public tumult during the 1964 Worlds' Fair in New York, within the confines of the Protestant-Orthodox Center. Maverick filmmaker Rolf Forsberg filmed one of the most controversial 'church' films, *Parable*, an allegory of Christ's suffering. The Messianic figure, however, was portrayed as a clown, who took on the sufferings, degradation and rejection of the oppressed, a woman and a black man, and was 'crucified' in the circus tent by the establishment.[54] Actor Fred Gwynne narrated Rolf Forsberg's allegorical *The Antkeeper* (1966) about the eponymous character taking on the form of an ant to communicate with warring red and black ants, eventually sacrificing his life. Other films stretched the dramatic limits of the status quo, particularly one controversial film that crossed over into the secular market. From the Lutheran Film Associates came William Jersey's *A Time for Burning* (1967), a cinema-verite, early Dogme '95, styled story of an attempted integration of a Lutheran minister's white church and the neighbouring black ghetto in Omaha, Nebraska.[55]

Young professional filmmakers emerged out of film schools and responded to a calling to create films from a Christian worldview, rather than produced Christian films. In 1988, Fred Holmes directed the melodramatic Kuntz Brothers' crossover film *Dakota* starring Lou Diamond Phillips, released through Miramax. The youth market was handled by servant filmmaker Eddie McDougal, whose *Never Ashamed* (1984) was one of the most widely seen youth films of the 1980s.

The apocalyptic phase of Christian filmmaking started in the early 1970s with Southern Baptist preacher Estes Pirkle and exploitation filmmaker Ron Ormond's gruesome *The Burning Hell* (1974), in which maggots crawl out of skulls. More popular was Russ Doughten and Shorty Yeaworth's classic end-times *Thief in the Night* (1972) a truly effective, albeit campy, film that sought to scare the hell out of spectators by focusing upon the tribulation. Doughten's production company, Mark IV Pictures, unleashed a legion of dispensational sequels such as *Distant Thunder* (1978) and *Image of the Beast* (1980). Canadians Peter and Paul Lalonde of Cloud Ten Pictures made the *Apocalypse* series and secured the rights to the Tim LaHaye runaway bestseller, *Left Behind*. Nepotistic Trinity Broadcasting Company employed Matt Crouch, producing *Omega Code* (1999) and *Megiddo* (2001) (along with the abysmal nadir of Christian films, *Carmen, the Champion*) seeking to exploit their diverse fundamentalist and charismatic audiences. TBN had previously underwritten the modestly successful *China Cry* (1990), the true story of Nora Lam who suffered under Mao's communist society.

For a brief period, the Christian graduate film school at Regent University competed with other national programmes, winning student Academy Awards for their University films (*Bird in a Cage, Turtle Races*), and marketing films to HBO, Cinemax and other television channels. After graduating from Regent's film school, Danny Caralles ventured into end-times films, a vanguard in the trend to shoot films on high definition video, releasing *Final Exit, Escape from Hell* and *Pilgrim's Progress*. The low cost of digital video cameras enabled such low-budget productions possible with churches producing new films. Such a phenomenon marked the cinematic debut of

Sherwood Baptist Church in Albany, Georgia, as they funded Alex Kendrick's feature length *Facing the Giants* in 2006 and their establishment of Sherwood Pictures, with *Flywheel* released in 2008.

Although complicated by financial decisions, Phil Vischer's Big Idea Productions possessed the ability to attract diverse audiences, resulting in the feature length Veggie Tale production of *Jonah*, with Bob the Tomato and Larry the Cucumber, a descendent of the Lutheran's Davey and Goliath series.

In 2001, Mel Gibson invested his own money in what appeared to be a fanatic's folly, producing *The Passion of the Christ*, essentially a foreign language film; marketed through grassroots organizations of local churches, it shocked industry insiders by its enormous profits, taking in over $370 million in domestic gross.

Christian businessman Phillip Anschutz purchased over one-fifth of America's theatres by acquiring Regal Cinemas, America's largest movie theatre chain, along with Edwards Theatres, and United Artists. Under the banner of his Walden Media film franchise, and in conjunction with Disney films, Anschutz released an adaptation of C. S. Lewis' *The Lion, The Witch and the Wardrobe*, which grossed almost $300 million domestically in 2005, Anschutz could play a major role in the distribution of Christian films theatrically. The theatres thus became a viable venue for feature films such as the Ken Wales' stunning production of *Amazing Grace*, the historical biopic of Wilberforce.

In the first decade of the 21st century, productivity and creativity in the Christian film industry seemed to be waxing, with economical filmmaking, numerous Christian colleges offering film programmes, young maverick Christian filmmakers, and the wary but willing media markets (FoxFaith films) to invest in films to religious audiences. In the 100 year anniversary of Reverend Herbert Jump, it appeared that church organizations and Christian groups may have finally realized the religious possibilities of the motion picture.

12 Catholic Movies

Peter Malone

When commentators mention the Catholic Church and cinema, the tendency is to speak of censoring, of the tradition of the Legion of Decency. However, the Catholic Church itself has been a constant in the moviemaking of Western industries. It has often been the subject of criticism. It has very often provided sentiment and humour. At other times, the focus has been on clergy, priests, bishops and popes. And many stars have portrayed nuns. In more recent times, the church has experienced a crisis because of sexual abuse by some clergy. That too has become the subject of the movies. And then, there was *The Da Vinci Code* (2006) with its absurd hypotheses about Jesus and Mary Magdalene, about secret cults in the Church and the sinister members of Opus Dei.

There is a classic text in English on the portrayal of the Catholic Church in cinema, very detailed, very thorough: *Hollywood and the Catholic Church* by Les and Elizabeth Keyser. However, it was published in the mid-1980s and the authors themselves lamented a little in their introduction that there were many explicit films about to be released. Their chapters considered the standard topics and their treatment was objective and fair.

Instead of repeating their work, or even supplementing it by adding the films on the Church since the publication of their book, this chapter takes a different approach.

One of the most significant theological books of recent decades for the study of the Catholic Church was Avery Dulles' *Models of the Church*, first published in 1976 and then revised and added to in 1986. What Avery Dulles did was to take key images from the scriptures and from the history of the Church to highlight quite different facets of theology, spirituality and Church activity. The tendency, especially for those who do not belong to the Church, is to see the Church as an *institution* and study it and judge it accordingly. But, for Dulles, this is only one model of the Church, a key model, certainly, but only one.

Where an emphasis is on the spiritual fellowship that bonds Catholics, there is consideration of prayer, community and charity. Dulles presents this model of the Church: *Mystical Communion*.

Commentators know, but often neglect to give due consideration, that the laity comprise the large body of the church, not the clergy. Church activity is on a worldwide scale but it is lived day-by-day for most Catholics in a local context, especially the local parish. Worship and the highlights of life in the church, baptisms, penance and reconciliation, marriage, care for the sick, funerals are all lived at parish level. This is where 'God's grace' is made manifest, so to speak. This making visible of the world of grace is the definition of what Catholics call *sacrament*. This is another model of Church for Dulles.

The Church has always had a sense of mission. This making known the Gospel message is called evangelization, the listening to God's word and preaching it. This means another model of Church which Dulles calls, *herald*.

When the activity of the Church, especially its justice and charity outreach, is mentioned, the Gospel notion of service becomes important. This can be day-by-day service or, in times of persecution, a laying-down-of-life for others as Jesus did. When the Church is looked at from this perspective, the model is that of *servant*.

During the 1980s, especially as the impact of the renewal of the Second Vatican Council was strengthened, a development of the previous models, especially that of servant, showed that in the contemporary world, there was a need for a greater witness to values even if they were countercultural. This led to the model of the Church as *Community of Disciples, Prophetic*.

This chapter will take these models in turn and illustrate them by films which dramatise them – offering a varied way of how cinema has presented the Catholic Church.

Institution

One of the best illustrations of the institution of the Catholic Church is seen in *The Shoes of the Fisherman* (1968). Based on the 1963 novel by Morris West, the film shows some of the workings of the Vatican in detail. Of particular interest is the conclave for the election of the pope, some of the bureaucratic rivalries, between Cardinals played by Vittorio de Sica and Leo McKern, and the ceremony of the crowning of the newly-elected pope (Anthony Quinn). The pomp, the ceremonial, the vestments, the rituals are quite meticulously presented.

In the background are both cold war tensions with Russia and a famine in China. The new pope is involved in shuttle diplomacy – at the time of the film's release, Pope Paul VI had been travelling the world for four years. One of the suggestions, a liberal gesture, is that the Vatican museum wealth be sold to find money for the Chinese. Also in the background is a learned Jesuit, played by Oskar Werner, who has some doctrinal difficulties with the Vatican Curia. This was based on the experiences of the scientist (and mystic) Teilhard de Chardin.

For more of the pomp and the diplomacy, historical films like *Becket* (1964) with its scene of the excommunication of King Henry II or *The Mission* (1986) where the papal nuncio recommends the advice of the Spaniards and Portuguese for the closure of the Jesuit missions in Paraguay or *Brother Sun, Sister Moon* (1973) and Pope Innocent III dealing with Francis of Assisi are prime examples. More negatively, John Gielgud portrays Pius V sending a priest hit man to attack the queen in *Elizabeth* (1998). In the sequel, *Elizabeth – the Golden Years* (2007), the Catholic Church is demonized (while Elizabeth herself is 'angelized'), especially through the monks and chants with Philip II of Spain and an assassin Jesuit sent to England.

On a more critical attitude towards the Vatican is *Monsignor* (1982), a florid melodrama where Christopher Reeve portrays a monsignor who is involved in managing Vatican finances, especially developing suspect links with the Mafia and losing his sense of vocation in the process. This character, portrayed by Donal Donnelly, is seen being murdered in *The Godfather III* (1990).

In an American setting, *The Cardinal* (1963) shows the life of the priest before World War II, the years of training, the hard parish work with a sympathetic priest in the sticks, the erratic commands of a bishop, an ordination ceremony in Italy, work in the Vatican, vocation crisis, time out and a return to the ministry. Director Otto Preminger received a papal medal for making this film.

One of the best films for looking at the strengths and weaknesses of the Church as institution and one of the best screen portraits of a priest is *True Confessions*, based on the novel of the same name by John Gregory Dunne (1981). Robert de Niro plays the chancellor of the diocese of Los Angeles in 1948. Becoming more worldly and ambitious as he has to deal with business matters, a haughty cardinal, covering up clerical scandals and caught in shady dealings by prominent lay Catholics, he is continually challenged by his detective brother and finally decides to retire from the institutional pressures to a life of simplicity in the desert.

More complex are the lives of the two central priests of *Priest* (1995) and their dealing with parish life, their struggles with their vow of celibacy and the attitude of their bishops and other clergy. Their bishop is presented as callous towards his priests – and the film opens with one of the local clergy charging a window in the bishop's house with a large crucifix. Other aspects of *Priest* will be considered in the section on the Church as a Sacrament.

Recent problems have raised questions about formation of clergy and members of religious orders. As early as 1976, Australian Fred Schepisi (basing his screenplay on his own memories in a Marist Brothers Juniorate in 1953) made an arresting insight film into this culture and aspects of its morbid sheltering of adolescent trainees, *The Devil's Playground*.

Since nuns are part of the institution of the Church, they must be considered. Often times they are presented as stereotypes or caricatures, convenient cinematic props, especially for school sequences with a cranky sister. However, the best film on nuns in the context of institution is still *The Nun's Story* (1959). It captures the atmosphere of the old-style convent and the details of the way of life, especially the strict regime of the nun's formation. Audrey Hepburn plays Sister Luke extraordinarily realistically. Sister Luke leaves the convent at the end of the film, a victim of a spirituality which equates the will of God with the whim of a superior – who, in this case, demands that Sister Luke fail her hospital exams as a sign of humility. The film was made during 1958 before the death of Pope Pius XII. At the time, Catholics would have assumed that this was how convent life would always be. However, in January 1959, the new Pope, John XXIII, called for a worldwide council of bishops which led to radical changes in the lives of nuns.

Mystical Communion

'Mystical' is not a word that immediately springs to mind when considering cinema. 'Transcendent' in style and content has been used of directors like Dreyer, Ozu, Bresson, Tarkovsky, Kieslowski. However, what Avery Dulles wanted to highlight in terms of the Church were the less formal, less juridical aspects of church life. It is the face to face association, even intimacy in community. At times, it can be anti-institution. This is the realm of piety and devotion. Church metaphors include the Body of Christ, the People of God. There is a ready language of the spirit, of the Holy Spirit.

Even though the example has irritated many nuns who saw it as caricature, *Sister Act* (1992) has a lot going for it in terms of entertainment and in terms of a spiritual communion that develops a spirit of love and care in a Church-convent setting. Whoopi Goldberg's Doloris is a catalyst for the sisters in the community, and the rather sour superior, to re-consider their enclosed lifestyle and to move towards greater friendship and to reach out to the neighbourhood. This is the light touch – which even has the Pope tapping his feet as the choir sings at the end of Mass.

This can happen in parish life. As early as *Going My Way* (1944), Father Bing Crosby was dispensing pastoral advice in his songs for a couple with marital troubles, the light emotional touch again. Over fifty years later, this kind of 'communion' was shared at interfaith level when friends from schooldays, Edward Norton as a young priest and Ben Stiller as a young rabbi, shared their spiritualities, their personal problems and their social outreach in *Keeping the Faith* (2001). A scene where the elderly parish priest sits in the comfortable rectory armchair and genially talks through problems with his young assistant is one example of this kind of 'communion'. One of the positive qualities of this model of Church is that it wants to communicate this spirituality.

In *Edges of the Lord* (2001), a young Jewish boy from Warsaw is hidden in a village as a Catholic to escape the Nazis. The villagers think he is a Catholic. He goes to Mass and to religion classes. The parish priest knows who he is. While the priest is cutting out the hosts for communion at Mass from the layer of bread – they are circles – the boy asks about the scraps. The priest says that they are 'the edges of the lord' and when the boy comes up to make his first communion, the priest respects his Jewish faith and gives him, instead of a consecrated host, a piece of the edges of the Lord.

A fine film that focuses completely on lay people is the Canadian film, *La Neuvaine* (*The Novena*) (2005). The central character is a lapsed Catholic doctor who has become embittered by the sadness in her life. She encounters a simple young man who prays at the shrine of St Anne de Beaupre outside Montreal. He is convinced that his ailing grandmother will be healed by a miracle. As their paths cross, the doctor comes to assist the grandmother professionally. There is no miracle – except that the faith and spirituality (plain and simple as it is) has a profound effect on the doctor, not to send her rushing back to Church, but giving her a more 'mystical' perspective on her life.

The danger, of course, is that the group can be too inward-looking and become exclusive, something of a sect. The grim 1960s Dublin convent life of *The Magdalene Sisters* (2002) shows tough and censorious attitudes towards the inmate girls who have found themselves in some kind of sexual trouble and have been committed there. This kind of community's lovelessness shows the absence of 'mystical communion'.

And for something completely different: evil spirit and evil spirits. There is a long tradition, from the time of Jesus himself, of people experiencing what is called 'diabolical possession'. Continued arguments question how much this is a real physical/spiritual condition or a psychosomatic condition. Whatever the conclusions, this phenomenon has fascinated many film-makers, especially since the release of *The Exorcist* (1973). *The Exorcist* is probably the best film illustrating this kind of diabolical mystical experience in a community. Despite the bile and blasphemies from the possessed girl, the screenplay uses the rituals and prayers of exorcism quite exactly. It is, according to the Gospel, by prayer and fasting that the evil spirit is cast out.

The Exorcism of Emily Rose (2005) is an interesting Hollywood version of possession and exorcism in a remote community and the subsequent court case where the parish priest is on trial, responsible for the death of the possessed girl. The screenplay raises all sides of the issue, the natural and the supernatural aspects. The film was based on an actual case in Germany in 1976. The German film version, more subdued and continental in its style, was called *Requiem* (2006).

Sacrament

The Church as Sacrament offers the local model of Church, especially in the Church's life in a parish. In many ways, cinema images of parish life are the most familiar. Particular rites of the Church are called 'the Seven Sacraments', particular symbols of God's grace at significant times of life: Baptism, Confirmation, Penance, Eucharist, Orders, Marriage and Anointing of the Sick. There are a number of baptisms in films. There are even more weddings. When one counts up the number of confessional sequences, there is a rather long list. Communion sequences are a short cut to let us know Catholic practice. An independent film, *Impure Thoughts* (1985) where some men reminisce about their 1960s Catholic school has some 'spot-on' sequences of a nun preparing the class for first communion – and then everything going awry on the day. There is a confession sequence which is worth seeing for its accuracy, except for the Latin which inevitably has mistakes in it.

Two fine films, not directed by Catholics, get to the core and to the spirit of parish life.

The first is *Raining Stones* (1994). The parish priest is a common-sensed, practical, spiritual man. He is dealing with many unemployed in Manchester, families with tough lives. The scenes of preparation for first communion and the subsequent, very funny for Catholics, meal scene where the father tries to explain what tradition calls the doctrine of Transubstantiation concerning Jesus' presence in the bread and wine, are well worth seeing. There is also a strong confession scene. This kind of parish life is part and parcel of the day-to-day lives of the people in the area. It is the local church.

There is something the same in *Mass Appeal* (1985). Based on a play by Bill C. Davis, *Mass Appeal* has a very Catholic feel about it. Quite a wide range of topics are covered, especially the difficulties of a 'liberal-minded' deacon, his sermons and his work in the parish and experiencing the disapproval of the seminary rector. The impetuous young man is also critical of the parish priest, a credible Jack Lemmon. The parish priest has been in the job a long time. His heart is in the right place but he has become weary, sometimes lazy, fond of a drop, relying on the esteem of the parishioners to keep going. His final Mass is preceded by his addressing his congregation, almost wanting to give up, confessing his complacency, reminding them of how he has been intricately connected to their lives. And he finds the strength to keep going.

This kind of thing is more dramatic in *Priest* (1995). Jimmy McGovern's screenplay shows a great deal of the ordinariness of the parish, parish meet-ings and discussions (and frustrations), the sacramental rituals, especially a confessional sequence where a young girl trusts the seal of confession and its confidentiality to confide that she has been abused by her father. The father also uses the confessional to threaten the priest. Sexuality is at the centre of the film. The parish priest has been a missionary in Latin America and has returned and is living with the presbytery housekeeper. The young assistant is homosexual, which gets him into trouble with his conscience, with the law and with the bishop. When he returns to the parish after time away, no one will come to him to receive communion. A number of parishioners have walked out in protest. It is only when the young, abused girl comes to receive from him that there is a moment of reconciliation in the church and communion.

Jimmy McGovern also wrote the screenplay for *Liam* (2000) which centres on a Liverpool Catholic family in the 1930s where the father is caught up in the anti-Semitic fascism of the time and the mother and children try to live out their Catholicism. Once again, the sequence where the little boy, Liam, goes to confession worried by sexual matters, is well worth seeing.

Alfred Hitchcock and Graham Greene were prominent English Catholics. The most explicitly Catholic of Hitchcock's films is *I Confess* (1953) which shows how a priest cannot break the seal of confession even when he is being tried for a murder and knows the identity of the killer. The most explicitly Catholic films of Graham Greene's novels were made at the same time, *The Heart of the Matter* (1952) and *The End of the Affair* (1955). A powerful image of sin and guilt is found in *Brighton Rock* (1946). As in his actual life, Greene struggled with sexual issues, with repentance, with confession, with grace and forgiveness and the possibilities of hell because of sinfulness. The films are dramatic theological cases where a central character, especially Trevor Howard's Scobie in *The Heart of the Matter* will choose to damn himself by a sacrilegious communion rather than hurt the two women he loves. *The End of the Affair*, remade by Neil Jordan (1999), advances the theological treatment that the repentant sinner, Sarah, has been so forgiven that she can work a miracle of healing. This theme was taken up by Brian Moore. His *Cold Heaven* (1992) was about sin, forgiveness and a miracle.

Herald

This is not as strong a model of the Church for Catholics as the previous models. The Catholic tradition is that of incarnation and image. It is the Churches of the Reformation who let go of (sometimes literally destroying) images and became Churches of the Word. This was especially true when the Catholic tradition retained Latin for its rituals permitting the use of the vernacular only from the mid-1960s and encouraging biblical studies at that time. This is very clear in the films which show Protestant and Evangelical church services which are principally the reading of scripture, prayer and the sermon. At the end of the service, the congregation congratulates the minister on his sermon.

Church as Herald also emphasizes discernment, an attentive listening to the Word so that a person is not merely a self-proclaimed preacher. The Word is accepted in faith. It is not a cause or an ideology.

In the Catholic tradition, films which illustrate the model of the Church as Herald are the films about missionary activity. Earlier, films about mission activity also provided meaty roles for Hollywood stars. A young Gregory Peck was a missionary, along with Vincent Price, in China in *The Keys of the Kingdom* (1944). Spencer Tracy, who was one of the first stars to visualize a Catholic priest on screen in *San Francisco* (1936), *Boys Town* (1938) and *Men of Boys Town* (1941) played a missionary in a leper colony on a Pacific Island in *The Devil at 4 O'Clock* (1961). At the same time, William Holden and Clifton Webb were priests in China in *Satan Never Sleeps* (1962).

However, three films offer more profound experiences of the missionaries as Heralds of the Word: *The Mission, Black Robe, Molokai*.

The Mission (1986) has become the classic. It is a story of the famous Paraguay Reductions of the eighteenth century which were targeted by the hostile Spanish and Portuguese governments, the Indians attacked by their forces and, in 1773, the Jesuit order was suppressed by the Pope.

There are two key missionaries in *The Mission*. Father Gabriel attracts the Indians by care, by music and by a self-sacrificing love which leads to his being killed with them. Rodrigo is a reformed slave-trader who becomes a Jesuit and who, when the soldiers attack, takes up arms against them against Jesuit orders and dies in battle. The film reflects different theologies, especially of the 1980s when the film was made. Father Gabriel represents the tradition, the preaching of God's word for conversion and for a Catholic life. Rodrigo embodies a theology of justice which is prepared to defend the oppressed. This was the language of 'Liberation Theology' which caused controversy at the time concerning the use of violence for justice.

Black Robe (1991) is based on a novel by Brian Moore. Again, it is a film about Jesuits but this time more than a century before *The Mission* and in Canada. Lothaire Bluteau, who had been *Jesus of Montreal* (1988), plays Fr Laforgue who travels from France to Quebec in 1634. He has come from Louis XIII's and Richelieus's France; for bizarre images of this period see *The Devils* (1970) and any of the *Three Musketeers* films and, by way of devout contrast, *Monsieur Vincent* (1947). Spirituality in France at that time was developing in two directions: a more personalized devotion focusing on the person of Jesus and a more austere, self-mortifying practice focusing on sin and repentance. Moore's screenplay shows the commitment of the missionaries to preach God's word but also shows the spiritual journey with the literal physical journey through hostile Iroquois territory where Fr Laforgue has to shed his rigidity and learn to love the Indians for themselves and not just as people to be converted.

Molokai (1999) is a down-to-earth look at the work of the nineteenth century Belgian Damien de Veuster who volunteered to work in the leper colony of

Molokai in the Hawaian Islands, eventually contracting the disease himself. This portrait is of a generous man with some gruff Flanders characteristics who, like Father Laforgue, learned, we might say, to move from the model of institution to the models of mystical communion and servant.

Not all missionary activity has been presented so positively on screen. At the end of *Apocalypto* (2006), missionaries arrive who will be a threat to the Mayan culture. In the film adaptation of Peter Shaffer's *The Royal Hunt of the Sun* (1970), the missionaries who accompany the conquistador, Pizzaro, are presented as embodying the zealot facets of the Herald.

Servant

While the model of the Church as servant has been a constant, it is only in recent decades that it has received strong theological attention. Jesus said that he had come not to be served but to serve. He also says that lording it over others is a pagan thing and 'that is not to happen among you' (Matthew 20: 24–28). Many a film shows a pompous bishop or a dominating priest or nun. It is easy to see how the model of servant has been neglected or abused. The Church is not meant to be privileged. It has to be open to care for and dialogue with everyone.

Though not written by a Catholic, Robert Bolt's play, *A Man for All Seasons*, is considered a classic. It has been filmed twice. The 1966 version was an Oscar-winner. The 1988 version made for television contained the entire text of the play. Thomas More is portrayed as the exemplary Catholic. He states the he is God's servant first and then the king's. He is a good household man of his times. He is diligent in his work. He is an adviser to the king. However, when Henry VIII wants to divorce Catherine of Aragon to marry Anne Boleyn and have a male heir and decides to reject the annulment decision from Rome, Thomas More can do nothing else but obey his conscience and allow himself to be executed by the king. A man for all seasons is a man of integrity.

In 1980, a story hit the headlines in the Western press. A group of women, including a lay missionary, Jean Donovan, and some nuns, were executed by government forces in El Salvador. Women martyrs make headlines, especially at times of criticism of oppressive authorities like those in El Salvador at this period. The film *Choices of the Heart* (1982) put a contemporary face on the care that these women were providing in the country as well as laying down their lives, like Jesus, for the good of the people. The film, starring Melissa Gilbert as Jean Donovan, showed her as an ordinary young American student who felt a call to do something with her life, willing to go back to Central America despite the dangers. This episode is also part of Oliver Stone's *Salvador* (1986).

One of the major war horror stories of the 1990s was the genocide in Rwanda. One of the films made by outsiders was *Shooting Dogs* (2006). The action takes place over the initial days of the uprising and the Hutus massacring Tutsis. The setting is a school in Kigali. Of Catholic interest and for the model of servant is the character of a priest played by John Hurt. It is one of the most convincing portrayals of a priest in recent films. Not only does the priest serve the children and the adults, he witnesses by his words to the meaning of suffering and the Eucharist, he also lays down his life.

This model of servant led to further reflection, especially in the 1970s and 1980s, leading to the model of Community of Disciples with a Prophetic dimension.

Community of Disciples, Prophetic

The Church is a communion. It is a community. Individuals are servants and can die for their faith. But, the communal dimension is important. We are not alone. The community is a communion. And, if it is to be a servant, then it has to bear witness to what it believes and believes in after listening to the word with discernment.

This means that this model of the Church shows how the Church community is to be a challenge to accepted values, sometimes has to be counter-cultural, sometimes has to be the avant-garde of the Church. That is not always easy, either within the Church or from outside.

Father Bud Keiser CSP, who originated the television *Insight* series, produced two feature films which highlighted contemporary versions of this model. The first was *Romero* (1989), the story of the final years of the life of Archbishop Oscar Romero of San Salvador, assassinated while celebrating Mass in April 1980. If the film had shown only Romero's death, he would clearly have been a servant. However, the bookish, somewhat conservative priest, had a change of heart on becoming archbishop and was outspoken in his criticism of social injustice, government ruthlessness in 'disappearing' and killing opponents. Raul Julia is memorable as Romero, especially in showing his growing in awareness of what was happening, his being supported by his community and his outspoken condemnations.

The other film was the story of New York activist Dorothy Day. The film was *Entertaining Angels* (1995). There is a great deal of discussion between Dorothy Day and her friend and adviser, Peter Maurin, regarding Catholic views of justice. A scene where Dorothy confronts the Cardinal of New York in a restaurant and stakes her claim to be a Catholic voice for justice summarizes this model.

Going back into the past and the community of dock workers and unions in the 1950s in *On the Waterfront* (1954) there is the sermon where Karl Malden as the local priest speaks out about justice and decency in the workplace. The scene is dominated by Malden and a crucifix, and represents a community of disciples who still needed to be goaded in conscience and action.

Other examples range from the nuns sheltering Jewish children in *Conspiracy of Hearts* (1960) and the same theme, more critically dealt with in Louis Malle's semi-autobiographical *Au Revoir, Les Enfants* (1987) to the devoutly Catholic Chico Mendez (Raul Julia again), the rubber tapper who led his people in protest, even to the UN, against the land exploiters in the Amazon jungles of Brazil, *The Burning Season* (1994).

One of the best films to illustrate this model is *Dead Man Walking* (1995). It portrays a community of nuns who have been trained in more traditional *Nun's Story* style but who have discerned that their mission as servants must take them into the community to teach underprivileged children in the neighbourhoods. A prisoner on death row contacts Sister Helen Prejean, asking her to be his spiritual director. She serves, against the wishes of the prison chaplain, as his spiritual companion in his final weeks, listening to him, enabling him to repent and to go to his execution in some peace, asking the forgiveness of the parents of his victims. The nuns in her community and the bishop join with her in protest against the death penalty, something that Sister Helen has continued to do for many years, becoming a world figure in the campaign. The final sequence where the audience glimpses Sister Helen praying with an angry father of one of the victims is quietly eloquent on reconciliation and forgiveness.

Epilogue

The films on sexual abuse need to be acknowledged. There have been many films about priests falling in love, *The Thorn Birds* Syndrome! But more recent films emphasize the exploitation by priests like *The Crime of Father Amaro* (2002), *The Magdalene Sisters* (2002). However, it is films about the abuse of minors that have been sad, sometimes shocking. Most of them are deeply-felt and are an occasion for an examination of conscience for the Catholic Church about these issues and what lies behind them: *Judgment* (1990), *Song for a Raggy Boy* (2003), *Mal Educacion* (2004), *Our Fathers* (2005).

At the end of John's Gospel, he says, 'there were many other things that Jesus said and did which are not recorded in this book . . . (John 20: 30–31). Well, there are many other films that portray the Catholic Church and are not recorded in this chapter, except with a regret that films like this did not find space here: for instance, *Angels with Dirty Faces* (1938), *Heaven Knows Mr Allison* (1956), *Ryan's Daughter* (1970), *From a Far Country* (1981), *The Scarlet and the Black* (1983), *Saving Grace* (1986), *Jesus of Montreal* (1988), *Dogma* (1999), *Amen* (2001), *The Statement* (2003), *Pope John Paul II* (2005), *Brideshead Revisited* (1981; 2008).

147

13 Buddhism and Film

Michele Marie Desmarais

Buddhism began as a practical path meant to alleviate suffering. One of its earliest teachings, likely given by the Buddha himself, is that everything that exists is characterized by: *anicca* (impermanence); *anattā* (no eternal essence) and *dukka* (suffering, unsatisfactoriness).[1] It would be odd then, to expect that the path founded upon these principles would not itself change. Such transformation occurs both diachronically as well as geographically. Despite changes, the Buddhist emphasis on practice, compassion and the relief of suffering do tend to persist, albeit often taking different forms. Film is a useful source for exploring these principles, practices and changes of Buddhism.

The presentation of Buddhism in film has changed over the last seventy years. Western filmmakers, entranced especially by the exoticism of Tibet and other Asian countries, presented a pristine, idealized view of Buddhism. This view largely persisted until Buddhist-born directors began presenting their own perspectives on Buddhism. Such perspectives humanize Buddhism and show how Buddhism tends to merge with other cultures and traditions as it moves from South Asia to East Asia and the West. Thus while the focus of this chapter will be largely on Hollywood movies, the chapter will also explore a few Asian movies to complement, and sometimes counter, the Hollywood images of Buddhism.

Hollywood Perspectives of Buddhism

One of the earliest Hollywood films to depict Buddhism, or at least its perspective on Buddhism, was Frank Capra's *Lost Horizon* (1937).[2] Capra's movie was based on James Hilton's 1933 novel of the same title. Both represent Tibet as Shangri-la, the mythological kingdom in the Himālayas where inhabitants are peaceful, enlightened and eternally young.[3] In the film, Robert Conway, a well-known humanitarian, is on a plane that is hijacked and brought to Shangri-la. The scenes representing the 'outside world', are visually dark, replete with nighttime images of war, panic, wind, snow and coldness. In contrast, when Conway and the others from the plane arrive in Shangri-la, it is daytime and the climate becomes sunny and temperate. Shangri-la is almost completely isolated, and in this isolation flowers bloom, wisdom and art are preserved and the inhabitants are almost all uniformly happy, young, peaceful and contented. This orientalist-influenced perspective of Shangri-la, while seemingly positive on the surface, divorces Buddhism and Tibet from the real world, from history and largely from humanity.[4]

Capra's film not only separates Buddhism from the world, but also separates Buddhism from itself. While the movie communicates some Buddhist principles quite effectively, it can neither credit these to Buddhism, nor can it allow Buddhism to be an evolving path that is engaged with the world. For example, Buddhist teachings on moderation and the Middle Way come in the movie, not from a lama, but rather a lama-like figure who is a Belgian Roman Catholic priest.

The Razor's Edge (1946) is another early film that draws upon Buddhist teachings and principles.[5] In it, Larry is a pilot back from World War I. Experiencing survivor guilt, Larry refuses to take part in the material plenty of his friends and fiancée, preferring instead to study in the library. He leaves the United States to live in France for a year. There, he meets a miner who tells him, 'You sound like a very religious man who doesn't believe in God'. The miner encourages Larry to go to India. In the original film, Larry goes to India where he receives a vaguely eastern mixture of teachings from Hinduism and Buddhism combined with a bit of Christianity. The 1984 re-make more clearly presents Larry as eventually travelling to Tibet. In both movies, Larry retires to a cave high in the mountains for isolated contemplation, during which time he undergoes a transformation.

While Buddhist teachings are obscured more in *The Razor's Edge* than in *Lost Horizon*, the film is still notable because Larry, after his transformative experience or insight, returns to Paris and works, successfully, to alleviate the suffering that he witnesses around him. In this respect, his path and aim is similar to the Buddha's. Furthermore, Larry's intermingling of his Western culture with Buddhist principles and practices anticipates the intermingling of Western culture with Buddhist principles that became a growing trend in Europe and the United States.

Other than re-makes of *Lost Horizon* and *The Razor's Edge*, the next popular Hollywood film to convey a sense of Buddhism was *The Karate Kid* (1984). In the original film, Buddhism merges with, and is partially disguised by, the martial arts tradition. Teachings of Mr. Miyagi to his student, such as 'if life has balance, everything is better', could reflect either karate teachings or Buddhism. This ambiguity changes in the sequels. In *The Next Karate Kid IV* (1994) Miyagi takes his latest troubled student to a Buddhist monastery in order to help bring her peace. The scenes, although representing pseudo-Zen or caricatures of Buddhist monks, are nevertheless enough that some conservative Christian web sites warn parents that viewers might be attracted to the false religion.[6] There is no denying that the films are 'fluff', and oriented to young viewers, but *The Karate Kid* and *The Next Karate Kid* illustrate the growing comfort of filmmakers in the United States to identify Buddhism as the source of the teachings and practices. Here though, as Jane Naomi Iwamura notes, the orientalist perception remains strong. Although characters such as Daniel in *The Karate Kid* belong to the dominant culture, they

> have an ambivalent relationship with that culture; this allows each to make a break with the Western tradition radical enough to embrace their marginalized half. The Oriental Monk figure seizes this half, develops it, nurtures it. As a result of this relationship, a transmission takes place: oriental wisdom and spiritual insight is passed from the Oriental Monk figure to the occidental West through the *bridge figure*. Ultimately, the Oriental Monk and his apprentice(s) represent future salvation of the dominant culture – they embody a new hope of saving the West.[7]

In other words, despite the passing of nearly fifty years, Shangri-la has merely arrived in Los Angeles.

Another popular film of the 1980s, *The Golden Child* (1986), reinforces what we might call the Shangri-la syndrome. In the movie, an Asian group hires a private detective to find a kidnapped Tibetan boy, the Golden Child, who possesses mystical powers. Through rescuing the boy, Murphy's character comes to believe in these powers, paralleling the East-comes-West themes of previous films. Furthermore, as the Golden Child is a saviour-style figure, who even has the power to bring people back from the dead, a westerner rescues Buddhism which is the source of peace and spiritual power in the world.

The 1990s marked a time when a number of major directors made serious films about Buddhism. Bernardo Bertolucci's 1993 movie *The Little Buddha*, combined two stories. In one, a lama comes to Seattle, Washington seeking the reincarnation of his teacher. A young American boy seems to be a candidate, so the lama, the boy and his father travel back to Bhutan in order to make a final determination about the reincarnation. This story is interspersed with scenes re-enacting the legend of the Buddha's life, particularly the moments leading to his enlightenment.

Bertolucci's film was soon followed by two more movies focusing on Tibetan Buddhism. Jean-Jacques Annaud's film *Seven Years in Tibet* was released in October 1997.[8] This film focused on the relationship between the young Dalai Lama and Austrian mountain climber Heinrich Harrer, whose book of the same name describes his years in Tibet between 1944 and 1951. Harrer became one of the Dalai Lama's tutors and eventually a friend of the young spiritual and political leader. The Chinese People's Liberation Army invaded Tibet in 1950, and Annaud's film includes these events that forced the parting of the Dalai Lama and Harrer.

The second film, *Kundun*, was directed by Martin Scorsese and released in December 1997. *Kundun*, based on the life and writings of the Dalai Lama, traces his life from childhood until his exile from Tibet in 1959. The film is beautifully shot and could almost be mistaken for a lush documentary. The early scenes of the movie are particularly valuable for their portrayal of how a Dalai Lama is identified. An oracle directs lamas to a village in which a two-year-old boy chooses articles belonging to the previous Dalai Lama. The film includes coverage of the intense and complicated events leading to the Dalai Lama's visit to China and meeting with Mao Zedong, along with the threats and violence that finally cause the Dalai Lama to leave Tibet.

Both *Seven Years in Tibet* and *Kundun* reflect the growing popularity of the Dalai Lama in the West. These films are an enormous improvement over the earlier films listed above as they do not disengage Tibet from history. They also employ ethnically Tibetan actors in lead roles. Both films are extremely reverential. This is not necessarily a flaw, and may, in fact, reflect the especially deep respect for both the Dalai Lama himself and Tibetan traditions. Responses to the films, however, were

> totally polarized, not just over their artistic merit, nor simply about Hollywood's involvement, but even about the politics of the Tibetan struggle. Both those who dismiss the films and those who praise them have accused the other side of political correctness . . . Ironically, in order to attack Hollywood, reviewers often mobilize the idealized fantasy about Tibet that Hollywood itself has fostered and promulgated.[9]

Reviewers complained that if they criticized the movies, it was perceived as tantamount to criticizing the struggles of the Tibetan people. At the same time, other reviews and articles focused on the materialist, spiritually bankrupt West versus the successes of a pure Tibetan Buddhist spirituality – another version of the Shangri-la syndrome. The real-life successes of a small group of Tibetan exiles to place their stories in the forefront of world-wide media, to mobilize support for their cause, and to succeed in bridging cultures through working strategically in film and other media, went largely unnoticed.[10]

Hollywood's fascination with Tibetan Buddhism is interesting in and of itself. This form of Buddhism, if we take into account solely the number of adherents, is greatly over-represented in film. Hollywood has sometimes made films referencing Ch'an/Zen Buddhism, but Pure Land forms of Buddhism, likely the most popular in the world, are almost completely unrepresented. More human perspectives on Buddhism which can include the human struggles and socio-cultural developments within it (or even comedy!) have largely come into the West through the films of Asian writers and directors.

Asian Perspectives on Buddhism

In contrast to the reverent focus upon the Dalai Lama in *Seven Years in Tibet* and *Kundun*, Tibetan filmmaker Khyentse Norbu's *Phörpu* (*The Cup*) (1999) is about the efforts of young Tibetan boys who are trying to see the World Cup Football (soccer) final broadcast from France. It is the first Tibetan-made feature film. From the beginning, film-goers catch a different view of Tibetan Buddhism, likely because the writer and director is a Bhutanese-born Tibetan lama and rinpoche. Known outside the film world as Dzongsar Jamyang Khyentse Rinpoche, he based *The Cup* on his experiences heading a monastery and boarding school filled largely with refugee monks and students who are 'consumed with an obsession for World Cup soccer'.[11]

The Cup gives us an insider's view of the monastery. Here the solemn monk in charge of discipline is somewhat weary of his role. The novices, intent on getting funds to rent a TV in order to watch the game, sneak soccer magazines in to their rooms and play tricks on the local Tibetan yogi. They even, as young boys would, pass notes, don't pay attention and make jokes during times when they should be chanting and praying. As Norbu notes,

> Usually there is an expectation that a monastery is pure, but it is not always like that. Because, after all, what is a monk? A human being. It's someone who is trying hard to do something, to practise. That doesn't mean that when he becomes a monk, ninety per cent of his emotion is gone.[12]

The human aspects of the film enchant, inform and engage the viewer, who is able to identify with the characters.

Furthermore, none of this diminishes the precarious situation of the Tibetan exiles. Norbu's crew largely consists of Tibetan monks, lamas and students who are refugees from Tibet. At the beginning of the film, the monastery's leaders express concern about the well-being of two Tibetan boys who are fleeing from Tibet. Beyond the political situtation, Norbu uses film itself as a way to teach Buddhist views. The Rinpoche says,

> 'I think there's no contradiction between film and teaching responsibilities. Any skilful means, any methods, have to be accepted, and that's the beauty of Vajrayana [Tibetan tantric] Buddhism. I think to refrain from such a strong and powerful skilful means is ignorance, cowardliness. Buddhism is

one philosophy or religion that really has this wealth of openness. And I think we should take advantage of that'.

Dzongsar Khyentse Rinpoche frequently teaches the subtleties of Buddhist philosophy, using the analogy of 'life as cinema'. 'There's a big difference between watching a movie without knowing it's a movie and watching a movie knowing it's a movie. If you don't know it's a movie, then you have a hard time rewinding it. Yet, if you know it's a movie and then watch it, there's leisure, there's humour, there's a readiness to let go'.[13]

Norbu continues to explore tradition, modernity and Buddhism. His most recent film is *Travellers and Magicians* (2003). In this film, a Bhutanese official from a village wants to travel to the United States, which to him represents the ideal place to live. Having missed his bus to the city, he joins a group of travellers that includes a story-telling monk who helps the official reflect on his choices.

Moving away from Tibetan Buddhism, Buddhism is particularly well presented in two South Korean movies, *Dharmaga tongjoguro kan kkadalgun* (*Why has Bodhi-Dharma Left for the East?*) (1989),[14] and *Bom yeoreum gaeul gyeoul geurigo bom* (*Spring, Summer, Autumn, Winter . . . and Spring*) (2003).[15] Both films are visually stunning, move at a meditative pace, largely take place at a hermitage and portray the way Buddhist masters in these traditions teach their students. However, the first primarily aims to get the viewer to *experience* the present moment (a Son/Zen Buddhist practice), while the second communicates key Buddhist teachings through its story.

Bodhidharma takes place in a hermitage high in the mountains. A young man joins a Son master and an orphan boy there. The film's plot is merely a reflection on their lives together, but *Bodhidharma* contains little action or dialogue. This is intentional, for it depends upon a key part of Son practice:

> In contrast to traditions of Buddhism that emphasize certain scriptures (sutras) or scholarly activity, or certain rituals, this type focuses on getting the point through one's own practice and direct transmission from a teacher. The transmission is not, however, through words. Often, Zen is said to be based on four notions: A special transmission outside the scriptures; Not based on words or letters; A direct pointing at the heart of reality; To see into your own nature and wake up.[16]

In an imagistic way, *Bodhidharma* draws upon these four principles, blending form and content seamlessly. The relationship between master and student illustrates the special transmission, as does the film's opening that tells the story of this intuitive experiential transmission between the Buddha and one of his disciples. A film full of dialogue would largely negate the second principle. Given this, the film's visual elements, often repeated, can be seen as a meditative device aimed at helping us to directly experience reality. Finally, the entire film presents us with the opportunity to reflect upon our own focus, or lack of focus, as we watch.[17] As William L. Blizek notes, the film can generate the opposite of the Buddhist 'being in the moment' experience:

> Watching a movie without dialogue, without the usual plot, with only natural sounds, makes the viewer uncomfortable. Since there is nothing in the movie to capture the viewer's attention, nothing to keep the viewer riveted, the viewer begins to think about other things, things that are either past or future.[18]

It is, according to Son/Zen Buddhism, largely this inability to concentrate and experience reality directly that prevents us from being awakened, from being a Buddha.

Director Ki-duk Kim's *Spring* (2003) also takes place at a hermitage, this time a floating hermitage on an isolated lake. As the title indicates, the film is a meditation on *saṃsāra*, literally 'wandering through', the cycle of birth, death and rebirth. This cycle is witnessed through the changes of the seasons and years and through the growth, mistakes and maturation of a young boy into a young monk, an adult and a master.

Spring begins with a young boy who lives with an old master (simply known as the Old Monk) in a hermitage. The Old Monk takes care of the Buddhist shrine, teaches his young charge and, in his role as healer, collects medicinal plants nearby. The boy, although learning from the Old Monk, has a mischievous streak that sometimes stretches to cruelty. He ties a stone to a fish, a snake and a frog. The master, having witnessed this, takes the opportunity to teach the boy about the universal nature of suffering (*dukka*). He ties a stone to the boy's waist and asks him to find and release the creatures he has tormented. While a seemingly harsh punishment, the Old Monk carefully watches over the boy to make sure that, while experiencing a bit of the suffering of the creatures, the boy comes to no real harm. Sadly, foreshadowing his future, the boy finds that two of the creatures have died. Only the frog, a symbol of transformation, survives.

In another season (*Summer*), a mother brings her ill teenage daughter to the hermitage for healing. The boy, now a monk and young adult, becomes attracted to the girl. Their relationship deepens, the girl recovers from her illness, and eventually they make love. The Old Monk discovers their relationship and sends the now healthy girl back to her city. At this point, the young monk, who is filled with passion, abandons the hermitage in order to follow after the girl and to pursue worldly life.

Before the young monk leaves the hermitage, he takes the Buddha statue from the shrine and carries it away with the head of the statue sticking out of his knapsack. The young man may be taking the statue for comfort, or to sell, but regardless, it is clear that his Buddhist practice and knowledge reaches only the surface – is stone image rather than life. In contrast, in the opening scene of the fall season, which follows directly after the young man leaves, we see the Old Monk rowing his boat towards the hermitage. A cat, rather than the Buddha statue, pokes his head up out of the knapsack. The difference in images between the fleeing young man and the Old Monk is striking. For the master, the Mahāyāna Buddhist doctrine that all things have Buddha-nature is fully actualized. For him, even the cat is a Buddha – a point reinforced when we see him painting verses from Buddhist scriptures with the end of the (sometimes complaining) cat's tail.

From a scrap of newspaper, the Old Monk learns that his former charge has committed murder – has, in fact, murdered a woman for falling in love with another man. The former monk, now a thirty-year-old fugitive, seeks refuge at the hermitage. The police eventually catch up with the young man and take him to prison, but not before the Old Monk gives them all a powerful and experiential lesson on the famous *Prajñā-paramitā* (Perfection of Wisdom) scriptures.[19] Through carving and painting the verses from these scriptures on the deck, the dichotomies between Old Monk and young man, between police officers and captive, are overcome. The experience allows the young man to accept imprisonment – the consequences of his action – with the beginnings of some calmness and dignity.

The Old Monk passes away, and, in the *Winter* season, the now mature man returns from prison to begin his spiritual practice again. A veiled, mysterious woman brings a baby boy to the shrine for him to look after. In leaving, she falls through the ice and dies. The film ends, appropriately, much as it began. Now on his way to becoming a master himself, the monk watches over and teaches his mischievous young charge.

In its presentation of Buddhist practice – including prayers, acts of charity, recitation of *sūtras* and an emphasis on compassion – the film is excellent. The human failings, it also shows, allow the viewer to reflect on the real difficulty and benefits of following the Buddhist path. Beyond that, it is fundamentally a beautiful portrayal of the universal nature of suffering within the cycle of *saṃsāra*. Even the Old Monk is not exempt from the experience of suffering. Indeed, it is the sorrow and concern he feels at the young boy's acts of cruelty towards creatures that give him the means for teaching the boy compassion and liberation. Thus the hermitage is not Shangri-la, but very much a part of the world, no matter its isolation.

Most of the films to this point have portrayed Buddhist monastic life in some form. Director Julia Kwan's lyrical film, *Eve and the Fire Horse* (2005), depicts Chinese lay Buddhist life. In addition to this, through the eyes of a nine-year-old girl, we see Buddhism's ability to blend with other cultures and religious traditions. The film is set in Vancouver, Canada in 1975. In it, Eve and her older sister become exposed to and even, in the older sister's case, attracted to the religion of Roman Catholicism. At home, the family continues on with Chinese Buddhist rituals such as making offerings to ancestors, burning joss and visiting the temple. The mother even makes a failed attempt at meditation. The girls, however, begin to attend Roman Catholic Sunday school. Their mother, knowing their interest in the religion, supports their attendance, reasoning that 'two gods in the house are better than one'.

Much of the film's magic and humour comes as Eve tries to reconcile Buddhist teachings, her imagination and Christianity. As Eve tries to sort through the various religious practices in her household and at Sunday school, she asks her mother, 'Would Jesus and Buddha get along?' 'Buddha and Jesus teach you to be a good person. Why wouldn't they get along?' her mother replies. At night, Eve watches as Jesus and the Buddha waltz together, and laughing, they lift her up to join them. The film, while being enjoyable, is valuable for its portrayals of Buddhist lay devotional practices and also for its whimsical depiction of Buddhism's ability to transform in different cultural contexts.

Using Buddhism to Interpret Films

Buddhism, while being portrayed in film, may also provide us with an interpretive strategy for non-Buddhist movies. The book *Cinema Nirvana* seeks Buddhist 'enlightenment lessons', from movies as diverse as *Snow White, Easy Rider* and *Casablanca*.[20] Others find Buddhist meanings in *Fight Club* and *The Matrix* series.[21] However, once we start using Buddhism to interpret movies, the situation becomes complicated.

From the early Hollywood, outsider perspective, Buddhism was easy to identify and portray – it was Shangri-la, or a timeless unchanging font of exotic Asian wisdom. However, if we eschew orientalist versions of Buddhism, we are confronted with highly diverse traditions that may appear remarkably different from each other depending upon time and culture. What form of Buddhism do we then use as the basis for our interpretation of film? If we decide that one tradition encapsulates the 'real Buddhism', we fall into the fault of essentialism, something that Buddhism itself decries. If we focus on foundational Buddhist teachings, such as the three attributes of existence, then we could potentially identify almost any film that tells a story of suffering, change, insight or release as Buddhist. Finally, if, as Mahāyāna Buddhists believe, we accept that all things have Buddha-nature, then every film also possesses it. In this respect, each film potentially provides us with an opportunity to experience that sound of one hand clapping.

14 Hinduism and Film

Michele Marie Desmarais and Birud Sindhav

Hinduism pervades Indian culture, including cinema. Its themes, beliefs, doctrines and practices are present in many films. These elements may influence non-Indian films as well. Hinduism can also be fruitfully employed as an interpretive device or strategy for both Hindu and western films. Despite such obviously rich material, any analysis or interpretation must first consider the nature of Hinduism itself. In other words, if film is to be used as a way of teaching or studying Hinduism, and Hinduism as a way of interpreting and critiquing film, then the question 'what is Hinduism?' must be answered, even in a rudimentary way.

The terms 'religion' and 'Hinduism' are problematic, given that both are of western origin. There is no term synonymous with 'religion' in Sanskrit, the language in which the primary scriptures of Hinduism are written. Some use 'darśana' as an equivalent for 'religion', but darśana (from the root dṛś, 'see') includes systems of thought equally well translated as 'philosophy', as well as the viewing of mūrtis (icons), or even the viewing of a holy person. 'Bhakti' (devotion), is narrower in meaning than 'religion'; dharma includes duty, truth and righteousness; and sādhana refers more specifically to practice.

The difficulties applying the term 'religion' to aspects of Hinduism have direct consequences for religion and film. For example, if we view the system of social classes (varṇa)[1] as part of the Hindu religion, then we will consider negative portrayals of brahmins, or of traditional village life in which class inequalities are shown, as critiques of Hinduism, or the Hindu religion, rather than Indian society.[2] Similarly, if the treatment of widows is viewed as practices mandated by religion, rather than law or social custom, then Deepa Mehta's film Water (2005) becomes a critique of the Hindu religion rather than Indian society.[3,4]

'Hinduism' is likewise difficult to define and apply in this context. Muslims introduced the term around the eighth century CE to refer to the indigenous peoples of the Indus river area.[5] In origin, therefore, 'Hindu' was a geographical term coined by outsiders. Orientalist scholars along with British rulers employing the term 'Hinduism', emphasized the primacy of the textual traditions over diverse regional practices, thereby giving a sense of a uniform 'religion'. Even this is an overly simplistic analysis, for as Viswanathan notes, although the Sanskritic tradition was likely dominant before colonialism, it contained strands of heterodox discourse.[6] Finally, post-colonial perspectives on Hinduism range from critiques of the term as artificial and meaningless, to attempted definitions and alternate nomenclature such as 'Sanātana Dharma' (eternal *dharma*).[7]

Again, this discussion is not peripheral to the field of religion and film. One must always be sensitive that both narrow and broad perspectives on who or what is 'Hindu' will affect the choices of what films to consider as well as the analysis of these films. While this is a similar situation for using western religion to explore films, and films to critique western religions, it is much more difficult to specify who or what is Hindu rather than who or what is Jewish, Christian or Muslim.[8] There is no doubt that restricting oneself to the themes, practices and beliefs found in Hindu scriptures will yield a wealth of information for considering films; however, even a brief consideration of this topic reveals that this is only a partial representation of the Hindu or Indian traditions. Indeed, 'Hinduism' or 'religion' pervades daily life so much that it is difficult to have an Indian movie without any religious references.

Having made some attempt at least to address these complexities, the exploration of Hinduism in film can begin. While Indian films depicting mythological stories are the most obvious choice, non-Indian films sometimes also reveal Hindu doctrines, practices, symbols and themes.

Apart from language categories (Hindi, Tamil, etc.), people tend to define Indian films as either 'art house', or '*masala*'. Art house films are often serious, less formulaic than *masala* movies, given to realism or neo-realism, and/or have controversial or largely unexplored topics in their plotlines.[9] '*Masala*' is a spice mixture, and '*masala*' (also known as 'Bollywood')[10] movies must blend a variety of elements and emotions such as joy, sadness, good fortune, suffering, comedy, music and dance. Either art house films or *masala* movies may fall into a variety of styles or genres, which include: historical; action; comedic; mythological; devotional or social drama.[11]

For religious elements within any of these categories or genres, we may find: that the story is based, at least partially, on a religious text; or that the characters' names are based on those of deities; that the song sequences include a devotional song or two; and that there are many religious symbols such as the letter OM, a *svastika*, holy verses that are written on a book or cloth, a *mālā* (rosary), or a dot on the forehead (*tilak*) to signify participation in a religious ritual. For example, Subhash Ghai, one of the most successful directors of the current generation, is a master of weaving his tale around religious myths. His characters' names are straight from religious books: Rādhā, Gītā, Tulsī and Lakṣmī for the female leads, while the male leads bear the names of variations of Kṛṣṇa, Rāma, Lakṣmana and Arjuna.[12] His film *Ram-Lakhan* (1989) drew on themes from the holy book *Rāmāyaṇa*. In the film, Ram (the elder brother), like Rāma himself, is a virtuous person upholding the family traditions, while Lakhan, a hot-blooded younger brother falling from the path of virtue, is not unlike the mythical younger brother of Rāma. Similarly, Ghai's film *Kisna: The Warrior Poet* (2005) draws on themes from the epic *Mahābhārata* and the *Purāṇas* (ancient scriptures).[13] In *Kisna*, like the god Kṛṣṇa, the main character fights the evil forces to perform his *dharma* (duty).

Ghai is not the only director influenced by great Indian epics. The *Rāmāyaṇa* and *Mahābhārata* provide us with many stories of heroes, deities, bravery, faithfulness, human failings, cautionary tales and, fundamentally, explorations of *dharma*. Although not classified as *śruti*, these epics often have the most impact on the religious lives of Hindus. Because of their dramatic value and religious impact, there are numerous interpretations and re-enactments of the epics in film.[14] Perhaps most recently, independent filmmaker and animator Nina Paley has set an animated and light-hearted take on the *Rāmāyaṇa* to 1920s jazz music. *Sita Sings the Blues* (2008) has moved from clips on the internet, to a full-length, animated film that has won a number of film festival awards.[15] Likewise, the *Mahābhārata* has inspired many films and, most famously, was serialized by B. R. Chopra and Ravi Chopra.[16] The English theatre director, Peter Brook, in emphasizing the universal themes of the epic, chose to use a multi-cultural and multi-racial cast in his 1989 adaptation.

Further analysis of Hinduism and film can be done by interpreting films using the well-known *tri-marga*, the three general paths to *mokṣa* (liberation). As explained in the *Bhagavad-Gītā* (*Gītā*), which is often called the 'Hindu bible' and considered one of the holiest scriptures in Hinduism, these three paths are: *jñāna-marga* (the path of knowledge); *karma-marga* (the path of action) and *bhakti-marga* (the path of devotion).[17] The paths are given in order of ease, from the most difficult (*jñāna-marga*) to the easiest and most common (*bhakti*). These paths are a beneficial way to analyze Hindu themes and practices in both Indian and non-Indian films.

Jñāna-marga, the path of knowledge, is an approach that focuses on attaining a veridical understanding of reality, particularly the nature of the *ātman* (Self/Soul), the Absolute, and the material world. Such an understanding necessitates a move beyond appearances or normal consensual reality. This path is difficult and often involves renunciation, philosophy and meditation. *Jñāna-marga* is often portrayed in Indian films through characters who are priests or sages. The difficulties of such an approach may be seen in disciplined but ultimately flawed characters such as Raibhya or Yavakri in director Arjun Sajnani's 2002 film *Agni Varsha* (*Fire and Rain*).[18]

Although *jñāna-marga* is difficult, *Guide* (1965) shows an unlikely character who succeeds at this path. In *Guide*, Raju, a tourist guide and conman meets and encourages Rosie, an unhappy wife, to become a dancer. She is successful, but even in a life of ease, Raju still commits a crime and is caught. After his jail term, he tries to find Rosie, but is eventually mistaken as a *sādhu* (holy person). Although in the beginning Raju uses his position as a *sādhu* merely to receive food, shelter and the esteem of villagers, he eventually becomes a true *sādhu*. As his fame spreads, particularly when he undertakes a fast to end drought in the region, Rosie finds him again. Despite the lure of a happy ending, Raju persists with his fast and the movie ends with Raju sitting in meditation, longing for that which is beyond dualities such as good and bad, pain and pleasure, love and hate. As Raju loses consciousness, the rains arrive.

Non-Indian films also portray the path of knowledge. Here, movies that portray normal reality as ultimately unreal or untrustworthy and that rely on a character renouncing what had been normal life in favour of truth contain the dominant doctrines, practices and goals of *jñāna-marga*.[19] For example, in Peter Weir's 1998 film *The Truman Show*, Truman Burbank leads a normal and happy life – really a perfect life surrounded only by a loving wife and friends in a beautiful seaside town. However, unbeknownst to Truman, his world is actually a soundstage and all the other people are actors in a hit television reality show. A studio floodlight unexpectedly crashing from the sky begins a series of events that cause Truman to question his 'reality'. His journey via boat to the edge of his world takes him to Christof, who has created the world. Through this journey and his stubborn quest to know the truth, Truman quite literally breaks through ignorance and artificiality, achieving knowledge and reality at the cost of his previous world and life.

Terry Gilliam's dark film *Brazil* (1985) portrays an apocalyptic and futuristic world in which everything is simultaneously monitored and falling apart. Within this fascistic world, an ordinary civil servant, Sam Lowry, becomes caught up in an increasingly tense and dangerous situation by trying to correct the arrest of an innocent man. In the course of doing so, he meets the woman he dreams about and ends up confronting authorities and trying to protect the woman. The end of the movie is ambiguous yet transcendent, as it is unclear whether Lowry's revolutionary response to the situation took place in reality or completely in his head. In either instance, Lowry escapes by liberating himself from the control and artificiality of his previous world.

Although *The Truman Show* provides the most easily understood portrayal of a quest for knowledge, *Brazil*, with its character who gradually becomes aware of the nature of his society and who pushes against and through this until he transcends it, also represents the primary aim of *jñāna-marga*. Other movies with similar themes include *The Matrix* series, *Fight Club* (1999) and *Twelve Monkeys* (1995).

Karma-marga is the path of action, which, according to the *Gītā*, involves the performance of *dharma* (duty) without attachment to the results of action.[20] The *Gītā* does not really differentiate between good and bad karmas, but maintains that all karmas (actions, whether internal or external) colour the consciousness of a doer, hence, a real yogin is one who performs karmas without getting attached to them. Arvasu, the protagonist in Arjun Sajnani's 2002 film *Agni Varsha* (*Fire and Rain*), provides a good example of *karma-marga* and a character who moves beyond attachment.[21]

Films on the life of Gandhi can also be included as sources for exploring the nature of *karma-marga*. It is well known that Gandhi read the *Bhagavad-Gītā* on a regular basis and learned verses from it by heart.[22] He was particularly fond of reciting a verse about the proper way to perform action:

> Place your mind upon your work
> not upon the results of your work.
> Never work for a reward/result,
> but never stop doing your work.[23]

We may thus use this verse, and *karma-marga*, as a lens through which to view any film on Gandhi's life. For example, in a pivotal scene in Attenborough's film *Gandhi* (1982), the *sarvodaya/satyagraha* marchers who are protesting the salt tax are beaten by military troops. Wave after wave of marchers come forward, with no aggression and no defence, in silent protest of the taxation of salt. It is an inspiring example of performing an action without attachment even to personal safety.

Western films that feature non-Indian characters can also contribute to our understanding of *karma-marga*. If we view the essential elements of *karma-marga* colloquially as 'doing the right or correct thing' and doing that regardless of personal interest or consequence, then many non-Indian movies explore similar themes. Indeed, westerns often feature a character who, while being an outsider, is drawn to a cause that brings him into contact with potential friends, allies and usually a love interest. Despite the temptation to give in to the personal desire to belong to society and to live a normal, comfortable life, the protagonist, in the end, holds true to his cause, to what should be done. This decision usually results in a just resolution for the townspeople, while the main character, having sacrificed his own interests, either dies or rides off, alone, into the distance. *Shane* (1953), the dark *High Plains Drifter* (1973), *My Name is Nobody* (1973)[24] and *They Call Me Trinity* (1970),[25] all fit this general pattern.

Moving out of the western westerns, one can also find similar themes in other genres. The classic and beautiful film *Roman Holiday* (1953), features Gregory Peck as Joe Bradley, a broke American reporter in Rome. He and his photographer friend Irving are thrilled when a disillusioned foreign princess escapes from the conservative protocol of royal life and unknowingly spends time with the two newsmen. Joe and Irving are thrilled with their unexpected luck as a scandalous story about the princess, along with accompanying photos, will bring them each a large amount of money. In the end though, and despite falling in love with Joe, the princess returns to her duties. Joe and Irving, in turn, also sacrifice their own interests, by returning the photos, not running the story and, in Joe's case, by walking away from romantic love. All the main characters uphold their duty, do the right thing, and do it despite personal wishes or inclinations otherwise. The film thus provides us with a gentle yet thorough western variation of *karma-marga*.

Bhakti-marga is the path of devotion. In the *Gītā*, Krsna, while affirming the other paths, upholds *bhakti-marga* as supreme. One reason for this is because it is easier for a person to build an emotional connection with a deity or some supreme thing than, in most cases, to abandon everything in order to understand the nature of reality (*jñāna-marga*), or to achieve perfect equanimity while performing action (*karma-marga*). Another reason is that *bhakti-marga* ensures liberation for anyone who undertakes it, no matter how unlikely the person.[26] Given these advantages, it is the easiest and most popular path. Not surprisingly then, the key aspect of *bhakti-marga* – intense devotion and love – is represented more often in film in comparison to the other two paths. Since devotion is thought to be the most accessible way for people to attain *moksa* or realize god, viewers are likely to identify with *bhakti* on film.

At times in Indian films, the portrayal of *bhakti* is symbolic and subtle, at least to non-Hindus. Nevertheless, these elements and symbols function to communicate to the viewer the elevation of romantic love to a divine level. For example, when a male character plays a flute, or holds his hands in that position while he dances, the viewer identifies him with Krsna-gopala – the young, flute-playing, flirtatious form of Krsna. The same holds true, as in the recent (2002) version of *Devdas*, when characters in love, like Devdas and Parvatī (Paro), sit together on a swing that is bedecked with flowers. This scene, which is common in Indian movies, is almost identical to popular images of Krsna and his love Rādhā on a swing. That humans, having reached such ideal love, sometimes cannot maintain that ideal only adds to the sense of drama. A more subtle suggestion of divine love is found in *Monsoon Wedding* (2001), when the very fallible character P. K. Dubey, a wedding planner, eats marigolds. Marigolds are flowers frequently offered to Hindu deities. By ingesting the marigolds, there is a suggestion or foreshadowing of the transformative and ideal love that will take place between Dubey and the servant Alice. All these examples given above then imply the transformative nature of divine love for a devotee.

The elevation of human love to divine is also a theme in movies that deal with grief and loss. *Kal Ho Naa Ho* (2003) is a popular *masala* movie with a twist on the standard boy meets girl paradigm. In the movie, Naina is a stressed-out and bitter young woman whose family is in disarray due to the death of her father. She has friends, namely Sweetu and Rohit, along with a loving mother, but no real joy or romantic love in her life. During a particularly difficult time, Naina's mother, who is a Christian, prays and tells her children, 'Our angel is watching us even now.' Immediately after this, Aman, the nephew of a neighbour, enters their lives. Naina at first finds Aman annoying, but eventually is charmed by him and falls in love. However, Aman tells Naina and her friends that he is married. Aman then works to get Naina to fall in love with Rohit, who has discovered his love for Naina.

Aman's efforts to bring Rohit and Naina together are partially successful, but the light-hearted movie turns serious when it is revealed that Aman is not married, but rather dying of a heart problem. At this point, Naina realizes that she cannot deny her deep love for Aman and Rohit is at first devastated by the knowledge that he will be 'second best'. For his part, Aman tries to deny his romantic love for Naina by telling her, 'I don't love you. I don't love anyone', but Naina understands the depth of his love and responds, 'You love me so much you want to leave love behind for me . . . even if it is someone else's love.' This is where love becomes elevated to selfless, all-encompassing, divine love. Indeed, all three characters achieve this as Naina and Rohit marry, with Aman's love and support throughout. On a human note though, Aman tells Rohit that while Rohit can have Naina in this life, in future lifetimes he (Aman) and Naina will be together. Rohit, transcending his own romantic love and attachment, agrees readily to this.

Anthony Minghella's sensitive film *Truly, Madly, Deeply* (1991) provides us with similar themes of a deep romantic love that, in moving beyond attachment, becomes akin to unconditional divine love. The protagonist in the film, Nina, is unable to overcome her grief at the sudden death of her boyfriend Jamie. She tries to maintain relationships with her friends and family, but overwhelming grief is a kind of living death for her.

In the midst of Nina's despair, Jamie appears. The two, woman and ghost, are ecstatic over their reunion and celebrate. Nina learns from Jamie about the afterlife and begins to prefer being with him rather than living her life. This reluctance to be part of the world, and even to love again, begins to wane when Jamie starts bringing home ghostly friends. Nina, lacking attention from Jamie as well as privacy, comes to appreciate her friends who are alive and even starts, tentatively, to respond to the romantic interest of another man. The film ends as Nina, starting to love again, realizes that Jamie has disappeared. This time Nina grieves, but attains some sense of closure. She leaves her apartment to go meet her boyfriend, while the viewer catches a glimpse, behind Nina, of the other ghosts comforting Jamie. Thus, while initially it is Nina's human love and devotion to Jamie that reunites them, it is ultimately Jamie's selfless love that restores Nina to life – a divine gift.

Some movies address devotion to a deity directly. These may or may not fall into the category of mythological film. The blind mother in Manmohan Desai's *Amar Akbar Anthony* (1977) instantly gets her vision back after devoting herself in a temple. In *Outsourced* (2001), the goddess Kālī, having been asked to destroy something in order to show that destruction can lead to creation, is quickly credited with blowing up a ferry, which then leads to the two main characters falling in love.

Devotion to a deity and the idea of an *avatāra* (incarnation), or at least the possession of a human by a deity, is at the heart of Satyajit Ray's film *Devī* (1960). The film is set in rural Bengal in 1860. In it, Kalikinkar Roy, a rich landlord, is a fervent devotee of the goddess (*devī*) Kālī. His son, however, is a modern thinker and a Christian. When the elder Roy receives a vision of his daughter-in-law Doyamoyee as an incarnation of Kālī, he becomes her devotee, much to the shock of the entire family. Kalikinkar Roy makes Doyamoyee sit upon an altar while a priest and other potential devotees offer incense, food and religious songs. When Doyamoyee/Kālī appears to cure a critically ill boy, the faith of Roy is confirmed and Doyamoyee/Kālī's fame spreads. She becomes the object of worship for thousands of people. Such attention causes antagonism between Kalikinkar Roy and other members of the family. This trouble only increases when Doyamoyee's husband returns home from his studies and tries to take Doyamoyee away, accusing his father of being deluded and manipulating Doyamoyee. Doyamoyee herself is either unwilling, or unable, to answer her husband's queries about whether or not she believes that she is Kālī. 'What if I am?' she asks. While her husband is away trying to sort through the problems at home, Doyamoyee/ Kālī is asked to heal her beloved nephew, who is sick. Up to this point, the boy has been kept away from Doyamoyee, but now she asks to take care of him for the night. Doyamoyee's husband returns again to find that his nephew died during the night, and that his father is having a crisis of faith. Meanwhile, the multitudes of believers have deserted the home temple and Doyamoyee has become in behaviour and appearance as wild and unpredictable as the goddess. The film ends ambiguously, as Doyamoyee/Kālī disappears into the fog, running from the demons who are pursuing her.

In addition to the plot and to the scenes in which religious rituals are shown, *Devī* is a beautiful visual exploration of the meanings of *darśana*. The film begins with the symbolic three eyes of Kālī, giving a sense of the goddess's intensity and presence. Throughout the film, the glance (another meaning of *darśana*) of Doyamoyee is lingered upon. Viewings (*darśana*) of, and offerings before, the *mūrti* (statue) of Kālī are shown repeatedly in the film. Finally, Doyamoyee/Kālī herself becomes an object of *darśana*, at least for a time.

Another interesting example of *bhakti* and film is the 1975 Indian hit movie *Jai Santoshi Maa*. While the scriptural origins of Santoshi Mā are not clear, popular images of her can be traced back to the 1960s and the film may be an adaptation of a prayer book devoted to her.[27] In the movie a woman, Satyavati, is a devotee of the little-known Hindu goddess, Santoshi Mā, the Mother of Contentment. Satyavati marries, but after the marriage her husband's family mistreats them both. One day Satyavati learns that her husband has died in a boating accident. She refuses, however, to act like a widow and takes a *vrata* (vow) to fast for sixteen Fridays to honour Santoshi Mā and to persuade her for help. In the end, Satyavati and her husband are reunited, while the mistreatment by the in-laws is severely punished, ultimately allowing both Satyavati and the goddess to show their mercy.

Jai Santoshi Maa is an intriguing film not merely for its strongly devotional plot, but also for the response of audiences to the film. Audiences engaged in ritual acts even in the theatre, throwing coins, petals and rice at the screen as religious offerings to Santoshi Maa. Temples and shrines were built in honour of this previously rarely worshipped *devī*. Increasing numbers of women undertook the sixteen week Friday fast, while movie theatres screened the movie on Friday afternoons in order to encourage and inspire the women (and, undoubtedly, to make money).[28]

While the three main paths to liberation as explained in the Gītā and portrayed through film have been examined, the paths should not be viewed as existing in isolation from each other. Some Indian films combine one or more paths and indicate their valuation of each. In *Ram Teri Ganga Maili* (1985), a *chandal*, someone who survives by collecting material off the dead bodies that arrive for cremation, is shown to be better than the priest who tries to rape the female lead. This lead is not subtly named Gangā, after the holiest river for Hindus, the Ganges. The message is clear: before the almighty, good karmas or actions are more valued than the pretentious knowledge that is combined with evil actions of the priest. Similarly, 'bad guys' often try to redeem their bad karma through the supposedly easy route of devotion. In *Sarkar* (2005), the main character is an underworld don who always carries a rosary with him, and has a *tilak* (sacred mark) on his forehead. Such films give a sense of the complexities and interactions of various religious paths, beliefs and duties.

Indian mythological films based especially on the *Mahābhārata* of course regularly portray the three paths to liberation along with their interactions.[29] Some non-Indian movies, however, might also be seen as expressing similar paths and practices. Here, the popular movie *V for Vendetta* (2006) is particularly appropriate. Evey, the main character, lives a normal life in a totalitarian society until that life is disrupted by the mysterious V. V, a magnetic freedom fighter – who is labelled a terrorist by the fascistic government – rescues Evey from the secret police, but also imprisons her to ensure that she will not give away his identity. Evey learns about the true nature of her government, including its cruelty toward citizens, its intense censorship of the arts, and highly conservative moral laws. Such knowledge, combined with insights from V and discoveries of her own strength, represent a path of knowledge. As Evey learns about V's plans to challenge the government, she comes to acknowledge the validity of such actions and plans to participate in the upcoming confrontation, even at the cost of her life (path of action). Throughout this time, Evey also starts to fall in love with V. Her love helps V overcome bitterness and hatred so that he can carry out his actions in a better frame of mind (path of devotion). In seeking to restore justice to a violent and unjust society, V's purpose parallels that of Kṛṣṇa in the *Mahābhārata*. Finally, the climax of the movie, in which the populace supports V by donning masks in his image, is reminiscent of the beautiful middle chapters of the *Gītā*, when Kṛṣṇa reveals himself to be all people and all things.

While some films might illustrate one or more paths, others give newcomers to the study of Hinduism general and gentle introductions to Hinduism and Indian culture. Particularly good here are *Outsourced* (2006), about an American's first trip to India; *Swadeś* (2004), about an NRI going home; or *Lagaan: Once Upon a Time in India* (2001), the Oscar-nominated story of villagers resisting taxation by challenging the British to a cricket game. Regardless of the path that is taken though, even a glimpse at some of these and other films reveals much about the richness of Hindu traditions.

15 Judaism and Jewishness in Film

Allison Smith

Jews have been a behind-the-scenes presence in film since the advent of the Hollywood system, but to suggest as much is to broach a complicated topic. The men who came to be known as the first and second generations of movie 'moguls', among them Carl Laemmle, Adolph Zukor, Louis B. Mayer, William Fox, the Warner brothers, Marcus Lowe, Samuel Goldwyn and Jesse Lasky were outsiders in American mainstream culture. They were, for the most part, Jewish immigrants or the children of immigrants from Central and Eastern Europe. Keenly aware of their marginalized status as members of an ethnic and religious minority in America, they sought to integrate and embrace the American Dream. The movie business provided a foray for them because it was a new industry not yet affected by the unspoken agreements which often barred Jews from advancing in other occupations in the early twentieth century.[1]

The Jewish movie moguls' rags to riches history calls forth the distinctively national mythology of the American Dream, but the story of Jewish involvement in Hollywood also evokes the uglier discourse of anti-Semitism that is, likewise, a part of the American past. The claims that Jews have 'controlled' Hollywood, wielded a disproportional power, and manipulated the medium of film to advance a 'subversive' ideology are part of a history of anti-Semitic propaganda that situates Jews as somehow posing a threat to the American nation and values.

When the history of the Jewish film studio heads is examined in light of the films that were produced, as Neil Gabler does in his text *An Empire of Their Own: How the Jews Invented Hollywood*, what becomes clear is that the moguls did not use the medium of film to advance distinctively Jewish ideas or narratives. Some films produced up until the end of the Silent Era in 1927 did focus on Jewish immigrant life in the ghettos of America, but most did not. Instead, Gabler suggests that the first and second generation of Jewish film producers, anxious to be viewed as mainstream Americans, established a cinematic world in which ethnic and religious differences were largely ignored in favour of a homogenous fantasy of America and the people who composed the nation. Like the studio heads who sought to redefine their identities, the Jewish presence in film has continually been redefined. As cinematic plots that featured

Jewish characters developed throughout the twentieth century and beyond, increasingly complex and nuanced depictions that explored both the religious and ethnic components of Jewish identities evolved.

Some of the earliest films that dealt with Jewish-subjects detailed the struggle between the Old World and the New. By the end of the Silent Era, if a Jewish plotline was introduced onscreen, it was often through the lens of an assimilationist narrative. 1927's *The Jazz Singer*, the first talkie, is perhaps the most famous of the early studio films to treat Jewishness in this way, and many surveys of Jewish identity in film begin with this Al Jolson vehicle. Set in New York's Lower East Side, the plot of *The Jazz Singer* hinges on a conflict between the protagonist Jack Robin (born Jakie Rabinowitz) and his Old World father, a cantor who wants his son to follow in his spiritual footsteps and cannot abide Jack's desire to enter into the secular world of show business. Jack achieves his American Dream and success as an entertainer only after he runs away, abandons his Jewish roots and becomes romantically involved with a Gentile woman. The son does return to his old neighbourhood, as his father lies on his deathbed, but it is only to momentarily fulfil his father's dream by chanting the Kol Nidre prayer at Yom Kippur services. The film concludes in the world outside of the ghetto, when Jack's mother comes to see her son perform. That Jack performs onstage in blackface, a uniquely American entertainment form, does not seem coincidental. He leaves behind religious music in favour of what had been a mainstream form of entertainment in the New World of America. By the closing scene of the film, the transformation of Jakie Rabinowitz from the Lower East Side is complete, and he has metamorphosed into Jack Robin, American.

The melting pot ideology endorsed by *The Jazz Singer* was taken to an extreme in the 1930s when Jewish characters and narratives seemed largely to disappear from the screen. Throughout the thirties, Jews were featured in minor roles, but plots about Jewish identity highlighting major Jewish characters were largely absent from the cinema. When historical dramas about non-fictional Jewish characters were produced, the Jewish heritage of those figures was often downplayed, even when that identity was integral to the actual historical narrative. One example is Warner Brothers' 1937 production of *The Life of Emile Zola*, a film which focuses on the biography of the well-known French writer. The film highlights Zola's involvement in the famous case of Alfred Dreyfus, the French Jewish military officer who was brought down by charges of treason. Based on an accusation that was the result of anti-Semitic propaganda, the charges against Dreyfus were later proven to be untrue. When *The Life of Emile Zola* comes to Zola's famous 1898 'J'accuse' editorial in which he denounced the French government for the anti-Jewish bias in its case against Drefyus, the portions of Zola's piece which attacked anti-Semitism are omitted from the film. Dreyfus' Jewish background is referred to only once in the film, when a general looks at a list of officers and sees Dreyfus's name along with the description, 'Religion: Jew'. Many scholars note that the word 'Jew' is never spoken by anyone in the film.[2]

Some film theorists and historians attribute the lack of Jewish content in 1930s films to the desire of Jewish producers not to disturb European markets under Nazi control, which in 1934 prohibited the showing of any film if the cast included Jewish actors. There are, however, two more plausible explanations for the virtual absence of Jewish content in the films of the 1930s. One is the impulse of Jewish producers to distance themselves from their immigrant and ethnic backgrounds in efforts to fully integrate.[3] The other is pressure brought to bear on studio executives by Jewish groups who were concerned that images of Jews in films might contribute to American anti-Semitism.[4]

A major shift occurred once America became involved in World War II. Hollywood contributed to the war effort, most notably by producing a number of combat films that were characterized by an ethnic and racial inclusiveness. In films like *Baatan* and *Action in the North Atlantic*, Jewish characters were members of ethnically and racially diverse integrated military units. The plots of such war films often linked the multi-ethnic group's ability to work together against the Nazis or Japanese to a protection of American values, marrying varied identities to those values and expanding the notion of who might be seen as 'American' in the cinema.[5] Still, Jewish along with African American and Latino characters occupied minor roles in ensemble casts in the war films. The main narrative action often centred on Gentile white protagonists, and plots did not revolve around issues of Jewish identity.

Many film critics and historians see the post-War 1940s as a moment when Hollywood began to envision narratives about issues affecting Jews as cinematically viable. It would take years before films about the Holocaust would be released.[6] Still, the devastation of the genocide began to affect whose stories were shown in the cinema. In the aftermath of the War, broader conceptions of American identity developed and perceptions of the Jew's place in America underwent a radical transformation in the wake of the Holocaust, amidst extensive revelations of the effects of Nazi racial policy in Europe. Post-war and post-Holocaust, Jews were no longer seen as others in America; they were increasingly understood to be assimilatable ethnics. Part of a wave of films with liberal social agendas, RKO's production of Edward Dmytryk's *Crossfire* (1947) and Twentieth-Century Fox's production of Elia Kazan's *Gentleman's Agreement* (1948), began to address these issues. Both films examined anti-Jewish bias, and they marked a shift from less than a decade earlier when, in 1939, Adolf Zukor, the architect behind Paramount, remarked, 'I don't think that Hollywood should deal with anything but entertainment. The news reels take care of current events'.[7] Anti-Semitism became the issue du jour in Hollywood as the two studios introduced the viewing public to narratives that centre on a matter that directly affected Jews. A film noir, *Crossfire* is a murder mystery involving members of a military unit who appear to be linked to the murder of a Jewish man. *Gentleman's Agreement*, the better known of the two films, follows Gentile journalist Phil Green who passes as Jewish to write an article about anti-Semitism in America.

Each film exposes the existence of anti-Semitism in America, while also suggesting that such bias is anti-American. The films are united in their ultimate goal of demonstrating the similarity and equality of all Americans, regardless of their ethnic or religious backgrounds. A telling moment occurs early in *Gentleman's Agreement* when, while contemplating how to approach the topic of anti-Semitism, Phil looks in a mirror and comments on just how alike he is to his Jewish friend, Dave Goldman. Phil remarks on their physical similarities in particular, saying, 'Dark hair, dark eyes . . . so has Dave, so have a lot of guys who aren't Jewish. No accent, no mannerisms. Neither has Dave . . .' Phil's confidence that he can easily pass for Jewish, coupled with his comments that Dave feels the way he, himself, feels 'as a man, as an American, as a citizen . . .' work to reveal one of the film's main messages – that Jews are no different than any other Americans. *Crossfire* also establishes a strong linkage between Jewish and national identities when the film reveals that the Jewish murder victim, Joseph Samuels, was a military man and had been wounded in Okinawa, while patriotically serving his country.

Both films interestingly include references to what might be called the duality of Jewish subjectivity. While at times Jewishness has been understood to be a religious identity, it's also been viewed as an ethno-racial identity, and sometimes, as both. The notion of 'Jewish' physical characteristics is key to understanding Jewishness in terms of ethnicity or race, and explicit and implicit references to the 'Jewish' physique can be found in the films. Depictions of Judaism as a religion in film are rarer than plots that touch upon ethnic markers of 'Jewishness'. The films significantly categorize Judaism as a religion and place it within a catalogue of other religions. Phil tells his son Tommy, 'See, you could be an American and a Catholic or an American and a Protestant or an American and a Jew . . . One thing is your country, see, like America or France or Germany or Russia. All the countries . . . But the other thing is religion, like the Jewish or the Catholic or the Protestant religions'. Late in *Crossfire*, the police officer investigating the murder, Detective Finley, discusses Judaism as a faith, like Phil, listing it among a number of other religions. He remarks, 'Hating is always the same, always senseless. One day it kills Irish Catholics, the next day Jews, the next day Protestants, the next day Quakers'. Each protagonist's framing of Judaism as a religion – Phil's explication that one can be an 'American and a Jew' and Finley's discussion of senseless hate – also work to support the overall message about social equality that they advocate.

Gentleman's Agreement and *Crossfire* were critically well-received and made important contributions to mainstream American cinema by introducing the hitherto unexamined subject of American anti-Semitism. Still, while the plots of the films centre on anti-Jewish bias, both movies troublingly devote little attention to Jewish characters, instead exploring anti-Semitism through the lenses of their Gentile characters. Samuels is killed in *Crossfire's* first scene and appears in the film only briefly through flashback sequences. The film's hero, Finley, is Gentile and time and time again in *Crossfire*, it is through his voice that viewers hear the strongest critique against anti-Jewish bigotry in America. *Gentleman's Agreement's* Phil does encounter many Jewish characters as he passes for Jewish in his investigation of anti-Semitism, but they are, for the most part, minor characters. The films of the 1940s nobly tackle the subject of anti-Jewish bias and suggest that Jewish Americans deserve parity, but do so by eschewing most markers of Jewish identity, and virtually erase Jews from the screen.

An era that was rather significant in terms of race relations and Jewish assimilation in America, the 1950s and 1960s expanded on the trend of inclusion begun by the social progress films. In 1959, Leslie Fiedler, writing about American popular culture, cast 'Zion as Main Street', arguing that 'for better or for worse, the time has come when each cultural level in America looks to some Jewish-sponsored myth for a justification of its existence and its dreams . . .'[8] From the late 1950s through the 1960s, Jewish cinematic protagonists became familiar in films such as *Marjorie Morningstar* (1958), *The Last Angry Man* (1959), *Exodus* (1960), *Funny Girl* (1968), and *Goodbye Columbus* (1969).

Produced during a time when the nation's attention was focused on the Civil Rights movement and identity issues, 1959's *The Last Angry Man* offers Jewish characters who are more ethnically specific than those in films made earlier in the post-War years. The film's protagonist Sam Ableman is marked as Jewish by stereotypical 'Jewish' mannerisms and gestures that characters in these earlier films lack. While all *Gentleman's Agreement's* Phil Green's 'gotta do is say' he is Jewish in order to pass, Sam never says it, but everything from his accent, to his appearance, to his slippage into Yiddish reveals his status as Jew. Even as these mid-century films do focus on the specifics of Jewish ethnic identity, they, like the earlier post-World War II productions pursue the same goal of establishing connections between Jewish and American national subjectivities. Ableman may toss around Yiddish words like 'nudnick', but he also quotes Thoreau. And the film links the Ablemans' appreciation for American authors to their status as immigrants. Sarah, Sam's wife, remarks that even though the couple came from Russia and were raised poor on the Lower East Side of New York, '. . . we felt it was important for us to identify with what was finest in American life, so we turned to American writers . . . These were our heroes'. Ableman, himself, observes, 'Thoreau had the right idea. He used to say, "Don't take any nonsense from anybody! The bigshots, the governments, nobody! Be your own man!" ' His discussion of Thoreau is significant for its evocation of both American tradition and the idea of difference. Ableman's admiration for Thoreau ostensibly works to reinforce the idea that the Jewish Ablemans are and can be both ethnic and traditional Americans, but his appreciation for a canonical American author can also be read as a gesture towards the ability of the Jewish Ablemans to fit into American society.

Other films from this era examine the tensions felt by upwardly mobile Jewish Americans who were leaving their old worlds behind in a wave of suburbanization. By the 1950s, Jews had begun to move into the American middle class, relocating from the mostly Jewish urban neighbourhoods that they had lived in and coming into closer proximity with Gentile neighbours in suburbia. For many Jews, the suburbanization heightened anxieties about the consequences of assimilation. This process brought with it two fears on the part of American Jews – that Gentiles would find them 'too Jewish' and that assimilation would mean that subsequent generations of Jews would lose any sense of Jewish identity.[9]

Like *The Jazz Singer*, *Marjorie Morningstar* presents the viewer with a narrative that revolves around intergenerational conflict, but in a marked twist, the later film links assimilation and abandonment of roots to failure. Marjorie Morgenstern, the daughter of a middle class Jewish family is caught between her Jewish bourgeois parents, who want her to marry well and settle down into suburbia, and her boyfriend, a singer and dancer whose rejection of his Jewish background and upper middle class family is symbolized by his changing of his name from Noah Ehrman to Noel Airman. The type of Jewishness that the Morgensterns represent is a particularly upper middle class, acculturationist Jewishness. They have moved away from their old neighbourhood in the Bronx and into a swanky high rise in Manhattan, but they are not completely assimilated and preserve ethnic and religious markers of Jewish identity. The film opens as Marjorie's family prepares to leave for her brother's bar mitzvah. Jewish ritual objects decorate the Morgenstern's home, and late in the film, the family is shown celebrating a Passover Seder.

A melodrama, this film takes the inclusionary models offered by the social progress films one step further, by suggesting that a preservation of Jewish difference is compatible with being members of the American middle and upper classes. Marjorie is both an all-American girl and very specifically Jewish, and much of the conflict in the film is wed to the idea that too much assimilation can have disastrous effects. Her boyfriend Noel differentiates himself from Marjorie, telling her, 'You're on a course charted by 5,000 years of Moses and the Ten Commandments. I'm a renegade'. Rushing out of the

Morgenstern's Seder, he tells Marjorie that he is distressed that he is not familiar with the ceremony and that what has been absent in his life is 'family – your kind of family – faith and tradition'. Abandoning both his father's Jewish name and his father's respectable chosen career as a lawyer in order to follow his dreams of making it big on Broadway, Noel fails miserably and the theatrical production he devotes a great deal of attention to is a flop. *Marjorie Morningstar* associates a rejection of Jewish particularity to a rejection of American middle class values and success.

A key component of *Marjorie Morningstar's* exploration of Jewish upward mobility is gender, and the film introduced audiences to the Jewish Princess and a particular rendition of the Jewish Mother that was a departure from the loving Yiddishe Mama depicted in films like *The Jazz Singer*. The depictions of the princess and the new Jewish mother were superficial constructions of Jewish womanhood and persist even in more contemporary films like *Private Benjamin* (1980), *Dirty Dancing* (1987), and *Clueless* (1995).

The women in *Marjorie Morningstar* and the later film *Goodbye Columbus* (1968) are surrounded by symbols of materialism and fail to reflect on their family's wealth until the men in their lives prompt them to do it. Marjorie comes from a financially comfortable family. Noel calls her a 'Shirley', explaining 'It's a trade-name for a respectable middle-class girl who likes to play at being wordly'. Brenda Patimkin from *Goodbye Columbus* similarly exemplifies a materialistic and shallow form of Jewish femininity. Brenda first appears onscreen swimming at her upscale country club. She lives in a mansion and reveals that she has experienced the luxury of having had her nose 'fixed'. The young women are also nagged by Jewish mothers who want to find socially and financially acceptable matches for their daughters. Reflecting on one of Marjorie's suitors, Mrs. Morgenstern says, 'From a mother's viewpoint he's a catch. It isn't every boy whose father owns a big department store'.

While particular venom is reserved for how Jewish women are imagined in such films, other members of the Jewish family do not fare much better. Mr. Morgenstern is an undeveloped character, ultimately depicted as over-powered by his aggressively ambitious wife who seeks increased social acceptance through her daughter's marriage. Mr. Patimkin, while loving to his children and family, is ill-mannered and materialistic. In perhaps one of the most famous scenes involving Jewishness in film, he is shown glorying in the excesses of the extravagant wedding he throws for his son. *Goodbye Columbus*, in particular, fell victim to criticism. Some reviewers and audiences saw it as offering only reductive anti-Semitic depictions of Jewish identity. Others recognized the film as part of new movement in Jewish cinema, highlighting ethnic identity and marking a break from earlier films which sought to do away with any sense of Jewish difference.[10]

The trend of exploring an emphasized sense of Jewish ethnic identity would continue into the 1970s. Jewish actors, who unlike their predecessors, did not try to hide their Jewish identities, were celebrated. Barbra Streisand and Dustin Hoffman were cast not as bit players but as stars, who played Jewish characters in dramas like *The Way We Were* (1973) and *Marathon Man* (1976). Jewish ethnic identity was highlighted and satirized in comedies like the films of Woody Allen. *Annie Hall*, Allen's masterpiece on the romantic relationship between a Jewish man and Gentile woman, took jibes at the Jewish male and the Jewish family. A famous split-screen scene comically reveals the differences between the boisterous Jewish family of Allen's Alvy Singer and the reserved WASPy family of his girlfriend, Annie. Mel Brooks contributed to this wave of Jewish comedies, interjecting Jewish-influenced humour into films like *Blazing Saddles* with its Yiddish-speaking Native American chief.

Filmmakers of the era also grew nostalgic and began to look to the Jewish past for plotlines. Perhaps one of the most celebrated and sentimental examinations of Jewish religious identity in cinema comes at the start of *Fiddler on the Roof* (1971). Set in 1905, the film opens with the Jewish townspeople of the Russian village Anatevka musically meditating on 'Tradition'. The film's protagonist, Tevye, a shtetl milkman, introduces the song with a lesson for the viewer on Jewish ritual garb, in particular yarmulkes and prayer shawls. Women sing about keeping a kosher home, girls sing about finding perfect matrimonial matches, and boys sing about attending Hebrew school. But, as the film's narrative unfolds, traditions are challenged and modified, and the people of Anatevka adapt their ways to modern life. The film interrogates shifting definitions of 'Jewishness', examines Jewish customs, highlights anti-Semitic threats, and explores the humour that has come to be seen as a trademark of the Jewish identity onscreen.

Like *Fiddler*, 1975's *Hester Street* also examines the massive changes that Jews endured in the early twentieth century. Based on a novella by Abraham Cahan, the film follows immigrant life in the tenements of the Lower East Side of New York and tackles religious issues and the tensions between assimilation and acculturation. The world of Jake, an immigrant sweatshop worker, is turned upside down when his wife Gitl arrives in America from the old country. Jake has relaxed his Old World piety in favour of becoming a true 'Yankee', but Gitl seems unwilling to let go of the traditional ways. She covers her hair in the religious style, wearing a wig and has difficulty learning English. Jake seems on his way to abandoning his wife and pursues an affair with the more assimilated Mamie. By the conclusion of the film, Gitl's story seems far from tragic. She grants Jake a divorce, begins to wear her hair and clothing in a more modern fashion, and settles with her religious neighbour, Bernstein. With plans to open up a grocery store, the more traditional of the two couples seems to come out on top, well on their way to pursuing the American Dream.

Another film to explore the Jewish past, 1981's *The Chosen* chronicles the story of two boys, one Hasidic and one who is from a Modern Orthodox background. Like *Hester Street* and *Fiddler on the Roof*, *The Chosen* offers a careful and sensitive depiction of Jewish religious customs. Focusing on the religious and secular worlds, the film significantly presents different ways of being Jewish.

Films of the eighties, while touching upon Jewish identity often saw a reduction in narrative threads that hinged upon Jewish issues. The gangster epic and *Once Upon a Time in America* (1983) and *Driving Miss Daisy* (1989) feature main characters who are Jewish, but their Jewish identity is neither explored in depth, nor does it seem integral to the plots.

Two exceptions to the trend are films that also feature women protagonists. *Crossing Delancey* (1988) focuses on an assimilated Jewish heroine, Isabelle who lives in Manhattan. When Isabelle's more traditional grandmother seeks the aid of a traditional shadchen, or matchmaker, to ensure that her granddaughter will wed, Isabelle is initially resistant. By the conclusion of the film, she sees the wisdom of her bubbie's traditional ways and begins a relationship with the shadchen's choice, a Lower East Side pickle peddler. Based on a story by Isaac Bashevis Singer, Barbra Streisand's musical *Yentl* (1983) follows the narrative of a young Jewish girl in Poland. Forbidden to study in a Jewish yeshiva because of her gender, she disguises herself, passing as a boy in order to learn the Talmud.

Films of the 1990s tend to look through nostalgic lenses to the Jewish past but expand the boundaries of that past from earlier films, reflecting on mid-century Jewish life and beyond. Barry Levinson's drama *Avalon* (1990) is a sentimentalized look at the journey of immigrant Sam Krichinsky and his descendants throughout the twentieth century. While Sam becomes a success in America, the film problematizes his American Dream by showing the family becoming increasingly distant from each other with each successive generation. At the close of the film, Sam laments the changes, telling his great-grandson, 'If I knew things would no longer be, I would have tried to remember better'. While *Avalon* was well-received, some critics faulted the film for seeming too generic an immigrant story. References to the Krichinsky's family's Jewish identity are limited. Older members of the family speak Yiddish in one significant scene when relatives who are refugees from World War II Europe arrive, but the words 'Jew' and 'Jewish' are never mentioned in the film. Levinson has produced a number of films that include Jewish characters living in mid-century Baltimore and its surroundings. His most recent instalment in the series, *Liberty Heights* (1999), touches more directly on Jewish issues, focusing specifically on anti-Semitism. Early in the film, the teenaged protagonist, Ben Kurtzman is barred from a country club by a sign that reads, 'No Jews, dogs, or coloreds'.

In its treatment of American anti-Semitism, *Liberty Heights* follows in the path of two earlier films from the 1990s, *School Ties* (1992) and *Quiz Show* (1993). Like *Gentleman's Agreement*, *School Ties* explores 'polite anti-Semitism'. David Greene, a Jewish teenager, wins a scholarship to a prep school where he is forced to contend with the bigotry of his classmates. *Quiz Show* recalls the government investigation of the game show scandals of the 1950s, examining how Jews were set up to lose against Gentiles on popular quiz shows. The film also investigates the complexity of mid-century Jewish identity when Jews had not yet achieved full acceptance in American society. The Jewish government investigator, Dick Goodwin, is reluctant to prosecute a cheating contestant, so drawn in is Goodwin by the magnetism of the contestant. The moment that Goodwin's wife calls him 'the Uncle Tom of the Jews', recalls Irving Howe's assessment of mid-century American Jews. Descendants of an East European immigrant mindset, these Jews, Howe suggests, 'still *felt* like losers. Being able to buy a home, or move into a suburb, or send kids to college could not quickly dissolve that feeling'.[11] Goodwin is compelled to face the fact that he views acceptance as linked to identifying and being identified with the Gentile establishment.

A great deal of critical attention has been devoted to the twenty-first century comedic films of actors, writers, and directors such as Ben Stiller, Adam Sandler and Judd Apatow. Works like *Meet the Parents* (2000), *Meet the Fockers* (2004) and *Knocked Up* (2007) hearken back to the comedies of the 1970s and recall earlier cinematic types and narrative formulas with plots that focus on the romantic involvement of Jewish men with Gentile women. Another recent film, *The Hebrew Hammer* (2003), about a Jewish superhero who saves Hannukah from destruction, similarly looks to the past for inspiration, satirizing Blaxploitation films.

Jewish identity is made up of an assortment of diverse subjectivities, and no single film adequately defines some imaginary 'quintessential Jewish experience'. The films included here comprise a survey that traces how the representation of Jewishness onscreen has developed and changed, but they by are no means a complete collection. As recent releases demonstrate, there are still many areas of Jewish identity that have yet to be explored on film. Notably, *Kissing Jessica Stein* (2001), the documentary *Trembling before G-d* (2001) and the film version of Tony Kushner's exploration of the AIDS crisis, *Angels in America*, all focus on Jewish identity and sexuality. As we look to the future, films that center on Jewish subjects and characters will importantly continue to expand upon the cinematic definition of Jewishness.[12]

16 Muslim in the Movies

Rubina Ramji

Orienting the Muslim in Hollywood

Over the past eighty years of American cinema, the image of Islam and the portrayal of Muslims have undergone a significant evolution. In early films, such as *The Unfaithful Odalisque* (1900), *The Palace of Arabian Nights* (1905), *The Arab* (1915), *The Sheikh* (1921), *The Desert Song* (1929) and *Thief of Damascus* (1952), the world of Islam is depicted as mysterious and exotic, filled with images of bejewelled, yet, veiled women in harems, bearded sheikhs and dark-skinned villains living in places in the desert landscapes surrounded by palm trees and camels. But the mysterious and exotic do not necessarily promote a positive image. The Arab Muslim male is portrayed as a backward and undeveloped heathen.[1] American film, in its projection of Arabs, consistently associates 'Arab' with 'Islam', thus all Arabs are Muslims and all Muslims are Arabs. American film does not offer depictions of Muslims as Indonesian, Malaysian or Pakistani, countries that have the highest Muslim populations. Even though approximately fifteen percent of all Arabs are Muslim, the two become one in American cinema. Muslims in American films speak Arabic, invoke the name of Allah and wear specifically Middle Eastern clothing: in the case of women one sees the burqa (Afghani) or the chador (Iranian) and the men usually wear the kafeyah (chequered scarf associated with Palestine). American cinema has created a homogeneous concept of what a Muslim is, and what a Muslim extremist is – he is an Arab.[2]

The Discourse of Terror Enters American Film

After Iranian militants took over the US embassy in Tehran and held sixty-five Americans hostage in 1979, Muslims/Arabs became identified with terrorism and Islam came to be understood as a radically militant religion at war with the West, especially the United States. The Islamic threat narrative, imagining impending terrorism, then became a constant on the Hollywood silver screen. *Into the Night* (1985) and *Iron Eagle* (1986) capitalized on the situation and portrayed Arab Muslims as terrorists, as ruthless killers threatening the American way of life. These movies were seen as tools to 'help the American public accept preparations for going to war against them (Arabs)'.[3]

Also in 1986, the US action thriller *The Delta Force*[4] was released, starring Chuck Norris and Lee Marvin. Stolen from headline news, the storyline was about the hijacking of an American Travelways (ATW) Boeing 707 jet airliner by Lebanese terrorists, based on the actual events of the hijacking of TWA flight 847 by the Hezbollah in 1985.[5] The beginning of the film also made reference to the original American military's attempt to free the hostages in the Iranian embassy in Tehran, thereby linking the story line of the film with historical events and giving it a sense of realism. The tagline for *The Delta Force* was 'they don't negotiate with terrorists . . . they blow them away!', illustrating how the United States would no longer be held hostage again by the threat of terrorism as it had in Iran. And this terrorist threat, visibly defined as 'Muslim' in the Iranian hostage taking, is clearly evidenced in *The Delta Force*. Not only are the terrorists suspicious looking dark skinned men who speak Arabic, they are in fact Shiite Muslims who are a pro-Ayatollah Khomeini group known as the New World Revolutionary Organization. Diverting from the historical truth of the botched rescue attempt in Iran and on the original TWA flight, where a US navy diver was murdered, the Delta Force dispatched to kill the terrorists and rescue the hostages in the movie are triumphant, thereby creating a hyper-reality[6] where the dominant Americans always save the day. This image becomes a 'floating signifier' in the movies, because it has no real connection to concrete or original events.[7] A heroic America becomes the simulation which is but a reflection of reality, and in itself, becomes 'real' for the viewer.

Television has played a large role in authenticating the storylines of movies. Clearly evidenced in *The Delta Force*, images which had been taken from the TWA hijacking were recreated in various scenes throughout the film. As news coverage of the Iranian hostage-taking became a daily reminder and reference of the event playing out, television has become the narrator of the memories of historical events. As the movie audience is reminded of the memories which television has given them, the role of the television in the movie itself is to authenticate the events unfolding on screen. This idea continues forward in a number of 'Muslim terrorist' films, showing footage of death, fear and disaster throughout the world, while also offering American statements that terrorism will not be tolerated by America.[8] Thus the superiority of the United States is always confirmed throughout the movies, as the Americans almost always end up victorious over the outside threat of terrorism from the Middle East and from Muslim extremists (at least in film).

Furthermore, the creation of the image of terrorism 'is a process of stimulating and feeding the imaginations of Americans with certain kinds of images that will serve as the foundation for a certain kind of social structure and governmental policy'.[9] At the exact same time as these movies were being released for American consumption, then Vice President George H. W. Bush stated in the public report on combating terrorism, that he wanted to 'launch a public awareness effort to better inform the American people about the nature of terrorism and the threat it represents to our national security interests and to the freedoms we so deeply cherish'.[10] Thus, when audiences watched as the American military invaded Beirut in *The Delta Force*, blew up buildings and destroyed the city, it seemed justifiable behaviour in the name of protecting America's 'freedoms'.

Navy Seals, released in 1990, carried forward the idea of a national fear, as it was one of the first instances in American popular film where Islamic 'terrorists' were now endangering the 'civilized world', by attacking Spain. A unique American elite force called the Navy Seals, specially assembled to deal with acts of terrorism and guerilla warfare, are sent in to stop the Islamic terrorist group, in order to protect the defenceless, innocent civilians. As the image of 'terrorist' Islam developed over the next ten years in Hollywood, Islam became feared as an invading threat specifically aimed at US interests. Even though this threat has proven real, not all Muslims are threatening. The Hollywood film industry, in many ways, continues to advance the fears of American viewers who have all but assumed that there is a mass Islamic conspiracy underway.[11]

The film *Not Without My Daughter* (1991) did not focus so much on Islamic terrorism but on the idea of protecting American freedoms in an Islamic country. The movie began filming in the summer of 1990 and was released in January 1991 while tension was mounting in the Middle East because Saddam Hussein had invaded Kuwait. The week the Persian Gulf War began was the movie's highest box office ranking and it made over 14 million dollars. This film claims to be a story based on fact and therefore offered a sense of authenticity, depicting women, especially American women, as victims of the savage, violent Islamic religion in Iran, in need of American protection. Islam, as a religion, is connected with ignorance. The only Muslims who were helpful in the film were those who had been exposed to Western influences. Movie reviews denounced it for exploiting the stereotype of the demonic Iranian Muslim but in the absence of other film representations of Iran and Islamic culture at the time, it was able to disseminate its particular perspective on Islam and Muslims to a wide audience.[12]

The Disney animated children's film *Aladdin* was released in 1992. The message conveyed through this medium continues to strengthen the violent image of Islam as well as the perceived injustice that Muslim women face by their own religion.[13] Many North American children have come to understand the 'cultural' laws of Islam through Princess Jasmine, a young girl forced by 'Islamic' law and her father to wed against her wishes, and only to a prince. When she escapes the palace, she finds that the 'threat' of Islam is greater outside the palace walls. This popular Disney film constructs the protagonist Jasmine as the subject of the viewer's pity. The barbaric rules of Islam keep her trapped in the palace, imprisoning her through primitive demands of forced marriage she herself, as a princess, cannot escape.

Executive Decision (1996) brought the threat of Islamic terror closer to the US people. Another hostage-taking film, *Executive Decision* was about a US 747 airliner taken captive by Muslim terrorist Nagi Hassan, wishing to destroy the plane and all of Washington, DC (the heart of America) in a suicidal mission as a form of revenge for the death of his family in the Middle East. *Air Force One* (1997),[14] was yet another movie about an Islamic terrorist hijacking of the American president's plane. *The Siege* (1998) is loosely based on the first bombing of the World Trade Centre. It continues to perpetuate Islam as violent and aggressive, but also crosses a new threshold by bringing Islamic terrorism directly into the United States and threatening its popular icons, the FBI building (One Federal Place) and New York City in order to gain the release of an imprisoned sheikh. Arabs living in America now become suspect. In response to the conflation of fundamentalism equalling terrorism, American Arabs felt vulnerable and discriminated within the film, so they requested a plot change to substitute 'militiamen' for 'Islamic fundamentalists', but the director released the film in its original form. Other films that continue to use this stereotype include *Three Kings*[15] (1999) and *Rules of Engagement*[16] (2000).

The image of the Muslim woman as terrorist has begun entering into American film recently. The remake of *The Manchurian Candidate* (2004), starring Denzel Washington, utilizes images of veiled Muslim women with writing on their faces as something to be feared and part of a brainwashing scheme happening to Americans. In the past ten years, over twenty-one major movies have been released in the United States that depict Arab Muslims as killers, films such as *Air Force One* (1997), *The Siege* (1998), *Rules of Engagement* (2000), *Black Hawk Down* (2001) and *The Kingdom* (2007).[17] The inevitable link between Islam and terrorism is reinforced through these films.

The Good Muslim in American Film

As with all stereotypes, the opposite does exist. In American film, there have been a handful of films that depict Muslims in a positive light. The movie *Robin Hood: Prince of Thieves* (1991) takes place in the twelfth century. Robin Hood is a prisoner in an Ottoman jail, where he is tortured by guards speaking Arabic. Robin escapes the jail, and in the process rescues a Muslim Moor, Azeem who vows to help Robin Hood, stating 'you saved my life Christian. I will stay with you until I have saved yours'. *The Thirteenth Warrior* (1999) is based on Michael Crichton's 1976 novel *Eaters of the Dead* and is set in the tenth century. Ahmed Ibn Fahdlan is thrown out of Baghdad for desiring another man's woman. He and his courier Melehisidek encounter a landed ship of 'Northmen' (Nordic warriors). While spending the evening with them, the Northmen are beckoned to help a northland village which is being attacked by an 'ancient evil'. Thirteen warriors are needed, and Ahmed is chosen as the thirteenth warrior, who fights valiantly alongside the Northmen. *Three Kings* and *The Siege* also offer up a few positive Muslim male characters, but both have been Americanized, and in a sense are considered rare.

The Immigrant Muslim Arrives in British Cinema

British Cinema, although considered to have been able to thrive on its own, unfortunately became dominated by Hollywood. From its earliest days, the British film market was saturated with English speaking movies from the United States. Under these conditions, the industry was restrained from producing films that reflected British culture.[18] Although British Cinema has started producing more films recently, 'the Britain that is being disseminated on cinema screens around the world is steeped in heritage, literary culture and conventional ideas of class relations. It is also overwhelmingly white, in sharp contrast to our workplaces, high streets and bedrooms which tell a different story'.[19]

Predominantly beginning in the 1980s, both American and British Cinema began including the portrayal of the Muslim as one of the leading characters in popular film, but with very diverging attributes. In British cinema, the issue of personal identity and community identity has begun to play a large role in the images portrayed. With an increase in immigration, the 1970s represented a period of second generation immigrants growing up in England. It was this generation that began producing literature and film that reflected their British as well as traditional identities. They grew up in a country that believed that 'British identity was seen as the most outstanding example of the "universal" identity, of civilization, justice and reason, that colonial "others" needed to aspire to. It was a fairly typical example of a privileged ethnic identity being produced through the subordination and differentiation of other identity'.[20] The 1990s saw an increase in movies being made by Asian immigrants about East Asian and Muslim families adjusting to life in the United Kingdom. Films such as *My Beautiful Laundrette* (UK, 1985), *My Son the Fanatic* (UK, 1997) and *East is East* (UK, 1999) explore the stories of immigrant life and the harsh realities of living with racism and tradition.

Although *My Son the Fanatic* was made with the backing of the BBC, it was not considered a box-office success, but nevertheless received wide audiences when screened on television. *East is East*, on the other hand, was considered one of the most successful British films of the decade, grossing more than £10 million at the box-office.[21]

The screenwriter, Hanif Kureishi, is a son of a Pakistani father and a British mother, who challenges traditional British standards about race, sexuality and class. 'He found himself observing the assimilation of "Asians" and other "Blacks" and foreigners into British society, while some newcomers in the Muslim community became attracted to religion and fundamentalism',[22] a confrontation deeply examined in the movie *My Son the Fanatic*.

Two other movies which included themes of Muslim identity in British culture were extrapolated from stories written by Kureishi. *My Beautiful Laundrette* explores issues of being Asian, gay and straight in English society, by telling the story of a young Muslim Pakistani immigrant who opens a Laundromat with his white, gay lover. Reviewers praised the film: 'here at last is a story about immigrants which shows them neither as victims or tradition-bound aliens. They're comprehensible, modern people with an eye to the main chance, no better or worse than the rest of us',[23] while on the American side, it was met with protests by some Pakistani organizations such as the Pakistan Action Front in New York because they felt that a character of Pakistani origin was held representative of the whole Pakistani community, and therefore should display a positive stereotype to American and British audiences.

In the film *Sammy and Rosie Get Laid* (UK, 1987), Kureishi examines the life of a racially mixed couple living in London during the race riots. Sammy is an accountant who has an open marriage with his wife Rosie. When Sammy's father Rafi makes a visit, Sammy finds that he has to reconcile his Muslim family duties with his progressive attitudes. In *My Son the Fanatic*, Parvez is an immigrant father who has lived in England for twenty five years driving a taxi to support his family. When his son Farid becomes a Muslim funda-mentalist, rejects acculturation and invites a Muslim leader to stay in his home, Parvez finds that he cannot understand his son's behaviour. Parvez does not follow traditional Muslim ways; he espouses interracial marriage, and has no qualms about indulging in whiskey and American jazz music. On the other hand, Farid represents a character that has become disillusioned with the British notion of capitalism, materialism and acculturation because British society is racist and keeps outsiders at the bottom of the social order. These two radically different personalities show how early immigrants tried to assimilate into western society, while second generation youth feel unwelcome, and therefore search for other alternatives to the prejudiced and immoral aspects of British society.

Set in working-class Manchester, the film *East is East* explores the lives of a Muslim Pakistani immigrant, his English wife and their seven children. Based on the autobiographical play by Ayub Khan-Din, it tells the story of

Khan-Din's life experiences growing up in a bicultural, working-class family. The film offers competing views of Muslim tradition versus western values through the generation gap of the first and second generation immigrant members of this family.

'British national culture still retains traces of "an imperial mentality" that saw "the white British as a superior race" and reveals itself "in projected fantasies and fears about difference, and in racialized stereotypes of other-ness" '.[24] Although many of these films offer a negative view of Islamic fundamentalism (especially those written by Hanif Kureishi[25]), they are capable of exploring the relationships between people, and offer an idea of what it means to live as a minority within a country where identity plays such a large part of integration and inclusiveness.

Who Documents the Documentary and Who Watches It?

The ethnographer, or documenter, 'occupies a position or structural location and observes with a particular angle of vision'.[26] Thus, when watching documentaries, the viewer tends to assume they are watching truth rather than fiction, but one needs to remember that the angle of vision of the documenter is also influenced by the lens of politics, gender, age, etc., and that the vision is often made for a particular public.

There are quite a few popular documentaries made by PBS which are used by many North American scholars of Islam to teach the basic fundamentals of Islam as well as to illustrate Muslim rituals and philosophy. An introductory documentary is the 2002 PBS documentary entitled *Muhammad: Legacy of a Prophet*. This film is considered a teaching tool to explain how Muslims understand the life of the Prophet Muhammad and thus has a supplementary website that can be used in the classroom.[27] A documentary that discusses pilgrimage is the 2007 PBS Wide Angle Special, *Pilgrimage to Karbala* which examines Muslims travelling to Iraq to visit a famous shrine. PBS has stated that 'due to the rise in interest following the September 11 terrorist attack' they have begun re-airing previously released documentaries.[28] One such documentary was the three-part series narrated by Ben Kingsley entitled *Islam: Empire of Faith*[29] which, PBS stated, provided a balanced and accurate report on Islamic history.

As well as offering documentaries to be used in the classroom, PBS also put forward a series of films in 2007 about Islam in America, Islam in the world and the extremist and terrorist elements of Islam, that pose a threat to America. Some of the titles within the series are *The Brotherhood* (2007) which examines the Muslim Brotherhood, 'a secretive, international movement dedicated to the spread of a fundamental version of Islam throughout the world';[30] *Jihad: The Men and Ideas Behind Al Qaeda* (2007) which examines

Islamic radical groups and the 'blood soaked careers' of the men who have 'created an ideology of violence and hatred towards the West';[31] and, *Homegrown: Islam in Prison* (2007) which examines the impact of teaching Islam's 'extremist ideologies' to American inmates.

As fear of Islam and Muslim extremists escalates, a handful of American documentaries have been produced that criticize the religion of Islam itself and its followers. Such films include *Islam: What the West Needs to Know* (2007) and *Obsession: Radical Islam's War Against the West* (2006) which uses television footage from Iran and other Arab countries to illustrate how radical Islam is inspired by Adolph Hitler's Nazism. *Obsession* aired on both CNN and the Fox Network, as well as screened at thirty university campuses throughout the United States.[32] Another such documentary aired by the Fox Network in 2006 was *Radical Islam: Terror In Its Own Words* in six parts, which reached a large American audience. This documentary not only depicted Muslims killing Americans in foreign countries, but also includes footage of Islamists at a University of California university campus threatening to 'burn American down', thereby illustrating how the threat of Islam was now on American soil. Fox News conducted a survey about the documentary in question and found that 64 percent of the 900 voters polled agreed that threats emitted on Arab television broadcasts 'should be taken very seriously'.[33]

In the same vein as the above American documentaries, those that openly elicit a fear of Islam as a radical force, one can find such films now emanating from European countries, reflecting the political situation that has arisen there. Since 2003, Europe has become much more aware of Islamic extremism. Bombings have occurred in Casablanca, Istanbul and Madrid, and London, England, all linked to Al Qaeda. In 2004 the Dutch film-maker Theo van Gogh was murdered in Holland by Mohammed Bouyeri, a Dutch Muslim. Based on a script written by Ayaan Hirsi Ali, van Gogh created a fictional short film entitled *Submission*[34] which focuses on Muslim women who are abused, assaulted and killed because of the misogynistic way the Qur'an is interpreted by Muslim men.

One of the most popular European short documentary films released during this time period is the Dutch film *Fitna* (2008)[35] by Dutch Parliamentarian Geert Wilders. This short film received a very wide audience because it was released on the internet in both Dutch and English, showing simultaneous images of the Qur'an next to images of 'terrorist' attacks carried out in the name of Islam. This film, Wilders states, illustrates how the Qur'an motivates acts of terrorism, violence and anti-democracy in modern Muslims, and therefore wishes to ban the Qur'an and remove Islam from European society.[36] The other film, a Swedish documentary entitled *Det svider i hjärtat* (*Aching Heart*),[37] was nominated by the Swedish Film Institute in the category of 'Best Documentary' for the Guldbagge Awards in 2007.[38] The basis of this film illustrates how ' "regular" European Muslim immigrants, who have grown up with the comforts of a European lifestyle, become Islamic radicals who dedicate themselves to jihad (holy war) as martyrs against their own European "homeland" '.[39]

North American Muslims have also offered up various documentaries to explain how they view their own religion and how they live within it while also being immigrants in their new homelands. *Stand Up: Muslim American Comics Come of Age*[40] is one of the most recent films following Muslim stand-up comedians. It was aired on PBS in May 2008 and offers five comedic perspectives on how American Muslims use humour to make the case for Arab and Muslim inclusion in the American 'public sphere'.[41] In Canada, Zarqa Nawaz has become popular for her short films and documentaries which examine the lives of Muslims living in Western countries as well as gender issues in the Islamic tradition. Two of Nawaz's popular short films are *BBQ Muslims* (1995) in which two brothers, having a barbeque, are accused of terrorism when it explodes, and *Death Threat* (1998) in which an author, looking to get a book published, claims to have received a death threat.[42] Nawaz has also made a full-length documentary entitled *Me and the Mosque* (2005), a personal exploration of women's role in Islam and the exclusion of women from public space in Canadian mosques.[43]

The Evolution of the Muslim and Muslim Film in Iran

While many countries in the Middle East have produced a variety of films that depict the lives of Muslims in the Muslim world, such as Lebanon, Egypt, Morocco and Turkey, the most popular films tend to come from Iran and many have achieved international stature.[44] Just as recent historical conflicts have affected the way Western films reflect various political situations, the same is true for Middle Eastern cinema. In order to better understand Iranian cinema and its evolution over the past thirty years, it is important to examine Iran's political context and the changes that took place in its culture and society.

The Iran–Iraq war broke out after the Iranian Islamic Revolution in 1979, and a new era of war-films evolved. The new Islamic state, under the rule of Ayatollah Khomeini, saw the media as a powerful tool to control the public: 'cinema is one of the manifestations of culture and it must be put to the service of man and his education'.[45] In Iran, the documentary *Revayat-e Fath (Witness to Glory)* became the longest running documentary made about the Iran–Iraq war and was aired on television nightly for almost a decade. Filmmaker Mohammad Avini, concerned about the way Iranian television was depicting the war, wanted to show the people of Iran what was really happening on the front lines. Although the Iranian government was trying to convince the public that Iran was winning the war because of Iraqi 'fear', Avini wanted to 'illustrate the beauty and true purpose of the war in order to encourage young men to volunteer at the front'.[46] In essence, Avini was creating a religious film, to entice Iranians to want to fight in order to get closer to God through martyrdom. In this way, film acted as a way of projecting a version of what 'a proper Islamic reality and the proper civic duties of an Islamic citizen' should be.[47]

By 1983, fictional films portraying the war were controlled by the Ministry of Culture and Islamic Guidance[48] because these films tended to be action-packed, had poor scenarios and were 'unable to show the truth about the sacred defense'.[49] The Ministry created a 'War Films Bureau for the Sacred Defense' at the Farabi Film Foundation and trained film directors, who had to be Muslim and had served at the frontlines of the war, to be war-movie directors – some of these filmmakers would later become internationally recognized feature film directors.[50] These films were meant to emphasize the soldier's experience as Muslim believers rather than the depictions of war. These movies became a war machine, 'holding the nation captive to a passion play that they were (and still are) intimately involved in, where they are made to believe that their very freedom and flesh was at stake'.[51]

One of the first action movies made with this initiative in mind was called *The Horizon* (1989) and illustrated Iranian soldiers as spiritual warriors and true martyrs. Even though the enemy, the Iraqis, was Muslim as well, they were depicted as infidels. They were characterized as 'clean cut, cigarette-smoking, suave Westernized strategists who sit in their highly technologized war machine watching and waiting for the Iranians'.[52]

Since the end of the war in Iran, emotions of anger and disillusionment have arisen and are reflected within its films. Many Iranian films that 'reach the West' involve children rather than adult situations, as they tend to be promoted at international film festivals.[53] Majid Majidi's film *Children of Heaven* (1997), which was nominated for an Oscar in 1999, is an excellent example of a popular Iranian film making it big in the West. The film focuses on the lives of two children in post-revolutionary Iran, who have to share a pair of shoes due to their family's financial difficulties. In telling the story, it depicts an enchanting yet superficial tale of the children rather than directly focusing on the real hardships endured by the family in Iranian society.

In contrast to this theme, Rakhshan Bani-Etemad's film *The May Lady* (1998) is a contemporary Iranian film that claims to be a true 'barometer of the reality of Iranian life'.[54] The film illustrates the struggling and frustrating relationship between secular life and the Islamic state by focusing on the life of a middle-class single mother trying to raise her adolescent son in Iran, while looking for love. This film is an outstanding illustration of how constantly changing societal values in Iran are being negotiated between those who are living in a 'modern urban' Iranian world in relation to a post-revolutionary Iranian Islamic state. Bani-Etemad is considered to be an oddity in Iranian cinema, as she is a female film-maker, who tends to focus on 'taboo' subjects in Iran such as divorce, polygamy, poverty, love and the repressiveness of Iran's social existence.[55] She began by making feature films in the 1980s.[56] Other popular Iranian films focus on the 'violent and empty effort that caused the country to lose a large segment of its future generation'.[57] Post-revolution Iranian films have now begun to focus on contemporary social issues that were once forbidden, as well as the injustices of war that produced martyrs to be mourned. Ironically, those filmmakers who trained for, fought in, and promoted the war, have become its loudest critics.[58] Most films in Iran are publicly funded by the state, and therefore still face censorship issues. Violence, profanity and romance are themes to be avoided; otherwise the films are banned by the government for moral and ideological reasons. But Iranian film-makers continue to provide thoughtful and critical social commentaries, perhaps making Iranian cinema the 'strongest medium for independent political voices in the Middle East'.[59]

Conclusion

The discourse of the Muslim identity has been formulated in a global context. Cinema itself is part of the message, in that it participates in the discourse of the society and culture in which it is situated. There is a multiplicity of publics, and thus the identity of Islam is manifold as well. Depending on which brand of Islam one 'consumes', one will expect that brand to behave in a universal way. Recent terrorist attacks attributed to Islamic extremists have left many in the Western world questioning whether they wish to live with Muslims for fear that immigration has let the terrorist threat into their homelands. But as the cinematic world continues, ever so slowly, to permit viewers to consume images of Muslims that are not based on terror, but rather on a multiplicity of lives and discourses, perhaps world cinema will lend more balanced representations of the many Islams that exist in the world.

17 Indigenous Religions and Film

Julien R. Fielding

'Indigenous' is an umbrella term used to designate the 'pockets of people (who) still follow local sacred ways handed down from their remote ancestors and adapted to contemporary circumstances'.[1] A few examples of indigenous people include Aborigines, Maori, Lakota Sioux, Hopi, Inuit, Aztec, Mayan, Yoruba and Zulu. In fact, of these people, which comprise four percent of the world's population, 'there are hundreds of different tribal traditions in North America alone, and at least fifty-three different ethnolinguistic groups in the Andean jungles. And Australian aboriginal lifeways, which are some of the world's oldest surviving cultures, traditionally included over five hundred different clan groups, with differing beliefs, living patterns and languages'.[2]

Scholars acknowledge that many problems confront the 'outsider who tries to describe indigenous religions today'.[3] For instance, in the West there is a tendency to split the sacred from the profane – indigenous people rarely see a difference – so when scholars talked about indigenous belief systems, they often imposed their own worldview, thereby misrepresenting what the indigenous people actually believed or, in some cases, denigrating it. Although some generalizations can be made as far as the religious practices and beliefs of indigenous people go, there is a tremendous amount of cultural diversity, especially since their beliefs are generally tied to a specific place. Another, very real problem is that as indigenous people have come into contact with the West, many have been forced to abandon their language, religion and culture, and adopt those of their 'conquerors'. This has presented problems for many indigenous cultures, especially tribes in North America, who keep their stories alive through storytelling. If the stories are not written down and the storytellers 'lose' their stories then it is possible that they will be lost forever. Some indigenous cultures had a written tradition. The Mayans, for instance, are well-known for their large libraries, which contained a range of books on various topics. However, only a handful of their books have survived. One reason is natural decay – they wrote on bark paper or deer skin – and the other was the book-burning zeal of the Spanish.

The representation of indigenous people in film poses yet another problem.

Seen through the 'white' lens, American Indians, especially prior to the 1960s, have often been depicted as primitive 'savages' who need to be killed or civilized. Although talking about museums and American Indian exhibitions, Tom Hill could very well be talking about early cinema:

'The public, educated about Indians by dime novels, the press, advertising, tourism, and later Hollywood, went to museums to see more of the same: the stereotype, the exotic, the scalp, the tomahawk – images and stories that excited European-Americans and confirmed their impressions of their own history. The noble savage, the bloodthirsty warrior, the "Vanishing American" . . . all were presented as unchanging realities, incapable of meeting the advance of civilization and progress, trapped in the time-warp of exhibition dioramas'.[4]

The same applies to the indigenous people of Africa, Australia and Mesoamerica. Christians saw them as savages with an inferior culture, believing that the only way to 'civilize' them was to convert them to Christianity and give them a Western education. As one scholar points out, in Africa 'the Christian scriptures were translated into hundreds of vernacular languages, and modern institutions of learning were established in virtually all of Africa'.[5] What is interesting about the effort to convert indigenous people is that even when they converted to monotheism, indigenous people often retained elements of their own culture, thereby creating something new. In Africa, for instance, there has been the creation of 'thousands of new movements among hundreds of African peoples'.[6]

Despite the fact that American Indians have become more politically active – during the 1960s and 1970s they called for 'cultural revitalization and self determination'[7] – Hollywood, with a few exceptions, continues to hold onto the past, having its biggest success with 'retro' films, including *Young Guns* (1988), *Dances with Wolves* (1990), *Last of the Mohicans* (1992), *Pocahontas* (1995) and the TNT mini-series *Into the West* (2005). As Vine Deloria wrote in *Custer Died for Your Sins: An Indian Manifesto*:

'The American public feels most comfortable with the mythical Indians of stereotype-land . . . These Indians are fierce, they wear feathers and grunt. Most of us do not fit this idealized figure . . . To be an Indian in modern American society is in a very real sense to be unreal and ahistorical'.[8]

American Indian filmmakers, most visibly Chris Eyre, are trying to offer a more realistic and contemporary view of indigenous people and their struggles with alcoholism, acculturation and poverty.[9] When it comes to the depiction of Africans, they have historically been shown to be a formidable enemy,

Zulu (1964) and *Shaka Zulu* (1986), as slaves, *Roots* (1977), or as the backward foil for comedy, *The Gods Must Be Crazy* (1980). More recently they have been cast as victims of incredible pain and suffering. A small sample of these films includes *Hotel Rwanda* (2005), *Blood Diamond* (2006), *The Last King of Scotland* (2006). *Shake Hands with the Devil* (2007) and *The Devil Came on Horseback* (2007).[10]

In the case of American Indians and religion, Hollywood can offer the viewer images of the Sun Dance (*A Man Called Horse*, 1970) and the peyote-induced vision quest (*Young Guns*, 1988), but are they true reflections of indigenous religion? As Eyre said in a 2003 interview:

> 'I would not do ceremony in my films because I do not know how to capture it. It is subjective. Those who exploit it, do a disservice to it. *A Man Called Horse* bastardized the Sun Dance, and vision quest sounds so cliché if it is not done in the right way. There is nothing that can capture it. Indian religion is not considered a real thing. People regard it as non-religion, not a real religion. I think we've fallen short of portraying Indians in the media. Indians have never been portrayed in a respectful way, someone always over romanticizes them or over glorifies them on an iconic level. They don't know how to portray them. We don't need to make another *Dances with Wolves*, because it is not an Indian movie. When Indians portray themselves, then we have a different perspective'.[11]

The question remains: Can the viewer learn about indigenous people and their religious traditions from film? Because Christianity has had such an impact on indigenous cultures, perhaps, the best place to start is the ways in which it has been incorporated with indigenous culture. For example, *Smoke Signals* (1998), which was the first movie to be written, directed and co-produced by an American Indian, is probably the most cited and lauded film about contemporary indigenous life, and many try to interpret it through American Indian spirituality. However, as its author Sherman Alexie admitted, he is still 'heavily Catholic and Christian influenced' and that a number of key scenes in his short story and in the film were inspired by Biblical stories.[12] For most movies about indigenous people, evidence of Christianity is typically present. It might just be a cross hanging on the wall or a missionary or priest standing in a crowd, but it is still there. This doesn't mean that indigenous practices are absent; quite the contrary. Indigenous people often find a balance between the 'new' religion and the old one. Santeria and Hoodoo, for example, are just two of the many syncretic religions born out of the mixture of Christianity and native beliefs systems. In her essay 'To Carry the Fire Home', Kathryn Lucci-Cooper demonstrates this necessary religious fusion. When she remembers her grandmother:

'I see her standing at the kitchen sink, washing the dishes and singing "Jesus Loves Me". It is the song that she would sing to us each morning as she pulled away our warm quilts and fed us bowls of rice and honey and melted butter. My grandmother was a devout member of the Church of God. My grandmother was Cherokee' . . . 'Growing up as a child, it was a reasonable coalescing of Christian principle woven into the warp and weft of Cherokee storytelling and handed down as a basket of mountain tradition. We never knew anything was different about us. We thought all people were . . . just a mixture of cultural identities'.[13]

Two films that capture well the 'conquest of the indigenous person's soul' are *Black Robe* (1991) and *The Other Conquest* (*La Otra Conquista*, 1998).[14] Set in 'New France' in 1634, *Black Robe* is about an idealistic yet theologically rigid French Jesuit missionary named Father Laforgue – the titular 'black robe' – whose mission it is to save the souls of the 'savage and godless' Huron and Algonquin Indians. Not long after his arrival Laforgue hires a group of Algonquin, led by Chomina, to escort him on a 1,500-mile trek up the St. Lawrence River. The missionary's objective is to relieve an ailing priest of his duties at a remote outpost. He is also joined by a young Frenchman, Daniel.

Laforgue is driven to convert the people, but the natives do not share his passion. They are suspicious, resentful and openly hostile to him. Mestigoit, a dwarf shaman calls him a demon, saying as he shakes a rattle over the man: 'Demons fear noise. I curse you, demon'. Later Mestigoit tells those who accompany Laforgue that: 'The spirits are angry with you for traveling with the demon Blackrobe. Listen. They are saying I must protect you . . . from his evil'. The longer the missionary stays with the native people, the more confused and conflicted he becomes. Especially troubling for him are his conversations with Daniel who initially says he wants to 'serve God', but as time goes on becomes increasingly entranced by the native people, especially Annuka, the chief's daughter, and their way of life.

As Daniel says to Laforgue, 'They are true Christians. They live for each other. They forgive things we would not forgive'.

But the missionary will have none of this. 'The devil makes them resist the truth of our teachings'.

'Why should they believe them', Daniel counters. 'They have an afterworld of their own'.

'They have no concept of one', Laforgue says, shaking his head. 'Annuka has told me, they believe that in the forest at night, the dead can see. Souls of men hunt the souls of animals'.

At this the missionary scoffs, 'Is that what she told you? It is childish, Daniel'.

'Is it harder to believe than a paradise where we all sit on clouds and look at God?'

Despite the similarities between their religions, the two sides continually experience conflict, either because of misunderstanding or lack of acceptance. After a baby dies, for example, the indigenous people place it in the crook of a tree. Not respecting their beliefs, the missionary takes the child and prays over it, making the sign of the cross on its forehead.

'See that sign', says one of the indigenous men. 'That's how they steal our spirit'. Not long after this, Laforgue's Indian companions abandon him, telling him to ask his Jesus to help him.

In another scene, a group of natives are sitting around a campfire.

One asks, 'In your paradise, would we have tobacco?'
'You will not need tobacco there. You will need nothing', he replies.
'No women', another queries.
'No, you will be happy just to be with God'. The men grumble.
'They don't seem to be very happy', Daniel remarks.
'They should be. I've told them the truth', Laforgue says, not acknowledging that his vow of chastity may seem strange to the indigenous people.

In this, and many other examples, we see that Laforgue is so dogmatic and fervent in his duties that he lacks objectivity. At the end of the film, when he arrives at the outpost, it is winter, and many people have died. Still he rings the bell, calling the natives to church. He offers them conversion; they need medicine.

One man approaches, 'demon, why are you here?'
'I am not a demon. I take the place of Father Jerome'.
'How long do you stay', the man asks.
'All of my life'.
'If we take the water sorcery – we will not get sick?'
'Baptism will not cure you'.
'The other Blackrobe said so'.
'He meant only that we must ask the help of Jesus. Perhaps he will answer your prayers'.

The man speaks to his people in their native language as they bring out their sick and ailing; the Father sheds tears. 'Many want to kill you Blackrobe . . . Demons cannot feel grief. Are you a man? You must help us Blackrobe. Do you love us?' The Father surveys the people, 'yes'.

'Then baptize us'. The Father does so, making the sign of the cross on their foreheads. The end titles explain that 'Fifteen years later, the Hurons, having accepted Christianity, were routed and killed by their enemies, the Iroquois. The Jesuit mission to the Hurons was abandoned and the Jesuits returned to Quebec'. Not only does this confirm the fears that some of the Algonquins had about conversion, but it also 'legitimizes' the dream that Chomina had about their impending doom.[15]

Adapted by Brian Moore from his novel of the same, *Black Robe* was released in cinemas one year after *Dances with Wolves* and, rather than romanticize either side of the conflict, it paints a more realistic, and sometimes uncomfortable, portrait of the intersection of cultures. As many reviewers have noted, the film refuses to take sides and it avoids easy answers. As John Simon wrote in a *National Review Online* commentary on (review of) *Black Robe*:

> Indians in movies, to this day, have been noble or ignoble savages, food for one or another kind of mendacity and sermonizing. Here they and their beliefs come to extraordinary, absorbing life, as do Catholicism and its representatives, though neither party gets the final nod.[16]

Written and directed by Salvador Carrasco, *The Other Conquest* depicts the conquest of Mexico by Spain. The story begins on May 19, 1520, one year after the arrival of Hernando Cortes. We watch as countless Aztecs, including priests and Aztec nobility, are massacred at the Great Temple of Tenochtitlan. A codex maker named Topilzin survives, asking the sun god, why he has abandoned them. He survives by hiding under a stack of dead bodies. Six years pass, and he is still trying to preserve the cult of Tonantzin, the Aztec Mother Goddess. Inside of a clandestine temple, a virgin is brought in, washed and given a mushroom to eat so that she doesn't feel what will happen next. A priest cuts out her heart. Spanish soldiers, led by Captain Cristobal arrive, and immediately replace the native mother goddess with a sculpture of the Virgin Mary. Father Diego is also present. His mission is to convert the 'savages' and make them civilized Christians; to replace their human sacrifices and feathered deities with public christenings and fealty to the Virgin Mary. Topilzin escapes from the temple, but is soon betrayed by his brother for a bag of money and taken before Cortes. Topilzin, who is the illegitimate son of Monctezuma, is then whipped thirty-three times and forced to renounce his religion.[17] To make sure that he does so, he is taken to and confined in the Franciscan Monastery of Our Lady of Light to be 'educated in the one true faith'; he is also taught Castilian Spanish.

Another five years pass, and the now named Tomas is struggling to reconcile two worlds. Later in the film, he has a vision in which the Virgin Mary is revealed as the Aztec Mother Goddess. When a statue of the Virgin arrives in the monastery, Tomas becomes increasingly obsessed with it, and attempts to 'appropriate her'. In the end, Father Diego comes to realize that deep inside, Tomas and he 'shared the same belief, even though they were from different worlds'; that all men are equal. With many holding the belief that native people were 'subhuman', Father Diego is 'converted' through his time with Tomas. The director's premise is that the indigenous people may have converted to Christianity, but they did so by appropriating familiar images, in this case the mother goddess, and made them their own, thus ensuring their survival. Furthermore, the director applies images and scenes from the passion of Jesus to the 'passion' of Topilzin/Tomas to demonstrate how similar were/are the Aztec and Christian concepts of sacrifice and suffering.[18] As it states on the film's official web site, '*The Other Conquest* is a drama of one man's quest to adapt to a hostile, new world and another man's journey toward tolerance and understanding. The film reveals the complex and ambiguous origins of a new, hybrid culture'. Not only is it about Aztecs and Spaniards, 'but also about other cultures throughout history that have been subjugated to colonization, conversion and ethnic cleansing'.[19]

Although religion, from the Aboriginal perspective, is not really depicted in *Rabbit-Proof Fence* (2002), the film demonstrates the harsh, and often inhumane, treatment that the indigenous people endured under a callous government. As the title cards read:

'Western Australia, 1931. For 100 years the Aboriginal people have resisted the invasion of their lands by white settlers. Now, a special law, the Aborigines Act, controls their lives in every detail. Mr. A. O. Neville, the chief protector of Aborigines, is the legal guardian of every Aborigine in the State of Western Australia. He has the power to "remove any half-caste child" from their family, from anywhere within the state'.

Based on Doris Pilkington's book, *Rabbit-Proof Fence* focuses on the abduction of three Aboriginal girls, who are taken to an internment camp so that they can be trained as domestic staff. They eventually escape, and trek 1,500 miles back to their home.

An exploration of post-colonialism in Australia can be found in Werner Herzog's *Where the Green Ants Dream* (*Wo Die Grunen Ameisen Traumen*, 1984), and in *Dead Heart* (1996). Filmed in Coober Pedy, the opal capital of the world, *Where the Green Ants Dream* shows the clash between Western 'development' and Aboriginal belief that the land is sacred. A mining company has employed a geologist to map the subsoil of the desert, prior to the extraction of uranium. His work, however, is interrupted by a group of Aborigine men. The elders Miliritbi and Dayipu explain that this is where the green ants dream; disruption of them will have dire consequences for the Aboriginal people, and for the earth itself. Negotiations begin between the two groups, and eventually, the two sides square off in court.[20] But the film is more than a court case. It reveals the clash of cultures that continues in Australia today. In one of the film's most poignant scenes, the geologist is in a supermarket when he sees several Aboriginal men sitting in the middle of an aisle. When asked about this, the supermarket manager tells him that before the store was built, on this spot stood the area's only tree. It is believed, he continues, that this is the only place where the tribe can 'dream' their children.[21]

Dreams also play an important role in Peter Weir's 1977 film *The Last Wave*.[22] The white protagonist, David Burton, is a tax and corporate lawyer who decides to represent five Aborigines at a murder trial. Their alleged victim has died from drowning in a small amount of water. The lawyer is drawn into the case because of his own prophetic dreams, which are mostly about water. In one scene he asks 'what are dreams?' Chris Lee, an Aboriginal man, replies: 'Like seeing, hearing, talking . . . the way of knowing things. Messages are sent in dreams. If my brother called me – part of my body would move. A dream is a shadow of something real'. Furthermore, *The Last Wave* demonstrates how important it is for the Aborigines to adhere to tribal law, and the punishment that occurs when they do not. 'People who still practice tribal law live one thousand miles from Sydney, up north and in the desert', a character says. In one case, a man who broke tribal law was punished by having a spear stuck into his leg three times.

This same punishment is found in *Dead Heart*, which takes place in the desert town of Wala Wala, an 'eight hour drive from Alice Springs'. When a jailed Aboriginal is found hanged in the police lock-up, the indigenous people are outraged, demanding justice. Against his white superior's wishes, an Aboriginal deputy steps forward and lets the dead prisoner's father stab him in the leg three times. 'The law has to apply equally to everyone', someone says. But the conflict between the whites and indigenous people does not end here. Tony, an indigenous man who is having an affair with Kate, a white woman, takes her to a sacred 'dreaming' site, where only men are allowed, and they engage in sexual relations. He is killed for breaking the law. The few whites inhabiting the town have 'good intentions', believing that they are 'making a difference out here'. They want to 'civilize' these people and are trying to accomplish that through white justice, education and, of course, Christianity. The hard-headed Aboriginal leader who has tremendous clout, however, does not want the whites there, and he is willing to do whatever it takes to get rid of them.[23]

Not many films about Maori life and culture have been released in the United States. *Her Majesty* (2001) and *Whale Rider* (2002) prove the exception. The former film is set in 1953, and is concerned mostly with Elizabeth

Wakefield and her fixation on Queen Elizabeth, who is planning a tour of New Zealand. When news surfaces that the queen might be stopping in Middleton, the townspeople make preparations. Trouble arises when the home of an old Maori 'witch', Hira is found to be in the middle of the parade route. During the course of the film, Elizabeth befriends Hira and learns about Maori practices, such as the coming-of-age ritual of getting a tattoo (*moko*) on one's chin. As the old woman explains, before the bone chisel was used, a pattern was drawn three times, and the person was asked 'are you willing to take the *moko*? Are you willing to bear the pain?'

'Why did you do it', Elizabeth queries.

'It was my identity as Maori', the old woman replies. When a person reaches adulthood, it shows that she is willing to take on responsibility. 'It's like having your name written on your face'. Hira also takes the girl into the 'bush' to see her father's grave. While there, Hira sings and washes her face. Hira's father, it is explained, was a 'great warrior', who tried for twenty years to keep the British from taking Maori land. He eventually brokered a treaty with them, which was supposed to allow the Maoris to keep 'what was already theirs', but two weeks after the British royal family left the country, her father was ambushed and the land was taken back. Although not available in the United States, the *River Queen* (2005) explores this uneasy and violent early period, during the British colonization of New Zealand. At its centre is Sarah O'Brien, an Irish woman who becomes pregnant by a Maori. Her son is eventually kidnapped by his Maori grandfather, and she spends much of the film trying to get him back. At the end, we watch Sarah enduring the *moko* ritual.

Based on the novel by Maori writer Witi Ihimaera, *Whale Rider* begins with the birth of fraternal twins. But any happiness they might have experienced is short lived, because the mother and her son die. Hope, too, has died for the tribe, because it is believed that this boy was destined to become their 'chief'. Porourangi goes against the wishes of Koro, the tribal chief and his father, and names his surviving daughter Paikea. (Paikea is reserved for boys and is the name of their ancestor who came to New Zealand on the back of a whale.) Filled with grief, Porourangi leaves for Europe, leaving the girl in her grandparents' care. As she grows up, she is excluded from the ancient teachings, simply because she is a girl. But she has a destiny that transcends gender. *Whale Rider* is probably the best film available about indigenous religion and culture. In it, we find evidence of both myth and ritual. For instance, Koro trains the local boys in the lessons of their people and teaches them how to use a *taiaha*, fighting stick, and how to perform the traditional 'dance', known as *haka*. *Whale Rider* also demonstrates how indigenous people have had to 'adapt or die'. This is a lesson that Koro must learn.

A Canadian film that is reminiscent of *Whale Rider* is *Luna: Spirit of the*

Whale (2007), which was inspired by a true story. Set in British Columbia, this film focuses on the Mowachaht/Muchalaht, a First Nations tribe that has 'lived here since the beginning; between the mountains and the sea'. Two animals are sacred to them – the wolf and the whale – and it is said that when the chief dies, he can choose to join with either one. The town's chief does die, which results in the return of his son, Mike Maquinna. Not long after the funeral, an uncharacteristically friendly orca is sighted in the cove, and many of the natives believe that it is the returning chief. 'The whale wants to be with his people', says one man. Conflict soon erupts between the local government, the fishermen, and the indigenous people. At first Mike is reluctant to believe. But the more he comes into contact with the orca, the more he finds it plausible. The emergence of the whale renews the indigenous people's 'faith' in themselves and reminds them of their identity, connecting them to the water, to their past, and to their traditions.

Using feature films to learn more about indigenous religion can prove challenging. Christianity has had a tremendous influence on indigenous traditions, so it is often difficult to extricate the two. There is also the challenge of definition. What is religion? For indigenous people, it is often inseparable from culture. Religion is very much a 'way of life'. Furthermore, it is only recently that non-native filmmakers have insisted on historical and cultural accuracy, and have made a concentrated effort to take characters beyond stereotypes. Indigenous filmmakers are usually considered more 'accurate' in their depictions. Their films, however, are often low-budget, independent films that can be difficult to find.

18 Religion, Spirituality and Film

Wendy M. Wright

It is something of an old saw at this point, the 'I'm spiritual, but not religious' mantra. It is a phrase that is frequently heard among college students and it is commonly used among men and women across America. But what does this phrase, 'spiritual, but not religious', mean? Although it is part of the contemporary discussion, does it have a history? And what does spirituality have to do with religion and film?

In his recent study, Restless Souls: the Making of American Spirituality from Emerson to Oprah, historian Leigh Schmidt argues that the phrase, 'spiritual, but not religious', and all that it represents on the current American scene, has a national pedigree.[1] Rather than being the product of the sixties counterculture or the recent invention of New Age adherents, the 'religion' of the spiritual seeker is a hallowed American tradition. Schmidt argues that the roots of modern American spirituality can be found in the nineteenth century rise and flourishing of Religious Liberalism.

Religion and Spirituality

Seeker spirituality – excitedly eclectic, mystically yearning, perennially cosmopolitan – is an artefact of religious liberalism, especially in its more radical stripes. Included in that company of non-conformists were Transcendentalists, romantic Unitarians, reform Jews, progressive Quakers, devout disciples of Emerson and Whitman, Spiritualists, questing psychologists, New Thought optimists, Vedantists and Theosophists, among sundry other wayfarers.... Almost from first to last, they charted a path – at least so they imagined – away from the old 'religions of authority' into this new 'religion of the spirit'.[2]

Ideals of individual spiritual liberty, an interest in mystical experience and meditative interiority, sympathetic appreciation of all religions and a belief in universal brotherhood are characteristics of this eclectic movement which was as much a vision of emancipated souls as a political theory of individual rights and civil liberties or an economic programme. Schmidt uses the term

Religious Liberalism as a catch-all phrase for an interlocking group of precepts and practices embraced by a wide spectrum of Americans from the early 1820s until the present. Individualistic in its understanding of authority, Religious Liberalism had and still has little sympathy with traditional religious, especially Western, creeds or scriptural texts that define truth for believers. It encourages its adherents to set out on an individualized, rather than a collective, search to find spiritual meaning in *this* life, rather than in an otherworldly salvation. Religious Liberalism values the ethical work of social reform and stresses the immanence of the transcendent discovered in each person and, notably, in nature. It views religious traditions, especially those from the 'East', as resources for the personal, if universally conceptualized, spiritual quest. Religious Liberalism especially promotes the idea that there are a set of universal spiritual values found in all religious traditions.

Another perspective on the 'spiritual, but not religious' mantra is suggested by Robert Orsi.[3] Orsi raised a scholarly red flag about the current spiritual renaissance when he challenged those engaged in the academic study of Spirituality by claiming that 'spirituality' is simply another name for what modern Americans deem 'good religion'. Orsi claims that the term 'religion' is now utilized as a label for all that is conceptualized as 'bad' in human religiosity. Constricting rules, eviscerated rituals, moribund or – worse yet – totalizing doctrines, institutional inertia, overbearing authority, exclusive truth-claims, fundamentalist world-views, superstitious devotional practices: these are 'bad' and they are 'religion'. Spirituality, then, equates with all that is 'good' about religiosity. One need not accept in its entirety either Schmidt's view or Orsi's perspective on spirituality, but both approaches provide insight into the idea of spirituality that is found in contemporary American culture. Spirituality may be seen as an American sort of Religious Liberalism cast in a contemporary mode. Or, it may be seen as a type of 'good' individualized religiosity that eschews dogma, authoritarianism and creeds. Or, Spirituality may be seen as some combination of these.

Yet another perspective on spirituality is an alphabetically arranged sequence of virtues, maxims, concerns, interests or commitments to things spiritual. Perhaps the most notable example comes out of sixteenth century Spain from the pen of Franciscan Fray Francisco de Osuna, a book much admired and mentioned in her own writings by revered Carmelite master of the contemplative life, Saint Teresa of Avila. More recent examples include: *Alphabet Treats: A to Z Nuggets of Nourishment for Spiritual Consumption*, a book of 'spiritual mind treatments' by Edward J. Lemberger, who claims the heritage of nineteenth century New Thought exemplars such as Ralph Waldo Emerson; a chapbook of alphabetically arranged spiritual maxims by turn of the twentieth century saint Thérèse of Lisieux, enhanced with quotations from the new Catechism of the Catholic Church; and alphabetical cyber 'jottings' from the desk of the priest-director of the national Catholic Shrine of Our Lady of Lourdes.

Spirituality and Film

One of the most interesting alphabetical spirituality lists can be found in *Spiritual Literacy: Reading the Sacred in Everyday Life*, a compilation of thirty seven spiritual practices 'from Attention to Zeal', by Frederic and Mary Ann Brussat.[4] This is an especially interesting alphabet because the Burssats also publish in a journal, *Spirituality and Health: the Soul Body Connection*, which includes a list of the 'Most Spiritually Literate Films' between the years 1997 and 2001.[5] The spiritual alphabet found in *Spiritual Literacy* does not claim to derive from a particular theological or ecclesial community, although there are some recognizable overlaps with Christian ideals – for example, the traditional theological virtues of Faith, Hope and Love. The Brussat's list is seen as representative of enduring and universally acknowledged 'practices' that evidence the presence of 'Spirit' (not the Holy Spirit of the Trinity) in everyday life and are found in all world religions. The list includes themes or topics such as Beauty, Mystery, Questing, Peace, Shadow, Yearning, Transformation, Imagination, Enthusiasm, Forgiveness, Grace, Gratitude, Joy, Listening, Nurturing, Openness, Play, Silence and You, among others.[6]

The examples above provide a reasonable account of the concept of the spiritual that is at work when people claim that they are 'spiritual, but not religious'. But, what does all of this talk about spirituality mean for the study of religion and film? When one talks about spirituality within the study of religion and film, there is a realization that 'the spiritual, but not religious' expands the horizons and the possibilities of discussion.

There is no single way to understand the Spiritual. How one describes or defines the Spiritual and which elements of the Spiritual will be emphasized differs from one individual to another. Given the nature of the Spiritual, this is exactly what we would expect. But, the descriptions of the Spiritual offered above do give a rough overview of what counts as Spiritual and how the Spiritual differs from our common understanding of particular religious traditions. These descriptions also provide some history of the idea of the Spiritual. This history indicates that the Spiritual is not simply a popular contemporary movement that sprang up out of nowhere. The Spiritual, in whatever form it takes, has deep roots and a close connection to a broad view of religion.

We may now ask what all of this talk about Spirituality means for the study of religion and film. Although the Spiritual goes beyond the religious, there is some significant overlap and the history of the Spiritual is closely connected to the religious. This means that we can see the Spiritual as an extension of the religious. In an important sense, 'religion and film' becomes 'religion/spirituality and film'. It follows then that by expanding the realm of the religious to include the realm of the Spiritual we expand the range of topics and themes that will be of interest to scholars of religion and film. Religion and film will be not only about redemption and salvation, but also about yearning and zeal. Religion and film will be not only about love and hope and forgiveness, but also about a wide range of themes and topics that come from the Spiritual, including being present, openness, questing, shadow, silence and others. The following paragraphs discuss some of the themes and topics of Spirituality and provide some examples of movies in which these themes are to be found.

Hope

Hope, of course, is one of the three 'theological' virtues enumerated in the Christian scriptures (the other two are faith and love). Hope, in such a classical context, is defined as the desire for a future good, that good being assumed to be God. More broadly in non-theological contexts, hope is generally conceived as confident desire, a feeling that something desirable is likely to happen. When identified in the Robert Zemeckis-directed film *Cast Away* (2000) starring Tom Hanks, hope emerges as a complex quality that allows a person to endure great difficulty while reshaping the horizon of meaning within which the person endures. *Cast Away* is the tale of Chuck Nolan, a driven FedEx systems engineer whose every moment is consumed with work. On Christmas Eve, hastily taking leave of his fiancée, he answers a call to board a FedEx plane taking cargo across the Pacific. A fierce storm blows the plane off course and it plunges into the ocean. The only survivor, Chuck is washed ashore on a deserted island where he is confronted with the spectre of his own demise. At first, he entertains the thought that he might be rescued but soon his attention is taken up with the sheer arduousness of surviving. Most of the film focuses on the ingenious ways Chuck utilizes native materials and the debris washed ashore from the crash to fashion shelter and feed himself as well as to devise means by which he might return to civilization. But the mental challenges he faces are highlighted as well: the terror of isolation and the threat of despair loom. Gradually he sheds the false, frantic consciousness acquired in his former life and learns to live attentively, focusing on the simple acts that make one human. After four years, a piece of plastic strong enough to form the platform for a sea-worthy craft floats up on the beach and Chuck takes the risk to set out onto the ocean. His tiny craft is spotted by a passing ship and he is rescued. When he returns home, he discovers that his fiancée has married another man and that he must refashion his life. Of course, he has already done that on the island. Chuck has become another person. Hope is what keeps his soul alive and enables him to give up illusions of control and open up to the mysteries of the present moment. Hope, in this interpretation, is not merely the capability to persevere in believing that the good will occur despite all appearances, it is also the relinquishment of a false consciousness. In this case, that meaning is discovered in the modern twenty-four hour, three hundred sixty-five day year enslavement to productivity.

Hope emerges as a spiritual practice in another film which treats of the capacity to surmount almost impossible odds. *The Hurricane*, directed by Norman Jewison and starring Denzel Washington, is based on the true story of middleweight boxing champion Rubin 'Hurricane' Carter who in 1966 was wrongly convicted of murder. The plot begins by setting up the bright future prospects of African American Carter then takes the viewer to the fateful night when he and a friend were stopped when driving home from a club in Paterson New Jersey. A triple murder in a nearby bar has brought the police out. Despite the fact that they had not visited the fated club, another suspect claims that Carter and his companion were indeed present. On the basis of this testimony the two are convicted and Carter sentenced to three consecutive life terms in prison. Even though his accuser recants and he continues to protest his innocence, claiming that racism and his record as a civil rights activist are to blame, Carter is reconvicted. A good deal of the action of the film features the efforts of a young African American teenager from Brooklyn, Lesra Martin, and a trio of Canadian activists to free Carter from his wrongful imprisonment. When Carter is finally freed as a result of their investigations and selfless dedication to seeing justice done, he claims, 'Hate got me into this place, love got me out'. Hope is spun out of the 'lifeline' of small acts of kindness, love and hard work on the part of the strangers that take Carter's cause on as their own.

Other movies that may be seen as addressing the virtue of hope include *Our Song* (2000), *The Shawshank Redemption* (1994) and *The Cider House Rules* (1999).

Love

Love is, with Hope, one of the Christian theological virtues and like its virtuous companion is traditionally understood to have an intrinsic connection with God, who is, according to Scripture, Love. As such, Love is understood to be a divinely infused habit orienting the person towards the divine and inclining him or her towards others for God's sake. Ancient Greek treatments of love saw it as having a variety of modalities: including idealized pure love, love of the good, true and beautiful, the bond of friendship and natural, familial affection. In common use today, love is variously identified as deep affection for another person or persons based on kinship, romantic or erotic attachment, or as more generalized sympathy for others. Two films that focus on the long-suffering care of spouses are excellent examples of the spiritually literate practice of Love. Both films, interestingly, are based on real life accounts. The first is Oscar winning *A Beautiful Mind,* the 2002 film directed by Ron Howard. It stars Russell Crowe and Jennifer Connelly as mathematical genius John Forbes Nash, Jr. and his wife Alicia. A brilliant mind is what Nash has and for much of the film the viewer sees the world through Nash's perspective. It follows the youthful prodigy from his early graduate career at Princeton where he is recognized for his accomplishments through his time teaching at MIT where he meets Alicia and marries. It also chronicles Nash's encounters with a former roommate Charles and his niece and a mysterious agent from the Department of Defence who enlists the brilliant scientist in cracking encoded Soviet secrets. Soon, Nash finds himself followed by hostile individuals and is given an assignment to decode secrets embedded in magazines and newspapers. Gradually, he becomes more paranoid and obsessively engrossed in his encryption project. When Alicia intervenes and Nash is sent to a psychiatric facility the viewer becomes aware, along with Nash himself, that Charles, the niece and the enigmatic agent are figments of his imagination skewed by schizophrenia. He submits to anti-psychotic medication but it impairs his intellect and so he ceases taking it, triggering a relapse. Through a series of harrowing incidents, during which Nash endangers their toddler son and is told by the reappearing agent to kill his wife, Alicia struggles to help her husband. His career flounders while he takes his medicine and so the couple decides to try and live with Nash's demons. Gradually, with her support, Nash learns painfully to distinguish between the real and the imaginary, is allowed to teach again and goes on to win the Nobel Memorial Prize in Economics for his revolutionary work on game theory. The film's last sequences, as Nash receives his award in Stockholm and Alicia tearfully watches from the audience underscores the extent to which this moment is the result of the selfless, long-suffering of Alicia who has loved him unsparingly.

Another devoted spouse earns the accolade of practicing the virtue of love in *Iris,* based on the poignant books by John Bayley about his wife Iris's descent into Alzheimer's. *Iris,* directed by Richard Eyre, featured Kate Winslet and Judi Dench as, respectively, the younger and older Iris Murdoch, noted British philosopher and writer. Set against the backdrop of the ardent youthful love affair between the vivacious, free-spirited Murdoch and her more awkward fellow student Bayley, the story comes to focus on the couple decades later, when Iris is at her height as a noted public figure. Gradually and painfully her powers begin to diminish and the two are made aware that she is suffering from Alzheimer's disease. The horror of the degeneration is experienced through both characters but especially through Bayley himself, who patiently carries the burden of his wife's deterioration, keenly aware of the intelligence, humor and relationship that is slipping away from him as Iris recedes into her own world. It is love expressed as spousal fidelity, both to the damaged woman Bayley came to live with as well as to the memory of the woman with whom he fell in love, that wins the film its designation as spiritually literate.

Other movies for which love is a topic include *Titanic* (1997), *Shakespeare in Love* (1998), *Children of Heaven* (1997), *Love Actually* (2003), *Breaking the Waves* (1996), *Moulin Rouge* (2001), *Dead Man Walking* (1995) and *Oscar and Lucinda* (1990).

Justice

Justice is one of the most prominent virtues of the ancient Greek philosophers. Although different philosophers give different descriptions of justice, there is a general sense that when justice is in place there is a kind of appropriate balance. Injustice, then, is a condition in which things are out of balance and seeking justice in such circumstances means something like 'making things right'. This idea of setting things right is a common theme in film.

Amistad (1997) is the story of a group of Africans who take over a Spanish slave ship bound for America. They are eventually captured and imprisoned. Then two abolitionists set out to free these slaves, thereby setting things right. The abolitionists hire a lawyer who thinks that he can free the slaves and, indeed, he does win their freedom in a lower court. But supporters of slavery are not ready to give up easily and eventually the lawyer must make his case before Supreme Court of the United States. Since the Africans were not originally slaves, taking away their freedom is an injustice and rectifying that injustice – making things right – requires giving them back their freedom.

Erin Brockovich (2000) is the story of a woman who goes to work for an attorney in order to pay off her debt to him. While working for the lawyer, Brockovich discovers that a large utility company has been dumping pollutants that have made people in the area sick. She convinces her boss that the utility company should pay for the behaviour that has harmed others and in the end her boss wins the case against the utility company. The utility company has been profiting from its harmful behaviour and setting things right means requiring the company to pay for the damage it has done to the families in the area. Since many people died, including children, from the dumping of the toxic material, the movie also raises the question of whether things can be set right by making the company pay a fine, even a large fine.

The Insider (1999) pits a former employee of the Brown and Williamson Tobacco Company against 'Big Tobacco'. Jeffery Wigand is asked by the people at *60 Minutes* to interpret for them documents about the tobacco industry that had been sent to the CBS show. Having signed a confidentiality clause while working for Brown and Williamson, Wigand is reluctant to get involved, but eventually he helps *60 Minutes* expose the tactics and practices of Big Tobacco. Contrary to their public claims, tobacco companies did include various chemicals that would make cigarettes more addictive. The exposure of these practices, brought about in part by Wigand's appearance on *60 Minutes* resulted in many states winning a huge settlement from the tobacco companies. Since Wigand was a tobacco insider, he was able to help 'set things right' in a way that outsiders would not have been able to do.

'Setting things right' is a popular story to put on film. The audience leaves with a good feeling. It may even be that justice on film is important because we see so little of it in the real world. It is to movies that we must turn if we are to see justice done and this makes movie going very attractive. Other movies that deal with justice include *The Rainmaker* (1997), based on the novel by John Grisham, and *A Civil Action* (1998), based on the novel by Johnathan Harr. Many superhero movies also deal with justice and making things right in the world.

Transformation

The maxim for transformation in *Spiritual Literacy* is: 'Welcome the positive changes that are taking place in your life. Open up the windows and let in some fresh air. Wholeness and healing waiting in the wings'.[7] Being open to change, as opposed to resisting change, and the consequent benefits of such change are also themes found in film. In Robert Duvall's *The Apostle* (1997), for example, Sonny lives what some might call a religious life. He is a preacher and has his own large congregation. His jealousy, however, causes him to kill a man and he must then run from the law. As he runs, we see the transformation take place. In one scene he drives his car in the river to hide it. As it sinks, we see the license plate with 'Sonny' on it sinking as well. He then begins to call himself the Apostle E. F. He starts a new church, much more modest than the first one and he begins to minister to his small congregation in a way that puts them first, not himself. The transformation is complete when the Apostle E. F. is arrested and taken to prison for the murder he had committed earlier. At this point, he has no interest in running, as he had before. Sonny has transformed himself to the point where he is now able to accept responsibility for his actions and in doing so he finds a peace that he had never experienced before.

Robert Duvall also appears in another transformation movie, *Tender Mercies* (1983). In this film Duvall is Mac Sledge, a hard drinking, womanizing country music performer and song writer. One night his friends leave him in the small motel cabin where they were partying. He is hung over and has no money and no friends to call. The woman who runs the motel, a widow named Rosa Lee, agrees to let him stay in the cabin and to get free meals in exchange for doing odd jobs around the motel. The one rule is 'no drinking'. Mac's work and sobriety, as well as his interactions with Rosa Lee and her son, who lost his father in Vietnam, transform Mac into a family man. He not only finds peace in the life of a family man, but he is able to show sympathy for his ex wife, also a country music star, when their only daughter is killed in an automobile accident. In the end, Mac is playing football with Sonny and the music that plays is: 'This is what love means to me'.

Other movies that deal with transformation include *Down in the Delta* (1998), *Good Will Hunting* (1997), *Nurse Betty* (2000), *The Shipping News* (2001), and *Life As A House* (2001).

Yearning

Another topic of spirituality is that of yearning. Yearning is not a typical religious virtue, although one might equate it to somewhat more traditional themes such as desire or aspiration. Nevertheless, yearning is an important aspect of spirituality and two movies that exemplify the practice of yearning are the Japanese release, *Shall We Dance?* (1997), and the British film, *Billy Elliot* (2000).

Shall We Dance?, directed by Masayuki Suo, features Koji Yakusho as hard working accountant Shohei Sugiyama. Shohei is caught up in the mind- and spirit-numbing routine of the Japanese businessman: endless work and the obligatory routines of conventional married life. One evening, riding home on the train he catches a glimpse of a beautiful face on the balcony of a dance school. She is Mai Kishikawa and the thought of visiting and dancing with her enters his mind. What follows is the story of a gradual awakening on many levels. Shohei learns to dance. As his body begins to express itself his spirit soars. He meets and interacts with a variety of characters who are his fellow students and he enters a dance competition with his teacher. But he is ashamed to admit his new delight to his family: dancing is frowned upon in his culture. It certainly is not an acceptable hobby for a respected business-man. When his wife hires a private investigator to find out what her strangely changed husband is up to, the truth comes out and Shohei opens his heart to his family.

Billy Elliot (2000) is set in a different cultural milieu yet it deals with a similar singular individual who finds himself yearning to be someone the culture cannot imagine him to be. Billy is the son of a poor miner who is caught up in the rough and tumble coal miners strike in 1984 in County Durham, UK. His dad enrols Billy in a local boxing school but the boy dislikes the brutal sport and is drawn instead to the girls' ballet class. Billy shows an incredible talent and the ballet mistress encourages him and helps him pre-pare for entrance exams at the Royal Ballet Academy. Incensed that his son should be involved in such an unmanly activity, the father interferes. But the ballet mistress, Billy's own yearning and the recognition that this unlikely profession might enable his son to climb out of the brutal life of a provincial miner, changes Billy's father's perspective.

Forgiveness

The small but memorable David Lynch film, *The Straight Story* (1999), is an example of the spiritual practice of forgiveness. Forgiveness is a virtue central to a number of religious traditions and currently espoused by elements of the medical community as an aid to psychological and even physical healing. The film focuses on seventy three year old widower, Alvin, who lives in rural Iowa and has not spoken to his older brother Lyle for a decade. Pride and alcohol, he says, are what the old feud is really about. When Alvin learns that Lyle has suffered a stroke and may not live long, he becomes determined to visit and reconcile with him. The trouble is Lyle lives hundreds of miles away, and Alvin has a bad hip, emphysema, little money, no car and no driver's license. He does, however, own a riding lawn mower and so hops on it and begins his snail's pace journey northeast to Wisconsin. The bulk of the film chronicles Alvin's sometimes painful, sometimes comical adventures on the road: including encounters with strangers of all sorts and frequent mechanical breakdowns. But the real momentum that drives the film and Alvin's stubborn persistence to keep going is the inner dynamism of the longing to forgive and be forgiven.

One of the interesting features of spirituality and film is that although any particular movie might be identified as an example of a particular spiritual topic or theme, that same movie might well serve as an example of other spiritual themes as well. *Tender Mercies*, for example, has been identified above as an example of transformation, but it just as well might be considered an example of love. *The Cider House Rules* has been identified as a movie about hope, but it might be seen equally as an example of yearning, or an example of love. *Dead Man Walking* has been identified as a movie about love, but it also could be seen as a movie about forgiveness. *The Rainmaker* is a movie about justice, but it also is a movie about zeal. Many more examples could be given but the point here is that many movies discuss or provide an example of more than one spiritual topic or theme.

Religion, Spirituality and Film

What does all of this mean for religion and film? One way to think about religion and spirituality is to think of expanding the category of the religious to include the category of the spiritual. If we do this, it explains why many people who are interested in spiritual topics and themes can be said to be interested in religion and film or why they see themselves as interested in religion and film. Expanding religion to include spirituality also explains why there are so many films that are seen as movies about religion and film. Unfortunately, if we define the spiritual too broadly, we find ourselves in a situation where almost every movie has something to say about one or another spiritual topic – we can find the spiritual in any film and the category of 'religion and film' becomes so broad as to be almost meaningless. Expanding religion to include spirituality also makes it difficult to talk about being 'spiritual, but not religious'. That is, since the religious and spiritual now coincide, you can no longer have the one (spiritual) without the other (religion).

It might be better, then, to think of religion as having an interest in things spiritual – love, hope, faith, mystery, grace, being present, compassion, forgiveness, transformation and so on. While religion also has an interest in rituals, institutions, creeds, authority and so on, much of religion has to do with the spiritual nature of human beings. Interest in the spiritual, then, is something shared by both religion and those interested in spirituality. Viewing the relationship between the spiritual and the religious in this way means that one can be 'spiritual, but not religious'. It also means that the spiritual themes and topics that are of interest to religion and film will be primarily those that are also of interest to religion. The farther we move in the realm of spirituality from the spiritual interests of religion, the less interest in spirituality there will be for religion and film. If we take the spiritual interests of the religions of the world into account, as opposed to the spiritual interests of only western religions, we will expand greatly the range of topics for religion and film without at the same time having to consider every spiritual interest a part of religion and film.

Part III

Religious Themes in Movies

19 Jesus Movies

Adele Reinhartz*

Since the advent of cinema in the late nineteenth century, 'Bible movies', that is, films that focus on biblical characters and retell biblical narratives, have been perennial favourites. Of all biblical subjects, it is Jesus of Nazareth who is the most popular biblical celebrity. From the very first short Jesus film in 1898 to the present day, more than a 100 feature and made-for-television films have been produced, many of which are readily available in DVD format. There is little doubt that the cinematic representations of Jesus and his life story have had, and continue to have, a profound influence on the ways in which the general public perceives Jesus visually and interprets his life and ongoing religious and cultural significance.

Jesus films are made in every genre of film, from comedy through animation, yet they have much in common. First, all use one or more of the canonical Gospels (Matthew, Mark, Luke and John) as sources to recount all or some of Jesus' life story as told in those Gospels, and all wrestle with the question of how to portray a man whom many believe to be the Messiah. Most important, they all address the intertwined issues of historicity, authenticity and fidelity to scripture. Should the cinematic Jesus have the physical characteristics often associated with men of middle-eastern and Semitic origin or should he resemble the iconic Christ figures of the European Renaissance? Should the major role that the Gospels assign to the Jewish leadership and the crowds in Jesus' Passion be replicated, in the interests of fidelity of the scriptural sources, or modified or even eliminated, in order to avoid the charge of anti-Semitism?

With a handful of exceptions, the Jesus movies are set in a historical place and time: the Galilee and Judea of the early first-century CE. Like other biographical films ('biopics'), however, Jesus films are not documentaries, but rather fictionalized accounts of a familiar story. Viewers have a mixed and paradoxical response to such films. On the one hand, they (we) recognize the fictional nature of the biopics and typically grant them a measure of artistic

* Parts of this chapter have been modified from, or previously published in, A. Reinhartz (2007), *Jesus of Nazareth*, New York: Oxford University Press, with the kind permission of the publisher.

license to flesh out the story and the character of their subjects. At the same time, however, they also view them as 'real' or historical and expect them to cohere with the familiar story as told in the Gospels, in church, and around the dinner table. This expectation is evident in the tendency of many viewers, including film critics and scholars, to assess the Jesus movies on the basis of their historicity.[1]

Expectations of historicity are actively encouraged by these films themselves. Through their choice of subject (someone who is known to have existed), and the use of costumes (the familiar bathrobe and sandals outfit of the biblical epics), settings (the Middle East or locations that resemble the Middle East) and language (biblical-sounding English, ancient languages), these films imply not only that they are telling a story about people who really existed, but also that they are telling a 'true' story. More than this, the Jesus movies explicitly assert their claim to historicity, often through the use of scrolled texts, titles and/or narration. The 1912 silent movie *From the Manger to the Cross*, for example, announces itself as 'a review of the saviour's life according to the gospel-narrative'. The 1961 film *King of Kings* begins with a lengthy and authoritative-sounding voice-over narrative, intoned solemnly by Orson Welles, that describes the historical situation of Judea in the time of Jesus.

Despite such assertions, these films have numerous non-historical elements. Every Jesus biopic contains scenes and/or dialogue that are not found in their primary sources, the Gospels of Matthew, Mark, Luke and John. Most invent speeches for Jesus, from everyday interactions with his mother and disciples, to cryptic sayings and pious discourses. Some films even attribute to Jesus the *bon mots* of other New Testament personalities, as when Max von Sydow's Jesus recites the apostle Paul's famous ode to love (1 Corinthians 13) in *The Greatest Story Ever Told* (1965). They may create fictional characters such as the scribe Zerah who masterminds Jesus' execution in Franco Zeffirelli's *Jesus of Nazareth* (1977). And some films present subplots that are nowhere to be found in the ancient sources. Nicholas Ray's *King of Kings* links Judas and Barabbas and places them among the leadership of a militant Jewish group that seeks to exploit Jesus' charisma for the good of the revolution. Robert Young's *Jesus* (1999) has the youthful saviour fall in love with Mary of Bethany. While some films consult the works of ancient historians such as Josephus Flavius, many draw heavily upon works of legend, liturgy and imagination such as the apocryphal gospels (*Infancy Gospel of Thomas*), liturgy (the Apostles' Creed), art (Michelangelo's *Pietàs*; Leonardo's *Last Supper*), fiction (*Ben-Hur*; *The Last Temptation of Christ*) and last but certainly not least, other Jesus movies.

Finally, Jesus films must contend with the contradictions among their canonical source texts as well as the narrative gaps within them. Most films follow the general outline that can be derived from a harmonization of the Gospel, and also utilize freely incidents from all four Gospels to achieve maximum impact. But at the same time, they adhere to the narrative template that is characteristic of the biopic genre. The biopic template situates its subject within a family and circle of friends to show how the hero's immediate circle as well as the broader social and political context either influences or responds to his or her growing capabilities and sense of mission. After establishing their subject's talents and accomplishments, biopics place him or her in an antagonistic relationship with an individual or group. Conflict ensues, inflicting physical and mental pain upon the hero. The conflict is resolved in a judicial trial that provides the occasion for an impassioned summation of the hero's primary message for the benefit of the viewing audience. Throughout, the principle of causality tightly links the story elements.[2] Jesus movies package Jesus' story into the same overall plot structure.

Finally, like other biopics and most other historical films, Jesus movies use the past as a vehicle for contemplating the present. The cinematic versions of Jesus' life story tell the story in a way that reflects the anxieties, concerns, hopes and aspirations of the era in which they were produced. Modern concerns are evident, for example, in the changing representations of women, reflecting changes in women's roles through the past century and more, and in the depiction of Jews and Judaism, in response to the events of the Holocaust as well as the growing recognition and acceptance of Jesus' own Jewish identity. It is the gaps in and contradictions among the Gospels that allow and even account for the variety and sheer number of cinematic Jesuses. The Gospels' silence allows film-makers to fill the void with their own creativity.

The fact that film-makers are engaged in reshaping Jesus' story to reflect the concerns of their own times should not be condemned as a distortion of the past merely for the sake of entertainment and box office appeal, though these factors are not irrelevant. Rather, the varieties of Jesus on the silver screen testify to the conviction that Jesus remains relevant to our society as well as to the ongoing need to tell and retell this story, in Hollywood and in other, international cinematic centres in which commercial films are made.

Chronological Survey

As we have noted, Jesus biopics span all eras and genres of cinema, on big screen and small. The majority provide a full biography of Jesus, others cover only a portion of Jesus' life, most frequently the events of Jesus' passion from the betrayal to the resurrection (e.g., *The Passion of the Christ* [2004]).[3]

Jesus also appears in two types of films that are not properly speaking Jesus biopics. One is the so-called peplum movie, otherwise known as the 'sword-and-sandal' movie.[4] In these films, Jesus appears briefly within the fictional story of another character who may be purely fictional (Demetrius, Judah Ben-Hur) or whose appearances in the Gospel provide us with virtually no information (Salome, Barabbas). Peplum films manage to insert pious Christian material while at the same time avoiding the problems associated with films purporting to tell the biography of the son of God. Examples include *Salome* (1923, 1953), *The Big Fisherman* (1959, featuring Peter), and *Barabbas* (1961/1962 in the US).

A second type is the 'Passion Play' movie. Passion Play films present a fictional frame narrative about the preparation and performance of a Passion Play; scenes from the Passion Play itself are usually presented as well. Examples include *Jesus of Montreal* (1989) and *The Master and Margarita* (1994). *Jesus Christ Superstar* (1973) technically belongs to this subgroup, in that occasional details remind us that we are watching a group of actors stage a passion play, but there is no narrative associated with the contemporary frame. At the opposite end of the spectrum is the 1957 French/Italian film, *Celui Qui Doit Mourir* (*He Who Must Die*), which focuses so intensely on the frame narrative that the actual Passion Play is never performed.

The Silent Era

The first known example of a Jesus movie is *The Passion Play at Oberammergau* (1898). While it claimed to be an authentic film of the periodic Passion Play performed at Oberammergau, Germany,[5] this nineteen-minute movie was actually staged and filmed on the roof of the Grand Central Palace in New York, using props and costumes that had been created for a New York stage production that was shut down before its first performance. Even after the public learned that this movie was a 'faked re-creation' of the Oberammergau production, the film remained immensely popular.[6]

The Passion Play at Oberammergau and other early silent films about Jesus such as *The Life and Passion of Jesus Christ* (1904), *From the Manger to the Cross* (1913) and *Christus* (1916/1917 in US), present a series of slow-moving tableaux.[7] These tableaux are often set up in imitation of popular devotional paintings or of famous paintings by Leonardo Da Vinci, Donatello and Rembrandt.[8] Jesus is invariably a tall, bearded, solemn and majestic figure whose piercing gaze is accentuated by a ring of black eye-liner. His white-robed figure is well-lit in contrast to his surroundings, creating a halo effect that reverently evokes Jesus' sanctity. These films presume the viewer's prior knowledge of the Gospels or at least the general outline of Jesus' life story. Their goal is not to create a complex or unified narrative, but to illustrate the relevant Gospel scenes.

Some silent Jesus movies move beyond such formulaic presentations to emphasize specific aspects of Jesus' life. The 1921 German film, *Der Galiläer* (*The Galilean*), goes further than most other movies of this period in its use of standard anti-Semitic tropes by presenting the Jewish characters as physically repugnant and laughable, hate-mongering and avaricious. The 1923 film *I.N.R.I.*, reissued as a 'talkie' entitled *The Crown of Thorns* in 1934, fleshes out the character of Jesus' mother, and transforms her from a virginal maiden to a resourceful, adventurous and assertive woman who will go to any lengths to be with her son in his moment of need.

The most interesting Jesus-related film in this period is D. W. Griffith's classic, *Intolerance: Love's Struggle Throughout the Ages* (1916). This film may have been intended to compensate for, or perhaps to undo, the damage done to Griffith's reputation by his magnum opus, *The Birth of a Nation* (1915), which, even as its brilliance was acknowledged, was also condemned for its blatantly racist point of view as evident in its highly positive portrayal of the Ku Klux Klan.[9] *Intolerance* weaves the story of Jesus together with three other narratives in order to illustrate the struggle between tolerance and intolerance through the ages. The most important narrative thread is 'The Modern Story', which relates the trials and tribulations that an intolerant, pious and meddling group of powerful women called 'The Uplifters' inflict upon a young, sweet couple, called The Boy and The Dear One. Though brief, the Judean Story of Jesus is crucial to Griffith's theme. Jesus' enemies among the Pharisees are portrayed as the prototype of the intolerant 'Uplifters' of the Modern story, while Jesus' crucifixion is directly compared to the travails of the Boy and the Dear One.[10]

The most famous Jesus film of the silent period is Cecil B. DeMille's *The King of Kings* (1927). In contrast to earlier films, DeMille's movie developed cause-and-effect, and had both a main plot and subplots. Its intertitles not only quote from scripture or provide background information, but convey dialogue and commentary that are often witty and aid considerably in the development of the plot and characters. DeMille's work had a major influence on the development of the Jesus biopic genre.

With the exception of DeMille's film, the silent Jesus is often not much more than an animated version of the illustrated Jesus found in Bible storybooks and devotional literature. No doubt the limitations of the silent genre itself, which was superseded soon after DeMille's film was released, contributed to this cardboard treatment. But reluctance to offend public mores also played a part. Film-makers met the challenge of portraying the son of God by stripping him of all human affect and robbing him of the ability to engage in normal human relationships and behaviours.

Early Sound Films

Curiously, not a single major movie about Jesus' life was made from 1927 (DeMille's *The King of Kings*) until 1961 (Nicholas Ray's *King of Kings*).[11] True, Jesus appeared as a cameo figure in the 'peplum' films discussed above, but Hollywood studiously avoided placing Jesus at the centre of any film.

Some commentators attribute this lengthy silence to the extraordinary success of DeMille's *The King of Kings*. This film, they argue, left no room for competitors until narrative and technological norms had undergone significant change.[12] While DeMille's success may have been one factor, surely the institution of movie censorship played a role.[13] In 1930, the Motion Picture Producers and Distributors of America in 1930 adopted a Production Code. The Code was endorsed and promoted by the powerful Catholic Legion of Decency in 1934.[14] From 1930 to 1966, no film could appear in American movie theatres unless it was certified by the Production Code Administration (PCA). Films which did not conform to the Code were subject to censorship.

The Code contained detailed guidelines on a wide range of issues.[15] For example, the Code forbade films to question marriage as an institution, or to portray 'impure' love as attractive and beautiful. Films were not permitted to depict 'ministers of religion' either as comic characters or as villains 'because the attitude taken toward them may easily become the attitude taken toward religion in general'. The Production Code required a high standard of reverence in any representations of Jesus, and forbade film-makers from 'throwing ridicule' on any religious faith. Similarly, the British Board of Film Censors, founded in 1912, banned the visual depiction of Jesus. The ban was not lifted until after World War II. DeMille's *The King of Kings* could be screened in London only after a special license was obtained; Jesus was edited out of films produced elsewhere but distributed in England, such as *Golgotha* (1935).[16]

The Epics

When Jesus reappeared as the star of epic films of the early 1960s, he was treated with the same solemnity and reverence as in the films of the silent era. What changed, however, was the drama and scope of his story and context. The epics were filled to the brim with people, colour and sound; the physical setting and the musical soundtrack were grand and majestic. The two major epics in this period were King of Kings, directed by Nicholas Ray[17] and *The Greatest Story Ever Told*, directed by George Stevens. Like DeMille's film, these movies emphasize causality; they fill in the gaps in the Gospel accounts in order to unify and clarify the plot. Their two Jesus figures, however, are very different from one another. The Jesus of *King of Kings* was an attractive youth

(Jeffrey Hunter) who broke the mold of solemn Jesus figures and thereby spawned the film's derisive nickname, 'I was a Teenage Jesus'.[18] The star of *The Greatest Story Ever Told*, Max von Sydow, was a gaunt, as yet unknown, European actor who took Son-of-Man solemnity to new heights. Along with *Ben-Hur*, and DeMille's 1956 *The Ten Commandments*, *King of Kings* and *The Greatest Story Ever Told* are the classics of the biblical epic genre as a whole.[19]

The Musicals

Most Jesus movies, both before and after the studio era, are dramas, in keeping with their tragic plot structure. The year 1973 saw two exceptions: the musicals *Jesus Christ Superstar* and *Godspell*.[20] Both of these films were sound recordings and Broadway stage productions before they appeared on the silver screen, and both were influenced by the Jesus movement of the 1960s and 1970s. They implicitly propose an answer to the question of how a 'hippie' Jesus would look and sound.

Jesus Christ Superstar depicts the staging of a passion play in the Negev desert in southern Israel. The film portrays Jesus as a (Super) star who, like Hollywood movie stars, is surrounded by a cult of celebrity that distorts his message, reduces it to superficiality, and renders it incapable of sustaining the burden of star-struck crowds. Stardom reduces Jesus to a publicity-driven Hollywood figure who, as Judas points out, is in danger of losing his sense of self and the raison d'être of his own mission. In this sense, even as it takes its place among other Jesus biopics, this musical can be seen as a critique of the Hollywood star system that both feeds and is fed by the biopic genre.

In contrast to the self-centred saviour of *Superstar*, the Jesus of *Godspell* is a winsome clown, brimming with warmth, friendship and ethical maxims. *Godspell* makes no attempt to be realistic. The clown Jesus is surrounded by a group of young men and women who frolic with him through the streets, parks and back alleys of a strangely quiet New York City. With the exception of Jesus, the figures in the film are not matched one on one with figures known from the Gospels; the same actor, for example, takes on the roles of John the Baptist and Judas while the others take on and cast off roles as needed. The narrative line is very loose; there is no clear causal development or plot.

While the songs might be catchy, the musical genre is ill-equipped to handle the drama of the Jesus story. It is therefore not surprising that there have been no mainstream additions to this list since 1973.[21]

Dramas

Most of the Jesus films made from 1966 to the present day have been feature dramas, produced for commercial release and/or television broadcast. While many are products of Hollywood, that is, the American movie machinery, some of the most compelling films have emerged in other countries. Perhaps the most highly regarded of the Jesus movies is Pier Paoli Pasolini's *Il Vangelo secondo Matteo* (*The Gospel According to Saint Matthew*; 1964). This Italian film, shot in black and white with a hand-held camera, takes all of its dialogue and most of its narrative from the Gospel of Matthew. Pasolini's Jesus is a passionate, angry young man who leads his group of peasant disciples in protest against the injustices of the established religious and political authorities. Most of the other actors, however, are non-professionals. The role of Jesus mother in her maturity is played by Pasolini's own mother; the disciples and crowds are played by rural villagers. Pasolini's Marxist perspective pervades the film, but for many viewers this does not detract from the power of its saviour figure.

A lesser known but fascinating Jesus movie is Roberto Rossellini's *Il Messias* (*The Messiah*; 1975), which due to distribution difficulties was never commercially released in North America.[22] Rossellini's film, like Pasolini's, evokes the simple rural life. Jesus, his mother, and his followers, both male and female, spend much of their time on the shores of the Sea of Galilee, where they fish, mend nets, bake and cook as they tell stories and share spiritual insights.

The American-made and/or produced feature films in the 1970s and later such as Franco Zeffirelli's lengthy made-for-TV series *Jesus of Nazareth* (1977), John Heyman's *Jesus* (1979) and Robert Young's miniseries by the same name (1999), exhibit the main features of the studio biopic. Similarly, the British made-for-TV 'claymation' (clay animation) movie *The Miracle Maker* (2000), though novel with regard to its medium, remains quite conventional in its narrative.[23] Its major innovation is to tell the story from the point of view of Jairus' daughter, a young girl whom Jesus raises from death or near death, according to Mark 5:22–43. This film borrows significantly from Zeffirelli's magnum opus, but attempts to tell the story in a way that is more accessible to children and more acceptable to their parents.

Spoofs of the Jesus Biopic Genre

The clichés of the Jesus movie genre inspired a number of spoofs, the best known and loved of which is *Monty Python's Life of Brian*. Though it is a 'Brian' movie and not a 'Jesus' movie, *Life of Brian* both uses and mocks the clichés of the genre.[24] The fictional Brian is an unintentional and reluctant messiah whose life parallels Jesus' biography in its public nature and tragic death, without the reverence, sanctity and perfection of the hero or the virginity of his mother. Despite its fictional premise, *Life of Brian* is meticulously researched and highly intelligent. Aside from Jesus himself, the film spares no one. Its hilarious darts are aimed at the conventions of Jesus' portrayal in film and popular culture, as well as at targets far removed from the Jesus biopic genre, notably the British school system.

A second, lesser-known spoof, Luis Buñuel's *La Voie Lactée* (*The Milky Way*, 1969), concerns two pilgrims from France who go on pilgrimage to Santiago de Compostela and have all manner of theological adventures along the way, including flashbacks to first-century Palestine.[25] Buñuel's main targets are Catholic theology and popular belief, but the biopic Jesus also comes in for his share of ridicule.

Recent Contributions to the Genre

The last twenty-five years have seen several additions to the corpus of Jesus films that differ considerably from one another and vary in relation to the conventions of the biopic genre. Martin Scorsese's *The Last Temptation of Christ* (1988) opens with a scrolling text asserting that the film is based not on the Gospels but on the novel by Nikos Kazantzakis. This claim is somewhat disingenuous, in that the film involves the same cast of characters and narrative line as other Jesus biopics. By disclaiming historicity, however, Scorsese is free to explore areas that conventional Jesus movies leave untouched. In the final section of the film, Jesus, while still alive, is led down from the cross by a young, red-haired girl claiming to be his guardian angel. He marries, has children and lives to a ripe old age. Only at the end do we learn that this sequence is a dream or hallucination; Jesus dies on the cross in this film as in every other Jesus biopic. But the mere suggestion that Jesus may have desired sexual intimacy and the domestic life was enough to trigger protests, angry letters and editorials even before the film was released.[26]

The following year saw the release of the Quebec-made *Jesus of Montreal*, directed by Denys Arcand. The film portrays a group of actors that has been commissioned by the priest of St Joseph's Oratory in Montreal to refresh the passion play that has been performed on the church grounds for decades. In the process of preparing and performing the play, the actors themselves take on the personas of the characters in the Gospel story.[27] Arcand's film is the most thoroughly allegorical of the genre. Virtually every detail of the Gospel stories, and many aspects of New Testament and historical Jesus scholarship are present, or, more accurately, concealed, in the frame for the knowledgeable viewer to discern.

More recently, Philip Saville directed *The Gospel of John* (2003). This film has the distinction of being the only full-length feature that utilizes every single word of a Gospel, in this case, the Good News Bible version of the Fourth Gospel. At the same time, it tries to overcome the liability of many Jesus movies, namely, an overabundance of words. This is a challenge particularly with regard to the Gospel of John, in which Jesus talks at extraordinary length virtually uninterrupted by any dialogue or action. Thanks to the skills of the camera operators and the actor, this Jesus manages not to bore the viewer to tears during the nearly five chapters of farewell discourses that John inserts between the final supper and the betrayal in the garden (John 13–17).

Saville's film was soon overshadowed by Mel Gibson's *The Passion of the Christ*.[28] Like *The Passion Play at Oberammergau*, *Golgotha* and *Jesus Christ Superstar*, Gibson's film is an account of Jesus' last hours. Its heavy-handed violence and its negative representations of the Jewish authorities touched off a major controversy that may well have contributed to its box office success. As was the case with respect to the early silent films, viewers who do not already know the story in some detail may well be puzzled by the plotline of the film. On its own, the film does not provide enough information for viewers to know what Jesus has done to raise the ire of Jews and Romans alike or why he is subjected to such violence culminating in death on the cross. From this point of view, Gibson's film is a throwback to the early silent films, where prior knowledge of the story and belief in Jesus were prerequisites for understanding the film, and no doubt for appreciating it as well.

The box office success of Gibson's film led to some anticipation of a revival of the biblical epic, or, at least, of an influx of Jesus and other biblical movies into the marketplace. To date, two feature films have appeared, both in 2006: Catherine Hardwicke's *The Nativity Story*, and Jean-Claude La Marre's *The Color of the Cross*. *The Nativity Story* is a charming and fairly literal account of Jesus' birth and early childhood, based on a harmonization of the infancy narratives of Matthew and Luke. It draws us into Mary's emotional turmoil and emphasizes the poverty of the Galileans in the early first century. Because it does not include Jesus' ministry or Passion, it also avoids the difficult issues surrounding the portrayal of Jewish society and Jewish authorities. *The Color of the Cross* is more ambitious, in positing a 'black' Jesus who is persecuted by Jews and Romans alike on account of his race. It departs from the biopic convention and sidesteps the issue of anti-Semitism by omitting the trial scenes. Dramatically, however, it is less successful; the dialogue is wooden and the plot moves along laboriously. Both of these films fall squarely into the biopic genre insofar as they use an ancient story to address contemporary concerns. This is most obvious in the case of *The Color of the Cross*, which is explicitly intended to show Christians of colour a Messiah to whom they can relate on the grounds of race and the experience of racism.

Conclusion

The fact that no major Jesus movies appeared in the years after the release of Scorsese's and Arcand's films led some scholars to speculate that the era of the Jesus film was over, 'because the humanist culture that assembled an image called "Jesus Christ" has disappeared'.[29] Subsequent events have required a revision of this expectation. Instead, it is likely, as Richard Wightman Fox has noted that it is Jesus' fate to be 'perpetually reborn in one culture after another'.[30] As new genres emerge, there is no doubt that they too will be used to tell Jesus' story, that is, to reshape the past in the image of the present, out of conviction that the past or their versions thereof, continues to be relevant for audiences today. Whether these will be limited to overly pious recreations, as we have seen in most films done thus far in the twenty-first century, or whether there will also be room for the comedies, musicals and iconoclastic films of the 1970s and 1980s remains to be seen.

20 Bible Movies

Richard Walsh

The following essay provides a brief history of the Bible in film and a suggested taxonomy of biblical films. It also provides an overview of the major interpretative questions posed of such films.

A Brief History of (Mostly American) Bible Films[1]

Given the theatre's questionable reputation, early critics worried about the propriety of portraying religious subjects in film; nonetheless, biblical stories ultimately helped make film respectable. Filmmakers stressed the reverence of their treatments with advertising that often depicted the theatre as a church and the film as a sermon.[2] Passion plays and the life of Moses were popular subjects. At first, film staged pictures from art or illustrated Bibles, rather than developing narratives with character or plot. Gradually, filmmakers began to create stories of the conversion or degradation of characters revolving around the sacred centre of the biblical stories they reprised.

Filmmakers like D. W. Griffith and Cecil B. DeMille developed the visual and narrative patterns of epic film, which offered a union of epic scale and human interest, exotic landscapes and times, grand vistas, casts of thousands, elaborate sets, melodramatic stories of conversions and degradations, and the ever-present claim of reverence. The Bible was attractive to marketers because of its prestige and because it was in the public domain. Biblical stories also allowed filmmakers to escape the production codes to a certain extent and to offer titillating sex, as long as morality triumphed in the end. Such films were prominent in the 1930s and had a golden age in the 1950s with many financially successful films, including *The Robe* (1953), *The Ten Commandments* (1956) and *Ben-Hur* (1959). The last was also critically acclaimed and held the record for the most Oscars won for one film until *Titanic* (1997) and *The Lord of the Rings* (2003) matched it.

Biblical spectacles in the United States catered to a largely Protestant audience, but filmmakers made deliberate, conscientious efforts to avoid anti-Semitism, to attract Catholics to the movies, and to mainstream Jews.[3] The films' melodramatic formulas generally combined Puritan theology, Victorian ethic and nationalistic propaganda.[4] In the 1950s, spectacles played an important role in propagating Cold War rhetoric. DeMille and others became adept at configuring biblical stories – whether from the Hebrew Bible, the New Testament, or religious fiction – as if they were precursors of the Free World. The bad guys were decadent tyrants and demagogues. The heroes provided early exemplars in the birth of freedom, the rule of law and the development of Christian Empires.[5] In fact, Michael Wood claims that such movies invented America and persuaded people to share that dream.[6]

The era of the spectacle ended, as television became popular, the society of the United States became more secular and pluralistic, foreign films became popular in art houses, the studio system ended, and a new ratings system took effect in 1968. Foreign films, often existentialist (e.g., the films of Bergman) or Marxist (e.g., Pasolini's *The Gospel According to St. Matthew*, 1964) in tone, encouraged cinematic experimentation, as did the competition of television. The spirit of the times was anti-establishment, but counter-culture movements were gradually mainstreamed, partly through the influence of Vietnam and Watergate and partly because the hippies grew up. While not Bergman or Pasolini films, films like *Barabbas* (1962) and *The Bible* (1966) experimented with new approaches to biblical stories even as the last great epics proved financial disasters (e.g., *The Greatest Story Ever Told*, 1965).

The end of the biblical spectacle did not mean the end of biblical films. It simply meant new markets and new styles. Television promoted the miniseries in the 1970s and biblical stories quickly became mainstays in that market. *Jesus of Nazareth* (1977) was the most successful of such movies, and NBC rebroadcast it several times. Instead of creating a new movie, ABC repeatedly aired DeMille's *The Ten Commandments* (1956). It was only in 2006 that ABC aired a 'remade' version of *The Ten Commandments*. Beginning with *Abraham* (1994), TNT became involved as well in the miniseries market and has since offered several biblical hero movies, referred to collectively as The Bible Collection. Some of the same interests eventually led to the *Jesus* movie first aired by CBS in 1999. Not incidentally, many of these films were jointly produced with Italian film companies and appeared in international versions.

The development of VHS technology in the 1980s, and subsequently of DVD technology, led to new markets for biblical movies. Various interests groups realized that they could use biblical movies to promote their theology and ethics and to provide venues for evangelism and spiritual education in the church/synagogue, academy and home. The movies produced by NEST entertainment and the Visual Bible series are examples, as is *The Jesus Film* (1979) of Campus Crusade for Christ. The widespread use of the last in churches and in missions has led to the claim that it has been shown to more people than any other movie in history. The creation and use of such biblical movies is analogous to modern publishing's development and use of biblical translations, with varying theologies, agendas and markets. Biblical film, like the Bible itself, is a commodity, and these market-niche movies represent the franchising of biblical film.

Filmmakers marketed both television and franchise movies as family entertainment, as well as opportunities for spiritual education. These movies also appealed in the United States to nostalgic, conservative desires for a return to the 'biblical America' of the spectacles (cf. the Moral Majority movement).[7] Paradoxically, these movies also spoke to a ghetto mentality. The movies responded, that is, to conservative fears about an increasingly pluralistic world.[8]

Meanwhile, mainstream filmmakers no longer expected a religiously homogeneous audience. What filmmakers' audiences now had in common was a superficial commitment to 'politically correct' thinking – to an acceptance and exploitation of ethnic identities (and diversity) – and more foundational commitments to individual economic success and self-expression. Generally speaking, filmmakers treated religion suspiciously and relegated it to the margins and to exotica.[9] As a result, mainstream film welcomed a vague Buddhism (or mysticism) and disparaged Western religions, particularly Christianity which many filmmakers associated with a repressive past. Only Islam fared worse, as Muslims largely replaced Nazis as the bad guys in film.[10]

Religion was still important to film audiences if and when it led practically to a better material life and as it engendered a spirit of awe in the face of a still somewhat inexplicable world. Nonetheless, a clear preference for a scientific worldview[11] typically rendered religion a matter of the (Freudian) uncanny. Thus, the Bible (and religion) continued to be an important element in horror films (as it had since *Frankenstein*, 1931 and *Dracula*, 1931). In addition to providing a source for taboos, interpretative depth or context, and talismans, biblical stories occasionally provided the story line this genre modified (e.g., *The Omen*, 1976; *The Rapture*, 1991; *Stigmata*, 1999; *End of Days*, 1999 and *The Reaping*, 2007).

Some biblical horror films also capitalized on millennial fears at the turn of the millennium. Perhaps, the most important was the franchise movie, *Left Behind* (2000). This movie version of the first in a series of extremely popular novels played out a premillennial interpretation of the apocalypse. It signalled something new in the world of biblical film, because it appeared in some mainstream theatres. A different, independent biblical film was the critically acclaimed *The Apostle* (1997), directed by and starring Robert Duvall. The different success of these two independent films was quickly eclipsed by *The Passion of the Christ* (2004), which revived the biblical spectacle. Financed by Gibson himself, *The Passion of the Christ* was aggressively marketed into a mainstream and international success. Cinematically, part of its success was its ability to combine elements from both of its major biblical film precursors, the spectacle and horror. In marketing terms, it aggressively exploited the franchise market. In broader cultural terms, the film spoke to the fears and fundamentalisms rampant in the early third millennium.[12]

The film's huge financial success augurs the return of other biblical spectacles to mainstream film. In the publicity surrounding the film, Gibson talked publicly about producing a film about the Maccabees, freedom fighters that he greatly admired, but later turned instead to *Apocalypto* (2006). *The Nativity Story* appeared in 2006, and other biblical films are in production.[13] At the same time, franchise films have continued unabated. CBS aired *Judas* in 2004 to capitalize on the media hype associated with *The Passion of the Christ*. As noted earlier, a new television version of *The Ten Commandments* also appeared in 2006. BBC One aired *The Passion* in 2008. The Bible also continues to play a role in horror films. While biblical stories have also appeared previously in comic form (e.g., *The Life of Brian*, 1979, *Wholly Moses*, 1980), one of the growing arenas for biblical stories in film appears to be in comedies (e.g., *Bruce Almighty*, 2003; *Evan Almighty*, 2007; *The Ten*, 2007, with others in production).

Film's Translation of the Bible: Stories Alongside

All biblical films are translations, offering biblical stories in a new medium, replete with visuals and sound (music accompanied the silent films), for a new age. While biblical knowledge varies widely and the very notion of a biblical story is an abstraction, all biblical films exist alongside a powerful precursor, the memory of a biblical story. Thus, biblical films inevitably exist in a comparative environment. The viewing experience for such film is analogous to that of an audience that goes to see a film version of a well-known children's story (e.g., *The Chronicles of Narnia*, 2005) or a popular novel (e.g., *The Da Vinci Code*, 2006).[14] If one thinks of biblical films as stories alongside this memorable precursor, several types of biblical films become discernible.

(1) The first and the most recognizable is the visualizing and retelling of a biblical story in the mode of historical realism. Well-known examples include *The Ten Commandments* (1956) and *Jesus of Nazareth* (1977). This style of film is the Jesus film, rather than Christ-figure film. While typically purporting to be a reverent, accurate reprise of the biblical story, it is inevitably creative and inherently modern. Such films depend upon scripts (at least, since Griffith and DeMille) that differ greatly from their biblical precursors in terms of rich visual details; in terms of heroic, romantic and melodramatic plots; and in terms of modernly conceived characters. Moreover, these films are modern not simply because of these cinematic patterns, but also because of their conception of history.[15] These films typically assume a 'great man' view of history. They tell the story of Abraham, Moses or Jesus, not the story of political or economic forces. Moreover, their historical recreations are

typically only dimly disguised analogies of the present. Their historical stories, that is, replay national or individual stories important to the audience
(e.g., the American Revolution). Thus, *The Ten Commandments* (1956) tells the
story of the Exodus during the Cold War as the story of the creation of free
societies. Thus, Moses poses at the film's end in a fashion strongly reminiscent
of the Statue of Liberty. Finally, these films treat history from a romantic,
nostalgic perspective. The films extol, for example, the goodness of a small
close-knit community vis-à-vis the evils of bureaucratic, civilized empires.

(2) A second type deliberately recreates a biblical story as a fiction. On
occasion, these fictions are clearly unrealistic or fantastic, as in the fantasy
temptation of Christ in *The Last Temptation of Christ* (1988). The deliberately
mythic aura of *The Bible* (1966) is another, lesser known example. Eschewing
historical realism, *The Bible* sets the first twenty-two chapters of Genesis in the
ethereal world of ancient myth.[16] Further, the film juxtaposes its scenes episod-
ically, rather than creating a linear narrative. Different parts of the film use
different visual techniques and different modes. The early Adam and Eve
scenes, for example, have a gold tint. The Noah scenes are broadly comic. The
Abraham scenes, particularly the sacrifice of Isaac, drip with pathos.

Musicals, like *Jesus Christ Superstar* (1973), *Godspell* (1973) and *Joseph and the
Amazing Technicolor Dreamcoat* (1999), also differ dramatically from the world
of the audience and that of the biblical story. By far, the most common
example of the fictional style in recent years, however, is animated family fare,
like *The Prince of Egypt* (1998) and the movies of NEST entertainment (e.g.,
Kids' Ten Commandments). The result is often comparable to Hawthorne's
sanitizing of classical myth in his *Tanglewood Tales*. Unlike their often disturbing biblical precursors, animated movies make biblical story acceptable for
children. Divine terror and troubling ethical dilemmas are largely absent.
Created and marketed for children (and their parents), the movies are also
often coming-of-age stories. *The Prince of Egypt* (1998), for example, transforms the story of the creation of Israel into fraternal rivalry and into an
individual's coming-of-age story.

The oldest example of the fictional style is film that creates a fiction on
the margins of biblical stories, like *Ben-Hur* in its various incarnations (the
most famous is 1959) (cf. *Quo Vadis?*, 1951; *The Robe*, 1953; *Demetrius and the
Gladiators*, 1954; *Barabbas*, 1962 and *The Life of Brian*, 1979). These films aim at a
historical realism like the films in category one, but their clear fictional status
allows far more creative freedom and flexibility than historical representation
of biblical story does. Of course, films in the first category fictionalize the
biblical story less obviously with their melodramatic plots and developed
characters.

Finally, the reprise of biblical stories in other settings and in non-historical
genres is a common example of this fictional style. The obvious Christ-figure

film is a clear example, but the use of biblical story, character, and themes in obvious, material ways in horror (e.g., *The Reaping*, 2007), millennial (e.g., *The Rapture*, 1991; *Left Behind*, 2000; *End of Days*, 1999), and comic films (e.g., *Bruce Almighty*, 2003; *Evan Almighty*, 2007) are also important examples of this style of film.

(3) A third style combines category one and two in one film. A minimalist depiction of biblical story provides an interpretative context for a richer, more fully developed modern story. Thus, D. W. Griffith's *Intolerance* (1916) weaves four stories, expressing the titular theme, together. The longest, most developed story is a modern story of a poor, romantic couple put into jeopardy by hypocritical, reforming do-gooders. The grand epic finale, in which the couple is saved, includes a chase scene and a last-minute stay of execution. The least developed story is a series of brief vignettes from the gospel emphasizing the intolerant, hypocritical religious leaders who killed Jesus.[17] The linkage of these two stories establishes a clear moral lesson castigating the Temperance Movement and other reformers of Griffith's own day.

Cecil B. DeMille's lesser known, early version of *The Ten Commandments* (1923) is similar. After titles explain that the recent World War was the result of modern disregard for the divine commandments, the film begins with a brief retelling of the Exodus, highlighting the Egyptian oppression of the Israelites slaves, the Exodus, and the giving of the commandments, replete with sinful, but titillating orgy. The film then cuts to its modern story as Mom reads this story to her two sons: Dan, the sceptic, and John, the devout. Subsequently, Dan breaks various commandments, marries Mary and becomes a rich builder while 'losing his soul' (a gospel variation on the Torah). By contrast, John is a poor, devout carpenter. Dan gives John a job on his latest contract, a church, for which Dan cuts corners to save costs. Eventually, the church and Dan's sinful life collapses. Trying to escape the law, Dan dies in a storm when his small boat, named *Defiance*, wrecks on cliffs that look like the tablets of the law. Meanwhile, John rescues Mary from the suicidal despair of her wrecked life with Dan and from her (psychosomatic?) leprosy simply by reading her gospel stories in which Jesus heals lepers.

The success of the historical spectacle effectively sidelined this style, but *Jesus of Montreal* (1989) is a fairly recent, critically acclaimed example. If the first two styles of biblical films create implicit comparisons with biblical stories, this style creates explicit comparisons by placing a reprised biblical story in clear counterpoint with a modern story. The move simultaneously antiquates and morally contemporizes the biblical story in question. The style resembles the homiletic use of historical criticism, which asserts simultaneously that a particular biblical story 'meant' and now 'means'. The move allows one to select those items from a biblical story which are of contemporary use, interest, or value.

(4) A fourth style uses a biblical story as a 'title' for a modern film. The effect is not unlike the titles provided for abstract art. The filmmaker employs the memory of a biblical story as a cultural resource to suggest certain interpretations. A recent example is Bruno Dumont's *The Life of Jesus* (1997) which tells the story of a young, unemployed adolescent who rides his motorcycle with his friends and has pornographic sex with his girlfriend. When an 'Arab' seduces his girl, the young man goes berserk and kills the 'Arab'. The story ends shortly thereafter with the boy lying in a field, looking up as clouds move across the face of the sun. Exactly what this particular film has to do with the gospel story is left for the (shocked) viewer to decide.

Other examples include *The Ten* (2007) and Krzysztof Kieslowski's critically acclaimed *The Decalogue* (1989). The last is a series of ten, one-hour episodes created for Polish television about the ethical quandaries of various, intersecting lives in a Warsaw apartment complex. The various episodes never cite the commandments (except for certain musical references) and do not clearly engage specific commandments. Nonetheless, the title encourages the viewer to make connections. Thus, the first episode relates the disturbing death of a young boy, the son of an atheist mathematician. The father's religious sister ameliorates his influence somewhat. In the climax, the boy drowns, while skating on a frozen lake, even though his father has calculated that the ice was thick enough to hold him. A mysterious young man who simply watches (and who appears in several of the episodes), the aunt's religious education and a computer which repeatedly, spontaneously says, 'I'm ready', all suggest mysterious, lurking powers demanding acknowledgement (the first commandment?). The other episodes are even more enigmatic and haunting and suggest, if anything, a modernity that is far too complex for the ancient commandments. The tenth episode, however, may suggest a more positive connection. Briefly, that episode is a Cain and Abel story that reaches a peaceful conclusion when the brothers work together to cope with their dead father's legacy. That episode may suggest that fraternal communion might be forthcoming if moderns learned to utilize the legacy of the (dead father's) Ten Commandments. If so, it is a conclusion that the viewer must draw on his or her own.

(5) A fifth style uses biblical stories even more incidentally or allusively. In the incidental version, the Bible itself appears as a talisman, as it does in various scenes in *The Apostle* (1997) and in some horror films, or appears otherwise as image or in quotation. Examples include the enigmatic rain of frogs and the frequent references to Exod. 8:2 in *Magnolia* (1999), the tattoos on the criminal and his references to scripture in *Cape Fear* (1991) and the citation of a (created) passage in Ezekiel to justify a hit man's actions in *Pulp Fiction* (1994).[18] The allusive version depends upon a particular viewer's interpretation. The most obvious examples are the ubiquitous claims that various

films are Christ-figure films, even though no definite, material connection is obvious. Scholars have extended the Christ-figure approach to other biblical stories. Larry Kreitzer, for example, has argued that various contemporary films provide insights into biblical texts, and Robert Jewett has read films as providing illumination about Pauline theology or ethics.[19] As such readings make allusive or heuristic connections, the claims convince some and do not convince others. Persuasion depends upon rhetorical force and fecundity, not upon material connections.[20] Material connections would move a particular film into category three or four.

Major Interpretative Questions

Biblical film demands interpretation. Despite such films' comparative-story situation, which would seem to invite literary comparisons, the most frequent assessments have to do with a film's theological accuracy. That judgment deals primarily with the film's coherence with the viewer's particular brand of theology. Here, of course, franchise films are most successful. Theological appraisals occur most often with respect to Jesus films, but they also speak to the reception of other biblical films. Thus, critics observe that a Protestant distrust of images retarded the development of early religious films in the United States. The general assumptions about the historicity of biblical stories may have had something to do with *The Bible*'s relative lack of success and with the generally dismissive critical responses to biblical horror, millennial and comic films.

In fact, the question of a film's historical accuracy is quite often a (theo-logical) concern. Given assumptions about biblical story's own historicity, films unsettle viewers if they do not offer a credible, historical story. Here, film's treatment of miracles is an obviously important and divisive issue. Critics often express more sophisticated historical concerns, evaluating a parti-cular film's reconstruction of a historical era in terms of their professional knowledge of history. Here, clothing, sets, language and social relations are important. Less often, viewers remark upon a film's literary accuracy. At least, they frequently note that films have omitted or added story elements. They are less likely to talk about more sophisticated literary matters (like genre or narrative perspective).

Beyond the question of accuracy, the major interpretative question asked of biblical film deals with its relationship to its own culture. Mainstream film and television movies function mythically, supporting the worldview and values of the largest possible audience. In the United States, the biblical epics advocated a civil religion that configured the nation as a religious entity in its own right. In the last third of the twentieth century, films have supported individual expression, understood primarily in terms of the freedom of economic choices and consumption. The commercials that punctuate television biblical movies, sometimes creating quite amusing disjoints with their biblical stories, provide a clear example. Such films support a culture of consumer capitalism, upon which the movies themselves depend. In fact, as many critics have remarked, religion itself has become, at least in the United States, primarily a capitalist commodity, consumed as a matter of individual preference and expression. Franchise movies are an important part of this capitalization. While they function mythically as they support the family values and religious theology of their particular market niche, their more important mythic work is their engagement with capitalism. The nostalgia implicit in biblical films is another major area of mythic work as the films thereby cater to and support conservative social desires.

In short, while biblical stories are foreign to modern society, film modernizes such stories so effectively that they seldom offer genuinely foreign, transformative visions.[21] The 'pet projects' of 'star' directors are different, as such directors see their work as art, rather than mere consumer entertainment, and as their work expresses their own private ideologies (e.g., John Huston's *The Bible*, 1966; Robert Duvall's *The Apostle*, 1997). The very different Jesus films of Martin Scorsese (*The Last Temptation of Christ*, 1988) and Mel Gibson (*The Passion of the Christ*, 2004) and their contrasting reception by opposed groups in society provides a clear example of such ideologies at work. These films function mythically in a fashion quite similar to franchise films. They allow people to express personal preferences and identities by choosing to pay to watch a particular film or by choosing to boycott another.

Critics have commented extensively on film's mythic work. Given their own cultural location, academic critics are more apt to critique than to praise both mainstream and franchise films. To do so, they often take one of a variety of ideological approaches to film (e.g., Marxist, feminist, cultural).[22] Such approaches call attention to biblical film's mythic work, by raising its support of the cultural dominant to consciousness and by striving to make such mythic issues matters of public, political debate. Of course, such critics have their own mythic identities, locations and agendas.

Academics have increasingly made biblical film a matter of academic concern in both biblical and theoretical studies. While such film has long been a venue for spiritual education and theological discussion, critics now utilize it to introduce students to the Bible as an academic subject or to various critical methods.[23] As such criticism becomes more adept, it will need to evolve more sophisticated interactions with film and film theory.

21 Holocaust Movies

Guy Matalon

The genre of holocaust films can be defined as follows, 'Let us say, simply, that it includes any films that reflect what historian Raul Hilberg describes as a step-by-step historical process, beginning with the laws of April 1933, which removed Jews from the civil services in Germany, and ending in 1945, when the last concentration camps were liberated and the war ended'.[1] The earliest images of the Holocaust that became well-known in the West were short documentaries and newsreel footage shot by American and European photojournalists to document Nazi atrocities. Some of these short films were expropriated from Nazi archives.[2] These early films provided the most gruesome and horrific images of the destruction of European Jewry. None of these early films, however, are motion picture footage of the actual murder of Jews.

There is only one film that has actual footage of German soldiers shooting Jews. The film was shot by Reinhardt Wiener in Latvia in 1941 and records the shooting of a truck load of individuals wearing yellow badges on their chests and backs. When the film was developed later, the filmmaker showed the film to six of his comrades who did not believe that Germans were murdering Jews.[3]

Since these early films, the genre of holocaust film has proliferated and grown in scope. According to Norman Finkelstein, Hollywood alone has produced more than one hundred and seventy-five Holocaust films since 1989.[4] The Holocaust film genre, however, truly begins with an abstract artistic French documentary, *Night and Fog* (*Nuit et brouillard*) (1954). *Night and Fog* shows the horrors of the concentration camps and it is still the most powerful film focusing on the experience of the concentration camp. Its title was based upon Hitler's December 1941 decree directing that all resisters would be sent to concentration camps. Although the film is very powerful it fails to identify the victims of the Nazis as Jews. This is a questionable distortion since most of the inmates at Auschwitz were Jews and while some non-Jews were also inmates, the concentration camps were part of the Final Solution to the Jewish problem.

Another immediate post-liberation film was the American film, *Death Mills* (1945). The 22-minute film was directed by Billy Wilder and produced by the

United States Department of War. Most of the film is a collage of footage of the allies liberating various concentration camps in Germany. It does not make mention of the Jewish victims of the Nazis but simply states that there were over 20 million people murdered by the Nazis.

Long is the Road (1945) was made in U.S. Occupied Germany. The film is based on a story by Israel Becker, a survivor himself, who plays the main character. The film tells the story of a Jew who is shipped from the Warsaw Ghetto to Auschwitz. Before the train reaches Auschwitz, however, Becker jumps from the train and finds his way to Jewish Partisans who help him escape. After the war, Israel Becker attempts to locate members of his family. As an immediate post-liberation film, this movie is unusual because it tells the Holocaust story from a Jewish perspective with actual survivors as cast members.

The Last Chance (1945, alternate titles *Die Letzte Chance* or *La Derniere Chance*) is a Swiss film that tells the story of three American officers who come to the aid of a group of Italian refugees. The entire group of soldiers and refugees encounter various difficulties as they seek refuge in Switzerland, all the while hunted by the Nazis who are hot on their trail. This film, too, is unique for its time because the American officers in the film were not portrayed by actors but by three Allied pilots who really had been shot down near the Swiss border. Likewise, the refugees were played by actual Italian refugees, giving the movie an odd authenticity.

Made in East Germany, *Murderers Are Among Us – Die Morder Sind Unter Uns* (1946) tells the story of Susanna Wallner, a concentration camp survivor who returns to her home only to find it occupied by another camp survivor, Hans Mertens. The film raises the issue of the collective guilt of ordinary Germans during the Holocaust. What it fails to address is the Jewishness of the Holocaust and particularly the effect of the war on Jewish survivors in Post-war Germany (East or West).

The next generation of Holocaust films can be identified as Hollywood Melodramas. In *The Diary of Anne Frank* (1959), Mr. Frank returns home after the war and finds a scarf that Anne gave him, which brings back memories of the past. The film uses the flashback technique to allow the audience to witness what took place in that past. The casting and musical score are two elements of the film that are examples of the 'Hollywoodization' of the Holocaust.[5]

Exodus (1960) is the story of the ship called Exodus and the founding of the State of Israel in 1948. Nurse Katherine (Kitty) Fremont is an American volunteer nurse at the Karaolos detention camp in Cyprus, where many Holocaust survivors are being held by the British. Ari Ben Canaan, a Haganah rebel, secures a cargo ship to smuggle 611 Jews out of the camp to sail to Israel. The act is discovered by the British, who block the harbour. The refugees then stage a hunger strike. The British finally allow Exodus safe passage to the Jewish homeland. The movie then sheds light on the Israeli War of Independence (Milchemet Tashach) where various characters interact with the survivors from the Exodus.

Judgment at Nuremberg (1961) is one of the most famous Hollywood Holocaust movies. Starring Spencer Tracy, Richard Widmark and Marlene Dietrich, *Judgment at Nuremberg* is the story of the trial of Ministry of Justice officials for their participation in the Holocaust. The movie raises not only the issue of how German judges facilitated the Holocaust, but also how much blame the German people themselves deserved. The movie takes place in 1948 in Nuremberg, Germany, where the Germans are trying to forget the war and move on. The eagerness to move beyond the past is encouraged by the United States because of the new confrontation with the Soviet Union but all of the officials are found guilty in the end.

These American melodramas were quickly followed by television network documentaries and interview films such as *Fighters of the Ghetto* (Israel, 1968), *The Warsaw Ghetto* (BBC-TV, U.K., 1968), *Genocide* (Thames-TV, U.K., 1975) and *The Eighty First Blow* (Israel, 1975). During this period, American television audiences also were exposed to survivors through various talk shows.[6]

The next phase of Holocaust film-making is comprised of European-made post realist films.[7] Among these post realist films is the Nazi sexploitation film, *Love Camp Seven* (1969), a rather stark contrast to the realistic films that preceded it. A German scientist has created a jet airplane that will give the Nazis greater power. The allies make contact with the scientist's secretary. When the scientist is killed, the secretary, who is Jewish, is sent to a concentration camp. The allies then send two women who pretend to be Jews behind enemy lines where they are captured and sent to the same camp as the secretary. The concentration camp, however, seems to be an excuse to show as much nudity, brutality, rape and depravity as the director could show without being censored. Although a sleazy sexploitation film, *Love Camp Seven* did take holocaust movies away from the realism of the previous phase of Holocaust films.

Another post realist film is the Italian film, *The Seven Beauties* (*Pasqualino Settebellezze*, 1975). The movie, directed by Lina Wertmüller, tells the story of two Italian Army deserters who are somewhere in Germany. The soldiers are captured and sent to a concentration camp where one of them seduces the female commandant to save his life. The plan works, but then the soldier is put in charge of the barracks and he now must kill six of the other inmates. If he does not kill the other inmates he and they all will be killed. What looked like a plan to save his life turns into the soldier's nightmare.

Ingmar Bergman's *The Serpent's Egg* falls into the category of post realist films, but it is a movie set in the 1920s. It is the story of Abel Rosenberg and his brother's widow, Manuela, who find themselves the unwitting subjects of medical experiments, including chemical gassing that results in psychotic states. Bergman's depiction of 1920s Berlin shows the city as a precursor of the medical experiments that were to become such an important feature of Nazi practices. What makes Bergman's film distinctive is its focus on the conditions in Berlin that made it possible for the Holocaust to take place.

One other film in this phase is Louis Malle's *Lacombe Lucien* (1974). In this story a young French peasant is rejected by the French Resistance and instead becomes a member of the German Police. He enjoys his position, until he falls in love with a Jewish girl and finds himself a part of the lives of those his employers are trying to oppress.

Several films from this phase have been described as 'European Art Films'. The European Art Films provide an aesthetic profile that was later adopted by Hollywood. Among these films is *Mr. Klein* (1976). In 1942, Robert Klein finds life in Paris to be very comfortable. Klein buys and sells works of art, and at this moment Jews are eager to sell valuable works of art at very low prices. This makes business good for Klein. This 'good life', however, takes a turn for the worse when Klein discovers there is another Robert Klein in Paris. The other Robert Klein is a Jew. For Klein, life changes when he becomes the object of police scrutiny, being confused with the other Klein. *Mephisto* (1981) is another of the European Art Films and an adaptation of Klaus Mann's novel of the same name. The main character, Hendrik Hofgen, abandons his conscience and his previous political views in order to ingratiate himself with the Nazi party. He does this in order to keep his job and to improve both his economic and social status. Hofgen does indeed sell his soul to the devil for economic well being and social standing.

The Assault (*De Aanslag*, 1986) is the story of Anton Steenwijk. At the age of 12, a man is shot and killed in front of Anton's neighbour's house. The neighbours move the body of the victim from their house to Anton's house. Because the body was found at Anton's house, his mother, father and brother are all killed by the Germans and his house is set on fire, Anton must come to grips with this horrible reality.

The European Art Films described above set an aesthetic tone for later Hollywood films, including *Sophie's Choice* (1982). One of the best known of the Hollywood Holocaust films, *Sophie's Choice* is the story of Stingo, who meets and befriends a beautiful Polish immigrant, Sophie Zawistowski. As Stingo gets to know Sophie better she begins to reveal secrets about herself to him and he begins to fall in love with her. Her final secret is that when she was taken to Auschwitz with her two children the Nazi officer forced her to choose which one of her children would live and which one would die. One of her children will be sent to the children's camp and the other to the crematorium and Sophie must make the choice or both of them will die.

A less well known Hollywood Holocaust film is *Jakob the Liar* (1999). A poor Jewish cafe owner, Jakob, overhears a German radio broadcast and tells his friends what he has heard. Rumours fly that there is a secret radio that provides the truth about the war and Jakob begins to use the mythical radio as the source of good news, thereby helping his fellow citizens have hope in an otherwise horrible situation. The movie provides an particularly interesting account of life in the ghetto.

The Grey Zone (2001) is based on a true story. It tells the story of the uprising of *Sonderkommandos* in the Auschwitz-Birkenau extermination camp. The *Sonderkommandos* were Jews who were forced to help the camp guards herd fellow Jews and others into the gas chambers and then dispose of the victims' bodies in the crematoria. The alternative to helping the guards was to be killed. In October of 1944, the *Sonderkommandos* of Auschwitz-Birkenau designed a plot to destroy at least one of the crematoria and one of the gas chambers, thereby limiting the number of Jews who could be killed. Polish citizens from a nearby village provide weapons for the insurrection, smuggling them into the camp. When the insurrection begins, the *Sonderkommandos* are able to destroy Crematoria I and III, thereby stalling the killing efforts of the Germans. However, all of the *Sonderkommandos* who survive the insurrection are captured and shot by the camp guards.

One other Hollywood Holocaust film that takes its cues from the European art films is Roman Polanski's *The Pianist* (2002). *The Pianist* is the story of Wladyslaw Szilman, a classical pianist who survives the Holocaust through stoicism and good luck. A survivor of the Holocaust himself, Polanski realized the extent to which fate and chance played in survival and Szpilman's story is one that exemplifies the role of accident in the process of surviving.[8]

Probably the best known Hollywood Holocaust film is Steven Spielberg's *Schindler's List* (1993). *Schindler's List* is the story of a clever, greedy Nazi-Czech businessman, Oskar Schindler, who tries to make his fortune by using Jews as cheap labour in his factories. By using Jews to work in his factories and paying them almost nothing Schindler is able to create better products at a lower cost. For a while he is very successful, but as the mistreatment and eventual fate of the Jews become clear Schindler has a change of heart and his factory becomes a refuge for Jews. Schindler spends his own money to rescue Jews from almost certain death in the camps and ends up penniless and on the run from the Nazis. It is thought that Oskar Schindler saved over one thousand Polish Jews from the gas chambers. At the end of the film, the survivors portrayed in the movie – and the actors who played those survivors – are shown placing stones on Schindler's grave in an expression of remembrance, appreciation and thanks for his efforts to save Jews from the Nazis. Although a widely known and popular film, *Schindler's List* raises a number of issues that must be addressed in evaluating Holocaust films.[9]

One such issue is how the requirements of Hollywood film-making affect the representation of the Holocaust in film. The first and obvious argument is that *Schindler's List* is a Hollywood product. As such it is circumscribed by the economic and ideological tenets of the film industry, with its unquestioned and supreme value of entertainment and spectacle; its fetishism of style and glamour; its penchant for superlatives and historical grasp at any and all experience ('the greatest Holocaust film ever made') and its reifying, levelling and trivializing effect on everything it touches.[10] The issue can be summed up by J. Hoberman's comment, 'Is it possible to make a feel-good entertainment about the ultimate feel-bad experience of the twentieth century?'[11]

A second issue is that of narrative. *Schindler's List* purports to be historically accurate, but it utilizes fictional narrative to discuss the Holocaust. Since the film claimed to tell the story of the Holocaust, 'the film's focus on the heroic exception, the Gentile rescuer and the miracle of survival, would indeed distort the proportions and thus end up falsifying the record'.[12]

The issue of subjectivity concerns the point of view of the film. Whose story is it? It turns out that the primary point of view is that of Oskar Schindler although on some occasions the point of view becomes that of Amon Goeth, the psychotic commandant. In either case, the audience sees the story through the eyes of the perpetrators, rather than the victims. Indeed, it might be argued that the Jews in the film are represented only superficially and that they are represented in stereotypic fashion. The subjectivity of a film controls the subjectivity of the audience and this means that *Schindler's List* is a movie told from the perspective of a corrupt businessman and a psychotic Nazi.

The issue of representation may be the most difficult problem raised by *Schindler's List*. The issue, simply put, is 'how can we provide an image of the unimaginable?' But this is not an issue only for *Schindler's List*. This is a problem for all Holocaust movies, whether they be documentaries, dramas, docudramas, comedies or feature-length films. Teri Ginsburg has described this as follows:

> Not widely discussed, however, is the fact that this cinematic cultural proliferation and expansion has been accompanied by a converse movement in cultural theory. That movement relies on a general consensus – fostered and encouraged by both popular and scholarly criticism as well as by many of the films themselves – of the proverbial assignation of the holocaust as beyond intelligibility or cultural representation.[13]

The Holocaust, as a historical reality, is understood to be so horrific, so unique that it cannot be understood by anyone. Since it cannot be understood, it cannot be imagined nor can it be represented. The consensus goes even further

and argues quite convincingly that there can be no 'adequate aesthetic repro-
duction' of any aspect of the Holocaust.[14] In the words of Elie Wiesel, one of
the most famous Holocaust survivors:

> The question inexorably asserts itself: Does there exist another way,
> another langugage, to say what is unsayable? The image perhaps? Can it
> be more accessible, more malleable, more expressive than the word? Can I
> admit it? I am wary of one as of the other. Even more of the image. Of the
> filmed image, of course. One does not imagine the unimaginable. And in
> particular, one does not show it on screen.[15]

Wiesel's call to avoid the imagining of the unimaginable is somewhat similar
to the biblical injunction against images of the Divine in Exodus 20:4. Film can
create a new reality, a new historical truth that challenges what took place in
the past. Moreover, film includes sounds and images that affect the audience
on an emotional level and do not require any intellectual reflection.

One can certainly argue that the appropriate genre for a Holocaust film is the
documentary. Yet even a documentary violates Wiesel's prohibition of images.
The recent BBC-TV series *Auschwitz* (2005), aired in the United States on PBS
suffered from the many problems other films of the Holocaust suffer, namely,
selective usage of footage and inability to transcend the image. In some sense,
one could return to Claude Lanzmann's *Shoa* (1981). *Shoa* succeeded in avoiding the image of the Holocaust because it was made up of interviews of survivors, perpetrators and bystanders. Yet the exploitation and manipulation of
the survivors in several scenes make the film quite problematic.

There are four main schools of thought with regard to Holocaust films and
the attempt to 'imagine the unimaginable'. The first school argues that any
attempt to depict the Holocaust through art (including film) is obscene. The
second school of thought claims that the possibility of the trivialization of the
Holocaust through popular film is a real issue but the disappearance of
the Holocaust from the Western cultural discourse and memory is a more
acute problem. Without Hollywood films and television programmes that
may at times raise some concern regarding the manner in which certain topics
or events are represented, the Holocaust might have remained in the past and
would have been forgotten. The third school of thought questions the very
assumption that Holocaust films must portray the Holocaust as realistically as
possible. This school of thought allows film directors to decide for themselves
what the appropriate cinematic style is for the portrayal they have in mind.
The fourth school argues that since the Holocaust was traumatic to the survivors and also in the collective memory of Western culture, ordinary conventions used in cinema to depict the Holocaust are insufficient. There is a need
for a new style.

The scholars and film critics who have been quite critical of films such as *Schindler's List* and Roberto Benigni's *Life is Beautiful* (Italy, 1997) contend that since the focus of these types of film is the quality of moral courage in the case of *Schindler's List* and the use of slap-stick humour in the case of *Life is Beautiful* Hollywood films distort and trivialize the Holocaust. Clearly juxtaposing Oskar Schindler as the good German to his alter ego Camp Commander, Amon Goeth, changes the message or the focus of the Holocaust. It is true that Schindler rescued more than a thousand Jews, but the reality for the majority of the Jews of Poland was quite different than the 'happy ending' that the film provides.[16]

The school of thought that restricts the depiction of the Holocaust in feature films does allow for the making of documentaries provided that they reflect as accurately as possible the events that occurred during the Holocaust. As noted by Lawrence Baron, however, this school of thought is based upon two assumptions: The Holocaust is unique and hence cannot be understood and secondly, that any depiction must present the reality of the Holocaust, namely that most Jews were starved, tortured, murdered, gassed and mutilated while most Germans were murderers, actively supported the murderers or passively supported them.

If the Holocaust is a unique event and hence incomprehensible then the Holocaust is mystical and irrelevant. That is, unless it was experienced there is no point in attempting to understand it. This sort of thinking turns a historical event into a supernatural event that is beyond human comprehension. Such an approach denies the historical fact that human beings planned, implemented and murdered millions of other human beings. And, some of the victims not only struggled and resisted but also survived. The second assumption which requires all representations of the Holocaust to reflect the historical reality of the event itself (despite the paradoxical claim that it cannot be understood) is problematic if one attempts to create a feature film. Must one truly mirror what took place in a particular ghetto or camp for an audience to understand some aspect of the Holocaust? Simply because the Hungarian film *Fateless* (*Sorstalanság*) (2005) does not show the beatings described by survivors of Auschwitz, this does not mean that one cannot learn a great deal from such a film about Auschwitz or what occurred in Hungry to its Jewish population.

It is an undeniable fact that Hollywood network television series and popular films have maintained the Holocaust as a part of Western culture. As Baron writes, 'If a director hopes to capture a semblance of the atrocities, sights, and sounds of the Holocaust effectively on the screen, then he or she must be a skilled as a story-teller and filmmaker rather than as an academic historian. Scholars should not dismiss the potential of feature films to convey a sense of the catastrophe that befell European Jewry'.[17] In short, one must seek a balance between the requirements of factual details of the Holocaust and artistic license that filmmakers must have to tell a story. This is expressed clearly by Toplin who writes, 'In sum we need a sensitive effort to judge integrity and an informed view of film that balances the defense of artistic liberties with the recognition that some dramatic flourishes can be problematic'.[18]

The third school pushes further than the second and grants almost unlimited artistic license to the artists, leaving it in their hands to decide what is tasteful and what is not. The key is that each filmmaker has a particular reaction that they are attempting to elicit from the audience and it is up to them to utilize whatever cinematic style they deem appropriate for their subject matter. Marcia Landy and Hilene Flazbaum are excellent examples of this perspective. Landy was quite critical of those who declared *Schindler's List* as overly theatrical and defended the right of the filmmaker to make his or her judgements as to how to tell the story.[19] The necessity of the use of realism as the only viable tool to portray the Holocaust is misguided because the horror and the grim reality of the Holocaust cannot be comprehended. Hence the limitation of the realistic representation of the Holocaust as the only aesthetic option is problematic. Moreover, Flazbaum explains the issue as follows:

> The very idea of lying, even lying within the clear realm of fiction, appears to run perilously close to Holocaust denial. And Holocaust etiquette demands that even the tiniest whisper of anything that might be used as fodder for deniers be exposed with due speed. I am not opposed to this in principle; I do, however, want to suggest that this avid policing of representations of the Holocaust has some troubling ramifications. It places the critic in treacherous political terrain, where following Holocaust etiquette threatens meaningful discussion of complex and controversial topics. Paradoxically, such careful observance of etiquette places caretakers in precisely the place they sought to flee. By paying such close attention to denial (consciously or unconsciously), many critics unwittingly pay tribute to Holocaust deniers by molding their standards of art out of fear, and so reduce their expectations for the power of imagination for the same reason.[20]

The fourth school of Holocaust scholars, such as Rothberg and Hirsch, explains that since there was no closure for the survivors, no end to the Nazi torture even with Hitler's death and the defeat of the Nazis, the only appropriate way to depict the Holocaust is through post-traumatic witness-ing, to use Hirsch's views as an example.[21] As explained by Rothberg, the cinematic style that is needed to imagine the unimaginable must be a mixture of styles. What is needed is 'a form of documentation beyond direct reference and coherent narrative, but do not fully abandon the possibility for some kind of reference and some kind of narrative'.[22] The problem of this fourth school is that most people are not victims of the Holocaust. Hence, one's ability to learn about an event through traumatic realism is quite limited. The manner in which people learn about the Holocaust is through books, films, exhibits, eye-witness reports, fictional narrative and art and as Baron explains, 'these sources communicate an artificially constructed approximation of how it might have felt to experience the Holocaust as a bystander, liberator, perpetrator or victim'.[23]

In sum, the Holocaust is visualized and will continue to be visualized through film and other mediums (photography, artwork, etc.) and the question that each of these schools tries to address is the limits of Holocaust representations. The dos and don'ts of representing one of the most horrific events in human history are not easy to list. Saul Friedlander did warn against trivializing certain aspects of the Holocaust, against distorting history through gross misrepresentation of the facts.[24]

Hanna Arendt described the facts or the reality of the Holocaust as follows:

> The facts are that six million Jews, six million human beings, were helplessly, and in most cases unsuspectingly, dragged to their deaths. The method employed was that of accumulated terror. First came calculated neglect, deprivation and shame, when the weak in body died together with those strong and defiant enough to take their own lives. Second came outright starvation, combined with forced labor, when people died by the thousands but at different intervals of time, according to their stamina. Last came the death factories – and they all died together, the young and the old, the weak and the strong, the sick and the healthy; not as people, not as men and women, children and adults, boys and girls, not as good and bad, beautiful or ugly – but brought down to the lowest common denominator of organic life itself, plunged into the darkest and deepest abyss of primal equality, like cattle, like matter, like things that had neither body nor soul, nor even a physiognomy upon which death could stamp its seal. It is in this monstrous equality without fraternity or humanity – an equality in which cats and dogs could have shared – that we see as though mirrored, the image of hell.[25]

The question is how does one visualize, represent, depict or imagine hell? What are the limits of depicting human suffering especially when the scene is recreated along with a set, costume, casting and a musical score?

To engage in the interpretation, understanding and criticizing of Holocaust film as a genre is to some extent to engage in 'The Discourse of Unknow-ability'.[26] What films do succeed in doing is depicting a 'shadow of the authentic object'.[27] The shadow certainly is different from the authentic object but the two are interconnected and interrelated and share some features. The authentic object is to some extent lost to us but the imprint, the outline, the shadow remains accessible to all through the medium of film.[28]

22 Redemption and Film

Julien R. Fielding

Redemption simply means to buy back, to free from what distresses or harms, to extricate from something detrimental, or to reform. We often see this term applied to a human being or divine agent who 'redeems' or saves someone else from a host of problems, including death, war, guilt, sin, poverty, crime, etc. This redeemer frequently sacrifices himself or herself for another person or for society. His or her rationale for doing this may or may not carry any religious significance; the person might simply be performing such acts because it is expected of him or her. For instance, in samurai culture, which was largely influenced by Confucianism and Zen Buddhism, it was believed that only by being ready and willing to die at any time could a warrior be loyal to one's master. In the modern era, Japanese soldiers willingly died for their emperor and for their country. Filial piety is the cornerstone of Confucianism, and it was believed that a son could only be considered filial if his father ordered him to die and he was willing to do so.[1]

When redemption is placed within a theological context, we find examples of redeemers in a variety of cultural traditions, from the Egyptian god Osiris to the Buddhist bodhisattvas, which are 'enlightenment beings' who dedicate themselves entirely to helping all other sentient beings toward relief from suffering. In Hinduism, too, we find a redeemer in the deity Vishnu, who assumes various avatars, from a fish to a rider on a white horse, with the aim of saving humans from calamity and demons. But nowhere is the concept of redemption so central to its theology as it is in the Judaeo-Christian tradition. As the *Oxford Companion to the Bible* explains, in the *Hebrew Bible* to redeem (*ga'al*) entails 'doing something on behalf of others because they are unable to do it for themselves'. The redeemer, in this case, is typically a family member, but in his or her absence, the king or God. Most commonly, redemption 'arises . . . when property or persons have been confiscated to reconcile a debt. A redeemer is the one who pays the debt for the debtor; prisoners can be redeemed through payment of a ransom'. Beyond financial transactions, redemption can mean taking revenge; being an avenger of blood. In the *Hebrew Bible*, God is the ultimate redeemer for it is he who frees his people from bondage.[2] For instance, Exodus 6.6 says that God tells Moses to say to the people of Israel that God 'will bring you out from under the burdens of the

Egyptians, and . . . will deliver you from their bondage, and . . . will redeem you with an outstretched arm and with great acts of judgment'. Moses, here, is merely acting as an instrument through which God works. In Jeremiah 15.21 God says: 'I will deliver you out of the hand of the wicked, and redeem you from the grasp of the ruthless'.

The *New Testament* authors build on the *Hebrew Bible*'s concept of redemption as ransom, now positing the idea that Jesus Christ is the ultimate redeemer.[3] And he does this by dying, 'in that he gives humanity the forgiveness that (it) could not give itself'.[4] Paul talks frequently about Jesus as redeemer. Ephesians 1.7, for example, states that in Jesus 'we have redemption through his blood, the forgiveness of our trespasses, according to the riches of his grace'. Colossians 1.13–14 explains that God 'delivered us from the dominion of darkness and transferred us to the kingdom of his beloved Son, in whom we have redemption, the forgiveness of sins'. Titus 2.14 says that Jesus 'gave himself for us to redeem us from all iniquity and to purify for himself a people of his own who are zealous for good deeds'. And Hebrews 9.11–14 explains that by taking 'his own blood', Jesus secured 'an eternal redemption'.

If we want to talk about cinematic characters as redeemers or their acts as redemptive, from which religious tradition should we draw – Judaism or Christianity? More often than not, when the topic of redemption arises, people are referring to 'Christ figures'; characters who sacrifice themselves so that others may live and be free from 'evil' or hardship.[5] Films about redemption are numerous and range from the 1945 Academy Award winner, *The Lost Weekend*, to the 2008 Keanu Reeves vehicle *Street Kings*. Based on the novel by Charles Jackson, the former chronicles the downward alcoholic spiral of Don Birnam, a writer plagued by self-doubt and depression. His faithful girlfriend is the one whose love offers him a chance at redemption. In *Street Kings*, Detective Tom Ludlow is a highly flawed officer who does whatever it takes to bring criminals to justice, even if that means planting evidence, lying or falsifying reports. After his former partner is gunned down, Ludlow decides to uncover the truth. Along the way, he gets a chance at redemption.[6] Cinematic redeemers are ubiquitous and can be found in just about every genre. This essay considers examples from westerns, horror, science fiction/ fantasy and drama.

Westerns

In *3:10 to Yuma* (2007), Dan Evans, a down-on-his luck rancher, Civil War veteran and father of two boys, volunteers to escort notorious outlaw Ben Wade to Contention, where Wade will board the 3:10 train to Yuma. In Yuma, Wade will be put on trial for his misdeeds and he is likely to be hanged for the crimes he has committed. But there are obstacles along the way, including Wade's greedy, cruel and blood-thirsty gang, led by Charlie Prince.

At the centre of the story is Dan Evans's 14-year-old son, Will. Rather than look up to his ethical father, he hero worships Wade, whose life seems dangerous and exciting.[7] Will's disdain for his father can be seen when Dan says, 'Someday, William . . . you walk in my shoes, you might understand'. Will's reply is 'I ain't ever walkin' in your shoes'. On the one hand Evans is a law-abiding man who is guided by moral, perhaps even Christian, principles. He is a man of his word. He is compassionate and he believes in doing what is right. Wade, on the other hand, has no moral code. Instead he simply kills anyone who gets in his way. Unlike Evans who has suffered in his life but remains a loving man, Wade takes his suffering (the result of his father's early death and his mother's abandonment) and turns it on others; believing that only he matters. But this will change.

At the end of the film, Evans and Wade arrive at the train station only to discover that Wade's gang is waiting for them. Despite this obstacle, Evans is determined to fulfil his obligation. He manoeuvres Wade through the streets, dodging bullets as they go and finally gets Wade onto the Yuma-bound train. For Evans this is an important triumph, even though Wade has assisted in his own capture and he tells Evans that he has been to Yuma twice and has escaped both times.

Sadly, Evans' victory is a short-lived. Charlie Prince shoots and fatally wounds Dan Evans. At this point in the story, Wade can join his gang – there is nothing to stop him. But instead, Wade takes his gun – called 'the Hand of God' – and shoots every member of his gang.[8] Director James Mangold says of this moment that he was hoping for a 'Biblical quality' in the end; a 'kind of washing clean of the earth, both the tragedy that had been Dan Evans' life and finding something redemptive in it and the misguided venture that had been Ben Wade's and trying to find a new chapter in that as well'.

Evans' son, Will, who has emerged from hiding during the shooting, now has the opportunity to retaliate, to kill Wade. But he does not. Will has learned compassion and justice from his father and he will not take revenge. In his final act of self-sacrifice, Evans not only becomes a role model for his son but also for Wade himself and Wade is ultimately 'redeemed' by Evans' example of sacrifice. The evidence for Wade's redemption is that he boards the train, hands over his weapon, and heads for Yuma. Will Wade escape again or will he finally accept responsibility for his many crimes? The answer may be found in Wade's own words. 'You do one thing decent, and I image it's habit forming . . . see that grateful look in their eye imagine it make you feel like Christ hisself'. Maybe Will was right when earlier in the film he said there was something good in Ben Wade. It only took one man, Dan Evans, to turn him away from his path of death and destruction.

Other Westerns that deal with redemption include *Knights of the Range* (1940), *Angel and the Badman* (1947), and Clint Eastwood's *Unforgiven* (1992).[9] Since Westerns in general are more frequently about revenge and the 'virtues of vengeance' than they are about redemption the movies noted above stand out among Westerns.[10]

Horror

Among horror films dealing with the concept of redemption, two movies stand out – *30 Days of Night* (2007) and *The Seventh Sign*.[11] Based on the graphic novel by Steve Niles and Ben Templesmith, *30 Days of Night* 'reinvigorates' the vampire genre with savage, blood-thirsty creatures that see 'humans as nothing more than something to feed on'.[12] The film's events take place in the remote town of Barrow, Alaska, where the sun will not shine for a month. Anticipating these 30 days of night is a group of vampires that arrives in town, preparing for a feast. The townspeople do their best to survive, and they are ably led by Sheriff Eben Oleson, but they are no match for the ferocity and strength of the vampires, and many die. His estranged wife, Stella, however, is still alive, and towards the end of the film, she finds herself and a girl trapped under an abandoned truck. They are freezing to death. To make matters worse, the hungry vampires have come out in full force so that they can burn down the town. One of the survivors realizes that the vampires want to destroy all evidence of their having been in Barrow, so that they can move on to the next town. Eben's younger brother, Jake, suggests that they can stay put, until the sun comes up. But Eben's thoughts are on Stella: 'He'll kill her if she runs. She'll burn if she stays'. 'You go out there, won't they come after all of us', Billy asks. A conflicted Eben whispers, 'Oh dear God' and then injects himself with some infected blood, so that he can become a vampire. Transformed, he fights with Marlowe, the leader of the vampires, and he wins. Without their leader, the other vampires leave. It is almost dawn, and Eben asks Stella if he should go after the vampires. Instead, he spends his last moments on a cliff top, sitting next to Stella. She holds him tightly as he incinerates. Ultimately, Eben's literal blood sacrifice not only saves the people of Barrow but possibly the world from 'the dominion of darkness'.

An end-of-times thriller, *The Seventh Sign* centres on Abby Quinn, a pregnant woman who rents out the room over her garage to a quiet boarder. As the film progresses we learn that Abby has had difficulty carrying a baby to term and in her despondency has tried committing suicide. But *The Seventh Sign* is far from a social drama. It is soon revealed that the boarder is the second coming of Christ, who by breaking a series of seals is bringing about the end of the world. Believing that the events have a connection to her unborn child, Abby teams with a Jewish teen and together they try to stop the countdown. In the end, this woman is called upon to sacrifice herself, and in giving her life, she redeems the world.

Science Fiction/Fantasy

Several recent fantasy films include redeemers. In the *Lord of the Rings* trilogy (2001–03), Frodo acts as a self-sacrificing 'Christ' figure, volunteering to carry the One Ring, which leads to certain madness and possibly death, to Mount Doom. He is joined on his treacherous journey by three other Hobbits – Merry, Pippin and Samwise – two humans – Aragorn and Boromir, an elf named Legolas, the dwarf Gimli, and Gandalf, the wizard. One might say that not only are the Hobbits and their companions saving Middle Earth but their actions will redeem the fallen human rulers, who succumbed to greed and lust for power.

Although J.R.R. Tolkien, the author of the *Lord of the Rings*, was a devout Roman Catholic, his religious symbolism is not as overt as that of his friend, C. S. Lewis, whose *Chronicles of Narnia* books were recently adapted as feature films. In both, *The Lion, the Witch and the Wardrobe* (2005) and *Prince Caspian* (2008), four saviour siblings – Lucy, Peter, Susan and Edmund – are led by Aslan, a lion redeemer who is the embodiment of Jesus. And nowhere is this more apparent than at the end of *The Lion, the Witch and the Wardrobe*, when he is shaved, mocked, bound and killed by the White Witch's minions. But like Jesus, he is 'resurrected' and vanquishes evil, and a never ending winter, from Narnia.

The Matrix trilogy (1999, 2003) also has its redeemers in Neo and Morpheus. The former is more in line with Jesus, while the later is more like John the Baptist. Neo is referred to as 'the One' who was prophesized to return so that he can free those in the Matrix from slavery and lead them to Zion. He, too, does battle with 'evil' forces and, during the first film, dies and comes back to life. Morpheus paves the way for Neo, spending his entire life searching for 'the One'. He also seems to die and come back to life in *The Matrix*. Together, Neo and Morpheus redeem a world that, because of hubris, overstepped its limits, unleashing a kind of unholy monster (in this case artificial intelligence) upon itself.[13]

In *Iron Man* (2008), Tony Stark is a womanizing, laissez-faire capitalist who earns his living as an arms manufacturer. While he is in Afghanistan demonstrating his company's latest weapon of mass destruction – the Jericho – he is wounded by his own bomb. Kidnapped by terrorists, he is taken inside a network of caves, where he is operated on by a fellow inmate named Yinsen. While convalescing, Stark is ordered to build a Jericho missile for his captors. He is aided by Yinsen, who becomes his literal and symbolic saviour and redeemer. With his eyes open to the misery he has brought to the world, Stark emerges from the cave a new man, determined to use his money and techno-logical acumen to rid the world of his weapons. A few additional science fiction/fantasy films that share the theme of redemption include *Terminator 2: Judgment Day* (1991), *Aliens* (1986), *Batman Begins* (2005), *What Dreams May Come* (1998) and *Spider-Man* (2002).

A redeemer does not necessarily have to be the main character. In *Star Wars IV: A New Hope* (1977), Obi-Wan Kenobi sacrifices himself so that Luke Skywalker, Han Solo, Princess Leia, C-3PO, R2-D2 and Chewbacca can escape from Darth Vader's clutches. Even though he is struck down during a light-saber battle, Obi-Wan later reappears as a guiding voice, which ultimately leads Luke Skywalker and the Rebel Alliance to victory. And as for Luke Skywalker, at the end of *Star Wars VI: Return of the Jedi*, his compassion and faith in Darth Vader, his father, redeems the dark lord.

Drama

One Flew Over the Cuckoo's Nest (1975) is a classic and oft-referenced exam-ple of redemption. Based on Ken Kesey's novel, the film focuses on R. P. McMurphy, a criminal who is transferred from a state penitentiary to a men-tal institution for evaluation. After arriving, he consistently challenges the rules and authority, and in his actions inspires the other inmates in a bid for freedom. The horribly repressive Nurse Ratched is less than impressed with McMurphy's horseplay, pranks and attitude, and she becomes his primary foe. In the end, McMurphy is silenced by being lobotomized. The strong, silent Chief then smothers him, pulls up the limestone sink, hurls it through a window, and escapes. McMurphy's life and ultimate death offer freedom, and redemption, to the other mental patients.[14]

Other dramas that deal with concepts of grace, justice, redemption, hope and forgiveness are *The Fisher King* (1991) and *The Shawshank Redemption* (1994). In *The Fisher King*, shock jock Jack Lucas goes too far on his radio program, and the result is disastrous. Years later, the guilt-filled man is sui-cidal; a shadow of his former self. His redemption comes in the form of Parry, a deranged, homeless man whose own life was destroyed by Lucas' words. *The Shawshank Redemption* focuses on Andy Dufresne, a banker who is wrongly convicted of killing his wife and her lover. Sent to Shawshank Prison, he is repeatedly victimized but he never loses hope. By using his financial skills, he manages to better his and his fellow inmates, helping them to obtain their high school diplomas. His ability to persevere in the face of adversity and have hope when all seems lost has a redemptive effect on Red, a long-timer in the prison system and Andy's best friend.

A considerable number of dramas that are based on historical events contain main characters whose deaths bring redemption to their people, including *Braveheart* (1995), *Gladiator* (2000) and *300* (2006). *Braveheart* tells the story of William Wallace, a commoner, who during the fourteenth century united the Scots in their war against the English. The English are led by the 'cruel pagan' Edward the Longshanks, who claimed the throne for himself, and who engages in theft, rape and murder. All Wallace wants to do is to free his people. 'They may take our lives', he shouts to the Scottish army, 'but they'll never take . . . our freedom!' Seen as a saviour (he is a Christ figure), William is betrayed and taken before the king to whom he refuses to kneel. As punishment he is hung within an inch of death, then drawn and quartered. His death, however, was not in vain. It allows Robert the Bruce to lead the decisive battle of Bannockburn, which resulted in the defeat of the English, the establishment of Robert the Bruce as Robert I, and ultimately, the redemption of the Scottish people from the tyrannical English.

Gladiator tells the story of Maximus, a heroic Roman general who because he stands between a corrupt prince, Commodus, and the throne, endures the murder of his wife and son and is himself enslaved and trained to be a gladiator. A fine warrior, Maximus gains celebrity with the Roman people. This enrages Commodus, now emperor, who challenges the general to a final duel. But Commodus betrays the general by stabbing him, literally, in the back. A wounded Maximus enters the ring and fights, but he is dying. Before he does, he kills Commodus, thereby exacting his revenge. He also tells Quintus to free his men and reinstate Senator Gracchus, a democratic-minded senator; 'There was a dream that was Rome. It shall be realized. These are the wishes of Marcus Aurelius'. When Maximus dies, he rejoins his family in the afterlife. 'Is Rome worth one good man's life? We believed it once. Make us believe it again', Lucilla, the sister of Commodus, says to Gracchus. In life and in death, Maximus serves as a moral guide for the Roman people. His qualities of honesty and bravery contrast strongly with Commodus' qualities of treacherous and cowardice, and in the end, he inspires his people to overcome the corruption that has been eating away at them and rediscover the values that they once embraced.

300 is based on the Battle of Thermopylae (480 BCE.), during which King Leonidas and 300 Spartan soldiers squared off against 'the Persian Empire', headed by the God-King Xerxes. They are ultimately betrayed not only by a corrupt politician named Theron but also by the hunchback Ephialtes, who wants to fight along the Spartans to redeem his family but is rejected by Leonidas when he cannot hold up a shield. The Spartans fight bravely even though they know they cannot win. Their ultimate sacrifice – all of them die – inspires the Greek people to come together and fight on the 'ragged patch of earth called Plataea'. As the Spartan Dilios says at the end of the film:

Just there the barbarians huddle, sheer terror gripping tight their hearts with icy fingers, knowing full well what merciless horrors they suffered at the swords and spears of 300. Yet they stare now across the plain at 10,000 Spartans commanding 30,000 free Greeks . . . This day we rescue a world from mysticism and tyranny and usher in a future brighter than anything we can imagine.

Additional historical dramas, and there are many, that deal with redemption include *Schindler's List* (1993), *Les Miserables* (1995), *Raging Bull* (1980) and *Redemption: The Stan Tookie Williams Story* (2004).

As we have seen even though redemption, theologically, is usually associated with Christianity, we also find characters in East Asian films who sacrifice themselves for the benefit of others. Several recent examples include *Fearless* (AKA: *Huo Yuan Jia*, 2006) and Hero (AKA: *Ying Xiong*, 2002). The former biopic focuses on Huo Yuanjia, the Chinese martial arts legend who founded the Jin Wu Sports Federation. Early on, he is presented as a prideful, self-centred youth who, despite his parents' protests, eschews learning for martial arts training. As he grows up, all he wants is to be crowned champion, and he regularly engages in fights. One day, he acts impetuously, challenging another master to a fight. During the heat of the battle, Huo kills him. In retaliation, his own family is slain. His life shattered, he leaves his village, and nearly dies, until he is rescued by a blind woman and her mother. Their example of hard work, compassion and simplicity redeems Huo, and when he leaves them, he is a changed man. When he returns to his hometown, he finds that not only are Westerners ubiquitous but so is their influence – from fashion styles to religion. Furthermore, they are calling the Chinese, 'the sick men of the East', which is something Huo cannot tolerate. He enters a tournament during which he will fight against four opponents, each representing a different country. But he no longer fights for himself, he fights for his people. In the last minutes of the film, Huo is poisoned by a Japanese businessman who has a lot of money at stake in the competition. But rather than bow out, the dying Huo asks his students to promise not to seek revenge, because it 'will only bring more bloodshed. Please, that's not what I want'. He fights to the end, proving himself to be a true hero of his people.

Hero, too, is based on historical truth. Set during pre-unified China, the film shows how one man, Nameless, defeated three assassins – Broken Sword, Flying Snow and Sky – thus preventing them from killing the King of Qin. Although he was a ruthless ruler, this warlord 'had a vision – to unite the land. To put an end, once and for all, to war'. Even though Nameless could probably have killed the ruler, he decides to lay down his sword. The ruler's advisors clamour, in unison, for the 'man to be made an example of'. The air is then filled with arrows, and Nameless is executed 'as an assassin but buried as a hero'. As the title cards read:

> The King of Qin went on to conquer all of the six Kingdoms and unite the country. As China's first Emperor, he completed the Great Wall to protect his subjects. This was more than 2,000 years ago. But even now when the Chinese speak of their country, they call it Our Land.

Some might say that Huo Yuanjia and Nameless are 'Christ figures', however; this would be inaccurate considering the fact that these films are coming not from a Christian tradition but from a Confucian one. Early in *Fearless*, Huo Yuanjia is encouraged by his father to copy the sayings of Confucius. Being concerned with *wushu*, he ignores his father, and instead, pays his friend, Nong Jinsun to do it for him. Because he fails to study, Huo Yuanhia never learns to be a 'superior man'. Instead he has to learn how to behave from role models around him, especially the loyal and benevolent Nong Jinsun. Confucianism is built on the premise that 'the people are the most important element in a nation', and the masses come before the individual. At its heart, Confucianism is about doing what is right no matter what. As Mencius said a great man practices the Way for the good of the people; he is benevolent, righteous and stands in propriety: 'A person's character is revealed in an emergency or crisis. During such times, a man insists on doing what he must and refuses to do what he should not, *even to the extent of sacrificing his life rather than compromising his principles*'.[15] One sees that both Huo Yuanjia and Nameless sacrifice themselves for the greater good. One might even say that these films draw upon the Mahāyāna Buddhist tradition of a person taking the *bodhisattva* or the enlightenment being a path.

> The person entering this path aspired to be a compassionate, self-sacrificing hero. His path would be long, as he would need to build up moral and spiritual perfections not only for his own exalted state of Buddhahood, but also so as to be able altruistically to aid others by teaching, good deeds, 'merit' transference, and offering response to prayers.[16]

Because redeemers 'save' others from harm, they might also be thought of as saviours.[17] The problem is that when these terms are used in the West, they typically carry Christian-specific connotations. And, redemption, in its original meaning, applies to a number of religious and non-religious actions. Nevertheless, most of the films that come out of the Hollywood system will be inspired by a Judaeo-Christian worldview. It is only by stepping outside of this system that the full definition of redemption in action can be found.

23 Filming the Afterlife

Christian Haunton

Given the human preoccupation with death and dying, it comes as no surprise that there have been many attempts made over the years to commit an interpretation of the afterlife to film. The question of why such stories are told seems simple enough to answer; they offer imagined glimpses of places and ideas that have dogged human curiosity for millennia. The more interesting question is *how* such stories are told. These are, after all, tales of what Hamlet calls that 'undiscovered country from whose borne no traveler returns', a place described by countless cultures, but seen by no living person. Filmmakers may feel constrained by the many, often deeply held, notions of the afterlife that exist in the audiences' minds, while simultaneously feeling liberated by the total freedom of describing a place that no one has ever seen. The product of this tension can be upsetting, humorous and frequently poignant.

Ultimately, every heaven, hell, reincarnation, ascension or oblivion that any religion or philosophy has ever offered is just a guess – a provisional response to the unanswerable question, 'what happens to me when I die?' This gives filmmakers an extraordinary opportunity to respond to this question in unexpected ways. One of the most common traits found in films about the afterlife is that they deviate somewhat from traditional religious descriptions. This deviation may be subtle, or it may involve the creation of an entirely new idea of what happens when humans die. In either instance, the filmmakers put their own ideas on the screen, inviting the viewer to examine himself or herself in light of this specific imagining of the afterlife.

Below are a dozen examples, divided by genre, of films which approach the issue of an afterlife from various angles and for various purposes. In each case a brief synopsis of the film's plot has been provided, along with a look at that particular film's unique approach to the afterlife.

The Afterlife in Thrillers

Perhaps the simplest place to start when discussing films about the afterlife is the thriller or horror genre. Because a great many such films include supernatural elements, and because supernatural elements frequently borrow from religious concepts, it is only natural that from time to time the afterlife would play a central role in such films. In thrillers about the afterlife, the tension usually comes from some element of the next world spilling over into the realm of the living in a threatening or disconcerting manner.

The Others (2001)

The Others, under the direction of Alejandro Amenábar, follows Grace Stewart and her children, a mid-twentieth-century family who live on a remote estate on the British island of Jersey. Throughout the film a variety of occurrences lead the family and the viewer to believe that the home is haunted by potentially hostile spirits. As the plot continues and the intensity and threat of the haunting grows, it is revealed that Grace and her children are in fact the ghosts who have been unable to leave their home, and the effects that they perceived as haunting were merely the actions of the living family that now inhabits the house. In the end, the family of ghosts accepts its fate and resolves to never leave the house, no matter who should come to inhabit it.

The Others is one of several stories (*The Sixth Sense, The Turn of the Screw*) that present an afterlife where ghosts are mistaken for the living and vice versa. Such stories rely on an afterlife that is indistinguishable from the world of the living. Often these stories suggest that unfinished business or unresolved tragedy is keeping the spirits attached to the world of the living, without ever explaining what happens to those souls who move on. This film is no exception, as it is Grace who ultimately killed her own children before killing herself and then awoke, as a ghost, believing the episode to have been a fantasy. Such versions of the afterlife seem eager to assign some element of consequence to the process of death, but often leave out any specific sense of judgment, salvation, punishment or other divine evaluation.

Dead Again (1991)

In *Dead Again*, Mike Church is a private detective who has been given the responsibility of learning the identity of an amnesic woman who has been left in his care. In searching for the details of her present life, the woman and Mike discover that in a past life they were husband and wife, as well as murderer and victim. Director Kenneth Branagh takes filmgoers through a series of twists and turns, and it becomes apparent that the real murderer responsible for the fifty-year-old crime is still at large and wants to kill his former victim again in her current incarnation.

This is one of three films discussed here that deal with the idea of reincarnation (the others being *What Dreams May Come* and *Defending Your Life*). However, only this film clearly deals with the issue from the side of the living – effectively portraying one's current life as someone else's afterlife. The film goes further by suggesting that with proper training and tools (in this case hypnotic regression), one can unlock past lives and carry knowledge and feelings through to the next life. This creates a world where the afterlife is, in fact, ever-present in the world of the living and vice versa.

Pulse (2001)

The plot of *Pulse* follows multiple characters through a collection of related events. These trace a gradual process wherein the realm of ghosts begins to seep into the world of the living. In some cases the dead enter the living world (typically through technology), and those exposed to the dead become 'sick' emotionally, resulting in depression, anxiety, alienation and eventually suicide, at which point the victims become physically absorbed into the world of the dead. The exact mechanism of what is happening is never fully explained. In fact several characters offer varying notions of what the afterlife is like. Regardless of the causes involved, the result is that the interaction of the world of the living with the world of the dead results in massive depopulation and what seems by the end of the film to be the end of the world.

The central cosmological concern of *Pulse*, directed by Kiyoshi Kurasawa, seems to be an essential conflict between the dead and the living – the notion that the former pose a threat to the latter. This is not a story about characters going to the afterlife, but about the afterlife coming to the characters, and literally poisoning their world. This film stresses, more than any other film discussed here, that the separation between the living and the afterlife is crucial to the success and stability of the living world. The afterlife is not merely the inevitable destination of all mortals, but the home of jealous and dangerous things that want to reclaim the mortal realm.

Stay (2005)

The plot of director Marc Forster's *Stay* is a complex and convoluted matter. After an initial scene of a car accident, the story follows the attempts of psychologist Sam Foster to find a young man named Henry Letham who has threatened to kill himself at 12:01 a.m. on the day of his twenty-first birthday. As Sam gets deeper and deeper into his search, it becomes evident that things are not as they seem. Time does not flow at a consistent pace, characters appear that are supposed to be dead, and even the boundary between the characters of Sam and Henry begins to dissolve. The final scenes return the viewer to the moment of the original car crash where Sam, a bystander and witness to the crash, attempts, and ultimately fails, to save Henry's life.

Though *Stay* is clearly a film that explores what happens to people when they die, its statement about the afterlife itself remains ambiguous. It may be best to see *Stay* as an atheistic exploration of the afterlife. Here the story is guided by the final spasms of the dying brain, attempting to construct meaning around the moment of annihilation. It takes place wholly in another world, separate from the realm of the living. Yet, this world does not exist in some theologically defined space, but within the human mind itself.

The Afterlife in Comedies

The arena of comedy provides some useful opportunities for telling stories about the afterlife. Because these movies are clearly intended to humour and amuse, they can offer interpretations of the afterlife without seeming dismissive in their irreverence. Often the comedy is based on how strange things would be in the afterlife from the point of view of the living.

Heaven Can Wait (1978)

Joe Pendleton is a professional quarterback who dies in a bicycle accident only to learn from heavenly officials that he was not scheduled to be dead for nearly fifty more years. Because Joe's own body has been cremated he is forced to reanimate another body, that of Leo Farnsworth, a recently murdered millionaire. In this form Joe is able to buy his old football team, repair Farnsworth's corrupt business practices, and ultimately train to become a quarterback again. Eventually, the Farnsworth body is successfully murdered, and Joe is moved to yet another body where he is able to win the Super Bowl and get the girl. Once his life is back on track, Joe forgets all the former bodies he has inhabited.

The afterlife outlined in the Warren Beatty and Buck Henry film *Heaven Can Wait* is notable for two reasons. The first is the presence of fallibility in the heavenly process of gathering and processing the dead. The beings that run the afterlife seem consistently well-intentioned, but entirely capable of error. The second aspect that stands out is the stark division between body and spirit that the film supposes. No matter what body Joe inhabits, he is still understood to be Joe. Even when Joe's memories are erased, it is because his new life is back on the track that his original life was on. In this afterlife, the soul and the self seem to be interchangeable concepts.

Beetlejuice (1988)

Beetlejuice, directed by Tim Burton, tells the story of a happy couple who die unexpectedly in a car accident and find themselves trapped as ghosts in the home they once inhabited. Chief among their challenges is the arrival of a new family whose presence in the house becomes a constant source of distress and aggravation for the ghostly couple. In their attempts to remove this new family, the couple endeavours to haunt their own house, consults with a bureaucracy of the dead, and eventually enlists the help of Beetlejuice, a self-described 'bio-exorcist'. In the end, the living and the dead learn to cohabit, developing a relationship that enriches the lives (and unlives) of all involved.

Tim Burton does an excellent job of establishing an afterlife that is in part comically similar to the world of the living and in part impenetrably obscure. On the one hand, there are scenes of ghostly secretaries, case workers and waiting room denizens all bearing the grotesque marks of the manners of their deaths. On the other hand, there are unexplained vistas of negative space populated by murderous sand worms that surround the couple's New England home. By combining the familiar with the outrageously strange, Burton effectively creates a sense of the afterlife that is both connected to our experience in the living world and radically different in ways that defy conventional explanation.

All Dogs Go to Heaven (1989)

In Don Bluth's *All Dogs Go to Heaven*, Charlie B. Barkin, a ne'er do well German Shepherd, is murdered by his villainous business partner and finds himself in heaven. Charlie has not earned a place in heaven by his deeds, but rather by default, because, as the title explains, all dogs go to heaven. Through trickery, Charlie returns to earth with the knowledge that he will no longer have a place in heaven waiting for him. Back on earth, Charlie meets Anne-Marie, an orphan girl whom Charlie uses to advance his own ends. Eventually, Charlie comes to love Anne-Marie and sacrifices his own life to save hers. This final act of self-sacrifice allows Charlie to return to heaven as a matter of merit, rather than species.

Though this is an animated children's film (or perhaps because of that fact), it is the only film here to take a very traditionally Christian view of a dual afterlife consisting of a rewarding heaven and a punishing hell. While the plot deals specifically with dog afterlives, it is explained in the film that, unlike dogs, not all humans go to heaven because humans are not inherently good. The afterlife described here is both traditional and simple; those who do good with their earthly lives will receive a reward, while those who do not will suffer eternally.

Defending Your Life (1991)

Defending Your Life, directed by Albert Brooks, follows Daniel Miller, a middle-aged yuppie who dies on his birthday after buying a new BMW. He finds himself in a place called Judgment City, where, for the next few days, he will take part in a sort of trial to determine his cosmic fate. During this time, he meets and falls in love with Julia, a bold and confident woman who brings out the better aspects of Daniel's nature. In the end, it is the bond Daniel forms with Julia that justifies his life.

The judgment that is central to *Defending Your Life* is not one of good versus evil, but one of courage versus fearfulness. Humans are among the lower forms of consciousness in the universe, and only by overcoming their fear and anxiety can they merit forward progression towards higher states of being. The afterlife exists to determine who are ready to move on and who need to return to earth to learn more lessons. Within this context, the afterlife is simultaneously a place of judgment, a mechanism of reincarnation, and an opportunity for enlightened ascension.

The Afterlife in Dramas

Dramatic treatment of the afterlife may be one of the most challenging approaches to this subject. The earnestness required to present a story on these terms puts the film at risk of coming across as corny or hokey. As such, great care is usually taken to ground these stories in deeply emotional situations, which is not particularly difficult, given that films about the afterlife must, by definition, also be films about death. The dramatic films tend to focus on the consequences of death for the survivors and the interplay of the dead and the living in reinterpreting their relationships.

Ghost (1990)

Ghost tells the story of Sam Wheat, a man who dies while trying to defend his girlfriend, Molly, from a mugger. Throughout the story, Sam attempts to make contact with his living girlfriend and protect her from the man who was ultimately responsible for Sam's own death. In trying to understand and function in his ghostly condition, Sam consults a violent and angry ghost who teaches him that with concentration he can physically affect the world of the living. Sam also makes use of a spirit medium who ultimately proves to be his best form of communication with Molly. Sam is eventually able to communicate with Molly and defeat his own killer's attempt to harm her.

In this film, directed by Jerry Zucker, the afterlife is depicted as having multiple distinct natures. Sam's story takes place here on earth, a fate reserved for those souls with unfinished business. The film makes clear that this is an upsetting and frustrating state of being that may eventually lead to madness. But the film also depicts souls leaving this state for either a bright and comforting or a dark and terrifying destination. The clear indication is that those who leave (or simply bypass) the status of ghosts end up in a more traditional heaven or hell.

Dragonfly (2002)

Dragonfly tells the story of Dr. Joe Darrow, whose pregnant wife Emily, also a doctor, dies in a mudslide in Venezuela where she has travelled to provide medical aid. Joe's grieving process is complicated by a series of experiences that convince him that his wife is trying to communicate with him from beyond the grave through symbols and images, as well as through patients who have suffered near-death experiences. Driven to the point of emotional collapse by this harrowing process, Joe eventually travels to Venezuela to try to make sense of the messages he has received. There he learns that though Emily died from her injuries in the mudslide, she first gave birth to a daughter who survived.

The themes director Tom Shadyac explores in *Dragonfly* are quite popular, both in fiction and in pseudo-scientific study of the paranormal. In this interpretation of the afterlife, souls who have unfinished business tend to remain in contact with the living. Though these souls are clearly able to affect and communicate with the mortal world, they invariably do so in vague and ambiguous ways that requite active interpretation by the living. This afterlife seems far better suited to keeping a sense of mystery in a story than it does to serving any useful cosmic function.

Death Takes a Holiday/Meet Joe Black (1934/1998)

Although there are several significant differences between *Death Takes a Holiday*, directed by Mitchell Leisen, and *Meet Joe Black*, directed by Martin Brest, their plots are essentially the same. Death, driven by loneliness and curiosity about the human condition, decides to take time off and disguise himself as a human for a time. In order to facilitate this plan, Death enlists the help of a wealthy man who is to act as Death's guide. The man is the only one who knows Death's true identity, but he must not reveal it, or there will be dire consequences. While Death is on earth he falls in love with a human woman and is driven to remain. In *Death Takes a Holiday*, the woman reveals that she has always seen Death for what he really is and loves him anyway. Death departs, and takes the woman with him. The end of *Meet Joe Black* is almost the opposite. Death realizes that the woman does not love him as he truly is and leaves alone, returning life to the body that he has inhabited.

Both films take some care to keep the afterlife itself out of the story – no scenes take place in other worlds, and overt discussions about what happens after death are quickly ended with vague responses like, 'There are no words by which to tell you'. Nonetheless, certain aspects of the afterlife may be inferred from these two movies. Perhaps the most significant aspect is that the afterlife is, to some extent, heedless of its effect on the realm of the living. Both stories involve the idea that Death is confused or curious about why people fear him so, though he uses this fear in a calculating manner to get his way from his guides. Also present in these stories is the clear implication that this anthropomorphized form of death is the cause of the mechanical process of dying. Both films show that without the entity of Death to fulfil his role, people cannot leave this world, no matter what happens to their bodies. In

Death Takes a Holiday this is dealt with casually and even somewhat comically, but *Meet Joe Black* more openly explores the idea that, for some, passage to the afterlife is a desperately sought release.

What Dreams May Come (1998)

This is the story of Dr. Chris Nielsen, who dies in an automobile accident years after his two children died in the same manner. After finding himself in a beautiful paradise and reconnecting with his dead children, Chris learns that his wife, unable to deal with the death of her last loved one, has committed suicide. The remainder of the movie shows Chris's epic quest to find his wife and rescue her from the grim fate that awaits suicide victims. Eventually Chris is able to stir recognition and hope in his wife's soul, and together they elect to be reborn on earth so that they can meet and fall in love again.

The afterlife described in director Vincent Ward's *What Dreams May Come* stresses the ability of the individual to fashion his or her own experience. Aspects that religion would characterize as heaven or hell are in fact products of the individual's imagination and self-perception. Despite this focus on individual control, the film seems to depict an overall sense of organization and even community. This leaves the viewer with the notion that the afterlife may simply be that place where everyone can be themselves and still be part of the whole.[1]

After Life (1998)

Hirokazu Kore-eda's film, *After Life*, is unique among those discussed here in that it is the only one to be set entirely in the afterlife. The story follows several civil servants whose job it is to process newly dead souls on their one week stop-over between the world of the living and the next world. The plot also involves the stories of the souls themselves as they consider their lives and the most important memories that they have. By the end of the film, one of the civil servants has chosen to move on to the next stage of his afterlife, while one of the souls remains behind to take his place.

This one week stay becomes a pivotal moment in defining the afterlife of each of the souls involved in the story. During the stay, each soul is tasked with selecting one memory from his or her life which will then be filmed by the civil servants whose job is to help with this process. Upon viewing this film, the soul will depart for the next world taking with it only this single memory. This afterlife stresses thoughtful re-examination of one's own life and consideration of the single most important or most treasured element. It is never made clear whether this single memory is carried forward into a new life, or if the memory becomes a sort of heaven that the soul lives out for eternity.[2]

It is worth noting that films about the afterlife are rarely *about* the afterlife. They are invariably about people (or dogs), with the afterlife serving as a setting or plot device that offers challenges or opportunities to the characters involved. Though this is not surprising, as virtually all films are about their characters, it does set up an interesting consequence that further distances cinematic afterlives from their religious counterparts. In films, the afterlife very often offers opportunities for change – a chance to correct past mistakes, to reconnect with living loved ones, or to transform as an individual. By contrast, in most religious interpretations, the afterlife is not a place of opportunity, but a place of consequence. Earthly life is the time for choice and change, and the afterlife is a place of singular consistency, whether that takes the form of reward, punishment, or some other manner of stopover between earthly lives. In this sense, the cinematic afterlife is particularly dynamic, making it a better place to tell stories about human nature.

24 Imaging God in the Movies

Christian Haunton

The focus of this chapter is the image of God in the movies. The image of God, however, is not the same kind in all movies. There are four rather different ways to provide an image of God on film: (1) the imageless image of God; (2) the use of another divine being as a surrogate for an aspect of God; (3) the use of a human character as a surrogate for God's capabilities and (4) the actual inclusion of God as an identifiable character in the film.

The Imageless Image

By far the most common expressions of God that have been put to film are those where God is presented not as an overt person or thing, but as a theme, an emotion or an experience. The fact that this is common should come as no surprise as this expression bypasses several problems. It escapes the need to fix the ineffable with a particular form. It avoids the issue of graven idols entirely, and it lends itself naturally to multiple interpretations. All this is gained, of course, at the cost of the overt 'image' of God, here replaced with a 'sense' of God. Such films are found in diverse genres and from varied countries.

For example, the 1951 film *Diary of a Country Priest*, directed by Robert Bresson, is clearly about the work of God in the lives of humans. It tells the story of a priest, newly arrived to his parish, who faces deep social resistance and open mockery by his new flock. His greatest struggles are centered on his interactions with the local noble family, a troubled group in need of salvation from a selfish and poisonous world they have created for themselves. The film's pivotal scene is a struggle between the peace of God and the turmoil of life played out in the interactions between the priest and the grim and obsessive countess.[1] Harsh words are exchanged, but ultimately the countess finds peace with herself and with God. This interaction, which is followed by the death of the countess, is further complicated by the fact that it is misinterpreted by the other characters that populate the film who see judgement and cruelty where there was, in fact, redemptive concern.

The 'sense' of God here is clear; the priest, and more broadly his interactions with a hostile environment, is intended to represent God's work among humankind. God is mocked, ignored and openly resented. Even when God's grace saves a soul, it goes unnoticed and unappreciated by the community. Though the message is clearly religious and told with a religious plot and a religious protagonist, the 'image of God' here is presented by impression only – in the image of the priest and his surroundings.

Babette's Feast[2] provides another look at God, here presented without the overt religious context of *Diary of a Country Priest*, but in clearly religious terms nonetheless. This film tells the story of two sisters raised by a conservative protestant pastor. The sisters have given up opportunities in their own lives to help maintain the life of the small, aging group who once followed their father. The film's title comes from the name of a French Catholic refugee from the Revolutionary War whom the sisters take in as their cook. When she unexpectedly wins the lottery she uses her newfound wealth to prepare a sumptuous meal for the sisters and their small community.

The denominational differences between the Protestant sisters and the Catholic Babette are not the focus of the film, which is more concerned with tensions and disappointments in the lives of the characters and the community. The extravagant meal of turtle soup and quails *en sarcophage* prepared by Babette becomes the point of transformation, not simply by cheering the townspeople, but by establishing a community of forgiveness and spiritual optimism.[3] Babette as God – as one who draws people together, unites them in celebration and nourishes their souls[4] – is no great stretch, but it does ask more of the audience in terms of filling in the blanks. The 'sense' of God presented here is more subtle, and perhaps more nuanced.

The 1990 film *Flatliners* revolves around a group of medical students who have banded together to do secret experiments about the limits of life and death. Their motivations are presented less as scientific hubris and more as dangerous thrill-seeking. As a result of their near-death experiments the various students become haunted by the nightmarish hallucinations that follow them back into the world of the living. In each case the characters are being haunted by choices they made at various points in their lives, which have now been brought back to the centre of their consciousnesses by the 'flatlining' trips.

God is presented here as a force of redemptive change. The students are confronted, by way of their flirtations with death, with what may be termed their 'sins'. Only be reconciling these issues are the students able to escape the living nightmares that plague them. God seems to be both in the horror of confronting one's mistakes and in the peace of seeking forgiveness and resolution.

As a final example of this strategy, Paul Schrader's 1980 drama *American*

Gigolo serves well. This is the story of Julian Kaye, the titular gigolo, who sees to the sexual desires of wealthy west coast women. After a series of poor choices and betrayals, Julian finds himself framed for murder, and dependent on the testimony of one of his customers to set him free – a customer who would rather spare her own reputation than save an innocent man. Though the story ends with Julian still in jail, the audience is assured that the woman has made the right decision in the end and that justice will be served.

Since pimps, prostitutes, liars and killers populate the film it may seem infertile ground for an image of God, but here God is painted less within the characters and more within the themes – righteousness and guilt, the relationship between earthly success and internal peace, and sacrifice for fellow humans. At this stage one must be looking for the sense of God to find it. The film functions successfully without any need to resort to the significance of the divine. (Compare to *Diary of a Country Priest*'s reliance on religious symbols and characters to evoke religious tones.) Here any image of God serves as a layer of depth, not as a showpiece or central figure.

The examples given above vary dramatically in their content, from subjects overtly religious to those only tangentially so, and here lies the difficulty of seeking the image of God in such films. Theoretically, there is no limit to this search. If God is infinite, and is also the source of all things, then it must hold that one can find the 'sense' of God in any circumstance, any theme, any character. One need not look to country priests or troubled souls. God should be equally accessible in war documentaries, pornography or even the test patterns used to focus a projector.

The fact that the faithful seeker can find God in such diverse circumstances (even where the filmmakers may have intended no such identification) should in no way be seen as a pitfall of either the film or the viewer, but the 'image' of God remains invisible – something that can be detected within the story, but not seen projected on the screen. It may be worth noting that though the image of God remains unseen on the screen, it can still be found reflected in the eyes of the beholder. When a viewer finds a sense of God in a pastoral landscape, or a private moment between loved ones, that viewer is expressing his or her own sense of where the image of God belongs. These may be spots designed by the filmmakers to evoke the sense of God, but more often, the 'images' that are seen (or not) are a manifestation of the viewers' expectations. God is seen where God is already imagined to exist.

Divine Surrogates

In some cases the 'sense' of God is not sufficient, but the image of God in his entirety is not desired either. In these instances it is possible to find aspects of

God depicted as individual entities – wholly separate from human beings and supernatural in nature, but limited in their role.

Perhaps the most iconic of these manifestations is Death, as famously depicted in Ingmar Bergman's 1957 classic, *The Seventh Seal*. The film is an existential study that follows the journey of a knight who tries to make his way back to his family after returning from war. He is confronted with death, both as a general concept – in the ravages of plague across the countryside, and as a specific being – personified as both frightening and inescapable, his pallid, hairless face setting him apart as something otherworldly. The ongoing conflict of the film is a chess match between Death and the knight, with the knight's life at stake.

Within the context of the film, Death serves as a touchstone for the various characters as they deal with the question of God's existence. Death can be interpreted as the personification of God's sovereignty over the issue of mortality, but this may be an oversimplification. Death seems to also represent the inescapable reality of the unknowable and in this capacity he serves as a counterpoint to the knight's agnosticism; though the knight cannot prove the existence of God, he can see how powers beyond his control directly shape his life.

It is worth noting that the character of Death personified is carried on in other films as well. For example, 1998s, *Meet Joe Black*[5] presents Death as a handsome and curious, but cold, man seeking to learn more about the world of humans. A considerably more light-hearted presentation of death is found in *Bill and Ted's Bogus Journey* (1991), directed by Peter Hewitt. Here Death is a direct parody of Ingmar Bergman's Death.

Another ubiquitous representation of God-by-proxy can be seen in the character of the angel, utilized in a variety of films. In *All That Jazz*,[6] the audience is presented with a wild and complex view of the life of director/ choreographer Joe Gideon, who after years of hard-living and workaholism has been hospitalized by a failing heart. As the future of Gideon's survival is determined on a surgical table, and the future of his career is debated by his Broadway backers, the future of his soul is negotiated in interactions between Gideon and the aptly named Angelique.[7]

Angelique may be seen as an angel of death, but she also seems to represent a force of judgement. Significantly, she is nothing like the pale and morose image of death from *The Seventh Seal*. She is depicted instead as an elegant and sexually attractive woman. Her role as messenger of God is not all that unusual, but her presentation most certainly is. Here God is a familiar force of fate, judgement and the inevitable, but he is also an object of desire, not merely spiritual, but physical as well.

Steven Spielberg's 1989 film *Always*, tells the story of a human who becomes an angel. Pete is a daredevil pilot who extinguishes forest fires. Shortly after deciding to give up his dangerous line of work in order to make a life with Dorinda, the woman he loves, Pete goes out on one last run where he is killed saving his friend's life. Pete is confronted with a female angel who tells him that he has been given the job of guardian angel to Ted, a pilot and suitor to Dorinda. Pete must ultimately overcome his own desire to be with Dorinda in order to promote the happiness and goodness that are now his responsibilities.

The image of God here is complicated by the fact that Pete changes as a character over the course of the film, something less evident in Death and Angelique. It is in Pete's final form, as a selfless agent of love and fate that the image becomes most clear. Pete represents God here as not only a guide to destiny, but as a self-sacrificing source of inspiration and support in the journey.

City of Angels (1998), directed by Brad Silberling, tells the story of an angel who becomes fascinated with a human doctor and eventually falls in love with her. Over the course of the story, the angel learns that it is within his power to cease being an angel and begin a life as a human being. He chooses to do so, only to have the woman he loves die in a car accident shortly after they begin their relationship together. Ultimately, the angel seems to take up his new human role and embrace it, tragedy and all.

This film uses the technique of the divine surrogate to illustrate the idea of God's desire to be closer to humanity. The audience is given a clear message that no matter how appealing and attractive the call of human companionship may be, it can prove to be a path towards loss and pain. Nonetheless, God, as represented by the angel feels this pull and ultimately submits, for better or for worse.[8] Here a traditional theme (humans seeking a way to heaven) is flipped to cast the divine in a different light.

What unites these diverse titles (and there are many others) is the use of the divine individual to illustrate the nature of God. In all of these instances, whether comedic or dramatic, these divine characters have some, but not all of the capabilities attributed to God. These are still not complete images of God, but images of aspects of God, overt in their presentation, but limited in their scope.

Human Surrogates

An alternative to having an overtly supernatural image that depicts an aspect of God is to have a human image that represents the function of God. This practice is easiest to find in genre films like science fiction, horror and westerns.[9] Where Babette may behave in ways that invite the viewer to draw parallels to God, the characters of these genre films are provided with capabilities generally reserved for God. Though God is not on screen, per se, he is present in effigy, and this representation bears the image.

Ridley Scott's 1982 masterpiece *Blade Runner* serves as an example. Here the viewer is introduced to a dystopian future where human beings have come to rely on slave-robots called 'replicants' to do jobs too difficult, dangerous or degrading for humans. The plot follows a detective whose job is to round up several replicants who have escaped their masters and come to earth seeking answers about their nature. At one point, Eldon Tyrell, a creator of the replicants, is confronted by Roy Batty, an angry, dying, ultimately powerless specimen of that breed. When Batty is given the opportunity to confront his owl-eyed maker[10] his questions are those of a human to God. Why must I die? Why won't you let me live longer?

What makes this exchange unusual, and this image of God so powerful, is that when the exchange is over, Tyrell's responses proving unsatisfying, Batty kills him by gouging out his eyes (which are an established metaphor for humanness in the context of the film). God is presented here as a creator, but not a caretaker, and it is as if Roy Batty is critiquing this image of God and demonstrating that it is lacking. The exchange ultimately raises the issue of the relationship between creator and creation, and the power struggle inherent in that connection.

Jacob's Ladder, a 1990 thriller directed by Adrian Lyne, is the story of a Vietnam veteran, named Jacob, who is badly wounded in battle. The events of the film take the form of memories and hallucinations about Jacob's life both before and after the war. Jacob eventually learns that he was the victim of secret government experiments designed to produce greater aggression in soldiers. Ultimately, the final scenes reveal that the entire film has taken place between Jacob's fatal wounding and his death.

God is represented by the character of Louis, a chiropractor. Though this character offers comfort and healing, it is ultimately his access to the secrets of the afterlife that give him the supernatural edge necessary to represent God. Louis explains that heaven and hell (and more particularly angels and demons) are a matter of self-perception more than they are opposite ends of a dichotomy.[11] It is not the sharing of this insight that defines Louis as God's surrogate, but the more fundamental fact that he knows this truth.

An example of the human surrogate in a western setting can be seen in George Cosmatos's 1993 film *Tombstone*. Though the story begins as a fairly familiar one of reluctant lawmen brining order to a troubled town, it turns to one of righteous retribution heavily painted in biblical hues. After the death of one brother and the severe injury of another, Wyatt Earp goes on a campaign of violence against the villainous gang responsible. He begins this war with quotations from the Book of Revelation, and this alone lends a certain theocentric air to the events that follow. What sets Wyatt apart as a special case, however, is his apparent invulnerability while on his quest for a reckoning. This is demonstrated in a scene where Wyatt fights and kills several outlaws in a creek, and even though they are only yards from their target, Wyatt's opponents cannot hit him.

God's role in this image is particularly apparent. He is the God that settles scores and balances accounts, as much a product of the *Hebrew Bible* as of the Book of Revelation. Wyatt, as God's surrogate, is given the ability to reach a reckoning with the violence that was done to the people he loved. Ultimately, it is only after this balance has been restored that Wyatt is allowed to find a measure of peace, suggesting a familiar notion that God's judgement must precede God's reward.

Stanley Kubrick's 1968 film, *2001: A Space Odyssey*, presents a complex and layered story which offers multiple impressions of God. Though the story spans millions of years, the bulk of the plot takes place in the near future during a manned mission to Jupiter. During this voyage the crew, and specifically the protagonist, Dave Bowman, are confronted with the likelihood that their ship's central computer, HAL, is critically malfunctioning. In an attempt to maintain control of the ship, Dave conspires against HAL, who eventually kills the crew. It is only after deactivating HAL that Dave is able to continue his mission and eventually encounter a black monolith floating in space, which ultimately gives Dave access to an existential journey of debatable meaning.

This film provides more than one possible locus for an image of God, but it is HAL that is being examined here. HAL is given several capabilities that fix him as a God-like figure. He is able to predict future events, maintain or extinguish human life, and see and hear the world around him from a nearly omniscient vantage. It is significant that Dave must destroy this conventional image of God in order to progress to the monolith which seems to hold images of its own, though these are warping, twisting spectrums that seem well outside traditional notions of human or divine.

These are images of God, but they are merely costumes, even within the context of the story. The characters are made God-like in some way – through supernatural power or insight in horror films, or through technological ability in science fiction – but they remain accessible on a human level to the characters and the audience. As such, they circumvent the issue of ineffability and idolatry quite neatly, but they also lack the unassailable supremacy upon which traditional interpretations of God depend. The God that can have his eyes gouged out is not entirely the God of monotheism.

God on the Screen

Finally, there are those films that do away with all of the tools and techniques described above and simply put God on screen for all to see. These films are somewhat rare, and not surprisingly, they are often comedies. The permissiveness of the comedic environment dilutes the irreverent into the ironic, the blasphemous into the merely unexpected.

Carl Reiner's 1977 film *Oh God!* (as well as its offspring, *Oh God! Book II* and *Oh God! You Devil*) played its comic notes on the idea of an unexpected image of God, here portrayed by George Burns as an unassuming old man in a golf hat. God chooses a grocery store manager named Jerry to serve as his prophet to the modern world, and the film revolves around Jerry's attempts to convince the world of his message and its divine source. In the end, Jerry takes the issue to the courts where God eventually makes an appearance and conveys his hopes for the future of humanity.

The message of the film is actually quite optimistic, but the premise of the bit is that this is not how one would expect God to look or act. In making God simple, small and elderly the film puts focus on his words and deeds rather than on his form or on his distance from humanity. The most important quality of this God may simply be his presence, not as a force or theme, but as a character that can be scrutinized and inspected.

Bruce Almighty[12] picks up the same cue a quarter century later by casting Morgan Freeman as God. The film tells the story of a man who believes that he can run the world better than God and who is given the opportunity to try. Aside from the myriad slapstick scenarios that develop from this premise, the film delivers the predictable message that only God can do God's job, and that human joy can only be found in taking responsibility for one's own life.

In this case the part itself, played by Freeman again in the sequel *Evan Almighty*,[13] is essentially that of straight man to the films' comedic leads, but the role of the unexpected is played up a notch by having an African American actor depict God. The result in this instance is not the punch line, but still uses the audiences expectations to set the tone of the film – in this case the idea that God's nature and function are considerably different than humans are inclined to imagine.

The theme of the unexpected image of God is used in a different (and somewhat more sophisticated way) by Kevin Smith in his 1999 film *Dogma*. This story involves two fallen angels who intend to make use of a divine 'loophole' to get a place in heaven; the problem being that in doing so, they will circumvent God's unerring will and consequently unmake creation. The bulk of the film is focused on the band of individuals who are trying to prevent this. God is present only at the beginning and end of the film, spending most of the time in a coma inflicted by demonic minions.

Here, God is played by Alanis Morissette. This God is not only female, but also mute and childlike, almost naïve. Smith creates an image of God that stands as a counterpoint to the violence and chaos that motivates the rest of the film. Morissette's God is sweet and fragile against a backdrop of evil, egos and faeces given physical form. Though the film is firmly in the realm of comedy, the image of God is in the realm of commentary, likely expressing Smith's own sensibilities about the relationship between a benevolent deity and the realities of the world of human experience.

To round out this discussion of literal presentations of God, it is worth considering the 2007 film, *The Nines*.[14] This film is not a comedy, and while it does overtly depict God as a living character,[15] it does not reveal this entirely to the viewer until late in the film.

The Nines is a complicated trio of interconnected plotlines focusing on three protagonists, Gary, Gavin and Gabriel, all played by the same actor. Each of these three characters is in some way a creator – actor, director and game designer – and each is dealing with some fundamental loss of control over their lives. Eventually, Gary/Gavin/Gabriel is revealed to be one being that has chosen various characters for himself to play in a universe of his creation.

The Nines deals with a theme more complex than simply God-as-joke or even God-as-commentary. *The Nines* explores God-as-character-study and ultimately reveals God to be essentially psychotic. John August, who wrote, as well as directed the film, seems to have been unwilling to commit entirely to the premise. At one point Gary asks if he is God and is told, 'Technically, no'. Still, we learn that he is the creator and perhaps the sustainer of the world that humans live in, and therefore 'God' by most conventional definitions.

The issue is less ambiguous when *The Nines* is paired with August's 1998 short film simply titled *God*. This film deals with one of the characters from *The Nines* and here she explains explicitly that she is pals with God and that they talk on the phone for hours.[16] She explains, 'The thing is, about God, he has the best gossip'. The decision to make the Gary/Gavin/Gabriel character less explicitly God in *The Nines* may well have been a result of shaping the film to appeal to a wider audience. Regardless, God he is, and when *The Nines* concludes, the viewer is left with the troubled, confused and unsatisfied sentiments that must go hand-in-hand with a genuine encounter with an earnest, unironic image of God in film.

Every scholar of religion knows that putting God into finite terms has been one of the greatest challenges of monotheism. To then take those finite terms and commit them to film, film that may be shot for the sake of art or the sake of profit, can only complicate the matter further. But complicated or not, the process leaves enduring images, – pallid spectres of death or owl-eyed creators of life. In viewing those images one is not reading religious texts, but watching social texts that acknowledge the role of religion. These texts are tempered by egos, limited by budgets and shaped by expectations about what the movie-watching public wants, or needs, to see. As such, it might be reasonable to assume that there is very little chance for 'God' to make it onto the screen in any meaningful way. But what one finds is quite the contrary; God – at least the metaphor called God, the social construct called God – is a frequently effective cinematic device. Whether presented implicitly or explicitly, as a theme or a character, God's image features prominently in the history of film.

25 The Saviour Figure

Matthew McEver

Insinuating that a film character is deliberately or inadvertently patterned after the biblical Moses or Jesus opens up a topic full of land mines. One camp finds religion and popular film incompatible and considers any attempt to link film with Moses or Jesus an act of sacrilege. Scholars of religion and film studies worry that, along with the last decade's surge of interest in the subject, overzealous viewers turn every theatre excursion into a game of pin the tail on the movie messiah. The culture's fascination with spirituality complicates matters even more. The communal conversation about spirituality does not depend on ecclesiastical validation, making the movie theatre a candidate for the surrogate church or synagogue. Barry Taylor even coined the phrase 'entertainment theology' to help describe how religious institutions no longer monopolize conversations about religion and spirituality, which by now are more likely to occur in alternative settings.[1] In his book *Cinematic Savior*, Stephenson Humphries-Brooks argues that today's university student brings to campus an already formed image of a filmic Saviour.[2] He writes of his experience teaching university courses in biblical literature.

> Eight years of graduate education had not prepared me for what the average college student brings to the study of Jesus. Those of my students who prided themselves on having ignored their religious upbringing still possessed firm opinions about who Jesus was and what his life meant. But most of what I heard came from the movies, not the Bible. Even those students who came from biblically informed backgrounds possessed similar opinions. My students believed in a Cinematic Savior. Where, I wondered had I been? How has Hollywood replaced the church as the producer of Jesus' image in our imaginations and our faith?[3]

The Saviour figure, a film character deliberately or inadvertently patterned after Moses or Jesus, is a direct reflection of how religion mutates to address new circumstances.[4] The Saviour is brought into the story to defeat the prevailing symbolic order, which may be political, sociological or religious in nature. The filmic Saviour is the lone individual who can defeat the dominant mythology. He or she may seem to have 'fallen from the sky' or may arise

internally, having reached a crossroads and called out of an ordinary existence. This plot formula, the mainstay of several Clint Eastwood Westerns,
largely has been imported into science fiction and comic hero films. Lloyd
Baugh writes

> The hero is a *deus ex machina*; his origins, his arrival, his powerful goodness
> and his departure and destiny are, by and large, unexplained and often
> defy the logic of the rest of the film. Little or nothing is revealed of his
> thoughts and feelings. He does not incarnate himself or put down roots in
> the world he came to save and his coming, his heroic action, his leaving, in
> fact cost him little.[5]

Pale Rider (1985) is an often cited illustration of what Baugh describes. In the
film, a community of poor miners is helpless to oppose a mining baron who
repeatedly sends his henchmen into the camp to terrorize the people into
leaving. We fully anticipate the hero to ride onscreen as if lowered by a crane
to decide the final outcome. The nameless drifter enters the camp on a
pale horse as a teenage girl reads from the Apocalypse of John. The film's title
refers to one of the seal visions of Revelation – the pale horse and its rider, a
symbol of death. However, that vision is but one cut of cloth in a patchwork of
biblical metaphors. The rider is revealed to have multiple bullet wounds in
his back; he wears a minister's collar. When the rich miner's gun for hire
is informed of the stranger, he comments that the 'Preacher' sounds like
someone he knows to be dead.

Would *Pale Rider* have been comparatively meaningless without the
allusions to Jesus? Probably not, but the film is illustrative of how Saviour
figures are crafted to deliberately parallel Moses or Jesus because the biblical
narrative seems to supply the right images, symbols and language. In most
instances, neither Jesus nor Moses will be overtly mentioned in the film, but
the vocabulary and symbolism are implicit.[6] The analogous relationship
the Saviour figure has with Jesus or Moses might be inadvertent in
some instances because, as Peter Malone says, the imagery is so embedded in
Western consciousness.[7]

Prerequisite to the arrival of the Saviour is the dystopian environment –
paradise lost. Such a setting is critical to the story because ultimately it
supplies the battleground for what Roman Catholic activist Ched Myers
calls 'the war of myths'.[8] The primary role of the Saviour figure will be to
destroy the prevailing symbolic order – which is assumed to be infallible.
The symbolic order in the Second Book of Moses is incarnated in the
Pharaoh and the surrounding institutions that serve the dominant mythology. In contrast to Genesis, Exodus begins not with the voice of God, but the
voice of Pharaoh – as if to say that creation slowly is being dismantled. In the

Apocalypse of John, largely a rewrite of Exodus, the symbolic order is allegorically called 'the Beast'. Numbed masses, in rote manner, garble and mutter that 'the Beast' is beyond critique. It is omnipotent. 'Who can fight against it?'

By its nature, the science fiction genre lends itself to dystopian settings complete with wars of myths. Such scenarios depend on our natural inclination to be apprehensive about the future. The genre continues to show the influence of *Blade Runner* (1982), which presents the future as claustrophobic, falling apart and managed by artificial intelligence. Reflecting the postmodern outlook, technology is not the saviour in today's sci-fi film – it is a controlling presence birthing a bleak existence that necessitates the Cinematic Savior. *Minority Report* (2002) depicts a future Washington, DC, in which the police have an experimental department called 'pre-crime'. Criminals are apprehended based on foreknowledge of a crime, with that knowledge provided by the visions of a holy trinity of 'precognitives' lying submersed in a chamber called 'the temple'. A political ad campaign promotes the system as infallible. The Saviour figure of the film illegally enters the holy of holies to dismantle the deified system, and several attempts are made to establish him in an analogous relationship with Jesus. There is a Judas figure, a metaphorical crucifixion, descent into Hell and a resurrection.

The Matrix (1999) has received a great deal of consideration for its Christological parallels, but its dependent relationship with the slavery motif of Exodus and John's Apocalypse usually is overlooked. The film presents a future in which humans are unaware that they have been harvested to bio-electrically generate sentient machines, known as 'the Matrix', which just as easily could have been called 'the Beast'. What humans believe to be everyday experience is a fabricated, virtual reality. Its henchmen, 'the Agents', act on the authority of the Matrix, performing signs and wonders on its behalf. Meanwhile, Morpheus leads a resistance movement, placing his hope in 'the One' who will free humanity of its enslavement to the illusion. When the chosen one morphs into his role, he appears wearing a long duster coat similar to ones worn by Clint Eastwood in films such as *Pale Rider*.[9]

In these films, the process of liberation begins when the Saviour arrives to defeat the symbolic order. The filmic Saviour is, to use Daniel Berrigan's analogy, 'the stick driven in the chariot spokes of empire'.[10] Just as the plagues in Exodus and John's Apocalypse are intended as a strike at the prevailing mythology, the Cinematic Savior reveals the dominant symbolic order is not divine and did not 'create the Nile'. The confrontation often is violent, as illustrated in films such as *Iron Man* (2008). The film opens with narcissistic weapons industrialist Tony Stark taken hostage by Afghan insurgents while Stark demonstrates the latest in war technology to American troops. Stark discovers the insurgents possess the weapons he invented to 'stabilize the peace'. The insurgents imprison Stark in a desert cave and order him to build sophisticated weaponry to their specifications. Stark feigns his way through the project and, instead, constructs a suit of armour outfitted with its own artillery to use in a dramatic escape. Returning to the United States, Stark publicly renders judgment on the military-industrial complex for its haughtiness, announcing plans to redirect his company's efforts to finding peaceable alternatives for its technology. He goes into seclusion and surreptitiously develops a more sophisticated version of his suit of armour, soon venturing to deliver an impoverished Afghan village from the grip of the insurgents who held him hostage. But Stark's attack on the military-industrial complex makes him a marked man, like somebody who has committed blasphemy. Stark's 'burning bush' experience and repentance (from 'Egyptian' to 'Hebrew') elicits ridicule from industry insiders who purport that Stark suffers from mental illness. His business partner conspires to construct an ironmonger suit of his own and kill Iron Man, thus destroying the blasphemer and his counter-myth.

Once the Saviour crosses the line and confronts the symbolic order, as he does in *Iron Man*, usually there is hell to pay. In these instances, the film's analogous relationship with biblical iconographies is rarely subtle. Superhero films in particular rely on the crucifixion motif. *Superman Returns* (2006) could have been titled *The Passion of Superman*. The film focuses on whether or not the world really needs Superman and includes a sequence in which Kal El is tortured by Lex Luthor, helplessly descending to the bottom of the ocean as he hears the voice of his Father, Jor El. *Spider-Man 2* (2004) focuses on the consequences of the hero's vocation. Peter Parker's vow to take up an impoverished life on behalf of the community has earned him mostly public derision, damaged his relationships, compromised his academic pursuits and even forced him to consider a vow of celibacy. When Parker decides that Spider-Man is better off in the trash, chaos ensues as a research scientist loses his wife in an experiment gone awry, developing the persona of Doctor Octopus. Parker re-embraces his alter ego and battles Doctor Octopus atop a runaway subway train. The sequence is layered with Christological symbols. During the mêlée, Spider-Man loses his mask, which in superhero vernacular is an ultimate humiliation. The unmasked hero then assumes a cruciform pose with the train at his back, as if Spider-Man is bearing the weight of the sins of his detractors. Once the fiasco is averted, the unmasked Spider-Man's lifeless body is found, and the witnesses to this crucifixion raise the hero above themselves, finally laying the body on the ground only to gape at it in astonishment. As Spider-Man regains consciousness, a child steps forward and presents Parker with his mask. The 'resurrected' Spider-Man returns to defeat 'the Beast' who is hurled into the sea like a millstone.[11]

Rarely does a film humiliate the Saviour and come to a grinding halt. In some instances, there will be the apocalyptic moment – the instant when the symbolic order learns its own claims about itself are not true.[12] Berrigan describes the defeat of the symbolic order as 'the toppling of thrones'.[13] The once colossal Beast is revealed to have feet of clay and is reduced to a parody of itself. In keeping with New Testament theology, the Saviour figure may return in justice and judgment. Although many film viewers reject a character as a Saviour figure because he or she wields a gun or dispenses destruction, Christopher Deacy argues that these heroes may be saviours precisely because they mete out judgment and destruction.[14] After all, in John's Apocalypse, Jesus is described to look like a warrior from *Lord of the Rings* (2001). It is appropriate that in *The Matrix* sequels, the 'resurrected' Neo's long, black duster coat looks more like a priestly robe, and his abilities have evolved.[15] Agent Smith, destroyed at the end of the first film, re-emerges as a grim parody of the resurrected Neo. He is the Beast whose mortal wound has been healed; Antichrist to Neo's Christ.[16] As the film's city of Zion falls under attack, Neo faces Agent Smith in a final decisive battle that concludes with a consummation of humanity and machine.

It seems fitting to reflect more intently on four films that feature a central character in an analogous relationship with Moses or Jesus, thus contributing to the communal conversation on spirituality. The films range from dark comedy to blockbuster superhero fare.

Fight Club (1999)

Fight Club lowers the Saviour figure into a dehumanizing dystopia of pervasive meaninglessness. The Beast is a capitalist cultural liturgy that indoctrinates the masses into embracing that the ideal human is the consumer, our greatest need is met in accumulation, and ultimate meaning is found in possessions. The film is narrated from the viewpoint of Jack, an insomniac who despises his job along with the sterile and bland existence he refers to as 'Planet Starbucks'. He spends his nights watching infomercials and browsing apartment furniture catalogues in the same way one might watch televised religion and read inspirational literature. As a last ditch effort in a desperate search for meaning, Jack finds a support group for men with testicular cancer. He finds the experience so emotionally cathartic that he begins frequenting support groups, feigning the corresponding illnesses to where the practice takes on an addictive quality. However, Jack regresses when he meets a mirror image of himself, a 'tourist' as he calls her. It is during a flight home from a business trip that Jack meets Tyler Durden, a self-described boutique soap manufacturer. The pair strike up a conversation and Tyler begins to suggest that Jack's despair is rooted in his inability to match the cultural definition of happiness. Jack returns home to discover that a fire in his apartment building has destroyed his trendy condo, along with all his belongings. Jack contacts Tyler, and the pair move into an abandoned, decaying house with no furniture and few possessions. Later, the film reveals that Tyler deliberately burned down the condo in order to initiate Jack's spiritual awakening. In other words, Jack's life does not properly begin until he renounces everything.[17]

Tyler then initiates a support group of his own called Fight Club, recruiting young men to engage in bare knuckle fistfights that leave them severely bruised and bloody. While the film began with support groups meeting in churches, Fight Club meets in the basement of a bar, where the gatherings take on characteristics of a church. Tyler in a pivotal monologue offers his sermon.

> I see in *Fight Club* the strongest and smartest men who have ever lived – an entire generation pumping gas and waiting tables; or they're slaves with white collars. Advertisements have them chasing cars and clothes, working jobs they hate so they can buy sh*t they don't need. We are the middle children of history, with no purpose or place. We have no Great War or Great Depression. Our great war is a spiritual war. Our Great Depression is our lives.

Tyler leads his followers to discover that negative emotions such as fear and horror, coupled with the passions of anger and rage, are the means to empower themselves to react against the Beast bleeding their souls dry.[18] In one of many symbolic acts, Tyler takes Jack to a convenience store, where Tyler manhandles the clerk at gunpoint, asking him, 'What did you really want to do with your life?' When the clerk responds that he wanted to be a veterinarian but dropped out of college, Tyler vows to return and kill him if he is not re-enrolled within six weeks. In the aftermath, he soliloquizes, 'Tomorrow will be the most beautiful day of his life'. Tyler is calling people to leave behind what causes them to feel so empty.

In keeping with the use of readily available religious symbols, there is a scene in *Fight Club* where the bar owner discovers the group meeting in his basement. Tyler invites him to 'join our club'. The exchange is suggestive of a narrative in the Synoptic gospels in which Jesus invites a man who has everything to 'sell all you have and follow me'. In mob-like fashion, the club owner responds to the offer by murderously humiliating and pummelling Tyler. He absorbs the blows in a cruciform pose, falls to the floor as if dead, then rises and washes his attacker in his own blood. Tyler then instructs his followers to 'go out' and follow his teachings. The support group gradually transforms from a gathering into a monastic order known as 'Project Mayhem' where Tyler's followers abandon all possessions, move into the dilapidated house and engage in several episodes of guerrilla street theatre aimed at collapsing the symbolic order: the destruction of corporate art, coordinating a torrent of bird excrement to fall on a lot of luxury cars and the demolition of credit card offices. The film's bizarre ending reveals that Tyler and Jack are the same character. Jack's need for meaning was so significant that he invented his own Saviour. Once Jack's transformation is complete, Tyler is 'sacrificed'.[19]

Donnie Darko (2001)

Initially ignored by mainstream audiences, *Donnie Darko* eventually gained cult appeal through a word of mouth following and the proverbial 'midnight showing'. The story revolves around a Virginia high school student given 28 days to save the people in his world when it is apparent there is little worth saving. Self-righteous villains and philosophical cheerleaders govern his world. Sane voices are ostracized. Donnie experiences a series of interrelated hallucinations and visits by Frank, a figure in a creepy rabbit costume, who tells Donnie the world soon will meet its demise. Frank the Rabbit's prophecy is part of a convoluted scenario revealed through a series of conversations and excerpts from a manuscript called *The Philosophy of Time Travel*. Early in the story, a jet engine falls from the sky and through Donnie's roof. According to Frank, the engine is an artefact from a parallel or tangent universe that travelled through a worm hole and fell into the Primary Universe, creating an unstable cosmos that will collapse in 28 days. Knowing the world is coming to an end, Donnie becomes somewhat of an apocalyptic prophet. The hallucination scenes and symbolic acts Donnie carries out on instruction from the voice he hears suggest parallels to the Prophet Ezekiel's engagement in bizarre and culturally vulgar behaviour.

Donnie stages two important public confrontations. His community has deified a self-empowerment guru, who sells motivational videos and speeches consisting of hackneyed phrases and banalities. After Donnie lampoons the triviality of this curriculum being introduced into one of his classes, he is banned from school activities. His mother is lectured by the teacher on how her son should 'follow the path of righteousness'. But Donnie soon gains an audience with the celebrated motivational speaker at a school assembly. Donnie walks over to a microphone, offers an indictment ('you're the f***ing anti-Christ'), and is forcibly escorted from the building. Shortly thereafter, again obeying Frank's voice, Donnie is led to the home of the self-empowerment specialist and told to burn it to the ground. The following day, investigators discover the owner was the head of a child pornography ring.

Once the Saviour figure in *Donnie Darko* dismantles the symbolic order, he turns his attention to the realigning of the universe, which ultimately will involve a sacrificial death on his part. Donnie is the lone figure who can guide the artefact – the jet engine – through a wormhole, thus restoring the world to its proper balance. To foreshadow the choice he faces, Donnie is pictured exiting a theatre showing *The Last Temptation of Christ* (1988). He laments to his psychiatrist that he is afraid to die alone, but peacefully retreats to his bedroom on the night of his impending death. The artefact is guided through a wormhole and crashes through Donnie's roof, killing him. As the song *Mad World* plays in the closing moments of the film, the camera captures many figures affected by Donnie Darko's actions – the teacher who spoke of the righteous path wakes from her sleep with a horrified expression, and the self-empowerment specialist weeps alone in his home. In the end, they carry a piece of what happened in Donnie Darko's alternate universe in the story.

Lars and the Real Girl (2007)

An illustration of how the Saviour figure cannot be confined to one type of character (a notion problematic to some viewers)[20] is found in *Lars and the Real Girl*. Like *Fight Club*, the film features a state of existence that necessitates the imagined saviour. Lars Lindstrom is 27, unmarried and lives in a garage behind his brother's house. The character's unspecified mental illness makes human interaction a source of tremendous anxiety. He holds an office job and attends church, but manages to avoid meaningful social interface. Lars cannot relate to Margo, who seeks a relationship with him, nor can he relate to his brother and sister-in-law, who literally must tackle Lars in the driveway to invite him to dinner. It is clear that the brothers have a distant relationship, which somehow relates to their deceased parents.

One day a delivery truck leaves a wooden crate in Lars' driveway. Arriving home, he shoves the crate into his living room, changes clothes and preens in the mirror as if going on a date. He visits his brother, announcing he is bringing over a girl he met online. Lars' girlfriend turns out to be an anatomically correct love doll, purchased online at the recommendation of a co-worker (though not for its intended purpose). Lars has invented a complete back story for his companion. 'Bianca', he explains, is a former South American missionary raised in a convent. Realizing the severity of Lars' problems, the family seeks professional help, coaxing Lars by suggesting that perhaps Bianca would like to have a routine exam. The attending physician explains that Bianca is 'a delusion he has created for himself' as a mechanism for working through his abandonment issues, and advises the family to go along. Knowing that Lars will insist on escorting Bianca to church, the couple meets with several parish leaders. Of course, one man cries 'golden calf'. A female parishioner counters by stating that everyone has their own neurosis, and the minister asks them to consider how Jesus would relate to the situation. Lars arrives to worship with Bianca, prompting others to gape in disbelief while one man 'rescues' his child from engaging with the couple. But a few women risk exclusion, presenting Bianca with gifts as if anointing her for the Saviour role.

Gradually, everyone begins to act as if Bianca is real. She is invited to social events, scheduled to volunteer and given a makeover. Bianca the sex doll progressively enables Lars to form relationships with others. But Lars soon begins to insist that Bianca needs medical attention, informing the physician that she has a weak heart. The physician plays along, and Bianca's condition worsens. After going bowling with Margo one night, Lars again insists that Bianca is ill, prompting a hospital visit. Bianca again is brought home and Lars takes her to a pond where he holds her in his arms in a *Pietà*-like manner, declaring that she is dead. A funeral is held for the community to mourn Bianca, with Lars insisting that nobody wear black clothing. In the closing scene, Lars and Margo meet at the grave, where he asks her if she would like to go on a walk.

The Dark Knight (2008)

The Dark Knight is best understood in relation to its predecessor, *Batman Begins* (2005), which hinted that the Batman's advent in Gotham City could lead to an escalation in destructive lunacy. The film introduces the Joker as an evolutionary consequence of the Batman, who is wanted by the police for his vigilantism. When the Gotham mafia's accountant flees to Hong Kong to avoid testifying against the mob, Batman travels to Hong Kong, abducts him and brings the accountant back to the United States for prosecution. The mob, in desperation, hires a bank robber known only for his bizarre theatrics to kill the Batman for them. The Joker sends a video file to the news media promising that if the Batman does not turn himself in to the police, 'people will die'. The Joker's initial murders make it clear that he is targeting high profile public officials, and his exploits grow increasingly outlandish. One film reviewer said of the character, 'He turns slaughter into a punch line; he's a homicidal comedian with an audience of one – himself'.[21] Revelling in the anarchy he has instigated, the Joker finds he cannot kill the Batman, confessing that 'a world without Batman' would cause his criminality to revert back to being petty and meaningless. The Joker insists the two are doppelgangers 'destined to do this forever'. When an employee for Wayne Enterprises appears on television to disclose his theory as to the identity of the Batman, the Joker makes an on-air declaration: if a member of the public does not murder the informant that afternoon, he will bomb a local hospital of his choosing.

Describing himself not as a madman but simply as 'ahead of the curve', the Joker conducts a number of 'social experiments' to prove that everyone is as deranged as he is. Film essayist Maurice Broadus suggests the Joker's attempt to bring about the moral collapse of District Attorney Harvey Dent (Aaron

Eckhart) is a parallel to the Hebrew Bible's story of Job.[22] The Joker, like the Accuser in Job, wagers that Dent's ideals are a matter of convenience that will fall by the wayside if he has a bad enough day.[23] The self-described 'agent of chaos' devises a plan to kidnap Dent and his assistant, D. A. Rachel Dawes, to whom Dent has proposed marriage. Both are placed in warehouses rigged with explosives at opposite ends of the city. The Batman speeds off to save Dawes, unaware that the Joker wittingly has led him to Dent. But, Commissioner Jim Gordon's unit does not arrive in time to save Dawes, and she is killed in the explosion. The Batman manages to save Dent's life, but explosions during the escape leave one side of Dent's face horribly burned. As it turns out, the Joker was correct about Gotham's 'white knight'. Dent becomes 'Harvey Two Face' and seeks vengeance on the system that failed him.

Throughout the film the hysterical public vilifies the Dark Knight, blaming him for inspiring the Joker's madness. When it appears that Gordon has been killed by the Joker, his widow screams at the Batman: 'You brought this craziness on us!' During an intense scene in which the Batman interrogates the Joker, the clown fiend remarks, 'To (the police), you're just a freak, like me. When they don't need you, they will cast you out like a leper'. The words prove prophetic. In the closing scene, Harvey Two Face holds Gordon, along with his wife and children, hostage at the place where Dawes died. Two Face obviously intends to murder Gordon's son in retribution for his unit failing to reach the woman he loved in time. The Batman arrives to save Gordon and his family, and Two Face falls to his death. In the aftermath, Gordon laments that the city will lose all hope when residents discover the Joker's wager was correct – Dent had one bad day and became a murderer. The Batman responds that people must never know of the fall of their white knight. The Accuser cannot prevail – so the Batman does the unthinkable. The Batman proclaims he will bear the weight of Harvey Two Face's sins. 'I'm not a hero. I killed those people. Hunt me. Condemn me. It's what needs to happen.' he says. 'Those people deserve to have their faith rewarded.' In the words of the Prophet Isaiah, the Batman is 'wounded for our transgressions, crushed for our iniquities; upon him was the punishment that made us whole, and by his bruises we are healed'. The Bat-signal is smashed with an axe. The Cinematic Savior initiates his own humiliation narrative in order to defeat the agent of chaos.

Conclusion

A common critique of epics that attempt to present Jesus or Moses 'as he was', such as *The Passion of the Christ* (2004), is that the genre presents a story meaningful to those already familiar with it, but typically fails to convey the significance of the story for the contemporary audience.[24] To paraphrase Taylor: in a post-secular world, biblical epics often seem disconnected from life and weighed down with concepts that no longer resonate.[25] On the other hand, transplanting Christological or Mosaic reference points into other genres makes the concepts more accessible. The process also allows filmmakers and viewers greater interpretive freedom. Because filmmakers are not bound to canonical tradition, the Cinematic Savior can be, as Humphries-Brooks put it, 'refashioned' in direct response to contemporary anxieties.[26] The filmic Savior truly can reflect the times in which we live. Film may not have entirely replaced synagogue and church as a mediator of Moses' or Jesus' image in our imaginations and faith, but it unquestionably has affected the conversation.

26 Karma and Film

Michele Marie Desmarais

Scholars of Indian drama often maintain that the category of tragedy does not exist due to the doctrine of karma. The word 'karma' means 'action'.[1] In Hinduism and Buddhism it refers, primarily, to a doctrine of cause and effect, or action (karma) and the fruit or results of action (karma, *karma-phala*).[2] Implicit in this understanding is a belief in rebirth (*punar-janman*) and the conviction that it is possible for a person to overcome or burn off karma in order to eventually attain liberation (*mokṣa, nirvāṇa*). While Indian films regularly employ karma as a primary or secondary theme, some non-Indian films, particularly super-hero and disaster movies, can be viewed as revealing the workings of karma.

'Karma' derives from the root *kṛ* 'do, make, act' (Monier-Williams). One of the earliest *Upaniṣads*, the *Bṛhadāraṇyaka Upaniṣad* (BU), explains that a person's actions and conduct lead to what he or she becomes, 'Doing good, one becomes good; doing evil, one becomes evil'.[3] Physical actions themselves are not the only concern though. Inner qualities such as motivation, and particularly desire and attachment, lead to karma – in the sense of consequences – as well.[4] Although this understanding of karma need not include belief in past and future lives, an explanation of rebirth precedes the discussion on karma, with karma determining the next type or form of birth.[5]

Beyond such generalities, the workings of karma are complex. According to the *Yoga-sūtra* (YS), the aggregate accumulation of karma determines a person's birth (i.e., what one is), life and worldly experience.[6] The main commentary on the YS, the *Yoga-bhāṣya* (YBh), states that while some karma ripens in a current lifetime, other karma carries over to another life.[7] Furthermore, the connection between an act and its consequence is not necessarily automatic or mechanistic. A person can normally mitigate or make up for past action, although this may sometimes be difficult since karma may lie in an unmanifest state until an appropriate external object or event (the instrumental cause) leads to the fruition of karma. Consequently, determining any one-to-one relationship between an act and its effect is largely impossible.[8]

Although it is common to view karma retrospectively, such as 'I must have been *x* in the past because *y* is happening now', this perspective alone is too fatalistic. The Indian tradition, whether Hindu, Buddhist or Jain (and each presents a slightly different view of karma and rebirth), maintains that it is crucial that we pay attention to what we are feeling, thinking and doing now, because all of these will have consequences in the future. Rather than being fatalistic, the Indian tradition is fundamentally optimistic and prospective, giving us control and choice over the future. The doctrine of karma therefore functions like an alarm clock, awakening us to future consequences and possibilities.

In the early *Upaniṣads* and later tradition, the ultimate goal or best choice that we can make is to be free from desires completely, as desire is the first in the chain of desire, resolve, action, attachment and consequence.[9] Such freedom from desire and its consequences leads to *mokṣa* (liberation).[10] Additionally, the *Bhagavad-Gītā* (*Gītā*) recommends the performance of one's *dharma* (duty) with equanimity or as an act of devotion.[11] In the Hindu tradition, *dharma* is in accordance with social class (*varṇa*) and stage of life.[12] Violation or refusal to do one's *dharma* results not only in demerit or 'bad karma', but also in chaos (*adharma*).

Thus the doctrine of karma, although fundamentally a law of cause and effect, also encompasses ideas about rebirth, traits, life experiences, triggering or instrumental causes, mitigating acts and the proper (or improper) performance of duty. Therefore, films that explore themes such as misbehaviour and its consequences and/or the overcoming of difficult life situations can provide useful illustrations of this central doctrine.

In director Arjun Sajnani's 2002 film *Agni Varsha* (*Fire and Rain*), each character fails to uphold *dharma* and suffers from the fruition of karma as a result. The film is based on the play of the same name by Girish Karnad, which in turn is based on a brief episode from the *Mahābhārata*, the great Indian epic on karma and *dharma*.[13] In the film, only one character, the protagonist Arvasu eventually transcends suffering and self-interest to finally do what is just.

The film opens as the people and land suffer from the effects of ten years of drought. A *brahmin*, Paravasu has stayed away from his wife for the previous seven years as he leads a fire sacrifice for the *deva* (God) Indra, who has power over the rains. In contrast, his brother Arvasu does not take part in the sacrifice, but rather wants to become an actor and also wants to marry a beautiful young tribal woman, Nittilai. Arvasu's decisions to pursue a career not deemed suitable for a *brahmin* and to marry outside his *varṇa* (social class) scandalize his brother and his father, the great sage Raibhya. Although he is a sage, Raibhya is attracted to Paravasu's wife Vishakha. Vishakha, in turn, was in love with Paravasu's cousin Yavakri, however Yavakri left her ten years earlier in order to carry out ascetic practices, and so she married the self-righteous Paravasu instead.

Each character succumbs to passion, self-interest and karmic consequences once Yavakri returns to the village. He and Vishakha make love, but the constantly suspicious Raibhya finds out and sends a demon to kill Yavakri. This murder delays Arvasu from meeting the elders of Nittilai's village and she is married to someone else instead. Paravasu makes an unexpected visit home to find his wife threatened by his father and he kills Raibhya. Paravasu returns to the fire sacrifice and blames his father's death on Arvasu, who is badly beaten. Nittilai leaves her husband to nurse Arvasu, thus rekindling their illicit love. At the climax of the film, Nittilai's husband kills her while she tries to protect Arvasu, who is giving an inspired performance in a drama that is taking place near the sacrifice. Paravasu admits his guilt and failures and performs a final act of self-immolation in the sacrificial fire, and Arvasu, bereft, tries to sacrifice himself as well.

In *Agni Varsha*, passion and attachment dominate each character. The extreme nature of their actions leads to the ripening of karma in the present rather than the future. There is a moment of transcendence at the end of the movie though, when Indra appears and tells Arvasu that he is pleased by Arvasu's performance, Nittilai's humanity and Paravasu's sacrifice. As a result, Indra gives Arvasu the choice of a boon. Arvasu knows that Nittilai would choose rain for the drought-stricken country, but he wants Indra to restore her to life instead. Indra questions this decision to turn back time, 'Won't the tragedy just repeat itself? Everyone will have to endure the same suffering all over again'. This reinforces the perspective that karma ultimately results in a person being trapped in a continuing cycle of birth, death and rebirth (*saṃsāra*).

Although Arvasu believes that he has learned enough to prevent the repetition of suffering, he still allows self-interest in the form of his love for Nittilai to dominate his decision. At this point, the demon conjured up by Raibhya appears and pleads with Arvasu to use the boon to secure *mukti*, release or liberation, for the demon. The demon reminds Arvasu that it was through Raibhya's actions that he was called into his tormented existence and also insists that Nittilai herself would care about him. The demon asks Arvasu, 'Would she want my soul to be damned, so that she can live?' Knowing that Nittilai would choose liberation for the demon, Arvasu finally rises above self-interest and the consequences of his family's actions, and chooses *mukti* for the demon as his boon. Indra, pleased, not only grants the demon *mukti*, but also brings the ten year drought to an end by unleashing the rain. Arvasu's karma is, quite literally, wiped clean.

Unlike Arvasu's character in *Agni Varsha*, the film *Devdas* reveals the consequences for the protagonist of failure to uphold either *dharma* or love. In India, *Devdas* has had enough resonance that there are several re-makes. P. C. Barua's Hindi/Bengali version (1935) inspired Bimal Roy's Hindi remake in 1955.[14] The most recent (2002) version by director Sanjay Leela

Bhansali features Bollywood superstars Shah Rukh Khan as Devdas, Aishwarya Rai as Parvati (Paro) and Madhuri Dixit as the courtesan Chandramukhi.[15]

Devdas and Paro are childhood sweethearts who, reunited after a separation once they are grown, fall deeply in love again. These early love scenes within the context of the village environment recall the divine love between Kṛṣṇa and Rādhā. The idyllic relationship changes when Devdas' father forbids Devdas from marrying Paro, who belongs to a lower social class. Unwilling to either elope with Paro, or to comply with his father's wishes and marry someone who has the family's approval, Devdas leaves the village for city life, where he indulges in drinking and attracts the devotion of courtesan Chandramukhi. Paro, in the meantime, marries a rich widower. Devdas eventually leaves the city for a last train ride through India. At the end of the journey, he takes a fatal dose of alcohol and lives just long enough to die at the front of the unhappy Paro's house.

Some view the films and the novel of *Devdas* as representing the difficulties of village feudalism along with the dangers of modernity or city life.[16] It is possible though to view the character Devdas as a cautionary figure. Rather than upholding his *dharma* as a son and a member of his social class, rather than navigating the difficult path of reconciling romantic love and tradition,[17] Devdas tries to run away, to literally drown his sorrows with alcohol and shallow sensuality. The *Gītā*, in cautioning against a lack of discipline, provides a fitting summary of the latter stages of Devdas' life:

> Brooding about sensuous objects
> makes attachment to them grow;
> from attachment desire arises,
> from desire anger is born.
>
> From anger comes confusion;
> from confusion memory lapses;
> from broken memory understanding is lost;
> from loss of understanding, he is ruined.[18]

Devdas, unlike Arvasu, ultimately fails to transcend his own self-interest and attachment. All the unfortunate consequences that befall each of the characters are a result of these flaws. A westerner may classify the film as a tragedy, but *Devdas* illustrates, albeit in a negative way, the integral connection of one's inner life of desires, thoughts and attachments with one's actions and the consequences of action in the form of karma.

Swadeś: We the People (2004) explores karma on individual and collective levels. The movie is aimed at the NRI (non-resident Indian) audience and follows Mohan Bhargav, a successful NRI who returns for a visit to his home country (*sva-deśa*). Once he is in India, Mohan's conscience and sense of individual duty and loyalty expand to an awareness of his duty to, and deep love for, his country.

Swadeś begins at Kennedy Space Center in Florida, where Mohan works as an engineer and project leader. Although he is wealthy and fortunate enough to receive American citizenship, Mohan is melancholic. His parents are deceased and he feels guilty about losing touch with Kaveri-amma, the woman who helped to raise him.[19] Determined to make amends and care for the elderly Kaveri, Mohan decides to take two weeks off of work to go to India, find Kaveri and return to the United States with her.

Mohan finds Kaveri living in a small traditional village in India. Kaveri is taking care of Gita, a young woman who runs the village school, and her brother. Mohan and Gita used to play together as children, but in the intervening years Mohan moved to America while Gita lost her parents and took over running their village school. Passionately devoted to educating the village children, Gita scolds and challenges Mohan regarding his knowledge of, and commitment to, India. Mohan falls in love both with Gita and village life. He encourages village people, regardless of their social class or wealth, to educate their boys and girls. Mohan also uses his engineering skills to bring electricity to the village. Despite all of this, Mohan sadly leaves Gita and Kaveri, who both refuse to move to America, and returns to his job in the States. In the end though, Mohan's sense of love and duty for family, friends, the village and India, bring him back to live in the village.

Swadeś is an interesting movie for while it upholds the traditional values of care for elderly family members and service to others, it also advocates more recent ideas such as education for all, love matches and the leadership of women.[20] Regarding karma, at the beginning of the movie Mohan, despite having great success and wealth, suffers emotionally from the consequences of leaving homeland and the only family that he has. Undoubtedly many NRIs will identify with this difficult situation. Overcoming his own opinions and agenda to experience village life in India helps Mohan transcend his guilt as well as any attachment to the modern 'successful' western lifestyle. His service and love at the end of the film reveal a strong sense of *dharma* and generosity of spirit. While *Swadeś* follows this individual character through his journeys, the issue of collective duty to country – along with the consequences of abandoning this duty – is a strong theme in the film.

The doctrine of karma is found in many Indian movies. Almost any version of the *Mahābhārata* will, by necessity, address karma and *dharma*. However, Peter Brook's multicultural version (*Mahabharata*, 1989) may be the most accessible to a non-Indian audience. Similarly, Mira Nair's *Monsoon Wedding* (2001) is an enjoyable and accessible introduction to Indian society and, in a secondary way, the idea of karma. Deepa Mehta's *Water* (2005), while controversial, nevertheless shows characters struggling with their own ideas of karma, *dharma*, fate and devotion. Finally, *Krrish* (2006) is a light-hearted film centred on a super-hero type character learning to balance duty and power while reconciling with the past.[21]

Indian films are not the only ones to provide us with examples of the workings of karma. *Groundhog Day* (1993) is a comedic but accurate look at *saṃsāra*, karma and *mokṣa*. *Saṃsāra* is the circuit or cycle of mundane existence, that is, the cycle of birth, death and rebirth. The term literally means 'going, or wandering through', in the sense of 'passing through a succession of states'.[22]

In *Groundhog Day*, a cranky weatherman Phil Connors, Rita, his producer and a cameraman travel to Punxsutawney, Pennsylvania for the annual Groundhog Day celebration. The cynical Connors mistreats everyone around him and suffers a whole series of minor annoyances. A blizzard forces him and his team to remain overnight in Punxsutawney. At 6 a.m. the next morning, Connors awakens to slowly realize that it is Groundhog Day again. As the cycle repeats itself each morning, Connors' reactions range from suspicion to panic and then to despair and fatalism. Finally, realizing that his knowledge of what will happen could be useful, Connors begins to take advantage of the situation to help other people and to learn new skills. He also falls in love and woos Rita. After many repetitions through the cycles, Connors breaks free of February 2 through his selfless love for Rita and kind acts on behalf of others.

Thus early in the film, Connors displays the consequences of negative acts and their fruition. Later in the film he acquires knowledge, performs good acts and eventually transcends his own self-interest through love. These latter qualities and actions, which eventually liberate him from the cycle in which he is stuck, parallel, albeit in a secular way, the *tri-margas* (three paths) to *mokṣa* in the *Gītā*.[23] *Jñāna-marga*, the path of knowledge, involves a correct understanding of the nature of self, the world and reality. *Karma-marga*, the path of action, requires proper performance of action (i.e. the performance of one's *dharma*) without attachment to the results. *Bhakti-marga*, the path of devotion, is the surrender and devotion to something greater than oneself.[24]

On a psychological level, the doctrine of karma helps people to view the universe as a just place where everyone ultimately gets what they deserve. Disaster movies tend to present characters and events in a similar manner. The protagonists must overcome some personal obstacles and work together in an effort to survive disaster(s). There are also usually one or more characters, operating only out of selfish motives, who end up dying. The movies commonly conclude with a sunrise, the end of a storm, or some other visual equivalent of purity and new beginning.

Twister (1996) is a good example of how the doctrine of karma can be used to analyse disaster movies. In the movie, Jo Harding and Bill Harding are meteorologists who specialize in the study of tornadoes. They once shared a volatile marriage and a passion for fieldwork, but now Bill is seeking a divorce and has become a weatherman. He joins Jo in the field in order to have her sign the divorce papers, but the test of an instrument they designed to collect data on tornadoes, along with a series of tornado touchdowns, results in the two renewing their commitment to each other and to the study of tornadoes.

Of the characters in the movie, Jo illustrates most clearly the effects of karma inherited from the past. Her father was killed by a tornado when she was a little girl and her interest in tornadoes consequently borders on obsession. She takes unnecessary risks because of this and after one danger-ous encounter with a tornado, Bill yells at her, 'Killing yourself won't bring your dad back!' Jo has also failed to move on with her life after the collapse of her marriage. Bill is perhaps less affected by events of the past, but his combined antipathy-attraction to Jo and her work shows that his new relationship and job are not what he should be doing in life. As a gifted scientist, his talents are better used in conjunction with Jo's to study tornadoes in order to be able to warn people about oncoming tornadoes and therefore save lives. As both characters overcome the karma of their past and work for a common cause, they attain love. The film ends with the two kissing, blue skies after storms and joy from their crew who have collected valuable data.

In contrast to Jo and Bill, the antagonist in *Twister*, Jonas Miller, is a storm chaser 'for the money, not the science'. He stole the design of his instrument for collecting data from the Hardings. Beyond this, he fails to help the Hard-ings and their crew when they need assistance after a clash with a tornado. Miller's love of media attention prompts Jo to comment, 'he really is in love with himself'. Remarkably, and to their credit, the Hardings overcome their own antipathy towards Miller and try to share their knowledge with him to help his own tests succeed. They also try, and fail, to save his life. As an arrogant, narcissistic, callous thief, Miller's death in the movie comes as a consequence of his actions and as no real surprise to the viewer. The ant-agonist's death, as in most disaster movies, is largely un-grieved because of the sense that it is a justified consequence of actions and attitudes. The ability of the protagonists to overlook or forgive the flaws of the antagonist only adds to their merit. Thus the relatively simple plot lines and stock characters of disaster movies such as *Twister* result in uncomplicated examples of how karma works. They also show the function of karma in satisfying the human need for an orderly and just universe. In this respect, *Dante's Peak* (1997) follows a plotline similar to *Twister*, although in this case the disaster involves a volcano.

Some movies, in addition to addressing personal karma, also reveal the consequences of collective greed, ambition or neglect through some human-caused disaster. *The Towering Inferno* (1974) is an early example of such a movie, while *Outbreak* (1995) and *The Day After Tomorrow* (2004) are more recent explorations of similar themes in different contexts.[25] Finally, almost any movie version of the Titanic disaster will have some relevance for karma and transcendence.

Along with disaster movies, we can use the doctrine of karma to interpret superhero movies such as *Spider-Man* and *Iron Man*. Superhero movies usually begin with a weak or otherwise flawed main character. This character often has an unfortunate past, even if he is wealthy.[26] There is, for example, a preponderance of orphans in superhero stories. Understandably, the protagonist is focused almost exclusively on himself in such circumstances. An accident then tends to be the cause of the main character's attainment of super powers. At first the protagonist uses these powers to gain money, fame or some similar advantage, but eventually he learns to overcome his past and self-centred orientation in order to use the powers for the benefit of good people. Using the conceptual framework of karma, the superhero progresses from a selfish person overwhelmed or embittered by past circumstances (karma), to a powerful person who is tempted to act only for the benefit of self rather than duty (in the Indian tradition, *dharma*). Finally, the superhero transcends self and past and, by acting without regard for self or the benefits of his actions, he attains, perhaps not liberation, but a form of equanimity in his commitment to work for the benefit of all.

The dominant theme of *Spider-Man* is, 'With great power comes great responsibility', and this theme holds true for superhero movies in general. In the film *Spider-Man*,[27] Peter Parker, an orphan, lives with his good, but working-class poor, aunt and uncle. Bullied at school and unable to win the affection of his pretty neighbour Mary Jane, Parker is delighted when he acquires extraordinary powers through an accidental bite by a genetically modified spider. Parker tries to raise money for a car to impress Mary Jane by winning a commercial wrestling match, but in the process of doing so, he lies about his activities to his uncle. Subsequently, his uncle is murdered by a criminal that Parker failed to stop. This represents the moment when Parker realizes that he must use his powers to protect others, even if that means endangering himself or foregoing the love of Mary Jane in order to protect her from enemies. Thus, much like Arjuna at the end of the *Gītā*, Parker learns to fulfill his duty and to perform necessary action without attachment.[28] Furthermore, by acting on behalf of something greater than himself, Parker attains some peace and release from his guilt over his uncle's death.

Unlike Parker's straitened circumstances, Tony Stark is an arrogant, spoiled millionaire at the beginning of *Iron Man*.[29] In some ways, his karma is both personal, particularly in terms of his attitude and treatment of others, and familial, as his inherited wealth comes from the largely indiscriminate sale of weapons.[30] Stark's life changes when he is seriously injured and taken captive in Afghanistan. Forced by his captors to create a devastating new weapon, he instead builds an armoured suit and becomes Iron Man. Stark's callousness and greed begin to crumble as he comes to know, though ultimately fails to save, Yinsen, a kind scientist who is his co-captive. Furthermore, Stark begins to realize (and care about) the effects of his technology on innocent people. As a result, his refusal to allow Stark Industries to manufacture weapons of destruction antagonizes Stark's paternalistic partner Obadiah Stane. Stark then learns of Stane's cruel disregard for anything other than wealth and power. Confronted with evil, Stark uses his resources – a brilliant mind, wealth, technology and the courage of good friends – to overcome Stane and the terrorists who traded with him. In effect, in a situation dominated by chaos or lawlessness (*adharma*) and suffering, Stark fights to restore order (*dharma*). Returning again to the *Gītā*, in this sense Stark acts both as the warrior Arjuna, and the restorer of *dharma*, Kṛṣṇa. Despite the violence apparent in *Iron Man* and the battlefield setting of the *Gītā*, we can view both film and epic poem as advocating not violence itself, but rather the necessity to overcome ignorance, suffering and selfish action. This, is the true battle. We can employ the same interpretive strategy for the *Batman*, *X-men* and *Fantastic Four* movies and their sequels. *The Shadow* (1994), in addition, contains some references to Tibetan Buddhism and control of the mind.

Thus although Indian movies provide us with a chance to explore the doctrine of karma within its cultural context, some popular movies made in the West can also reveal themes related to karma. We can use karma as an interpretive device for any movie that emphasizes the consequences of action, the need to fulfill duty, the temptation to succumb to self-interest and the subsequent transcendence of selfish motives and actions in order to benefit others. In this respect, popular films such as disaster movies or superhero movies are particularly valuable due to their clearly delineated characters, uncomplicated plotlines, and presentation of an ultimately just world.

27 The End of Days

Conrad E. Ostwalt

A decade ago, people around the world anxiously watched Y2K approach, arrive and exit largely without incident. While the event itself was a non-event, the anticipation surrounding it created uncertainty and sometimes fear. From the mundane (how will my computer react?), to the dangerous (will airplanes fall from the sky?), to the catastrophic (will a worldwide depression ensue?), to the horrific (will the year 2000 usher in the 'End of Days?'), people awaited the date with a mixture of curiosity, anxiety, and, sometimes, religious expectation. And while the end of the second millennium was a special time marker, similar phenomena occurred in the West throughout the ancient, Medieval, and modern worlds. The end of centuries and the two millennia since the birth and death of Christ have been marked with significance, sometimes by anticipations of the end of things. Even in secular history and discourse, modern westerners coined a phrase to mark attributes of western society at the end of the nineteenth century and beginning of the twentieth. The dawn of the twentieth century became fin de siècle society, as if somehow the placement of culture in time affected the character of society.

While centuries and millennia might heighten our awareness of the looming future 'End of Days', human beings in general are fascinated, and perhaps terrified, with the idea of the end of existence as we know it. The abstraction of the 'End of Days' exists in literature, popular culture, religious apocalypticism, and, yes, in the movies. When it comes to popular film, there is no shortage of movies that explore the possibility of our world coming to an end. Some of these movies are religious in character, so the connection between religion and film is obvious. Such films as *Left Behind* (2000) not only have an obvious religious content, but they also are made to dramatize a particular religious ideology about the end, in this case pre-millennial dispensationalism. Films such as *The Seventh Sign* (1988) or *The Rapture* (1991) are based upon religious traditions, language and images but are not necessarily promoting a particular tradition's theology. Rather, these films use religion as the entrée into exploration of religion and its relation to belief about the 'End of Days'. With films like these, the relationship between religion and film around the theme of the end is apparent and gives rise to discussion about religious belief, religious radicalism, and even religious truth. Yet, there are also a host of films about the 'End of Days' that seem to have nothing to do with religion such as *12 Monkeys* (1995), *Cloverfield* (2008), *Sunshine* (2007) and even *An Inconvenient Truth* (2006). However, I believe that these films should also be considered in an examination of religion and film because while they might not be *about* religion's theories or beliefs about the end, they *function religiously* in our culture when it comes to beliefs about the end. Thus, it is important to *define* what it means to be an 'End of Days' film by identifying the *characteristics* and *genre* of such films. With this foundation, this essay more fully develops what it means to be an 'End of Days' film by exploring how these films *function* in our popular culture. Thus, this article explores a two-part definition of 'End of Days' films based on characteristics and function, and the reason being that in both characteristic and purpose, these films function in our popular culture religiously.[1]

For the purposes of this discussion, 'End of Days' movies are movies that deal with the prospect of the annihilation of humanity, the world, or civilization wrought by a source more powerful (or seemingly so) than humanity. Some commentators attempt classification by the agent of destruction. For example, is the agent God or some other supernatural force (*Left Behind*, 2000; *Left Behind: World at War*, 2005; *The Omega Code*, 1999; *Megiddo: The Omega Code 2*, 2001), nuclear disaster (*Dr. Strangelove*, 1964; *The Day After*, 1983), alien invaders (*Independence Day*, 1996; *War of the Worlds*, 1953/2005), environmental collapse (*An Inconvenient Truth* and *Waterworld*, 1995), disease or mutation (*12 Monkeys* and *I Am Legend*, 2007), or some other natural catastrophe (*Armageddon*, 1998; *Deep Impact*, 1998; *Sunshine*). While such a typology based on agency might be helpful, it misses the crucial element for a discussion on religion and film. The crucial element is that humanity faces a situation of annihilation by a more powerful force. This reminds humanity of the reality of its contingent situation, its existential fragility, in the face of something more powerful, whether natural, human produced or supernatural. The 'End of Days' scenario is necessarily based on human contingency in relation to a more powerful or ultimate 'Other'. This contingent situation in and of itself is the religious existential quandary. One of the curious items about films with 'End of Days' characteristics is that humanity almost always defies the odds and survives in some fashion.[2] This seems true to a degree even in the films with a supernatural element as the 'Other' (*The Seventh Sign*, *Left Behind*). So, 'End of Days' movies, by definition, are those films that dramatize the existential religious condition for humankind of contingency in the presence of 'otherness' and that carry the threat of annihilation. One might also add that since most of these movies end with deliverance from destruction (often due to human effort), that the religious category of deliverance and redemption are a central element to the plots. These films are replete with religious themes and categories of contingency, apocalypse, and redemption, and one might add that they are exercises in confronting Fear with Hope.

'End of Days' films can also be examined in relation to religion based on their type or genre. Again, many commentators tend to categorize such films based on genres and subgenres: science fiction, zombie films, nuclear disaster films, fantasy films, etc. A simple typology will suffice. By definition, all 'End of Days' films fall into the 'fantasy' genre. 'End of Days' films operate on the assumption of extrapolation – they are based on the 'what if' question: What if global warming continues? What if aliens attack? What if a virulent disease agent mutates and spreads? What if God initiates the apocalypse? With 'End of Days' films, one should not get sidetracked debating the 'truth' of a film – Is the series of events depicted in *Left Behind* the truth as outlined in the Bible? Does Al Gore speak the truth of science in *An Inconvenient Truth*? Rather, the film critic and religious studies critic must start with the assumption that all these films are fantasy films based on extrapolation. It is this extrapolation itself that makes fantasy religiously significant, because religion is born with the great 'what if' questions. According to some theories about religion, (particularly psychological theories), belief in transcendence is an answer to the great 'what if' question of humanity, the question of alienation, and the horror of existential aloneness. Religion, like fantasy, proceeds into the realm of the transcendent, the unknown beyond, rather than the realm of the imma-nent and known. Fantasy film and religious questioning are partners of a kind in exploring the great 'what if' questions. And it is this 'what if' functioning of both religion and fantasy film that leads to the main point of this essay: 'End of Days' films function religiously to bring meaning to existential and religious questions of life. Ultimately, the question is: 'Is life meaningful given its seemingly contingent and temporary nature?' or 'Can temporality bear forth truth and meaning?'

When dealing with religion, film and 'End of Days' films, because of the wide variety of types and topics represented by this genre, it is probably best to pursue a functional definition of religion. To keep from getting bogged down in questions about truthfulness and factualness, we can avoid questions concerning whether or not a particular film represents some religious truth (as, for example, the *Left Behind* films are meant to do) or even a scientific truth (as, e.g., *An Inconvenient Truth* is meant to do). While these questions are fascinating, they are unproductive and take us away from the intersection of religion and film into other realms of inquiry such as theology and science. To avoid this pitfall, a functional definition of religion can provide a productive means for exploring how religion and film interact in culture. Functional definitions require us to ask how religions, beliefs and films function in the lives of individuals and cultures. Such a question applied to 'End of Days' films reveals that such films almost always function religiously in that they respond to the religious questions concerning finitude. 'End of Days' films in contemporary culture help humans cope with existential horror, with the possibility of alienation and non-existence. 'End of Days' films bring the viewer face-to-face with temporal contingency and potential non-existence, and like so many other aspects of cultural and political context, help one deal with powerlessness. Different films do this in different ways: traditional religious films (e.g., *Left Behind*, *The Omega Code*) give meaning by positing a divine context; others (e.g., *I Am Legend*, *Armageddon*) do this by celebrating the efforts and abilities of humanity. In fact, many contemporary 'End of Days' films rely on a plot that has humanity avoiding the end altogether. Heroes bond together to defeat the threat and humanity emerges with a new lease on life, so to speak.[3] From a functional standpoint, these films allow relief from the fear of non-existence and instil confidence that the future, indeed, will bring about a better day, not the horror of annihilation.

So, 'End of Days' films function to provide meaning given the threat of meaningless non-existence and courage in light of the fear of the unknown. They provide markers in time that place the present in light of an unknown future and, thus, by granting meaning to our notion of time, particularly in relation to the future. Such markers of time create artificial ends and beginnings and illustrate, perhaps, a human tendency (or at least a western one) to organize the abstract march of time into meaningful packets (centuries, millennia, creation-apocalypse). The ends of these packets of time catch the collective attention and give meaning to what went before and what comes after. But the 'ends' of these packets also raise the spectre of the possibility of the 'End' – will one of these ends be the End; the End of time or the end of space as we know it; the 'End of Days?' Westerners, bound by the abstraction of time, are fascinated by beginnings and ends, and Western religion is often consumed by creations and cosmic cataclysms. Creation and cataclysm not only bind and describe time, they give time meaning for western religion and society. Frank Kermode observed this in his 1967 seminal work, *The Sense of an Ending: Studies in the Theory of Fiction*, in which he describes how the sense of 'ending' helps organize meaning by ordering time – by structuring past, present and future in meaningful ways. While couching his work in a study of literary plot, Kermode's lessons demonstrate that human beings need to organize time using beginnings and ends in order to extract meaning from time. Kermode's illustration of a ticking clock brings the lesson home. Those old enough to remember when clocks ticked remember hearing a 'tick-tock' sound as if clocks marked time through a series of 'tick-tock' packets of time. In reality, clocks had a constant 'tick-tick-tick-tick', but our human need to create meaning from this constant march of time organized the 'tick-tick' into a 'tick-tock' – into, to use Kermode's words, 'a humble genesis . . . a feeble apocalypse'.[4] As the ear tends to hear a tick and a tock prior to another tick and a tock, so does the 'western religious ear' need to hear a creation and cataclysm, a Beginning and an 'End of Days'.

A fundamental aspect of western worldviews has to do with this linear bound concept of time. Perhaps any worldview must somehow deal with time and space. Just as physics and science have theorized that we inhabit time and space, our abstractions have led to the attempt to organize time and space. Part of this human abstraction leads to perhaps the most fundamental attribute of human existence, the ability to abstract and imagine non-existence. This abstraction leads to existential terror – human beings can imagine their own deaths and are frightened, and they can imagine the 'End of Days' and are horrified by what non-existence might mean. Some theorists suggest that the birth of religion lies in this ability to abstract non-existence and that the greatest existential fear lies in the ability to imagine death or perhaps the annihilation of the world and time. According to such theories, religion provides a particularly efficacious way of dealing with fear of non-existence.[5] While the fear of death is often seen to lie at the beginning of humanity's religious imagination, it seems the concomitant abstraction of the end of time promises an equal or even greater existential crisis. The ability to imagine one's own death is one thing, the ability to imagine complete and utter non-existence is quite another. If religion helps to lessen the human fear of death through ritual and belief, then perhaps 'End of Days' scenarios help to lessen the anxiety about non-existence of space and time. For example, Christianity is filled with resurrection rituals stories that help take away the fear of the finality of death. Might not stories of the end of time and space help take away the anxiety associated with non-existence?

If theorists are correct and the fear of death and non-existence lie shallow in the subconscious, then we might imagine that humans produce many ways to cope with those fears not only in our religions but also in culture. One way human beings battle such fears is by appropriating religious or cultural myths that provide meaning even against the threat of annihilation. Religious faith and religious communities provide such a buffer from fear by legitimating reality within a sacred context.[6] But in addition to religious beliefs, religion operates alongside of and sometimes in concert with cultural myths that give courage, stability and the ability to overcome the potentially paralyzing fear of destruction. Civil religion, for example, includes and supports a patriotic promise of protection in the form of national security and defence. National and cultural myths promise victory against outside threats and continued existence of a national way of life. Such myths give impetus and legitimacy to actions to ensure such victory. In the same way, religious myths provide assurances of life after death that are reinforced through ritual action. Perhaps, also, religious apocalyptic stories and other 'End of Days' myths provide a hedge against the terror lying shallow in the subconscious, that the world, time, space and universe are contingent as well. Human beings engage these fears to overcome them, and the rules of engagement play themselves out on our cultural stage. It is therefore no surprise to see culture, religious and popular, reflecting on religious and existential questions.

How does our culture deal with this most perplexing and frightening existential fear – the fear of non-existence itself – the fear that humanity will reach the 'End of Days' and that all life and indeed the world will cease to continue? A quick survey of bookstores and movie rental outlets reinforces the suspicion that the 'End of Days' is a topic rampant in popular culture. Movies that deal with the end run the gamut from religious movies (*Left Behind*) to documentaries (*An Inconvenient Truth*) to comedy (*Independence Day*) to science fiction (*Armageddon*). The variety of these movies is staggering, and many critics have attempted to classify them. Some follow traditional apocalyptic formulae, others have little to do with religious apocalyptic types but follow more secular, modern or post-modern patterns in imagining the end of time. But virtually all of them have one thing in common: they do not deal with the 'end' as much as they do the 'avoidance' of the end either imagined as life after the end or delaying or avoiding cataclysm altogether. In this sense then, the 'End of Days' is a misleading moniker for movies whose topic is the annihilation of humankind, the earth, or even the known universe. Rather, virtually all these movies function to allay existential terror accompanying subconscious fear of non-existence.

Because movies that deal with the end of time are based on fear, they become a tool for managing fear. Sometimes such movies are consciously used as a tool to not only manage fear but to manage a certain response to fear. For example, *Left Behind* becomes a tool of a certain religious persuasion to encourage a certain evangelical response to the movie.[7] *Dr. Strangelove* could be viewed as a political tool designed to play off fear of nuclear annihilation to produce a certain political response in the context of the Cold War.[8] Even Al Gore suggests addressing the fear of climate change by exercising political will in *An Inconvenient Truth*. But even when 'End of Days' movies do not carry with them the purposeful manipulation of fear, they play a cultural role in allowing human beings to come to grips with the horrific, even if subliminal, abstraction of non-existence. This is one reason 'end of days' films often reflect fears that are contemporary to cultural circumstances.[9]

Some Examples

Reflecting existential fear of non-existence – this is what the 'End of Days' films do. For example, nuclear Armageddon films reflect political tensions; *Waterworld* (1995) and *An Inconvenient Truth* raise the spectre that environmental degradation can not only impact quality of life but bring about the end of life; *12 Monkeys* or *Outbreak* (1995) or *I am Legend* make the viewer squeam-ish in an age of SARS, biological war agents and genetic manipulation; the existential fear is constant, the source of that fear shifts.[10] Since 'End of Days' films originate from fear, they can become a tool (religious or political) helping manage this fear, or an exercise to come to grips with this fear. Movies operate in popular culture as a means to manage the terror associated with the abstraction of time. As mentioned earlier, some movies do this theologic-ally (*Left Behind* and other traditional religious movies); some with humour (*Independence Day*); some with science (*An Inconvenient truth* or *Contact*, 1997), some with science fiction (*The Matrix*, 1999) – but almost all 'End of Days' films tap into this fear and provide a hope (whether religious, political, satir-ical, etc.). Fear and hope, terror and deliverance mark the way contemporary films operate within popular culture to help human beings deal with the threat of non-existence, organize time and create meaningful units that sup-port the passage from past to future. In this way, movies that deal with the 'End of Days', while potentially frightening, in reality function to allay the most fundamental of human fears – that of annihilation and subliminally of existential abandonment.

Steven Spielberg's 2005 *War of the Worlds*, based on H.G. Wells' 1898 science fiction classic illustrates this phenomenon well. One of the characters in the story, a half-mad survivor of the initial alien attack, expresses the funda-mental terror of the story in his commentary on the alien intentions with his comment, 'this is not a war . . . this is an extermination'. Indeed, the alien invasion depicted in this film appears to be just that – a complete and utter killing off of human species and human artifacts for no other reason than to satisfy the hunger of the alien species. The aliens attack in horrific machines (tripods) that vaporize people and objects or that capture humans for bloody snacks. The machines seem invincible, are impenetrable to human defences, and are almost innumerably spread across the urban and even rural land-scape. Everywhere they appear, they create utter and complete annihilation and leave hellish landscapes in their wake, accompanied by panic, terror and chaos. The first cinematic production of Wells' story was released in 1953 and directed by Byron Haskin. It probably reflected Cold War fears of destruction and atomic weaponry as much as anything. In a bit of frightening irony, even the atomic bomb is ineffective against the aliens. But by 2005, the film's fear factor eclipses that of 1953 and is more universal – there seem to be no hidden political agendas here, just pure subliminal and visceral fear. Humanity seems to be totally and helplessly powerless to do anything to curtail the complete destruction of earth and its inhabitants.

The alien efficiency at annihilation provides the fear factor for this movie, but where does the hope come from? Since the formula for most 'End of Days' movies balances the Fear with Hope, it must be somewhere buried in the plot.

Hope lies not with human ability or ingenuity – that fails. Neither does hope lie with religion – religion is virtually absent, except in one scene where religion appears as ineffective as human beings. When the tripods initially appear in the movie, they emerge from their subterranean hiding places. When the first machine appears, it does so at the door step of a church. As the steeple falls and church breaks apart, the ground before this sacred spot opens up, the horrific machine arises, and the cross topples to the ground before the evil agent of destruction. In one symbolic yet powerful image, the church is rendered powerless, and humanity is left abandoned to confront the alien threat. Hope seemingly dies in the beginning, yet it emerges (is resurrected) at the very end of the film when the aliens suddenly die from exposure to earth-bound germs for which they had no immunity. Hope bursts forth in one of the final images of the film with a green bud (life) focused against a stark, grey background (death). Thus, existential horror is replaced by hope, and the function of the 'End of Days' film is complete. And while religion plays no part in this film's redemptive element, the film is functionally religious in that it provides for the redemption of humankind.

Religion is not always a powerless agent in the 'End of Days' film, however. In fact, in *Left Behind* and other films by evangelical filmmakers, the 'End of Days' plot is not only patterned after certain apocalyptic views within Christianity, but the events surrounding the fear and hope pattern of the film are firmly in control of God. For example *Left Behind* is based on the apoca-lyptic tradition within Christianity. For the most part, these movies recreate on film depictions of events some Christians believe will accompany the 'End of Days'. Interest in apocalyptic visions of the future has proven to have significant staying power and impact in today's culture as evidenced by the continuing popularity of the *Left Behind* book series. While these films are not only religious in function, they also incorporate religious content and message. The basic message for these films, and indeed for the apocalyptic trad-ition in general, is that God is the author of time and, therefore, in control of time, history and the end of history. It is God, not aliens, not the environment, not disease, not warfare who will initiate the 'End of Days' and the judgment associated with it, and the main source of information concerning God's management of the 'End of Days' comes from biblical books like John's Revelation. And more often than not, scenes from these films are horrific, as scenes from the Book of Revelation are horrific, and are accompanied by the additional threat of eternal punishment.

Fear in these films is based on fear of judgment, and management of this fear is based on God's grace. So the films reinforce a traditional theology that comforts believers and seeks to gain adherents. For example, *Left Behind* is based upon the premise that faithful Christians will be raptured (or removed) to heaven and will miss the period of suffering known in some forms of dispensationalism as the tribulation. Those left behind after the rapture will suffer the trials of tribulation but will have opportunities to find redemption prior to the final judgment. However, the final judgment is just that – a final day of reckoning that seals the fate of all humanity, time and eternity. In traditional apocalyptic scenarios, the 'End of Days' happens at God's discretion as part of God's plan and determines the eternal status of all humanity living and dead. Fear of non-existence, or worse an eternal existence of suffering, is overcome through the Hope of grace that redeems those who seek it. It is worth noting that in these films, it is God who is the author of time and eternity and, thus, the end of time. It is God who initiates the end, and it is God who sees it through. There is no force that can overcome or stop divine events. However, it is human effort that allows individuals to avoid eternal punishment. While human effort cannot stop the 'End of Days', human acceptance of God's grace can allow avoidance of punishment following the 'End of Days'.

Aliens and God (transcendent beings both) are not always the source of Fear and Hope. Sometimes it is nature that acts as the source of otherness, and sometimes it is humanity itself. Some 'End of Days' films play on the relationship between humanity and nature to produce a contemporary type of fear that suggests the end of civilization, of earth, based on environmental degradation. Al Gore's 2006 documentary film, *An Inconvenient Truth*, might seem an odd choice as an example for a religion and film article. After all, this film is a scientific documentary film, right? Perhaps, but that does not preclude this film from functioning religiously as an 'End of Days' film. The film creates Fear about the future of the earth and implies that if humanity does not take action, and soon, then the earth will be beyond hope, its coastal cities inundated and interior areas facing environmental collapse. *An Inconvenient Truth* is almost the flipside of *Waterworld*, providing as it does a look at environmental collapse from this side of catastrophe. While Gore's presentation is filled with charts and reminiscences from his childhood and life, it also presents a grim picture of what our future might hold if action is not taken. Gore's presentation, like the other 'End of Days' movies mentioned here, is extrapolation. It may be based on hard data, but it is extrapolation about the future of earth and civilization, and the extrapolation does not paint a pretty picture.

The picture Gore paints is dramatic: as narrator, he warns that the extreme weather events witnessed around the world in 2005 will become more commonplace if global warming continues. Massive storms, record breaking floods, expanded drought areas and increased disease are ways that the environment out of control will seem 'like a nature hike through the book of Revelations'. Gore's allusion to the apocalyptic book in the Christian Bible brings forth images of biblical plagues and makes the connection between environmental catastrophe and the 'End of Days'. The catastrophe of Hurricane Katrina is invoked to suggest the societal collapse that will accompany environmental collapse. These frightening images based on science's assumption of a 'vulnerable' atmosphere make the viewer worry that this 'End of Days' extrapolation, unlike others, might really be based on a true vision of the future of earth. Because of this, Gore claims that action is required because the environmental crisis, which human activity helped bring about, presents humanity with a 'moral imperative' with high consequences accompanying failure. The consequence at stake is none other than 'our ability to live on planet earth'. But Gore leaves no doubt that this problem of climate crisis can be solved, thus the movie not only taps into Fear of non-existence but also offers Hope for solution, for a future for humanity and planet earth. This Hope lies in human ability, new patterns of behaviour and the employment of new technologies to solve existing problems. Gore calls for a moral, technological and political solution to the problem and makes his case that human beings can save the planet. *An Inconvenient Truth*, like many 'End of Days' films taps into the subliminal fear of non-existence and proposes that a means of redemption provides hope for deliverance. But in this film, redemption comes not from transcendent powers beyond control but rather from human effort and, more importantly, will.

Conclusion

'End of Days' films are those films that dramatize threats to human existence as we know it. They come in many forms, yet function in similar ways. While they seem to create fear, in reality they aid in dealing with fear. These films raise the spectre of human annihilation and in doing so bring human beings face to face with fundamental insecurities about human contingency. Existential Fear lies at the heart of the 'End of Days' film. Nevertheless, more often than not, 'End of Days' films also provide a means to deal with our contingency and horror of non-existence. There is usually Hope in these films: divine hope; hope in serendipity; confidence in human ability. Fear and Hope constitute the two sides of the cinematic 'End of Days', and they allow these movie dramas to function religiously in culture whether explicitly about religion or not. For that reason alone, it is likely that the cultural fascination with these fantasy films will continue until the 'End of Days'.

28 Satan in the Movies

Kelly J. Wyman

Filmmakers have explored the character of Satan since the advent of motion pictures. Within religious films, Satan, or the representation of evil, is often a prominent character. Because of his evil nature and established history in Western religion, Satan is the ultimate antagonist. His exact role within religion is in constant flux, and film serves as the perfect medium for exploration of his character. Many movies, not only religiously themed, focus on a battle between good and evil. Films frequently incorporate conflict, and Satan is definitely an engine of conflict. He is almost always a source of suffering and torment. Even in comedies, Satan is rarely represented as a positive force. However, in the majority of Devil movies, Satan is not particularly frightening because he is usually easily overcome.

Exploration into the depiction of Satan in movies is difficult because cinematic interpretations are varied and the numerous representations can become unintelligible. Differing definitions in film, literature, academe and religion contribute to a basic theological ignorance about Satan, who he is, what he stands for and what he looks like. In the Bible, he plagues humankind with temptations and hardships and tests basic belief in God, but not much more is known about his person. No one has been able to prove who he is, where he came from, if he exists, if he is an end result of God's creation or if he himself is one of the creators.

The overall debate about Satan allows filmmakers the opportunity to illustrate varying interpretations. Films are a way to investigate his character and to fill a void of knowledge about the Devil. Since the topic of Satan in film is vast, creating a typology from which to study his cinematic history is complicated. No category is perfectly distinct. Some films will fit into more than one group; some might fit into a class not mentioned here. Still other films, such as Rob Zombie's remake of *Halloween* (2007), make reference to the Devil, but never overtly portray him. For purposes here, the most frequent illustrations of the Devil in cinema will be discussed and are limited to films which have an obvious portrayal of Satan. Types of Devils presented in these movies include the sympathetic Satan, Satan as comedic hero, tempter, deceiver and Satan as concept and/or metaphor. Some themes present in Devil movies are the procreation and lineage of Satan, sexual imagery, the retelling of the Faust legend, the struggle against God and/or some other benevolent force, the characterization of Satanists, and possession and exorcism. In addition, names and symbolism are important in Devil movies. One can certainly find patterns in the way the Devil is presented cinematically; however, the only real constant in films with diabolical subject matter is that there is no consistency.

Any study of Satan in cinema would not be complete without mentioning the short films of Georges Méliès. Méliès' 1896 film *La Manoir du Diable* is the oldest cinematic representation of Satan still in existence. Throughout his career, Méliès wrote, directed and/or starred in more than 500 short films, many of which have diabolical themes. Other popular Méliès' films include *Le Cabinet de Méphistophélès* (1897), *Damnation du Docteur Faust* (1898), *Le Diable au Couvent* (1899), *Les Filles du Diable* (1903), *Le Chaudron Infernal* (1903), *Le Cake-walk Infernal* (1903), *Les Quatre Cents Farces du Diable* (1906) and *Satan en Prison* (1907). Before translating his tricks into cinematic magic, Méliès was a popular stage magician in France. Once he discovered the world of motion pictures, he eventually abandoned his stage shows and became the father of Devil movies. For Méliès, the new celluloid medium became a way for him to experiment with and expand his magic, and the Devil made for the perfect magician.

Many films, including several of Méliès', portray the Devil sympathetically. In these movies, Satan has a problem that needs to be solved, whether it is to procreate or to gather souls. In some way, the audience either ends up identifying with the Devil or, at the very least, understanding his position. The Satan in *Rosemary's Baby* (1968) simply wants to be a father. In Ingmar Bergman's *Djävulens Öga* (1960), Satan is plagued by a sty in his eye caused by a young woman's refusal to give up her virginity. In *The Prophecy* (1995), the archangel Gabriel is trying to overthrow God's power, but Satan wants nothing more than to stop the takeover. In this film, the viewer sympathizes with the Devil when he proclaims, 'Heaven will become just another Hell, and two Hells is one Hell too many'. The simple use of the name John Milton by the writers of *The Devil's Advocate* (1997) implies that they intended for the audience to feel some kind of sympathy for the Devil. *The Ninth Gate's* (1999) portrayal of Satan is sympathetic because the Devil assists the main character and leads him to a passageway of spiritual enlightenment. *Little Nicky's* (2000) Satan has problems with his rebellious children, a theme with which many parents can identify. The 1967 film *Bedazzled* features Peter Cook as a likable Devil, and the 2000 remake with Elizabeth Hurley makes the Devil more desirable than ever.

Jeffrey Burton Russell describes the Devil in medieval mythology as being 'ridiculous or unimportant, probably in order to tame him and relieve tension and fear'.[1] In Dante's *Divine Comedy*, Satan was deliberately 'empty, foolish, and contemptible'.[2] These ideas translate into modern movies where Satan is regularly mocked. *L'Inferno* (1911) is based on the *Divine Comedy*. *Bedazzled* (2000) is a classic retelling of the Faust story as well as a film in which the Devil can be seen as a prankster and somewhat of a comedic hero. While sitting in a bar one night, Elliot Richards proclaims, 'Dear God, I'd give anything to have that girl in my life', referring to his female co-worker. Elliot gets his wish, but it is not God who shows up to grant it. Throughout the film, the Devil is portrayed as a nuisance and humorous prankster.

Little Nicky, even though it has a procreation theme, is grounded in comedy. In this film, Satan and Lucifer are shown as two separate entities. Satan is the current ruler of hell, and Lucifer is Satan's father. Satan is physically representative of what some might view as a typical Devil. He has horns, pointed ears and a goatee. His physical appearance resembles a medieval satyr-style Satan. This film illustrates a Devil who is more funny than evil. He has difficulty controlling his sons and routinely assigns and administers laughable punishments to the souls in hell. The movie makes light of eternal damnation by basing its plot around juvenile behaviour and stand-up comedy routines.

Another comedic Devil is in *The Witches of Eastwick* (1987). Daryl Van Horne, otherwise known as Satan, is a mysterious, charismatic man. Van Horne has the ability to seduce women by altering his behaviour to suit any lady's desires. Van Horne is what Luther Link calls the wild man. 'Wild men', according to Link, 'were sexually aggressive and abducted women'.[3] Throughout the film, Van Horne switches back and forth between being a fun-loving guy and a demonic creature. The small town of Eastwick gradually becomes corrupted by Van Horne's presence, and the only voice of opposition is a woman named Felicia. Felicia is eventually murdered, but not before she reveals to the audience that Van Horne is the Devil and his mission is to procreate.

As has been mentioned before, the idea that Satan must procreate in order to continue his reign (assuming he has a reign), is thoroughly explored in Devil movies. In *The Witches of Eastwick*, Van Horne manages to father three children from three different human mothers. A half-human, half-Devil antichrist is born at the conclusion of *Rosemary's Baby*. In *The Omen* (1976), the viewer sees the antichrist first as a baby and then as a small child but never knows his exact parentage, only that his father is the Devil. The goal of Satan in *The Devil's Advocate* is to create an antichrist through the mating of his already existent half human, half satanic children. Thus, Satan in *The Devil's Advocate* wishes to create the antichrist through incest. Being the child of an incestuous relationship is one reason why Peter Kelson is targeted for being the antichrist in the film *Lost Souls* (2000). *End of Days* (1999) begins with the birth of Christine, who has been either chosen or destined to be the mother of the antichrist. In *Little Nicky*, Satan has three sons.

Of course, in order to procreate, the Devil must have intercourse. In *Rosemary's Baby*, Satan rapes Rosemary in order to create the antichrist. In *The Devil's Advocate*, Satan is not the one who needs to have sex in order for the antichrist to be created; however, he does rape Mary Anne, and the theme of sexual temptation is laced all throughout the film. In *The Ninth Gate*, Satan is portrayed by a woman who is not deliberately sexy, but one could argue that there is an implied sexual tension between her and the main character, Dean Corso. She never threatens Corso with harm or sexual temptation. However, she does transform into a sexual being in the final scene of the film when she and Corso engage in intercourse. During the 1970s, there were many Devil films which combined the genre of horror with pornography by expanding on the idea of Satan and his minions being incubi and succubi demons. Some of these films include *The Devil in Miss Jones* (1973), *L'Ossessa* (1974), *L'Antichristo* (1974), *The Devil Inside Her* (1977), *Devil's Ecstasy* (1977) and *Alucarda, la Hija de las Tinieblas* (1978).

Sexual temptation is also a commonality between Devil movies and Faustian themes. In Goethe's *Faust*, Mephistopheles 'corrupts [Faust's] imagination with a series of romantic visions'.[4] As well, in *The Devil's Advocate*, Satan invades Kevin's (Keanu Reeves) mind with arousing hallucinations of beautiful women who desire him. Davidson writes, 'Mephistopheles' aim is to make Faust fall headlong into a vulgar, sensual passion for a common, degraded woman'.[5] The object of Kevin's desire, Christabella, is not common, but her character is degraded. Her sexual nature presents her as being unclean and spoiled. Davidson asserts that Goethe's incentive is to 'show that the mere sensual passion is, in man, the result of the devil in him'.[6] The same conclusion can be reached for why these images are presented in *The Devil's Advocate*.

In Devil movies, sexual desire is sometimes translated into the battle between the virgin and the whore. In Goethe's *Faust*, Gretchen is the virgin. He presents her as a pure and innocent object of desire for Faust, representing more than sex. Gretchen is a symbol of goodness and piety. In *The Devil's Advocate*, Kevin's wife, Mary Ann, is the virgin. She is a soft-spoken, kind-hearted southern girl who comes from a middle-class family (as did Gretchen). Successful in her own job, she gives up her work for Kevin so he can pursue his dreams in New York. Her dream becomes synonymous with his.

In Goethe's *Faust*, Gretchen's neighbour, Martha, serves as her opposite. She is seductive, dishonest and corrupt. The whore in *The Devil's Advocate* is most certainly Christabella. Her purpose in the movie is to serve as an object of desire for Kevin. In *Faust*, Mephistopheles wants Faust and Gretchen to become lovers so he can corrupt both of them, and he uses Martha as a tool for carrying out his plan. In *The Devil's Advocate*, Satan wishes for Kevin and Christabella to become lovers. Like Martha, Christabella serves as a means to an end for the Devil. If he can get Kevin to impregnate Christabella, the Devil will have his antichrist.

Ultimately, Mary Ann leads Kevin to salvation. Close to the conclusion of the film, she commits suicide, just as Gretchen wants to do in *Faust*. Mary Ann becomes lost in her own world, confused and tormented by Satan's tricks. Having been driven to madness, Mary Ann finds herself without the strength to continue living. It is her suicide that makes Kevin realize his horrible error. His love for Mary Ann is so great that he finally recognizes his misdeeds. Just as Faust was influenced by Gretchen, Kevin comes to understand that 'salvation for a man depends not upon what he outwardly accomplishes, but upon the earnestness of his aspiration and struggle, and above all, upon his love'.[7] After Mary Ann's death, Kevin confronts the Devil and chooses free will as his way out. He makes a self-determined action by deciding to kill himself so the antichrist cannot be created.

Probably the most prevalent commonality between Satan movies and classic retellings of the Faust legend is the Devil's contract. In *Bedazzled* (both the 1967 and 2000 versions) the main character signs over his soul for seven wishes. At the end of the 2000 version of *Bedazzled*, after making his final wish, the Devil informs Elliot of a contractual loophole that allows him to regain possession of his soul. Elliot used his last wish to benefit his female co-worker by wishing that she find love and live a happy life. Goethe's *Faust* has a similar theme. Davidson explains that 'in the very last moment, [Faust] calls upon Mephistopheles . . . to do a piece of universal work which shall help to create a paradise of free men. In this very request Mephistopheles is already overcome'.[8] In the classic Faust story, 'the Devil claims that he is entitled to the soul because of the contract, but the contract is void because Faust has learned to love'.[9]

In *The Devil's Advocate*, Kevin 'sells his soul' to the Devil in return for power and notoriety. Kevin's deal with the Devil is not as blatant as Faust's contract with Mephistopheles, but Kevin still gives in to all the physical pleasures of the world – fabulous living quarters, an excellent job, more money than he can spend, any woman he desires. *Oh, God! You Devil* (1984) is a comedy in which Bobby Shelton promises his soul to the Devil in return for seven years of fortune and fame. Some other films which explore the 'deal-with-the-Devil' theme are *The Black Crook* (1916), *Faust* (1926), *The Devil and Daniel Webster* (1941), *La Beauté du Diable* (1950), *Damn Yankees!* (1958), *The Devil and Max Devlin* (1981), *Angel Heart* (1987), *Thank You Satan* (1989), *Faust: Love of the Damned* (2001) and *Canes* (2006).

Another incredibly popular theme in Devil movies is possession and exorcism. Michael W. Cueno believes 'the biggest promoter of Catholic exorcism remains the popular entertainment industry'.[10] Perhaps the most widely recognized American film with this theme is *The Exorcist* (1973). *The Exorcist* is a slow progression of events leading up to the possession and exorcism of a young girl named Regan. This film presents the Devil as a horrid, evil creature and a spirit skilled at possession. *The Exorcist* presents Pazuzu, a Babylonian demon who is not frightening to most Americans; however, once he is placed inside a Catholic framework, he automatically becomes identified with Satan. Peter L. Berger's process of legitimation draws on the idea that people within a culture hold widely accepted societal beliefs that serve as a basis for interpreting their surroundings.[11] *The Exorcist* draws on knowledge the audience has about the nature of Catholicism and the definition it provides of Satan. Therefore, whether or not explicitly mentioned, the demon possessing Regan becomes the Satan of the Christian Bible. Other films which include the possession and exorcism premise are *La Possession de L'enfant* (1909), *The Devils* (1971), *Seytan* (1974), *Amityville II: The Possession* (1982), *Prince of Darkness* (1987), *Repossessed* (1990), *Teenage Exorcist* (1994), *End of Days* (1999), *Exorcism* (2003), *Exorcist: The Beginning* (2004), *The Exorcism of Emily Rose* (2005) and *Dominion* (2005).

Despite claims by some religious leaders that Devil movies show their congregations in a negative light, much power is given to religion in many of these films. If the Devil has the ability to possess humans, then someone else must have the power to exorcise him. In most Devil movies, this power is given to the Catholic Church. In the Bible, God has the power to exorcise negative spirits. In Satan movies, anyone who has the power to exorcize demons is in a class with God. For example, a Catholic priest who has the knowledge and power to perform an exorcism is somewhat Christ-like. Cueno argues that in *The Exorcist* 'Karras and Merrin became full-fledged heroes ... when they entered the diabolic pit armed with nothing but faith and love and the mysterious powers conferred on them by priestly ordination'.[12] Not only does the film show the priests in a favourable light, it demonstrates the Catholic Church's authority and portrays it as having dominance over evil. The possession of Regan signifies a loss of control, and the Catholic Church can restore that control. When it is deemed that the Catholic Church is the only entity that possesses the ability to save Regan, it becomes a pillar of salvation and hope. This positioning of the Church leads the audience to conclude that deliverance is only available and attained through faith in God.

In *End of Days*, the Church is divided into two groups: (1) those who want to stop the antichrist's conception and save the mother's life; and (2) a secret order of Catholic officials who want to stop the birth of the antichrist by killing the mother. This is yet another theme which can be seen in Devil movies – the idea that the Catholic Church has been hiding knowledge in an effort to save society from itself. Whether or not the Church is presented in a positive light, it is still given the power and authority to stop the Devil's evil deeds. In these movies, the Church is mysterious, controlling and in possession of knowledge that the average person cannot be trusted with because it would upset a balance of power. Ultimately, in *End of Days*, it is the Church that restores faith to Jericho Cane (Arnold Schwarzenegger), who becomes the savoir in the movie. In *The Omen*, the Church knows about a Biblical prophecy that has foretold the arrival of the antichrist, and it is a shadowy priest who delivers the young Damien (Harvey Stephens) to his adoptive father. Viewers, along with the characters in the movie, come to know that Damien is truly the antichrist because the Catholic Church says he is. Even though there is some allusion as to wrong doing by the priest in the beginning of the film, the Church is still portrayed as having the knowledge and power to stop Damien.

In *Rosemary's Baby*, Satan is a primal force removed from the realm of Christianity. He functions on his own and invades the culture through the human characters in the film instead of through conventional religion. His infiltration of society is peaceful and calm. The Satanists shown in this film are the neighbours next door, and are not particularly horrible people. However, it is the humans in this film, not the Devil, who are corrupt and lie to get what they want. In the end, Rosemary does give birth to the son of Satan, and the audience is left wondering if her human influence on the child will stop it from fulfilling its destiny. In this film, the Church is positioned in neither a positive nor a negative light, but the conclusion is left open-ended for possible later intervention.

Rosemary's Baby is not the only Devil movie to incorporate the use of ritual Satanists. In fact, hundreds of films explore the theme of Satanists invoking the Devil. The opening scene of *End of Days* shows the demonstration of a ritual where the leader of a satanic cult slices a snake open and pours its blood into the mouth of a child. Although seemingly Satanic, there is no foundation for the ritual in the Satanism of the Church of Satan or First Church of Satan.

Instead, the ceremony parallels the Christian precept of blood sacrifice, and the visual reference comes directly from the Bible.[13] The inclusion of the serpent in the opening scene leads the audience to believe that something diabolical is happening or is about to happen. The ritual sacrifice of a snake foreshadows the arrival of Satan.

The Ninth Gate also portrays ritual Satanists. The motivation of the Satanists in this film is to acquire a copy of the book *The Nine Gates of the Kingdom of Shadows* so they can call upon Satan. The trouble is, some of them have been in possession of the book, but unable to conjure any demons, let alone the Devil. Authentication of the book is imperative to the goals of the Satanists because once the legitimate copy is found Satan can be called upon to come to Earth. The Satanists in *The Ninth Gate* are surprisingly distant from one another. Most Satan movies show worshippers banded together and trying to work for a larger cause, but the Satanists in this film compete with and loathe each other. Unfortunately, without prior knowledge of the underpinnings of Satanism, some audience members are likely to take the portrayal of Satanists in any Devil movie as a true representation. If people wish to explore the world of Satanism, it is recommended that they do not obtain their facts from Devil movies because they are rarely, if ever, accurate.

In many Devil movies, Satan is presented as a tempter. He is clearly shown this way in *End of Days*. At one point in the movie, Satan offers Cane his former life back. If Cane will cease his attempt to stop the Devil from mating with Christine, the Devil will return Cane's wife and daughter, whose murders were the main reason for Cane's loss of faith in God. This is an obvious parallel to the temptation of Christ. In this film, Cane is presented as Christ-like because he is not only sacrificing himself for the sake of humanity, but also refusing to give in to the temptations of the Devil.

The Ninth Gate presents the Devil as a temptress. In this form, Satan takes on the biblically themed characteristics of beauty and illumination. Satan does not disguise herself in this movie, but tempts Corso with an offer of truth, which she does eventually provide. When Corso accepts Satan's proposal and descends into *The Ninth Gate*, it is not a frightening realm of fire and brimstone, but instead an inspirational ascent into the realm of truth and enlightenment. The movie reinforces the idea that knowledge, power and truth are attainable through the forces of evil. Most Devil movies which incorporate Faustian themes also show Satan as a tempter. A few other films to present Satan in this manner are *The Temptations of Satan* (1914), *The Sorrows of Satan* (1926), *Angel Heart* (1987) and *The Last Temptation of Christ* (1988).

Satan is also presented as a deceiver in many Devil movies. In *Hellbound: Hellraiser II* (1988),[14] the individuals in the movie are selling themselves to Leviathan, in exchange for pleasure or pain. Those who open what is known as the L'Merchant box are searching for knowledge and pleasure, but they end up getting unintended results by receiving physical and mental torture. In this way, Leviathan is a great deceiver. In *Bedazzled*, Satan deceives Elliot by unfavourably altering his wishes. In *The Witches of Eastwick*, Satan deceives his love interests by transforming himself into whatever the women want at the time. Again, many of the Devil films which present a retelling of the Faust story also show Satan as a deceptive character.

In Devil movies, the use of symbolism abounds. One common form is the significance of character names. Many of the names in *The Devil's Advocate* have symbolic meaning. Anyone familiar with *Paradise Lost* immediately knows the significance of the name John Milton. The use of the name Mary Ann for Kevin's wife does not only imply virginity; the name parallels her to the Virgin Mary. Most horror films use the name Christy or some variation of it. *The Devil's Advocate* uses Christabella, which means beautiful Christ. The film also has fun with its own title. Lawyers are advocates. Kevin is a lawyer working for Satan; he is the 'Devil's advocate', a title with very specific significance in the Roman Catholic tradition.

In *End of Days*, the name Jericho Cane is symbolic and biblically significant. In the Bible, Cain kills his brother and is cast out by God. His punishment is to roam the earth as a vagabond, similar to how Cane is presented in *End of Days*. Jericho is not only the name of a modern-day city in the Middle East; it is also a city that is mentioned numerous times throughout the Bible. The biblical Jericho was a city the Israelites were determined to conquer. A prostitute named Rahab[15] assisted the Israelites in exchange for the protection of her family when the city was conquered. In the Bible, both Cain and Rahab are sinners and outcasts. Again, in *End of Days*, Jericho Cane is presented as a loner, sinner and outcast.

In *Hellbound: Hellraiser II*, hell is a physical place ruled by an entity named Leviathan. This can be seen as an obvious reference to the Leviathan Hell Mouth of the Last Judgment. The Leviathan in *Hellbound: Hellraiser II* is a type of hell where souls are captured and collected by coenobites. The coenobites are minions of Leviathan who work on Earth. In Catholicism, coenobites are monks who live 'life together according to a rule under the supervision of a recognized religious superior'.[16] The coenobites in *Hellbound: Hellraiser II* and the coenobites of Catholicism are closely paralleled and are almost opposites of each other. *Hellbound: Hellraiser II* also uses the name Kirsty for its main character, a close resemblance to Christy or Christ.

The use of dogs is another form of symbolism seen in Devil movies. In *The Exorcist* and *The Omen*, dogs are seen as representing evil forces. *The Exorcist* uses dogs at the beginning of the film when the priest is in the Iraqi desert. The dog fight symbolizes impending doom. In *The Omen*, Damien is protected by an evil dog. The dog not only symbolizes evil, but also serves as a protector for Damien. As well, *Little Nicky* contains a diabolical dog. The use of dogs as a diabolical aid has its roots in Greek mythology where Cerberus was an evil dog with three heads. Russell explains that the most recurrent creature forms of Satan during the medieval period were 'serpent (dragon), goat and dog'.[17]

An animalistic characteristic usually given to Satan is horns and red is the colour most frequently associated with him, whether it is used as the colour of the Devil's skin, in costuming, or in the background. Historically, horns have 'carried the ancient connotation of power'.[18] In *Little Nicky*, the Devil's horns are undeniably symbolic of his power. Lucifer (the retired Devil) has no horns, signifying his lack of power. Later in the film when one of Satan's sons almost usurps his father's throne, he grows horns, denoting his newly acquired authority. The colour red is also used in these films to indicate the fires of hell and the blood of humanity.

Characterizations of Satan in Devil movies range from humanoid to beast to spirit to a metaphor for all-encompassing evil. As has been illustrated, images of the Devil in film are wide-ranging. Unfortunately, it is not possible to list here all the films in history which have personified or characterized Satan,[19] nor is it possible to discuss every way in which he has been represented. Surprisingly though, there have not been any advancements in Satan's character or physical appearance since the Middle Ages. All of the imagery and themes discussed here can be traced to literature and/or art created throughout the Medieval period. It is also worth noting again that Satan is typically presented as being easy to defeat. Therefore, most movies present a relatively conservative picture of the Devil. Since there has been little academic study into the nature and character of the Devil as presented in cinema, this is undoubtedly an area which merits more investigation.

29 Evil on Film[1]

Bryan Stone

Cicero once said that 'the function of wisdom is to discriminate between good and evil'.[2] For over a hundred years, the cinema has provided storytellers a formidable means for doing just that. The purpose of this chapter is to survey the landscape of evil in film, to explore popular images, narratives, intertextual patterns and cinematic codes for constructing evil on screen, and to trace important ways that this landscape has shifted and altered over time. Cinema, like other forms of popular culture, draws heavily upon a wealth of inherited religious, philosophical and mythological notions of evil, many of which are quite ancient and deeply engrained in our cultural consciousness. But while evil may be just as prominent and recognizable a theme as it ever was in motion pictures today, its meaning in films is far from stable and under constant negotiation.

In traditional morality tales, good and evil were fixed, absolute and the binary opposites of one another. This is especially true in the classical Western, in monster movies, or in fantasy films where we get Dorothy and the Wicked Witch, Luke Skywalker and the Emperor, or Snow White and the Evil Queen. A combination of narrative devices, music, colour schemes, framing, symbols and other aural and visual clues help establish and alert us to these contrasts. So, for example, the presence of evil might be signalled by a scene shot at night, in shadows, or in twilight half-tones; in forbidden or liminal settings such as alleys, graveyards, abandoned castles or wastelands; by the use of particular glares, grimaces or masks; or by employing bodily features such as pale skin, warts, horns, claws, sharp or rotted teeth, or dark circles under the eyes.

But in many films, just as in life, evil is less absolute and its source less clearly traceable. More complex and subtle portrayals are required when a villain possesses a mixture of character traits and motivations, or when that villain is a tragic figure, as much the product as the source of evil. This is all the more true when the evil in question is associated with a complex social or economic system, an interior psychological state, or the routine harm perpetuated by those who are 'just doing their job'.[3] In the cinema of late modernity, moreover, while portrayals of evil on screen have become more sensational, excessive and violent, evil is increasingly presented as meaningless and hollow,[4] as impossible to explain or to trace so that the cinema of evil has become a cinema of paranoia and spectacle.[5] No longer is evil as likely to be constructed in relation to a fixed moral centre or absolute good, nor is it possible to locate a single definable 'Hollywood' pattern or genre for constructing evil.[6] But evil will not go away as a subject matter in motion pictures. Whatever its shape or source, evil continues to show up conspicuously in cinema, both shaping and serving complex and interlocking social, political, religious and economic interests.

One way to approach the topic of evil in film is to begin with a distinction philosophers and theologians have often made between two types of evil: (1) *moral evil* – that which is caused by the action or inaction of moral agents (whether human beings or supernatural beings) who are presumably free to act otherwise and (2) *natural (or non-moral) evil* – that which we experience or perceive as negative, harmful and threatening, but with no moral agents as its source and instead arising from physical, inanimate or natural forces.

Evil and Nature

Volcanoes, asteroids, fires, tornadoes, earthquakes, cancer, icebergs, 'perfect storms' – all these and more have appeared with an impressive frequency in the last quarter century of popular cinema; and while each is an otherwise natural phenomena for which moral blame cannot be assigned,[7] the damage and harm inflicted is often narrated as evil by the human bystanders who are their victims. While many films have featured natural disasters or calamities as a foil against which the triumph of the human spirit is exalted or moral choices need to be made, nature is never so 'evil' as when it is altered, transgressed or exploited by moral agents, resulting in something like a 'revolt' of nature against us. This fact alone already complicates any oversimplified distinction between 'moral' and 'natural' evil.

Cinema has long constructed evil by working with a storehouse of cultural symbols borrowed from the natural order such as snakes, crows, spiders, owls, bats, black cats or hyenas. But even beyond these more conventional symbols, motion pictures from as far back as *King Kong* (1933) capitalized on human fears of the natural order turning on us, whether that is plants, monkeys, ants, scorpions, leeches, sharks, birds, dogs, bats, rats, bees, fish, earthworms, alligators, spiders, snakes, cockroaches, dinosaurs, worms or even swamp bacteria – all of which have been constructed as perpetrators of injury and destruction in the last century of film. The twentieth century witnessed advance after advance in our ability to understand and control nature, to harness and direct it. And yet for all that, nature remains unpredictable – a place of transcendence and mystery that can, with no advance notice, dwarf our intellects and punish our arrogance. Films where evil is constructed as nature in revolt often capitalize on our growing sense of alienation from the ecosphere embodied especially in an escalating ecological crisis. The message here is that when nature is abused, it will spin out of control and harm us.

This construction of evil undoubtedly 'works' in film because of our primal confidence that while nature is itself not evil and actually quite benign, it cannot ultimately be predicted, harnessed or exploited without destructive consequences. Accordingly, the moral subtext in many such films is that when and if nature goes out of control, that is generally the fault of human beings who, through their own greed, evil machinations (*Willard*, 1971; *Ben*, 1972), scientific experiments gone awry (*Piranha*, 1978; *Bats*, 1999), nuclear detonations (*Godzilla*, 1954), radiation (*Them!*, 1954) or pollution (*The Day After Tomorrow*, 2004), mistakenly attempt to alter, exploit or contain and market nature (*King Kong*, 1933; *Jurassic Park*, 1993). The arrogance of self-described 'advanced' civilizations is that we forget our own ties to nature and inevitably do little more than plunder creation, turning it into our enemy.

But not all evil constructed in relationship to nature originates in the humans who have altered or exploited it. Perhaps we will simply find ourselves in the wrong place at the wrong time, as when a hoard of migrating tarantulas are heading through town (*Kingdom of the Spiders*, 1977) or when our pet St. Bernard has been bitten by a rabid bat (*Cujo*, 1983). Some of the most powerful horror films in history, such as Alfred Hitchcock's *The Birds* (1963) and Steven Spielberg's *Jaws* (1975), simply refuse to offer us any kind of explanation whatsoever for why their subjects go so uncharacteristically out of control. The net effect can be powerful. There are people who, three decades after seeing *Jaws*, are still afraid to wade too far out into the ocean.

In contrast to the moral nature of evil that originates within the realm of the free will, the evil associated with nature is fundamentally amoral, and for that reason Western religions have proven to be relatively impotent on nature's turf in film.[8] For while religious images, narratives, figures and motifs are otherwise able to thematize moral evil and symbolize resistance against it, they provide no help against threats posed by hurricanes, tsunamis or approaching asteroids. Science and the military, by contrast, as the secular counterparts to religion, are often portrayed as capable of bringing nature into check, even if they are just as often responsible for nature's revolt in the first place.

Science has provided an especially fertile soil for the construction of evil in popular cinema over the last century precisely because it is one of the primary vehicles by which humans trespass against nature. Thus, the threat we experience from nature is closely associated with a threat from science. Here the classic construction is the gothic morality tale featuring a 'mad' scientist who inevitably oversteps his bounds and stands accused of attempting to 'play God', the archetypal instance of which is *Frankenstein* (1931). The mad scientist was extremely popular during the thirties and early forties in a number of low budget films such as *Island of Lost Souls* (1932), *Doctor X* (1932), *The Invisible Man* (1933), *The Raven* (1935), *The Man Who Changed His Mind* (1936), *Black Friday* (1940), or *Man Made Monster* (1941). Though this particular sub-genre would become far less common after the 1950s, it was a staple in *James Bond* films and would continue to show up in later films such as *The Fly* (1958), *The Brain that Wouldn't Die* (1963), *The Abominable Dr. Phibes* (1971), *The Rocky Horror Picture Show* (1975), *Re-Animator* (1984), *Flatliners* (1990), *Hollow Man* (2000), or in *Spider-Man* (2002) and *Spider-Man 2* (2004).

Though the mad scientist could be merely seeking revenge or using science as a means to some other evil end, many on-screen scientists operate out of the most humane of intentions and are merely misguided in their search for truth, oblivious to the divinely imposed limits that have been placed upon knowledge. The anxiety about science reflected in classic Gothic horror films tended to focus on those sciences that transgressed nature, usurped the power of God over matters of life and death, or failed to appreciate the reality of a divinely created and immortal soul. In fact, in an age when psychological explanations of the human self were beginning to gain ascendancy, what made the 'mad psychiatrist' as suspicious a character as the 'mad doctor' is precisely his failure to recognize that what psychiatry calls the mind is really the soul (*Dr. Jekyll and Mr. Hyde*, 1931; *Cat People*, 1942).

Despite the ubiquity of explicitly religious images, symbols and metaphors within Gothic horror films, in later cinema these would increasingly become little more than external markers or conventions for helping viewers identify evil, while the self – and therefore the threat to the self – was being relocated from metaphysics to psychology. Of course, the Freudian model did not escape a similar fate, as Linda Badley notes, with its notion of the 'buried' self that, in place of God and the Judeo-Christian scriptures, had become 'the sacred text to be studied, translated, invoked, and consulted'.[9] In the cinema of the post-Freudian era, as the grand narrative of psychiatry itself would prove to be a quasi-religious explanation that must be rejected in the name of the embodied self, a new openness to religious symbolism and imagery emerged despite a loss in its narrative or interpretive power relative to evil. Thus, films today may well feature a heavy reliance on religious iconography in their construction of evil, but this is often little more than a way of marking the presence of evil on screen by providing it a dark, supernatural halo rather than rendering a coherent framework for constructing its meaning.

In more recent cinema, new forms of non-moral evil continue to surface in relation to science based on our insecurities and uncertainties about the promise of computer, video and internet technology. In films like *The Stepford Wives* (1975), *Lawnmower Man* (1992), *The Thirteenth Floor* (1999), *Existenz* (1999), *The Matrix* (1999), *The Ring* (2002), *Feardotcom* (2002) or *Pulse* (2006), evil is constructed against the backdrop of a post-modern negotiation of identities in the context of technologies upon which we have become increasingly dependent and which, like nature itself, threaten to go out of control and turn on us.

As science-horror moved away from the humanistic impulses of Gothic horror films, a whole new generation of films brought us face to face with evil in the form of entities from outer space: *The Thing From Another World* (1951), *The War of the Worlds* (1953), *Invasion of the Body Snatchers* (1956) and *The Blob* (1958). These films were especially popular in the 1950s, often signalling geo-political anxieties arising from a cold war mentality. They re-appeared with the blockbuster *Alien* in 1979, which set off a renewed interest in the alien-horror genre that has yet to diminish. The threat from outer space continues to capture the public imagination and to function as a battleground for our engagement with the transcendent dimensions of evil. By portraying the inbreaking of alien forces, films such as *The Thing* (1982), *The Hidden* (1987), *The Borrower* (1991), *Screamers* (1995), *Species* (1995), or *The Astronaut's Wife* (1999) symbolize a persistent supernatural dimension to evil – a threat from forces above us and beyond us (or even 'below us' in the sea, as with *Leviathan*, 1989), about which we know practically nothing and over which we have little or no control.

As in the case of nature's revolt, religious themes and symbols have generally played only a marginal role in films that construct evil with reference to space aliens. While religious figures and institutions may well comfort victims of alien invasions or offer a sanctuary in which to hide, shudder together and pray for help (for example, *War of the Worlds*, 1953), broadly speaking, religion offers few resources to guide us in an encounter with aliens. After all, aliens just do not play by the same rules as we do. For example, what effect could be had by waving a cross in front of 'the Blob'? What evil lies within 'the Thing' that a priest could exorcize? Would the creature from *Alien* shrink back and wince in pain if holy water were thrown its way? The futility of such actions also demonstrates, by the way, why religious iconography virtually disappears in psychotic 'slasher' films where monsters with ordinary names like Jason, Freddie or Michael belong to an extraordinary and even alien world where traditional conventions of sin and morality, good and evil, do not even come into play.

'Moral' Evil

From even this brief overview of natural evil, we can begin to see that the distinction between 'natural' and 'moral' evil is rather slippery, for the two are frequently entangled with one another. Though 'natural' evil refers to that which is experienced as negative or destructive without moral agency as its

South Park: Bigger, Longer, and Uncut (1999), or *Little Nicky* (2000). At least one reason for the resiliency of symbols such as Satan or demons is their capacity for capturing the transcendent dimensions of evil that exceed our individual choices.[11]

But supernatural accounts of evil, especially those that feature Satan and the demonic, have undergone their own permutations, becoming far more invasive, thereby paralleling the turn to the body that gave rise to slasher films. As Jonathan Lake Crane notes, supernatural horror films, though not as popular as slasher films, 'seem more concerned with demonstrating that Satan and his cohorts can be just as violent as killers who have not directly ascended from the pit of Hell. Now, the Devil must compete for our attention not with God but with serial assassins'.[12] *The Exorcist* is an especially fitting example of this, for while the references to Satan are chilling, they are made so by being located in the body of twelve-year-old Regan. As Badley says, 'In the 1980s, horror (whatever the medium) became a spectacle, offering not mere transcendence *of* the body but transcendence *through* the body'.[13]

In a number of ways, vampire movies have followed this same trajectory. Along with Frankenstein's creature, the vampire is one of the two most powerful archetypal monsters of cinema, having appeared in early classics like *Nosferatu* (1922) and Tod Browning's *Dracula* (1931) as well as no less than 100 other such films in the past century. As C. Fred Alford argues in *What Evil Means to Us*, given a dearth of symbolic resources for envisioning evil in our time, 'the vampire has replaced Satan as the leading figure of evil'.[14] The vampire not only sucks from us our blood (and thereby our life), but wilfully embraces evil, inverts normative patterns of valuation, and violates established institutions of family, religion, science and law. The vampire defies cultural norms of femininity and masculinity and transgresses heterosexual desire with an exchange of bodily fluids that is no respecter of gender. By luring women away from the men who control them, the vampire threatens the patriarchal structures of family, marriage and religion.[15] At the same time, the vampire offers his victims a new birth – a new and immortal patriarchy in which he not only is the husband of numerous brides but father of countless 'children of the night'. Not surprisingly, as cinematic evil has become more ambiguous and less anchored to fixed religious coordinates and moral absolutes, the vampire has also become increasingly ambiguous as more and more films augment the humanity of the vampire while attempting to retain his or her destructive power. Likewise, conventional means for stopping supernatural evil (holding forth a crucifix, retreating into a church building, etc.) rarely work anymore at the movies.

Evil and the Psyche

Perhaps the most frightening of all representations of evil on film are those where there are no monsters and no demons other than the psychological states of the characters. As early as *The Cabinet of Dr. Caligari* (1919) or *West of Zanzibar* (1928), evil had been constructed in relation to psychosis, inner compulsions or insanity. Unlike the 'mad scientist' of early horror films, however, the 'madman' of later psychological horror films was not a knowledge-seeking compulsive but a raging psychotic – the victim, says Andrew Tudor, of 'monsters brought forth by the sleep of reason, not by its attraction'.[16] In fact, it was precisely as the mad scientist was becoming less prominent in the 1960s that the tortured minds in *Psycho* (1960), *Peeping Tom* (1960) and *Repulsion* (1965) were becoming more prominent. This shift would accelerate in the 1970s and 80s, inevitably bringing forth the 'mad slashers' of *Halloween* (1978), *Friday the 13th* (1980), and *A Nightmare on Elm Street* (1984).

This turn to the psychological in filmic constructions of evil is closely related to significant alterations in religious meaning in American culture. In an earlier time, evil was absolute and threatened us from distant castles, haunted graveyards or remote laboratories. As Jonathan Lake Crane says, 'the majority of monsters were enemies who helped men gain confidence in their ability to control and understand the world'.[17] Religion provided the 'sacred canopy' under which the rational and moral exercise of human freedom could be counted on to defeat evil. But the turn to the psyche as the site of the sacred required that evil be reoriented to new and more familiar contexts (schools, families, the suburbs). Now our next-door neighbour might be the monster.

Given this transformation of meaning, not only was the sacred no longer 'out there' but rather 'in here', so also evil is no longer 'out there' but 'in here'. The monstrous dwells within the dark corners of the mind, repressed urges and divided personality. One of religion's primary functions in establishing meaning and assigning value had been its ability to stake out the boundaries of good and evil, sacred and profane, saint and sinner (often by literally 'staking' that which it deemed monstrous – the witch, the communist the homosexual[18]). Western religions traditionally did this in cosmological and theological terms with the net result that morality was imposed onto the human from outside. Thus, science had its divinely sanctioned limits, and the sacredness of certain 'places' (the church, the home, the body, the family, etc.) was established by reference to the transcendent. But now with the turn from soul to ego, from priest to psychiatrist, from religious discourse to psychoanalysis, all religious bets are off. Some of the greatest cinematic villains in modern film are those who are psychologically disturbed, such as Norman Bates in *Psycho* (1960), Baby Jane Hudson in *Whatever Happened to Baby Jane?* (1962), Travis Bickle in *Taxi Driver* (1976), Joan Crawford in *Mommie Dearest*

(1981), Frank Booth in *Blue Velvet* (1986), Alex Forrest in *Fatal Attraction* (1987), Annie Wilkes in *Misery* (1990), and both 'Buffalo Bill' and Hannibal Lecter in *The Silence of the Lambs* (1992).

Evil and the Body

As the preceding brief survey has shown, the source of evil on screen might be natural or supernatural, social or psychological, institutional or spiritual. But whatever the source, in the last several decades it is the body that was made to pay the price. For one thing, death, once the special province of religion, changed hands in the twentieth century and became the province of science and medicine, with important consequences for how evil is constructed on screen in relation to the body. As Badley says, 'once intimately connected with the life of the community, death became separated from life by medical technology, which confined it to the hospital and the funeral home'.[19] The symbols, the myths, and, indeed, the institutions that guided us in coping with and understanding death were transformed before our eyes. Cinematic constructions of evil parallel this repression and eroticization of, and inevitable fascination with, death. The assaults on the human body heralded by George Romero's *Night of the Living Dead* (1968) and, later, *Halloween* (1978) can be read as providing the new body language, the iconography, the communal rituals, if you will, for disposing of bodies that had been hygienically removed from public view. Romero, for example, consciously understands himself to be bringing home the corpses from Vietnam and depositing them on screen in front of us. He calls his zombies 'the blue collar monster' – 'they're us', says one of his characters. And their bodies – our bodies! – become 'the central marker upon which we articulate the spectacular degradation of everyday life'.[20]

It is not as though the human body had never been disfigured before in cinema, of course. But while these disfigurations could be created by mutations or by an inappropriate splicing of the human soul with alienated nature (*The Fly*, 1958; *The Alligator People*, 1959), more often than not these disfigurations emphasized the human spirit and were in reality disfigurations of the soul that made their way out onto the human form (*Cat People*, 1942, 1982; *Dr. Jekyll and Mr. Hyde*, 1931, 1941), thus providing the imaginative foil for a morality tale. One of the most interesting films in this regard is Tod Browning's *Freaks*, released in 1932, which requires that we identify not with those who are beautiful and otherwise 'normal'-looking, but whose souls are clearly bent and misshapen. Rather we are directed to identify with Browning's real-life collection of bearded ladies, human worms, Siamese twins, midgets and pinheads who, though disfigured outwardly, point us toward the beauty and truth of the human spirit.

In contemporary cinema, however, the threat to and torture of the human body has no such purpose. Indeed, as this fascination with bodies has continued to develop over time, what is most important about the evil we see on screen is no longer the villains, monsters, or other agents of evil, but the mere spectacle of evil, choreographed almost poetically as it lays waste to the bodies of those who are its victims. Vampire movies, for example, must now be much more public about their bloodletting. Two little pin-point punctures in a neck during the middle of the night just does not work. The body must be torn apart. Another good example of this phenomenon is the film *Se7en* (1995), in which the villain is not ultimately the focus of the film but rather the inventive ways the bodies of his prey are ravaged. In contemporary filmmaking, as Bather notes, by showing us 'bullet impacts, impaling, drowning, burning, eviscerations and so on – an eroticism of violence is created that compels audiences to watch when they normally would not'.[21]

The Future of Evil in Post-Modern Film

If the post-modern is characterized by a scepticism as to universal, neutral or objective knowledge and an emphasis on fragmented and multiple narratives, a relativizing of meaning in favour of image, then for post-modern film, the visual aesthetic used to construct evil is more important than the meaning of evil itself. Rather than the attempt to construct evil within a fixed moral framework around which there is no longer a consensus and within which good and evil are opposed to one another as absolutes, post-modern film veers instead toward the spectacular depiction of evil on screen. Of course, because of the primacy of image over substance, evil must still be recognized as evil; so filmmakers still find themselves 'playing' with an arsenal of narratives, paradigms, and symbols for evil intentionally borrowed from religion, philosophy and mythology. This borrowing is performed freely and with abandon by mixing multiple narratives and splicing together symbols that would otherwise have no relation to one another into a post-modern pastiche: a little apocalyptic here, a little paganism there, perhaps a spellbook, a ghost, some holy water and an explosion thrown in for good measure. The net result is, as Bather says, that 'while we may be unable to define specifically what evil is, we are still able to recognise it when we see it'.[22]

Yet, even while working within this post-modern aesthetic, a film may still successfully lay bare the reality of evil and even offer a vision of redemption in profound ways, as, for example, with *Pulp Fiction* (1994), directed by Quentin Tarantino.[23] While it is true that *Pulp Fiction* is structured by an almost frenzied attempt to implicate its characters in every evil, violent and chaotic aspect of contemporary culture, at the same time, as Thomas Leitch notes, 'beneath the film's veneer of lawlessness, violence, and casual cruelty is a deeply moral story, a story the film enacts three times, once in each of its separate stories'.[24] Tarantino accomplishes this not by providing comprehensive answers to moral questions, but through the skilful use of non-linear plot structure, unrestrained cross-currents of dialogue and action that take us in two directions at once, and by humanizing his criminals, thereby redeeming their violent cliché. *Pulp Fiction* demonstrates that the mere appearance of violent images in film is not necessarily a moral negative. As Sarah Kerr reminds us, 'violence can be used to frighten, to titillate, to provoke pity or outrage; its mere appearance has no fixed moral shading'.[25] In fact, one could even say that Tarantino is mocking violence while redeeming it. Tarantino puts an absurd twist on macho violence and standard heroic plot devices. He 'refuses to patronize, glamorize or judge his band of outsiders. Instead, he lets us see the glimmers of humanity that emerge when they drop their masks of control'.[26] The ultimate moral victory gained by Tarantino is the redemption of violence by three resurrections that appear in the film.

As the iconography for constructing evil on screen is increasingly unhinged from a compelling moral vision and reduced to mere conventions for marking the spectacle of evil, the downside is that only the rarest of films will have the symbolic power required to engage us at the deepest level of our being and thereby challenge and shape our responses to evil in the world rather than anesthetizing us to the destruction and violence around us. Yet within a postmodern universe, even if established paradigms for constructing the meaning of evil have less and less hold on us, the invincible presence of miracle and mystery persists, as does the possibility of redemptive encounters that refuse to give evil the last word.

Part IV

Resources

Film Index

Devil Came on Horseback, The	2007	Ricki Stern, Anne Sundberg
Devil in Miss Jones, The (Teufel in Miss Jonas, Der)	1973 (1974)	Erwin C. Dietrich
Devil Inside Her, The	1977	Zebedy Colt
Devil's Advocate, The	1997	Taylor Hackford
Devil's Backbone, The	2001	Guillermo del Toro
Devil's Ecstasy	1977	Brandon G. Carter
Devil's Playground, The	1976	Fred Schepisi
Devils, The	1970 (1971)	Ken Russell
Diary of a Country Priest	1951	Robert Bresson
Diary of Anne Frank, The	1959	George Stevens
Dinner with the President: A Nation's Journey	2007	Sachithanandam Sathananthan, Sabiha Sumar
Dirty Dancing	1987	Emile Ardolino
Dirty Pretty Things	2002	Stephen Frears
Distant Thunder	1978	Russ Doughten
Divine Intervention (Yadon ilaheyya)	2002	Elia Suleiman
Djävulens Öga	1960	Ingmar Bergman
Doctor X	1932	Michael Curtiz
Dogma	1999	Kevin Smith
Dominion	2005 (2006)	Larry Anderson, Greg Myers
Don't Die Without Telling Me Where You're Going	1995	Eliseo Subiela
Donnie Darko	2001	Richard Kelly
Doomsday	2008	Neil Marshall
Down in the Delta	1998	Maya Angelou
Dr. Jekyll and Mr. Hyde	1931	Rouben Mamoulian
Dr. Jekyll and Mr. Hyde	1941	Victor Fleming
Dr. Strangelove: Or How I learned to Stop Worrying and Love the Bomb	1964	Stanley Kubrick
Dracula	1931	Tod Browning
Dragonfly	2002	Tom Shadyac
Dreams	1990	Akira Kurosawa
Driving Miss Daisy	1989	Bruce Beresford
Early Autumn	1961	Yasujiro Ozu
Early Spring	1956	Yasujiro Ozu
Earth	1998	Deepa Mehta
East is East	1999	Damien O'Donnell
Easy Rider	1969	Dennis Hopper

Bibliography

Ahmed, L. (1992), *Women and Gender in Islam: Historical Roots of a Modern Debate.* New Haven, CT: Yale University Press.

Aichele, G. and Walsh, R. (2002) (eds), *Screening Scripture: Intertextual Connections Between Scripture and Film.* Harrisburg: Trinity Press International.

Alasuutari, P. (1995), *Researching Culture: Qualitative Methodology and Cultural Studies.* London: Sage.

Alexander, K. (2000), 'Black British cinema in the 90s: Going, going, gone' in Murphy, R. (ed), *British Cinema in the 90s.* London: British Film Institute.

Alford, C. F. (1997), *What Evil Means to Us.* Ithacy, NY: Cornell University Press, p. 13.

Anderson, D. and Lindvall, T. (1981), *We've Come A Long Way*, Video-documentary. Virginia Beach, VA: CBN (Regent) University Library.

Arendt, H. (1963), *Eichmann in Jerusalem: A Report on the Banality of Evil.* London: Penguin.

Arendt, H. (1994), 'The image of hell' in Kohne, J. (ed.), *Essays in Understanding, 1930–1954.* New York: Harcourt, Brace & Co., pp. 197–205.

Arenson, K. W. (2007, 26 February). 'Film's view of Islam stirs anger on campuses'. *New York Times.* http://www.nytimes.com/2007/02/26/movies/26docu. html?_r=1&ei=5087%0A&em=&en=a4062496f8729e35&ex=1172638800 &pagewanted=print&oref=slogin.

Arnheim, R. (1957), *Film as Art.* Berkeley: University of California Press.

Auty, M. and Roddick, N. (1985), *British Cinema Now.* London: British Film Institute.

Avila, W. (2006), '*Diary of a Country Priest*: The transcendent on film', *Journal of Religion & Film*, 10 (2). Omaha, NE: University of Nebraska. http://www.unomaha.edu/jrf/Vol10No2/Avila_CountryPriest.htm.

Avisar, I. (1997), 'Holocaust movies and the politics of collective memory', in Rosenfeld, A. H. (ed.), *Thinking about the Holocaust After Half a Century.* Bloomington: Indiana University Press, p. 53.

Aylmer, K. J. (1998), 'Towering babble and glimpses of Zion: Recent depictions of Rastafari in cinema', in Murrell, N. S., Spencer, W. D., and McFarlane, A. A. (eds), *Chanting Down Babylon: The Rastafari Reader.* Philadelphia: Temple University Press.

Babington, B. and Evans, P.W. (1993), *Biblical Epics: Sacred Narrative in the Hollywood Cinema.* New York, USA: Manchester University Press.

Bach, A. (ed) (1996), 'Biblical glamour and Hollywood glitz', *Semeia* 74, Atlanta: Scholars.

Badley, L. (1995), *Film, Horror, and the Body Fantastic*. Westport: Greenwood Press, p. 21.

Baker, G. (2006), 'Portraying the quest for Buddhist wisdom?: A comparative study of *The Matrix* and *Crouching Tiger, Hidden Dragon*', *Journal of Religion & Film*, 10 (1). Omaha, NE: University of Nebraska. http://www.unomaha.edu/jrf/vol10no1/BakerQuest.ht.

Balázs, B. (1952), *Theory of Film: Character and Growth of a New Art*. London: Dobson.

Bandy, M. Ll and Monda, A. (eds) (2003), *The Hidden God: Film and Faith*. New York: The Museum of Modern Art.

Baron, L. (2005), *Projecting the Holocaust into the Present: The Changing Focus of Contemporary Holocaust Cinema*. New York: Rowman & Littlefield, p. 4.

Barsotti, C. M. and Johnston, R. K. (2004), *Finding God in the Movies: 33 Films of Reel Faith*. Grand Rapids: Baker Books.

Bather, N. (2006), *'There is evil there that does not sleep . . .:' The Construction of Evil in American Popular Cinema from 1989 to 2002*. New Zealand: University of Waikato.

Bathrick, D.; Prager, B., and Richardson, M. D. (2008), *Visualizing the Holocaust: Documents, Aesthetics, Memory*. Rochester, NY: Camden House.

Baudrillard, J. (1983), *Simulations*. New York: Semiotext(e)

Baudrillard, J. (2002), *The Transparency of Evil: Essays on Extreme Phenomena*. London: Verso, p. 6.

Baugh, L. (1997), *Imaging the Divine: Jesus and Christ Figures in Film*. Kansas City, MO: Sheed & Ward.

Bazin, A. (1967 and 1971), in Hugh Grey (trans.), *What is Cinema?* 2 volumes. Berkeley: University of California Press.

Beck, A. C. (1995), 'The Christian Allegorical Structure of Platoon', in Martin, J. W. and Ostwalt, C. E., Jr. (eds), *Screening the Sacred: Religion, Myth, and Ideology in Popular American Film*. Boulder, CO: Westview Press, Inc.

Berger, P. (1967), *The Sacred Canopy: Elements of a Sociological Theory of Religion*. Garden City, NY: Doubleday.

Berger, P. L. (1990), *The Sacred Canopy: A Sociological Theory of Religion*. New York: Anchor Books.

Bergesen, A. J. and Greeley, A. M. (2005), *God in the Movies*. New Brunswick: Transaction Publishers.

Berrigan, D. (2008), *Exodus: Let My People Go*. Eugene, OR: Cascade Books.

Berrigan, D. (2008), *The Kings and Their Gods: The Pathology of Power*. Grand Rapids, MI: William B. Eerdmans.

Bhagavad-Gītā.

Bhaskar, Ira (1998), 'Allegory, Nationalism, and Cultural Change in Indian Cinema: Sant Tukaram', *Literature and Theology*, 12 (1), pp. 50–69.

Bishop, P. (2000), 'Caught in the Cross-Fire: Tibet, Media and Promotional Culture', *Media, Culture & Society*, 22(5), pp. 647–648.

Black, G. D. (1994), *Hollywood Censored: Morality Codes, Catholics, and the Movies*. Cambridge: Cambridge University Press.

Black, G. D. (1997), *The Catholic Crusade Against the Movies, 1940–1975*. Cambridge: Cambridge University Press.

Blizek, W. L. (1999), 'Report from Sundance 1999: Religion in Independent films', *Journal of Religion & Film*. Omaha, NE: University of Nebraska, http://www.unomaha.edu/jrf/sundance.htm.

Blizek, W. L. and Desmarais, M. M. (2008), 'What Are We Teaching when We Teach "Religion and film?" ', in Watkins, G. J. (ed.), *Teaching Religion and Film*. New York: Oxford University Press.

Book 3, Vana Parva, Tīrtha-yatra Parva, CXXXVI.

Bordwell, D. and Thompson, K. (1997), *Film Art: An Introduction* (5th edn). Columbus, OH: McGraw-Hill Companies.

Bordwell, D. and Thompson, K. (2003), *Film Art: An Introduction* (7th edn). Columbus, OH: McGraw-Hill Companies.

Bordwell, D., Staiger, J. and Thompson, K. (1985), *The Classical Cinema*. London: Routledge.

Boskin, J. (1980), 'Denials: The Media View of Dark Skins and the City', Rubin, B. (ed.), *Small Voices and Great Trumpets*. New York: Praeger.

Bounds, P. (1999), *Cultural Studies*. Plymouth, MA: Studymates.

Bowman, D. (2001), 'Faith and the Absent Savior in *Central Station*', *Journal of Religion & Film*, 5(1: April). Omaha, NE: University of Nebraska, http://www.unomaha.edu/jrf/centstat.htm.

Brady, M. B. (1935), 'A New Era for the Church', *TES* (December).

Brintnall, K. L. (2004), 'Tarantino's Incarnational Theology: *Reservoir Dogs*, Crucifixions and Spectacular Violence', *Cross Currents*, 54(1: Spring), pp. 66–75.

Broadus, M. 'To Job or Not to Job: A Review of *The Dark Knight*', *Hollywood Jesus*, www.hollywoodjesus.com.

Brown, C. G. (2000), *The Death of Christian Britain*. London: Routledge.

Brown, J. (2001), 'Movies of the Middle East', *Salon.com* (9 October). http://archive.salon.com/mwt/feature/2001/10/09/film/print.html.

Bruce, D. (2007), 'The Matrix: A Hollywood Jesus Review', *Hollywood Jesus*, http://www.hollywoodjesus.com/matrix.htm.

Carnes, M. C. (ed.) (1996), *Past Imperfect: History According to the Movies*. New York: H. Holt, pp. 136–141.

Carroll, N. (1988), *Philosophical Problems of Classical Film Theory*. Princeton, N.J.

Carter, E. (1983), 'Cultural History Written with Lightning: The Significance of *The Birth of a Nation*', in Rollins, P. C. (ed.), *Hollywood as Historian: American Film in a Cultural Context*. Lexington: University Press of Kentucky, pp. 9–19.

Cavell, S. (1979), *The World Viewed: Reflections on the Ontology of Film*. Cambridge, MA: Harvard University Press.

Cawkwell, T. (2004), *The Filmgoer's Guide to God*. London: Darton, Longman and Todd Ltd.

Chaney, D. (1994), *The Cultural Turn: Scene-Setting Essays on Contemporary Cultural History*. London: Routledge.

Chatterjee, G. (2008) 'Designing a Course on Religion and Cinema in India', in Watkins, G. J. (ed.), *Teaching Religion and Film*. Oxford: Oxford University Press, p. 89–90.

Chen, L. F. (1972), in Shih Shun Liu (trans.), *The Confucian Way: A New and Systematic Study of the Four Books*. Republic of China: The Commercial Press.

Cheney, H. (1983), 'The Prodigal', *Christianity Today* (7 October).

Chmiel, M. (2001), *Elie Wiesel and the Politics of Moral Leadership*. Philadelphia, PA: Temple University Press.

Cho, F. (1999) 'Imagining Nothing and Imaging Otherness in Buddhist Film', in Plate, S. B. and Jasper, D. (eds), *Imag(in)ing otherness: Filmic Visions of Living Together*. Oxford: Oxford University Press: pp. 169–195.

Cho, F. (1999), 'Imagining Nothing and Imagining Otherness in Buddhist Film', in Plate, S. B and Jasper, D. (eds), *Imag(in)ing Otherness: Filmic Visions of Living Together*. Atlanta, GA: Scholars Press.

Cho, F. (2003), 'The Art of Presence: Buddhism and Korean Films', in Plate, S. B. (ed.), *Representing Religion in World Cinema*. New York: Palgrave Macmillan.

Cho, F. (2008), 'Buddhism, Film, and Religious Knowing: Challenging the Literary Approach to Film' in Watkins, G. (ed.), *Teaching Religion and Film*. New York: Oxford University Press.

Christ, C. P. and Plaskow, J. (1979), *Womanspirit Rising*. New York: HarperCollins Publishers.

Cicero, M. T. (1913), *De Officiis*, translated by Miller, W. Cambridge, MA: Harvard University Press, p. 341.

Clines, D. J. A. (1993), 'Job, the Book of', in Metzer, B. M. and Coogan, M. D. (eds), *The Oxford Companion to the Bible*. New York: Oxford University Press.

Coard, R., 'Wired to Kill' and 'Wired to Kill real, not reel-Sci-Fi!', *Portsmouth Review and Chesapeake Chronicle* XXVI (October).

Conroy, M. (2007), 'Seeing with Buddha's Eyes: *Spring, Summer, Autumn, Winter . . . and Spring*', *Journal of Religion & Film*, 11 (2). Omaha, NE: University of Nebraska, http://www.unomaha.edu/jrf/vol11no2/ConroyBuddha.htm.

Cornick, M. (2008), 'Modern Film Censorship: Television, Airlines, and Home Entertainment', Master's thesis, Department of History. Omaha, NE: University of Nebraska.

Cort, J. (1996), 'Art, Religion, and Material Culture. Some Reflections on Method'. *Journal of the American Academy of Religion*, 64 (3), pp. 613–632.

Cosandy, R.; Gaudreault, A. and Gunning, T. (eds) (1992), *Un Invention Du Diable?* Sainte-Foy: Les Presses De L'Université Laval.

Crane, J. L. (1994), *Terror and Everyday Life: Singular Moments in the History of Horror Film*. Thousand Oaks, CA: Sage Publications, p. 21.

Cryderman, L. (1990), 'The Taming of the VCR', *Christianity Today* (24 September).

Cueno, M. W. (2001), *American Exorcism: Expelling Demons in the Land of Plenty*. New York: Doubleday.

Custen, G. F. (1992), *Bio/Pics: How Hollywood Constructed Public History*. New Brunswick, NJ: Rutgers University Press, p. 44.

Daly, M. (1973), *Beyond God the Father*. Boston, MA: Beacon Press.

Dark, D. (2002), *Everyday Apocalypse*. Grand Rapids, MI: Brazos Press, p. 19.

Davidson, T. (1969), *The Philosophy of Goethe's Faust*. New York: Haskell House Publishers.

De Groot, Dr. A. T. (1954), 'Scenes of the Protestant Reformation', *The Christian-Evangelist*, 92. Bloomington, MN: Bethany Press.

De Lauretis, T. (1984), *Alice Doesn't: Feminism, Semiotics Cinema*. Bloomington, IN: Indiana University Press.

Deacy, C. (2005), *Faith in Film*. Aldershot: Ashgate.

Deacy, C. and Ortiz, G. W. (2008), *Theology and Film: Challenging the Sacred/Secular Divide*. Malden, MA: Blackwell Publishing, 28.

DeBona, G. (1999), *Savior on the Silver Screen*. New York: Paulist Press, p. 62.

Deloria, V. (1988), *Custer Died for Your Sins: An Indian Manifesto*, reprint. Norman, OK: University of Oklahoma Press, p. 2.

DeMille, C. B. and Hayne, D. (1985), *The Autobiography of Cecil B. Demille*. New York: Garland Publisher, p. 282.

Dicker, R. C. (2008), *A History of U.S. Feminisms*. Berkeley: Seal Press.

Doane, M. A. (1987), *The Desire to Desire: The Woman's Film of the 1940s*. Bloomington, IN: Indiana University Press.

Doneson, J. E. (2002), *The Holocaust in American Film* (2nd edn). New York: Syracuse University Press.

Dönmez-Colin, G. (2006), *Cinemas of the Other: A Personal Journey with Film-Makers From the Middle East and Central Asia*. UK: Intellect Ltd.

du Gay, P., Hall, S., Janes, L., Mackay, H. and Nagus, K. (1997), *Doing Cultural Studies: The Story of the Sony Walkman*. London: Sage, in association with the Open University.

Dudley, A. J. (1976), *The Major Film Theories: An Introduction*. Oxford University Press.

Dwyer, R. (2006), *Filming the Gods: Religion and Indian Cinema*. London: Routledge.

Dwyer, R. and Patel, D. (2002), *Cinema India: The Visual Culture of Hindi Film*. New Jersey: Rutgers University Press.

Edwards, C. (1989), 'Recorded Interview with Candice Hunt, Director of Marketing, Cathedral Films'. Virginia Beach, VA: Regent University (Transcript 3).

Ehrlich, Linda C. (2007), *The Cinema of Victor Erice: An Open Window*. Lantham, MD: Scarecrow Press.

Eisenstein, S. (1969), *Film Form: Essays in Film Theory*. New York: Harcourt Trade Publishers/Harvest Books.

Ekman, I. (2007), 'Swedish Documentary Follows "Regular" Europeans Who Turn to Jihad.' *International Herald Tribune* (15 October). http://www.iht.com/articles/2007/10/15/africa/sweden.php.

Erens, P. (1984), *The Jew in American Cinema*. Bloomington: Indiana University Press.

Erickson, S. (2007), 'The Middle East Side', *The Reeler: New York City Cinema, from the Art House to the Red Carpet* (25 April). http://www.thereeler.com/features/the_middle_east_side.php.

Exum, J. C. (1996), *Plotted, Shot, and Painted: Cultural Representations of Biblical Women*. Sheffield: Sheffield Academic Press.

Exum, J. C. (ed.) (2006), *The Bible in Film – The Bible and Film*. Leiden: Brill; and the selection of essays of both types in Christianson, E. S., Francis, P. and Telford, W.R. (eds) (2005), *Cinéma Divinité: Religion, Theology and the Bible in Film*. London: SCM.

Ezrahi, S. D. (2004), 'Questions of Authority', Hirsch, M., Kacandes, I. (eds), *Teaching the Representation of the Holocaust*. New York: Modern Language Association, pp. 52–67.

Faber, A. (2003), 'Redeeming Sexual Violence? A Feminist Reading of *Breaking the Waves*', *Studies in Religion*, 17(1 March), pp. 59–74.

Faber, A. (2006), '*Dancer in the Dark*: Affliction and the Aesthetic of Attention', *Studies in Religion*, 35(1), pp. 85–106.

Fielder, L. (1971), *The Collected Essays of Leslie Fiedler*. New York: Stein and Day Publishers.

Fielding, J. (2008), *Discovering World Religions at 24 Frames Per Second*. Lanham, MD: Scarecrow Press, Inc.

Fielding, J. R (2003), 'Reassessing *The Matrix/Reloaded*', *Journal of Religion & Film*, 7(2: October). Omaha, NE: University of Nebraska, http://www.unomaha.edu/jrf/Vol7No2/matrix.matrixreloaded.htm.

Fielding, J.R. (2003), 'Native American Religion and Film: Interviews with Chris Eyre and Sherman Alexie', *Journal of Religion & Film*, 7(1: April). Omaha, NE: University of Nebraska, http://www.unomaha.edu/jrf/Vol7No1/nativefilm.htm.

Finkelstein, N. G. (2005), *Beyond Chutzpah: On the Misuse of Anti-Semitism and the Abuse of History*. Berkeley and Los Angeles: University of California Press.

Fischer, M. M. J. (2001), 'Filmic Judgment and Cultural Critique: The Work of Art, Ethics, and Religion in Iranian Cinema', de Vries, H. and Weber, S. (eds), *Religion and Media*. Stanford, CA: Stanford University Press, pp. 456–486.

Fisher, M. P. (2008), *Living Religions*, seventh edition. Upper Saddle River, NJ: Pearson/Prentice Hall.

Flannery-Dailey, F. (2003), 'Robot Heavens and Robot Dreams: Ultimate Reality in A.I. and Other Recent Films', *Journal of Religion & Film*, 7 (2: October), paragraph 5. Omaha, NE: University of Nebraska, http://www.unomaha.edu/jrf/Vol7No2/robotHeaven.htm.

Flannery-Daily, F. and Wagner, R. (2001), 'Wake up! Gnosticism and Buddhism in *The Matrix*', *Journal of Religion & Film*, 5 (2: October). Omaha, NE: University of Nebraska, http://www.unomaha.edu/jrf/gnostic.htm.

Flanzbaum, H. (2001), 'But Wasn't It Terrific: A Defense of Liking *Life Is Beautiful*', *Yale Journal of Criticism*, 14 (1: Spring), pp. 273–286.

Forshey, G. E. (1992), *American Religious and Biblical Spectaculars*. Westport, CT: Praeger.

Fox News (2007), 'New Poll Shows Worry over Islam terror threat, to be detailed in specific FNC report'. *Fox News Website* (3 February). http://www.foxnews.com/story/0,2933,249521,00.html.

Fox, R. W. (2004), *Jesus in America: Personal Savior, Cultural Hero, National Obsession* (1st edn). San Francisco: Harper San Francisco, p. 11.

Freedman, E. (2002), *No Turning Back: The History of Feminism and the Future of Women*. New York: Ballantine Books.

Freeland, C. A. (2000), *The Naked and the Undead: Evil and the Appeal of Horror*. Boulder, CO: Westview Press, p. 143.

French, P. (1997), *Cowboy Metaphysics: Ethics and Death in Westerns*. Lanham, MD: Rowman & Littlefield Publishers, Inc.

Friedlander, S. (1997), *Probing the Limits of Representation: Nazism and the 'Final Solution'*. Cambridge: Harvard University Press.

Friedman, L. D. (1987), *The Jewish Image in American Cinema: 70 Years of Hollywood's Vision of Jewish Characters and Themes*. Secaucus: Citadel Press.

Fuery, P. (2000), *New Developments in Film Theory*. New York: Palgrave Macmillan.

Furhammar, L. and Isaksson, F. (1968), *Politics and Film*. London: Studio Vista.

Gabler, N. (1989), *An Empire of Their Own: How the Jews Invented Hollywood*. New York: Anchor Books.

Gallagher, T. (1998), *The Adventures of Roberto Rossellini: His Life and Films*. New York: Da Capo Press.

Gandhi, M. K. (1927), *An Autobiography: or The Story of My Experiments with Truth*.

Garbowski, C. (2002), 'Film Review: *The Pianist*', *Journal of Religion & Film*, 6 (2). Omaha, NE: University of Nebraska, www.unomaha.edu/jrf/pianist.htm.

Gaut, B. (2007), *Art, Emotion and Ethics*. Oxford: Oxford University Press, pp. 72–76, 107–108.

Gillespie, M. L. (1997), 'Picturing the Way in Bae Yong-kyun's *Why Has Bodhidharma Left for the East?*', *Journal of Religion & Film*, 1 (1: April), 7. Omaha, NE: University of Nebraska, http://www.unomaha.edu/jrf/gillespi.htm.

Ginsburg, T. (2007), *Holocaust Film: The Political Aesthetics of Ideology*. Newcastle, U.K.: Cambridge Scholars Publishing, p. 2.

Gleiberman, O. (2008), '*The Dark Knight* Movie Review', *Entertainment Weekly*, 1003 (25 July), 47.

Gokulsing, K. M. and Dissanayake, W. (1998), *Indian Popular Cinema: A Narrative of Cultural Change*. Staffordshire: Trentham Books, p. 23.

Gomery, D. (1991), *Movie History: A Survey*. California: Wadsworth Publishing Co.

Goodacre, M. (2007), *Mel Gibson's Passion: The Film, the Controversy, and Its Implications*, in Garber, Z. (ed.), Review of Biblical Literature, Society of Biblical Literature, http://www.bookreviews.org/bookdetail.asp?TitleId=5161&CodePage=5161.

Greeley, A. M. (1997), 'Images of God in the Movies', *Journal of Religion & Film* 1(April). Omaha, NE: University of Nebraska, http://www.unomaha.edu/jrf/greeleya.htm.

Greene, R. (2005), 'Y movies: Film and the Modernization of Pastoral Power', *Communication and Critical/Cultural Studies*, 2(1: March).

Grossberg, L. (2006), 'Does Cultural Studies have Futures? Should it? (or What's Wrong with New York?) Cultural Studies, Contexts, and Conjectures', *Cultural Studies*, 20 (1), 1–32.

Guneratne, A. Y. and Dissanayake, W. (2003), *Rethinking Third Cinema*. London: Routledge.

Haber, K. (ed.) (2003), *Exploring The Matrix*. New York: Macmillan.

Haines Lyon, C. and Marsh, C. (2007), 'Film's Role in Contemporary Meaning-Making: A Theological Challenge to Cultural Studies', in Knauss, S. and Ornella, A.D. (eds), *Reconfigurations: Interdisciplinary Perspectives on Religion in a Post-Secular Society*. Vienna and Münster: LIT Verlag, pp. 113–25.

Hall, S. (1997), 'Introduction', in Stuart Hall (ed.), *Representation: Cultural Representations and Signifying Practices*. London: Sage, in association with the Open University, pp. 1–11.

Haneke cited in Vogel, A. (1996), 'Of Nonexisting Continents: The Cinema of Michael Haneke', *Film Comment*, 32 (2 July/Aug), 74.

Haneke, M. (1992), 'Film als Katharsis', in Bono, F. (ed.), *Austria (in)felix: zum Österreichischem Film der 80er Jahre*. Graz: Blimp.

Hansen, M. B. (2001), '*Schindler's List* is not Shoah', Zelizer, B. (ed.), *Visual Culture and the Holocaust*. New Brunswick: Rudgers University Press, pp. 127–151.

Harris, S. L. (2007), *Understanding the Bible* (7th edn). New York: McGraw Hill.

Harvey, P. (2002), *An Introduction to Buddhism: Teachings, History and Practices*. New York: Cambridge University Press.

Hawthorne, S. (1993), 'Diotima Speaks through the Body', in Bar On, B.(ed.), *Engendering Origins: Critical Feminist Readings in Plato and Aristotle*. Albany, NY: SUNY Press.

Hayne, D. (1985), *The Autobiography of Cecil B. DeMille*. New York: Garland Publisher.

Hayward P.R. (1928), 'The King of Kings', *International Journal of Religious Education* (April).

Hellbeck, R. (1931), 'The Film and Protestantism', *International Review of Educational Cinematography* (3 October).

Herman, F. (2001), 'Hollywood, Nazism, and the Jews, 1933–41', *American Jewish History*.

Hill, T. (1994). 'Introduction: A Backward Glimpse through the Museum Door', in Hill, T. and Hill Sr., R. W. (eds), *Creation's Journey: Native American Identity and Belief*. Washington, D.C: Smithsonian Institution Press.

Hills, M. T. (1956), '500ᵗʰ Anniversary of the Gutenberg Bible', *Bible Society Record*, 101. New York: American Bible Society.

Hirsch, J. (2004), *Afterimage: Film, Trauma, and the Holocaust*. Philadelphia: Temple University Press, pp. 1–3.

Hoberman, J. (1993), 'Spielberg's Oskar', *Village Voice* (21 December), 65.

Hoberman. J. (2003), 'Flaunting It: The Rise and Fall of Hollywood's "Nice Jewish (Bad) Boys" ', in Hoberman, J. and Shandler, J. (eds), *Entertaining America: Jews, Movies, and Broadcasting*. New York and Princeton: The Jewish Museum, New York and Princeton University Press.

Holloway, R. (1977), *Beyond the Image: Approaches to the Religious Dimension in Cinema*. Geneva: World Council of Churches.

Hoover, S. (2006), *Religion in the Media Age*. New York and London: Routledge.

Hopkins Jr., R. M. (1937), 'Where Materials in Visual Education may be secured', *IJRE*, 14 (November).

Howe, I. (1976), *World of Our Fathers: The Journey of the east European Jews to America and the Life They Found and Made There*. New York: Galahad Books.

http://preview.gospelcom.net/rev.php3?1291.

http://www.cbsnews.com/stories/2007/06/15/opinion/main2934136.shtml.

http://www.sitasingstheblues.com/.

http://www.trinidadandtobagonews.com/selfnews/viewnews.cgi?newsid1028966817,58558,.shtml.

http://www.mediaculture-online.de/fileadmin/bibliothek/stafford_black/stafford_black.pdf.

http://www.nytimes.com/2008/08/10/magazine/10politics-t.html.

Hughes, Stephen and Birgit Meyer (eds) (2006), *Postscripts* 1, pp. 2–3. Special issue on film.

Hulsether, M. (2005), 'Religion and Culture', in Hinnells, J.R. (ed.), *The Routledge Companion to the Study of Religion*. London: Routledge, pp. 489–508.

Humphries-Brooks, S. (2006), *Cinematic Savior: Hollywood's Making of the American Christ*. Westport, CT: Praeger, p. 4.

Hurley, N. (1970), *Theology through Film*. New York: Harper and Row.

Hussain, A. (2008), 'Film and the Introduction to Islam Course', in Watkins, G. J. (ed.), *Teaching Religion and Film*. New York: Oxford University Press.

Ingebretsen, E. J. (1998), 'Staking the Monster: A Politics of Remonstrance', *Religion and American Culture*, 8 (1: Winter), 91–116.

Insdorf, A. (1983), *Indelible Shadows: Film and The Holocaust*, New York: Random House.

Irwin, W. (ed.) (2002), *The Matrix & Philosopy: Welcome to the Dessert of the Real*. Chicago: Open Court Publishing Company.

Iwamura, J. N. (2000, 2005 rev. edn), 'The Oriental Monk in American Popular Culture', in Forbes, B. D. and Mahan, J. H. (eds), *Religion and Popular Culture in America*. Berkeley: University of California Press, pp. 33–32.

Jack, I. *Hanif Kureishi: Biography*, http://www.emory.edu/ENGLISH/Bahri/Krueishi.html.

James, D. (2002), James, D. E. and Kim, K. H. (eds), *Im Kwon-Taek: The Making of a Korean National Cinema*. Detroit: Wayne State University Press.

Jameson, Fredric (1992), *The Geo-Political Aesthetic: Cinema and Space in the World System*. Bloomington, IN: Indiana University Press.

Jewett, R. (1993), *Saint Paul at the Movies: The Apostle's Dialogue with American Culture*. Louisville: Westminster; idem. (1999), *Saint Paul Returns to the Movies: Triumph over Shame*. Grand Rapids: William B. Eerdmans.

Jewett, R. (1997), 'Stuck in Time: Kairos, Chronos and the Flesh in *Groundhog Day*', in Marsh, C. and Ortiz, G. (eds), *Explorations in Theology and Film*. Oxford and Malden, MA: Blackwell, p.155–65.

Johnson, C. (2002), 'The Dilemmas of Ethnic Privilege: A Comparison of Constructions of "British", "English" and "Anglophone Celtic" Identity in Contemporary British and Australian Political Discourse', *Ethnicities*, 2 (2).

Johnson, R. (1986–1987), 'What is Cultural Studies Anyway?', *Social Text*, 16 (Winter), 38–80.

Johnson, R. K. (2000), 'Responding to Film Ethically: Moving beyond the Rating System', *Reel Spirituality: Theology and Film in Dialogue* (2nd edn). Grand Rapids, MI: Baker Academic, pp. 217–237.

Johnson, R., Chambers, D., Raghuram, P. and Tincknell, E. (2004), *The Practice of Cultural Studies*. London: Sage.

Johnston, R. K. (2000), *Reel Spirituality: Theology and Film in Dialogue*. Grand Rapids, MI: Baker.

Jonas, E. and Fischer, P. (2006), 'Terror Management and Religion: Evidence that Intrinsic Religiousness Mitigates Worldview Defense Following Mortality Salience', *Journal of Personality and Social Psychology*, 91, pp. 553–567.

Kaplan, E. A. (1983), *Women and Film: Both Sides of the Camera*. New York: Routledge.

Keefer, K. and Linafelt, T. (1998), 'The End of Desire: Theologies of Eros in the *Song of Songs* and *Breaking the Waves*', *Journal of Religion & Film*, 2 (1), Omaha, NE: University of Nebraska, http://www.unomaha.edu/jrf/endofdes.htm.

Kermode, F. (1967), *The Sense of an Ending: Studies in the Theory of Fiction*. London: Oxford University Press.

Kerr, S. (1995), 'Rain Man', *The New York Review* (6 April), 23.

King, G. (2002), *New Hollywood Cinema. An Introduction*. London: I. B. Tauris.

Kinnard, R. and Davis, T. (1992), *Divine Images: A History of Jesus on the Screen*. New York, NY: Carol Publishing Group, p. 20.

Kozlovic, A. K. (2002), 'Superman as Christ-Figure: The American Pop Culture

Movie Messiah', *Journal of Religion & Film*, 6 (1). Omaha, NE: University of Nebraska, http://www.unomaha.edu/jrf/superman.htm.

Kozlovic, A. K. (2002), 'The unholy, Non-Christic Biblical Subtexts in *Superman: The Movie* (1978) and *Superman II* (1981)', *Journal of Religion & Film*, 6 (2). Omaha, NE: University of Nebraska, http://www.unomaha.edu/jrf/supergood.htm.

Kozlovic, A. K. (2003), 'The Unholy Biblical Subtexts and Other Religious Elements Built into *Superman: The Movie* (1978) and *Superman II* (1981)', *Journal of Religion & Film*, 7 (1: April). Omaha, NE: University of Nebraska, http://www.unomaha.edu/jrf/Vol7No1/unholy.htm.

Kracauer, S. (1960), *Theory of Film: The Redemption of Physical Reality*. New York: Oxford University Press.

Kreitzer, L. J. (1993), *The New Testament in Fiction and Film: On Reversing the Hermeneutical Flow*. Sheffield: Sheffield Academic Press; idem. (1994), *The Old Testament in Fiction and Film: On Reversing the Hermeneutical Flow*. Sheffield: Sheffield Academic Press; idem. (1999), *Pauline Images in Fiction and Film: On Reversing the Hermeneutical Flow*. Sheffield: Sheffield Academic Press.

Krows, A. E. (1936), 'A Quarter-Century of Non-Theatrical Films', *TES* (June), 169–173.

Krows, A. E. (1938), 'So the Pictures Went to church', *TES* (October).

Krows, A. E. (1942), 'Motion Pictures – Not for Theatres', *TES* (May), 180–182.

Kureishi, H. (2002), *Collected Screenplays*. UK: Faber and Faber.

LaFleur, W. R. (2002), 'Suicide Off the Edge of Explicability: Awe in Ozu and Kore-eda', *Film History*, 14 (2).

Landy, M. (2000), 'Cinematic History, Melodrama, and the Holocaust', in Signer, M. A. (ed.), *Humanity at the Limit: The Impact of the Holocaust Experience on Jewish and Christians*. Bloomington: Indiana University Press.

Larsson, D. (2001), 'Kureishi in Dialogue', *CineScene.Com*, http://www.cinescene.com.

Le Cain, M., 'Do the Right Thing: The Films of Michael Haneke', *Senses of Cinema*, http://www.sensesofcinema.com/contents/03/26/haneke.html.

Leff, L. J. and Simmons, J. L (1990), *The Dame in the Kimono: Hollywood, Censorship, and the Production Code from the 1920s to the 1960s*. New York: Grove Weidenfeld.

Leff, L. J. and Simmons, J. L. (1990), 'Appendix', *The Dame in the Kimono: Hollywood, Censorship, & the Production Code From the 1920s to the 1960s*. New York: Grove Weidenfeld Publishers.

Leff, L. J. and Simmons, J. L. (1990), *The Dame in the Kimono: Hollywood, Censorship, and the Production Code from the 1920s to the 1960s*. New York: Doubleday, pp. 283–92.

Leitch, T. M. (1997), 'Know-Nothing Entertainment: What to Say to Your Friends on the Right, and Why it Won't Do Any Good', *Literature/Film Quarterly*, 25, 3.

Leitch, V. B. (1991), 'Birmingham Cultural Studies: Popular Arts, Post Structuralism, Radical Critique', *The Journal of the Midwest Modern Language Association*, 24 (1: Spring), 74–86.

Leonard, R. J. (2003), *The Cinematic Mystical Gaze: The Films of Peter Weir*. University of Melbourne, PhD Thesis, http://dtl.unimelb.edu.au/dtl_publish/6/65996.html.

Lerner, G. (1986), *The Creation of Patriarchy*. New York: Oxford University Press.

Lindvall, T. (2001), *The Silents of God*. Lanham, MD: Scarecrow Press.

Link, L. (1995), *The Devil: the Archfiend in Art From the Sixth to the Sixteenth Century*. New York: Harry N. Abrams.

Litwack, L. F. (1996), '*The Birth of a Nation*', in Carnes, M. C. (ed.), *Past Imperfect: History According to the Movies*. New York: H. Holt, pp. 136–141.

Lott, T. (1958), 'The Radio and Television Commission,' *Encyclopedia of Southern Baptists Volume II*. Nashville: Broadman Press.

Loughlin, G. (2004), *Alien Sex: The Body and Desire in Cinema and Theology*. Oxford: Blackwell Publishing.

Loughlin, G. (2005), 'Cinéma Divinité: A Theological Introduction', in Christianson, E. S., Francis, P. and Telford, W. R. (eds), *Cinéma Divinité: Religion, Theology and the Bible in Film*. London: SCM Press, pp.1–12.

Lucci-Cooper, K. (2003), 'To Carry the Fire Home', *Genocide of the Mind: New Native American Writing*. New York: Thunder's Mouth Press/Nation Books.

Lutgendorf, P. (2002), 'A Superhit Goddess: Jai Santoshi Maa and Caste Hierarchy in Indian Films' (part one), *Manushi: A Journal About Women and Society*, 131 (October–November), 10–16.

Lyden, J. (2003), *Film As Religion: Myths, Morals, and Rituals*. New York: New York University Press.

Lyden, J. C. (2003), *Religion as Film: Myths, Morals and Rituals*. New York and London: New York University Press.

MacDougall, D. (1998), *Transcultural Cinema*. Princeton: Princeton University Press.

Makarushka, I. S. M. (1998), 'A Picture's Worth: Teaching Religion and Film', *Religious Studies News Spotlight on Teaching*, 6 (1 May). Atlanta, GA: American Academy of Religion, http://www.aarweb.org/Publications/spotlight/previous/6-1/06-01-07apic.asp.

Makarushka, I. S. M. (1998), 'Transgressing Goodness in *Breaking the Waves*', *Journal of Religion & Film*. Omaha, NE: University of Nebraska, http://www.unomaha.edu/jrf/breaking.htm.

Makarushka, I. S. M. (1998), 'Tracing the Other in household Saints', *Literature and Theology, 12 (March)*. Oxford: Oxford University Press.

Malone, P. (1990), *Movie Christs and Antichrists*. New York, NY: Crossroad Publishing.

Marks, H. (1985), 'A Brief History of Church Films', *Christian Film & Video Review* (January–February).

Marsh, C. (2004), *Cinema and Sentiment: Film's Challenge to Theology*, Milton Keynes and Waynesboro, GA: Authentic Media.

Marsh, C. (2007), *Theology Goes to the Movies: An Introduction to Critical Christian Thinking*. London: Routledge.

Marsh, C. (2009), 'Audience Reception', in Lyden, J. (ed.), *The Routledge Companion to Religion and Film*. New York and London: Routledge.

Marsh, C., and Ortiz, G. (eds) (2001), *Explorations in Theology and Film*. Chippenham: Blackwell Publishers.

Marthaler, B.L. et al. (eds) (2003), *New Catholic Encyclopedia* (2nd edn), 3, 'Cenobites'. New York: Gale Group.

Martin, J. W. and Ostwalt, C. E. (eds) (1995), *Screening the Sacred: Religion, Myth, and Ideology in Popular Film*. Boulder: Westview Press.

Mast, G. and Cohen, M. (eds) (2004), *Film Theory and Criticism: Introductory Readings*. Oxford University Press.

Matalon, G. (2001), 'Esther and the Mexican', *Journal of Religion & Film*, 5 (1: April). http://www.unomaha.edu/jrf/esther.htm.

Matthew, W. *World Religions*. Belmont, CA: Wadsworth Publishing 2004.

May, J. R. and Bird, M. (eds) (1982), *Religion in Film*. Knoxville, TN: The University of Tennessee Press.

McAlister, M. (2005), 'Iran, Islam, and the Terrorist Threat, 1979–1989', Slocum, J. D. (ed.), *Terrorism, Media, Liberation*. New Jersey: Rutgers University Press.

McDannell, C. (1995), *Material Christianity: Religion and Popular Culture in America*. New Haven: Yale University Press.

Medved, M. (1992), *Hollywood Vs. America: Popular Culture and the War on Traditional Values* (1st edn). New York, NY and Grand Rapids, Mich.: HarperCollins.

Meggitt, J. J. (2004), 'Sources: Use, Abuse, Neglect. The Importance of Ancient Popular Culture', in Horrell, D. and Adams, E. (eds), *Christianity at Corinth: The Scholarly Quest for the Corinthian Church*. London: Westminster John Knox Press, pp. 241–253.

Mehta, S. (2004). *Maximum City: Bombay Lost and Found*. New York: Vintage, p. 349–350.

Mercandante, L. (2001), 'Bess the Christ Figure?', *Journal of Religion & Film*, 5 (1). Omaha, NE: University of Nebraska, http://www.unomaha.edu/jrf/bessthe.htm.

Merrill, R. (2005), 'Simulations and Terrors of Our Time', in Slocum, J. D. (ed.), *Terrorism, Media, Liberation*. New Jersey: Rutgers University Press.

Meyer, Birgit (2001), 'Money, Power, and Morality: Popular Ghanian Cinema in the Fourth Republic', *Ghana Studies*, 4, 65–84.

Meyer, Birgit. (2002), 'Occult Forces on Screen: Representation and the Danger of Mimesis in Popular Ghanian Films', *Etnofoor*, 15 (1/2), 212–221.

Miles, M. (1996), *Seeing and Believing: Religion and Values in the Movies*. Boston: Beacon Press.

Miles, M. and Plate, S. B. (2004), 'Hospitable Vision: Some Notes on the Ethics of Seeing Film', *Cross Currents*, 54 (1: Spring), 30.

Miller, B. S. (trans.) (1986), *The Bhagavad-Gita: Krishna's Counsel in Time of War*. New York: Bantam Books, verses 2.62–63.

Mitchell, J. (2004), 'From Morality Tales to Horror Movies: Towards and Understanding of the Popularity of West African Video Film', Horsfield, P. et al. (eds), *Belief in Media: Cultural Perspectives on Media and Christianity*. Aldershot: Ashgate, pp. 107–121.

Mitchell, J. and Plate, S. B. (eds) (2007), *The Religion and Film Reader*. London: Routledge.

Monier-Williams, M. (1899/1995), *A Sanskrit English Dictionary* (new edn). Delhi: Motilal Banarsidass.

Mullen, E. L. (1998), 'Oriental Commercializations: Tibetan Buddhism in American Popular Film', *Journal of Religion & Film*, 2 (2: October). Omaha, NE: University of Nebraska, http://www.unomaha.edu/jrf/OrientalMullen.htm.

Mulvey, L. (1989), *Visual and Other Pleasures*. Bloomington, IN: Indiana University Press.

Münsterberg, Hugo. (1916), *The Photoplay: A Psychological Study*. New York: D. Appleton and Company.

Murray, D. (2008), 'A Film-Maker Who Lives in the Shadow of a Fatwa', *The*

Spectator, 12 March, http://www.spectator.co.uk/print/the-magazine/features/553681/a-filmmaker-who-lives-in-the-shadow-of-a-fatwa.thtml.

Myers, C. (1988), *Binding the Strong Man: A Political Reading of Mark's Story of Jesus.* Maryknoll, NY: Orbis Books.

Naficy, H. (2002), 'Islamizing Film Culture in Iran', in Tapper, T. (ed), *The New Iranian Cinema: Politics, Representation and Identity.* London: I.B. Tauris.

Nelson, C. (1991), 'Always Already Cultural Studies: Two Conferences and a Manifesto', *The Journal of the Midwest Modern Language Association*, 24 (1: Spring), 24–38.

Nigosian, S. A. (2008), *World Religions: A Historical Approach* (4th edn). Boston: Bedford/St. Martin's, 112–113.

Nixon, J. (2007), 'Richard Hoggart's Legacy for Democratic Education', *International Journal of Cultural Studies*, 10 (1: March), 63–71.

Nolan, S. (2003), 'Towards a New Religious Film Criticism: Using Film to Understand Religious Identity Rather than Locate Cinematic Analogue', Mitchell, J. and Marriage, S. (eds), *Mediating Religion: Conversations in Media, Religion and Culture.* London and New York: Continuum, 169–78.

Norton, A. J. (1998), 'De-Icing the Emotions: Michael Haneke's Retrospective in London', *Central Europe Review* (26 October), http://www.ce-review.org/kinoeye/kinoeye5old.html.

Noss, D. S., *A History of the World's Religions.* Upper Saddle River, NJ: Pearson/Prentice Hall.

Nowell-Smith, Geoffrey (ed.) (1996), *The Oxford History of World Cinema.* Oxford: Oxford University Press.

Nye, M. (2003), *Religion: The Basics.* London and New York: Routledge.

O'Brien, T. (1990), *The Screening of America: Movies and Values from Rocky to Rain Man.* New York: Continuum.

Ortiz, G. (2007), 'World Cinema: Opportunities for Dialogue with Religion and Theology', Johnston, R. (ed.), *Reframing Theology and Film: New Focus for an Emerging Discipline.* Grand Rapids: Baker, pp. 73–87.

Ostwalt, C. (1995), 'Hollywood and Armageddon: Apocalyptic Themes in Recent Cinematic Presentation', in Martin. J. and Ostwalt, C. (eds.), *Screening the Sacred: Religion, Myth, and Ideology in Popular American Film.* Boulder: Westview.

Ostwalt, C. (2003), *Secular Steeples: Popular Culture and the Religious Imagination.* Harrisburg: Trinity Press.

Oxtoby, W. G. and Segal, A. F. (eds), *A Concise Introduction to World Religions.*

Pearson, J. (2002), ' "Going native in reverse": The Insider as Researcher in British Wicca', in Arweck, E. and Stringer, M.D. (eds), *The Insider/Outsider Problem in the Study of Religion.* Birmingham: University of Birmingham Press, pp. 97–113.

Penley, C. (1989), *The Future of an Illusion: Film, Feminism and Psychoanalysis.* Minneapolis, MN: University of Minnesota Press.

Perez, M. (1972), 'The Puritan Despair', *Focus on the Horror Film.* Englewood Cliffs, NJ: Prentice-Hall, p. 134.

'*Phorpa/The Cup*: An Interview with the Film's Director Khyentse Norbu', *Gentle Voice: A Newsletter of Siddhartha's Intent* (March 1999), http://www.siddharthasintent.org/gentle/GV11-3.htm.

Picart, C. J. (2004), *The Holocaust Film Sourcebook* (vols. 1 and 2). Westport, CT.: Praeger.

Plate, S. B. (ed.) (2003), *Representing Religion in World Cinema: Filmmaking, Mythmaking, Culture Making*. New York and Hampshire, England: Palgrave Macmillan, pp. 3–10.

Plate, S. B. (2008), *Religion and Film: Cinema and the Re-Creation of the World*. London: Wallflower Press.

Plate, S. B. and Jasper, D. (eds) (1999), *Imag(in)ing Otherness: Filmic Visions of Living Together*. Oxford: Oxford University Press.

Plate, S. B. (2005), 'Religion and Film', *Encyclopedia of Religion* (2nd edn). Macmillan, pp. 3097–3103.

Plate. S. B. (2003), 'The Re-creation of the World: Filming Faith', *Dialog*, 42 (2: Summer), 155–160.

Pope, L. (1985), 'Flickers of Our Anti-Islam Bigotry', *Los Angeles Times* (1 March).

Pope, R. (2007), *Salvation in Celluloid: Theology, Imagination, and Film*. London: T&T Clark, p. 106.

Quinones, R. J. (1991), *The Changes of Cain: Violence and the Lost Brother in Cain and Abel Literature*. Princeton, NJ: Princeton University Press.

Qumsiyeh, M. B. (2003), '100 Years of Anti-Arab and Anti-Muslim Stereotyping', *The Prism*, http://www.ibiblio.org/prism/jan98/anti_arab.html.

Rajadhyaksha, A. and Willemen, P. (1999). *Encyclopaedia of Indian Cinema* (rev. edn), Oxford: Oxford University Press.

Ramji, R. (2003), 'Representations of Islam in American News and Film: Becoming the "Other" ', Mitchell, J. and Marriage, S. (eds) (2003), *Mediating Religion: Conversations in Media, Religion and Culture*. London: T&T Clark.

Ramji, R. (2005), 'From "Navy Seals" to "The Siege": Getting to Know the Muslim Terrorist, Hollywood Style', *Journal of Religion & Film*, 9 (2: October). Omaha, NE: University of Nebraska, http://www.unomaha.edu/jrf/Vol9No2/RamjiIslam.htm.

Ravetto, K. (2001), *The Unmaking of Fascist Aesthetics*. Minneapolis and London: University of Minnesota Press.

Read, C. (2001), 'Terror Movies Surging in Popularity: Viewers Seeking Insight', *National Post* (19 September).

Reimer, R. C. and Reimer, C. J. (1992), *Nazi-Retro Film: How German Narrative Cinema Remembers the Past*. New York: Twayne.

Reinhartz, A. (2003), *Scripture on the Silver Screen*. Louisville: Westminster John Knox.

Remark, S., '*Fight Club*: A Hollywood Jesus Movie Review', *Hollywood Jesus*, http://www.hollywoodjesus.com/fight_club.html.

Reuther, R. R. (1983), *Sexism and God-Talk*. Boston, MA: Beacon Press.

Richie, D. and Mellen, J. (1999), *The Films of Akira Kurosawa* (3rd updated and expanded edn). Berkeley: University of California Press.

Robbins, G. A. (1997), 'Mozart & Salieri, Cain & Abel: A Cinematic Transformation of Genesis 4', *Journal of Religion & Film*, 1 (1: April). Omaha, NE: University of Nebraska, http://www.unomaha.edu/jrf/robbins.htm.

Robbins, M. (1947–48), 'Films for the Church', *Hollywood Quarterly*, 3 (2: Winter).

Rodríguez, H. (1997), 'Ideology and Film Culture', in Allen R. and Smith, M. (eds), *Film Theory and Philosophy*. Oxford: Oxford University Press.

Rodríguez-Mangual, E (2002), 'Driving a Dead Body through the Nation: Death and Allegory in the Film *Guantanamera*', *Chasqui*, 31 (1), 50–62.

Rodríguez-Mangual, E. (2003), 'Santeria and the Quest for a Postcolonial Identity', in Plate, S. B. (ed.), *Representing Religion in World Cinema*. New York: Palgrave Macmillan, pp. 219–237.

Rollins, P. C. (ed.), *Hollywood as Historian: American Film in a Cultural Context*. Lexington: University Press of Kentucky, pp. 9–19.

Romanowski, W. and Vander Heide, J. L. (2007), 'Easier Said than Done: On Reversing the Hermeneutical Flow in the Theology and Film Dialogue', *Journal of Communication and Religion* (March), pp. 40–64.

Rosaldo, R. (1993), *Culture and the Truth: The Remaking of Social Analysis*. Boston: Beacon Press.

Rothberg, M. (2000), *Traumatic Realism: The Demands of Holocaust Representation*. Minneapolis: University of Minnesota Press.

Runions, E. (2003), *How Hysterical: Identification and Resistance in the Bible and Film*. New York: Palgrave Macmillan.

Russell, J. B. (1984), *Lucifer: The Devil in the Middle Ages*. Ithaca, New York: Cornell University Press.

Russell, J. B. (1986), *Mephistopheles: The Devil in the Modern World*. Ithaca, NY: Cornell University Press.

Sachar, H. (1992), *A History of the Jews in America*. New York: Alfred A. Knopf.

Said, E. (1979), *Orientalism*. New York: Vintage.

Schaeffer, F. (2007), *Crazy for God: How I Grew Up As One of the Elect, Helped Found the Religious Right, and Lived to Take All (Or Almost All) of It Back*. Cambridge, MA: DeCapo Press (Perseus Books Group).

Schrader, P. (1972) *Transcendental Style in Film: Ozu, Bresson, Dreyer*, Berkeley: University of California Press; reprinted 1988, DaCapo Press.

Schrader, P. (1988), *The Transcendental Style in Film*. Da Capo Press.

Schreck, N. (2000), *The Satanic Screen: An Illustrated Guide to the Devil in Cinema*. London: Creation Books.

Schuler, J. (1997), 'Kierkegaard at *Babette's Feast*: The Return to the Finite', *Journal of Religion & Film*, 1 (2). Omaha, NE: University of Nebraska, http://www.unomaha.edu/jrf/kierkega.htm.

Schüssler Fiorenza, E. (1992), *But She Said: Feminist Practices of Biblical Interpretation*. Boston, Massachusetts: Beacon Press.

Scott, A. O. (2002), '*The Pianist*: Surviving the Warsaw Ghetto against Steep Odds', *New York Times* (27 December), http://movies.nytimes.com/movie/review?res=9E0DE1DA113CF934Ai5751C1A9649C8B63.

Sen, K. (1994), *Indonesian Cinema*. London: Zed Books.

Senter III, M. H. (1981), 'Bringing Back Cinema Serials: Christian Style', *Christianity Today* (20 November).

Shaheen, J. G. (1987), 'The Hollywood Arab (1984–1986)', *Journal of Popular Film and Television*, 14 (4).

Shaheen, J. G. (2001), *Reel Bad Arabs: How Hollywood Vilifies a People*. New York: Olive Branch Press.

Shandler, D. (1999), *While America Watches: Televising the Holocaust*. New York: Oxford University Press.

Shapiro, J. S. (2000), *Oberammergau: The Troubling Story of the World's Most Famous Passion Play* (1st edn). New York: Pantheon Books.

Shapiro, M. (1986), '*Booby Trap*: A Cross between *The Road Warrior* and *Death Wish*', *Cinefantastique*.

Shepherd, D. (2008), 'Prolonging *the Life of Moses*: From Spectacle to Story in the Early Cinema', in Shepherd, D. (ed.), *Images of the Word: Hollywood's Bible and Beyond*. Atlanta: Society of Biblical Literature.

Shohat, E. (1990), 'Gender in Hollywood's Orient', *Middle East Report, 162* (1: January–February), 20.

Shohat, E. and Stam. R. (1994), *Unthinking Eurocentrism: Multiculturalism and the Media*. London: Routledge.

Short, K. R. M., and Dolezel, S. (1988), *Hitler's Fall: The Newsreel Witness*. London: Croon Helm.

Silverman, K. (1988), *The Acoustic Mirror: The Female Voice in Psychoanalysis and Cinema*. Bloomington, IN: Indiana University Press.

Silverman, K. (1996), *The Threshold of the Visible World*. New York: Routledge.

Simon, J. (1992) 'Black Robe', *National Review* (3 February), http://findarticles. com/p/articles/mi_m1282/is_n2_v44/ai_11860858/pg_2.

Sison, Antonio (2006), Screening Schillebeeck: Theology and Third Cinema in Dialogue. New York: Palgrave.

Sluyter, D. (2005), *Cinema Nirvana: Enlightenment Lessons from The Movies*. New York: Three Rivers Press.

Smith, B. (2000), *Global Feminisms Since 1945: A Survey of Issues and Controversies (Re-Writing Histories)*. London: Routledge.

Solano, J. R. (2004), 'Blessed Broken Bodies: Exploring Redemption in *Central Station* and *Breaking the Waves*', *Journal of Religion & Film*, 8 (1). Omaha, NE: University of Nebraska, http://www.unomaha.edu/jfr/Vol8No1/Bessed Broken.htm.

Solomon, J. (2001), *The Ancient World in Cinema: Revised and Expanded Edition*. New Haven, CT: Yale University Press.

Solomon, N. (1996), 'The Danger in Stereotyping', *St. Louis Post-Dispatch* (14 January).

Soukup, P. A. (2004), 'Transforming the Sacred: The American Bible Society New Media Translation Project', *The Journal of Media and Religion*, 3 (2), 101–118.

Stafford, R. (2002), 'Where's the Black in the Union Jack?', *Mediaculture Online*.

Stanton, E. C. (2003), *The Woman's Bible: A Classic Feminist Perspective*. Mineola, NY: Dover Publications.

Steele, T. (1997), *The Emergence of Cultural Studies. 1945–1965. Cultural Politics, Adult Education and the English Question*. London: Lawrence and Wishart.

Stern, R. C., Jefford, C. N., and DeBona, G. (1999), *Savior on the Silver Screen*. New York: Paulist Press, p. 62.

Stone, B. (2001), 'The Sanctification of Fear: Images of the Religious in Horror Films', *Journal of Religion & Film*, 5 (2: October). Omaha, NE: University of Nebraska, http://www.unomaha.edu/jrf/sanctifi.htm.

Stone, B. P. (2000), 'Theology and Film in Postmodern Culture: A Dialogue with *Forrest Gump* and *Pulp Fiction*', *Wesleyan Theological Journal*, 35 (1), 149–164.

Storey, J. (2006), *Cultural Theory and Popular Culture: An Introduction* (4th edn). London: Prentice-Hall.

Stucky, M. (2005), 'He is the One: *The Matrix* Trilogy's Postmodern Movie

Messiah', *Journal of Religion & Film*, 9 (2: October), http://www.unomaha.edu/jrf/Vol9No2/StuckyMatrixMessiah.htm.

Swedish Film Institute (2008), '2007 Nominations for Guldbagge – The Swedish National Film Award', *Swedish Film Institute Website* (8 January), http://www.sfi.se/sfi/smpage.fwx?page=8794&NEWS=21205.

Tapper, R. (ed.) (2002), *The New Iranian Cinema: Politics, Representation and Identity*. London: I. B. Tauris.

Tatum, W. B. (2004), *Jesus at the Movies: A Guide to the First Hundred Years*. Santa Rosa, CA: Polebridge Press, pp. 58–59.

Taylor, B. (2008), *Entertainment Theology: New Edge Spirituality in a Digital Democracy*. Grand Rapids, MI: Baker Academic, p. 19.

The Holy Bible, King James Version.

Thomas, J. B. (2007), '*Shukyo Asobi* and Miyazaki Hayao's *Anime*', *Nova Religio*, 10 (3).

Thompson Klein, J. (1996), *Crossing Boundaries: Knowledge, Disciplnarities and Interdisciplinarities*. Charlottesville: University Press of Virginia.

Thompson quoted in Meggitt, J. J. (2004), *Sources: Use, Abuse, Neglect. The Importance of Ancient Popular*, p. 242.

Thompson, J. B. (1990), *Ideology and Modern Culture*. Cambridge: Polity Press.

Tinkcomm, M. and Villarejo, A. (eds) (2001), *Keyframes: Popular Cinema and Cultural Studies*. London: Routledge.

Toplin, R. B. (2002), *Reel History: In Defense of Hollywood*. Lawrence: University of Kansas Press.

Travers, P. (1992), 'Tarantino's Twist', *Rolling Stone*, 692 (4 October), 80.

Trible, P. (1978), *God and the Rhetoric of Sexuality (Overtures to Biblical Theology)*. Minneaplis, MN: Fortress Press.

Trinh, T. M. (1989), *Woman, Native, Other: Writing Postcoloniality and Feminism*. Bloomington, IN: Indiana University Press.

Tudor, A. (1989), *Monsters and Mad Scientists: A Cultural History of the Horror Movie*. Oxford: Blackwell, p. 185.

Turner, G. (2000), 'Cultural Studies and Film', in Hill, J. and Gibson, P. C. (eds), *Film Studies: Critical Approaches*. Oxford: Oxford University Press, pp. 193–199.

Tusher, W. (1985), 'SB Prods. Plans Move from Dox to Feature Pix', *Variety*, 208 (1 September), (64) 5.

Unattributed (1919), 'Motion Pictures at the New York Labor Temple', *Film Educational Magazine*, 2 (2: August).

Unattributed (1920), 'The Church's Duty to the Movies', *Literary Digest*, 64 (21 February).

Unattributed (1949), 'Visual Aids for the Church', *CH* (October).

Unattributed (1950), 'Family Films Offer Moral Teaching Messages: Effective and Entertaining', *IJRE* (March).

Unattributed (1954), 'Movies for the Family – *John Wesley*', *Christian Advocate*, 129 (19: 13 May).

Unattributed (1954), 'Museum of Modern Art', *Christian Advocate*, 129 (12: 15 March).

Unattributed (1960), 'The Bible Goes to Press: From the Motion Picture, *Our Bible – How It Came to Us*', in Maus, C. (1960), *The Church and the Fine Arts*. New York: Harper and Brothers.

Unattributed (1981), *Family Films Is 35 and Proud Of It*. Family Films Promotional Guide.

Unattributed (1990), 'The Return of Franky Schaeffer', *Christianity Today* (19 November), 37–38.

Unattributed (2003), 'The World that is Known', *Cineaste*, 28 (3: Summer), 28–31.

Unattributed (2004), 'The Passion of the Christians', *The Economist*, 2nd October, 50.

Varzi, R. (2002), 'A Ghost in the Machine: The Cinema of the Iranian Sacred Defense', in Tapper, R. (ed.), *The New Iranian Cinema: Politics, Representation and Identity*. London: I. B. Tauris.

Varzi, R. (2006), *Warring Souls: Youth Media and Martyrdom in Post-Revolutionary Iran*. Durham: Duke University Press.

Vaux, S. A. (1999), *Finding Meaning at the Movies*. Nashville, TN: Abingdon.

Vaux, S. A. (2007), 'Letters on Better Movies', in Johnston, R. (ed.), *Reframing Theology and Film: New Focus for an Emerging Discipline*. Grand Rapids: Baker, pp. 88–107.

Viswanathan, G. (2003/2005), 'Colonialism and the Construction of Hinduism', *The Blackwell Companion To Hinduism*. Malden: Blackwell Publishing, 28.

Vollmer, U. (2007), *Seeing Film and Reading Feminist Theology*. New York: Palgrave Macmillan.

Vollmer, Ulrike (2007), *Film and Feminist Theology in Dialogue*. New York: Palgrave.

Walker, J. (2005), *Trauma Cinema: Documenting Incest and the Holocaust*. Berkeley: University of California Press.

Walsh, F., *Sin and Censorship: The Catholic Church and the Motion Picture Industry*. New Haven & London: Yale University Press.

Walsh, R. (2005), *Finding St. Paul in Film*. New York: T & T Clark.

Watkins, G. J. (ed.) (2008), *Teaching Religion and Film*. New York: Oxford University Press.

Webster, F. (2004), 'Cultural Studies and Sociology at, and after, the Closure of the Birmingham School', *Cultural Studies*, 18 (6 November), 847–862.

Wells, H. G. (1898), *War of the Worlds*. William Heinemann.

White, M. (1983), 'Does Christian Film Work in the Neighborhood Theater?', *Christianity Today* (7 October).

Wiesel, E. (2003), 'Forward', Insdorf, A., *Indelible Shadows: Film and the Holocaust* (3rd edn). New York: Cambridge University Press.

Willemen, P. (1994), *Looks and Frictions: Essays in Cultural Studies and Film Theory*. London: British Film Institute.

Williams, P. (2000), 'Review Essay: Religion Goes to the Movies', *Religion and American Culture*, 10 (2), 225–239.

Williams, R. (1985), *Keywords. A Vocabulary of Culture and Society* (rev. edn). Oxford: Oxford University Press.

Williams, R. (2000), *Lost Icons: Reflections on Cultural Bereavement*. Harrisburg: Morehouse Publishing.

Willis, T. M. (1993), 'Redeem', in Metzger, B. M. and Coogan, M. D. (eds), *The Oxford Companion to the Bible*. New York: Oxford University Press.

Wood, M. (1989), *America in the Movies* (2nd edn). New York: Columbia University Press.

Wright, M. J. (2007), *Religion and Film. An Introduction*. London: I. B. Tauris.

Wright, W. M. (1997), '*Babette's Feast*: A Religious Film', *The Journal of Religion & Film*, l (1: October), http://www.unomaha.edu/jrf/BabetteWW.htm.

Wyke, M. (1997), *Projecting the Past: Ancient Rome, Cinema, and History, The New Ancient World*. New York: Routledge.

Yao, X. (2000), *An Introduction to Confucianism*. Cambridge, UK: Cambridge University Press.

Young, W. A. (2005), *The World's Religions: Worldviews and Contemporary Issues* (2nd edn). Upper Saddle River, NJ: Pearson/Prentice Hall, p. 27.

Zerelli, L. (2005), *Signifying Woman*. Ithaca and London: Cornell University Press, p. 1.

Zondervan, p. 37–49.

Notes on Contributors

William L. Blizek is Professor of Philosophy and Religion at the University of Nebraska at Omaha. He is presently serving as Chair of the Religious Studies Program. He is one of the co-founders of the *Journal of Religion & Film*, first published in 1997. He holds a Ph.D. in philosophy from the University of Missouri-Columbia.

Michele Marie Desmarais is Associate Professor of Religious Studies at the University of Nebraska at Omaha. She is presently serving as editor of the Journal of Religion & Film. Her book, *Changing Minds: Mind, Consciousness and Identity in Patañjali's Yoga Sūtra and Cognitive Neuroscience* was published in 2008 by Motilal Banarsidass. She has a Ph.D. in Asian studies from the University of British Columbia.

Alyda Faber is Associate Professor of Christian Theology and Ethics at the Atlantic School of Theology. Her research interests are religion and film; Virginia Woolf and religious subjectivity; feminist theory and theology; and religion and violence. She received her Ph.D. from McGill University.

Julien R. Fielding is Lecturer in Religious Studies at the University of Nebraska at Omaha. She is the author of *Discovering World Religions at 24 Frames Per Second* (2008). Her Master's degree in religion is from the University of Kansas.

Christian Haunton is Lecturer in Religious Studies at the University of Nebraska at Omaha where he is the recipient of the College of Arts & Sciences Excellence in Teaching Award. He holds a Master's degree in religion from the University of Iowa.

Terry Lindvall is the C.S. Lewis Professor of Communication and Christian Thought at Virginia Wesleyan College. Among his publications are *The Silents of God: Selected Issues and Documents in Silent American Film and Religion, 1908–1922* (2001), *Sanctuary Cinema: The Origins of the Christian Film Industry* (2007). He received his Ph.D. from University of Southern California.

371

Fr. Peter Malone, MSC mans the Cinema Desk for SIGNIS, World Catholic Association for Communication, which is headquartered in Bussels, Belgium. His many books are *Through a Catholic Lens* (2007), *Film and Faith* (2008), *Lights, Camera . . . Faith! A Movie Lover's Guide to Scripture Cycle A* (2001), and *Lights, Camera . . . Faith! A Movie Lover's Guide to Scripture Cycle C* (2003). He holds an honorary doctorate from the Melbourne College of Divinity.

Matthew McEver, Spiritual Formation Pastor, is the teaching pastor and director of the Ancient Future gathering at McEver Road United Methodist Church. His publications include film reviews of *Planet of the Apes* (2001) and *Gladiator* (2000), and 'The Messianic Figure in Film: Christology Beyond the Biblical Epic' (1998), all in the *Journal of Religion and Film*. He is an alumnus of the University of Georgia and Southern Seminary.

Irena S. M. Makarushka is Associate Dean, College of Liberal Arts at Towson University in Towson, Maryland. Her publications include *Religious Imagination and Language in Emerson and Nietzsche* (1994) and over a dozen articles in collections of essays and professional journals on subjects including philosophy of religion and feminist interpretations of literature, art and film. She received her Ph.D. from Boston University.

Clive Marsh is Special Lecturer in the Department of Theology & Religious Studies in the School of Humanities at the University of Nottingham. His books include *Theology Goes to the Movies* (2007), *Jesus and the Gospels* (2006), *Cinema and Sentiment: Film's Challenge to Theology* (2004), and *Explorations in Theology & Film* (1998). He holds a D.Phil. (Oxon.) from the University of Oxford.

Guy Matalon is the Director of the Natan and Hannah Schwalb Center for Israel and Jewish Studies at the University of Nebraska at Omaha where he teaches a course on The Holocaust Through Film and a course on Judaism Through Israeli Film. He received his Ph.D. in Hebrew and Judaic Studies from New York University.

Conrad E. Ostwalt is Professor of Religion and Chair of the Department of Philosophy & Religion at Appalachian State University. His books include *Screening the Sacred: Religion, Myth, and Ideology in Popular American Film* (1995) and *Screening the Sacred: Popular Culture and the Religious Imagination* (2003), among others. He has a Ph.D. from Duke University.

S. Brent Plate is Associate Professor of Religious Studies at Hamilton College. His books include *Religion and Film: Cinema and the Re-Creation of the World* (2008), *The Religion and Film Reader* (2007), and *Representing Religion in World Cinema : Filmmaking, Mythmaking, Culture Making* (2003), among others. He holds a Ph.D. from Emory University.

Rubina Ramji is an Assistant Professor in the Department of Philosophy and Religious Studies at Cape Breton University. She is the Senior Editor (August 2007) of the online peer-reviewed journal *Golem: Journal of Religion and Monsters* and Film Review Editor for the *Journal of Religion and Film*. She received her Ph.D. at the University of Ottawa.

Adele Reinhartz is the Associate Vice-President for Research at the University of Ottawa. Her books include *Jesus of Hollywood* (2007) and *Scripture on the Silver Screen* (2003), and *Jesus, Judaism, and Christian Anti-Judaism: Reading the New Testament After the Holocaust* (2002), among others. Her Ph.D. is from McMaster University.

Birud Sindhav is Associate Professor of Marketing at the University of Nebraska at Omaha. He has published in such journals as *Journal of Marketing Theory and Practice*, *Journal of Retailing*, *Journal of Marketing Channels*, and *Journal of Market-Focused Management*. He is also an expert on the movies of India. He holds a Ph.D. from the University of Oklahoma.

Allison Smith is a lecturer in English at Yeshiva College of Yeshiva University where she teaches film and American Literature. She has an M.A. from, and is currently completing her Ph.D. in English at, the University of California at Riverside.

Bryan Stone is E. Stanley Jones Professor of Evangelism at the Boston University School of Theology. His publications include *Evangelism After Christendom: The Theology and Practice of Christian Witness* (2007), *Thy Nature and Thy Name is Love: Wesleyan and Process Theologies in Dialogue* (2001), *Faith and Film: Theological Themes at the Cinema* (2000), and *Compassionate Ministry: Theological Foundations* (1996) among others. His Ph. D. is from Southern Methodist University.

Richard Walsh is Professor of Religion and Co-director of the Honors Program at Methodist University in Fayetteville, North Carolina. He is author of *Finding St. Paul in Film* (2005), *Reading the Gospels in the Dark* (2003), *Mapping Myths of Biblical Interpretation* (2001) and *Jesus, the Gospels, and Cinematic Imagination: A Handbook to Jesus on DVD* (2007). His Ph.D. is from Baylor University.

Gregory Watkins is a Resident Fellow and Lecturer in Structured Liberal Education at Stanford University. He is the editor of *Teaching Religion and Film* (2008) and the director of two films, *A Little Stiff* (1991) and *A Sign From God* (2000). Watkins has a Ph.D. in religious studies and humanities from Stanford University and a MFA in film from the University of California at Los Angeles.

Melanie J. Wright was a Lecturer at the Open University, UK. Among her publications are *Religion and Film: An Introduction* (2007), *Understanding Judaism* (2003), and *Moses in America: The Cultural Uses of Biblical Narrative* (2002). Her D.Phil. is from the University of Oxford (Christ Church).

Wendy M. Wright is Professor of Theology and holder of the John C. Kenefick Faculty Chair in the Humanities at Creighton University. Her books include *Bond of Perfection: Jeanne De Chantal and Francois De Sales* (1985), *Sacred Dwelling: A Spirituality of Family Life* (1994), *The Vigil: Keeping Watch in the Season of Christ's Coming* (1992), and *Frances de Sales, Jane de Chantal: Letters of Spiritual Direction* (1988). She holds a Ph.D. from the University of California at Santa Barbara.

Kelly G. Wyman is a part-time speech and drama faculty member of Longview Community College. She has published an article, 'The Devil We Already Know: Medieval Representations of a Powerless Satan in Modern American Cinema', in the *Journal of Religion & Film*. She has a masters degree from the University of Missouri – Kansas City.

Notes

Introduction

1   *5 Minuti* is available online at a variety of websites, including the Internet Archive, http://www.archive.org/details/5_Minuti and youtube, http://www.youtube.com/watch?v=oYoUYFvKd5U.

2   Published by Scarecrow Press, Inc. in 2008.

3   Published by Palgrave Macmillan in 2003.

4   The first article published in the *Journal of Religion & Film*, Vol. 1, no. 1 (1997) was Andrew Greeley's *Images of God in the Movies* (April), accessed online at http://www.unomaha.edu/jrf/greeleya.htm.

Chapter 1

1   While Hollywood has been, for many years, the largest producer of motion pictures, India's Bollywood now has surpassed Hollywood in the number of motion pictures produces annually. Thus, when this chapter appears in a revised edition of this volume the category under consideration probably will be called 'Bollywood/Hollywood blockbusters'.

2   See Flannery-Dailey, F. and Wagner, R. (2001), 'Wake up! Gnosticism and Buddhism in *The Matrix*', *Journal of Religion & Film*, 5 (2). Retrieved from 18 August 2008 from http://www.unomaha.edu/jrf/gnostic.htm.

3   Ibid.

4   See Fielding, J. (2003), 'Reassessing *The Matrix/Reloaded*', *Journal of Religion & Film*, 7 (2). Retrieved from 20 August 2008 from http://www.unomaha.edu/jrf/Vol7No2/matrix.matrixreloaded.htm. *The Matrix* also is sometimes associated with Plato's *Allegory of the Cave*. See Irwin, W. (ed.) (2002), *The Matrix & Philosophy: Welcome to the Desert of the Real*. Chicago: Open Court Publishing Company or Haber, K. (ed.) (2003), *Exploring the Matrix*. New York: Macmillan.

5   See Blizek, W. L., 'Using Movies to Critique Religion' (Chapter 3) in this volume.

6   For other feature length narrative films that were not blockbusters, see Filmography at the end of this volume.

7   See Adele Reinhartz', 'Jesus Movies' (Chapter 19) in this volume.

8   For more on *Breaking the Waves*, see 'Bess the Christ Figure? Theological Interpretation of *Breaking the Waves*', by Mercandante, L. (2001), *Journal of Religion & Film*, 5 (1). Retrieved from 22 August 2008 from http://www.unomaha.edu/jrf/bessthe.htm; 'Transgressing Goodness in *Breaking the Waves*', by Makarushka, I. S. M. (1998), *Journal of Religion & Film*, 2 (1). Retrieved from http://www.unomaha.edu/jrf/breaking.htm; and Keefer, K. and Linafelt, T. (1998). 'The End of Desire: Theologies of Eros in the *Song of Songs* and *Breaking the Waves*',

Journal of Religion & Film, 2 (1). Retrieved from 25 August 2008 from http://www.unomaha.edu/jrf/endofdes.htm.

9 For more on *Babette's Feast*, see Wright, W. M. (1997), '*Babette's Feast*: A Religious Film', *Journal of Religion & Film*, 1 (2). Retrieved from 20 August 2008 from http://www.unomaha.edu/jrf/BabetteWW.htm and Schuler, J. (1997), 'Kierkegaard at *Babette's Feast*: The Return to the Finite', *Journal of Religion & Film*, 1 (2). Retrieved from 20 August 2008 from http://www.unomaha.edu/jrf/kierkega.htm. Also see Haunton, C., 'Imaging God in Movies' (Chapter 24) in this volume.

10 See Bowman, D. (2001), 'Faith and the Absent Savior in Central Station' in the *Journal of Religion & Film*, 5 (1). Retrieved from 9 September 2008 from http://www.unomaha.edu/jrf/centstat.htm and Solano, J. R. (2004), 'Blessed Broken Bodies: Exploring Redemption in Central Station and Breaking the Waves' in the *Journal of Religion & Film*, 8 (1). Retrieved from 9 September 2008 from http://www.unomaha.edu/jrf/Vol8No1/BlessedBroken.htm.

11 See Blizek, W. L. (1999) 'Report from Sundance 1999: Religion in Independent Films' (review of this film), *Journal of Religion & Film*, 3 (1). Retrieved from 9 September 2008 from http://www.unomaha.edu/jrf/sundance.htm.

12 See Bordwell, D. and Thompson, K. (1997), *Film Art: An Introduction* (5th edn). Columbus, OH: McGraw-Hill, p. 42.

13 Ibid., p. 44.

Chapter 2

1 See the Appendix to Leff, L. J. and Simmons, J. L. (1990), *The Dame in the Kimono: Hollywood, Censorship, & the Production Code From the 1920s to the 1960s*. New York: Grove Weidenfeld.

2 Ibid.

3 See Chapter 9 on 'Religion, Film and Cultural Studies' by Melanie Wright; Chapter 6 on 'Retelling Religious Stories' by William L. Blizek and Julien Fielding; Chapter 26, 'Karma and Film', by Michele Marie Desmarais, and Chapter 22 on 'Redemption and Film' by Julien Fielding in this volume.

4 These two movies are discussed in greater detail in other chapters of this volume, including the essays by William L. Blizek in 'Religion and the Movies' (Chapter 1), and Blizek's and Julien R. Fielding's 'Redemption and Film' (Chapter 22).

5 See Flannery-Dailey, F. and Wagner, R. (2001), 'Wake up! Gnosticism and Buddhism in *The Matrix*', *Journal of Religion & Film*, 5 (2), http://www.unomaha.edu/jrf/gnostic.htm.

6 Nurse Ratched has become a cultural symbol of evil.

7 Lyden, J. (2003), *Film As Religion: Myths, Morals, and Rituals*. New York: New York University Press, p. 5.

8 Whether this requires training in abstruse methods of analysis or not seems an open question. Even when viewers themselves do not find religion in the movies, they enjoy reading about what religion or religious themes others have found in films.

9 Robbins, G. A. (1997), 'Mozart & Salieri, Cain & Abel: A cinematic transformation of Genesis 4', *Journal of Religion & Film*, 1 (1). http://www.unomaha.edu/jrf/robbins.htm.

10 Quinones, R. J. (1991), *The Changes of Cain: Violence and the Lost Brother in Cain and Abel Literature*. Princeton, NJ: Princeton University Press.

11 It is interesting in this context to imagine different denominations of the same faith as children in competition for the favour of God. This might explain the bitterness of rivalry between different denominations.

12 Robbins (1997), *Journal of Religion & Film*, 1 (1).

13 Ibid.

14 See Kozlovic, A. K. (2002), 'Superman as Christ-Figure: The American Pop Culture Movie Messiah', *Journal of Religion & Film*, 6 (1). http://www.unomaha.edu/jrf/superman.htm; Kozlovic, A. K. (2002), 'The unholy, non-Christic biblical subtexts in *Superman: The Movie* (1978) and *Superman II* (1981)', *Journal of Religion & Film*, 6 (2). http://www.unomaha.edu/jrf/supergood.htm; and Kozlovic, A. K. (2003), 'The unholy biblical subtexts and other religious elements built into *Superman: The Movie* (1978) and *Superman II* (1981)', *Journal of Religion & Film*, 7 (1). http://www.unomaha.edu/jrf/Vol7No1/unholy.htm.

15 When Kal-El first appears on earth, naked at the bottom of the crater his star ship has created, he stands with arms outstretched in cruciform posture. Not everyone who adopts a cruciform posture is intended to be a Christ figure, but in this case the cruciform posture adds evidence to other indications that Superman is to be thought of as a Christ figure.

16 See Beck, A. C. (1995), 'The Christian allegorical structure of *Platoon*', in Martin, J. W. and Ostwalt, C. E., Jr. (eds), *Screening the Sacred: Religion, Myth, and Ideology in Popular American Film*. Boulder, Colorado: Westview Press, Inc.

17 Beck, p. 44.

18 Ibid., p. 46.

19 Ibid., p. 47.

20 Ibid., p. 53.

21 There is more in Beck's essay to show a correlation between the movie and the Christian story writ large, but the examples given here should suffice to show how one can apply the Christian story to a movie like *Platoon*.

22 Matalon, G. (2001), 'Esther and the Mexican', *Journal of Religion & Film*, 5 (1). http://www.unomaha.edu/jrf/esther.htm.

23 See Blizek, W. L. and Desmarais, M. M. (2008), 'What are we teaching when we teach "Religion and film?" ', in Watkins, G. J. (ed.), *Teaching Religion and Film*. New York: Oxford University Press, p. 20.

Chapter 3

1 See Blizek, W. L. and Burke, R. (1998), '*The Apostle*: an interview with Robert Duvall', *Journal of Religion & Film*, 2 (1). http://www.unomaha.edu/jrf/apostle.INTERVIEW.htm.

2 For further discussion of movies that address religious themes, see Chapters 2 through 29 in this volume.

3 *Godfather III* has a more extensive criticism of the Catholic Church.

4 Army General Musharraf staged a coup in 1999 and took over the Presidency of Pakistan in 2001.

5 'You'll Never Walk Alone' is a show tune from the 1945 Rodgers and Hammerstein musical, *Carousel*.

6 See Christian Haunton's Chapter 24 on 'Imaging God in the Movies' in this volume.

7 The institutional church is identified as hierarchical, rule governed and image conscious.

8 Music for 'Would You Like to Swing on a Star' was actually written by Jimmy Van Heusen with words by Johnny Burke.

9 For a discussion of film and experience, see Alyda Faber's Chapter 4 on 'Religion, Ethics and Film'. Also see Greg Watkins' Chapter 7 on 'Religion, Film and Film Theory' in this volume.

10 See Brent Plate's Chapter 8 on 'Religion and World Cinema', in this volume.

Chapter 4

1 Ethical approaches to film are emerging after, and sometimes in response to, significant criticisms within the area of religion and film. This includes the criticism that religious scholars tend to search for religious meaning, themes and content in films using a narrative approach, thereby neglecting any serious engagement with the distinct visual and aural medium of film as film. The 'Hollywood centrism' (Plate, S. B.) and the Christian-centrism of theological and religious film studies is also criticized. See Greg Watkins's Chapter 7, 'Religion, Film and Film Theory', in this volume.

2 Within the Christian tradition, the moral agent is understood as the person of conscience, although research in the historical and contemporary forms of Christian asceticism (which includes the work of Margaret Miles and Rowan Williams), has augmented this predominantly rational image of the moral agent to include inchoate bodily sensations and unconsciousness.

3 This term originated with a working group at Case Western Reserve University, and was the subject of an interdisciplinary symposium held there in April 2007.

4 Black, G. D. (1994), *Hollywood Censored: Morality Codes, Catholics, and the Movies*. Cambridge: Cambridge University Press, pp. 39, 299. See also Black, G. D. (1997), *The Catholic Crusade against the Movies, 1940–1975*. Cambridge: Cambridge University Press and Leff, L. J., and Simmons, J. L. (1990), *The Dame in the Kimono: Hollywood, Censorship, and the Production Code from the 1920s to the 1960s*. New York: Grove Weidenfeld.

5 Black, *Hollywood Censored*. p. 1. He argues that box office profits were a primary reason for Hollywood's compliance with the PCA's censorship of ideas and support of the status quo. For an account of censorship in film for airline use and home consumption see Cornick, M. (2008), 'Modern Film Censorship: Television, Airlines, and Home Entertainment'. Master's thesis, Department of History, University of Nebraska, Omaha, NE, April.

6 Walsh, F. (1996), *Sin and Censorship: The Catholic Church and the Motion Picture Industry*. New Haven & London: Yale University Press, p. 309.

7 Black, *Hollywood Censored*, pp. 299–300. See also pp. 5, 173–4, 296–7.

8 Johnson, R. K. (2000), 'Responding to Film Ethically: Moving beyond the Rating System', *Reel Spirituality: Theology and Film in Dialogue* (2nd edn). Grand Rapids, MI: Baker Academic, pp. 217–37.

9 Ibid., pp. 219–20.

10 Rodríguez, H. (1997), 'Ideology and Film Culture', in Allen R. and Smith, M. (eds), *Film Theory and Philosophy*. Oxford: Oxford University Press, p. 260.

11 Miles, M. R. (1996), *Seeing and Believing: Religion and Values in the Movies*. Boston: Beacon Press. For an elaboration of the ideological approach within a typology of three religious approaches to film, see Martin, J. W., and Ostwalt, C. E., Jr. (eds) (1995), *Screening the Sacred: Religion, Myth, and Ideology in Popular American Film*. Boulder, San Francisco, Oxford: Westview Press, pp. 10–12, 119–51.

12 Ibid., p. 10.

13 Silverman, K. (1996), *The Threshold of the Visible World*. New York: Routledge.

14 Vollmer, U. (2007), *Seeing Film and Reading Feminist Theology*. New York: Palgrave Macmillan.

15 Loughlin, G. (2004), *Alien Sex: The Body and Desire in Cinema and Theology*. Oxford: Blackwell.

16 Johnson, *Reel Spirituality*, pp. 217–37.

17 Miles and Plate (2004), 'Hospitable Vision: Some Notes on the Ethics of Seeing Film'. *Cross Currents*, 54 (1: Spring), 30. See also Plate (2003), 'The Re-creation of the World: Filming Faith'. *Dialog*, 42 (2: Summer), 155–60.

18 See Brintnall, K. L. (2004), 'Tarantino's Incarnational Theology: *Reservoir Dogs*, crucifixions and spectacular violence'. *Cross Currents*, 54 (1: Spring), 66–75. See also Faber, A. (2003), 'Redeeming Sexual Violence? A Feminist Reading of *Breaking the Waves*'. *Literature and Theology*, 17 (1), 59–74; and (2006) '*Dancer in the Dark*: Affliction and the aesthetic of attention'. *Studies in Religion*, 35 (1), 85–106.

19 Murdoch, I. (2001), *The Sovereignty of Good*. London: Routledge, p. 43.

20 Williams, R. (2000), *Lost Icons: Reflections on Cultural Bereavement*. Harrisburg: Morehouse.

21 Ibid., p. 149.

22 Ibid., p. 148.

23 Ibid., p. 175.

24 Ibid., p. 70.

25 Sharrett, C. (2003), 'The World that is Known: An Interview with Michael Haneke'. *Cineaste* 28 (Summer), 28–31.

26 Le Cain, M., 'Do the Right Thing: The Films of Michael Haneke', *Senses of Cinema*. Accessed on 14 December 2007 from http://www.sensesofcinema.com/contents/03/26/haneke.html.

27 Haneke, M. (1992), 'Film als Katharsis', in Bono, F. (ed.), *Austria (in)felix: zum Österreichischem Film der 80er Jahre*. Blimp, Graz, p. 89.

28 Gaut, B. (2007), *Art, Emotion and Ethics*. Oxford: Oxford University Press, pp. 72–6, pp. 107–8.

29 Due to his failure to communicate his whereabouts.

30 'The World that is Known'. *Cineaste*, 29–31.

31 Haneke cited in Vogel, A. (1996), 'Of Nonexisting Continents: The Cinema of Michael Haneke', *Film Comment*, 32 (2), 74.

32 Norton, A. J. (1998), 'De-icing the Emotions: Michael Haneke's Retrospective in London'. *Central Europe Review*, 26 October, accessed 10 April 2006 from http://www.ce-review.org/kinoeye/kinoeye5old.html.

33 Brintnall, 'Tarantino's Incarnational Theology', p. 67.

34 Related to this point, albeit from an anthropological perspective, see Fischer, M. M. J. (2001), 'Filmic Judgment and Cultural Critique: The Work of Art, Ethics, and Religion in Iranian Cinema', in de Vries, H. and Weber, S. (eds), *Religion and Media*. Stanford, CA: Stanford University Press, pp. 456–86.

Chapter 5

1 For example, what is meant by 'creation'? What are human beings like? What kinds of human community should be sought? How is evil to be understood? What is meant by 'redemption'? What hope is there?

2 Hurley, N. (1970), *Theology through Film*. New York: Harper and Row, p. ix.

3 Ibid., p. 8.

4 Ibid., pp. 12–13.

5 Schrader, P. (1972), *Transcendental Style in Film: Ozu, Bresson, Dreyer*. Berkeley: University of California Press; reprinted 1988, DaCapo Press.

6 Ibid., p. 3. See also Watkins, G., 'Religion, Film and Film theory' (Chapter 7) in this volume for additional discussion of Schrader.

7 Schrader, P. (1972), *Transcendental Style in Film: Ozu, Bresson, Dreyer*. Berkeley: University of California Press; reprinted 1988, DaCapo Press, p. 6.

8 Loughlin, G. (2004), *Alien Sex: The Body and Desire in Cinema and Theology*. Oxford and Malden, MA: Blackwell, p. xxix.

9 Miles, M. R. (1996), *Seeing and Believing: Religion and Values in the Movies*. Boston: Beacon Press.

10 Ibid., p. 10.

11 Jewett, R. (1997), 'Stuck in time: Kairos, Chronos, and the flesh in *Groundhog Day*', in Marsh, C. and Ortiz, G. (eds), *Explorations in Theology and Film*. Oxford and Malden, MA: Blackwell, p. 156.

12 Kreitzer, L. (1993), and many later works.

13 Romanowski, W. and Vander Heide, J. L. (2007), 'Easier said than done: On reversing the hermeneutical flow in the theology and film dialogue' *Journal of Communication and Religion* (March), pp. 40–64.

14 At the end of the day, it is clarity about God, who God is, and what God means for contemporary living that matters.

15 Marsh, C. and Ortiz, G. (eds) (1997), *Explorations in Theology and Film*. Oxford and Malden, MA: Blackwell.

16 Loughlin, G. (2005), 'Cinéma Divinité: A theological introduction', in Christianson, E. S.; Francis, P., and Telford, W. R. (eds), *Cinéma Divinité: Religion, Theology and the Bible in Film*. London: SCM Press, pp. 1–12.

17 Lyden, J. (2003), *Film as Religion: Myths, Morals, and Rituals*. New York and London: New York University Press.

18 Marsh (2004).

19 Marsh, C. (2009), 'Audience reception', in Lyden, J. (ed.), *The Routledge Companion to Religion and Film*. New York and London: Routledge, pp. 87–95.

20 Miles, M. R. (1996), *Seeing and Believing: Religion and Values in the Movies*. Boston: Beacon Press, p. 13.

21 I have written on this topic elsewhere. See Marsh, C. (2009), 'Audience reception', in Lyden, J. (ed.), *The Routledge Companion to Religion and Film*. New York and London: Routledge.

22 Hoover, S. (2006), *Religion in the Media Age*. New York and London: Routledge.

23 Haines Lyon, C., and Marsh, C. (2007), 'Film's role in contemporary meaning-making: A theological challenge to cultural studies', in Knauss, S. and Ornella, A. D. (eds) (2008), *Reconfigurations: Interdisciplinary Perspectives on Religion in a Post-Secular Society*. Vienna and Münster: LIT Verlag, pp. 113–25.

24 Cognitive, aesthetic and affective, not to mention the fact that all these are experienced in embodied form, and can actually then affect the ethics of daily life.

25 Pope, R. (2007), *Salvation in Celluloid: Theology, Imagination and Film*. London and New York: T & T Clark.

26 As, for example, in the work of Gregory Currie and Berys Gaut.

27 Carey, J. (1996), cited in Miles, M. R., *Seeing and Believing: Religion and Values in the Movies*. Boston: Beacon Press, xv.

28 See Faber, A. 'Religion, Ethics and Film' (Chapter 4) in this volume.

Chapter 6

1 One criticism of contemporary comedic films is that they do not tell stories but rather only string together a collection of skits.

2 See Adele Reinhartz' Chapter 19 on 'Jesus Movies' in this volume.

3 See the essay on Cain and Abel by Robbins, G. A. (1997), 'Mozart & Salieri, Cain & Abel: A Cinematic Transformation of Genesis 4', *Journal of Religion & Film*, 1 (1). http://www.unomaha.edu/jrf/robbins.htm. See Conrad Ostwalt's Chapter 27 on 'The End of Days' in this volume. See also Ostwalt's 1998 essay, 'Visions of the end. Secular apocalypse in recent Hollywood film'. http://www.unomaha.edu/jrf/OstwaltC.htm in the *Journal of Religion & Film*, 2 (1) and his 2000 essay, '*Armageddon* at the millennial dawn' in the *Journal of Religion & Film*, 4 (1). http://www.unomaha.edu/jrf/armagedd.htm.

4 See Martin, J. and Ostwalt, C. (1995), *Screening the Sacred: Religion, Myth, and Ideology in Popular American Film*. Boulder: Westview Press.

5 Quotes are from the the Holy Bible, King James Version.

6 *Hoosiers* is also a story about redemption, as the coaches redeem their pasts by creating a winning team. For more about redemption in film, see Julien Fielding's Chapter 22 on 'Redemption and Film' in this volume.

7 Quotes from the Book of Job are from the Holy Bible, King James Version.

8 Harris, S. L. (2007), *Understanding the Bible* (7th edn). New York: McGraw-Hill, p. 256.

9 Clines, D. J. A. (1993), 'Job, the Book of', in Metzer, B. M. and Coogan, M. D. (eds), *The Oxford Companion to the Bible*. New York: Oxford University Press, p. 368.

10 Writers have long made an association between the events in the Book of Job and the Holocaust. In 1951, Martin Buber spoke of 'the Job of the gas chambers', and Elie Wiesel, a Holocaust survivor and Nobel Peace Laureate, has himself invoked 'his Job-like status and connection to the murdered six million Jews'. He has 'reconstituted himself as their humble defender, as he reprimanded those who deemed to be the contemporary successors of Job's supposed friends who pontificated and proffered easy but insulting answers'. See p. 26 in Mark Chmiel's (2001) *Elie Wiesel and the Politics of Moral Leadership*, which is published by Temple University Press.

11 Interesting enough, the coat nearly gets him killed. Polish troops who are liberating Warsaw mistake him for a German officer and threaten to kill him.

12 Garbowski, C. (2002), 'Film Review: *The Pianist*', *Journal of Religion & Film*, 6 (2). Online at www.unomaha.edu/jrf/pianist.htm.

13 Scott, A. O. (2002), '*The Pianist*: Surviving the Warsaw Ghetto Against Steep Odds', *New York Times* (December 27). Found online at http://movies.nytimes.com/movie/review?res=9E0DE1DA113CF934Ai5751C1A9649C8B63.

14 See A. O. Scott's article, '*The Pianist*: Surviving the Warsaw Ghetto Against Steep Odds'.

15 Twenty minutes before the end, Gardiner takes his son to a church service, and, while clutching his son to him, he cries while a choir sings.

16 For a discussion on the religious hero, especially with reference to 'Christ figures', see pp. 385–7 in Fielding, J. (2008), *Discovering World Religions at 24 Frames Per Second*, Lanham, MD: Scarecrow Press, Incorporated.

17 See Adele Reinhartz's Chapter 19 on 'Jesus Movies'; Julien Fielding's Chapter 22 on 'Redemption and Film', and Matthew McEver's Chapter 25 on 'The Saviour Figure in Film', all in this volume.

18 *The Omen* (1976) is about an American ambassador who learns that after his wife gave birth, their child was killed and switched for the literal Antichrist. The evil forces will stop at nothing to manoeuvre this child into the highest political office. *Damien: Omen II* (1978) picks up the story when Damien is 13. The trilogy 'ends' with *The Final Conflict* (1981), with a 30-something Damien vying for world domination. In reality, the Omen films continued with *Omen IV: The Awakening* (1991), which was made for TV; and a 2006 remake of the original film titled *The Omen*.

19 A super computer rapes the wife of its creator in a bid to recreate itself.

20 An unstoppable cyborg is sent into the past to kill Sarah Connor, the mother of John, the future leader of the human resistance movement against the diabolic machines that have enslaved humanity.

21 A robot threatens the peace of an outpost where a man and a woman grow food for the starving Earth.

22 In *Resident Evil* (2002), an unscrupulous international corporation, known as the Umbrella Corporation, has a massive underground bioengineering facility known as the Hive, which has accidentally unleashed a deadly virus. To contain the leak, the supercomputer, known as the Red Queen, has sealed up the facility.

23 Just a few notable female 'saviours' include Ripley in the *Alien* quadrilogy, the

Doctor's Wife in *Blindness*, Trinity in *The Matrix*, Leeloo in *The Fifth Element*, Alice in the *Resident Evil* quadrilogy, Violet in *Ultraviolet* and Maj. Eden Sinclair in *Doomsday*.

24 Set in 2027, *Children of Men* shows us a future in which humans are no longer capable of procreation. Hope seems restored when a former activist is asked to transport a miraculously pregnant woman to an awaiting ship.

25 Based on Richard Matheson's novel, *I Am Legend*, the film focuses on a scientist who has survived a devastating plague that has killed most of humanity. Those who did not die are now light-shunning 'monsters'. Trying to no become a victim himself, the scientist works to find a cure.

26 A pregnant woman finds herself in a race against time in this end-of-times thriller. The 'lamb' has returned to earth so he can break the seven seals, thus bringing about the end of the world. Can she make the sacrifice needed to save humanity?

27 Once a Catholic missionary, Katherine now makes her living using science to debunk religious phenomena. She is put to the test when she arrives in the small town of Haven, Louisiana, and encounters the 10 plagues of the Bible. *The Reaping* is unusual in that it draws upon imagery found not in the New Testament's Book of Revelation but from the Hebrew Bible's Book of Exodus 7:14–12:36. These plagues include blood, frogs, gnats, flies, pestilence, incurable boils, storm, locusts, darkness and the death of the firstborn.

28 A deadly virus breaks out in Great Britain killing hundreds of thousands of people. The government quarantines the area by erecting a wall around the infected. Thirty years later, the virus reemerges in the non-infected areas. Hoping to find an antidote, the government sends a group of military specialists into the walled city.

29 Based on the novel by Jose Saramago, *Blindness* begins in an unnamed town. A Japanese man suddenly goes blind in the middle of an intersection. As he comes into contact with other people – an ophthalmologist, his patients and other casual bystanders – his disease spreads. Hoping to quarantine the outbreak, the government places the afflicted into a prison-like barracks and leaves them to fend for themselves. Miraculously, the ophthalmologist's wife has joined her husband in quarantine, and she emerges as a fearless leader.

30 The young protagonist, Sara, entertains the other girls in her boarding school with tales of Rama, Sita and Ravana. For more on this, see the Conrad Oswalt's Chapter 27, 'End of Days', on apocalyptic films.

Chapter 7

1 Another indispensable text for people interested in the general history of film theory is the 2004 *Film Theory and Criticism: Introductory Readings*, which is a collection of many important works in the field edited and skillfully introduced by Gerald Mast and Marshall Cohen. New York, NY: Oxford University Press USA.

2 Architecture and music, for example.

3 Münsterberg, H. (1916), *The Photoplay: A Psychological Study*. New York, NY: D. Appleton and Company.

4 Arnheim, R. (1957), *Film as Art*. Berkeley: University of California Press (first published in 1932 as *Film als Kunst* (*Film as Art*) and expanded upon for the 1957 republishing).

5 See Eisenstein, S. (1969), *Film Form: Essays in Film Theory*. New York: Harcourt Trade Publishers 124 Harvest Books.

6 See the collection of writings listed below in Balázs, B. (1952), *Theory of Film: Character and Growth of a New Art*. London: Dobson.

7 See the collection Bazin, A. (1967 and 1971), *What is Cinema?* 2 volumes, translated by Hugh Grey. Berkeley: University of California Press.

8 Kracauer, S. (1960), *Theory of Film: The Redemption of Physical Reality*. New York: Oxford University Press.

9 Erwin Panofsky, Susanne Langer, Maurice Merleau-Ponty, Gabriel Marcel and André Malraux.

10 Founded in 1951 by André Bazin and others.

11 Simpson, P., Utterson, A. and Shepherdson, K. J. (eds) (2003), *Film Theory: Critical Concepts in Media and Cultural Studies*. New York: Routledge.

12 Which takes film as a cultural product, which expresses theological views or which can be taken as the object of theological criticism.

13 A fuller analysis of the general landscape of religion and film work can be found in the volume of essays, Watkins, G. (ed.) (2008), *Teaching Religion and Film*. New York: Oxford University Press.

14 Feminism, Marxism and psychoanalysis, for example.

15 Singer, I. (2000), *Reality Transformed: Film as Meaning and Technique*. Cambridge, MA: MIT Press.

16 Schrader, P. (1988), *The Transcendental Style in Film*. Cambridge, MA: Da Capo Press.

17 Schrader, p. 7.

18 An explicit anthropological assumption made by Schrader.

19 Schrader, p. 8.

20 Ibid., p. 41.

21 Schrader points to Warhol, for example.

22 Ibid., p. 42.

23 Ibid., p. 42.

24 Ibid., p. 48.

25 Ibid., p. 48.

26 Ibid., p. 51.

27 Cho, F. (1999), 'Imagining nothing and imagining otherness in Buddhist film', in Plate, S. B. and Jasper, D. (eds), *Imag(in)ing Otherness: Filmic Visions of Living Together*. Atlanta, GA: Scholars Press. p. 169.

28 Ibid., p. 177–8.

29 Franscious Cho (2008) develops this argument in a more recent article, 'Buddhism, film, and religious knowing: Challenging the literary approach to film', in Watkins, G. (ed.), *Teaching Religion and Film*. New York: Oxford University Press.

30 Watkins, G. (1999), 'Seeing and Being Seen: Distinctively Filmic and Religious Elements in Film' *Journal of Religion & Film*, 3 (2), http://www.unomaha.edu/jrf/watkins.htm.

31 Persuasively, in my opinion.

32 Cavell, S. (1979), *The World Viewed: Reflections on the Ontology of Film*. Cambridge, MA: Harvard University Press, pp. 40–1.

33 Watkins, G. (1999), 'Seeing and Being Seen: Distinctively Filmic and Religious Elements in Film', *Journal of Religion & Film*, 3 (2), para. 7, http://www.unomaha.edu/jrf/watkins.htm.

34 Indeed, this book by Singer is recommended in part for Singer's efficient and relatively plain-language account of the basic terrain of film theory.

35 Singer, p. xi.

36 Ibid., p. xii.

37 Ibid., p. xiii.

38 Ibid., p. 5.

39 That is, the degree to which we need a 'theory of film'.

40 Singer, p. 6.

41 Ibid., p. 10.

42 Ibid., pp. 10–11.

Chapter 8

1 Shohat, E. and Stam, R. (1994), *Unthinking Eurocentrism: Multiculturalism and the Media*. London: Routledge, p. 7.

2 See, for example, Schrader, P. (1972), *Transcendental Style in Film*. New York: Da Capo Press; May, J. R. and Bird, M. (eds) (1982), *Religion in Film*. Knoxville, TN: The University of Tennessee Press.

3 Schrader, P. (1972), *Transcendental Style in Film*. New York: Da Capo Press, pp. 10–11.

4 See LaFleur, W. R. (2002), 'Suicide Off the Edge of Explicability: Awe in Ozu and Kore-eda', *Film History*, 14 (2), 159–64.

5 See Thomas, J. B. (2007), '*Shukyo Asobi* and Miyazaki Hayao's *Anime*', *Nova Religio*, 10 (3), 73–95.

6 See James, D. (2002), James, D. E., and Kim, K. H. (eds), *Im Kwon-Taek: The Making of a Korean National Cinema*. Detroit: Wayne State University Press; Conroy, M (2007), 'Seeing with Buddha's Eyes: *Spring, Summer, Autumn, Winter . . . and Spring*', *Journal of Religion & Film*, 11 (2), http://www.unomaha.edu/jrf/vol11no2/ConroyBuddha.htm.

7 Cho, F. (1999), 'Imagining Nothing and Imaging Otherness in Buddhist Film', in Plate, S. B. and D. Jasper (eds), *Imag(in)ing Otherness: Filmic Visions of Living Together*. Oxford: Oxford University Press: 169–95, 177–8; See also Cho (2003), 'The Art of Presence: Buddhism and Korean films', in Plate, S. B. (ed.), *Representing Religion in World Cinema*. New York: Palgrave Macmillan: 107–20.

8 Leonard, RR, S.J. (2003), *The Cinematic Mystical Gaze: The Films of Peter Weir*. University of Melbourne, PhD Thesis. Accessible at http://eprints.enimelb.edu.au/archive/00000471.

9 See MacDougall, D. (1998), *Transcultural Cinema*. Princeton: Princeton University Press.

10 That is, many of these films do *not* work as 'introductions to Islam' for Western audiences.

11 See Dwyer, R (2006), *Filming the Gods: Religion and Indian Cinema*. London: Routledge.

12 See Phalke, D. G. entry in Mitchell, J., and Plate, S. B. (eds) (2007), *The Religion and Film Reader*. London: Routledge.

13 See Lutgendorf, P. (2002), 'A Superhit Goddess', *Manushi*, 131, 10–16.

14 See Naficy, H. (2002), 'Islamizing film culture in Iran', in Tapper, R. (ed.), *The New Iranian Cinema: Politics, Representation and Identity*. London: I.B. Tauris: 26–65; Fischer, M. J. (2001), 'Filmic judgment and cultural critique: The work of art, ethics, and religion in Iranian cinema', in Hent de Vries, H. and Samuel Weber, S. (eds), *Religion and Media*. Stanford: Stanford University Press, 456–86.

15 See Kiarostami, A. (2007), in Mitchell, J., and Plate, S. B. (eds), *The Religion and Film Reader*. London: Routledge.

16 See Makhmalbaf, M. (2007), in Mitchell, J., and Plate, S. B. (eds), *The Religion and Film Reader*. London: Routledge.

17 See Mitchell, J., and Plate, S. B. (eds) (2007), *The Religion and Film Reader*. London: Routledge; and Mitchell, J. (2004), 'From morality tales to horror movies: Towards and understanding of the popularity of West African video film', in Horsfield, P. et al. (eds), *Belief in Media: Cultural Perspectives on Media and Christianity*. Aldershot: Ashgate, pp. 107–21.

18 See Sembene, O. (2007), in Mitchell, J., and Plate, S. B. (eds), *The Religion and Film Reader*. London: Routledge.

19 See Rodríguez-Mangual, E. (2002), 'Driving a dead body through the nation: Death and allegory in the film *Guantanamera*', *Chasqui* 31 (1), 50–62; Rodríguez-Mangual, E. (2003), 'Santeria and the quest for a postcolonial identity', in Plate, S. B. (ed.), *Representing Religion in World Cinema*. New York: Palgrave Macmillan: 219–37.

Chapter 9

1 Steele (1997), 2.
2 On Hoggart's contribution to liberal education, see Nixon (2007).
3 Webster (2004).
4 For North American perspectives on the character of cultural studies and the international significance of the British theorists discussed here, see Nelson (1991) and Leitch (1991).
5 Marsh (2007), pp. 161–9.
6 Ibid., pp. 4–8; 43–6.
7 Ibid., p. 3.
8 Ibid., p. 44. For a near-contemporary treatment that also takes interest in viewer experience see Deacy (2005), especially pp. 6–10.
9 Wright (2007), pp. 22–5.
10 Williams (2000), p. 237.
11 See the remarks in Marsh (2007), p. 1 and Wright (2007), p. 13.
12 In this view, I follow the suggestions of Johnson et al. (2004), p. 3, in their discussion of method in cultural studies.
13 See, for example, the varied approaches in Tinkcomm and Villarejo (2000), Turner (2001) and the questioning stance adopted by Willemen (1994).
14 For typical historical overviews of cultural studies, see Bounds (1999), Chaney (1994), pp. 10–13 and Grossberg (2006).
15 For an example of this strategy, see Storey (2006).
16 Williams (1985), pp. 87–93.
17 Johnson (1986), p. 41.
18 Williams (1985), p. 91.
19 Chaney (1994); Grossberg (2006), p. 2.
20 Brown (2001), especially pp. 12–13.
21 McDannell (1995), pp. 1–2.
22 The phrase here is E. P. Thompson's, quoted in Meggitt (2004), p. 242.
23 Nye (2003), p. 21. For a rather more cautious approach to cultural studies and the study of religion see Hulsether (2005).
24 Nye (2003), p. 24.
25 Cort (1996), p. 631.
26 Miles (1998), pp. xi and 195–7.
27 Ibid., p. xiii.
28 Ibid., p. xv.
29 Ibid., p. 191.
30 Ibid., pp. xiii–xiv.
31 See for example Pearson (2002), p. 106 or Knott (2005), p. 255.
32 Johnson et al. (2004), p. 18.
33 Wright (2007), pp. 100–6.
34 Miles (1998), pp. xiii, 191.
35 On interdisciplinarity generally, see Thompson Klein (1996), pp. 212–16; and with reference to religion and film, see Wright (2007), p. 24.
36 Cary (1991), p. 25.
37 m.Avot 2.16.
38 du Gay et al. (1997).
39 Johnson (1996), p. 48.
40 To view the diagram in its original context, see du Gay et al. (1997), p. 3.
41 Hall (1997), p. 2.
42 Compare the remarks of Johnson et al. (2004), p. 141.
43 Johnson (1986), p. 48.

44 Goodacre (2007).
45 Unattributed article in *The Economist*, 2 October 2004, p. 50.
46 Wright (2007), p. 25.
47 King (2002), p. 161.
48 Wright (2007), p. 169.
49 Alasuutari (1995), p. 2.
50 For the articulation of this point I draw on the remarks made concerning cultural studies as a whole in Johnson et al. (2004), p. 42.
51 Wright (2007), p. 26.

Chapter 10

1 Zerilli, L. (2005), *Signifying Woman*. Ithaca and London: Cornell University Press, p. 1. (Hereafter SW).
2 Lyden, J. C. (2003), *Religion as Film: Myths, Morals, and Rituals*. New York and London: New York University Press. In Chapter 1, 'Existing Approaches to Religion and Film', Lyden offers a summary of the range of interpretative frameworks engaged in the study of religion and film.
3 For a discussion of the formal structures common to religion and film, see Plate, S. B. (ed.) (2003), *Representing Religion in World Cinema*. New York and Hampshire, England: Palgrave Macmillan, pp. 3–10.
4 In *Screening the Sacred: Religion, Myth, and Ideology in Popular American Film*, Joel Martin describes three interpretative frameworks through which to engage religion and film: theological, mythological and ideological. He writes, 'Race, class, gender, and the postmodern are a few of the central interpretative categories for ideological critics'.
5 Feminism at the beginning of this century is very different from the feminisms of the sixties and seventies. If Barack Obama's Democratic presidential bid has raised the possibility of post-race politics (http://www.nytimes.com/2008/08/10/magazine/10politics-t.html), the Hillary Clinton campaign raised similar issues with regard to gender politics (http://www.cbsnews.com/stories/2007/06/15/opinion/main2934136.shtml). Just as the Civil Rights movement no longer defines the dominant attitudes of the new generation of African-American politicians, so too sixties feminism no longer defines how many women today see women's rights and choices. It would be an overstatement to say that just because some speak of post-race and post-gender; neither racism nor sexism has disappeared.
6 For recent works on the history of feminism/s, see Freedman, E. (2002), *No Turning Back: The History of Feminism and the Future of Women*. New York: Ballantine Books; Dicker, R. C. (2008), *A History of U.S. Feminisms*. Berkeley: Seal Press, and Smith, B. (2000), *Global Feminisms Since 1945: A Survey of Issues and Controversies (Re-Writing Histories)*. London: Routledge.
7 Celebrated original thinkers instrumental in validating the history and religious identity of women include Christ, C. P. and Plaskow, J. (1979), *Womanspirit Rising*. New York: Harper Collins Publishers; Daly, M. (1973), *Beyond God the Father*. Boston, MA: Beacon Press; Lerner, G. (1986), *The Creation of Patriarchy*. New York: Oxford University Press; Reuther, R. R. (1983), *Sexism and God-Talk*. Boston, MA: Beacon Press; Schüssler Fiorenza, E. (1992), *But She Said: Feminist Practices of Biblical Interpretation*. Boston, Massachusetts: Beacon Press; Stanton, E. C. (2003), *The Woman's Bible: A Classic Feminist Perspective*. Mineola, NY: Dover Publications, and Trible, P. (1978) *God and the Rhetoric of Sexuality (Overtures to Biblical Theology)*. Minneapolis: MN: Fortress Press. Feminist film scholars include De Lauretis, T. (1984), *Alice Doesn't: Feminism, Semiotics Cinema*. Bloomington, IN: Indiana University Press;

Doane, M. A. (1987), *The Desire to Desire: The Woman's Film of the 1940s*. Blooming-ton, IN: Indiana University Press; Kaplan, E. A. (1983), *Women and Film: Both Sides of the Camera*. New York: Routledge; Mulvey, L. (1989), *Visual and Other Pleasures*. Bloomington, IN: Indiana University Press; Penley, C. (1989), *The Future of an Illusion: Film, Feminism and Psychoanalysis*. Minneapolis, MN: University of Minnesota Press; Silverman, K. (1988), *The Acoustic Mirror: The Female Voice in Psychoanalysis and Cinema*. Bloomington, IN: Indiana University Press; and Trinh, T. M. (1989), *Woman, Native, Other: Writing Postcoloniality and Feminism*. Bloomington, IN: Indiana University Press.

8 Countless women mystics, healers, herbalists, scientists and artists have spoken from the margins against male domination and have played a role in bringing about the changes that benefited women in a variety of historical and cultural contexts.

9 Makarushka, I. S. M. (1998), 'A Picture's Worth: Teaching Religion and Film', *Religious Studies News Spotlight on Teaching*, 6 (1 May). Atlanta, GA: American Academy of Religion (http://www.aarweb.org/Publications/spotlight/previous/6-1/06-01-07apic.asp) (members only).

10 Zerilli, SW, pp. 1–15.

11 Zerilli, Ibid., p. 2.

12 *Metaxu* is a concept introduced by Diotima in Plato's *Symposium*. Commenting on Diotima's speech, Hawthorne writes: '*Metaxu* is conceived of as a point on a continuum, a bridge between things that are separated, or between qualities that appear irreconcilable. . . . What Diotima attempts, through the use of the *metaxu* metaphor, is to establish links between separated elements, by doing so, she breaks down the separation . . .'. See, Hawthorne, S. (1993) 'Diotima Speaks Through the Body', in Bat-Ami Bar On, *Engendering Origins: Critical Feminist Readings in Plato and Aristotle*, Albany, NY: SUNY Press, pp. 88–9.

13 For a feminist reading of Nancy Savoca's *Household Saints*, see Makarushka, I. (1998), 'Tracing the Other in Household Saints', *Literature and Theology*, Oxford, UK: Oxford University Press, 12.

14 The phrase, women on the verge, was popularized by the 1988 film, *Women on the Verge of a Nervous Breakdown* which *Pedro Almodóvar* wrote and directed.

15 Campion examines the question of what women want and desire in all her films. In *The Portrait of a Lady*, however, what Isabel Archer desires remains ambiguous. Nevertheless, Isabel will inevitably pay a price for her independence.

Chapter 11

1 Krows, A. E. (1938), 'So the Pictures Went to Church', *TES* (October), 252–3.

2 Lindvall, T. (2001), *The Silents of God*. Lanham, MD: Scarecrow Press.

3 Greene, R. (2005), 'Y Movies: Film and the Modernization of Pastoral Power', *Communication and Critical/Cultural Studies*, 2 (1: March), 20–36.

4 'Motion Pictures at the New York Labor Temple' (1919), *Film Educational Magazine*, 2 (2: August), 18, 20.

5 'The Church's Duty to the Movies', *Literary Digest*, 64 (February 21, 1920), 38.

6 Krows, A. E. (1936, 1942), 'A Quarter-Century of Non-Theatrical Films', *TES* (June), 169–73; 'Motion Pictures – Not for Theatres', *TES* (May), 180–2.

7 Brady, M. B. (1935), 'A New Era for the Church', *TES* (December), 289–90.

8 Hellbeck, R. (1931), 'The Film and Protestantism', *International Review of Educational Cinematography* (3 October), 923–25.

9 Cited by Hopkins Jr., R. M. (1937), 'Where Materials in Visual Education may be Secured', *IJRE* 14 (November), 16–17.

10 His General Manager, George Reid Andrews divided them as the Bible, Religious

Biography, Church History, World Friendship or Missionary, Religious Pedagogical Pictures and a large class of wholesome pictures for Sunday night services. 'The Church and the Motion Picture', *National Board of Review Magazine* op. cit 10.

11 Hayward P.R. (1928), 'The King of Kings', *International Journal of Religious Education* (April), 7.

12 Anderson, D. and Lindvall, T. (1981), *We've Come A Long Way*, Video-documentary. Virginia Beach, VA: CBN (Regent) University Library.

13 Ibid., p. 401.

14 'James K. Friedrich Interview', BFC/NCC Fourth International Christian Film Workshop in Green Lake, Wisconsin (1947), Collection 327 at Billy Graham Center Archives, Wheaton College, Illinois.

15 'I called it *The Great Commandment* because that was its subject: "Thou shalt love the Lord thy God with all thy heart and all thy strength and thy neighbor as thyself" '. 'A producer serves the church', 400.

16 Edwards, C. (1989), 'Recorded Interview with Candice Hunt, Director of Marketing, Cathedral Films'. Virginia Beach, VA: Regent University (Transcript 3).

17 See 'Church builder: 16mm sound motion pictures', *CH* (16 November 1950), 20; and Hockman W. (1950), 'How to Visualize Your Teaching', *CH* (16 November), 19–23. In the same issue, a photograph of children, a few men and women in hats watching films in church was captioned: 'What enters the eyes is usually better retained than that which enters the ears'. The Protestant Film Commission also advertised themselves as 'Again . . . Pioneers' with the film *South of the Clouds*, available through the RFA libraries (23).

18 Ibid. Such a film gave rise to a wag quipping that Alexandra Astruc's phrase of film auteurs using the medium as a pen, *un camera stylo*, was realized in Baptista's *un camera stylo fountain*. Baptista said: 'Although mediocre, it was the first clear indication from the Lord that we could put the Gospel on film', *Baptista*, 22.

19 Anderson, op. cit.

20 Miller, op. cit.

21 Marks, H. (1985), 'A Brief History of Church Films', *Christian Film & Video Review* (January–February), 4.

22 Cooperative film libraries had been set up by a number of city councils of churches (Louisville, Kentucky; Oak Par, Illinois; Denver, Colorado) that provided mainline churches with religious education films. See Hockman op. cit. 349.

23 'Free Films: Gospel Films', *CH* (October 1951), 73.

24 Nelson, A., op. cit.

25 Zeoli's close connection to Republican politics would be satirized in *The Wittenburg Door*. See 'Wanda Ritchie's Body Life' column in which movie mogul Billy Zeoli cashes in on the Vietnam war movies, using the 'entire student body of Moody Bible Institute as the Viet Cong'. *The Wittenburg Door*, 50 (August–September 1979), 10.

26 Mel White claims that he 'ghost-wrote and directed the final version' of Schaeffer's *How Should We then Live* film series. See White, op. cit., p. 144.

27 Schaeffer, F. (2007), *Crazy for God : How I Grew Up As One of the Elect, Helped Found the Religious Right, and Lived to Take All (Or Almost All) of It Back*. Cambridge, MA: DeCapo Press (Perseus Books Group).

28 The truly odd story of Francis Schaeffer's son, Franky, followed his work on his father's series. As an angry young man, Franky castigated Christians for their mediocrity and hypocrisy, wrote and directed a Nietzchean tale of 'kicking some butt' in *Wired to Kill*. Franky described the Schaeffer/Buchfuehrer film as an action-adventure and social commentary, emphasizing that 'individuals can stand up and make a difference: "If you want history, you've got to make your own" ',

presumably by castrating a villain with a knife up his motorcycle seat. (*Wired to Kill, A Conversation With Writer*/Director Fanky Schaeffer. Hollywood: American Distribution Group, 1987). See it as *Booby Trap* in *Variety* (May 28, 1986), 5. According to Executive Producer Paul McQuire, the film won the best director award from the Academy of Science Fiction, Fantasy, and Horror Films. See Shapiro, M. (1986), 'Booby Trap: A Cross Between *The Road Warrior* and *Death Wish*', *Cinefantastique*; Coard, R., '*Wired to Kill*' and '*Wired to Kill* real, not reel-Sci-Fi!', *Portsmouth Review and Chesapeake Chronicle*, XXVI (October), pp. 1, 10–11, 13 and Tusher, W. (1985), 'SB prods. Plans Move from Dox to Feature Pix', *Variety*, 208 (64), 5 September, 1. He then produced a few other edgy films in the vein of Roger Corman such as *Headhunter* (See *Premier Magazine*, October 1989, 103) and *Rebel Storm*, in which Rock and Roll help to defeat a fascist television evangelist. His continental taste in film (Bergman, Fellini, etc.) and his call for a radical Christian filmmaking were not easily evident in his own works. His *Sham Pearls for Real Swine: Beyond the Cultural Dark Age – A Quest for Renaissance* (Wolgemuth and Hyatt, 1990) expresses his polemic against bourgeoisie Christians. See 'The Return of Franky Schaeffer', *Christianity Today* (November 19, 1990), 37–8.

29 Senter III, M. H. (1981), 'Bringing Back Cinema Serials: Christian style', *Christianity Today* (20 November), 37–8.

30 Many individuals enhanced their ministries through Gospel Films and found that moot gift of celebrity: Bob O'Donnell (*Unshackled*); a young evangelist named James Kennedy, *Like a Mighty Army* (1970); Raul Ries, *Fury To Freedom* (1985); and Clebe McClarey, *Clebe McClarey: Portrait on an American Hero* (1985).

31 Carpenter, F. (1986), 'When Are You Going to Make *Real* Movies?', *Mediator*, 1 (1: Fall), 1, 3.

32 Marks, H. (1985), 'A Brief History of Films in the Church, Part II', *Christian Film and Video Review* (January–February), 2.

33 *Family Films Is 35 and Proud Of It*, Family Films Promotional Guide, 1981.

34 'Visual Aids for the Church', *CH* (October 1949), 42; 'Family Films Offer Moral Teaching Messages: Effective and Entertaining', *IJRE* (March 1950), 91.

35 Cryderman, L. (1990), 'The Taming of the VCR', *Christianity Today* (24 September), 65.

36 Cecil B. DeMille posed with Billy Graham over a copy of the Ten Commandments as he was preparing to film his spectacle and was cited as remembering 'the record-breaking premier he attended in the Hollywood Bowl in 1951 to see the first Billy Graham feature film, *Mr. Texas*. The evangelist remembered the projector breaking down, and wondered at his audacity to invite the film capital's greats to a production that cost only $25,000. 'It took that amount of money just to turn on their lights', he once said. *20 Years under God: A pictorial review of the Billy Graham ministries* (Minneapolis: World Wide Pictures, 1970), 122.

37 Many records of the WWP are stored at the Archives of the Billy Graham Center on the campus of Wheaton College, in Wheaton, Illinois. The best-documented (and most successful) film in the collection is *The Hiding Place*, covering everything from strategies of fundraising to personal testimonial responses.

38 DH 'Interview with Ken Engstrom' (Virginia Beach: Regent University, July 1992), 3. Like Alfred Hitchcock, Graham would make cameos in all of his films, usually at a crusade.

39 *Christianity Today* (October 14, 1966).

40 Director James Collier believed that *The Hiding Place* would actually be nominated for several Academy Awards, for Jeanette Clift and Julie Harris' performances. Las Vegas gave both actresses odds for being nominated. However, Hollywood continued to be uneasy with Christian films, as they were outside the 'club'.

Nevertheless, Jeannette Clift was nominated for Best Newcomer for the Golden Globes. White, M. (1983), 'Does Christian Film Work in the Neighborhood Theater?', *Christianity Today* (7 October), 14–20.

41 Rochester, op cit, 3.

42 Cheney, H. (1983), *'The Prodigal', Christianity Today* (7 October), 16.

43 White, op cit, 14–20.

44 Ibid., p. 15. Ken Wales defined an 'explicitly evangelistic film' as one that contained a crusade and showed how 'people's lives are changed by a crusade and primarily by hearing the word of God through Billy's preaching'.

45 Ibid., p. 18.

46 'Programming with visual aids', *CH* (October 1947), 40–5.

47 Ibid. Keyed to the 1947–48 theme of the PFC emphasis on evangelism, the film presents a story of man who loses his soul in an addiction to business, but finds the Light through his missionary brother. See 'Religious Pictures on the Way', *CA*, 123 (14: 1 April 1948), 419.

48 Robbins, M. (1947–48), 'Films for the church', *Hollywood Quarterly*, 3 (2: Winter), 178–84.

49 'Visual Aids for the Church', *CH* (October 1948), 64.

50 Lott, T. (1958), 'The Radio and Television Commission'. *Encyclopedia of Southern Baptists*, Vol. II. Nashville: Broadman Press, p. 1131.

51 'The Bible goes to press: From the motion picture, *Our Bible – How It Came to Us'* in Maus, C. (1960), *The Church and the Fine Arts*. New York: Harper and Brothers, 410–42; 'Here I Stand' from the Motion Picture *Luther*, 412–16; see Hills, M. T. (1956), '500ᵗʰ Anniversary of the Gutenberg Bible' in *Bible Society Record*, Vol. 101. New York: American Bible Society, pp. 104–5; De Groot, Dr. A. T. (1954), 'Scenes of the Protestant Reformation', *The Christian-Evangelist*, 92. Bloomington, MN: Bethany Press, pp. 1032–40.

52 http://www.jesusfilm.org/

53 'Movies for the family – *John Wesley'*, *Christian Advocate*, 129 (19: 13 May 1954), 602; 'Museum of modern art', *Christian Advocate*, 129 (12: 25 March 1954), 378.

54 See Schillaci, A. O. P., *Movies and Morals*, 122–7.

55 Ibid., p. 73.

Chapter 13

1 These are the three marks or attributes of existence, cf. *Anguttara-nikāya*.

2 The film was re-made as a musical of the same name in 1973.

3 'Shangri-la' is based on the Sanskrit word '*śambhala'*.

4 In Eve L. Mullen's article (1998), 'Oriental commercializations: Tibetan Buddhism in American popular film', *Journal of Religion & Film*, 2 (2: October). Omaha, NE: University of Nebraska at Omaha, http://www.unomaha.edu/jrf/OrientalMullen. htm, she describes orientalism as 'Western distortions, purposeful or not, of Eastern traditions and culture, distortions which ultimately can be patronizing or damaging to the studied cultures'.

5 Much like *Lost Horizon*, *The Razor's Edge* was based on a novel, in this case by Somerset Maugham (1944) and was re-made in 1984.

6 http://www.crossroad.to/articles2/05/karate.htm.

7 Iwamura, J. N. (2000, 2005 rev. edn), 'The Oriental Monk in American Popular Culture', in Forbes, B. D. and Mahan, J. H. (eds), *Religion and Popular Culture in America*. Berkeley: University of California Press, pp. 33–2.

8 The original version of *Seven Years in Tibet* was directed by Hans Nieter in 1956. Heinrich Harrer, who wrote the book about his experiences in Tibet, contri-

buted his documentary footage to the film and was directly involved with its production.
9 Bishop, P. (2000), 'Caught in the Cross-Fire: Tibet, Media and Promotional Culture', *Media, Culture & Society*, 22, 647–8.
10 Ibid., p. 651.
11 '*Phorpa/The Cup*: An interview with the film's director Khyentse Norbu', *Gentle Voice: A Newsletter of Siddhartha's Intent*. March 1999.
12 http://www.siddharthasintent.org/gentle/GV11-3.htm.
13 Ibid.
14 *Bodhidharma* from here after. Tradition says that Bodhidharma was the Indian monk who brought the Ch'an (Son/Zen) school to China. It spread from there to Korea and Japan.
15 *Spring* from here after.
16 Gillespie, M. L. (1997), 'Picturing the Way in Bae Yong-kyun's *Why Has Bodhidharma Left for the East?*', *Journal of Religion & Film*, 1 (1: April), 7. Omaha, NE: University of Nebraska at Omaha, http://www.unomaha.edu/jrf/gillespi.htm.
17 For an example of how students in a religion and film class react to this experience, see Blizek, W. L. and Desmarais, M. M. (2008), 'What Are We Teaching When We Teach Religion and Film?', in Watkins, G. J. (ed.), *Teaching Religion and Film*. New York: Oxford University Press, pp. 23–4.
18 See Blizek, W. L., 'Using Movies to Critique Religion', (Chapter 3) in this volume.
19 Briefly, the *Prajñā-pāramitā* scriptures are early Mahāyāna texts that discuss the *bodhisattva* path. They also teach that everything is empty of 'own-nature', therefore, all existents are characterized by interdependence. That is, because nothing has its own eternal, unchanging essence, each thing comes into existence through a host of other factors. Although normal perception presents us with a view of independent, separate 'things', this is a mistake. This teaching, combined with the *bodhisattva* path, means that all are interconnected and the welfare or suffering of one is the welfare or suffering of all.
20 Sluyter, D. (2005), *Cinema Nirvana: Enlightenment Lessons from the Movies*. New York: Three Rivers Press.
21 See, for example: Geoff Baker's (2006) 'Portraying the Quest for Buddhist Wisdom?: A Comparative Study of *The Matrix* and *Crouching Tiger, Hidden Dragon*' *The Journal of Religion & Film*, 10 (1: April).Omaha, NE: University of Nebraska at Omaha, http://www.unomaha.edu/jrf/vol10no1/BakerQuest.htm; Frances Flannery-Dailey, F. (2003), 'Robot Heavens and Robot Dreams: Ultimate Reality in *A.I.* and Other Recent Films' in *The Journal of Religion & Film*, 7 (2: October). Omaha, NE: University of Nebraska at Omaha, http://www.unomaha.edu/jrf/Vol7No2/robotHeaven.htm. For the difficulties in using Buddhism as the solo interpretive device for *The Matrix*, see Fielding, J. (2003), 'Reassessing *The Matrix Reloaded*' in *The Journal of Religion & Film*, 7 (2: October). Omaha, NE: University of Nebraska at Omaha, http://www.unomaha.edu/jrf/Vol7No2/matrix.matrixreloaded.htm.

Chapter 14
1 The system of four *varṇas* (*brāhmaṇas/brahmins; kṣatriyas; vaiśyas; śūdras*) is commonly called the 'caste system'. However, there are only four *varṇas* while there are numerous *jātis* (castes).
2 This is not to deny that some Hindu scriptures refer to the *varṇa* system (cf. *Ṛg-veda* X.90; *Bhagavad-Gītā* 18.41; *Manu-smṛti*). However, Hindu reformers such as Gandhi or Ram Mohan Roy tend to take their inspiration and mandate from the same scriptures, so we might argue that support for the *varṇa* system is not an integral

part of being Hindu. Furthermore, the class/caste system is not exclusive to Hinduism. For example, we might take either perspective – that class/caste is part of Hindu religion, or that class/caste is not part of Hinduism but rather Indian society – when viewing the film *Swadeś: We the People* (2004). In this film a non-resident Indian returns from America and reforms some of the traditional class/caste restrictions in a small village in India.

3 *The Manu-smṛti (Laws of Manu)*, which is quoted at the beginning of Mehta's *Water*, includes not only 'religious' instruction, but also information on hygiene and many other aspects of etiquette and behaviour. Therefore, the entire text can not be considered to be 'religious' in nature nor, necessarily, the sections that refer to the treatment of widows as such. Furthermore, it was the British who made *Manu-smṛti* the law of the land in India.

4 Kim Kronschnabel, a Religious Studies major and scholar at the University of Nebraska at Omaha, drew my attention to these important points regarding *Water*. Mehta, in fact, denies that the film is a critique of Hinduism.

5 This area is now part of Pakistan.

6 Viswanathan, G. (2003/2005), 'Colonialism and the Construction of Hinduism', 28, in *The Blackwell Companion To Hinduism*. Malden: Blackwell Publishing.

7 The Supreme Court in India has affirmed that Hinduism does not fit the conventional sense of the term 'religion', but rather refers to an 'all-embracing way of life', http://www.trinidadandtobagonews.com/selfnews/viewnews.cgi?newsid1028966817,58558,.shtml.

8 In addition to the reasons for the difficulty given above, some beliefs and practices, while originating within Hinduism, become pan-Indian and even international or multi-religious practices. Examples of these include: yoga; karma; meditation; some ascetic practices; the *mālā* or rosary; and certain ideas of ritual purity. Given this situation, are we then examining Hindu themes or practices in movies, or Indian themes?

9 Gokulsing, K. M. and Dissanayake, W. (1998), *Indian Popular Cinema: A Narrative of Cultural Change*. Staffordshire: Trentham Books, p. 23.

10 The popular term Bollywood is not synonymous with Indian cinema, particularly since Indian cinema is much older and more diverse than Bollywood connotes. See Mehta, S. (2004). *Maximum City: Bombay Lost and Found*. New York: Vintage, p. 349–50.

11 See for example, Gouklsing and Dissanayake *op. cit.*, or Dwyer, R. (2006), *Filming the Gods: Religion and Indian Cinema*, New York: Routledge.

12 Similarly, in Manmohan Desai's *Gaṅgā, Jamnunā, Saraswatī* (1988), the main characters are named after the goddesses and three holiest rivers in India.

13 Hindu scriptures are divided into two categories: *śruti*, which are the most sacred, revealed scriptures (these are the four *Vedas, Brāhmaṇas, Araṇyakas*, and *Upaniṣads*); and *smṛti*, which are other important scriptures and texts.

14 See Gokulsing, K. M. and Dissanayake, W. (1998), *Indian Popular Cinema: A Narrative of Cultural Change*. Staffordshire: Trentham Books, p. 17. An example of a re-telling would be Bahubhai Mistri's *Sampoorna Ramayan* (1961). Newer interpretations of the epic include Ritwik Ghatak's 1964 film *Subernarekha* and Rajkumar Santoshi's 2001 film *Lajja*, which focuses on a modern woman learning about Indian women and Sītā through a journey across India (Chatterjee, G., 'Designing a Course on Religion and Cinema in India', p. 89–90, in Watkins, G. J. (ed.) (2008), *Teaching Religion and Film*, Oxford: Oxford University Press.

15 See http://www.sitasingstheblues.com/

16 See, for example Babubhai Mistri's 1965 film *Mahabharat*.

17 The *Bhagavad-Gītā* is a small, but enormously influential, portion of the *Mahābhārata*.

18 See Michele Marie Desmarais' 'Karma and Film' (Chapter 26) in this volume.

19 See Flannery-Dailey, F. (2003) *'Robot Heavens and Robot Dreams: Ultimate Reality in A.I. and Other Recent Films'*. *Journal of Religion and Film*, 7 (2: October), paragraph 5. Omaha, NE: University of Nebraska at Omaha, http://www.unomaha.edu/jrf/Vol7No2/robotHeaven.htm.
20 See Desmarais, Chapter 26, 'Karma and Film', in this volume.
21 Ibid.
22 See, for example, Gandhi, M. K.(1927), *An Autobiography: or The Story of My Experiments with Truth*.
23 *Bhagavad-Gītā*, 2.47.
24 *Il Mio Nome E' Nessuno*.
25 *Lo chiamavano Trinita*.
26 See *Gītā* 9.30–32.
27 Dwyer, *op. cit.*, p. 46.
28 Lutgendorf, P. (2002), 'A Superhit Goddess: Jai Santoshi Maa and Caste Hierarchy in Indian Films' (part one) in *Manushi: A Journal About Women and Society*, 131 (October–November), 10–16.
29 See above.

Chapter 15

1 Gabler, N. (1989), *An Empire of Their Own: How the Jews Invented Hollywood*. New York: Anchor Books, p. 5.
2 Friedman, L. D. (1987), *The Jewish Image in American Film: Seventy Years of Hollywood's Vision of Jewish Characters and Themes*. Secaucus: Citadel Press, p. 120.
3 Erens, P. (1984), *The Jew in American Cinema*. Bloomington: Indiana University Press, pp. 150–1.
4 Herman, F. (2001), 'Hollywood, Nazism, and the Jews, 1933–41', *American Jewish History*, New York: American Jewish Historical Society (AJHS), 62–3.
5 Erens, p. 171; Friedman, p. 43.
6 A number of important films about the Holocaust have been produced. They are the subject of Chapter 21 in this volume.
7 Quoted. in Gabler, p. 340.
8 Fielder, L. (1971), *The Collected Essays of Leslie Fiedler*. New York: Stein and Day Publishers, p. 97; Fiedler, p. 111.
9 Sachar, H. (1992), *A History of the Jews in America*. New York: Alfred A. Knopf, p. 680.
10 Erens pp. 275–6; Hoberman. J. (2003), 'Flaunting it: The Rise and Fall of Hollywood's "Nice Jewish (Bad) Boys" ', in Hoberman, J. and Shandler, J. (eds), *Entertaining America: Jews, Movies, and Broadcasting*. New York and Princeton: The Jewish Museum, New York and Princeton University Press, 232–5.
11 632, emphasis in the original.
12 A subset of the larger category of films related to Jewish identity are Israeli films. Most Israeli films that focus on Jewish characters address Judaism as a religion and/or Jewish identity in terms of ethnicity. Recent films such as Amos Gitai's *Kadosh* (1999) and Giddi Dar's *Ushpizin* (2004) examine Jewish religious identity. Other works like Joseph Cedar's *Beaufort* (2008), Eran Kolirin's *The Band's Visit* (2007), Gitai's *Free Zone* (2006) and *Kippur* (2000), and Eytan Fox's *Walk on Water* (2004) touch upon Jewish identity as it relates to Israeli nationality and Middle East politics. Israeli films may not be as widely known as American films, but as contemporary Israeli releases gain more and more attention, they will surely play an increasing role in our cinematic understanding of Judaism and Jewish identity. There are many films about Jewish identity that fell outside the scope of this essay.

Some of the more well-known include *Body and Soul* (1943), *The Ten Command-ments* (1956), *Ben-Hur* (1959), *Exodus* (1960), *The Way We Were* (1973), *Zelig* (1983), *Brighton Beach Memoirs* (1986), *Biloxi Blues* (1988), *Crimes and Misdemeanors* (1989), *Homicide* (1991), *The Prince of Egypt* (1998) and *The Life and Times of Hank Greenberg* (1998).

Chapter 16

1 Ibid. The way in which the Orient has been depicted in Hollywood is often a product of the colonialist imagination as well as the Western male gaze. See Shohat, E. (1990) 'Gender in Hollywood's Orient', *Middle East Report*, 20 (162: 1 January–February), 40–2.

2 Shaheen, J. G. (2001), *Reel Bad Arabs: How Hollywood Vilifies a People*. New York: Olive Branch Press.

3 Solomon, N. (1996), 'The Danger in Stereotyping', *St. Louis Post-Dispatch*, 14 January.

4 *The Delta Force* (1986) was produced and entirely filmed in Israel. It was directed by Menahem Golan.

5 The plane hijacking that took place in 1985 by the Hizbollah lasted seventeen days and the news media showed daily images of hooded hijackers holding guns on innocent Americans.

6 In this sense, hyper-reality refers to Jean Baudrillard's explanation of the hyperreal in media simulations. He states that 'simulation is no longer that of a territory, a referential being or a substance. It is the generation by models of a real without origin or reality: a hyperreal'. As cited in Baudrillard, J. (1983), *Simulations*. New York: Semiotext(e), p. 2.

7 Baudrillard, J. (1983), *Simulations*. New York: Semiotext(e).

8 *Navy Seals* (1990) and *The Siege* (1998) are two excellent examples where television footage is interspersed throughout the movie to add credibility to the storyline.

9 Merrill, R. (2005), 'Simulations and Terrors of our Time', in Slocum, J. D. (ed.), *Terrorism, Media, Liberation*. New Jersey: Rutgers University Press, p. 173.

10 George H. W. Bush's remarks, made in 1987, were included in the introduction of the Vice President's Task Force on Combating Terrorism report entitled *Terrorist Group Profiles*, Washington, D.C.: US Government Printing Office, released in 1988.

11 This argument has been put forward by the author in previous papers. See Ramji, R. (2003), 'Representations of Islam in American News and Film: Becoming the "Other" ', in Mitchell, J. and Marriage, S. (eds), *Mediating Religion: Conversations in Media, Religion and Culture*. London: T&T Clark, and Ramji, R. (2005) 'From "Navy Seals" to "The Siege": Getting to Know the Muslim Terrorist, Hollywood Style', *Journal of Religion and Film*, 9 (2). Omaha, NE: University of Nebraska. For more details see http://www.unomaha.edu/jrf/Vol9No2/RamjiIslam.htm.

12 Miles, M. (1996), *Seeing and Believing: Religion and Values in the Movies*. Boston: Beacon Press.

13 Caricatures that portray Islamic women as weak and oppressed have become more pervasive in recent years. See Ahmed, L. (1992), *Women and Gender in Islam: Historical Roots of a Modern Debate*. New Haven, CT: Yale University Press.

14 *Air Force One* (1997), directed by Wolfgang Peterson (USA). This movie made over $172 million.

15 *Three Kings* (1990, Director: David O. Russell [USA]). This movie continues the trend that the only helpful Muslims are those who have had exposure to the West.

16 *True Lies* (1994) made over $146 million at the box office in the United States. The

movies *True Lies*, *Executive Decision* and *Rules of Engagement* have all been assisted by the United States Department of Defense and the US Marine Corps. More than fourteen feature films which depict Americans killing Arabs have credited the Department of Defense for their assistance in the making of these films. As cited in Shaheen, J. G. (2001), *Reel Bad Arabs: How Hollywood Vilifies a People*, New York: Olive Branch Press.

17 Parts of the Arab-American community refer to such movies as part of the 'Three B Syndrome: Arabs are portrayed as either Bombers, Billionaires or Belly dancers'. Mazin B. Qumsiyeh, M. B. (2003), '100 Years of Anti-Arab and Anti-Muslim Stereotyping', *The Prism*, accessed on 26 March (2008).

18 Auty, M. and Roddick, N. (1985), *British Cinema Now*. London, British Film Institute, p. 5.

19 Alexander, K. (2000), 'Black British Cinema in the 90s: Going, Going, Gone', in Murphy, R. (ed.), *British Cinema in the 90s*. London, British Film Institute, p. 113.

20 Johnson, C. (2002), 'The Dilemmas of Ethnic Privilege: A Comparison of Constructions of "British", "English" and "Anglophone Celtic" Identity in Contemporary British and Australian Political Discourse', *Ethnicities*, 2 (2), 171.

21 Stafford, R. (2002), 'Where's the Black in the Union Jack?', *Mediaculture Online*. http://www.mediaculture-online.de/fileadmin/bibliothek/stafford_black/stafford_black.pdf.

22 Larsson, D., 'Kureishi in Dialogue', in *CineScene.Com*, http://www.cinescene.com/don/kureishi.html.

23 Jack, I. as cited in *Hanif Kureishi: Biography*, Http://www.emory.edu/ENGLISH/Bahri/Krueishi.html.

24 Johnson, C. (2002), 'The Dilemmas of Ethnic Privilege: A Comparison of Constructions of "British", "English" and "Anglophone Celtic" Identity in Contemporary British and Australian Political Discourse', *Ethnicities*, 2 (2), 168.

25 Hanif Kureishi states that fundamentalism, like racism, is a diminisher of life. 'Islamic fundamentalism is a mixture of slogans and resentment; it works well as a system of authority that constrains desire, but it strangles this source of human life too. But of course in the Islamic states, as in the West, there are plenty of dissenters and quibblers, and those hungry for mental and political freedom. These essential debates can only take place within a culture; they are what a culture is, and they demonstrate how culture opposes the domination of either materialism or Puritanism. If both racism and fundamentalism are diminishers of life – reducing others to abstractions – the effort of culture must be to keep others alive by describing and celebrating their intricacy, by seeing that this is not only of value but of necessity.' This text originally appeared in the introduction to Kureishi, H. (2002), *Collected Screenplays*. UK: Faber and Faber.

26 Rosaldo, R. (1993), *Culture and the Truth: The Remaking of Social Analysis*. Boston: Beacon Press, p. 19.

27 Hussain, A. (2008), 'Film and the Introduction to Islam Course', in Watkins, G. H. (ed.), *Teaching Religion and Film*. New York: Oxford University Press.

28 The PBS statement about the documentary *Islam: Empire of Faith* was found on About.com: Islam at http://islam.about.com/library/weekly/aa050701a.htm.

29 *Islam: Empire of Faith* (2001) is produced and directed by Robert Gardner and narrated by Ben Kingsley. It originally aired on PBS in May 2001, and was re-aired in October 2001 after the 9/11 attacks on the United States.

30 PBS, 'The Brotherhood', *PBS Website* (2007), http://www.pbs.org/weta/crossroads/about/show_the_brotherhood.html.

31 PBS, 'Jihad: The Men and Ideas Behind Al Qaeda', *PBS Website* (Paladin InVision, 2007), http://www.pbs.org/weta/crossroads/about/show_jihad.html.

32 Arenson, K. W. (2007), 'Film's View of Islam Stirs Anger on Campuses', *New York Times*, 26 February, http://www.nytimes.com/2007/02/26/movies/26docu.html?_r=1&ei=5087%0A&em=&en=a4062496f8729e35&ex=1172638800&pagewanted=print&oref=slogin.

33 Fox News (2007), 'New poll shows worry over Islam terror threat, to be detailed in specific FNC report', *Fox News Website*, 3 February, http://www.foxnews.com/story/0,2933,249521,00.html.

34 *Submission* (2004) was written by Ayaan Hirsi Ali and Theo van Gogh and directed by Theo van Gogh.

35 *Fitna* is written by Geert Wilders and Scarlet Pimpernel and directed by Scarlet Pimpernel (Scarlet Pimpernel Productions, 2008). The Dutch public broadcasting network companies did not air the film so it was posted on the Liveleak website.

36 Murray, D. (2008) 'A Film-Maker Who Lives in the Shadow of a Fatwa', *The Spectator*, 12 March, http://www.spectator.co.uk/print/the-magazine/features/553681/a-filmmaker-who-lives-in-the-shadow-of-a-fatwa.thtml.

37 *Det svider i hjärtat (Aching Heart)* is written and directed by Oscar Hedin, Danmarks Radio, 2007.

38 Swedish Film Institute, '2007 nominations for Guldbagge – The Swedish national film award', *Swedish Film Institute Website* (January 8, 2008), http://www.sfi.se/sfi/smpage.fwx?page=8794&NEWS=21205. 15 August 2007.

39 Ekman, I. (2007), 'Swedish Documentary Follows "Regular" Europeans who Turn to Jihad', *International Herald Tribune*, 15 October, http://www.iht.com/articles/2007/10/15/africa/sweden.php.

40 *Stand Up: Muslim American Comics Come of Age* (2007) is directed by Glenn Baker and Omar Naim and produced by Glenn Baker and Lauren Cardillo, Potomac Media Works.

41 PBS, 'Stand Up: Muslim American Comics Come of Age', *PBS Website*. http://www.pbs.org/weta/crossroads/about/show_standup.html.

42 Two more recent short films by Zarqa Nawaz are *Random Check* (2005) where a young man is arrested at the airport due to racial profiling, and *Fred's Burqa* (2005), a humorous story about a stolen burqa and mistaken identity.

43 Zarqa Nawaz has her own website based on her production company, FUNdamentalist Films, which she describes 'puts the fun back into fundamentalism'. It also includes information about her current Canadian based television show *Little Mosque on the Prairie*. See http://www.fundamentalistfilms.com.

44 Erickson, S. (2007) in his article 'The Middle East Side', *The Reeler: New York City Cinema, From the Art House to the Red Carpet* (25 April), states that Iranian cinema became popular in the film festival circuit in the late 1980s, with the 'Western' discovery of film-maker Abbas Kiarostami. Considered Iran's most famous director, Kiarostami's movies focus on universal human dilemmas. For more information, see Brown, J. (2001), 'Movies of the Middle East', *Salon.com*, 9 October, http://archive.salon.com/mwt/feature/2001/10/09/film/print.html.

45 Tapper, R. (2002), 'Introduction', in Tapper, R. (ed.), *The New Iranian Cinema: Politics, Representation and Identity*. London: I.B. Tauris, p. 6.

46 Varzi, R. (2006), *Warring Souls: Youth Media and Martyrdom in Post-Revolutionary Iran*, Durham: Duke University Press, p. 77.

47 Ibid., p. 79.

48 The Ministry of Culture and Islamic Guidance was created to regulate all forms of communications media. The cinema, music, theatre, television and radio media were controlled by the state now. As cited in Tapper, R. (2002), 'Introduction', in

Tapper, R. (ed.), *The New Iranian Cinema: Politics, Representation and Identity*. London: I.B. Tauris.

49 Varzi, R. (2006), *Warring Souls: Youth Media and Martyrdom in Post-Revolutionary Iran*. Durham: Duke University Press. p. 97.

50 Varzi, R. (2002), 'A Ghost in the Machine: The Cinema of the Iranian Sacred Defense', in Tapper, R. (ed.), *The New Iranian Cinema: Politics, Representation and Identity*. London: I.B. Tauris.

51 Varzi, R., *Warring Souls*, p. 98.

52 Ibid., p. 99.

53 Dönmez-Colin, G. (2006), *Cinemas of the Other: A Personal Journey with Film-Makers From the Middle East and Central Asia*. UK: Intellect Ltd., p. 20.

54 Varzi, R. (2006) *Warring Souls*, p. 148.

55 Dönmez-Colin, G. (2006), *Cinemas of the Other*.

56 In 1992, Bani-Etemad made a film based on research she had conducted making documentaries entitled *Nargess*, which focuses on the problems women face with societal expectations in Iran. Her next film, *Rusariye Abi (The Blue Veiled)* was made in 1995 examines the idea of forbidden love through extramarital affairs. As cited in Gönül Dönmez-Colin, G. (2006), *Cinemas of the Other: A Personal Journey with Film-Makers From the Middle East and Central Asia*. UK: Intellect Ltd.

57 Varzi, R. (2006), *Warring Souls*, p. 176.

58 One such filmmaker is Hatamikia. Some of his most successful and controversial films are *Kharkeh to Rhine* (1994), *The Scent of Yusef's Shirt* (1996), *The Glass Agency* (1998) and *The Red Ribbon* (2000).

59 Brown, J. (2001), 'Movies of the Middle East', *Salon.com*. (9 October), http://archive.salon.com/mwt/feature/2001/10/09/film/print.html.

Chapter 17

1 Fisher, M.P. (2008), *Living Religions* (7th ed.). Upper Saddle River, NJ: Pearson/Prentice Hall, p. 32. When it comes to the discussion of indigenous groups, religious studies' scholars differ on which ones to include and exclude in their introductory texts. In *World Religions: A Historical Approach*, Nigosian, S. A., considers African and American religions in separate sections under the larger topic Religions of Oral People. Mayans and Aztec religions are found under Religions of the Past. Warren Matthews also separates religions of the Americas and of Africa, but includes them under the topic Religions of Tribes and City-States in *World Religions*. *A History of the World's Religions* by Noss, D. S., discusses 'Mesoamerica: The Maya under Bygone Religions That Have Left Their Mark on the West', and includes case studies of the Dieri of Southeast Australia, the BaVenda of South Africa and the Cherokee of the Southeastern Woodlands under the chapter 'Religion in Prehistoric and Primal Cultures'. The most comprehensive text, *A Concise Introduction to World Religions*, Oxtoby, W. G., and Segal, A. F. (eds), has a chapter on indigenous religious traditions, in which one finds discussion of Africa, North and Central America, Northeast Asia, focusing on Siberia; Australasia, and finally Western Pacific Islands. This essay discusses Native American, Aborigine, Mayan and Maori, because those are the traditions most readily found in film.

2 Fisher, M. P. (2008), *Living Religions* (7th edn). Upper Saddle River, NJ: Pearson/Prentice Hall, p. 36.

3 Young, W. A. (2005), *The World's Religions: Worldviews and Contemporary Issues* (2nd ed.). Upper Saddle River, NJ: Pearson/Prentice Hall, p. 27.

4 Hill, T. (1994), 'Introduction: A Backward Glimpse through the Museum Door', in

Hill, T., and Hill Sr., R. W. (eds), *Creation's Journey: Native American Identity and Belief*, Washington, D.C: Smithsonian Institution Press, p. 16.

5 Nigosian, S.A. (2008), *World Religions: A Historical Approach* (4th ed.), Boston: Bedford/St. Martin's, p. 112.

6 Nigosian explains some developments on p. 113.

7 Hill, T. (1994), 'Introduction: A Backward Glimpse through the Museum Door', in Hill, T. and Hill Sr., R. W. (eds), *Creation's Journey: Native American Identity and Belief*. Washington, D.C: Smithsonian Institution Press, p. 17.

8 Deloria, V. (1988), *Custer Died for Your Sins: An Indian Manifesto*, reprint, Norman, Oklahoma: University of Oklahoma Press, p. 2.

9 Films by Chris Eyre include *Skins* (2002), *Skinwalkers* (2002), *Edge of America* (2003), *A Thief of Time* (2004), *Smoke Signals* (1998) and *A Thousand Roads* (2005).

10 Few if any of these films can teach us much about religion. A more realistic portrait would undoubtedly be found in films produced in Africa. However, few are released in the West, and even fewer are available on DVD. A few exceptions include *Sia, the Dream of the Python* (2001), which is an adaptation of a seventh-century African legend about a woman who is selected to be sacrificed to a snake god; *Yeelen* (1987), which tells the story of one man's search for his evil, all-powerful shaman father; and *Masai: The Rain Warriors* (2004), which is a coming of age film about the Masai.

11 Fielding, J.R. (2003), 'Native American Religion and Film: Interviews with Chris Eyre and Sherman Alexie', *Journal of Religion & Film*, 7 (1). Omaha, NE: University of Nebraska at Omaha, http://www.unomaha.edu/jrf/Vol7No1/nativefilm.htm.

12 Fielding, J.R. (2003), 'Native American Religion and Film: Interviews with Chris Eyre and Sherman Alexie', *Journal of Religion and Film*, 7 (1). Omaha, NE: University of Nebraska at Omaha, http://www.unomaha.edu/jrf/Vol7No1/nativefilm.htm.

13 Lucci-Cooper, K. (2003), 'To Carry the Fire Home', *Genocide of the Mind: New Native American Writing*. New York: Thunder's Mouth Press/Nation Books, p. 3–4.

14 A few other films that depict missionaries and indigenous people are *The Mission* (1986), *At Play in the Fields of the Lord* (1991), and *End of the Spear* (2005).

15 In the dream a raven (symbolizing the Blackrobe) attacked Chomina but he could not move. This raven also plucked the eyeball out of a dead man. What does the dream mean? That Laforgue would bring death and destruction to the Algonquin, which is what happened. Because they led Laforgue on his journey, they came into contact with the hostile Iroquois, undoubtedly enflaming pre-existing tensions. When Chomina tells his companions about the dream they said that they should 'respect it'. Dreams, they said, are more real than life and even war. But they didn't respect it, and choose to ignore its warning.

16 Simon, J. (1992), 'Black Robe', *National Review* (Feb. 3), http://findarticles.com/p/articles/mi_m1282/is_n2_v44/ai_11860858/pg_2.

17 This is, of course, a reference to Jesus of Nazareth's own 'passion'.

18 Mel Gibson's *Apocalypto* (2006), which deals with Mayan civilization 'prior to the arrival of the Spanish', provides an interesting contrast to *The Other Conquest*. Whereas *The Other Conquest* has been praised for its accuracy, *Apocalypto* has, along with Gibson's other films *Braveheart* and *The Patriot*, been 'named and shamed among the most historically inaccurate films ever made'.

19 From www.theotherconquest.com, found under Production Information. The director claims that he conducted extensive research and shot at archeological sites, using authentic costumes and props. He was also careful to have his characters speak in Nahuatl – a language still spoken by one and one-half million people – and have a soundtrack that used authentic music. As the director said on the audio DVD commentary, between fifteen million and twenty million Indians lived in

Mexico prior to the arrival of the Spaniards. Afterwards, there were only about one million. Many of the survivors, he said, believed that they were abandoned by their gods.

20 In the DVD audio commentary, Herzog said that the film was inspired by a real court case. An Aboriginal group had sued a mining company, in the film the Ayers Mining Company, in reality, Nabalco, because it was threatening sacred ground.

21 Herzog admits that this scene was inspired by a real event. He also said that although 'dreamtime' and 'the dreaming' exist in Aboriginal thought, he made up the story of the green ants.

22 In the film, Aboriginal characters talk about 'dreamtime' and 'dreaming', but the director has taken liberties with the concept. He explained in the DVD audio commentary that 'dreamtime is another perception; another way of seeing things. I never got a full understanding of it'.

23 *The Tracker* (2002) also demonstrates the clashes between Aborigines and the white settlers. Set in 1922, *The Tracker* is about three white law men and their Aboriginal tracker who set off across the 'bush' to find an Aboriginal man who is accused of killing a white woman. The film exposes us to the racist attitudes and savagery characteristic of early white settlers. One character sees nothing wrong in shooting innocent women and children, because, after all, all these 'blacks' are 'cannibals, treacherous and dirty'. In fact, viewers will probably find parallels between the ways in which Aborigines and American Indians were treated.

Chapter 18

1 Schmidt, L. E. (2007), *Restless Souls: The Making of American Spirituality from Emerson to Oprah*. San Francisco: Harper San Francisco.

2 Ibid.

3 Orsi, R. A. (2006), '2 + 2 = 5, Or the Quest for an Abundant Empiricism', in *Spiritus: A Journal of Christian Spirituality*, 6, 113–21. This essay is part of a review symposium on Orsi's 2005 *Between Heaven and Earth: the Religious Worlds People Make and the Scholars Who Study Them, Princeton University Press*. Orsi's main point in *Between Heaven and Earth* is that scholars of religion have limited their study to aspects of religion that fit the bias of a scholarly liberal Protestant tradition which has a built in anti-Catholic approach. In the review symposium he takes on the newly emerging academic field of spirituality.

4 Brussat, F., and Brussat, M.A. (1996), *Spiritual Literacy: Reading the Sacred in Everyday Life*. New York: Scribner.

5 Brussat, F. and Brussat, M. A. (eds.) (1997–2001), *Spirituality and Health: the Soul Body Connection*. Traverse City, Mich: Spirituality & Health Media, LLC. The examples of 'spiritually literate films' is taken from the Brussat's listing.

6 Ibid., pp. 19–25.

7 Ibid., p. 24.

Chapter 19

1 Lloyd Baugh, for example, comments extensively on the historical distortions of the films as part of his critique of their lack of historicity. Cf. Baugh, L. (1997), *Imaging the Divine: Jesus and Christ-Figures in Film, Communication, Culture & Theology*. Kansas City, MO: Sheed & Ward, pp. 18–19.

2 Custen, G. F. (1992), *Bio/Pics: How Hollywood Constructed Public History*. New Brunswick, NJ: Rutgers University Press, p. 44.

3 The survey covers only full-length feature films and the most widely circulated

television miniseries. It should be noted, however, that in addition to these lengthy renditions, numerous short films and videos tackle all or part of Jesus' life in both conventional and innovative ways. Among these are the six videos produced by the American Bible Society's New Media translation project as part of a projected 12-part 'Life of Christ' series. For description and discussion, see Soukup, P. A. (2004) 'Transforming the Sacred: The American Bible Society New Media Translation Project', *The Journal of Media and Religion*, 3 (2), 101–18. Another creative video that does not depict a scene from Jesus' life but portrays the salvific role of faith, is *5 Minuti* (*5 minutes*), an 11-minute Italian film that won the 2006 Best Film Award at 168 Hour Film Project. The film can be viewed at http://www.archive.org/details/5_Minuti.

4 According to Baugh, the term 'peplum' refers to the loose-fitting clothing worn by the women in these films. Cf. Baugh (1997), *Imaging the Divine*, p. 241. For detailed study of this genre, see Forshey, G. E. (1992), *American Religious and Biblical Spectaculars*. Westport, CT: Praeger; Solomon, J. (2001), *The Ancient World in Cinema: Revised and Expanded Edition*. New Haven, CT: Yale University Press; and Wyke, M. (1997), *Projecting the Past: Ancient Rome, Cinema, and History, The New Ancient World*. New York: Routledge.

5 For an excellent discussion of the Passion Play at Oberammergau, see Shapiro, J. S. (2000), *Oberammergau: The Troubling Story of the World's Most Famous Passion Play* (1st edn). New York: Pantheon Books.

6 Kinnard, R. and Davis, T. (1992), *Divine Images: A History of Jesus on the Screen*. New York, NY: Carol Publishing Group, p. 20.

7 The earliest available Jesus movie on DVD is *The Life and Passion of Jesus Christ* (1905).

8 Kinnard and Davis, *Divine Images*, p. 32.

9 For example, Carter, E. (1983), 'Cultural History Written with Lightning: The Significance of *The Birth of a Nation*', in Rollins, P. C. (ed.), *Hollywood as Historian: American Film in a Cultural Context*. Lexington: University Press of Kentucky, pp. 9–19; Litwack, L. F. (1996) 'The Birth of a Nation', in M. C. Carnes (ed.), *Past Imperfect: History According to the Movies*. New York: H. Holt, pp. 136–41.

10 Originally, this story was to occupy a considerable portion of the film as a whole. Following upon strong protests by the Anti-Defamation League of the B'nai Brith, however, Griffith removed a number of segments that clearly depicted the Jewish leaders as crucifying Jesus. These changes reduced the Judean story to seven brief segments occupying a total of twelve minutes of this three and half hour opus. Tatum, W. B. (2004), *Jesus at the Movies: A Guide to the First Hundred Years*, pp. 58–9; DeMille, C. B. and Hayne, D. (1985), *The Autobiography of Cecil B. DeMille*. New York: Garland Publisher, p. 282.

11 Custen (*Bio/pics*) examines all biographical movies made in the studio era of Hollywood. Yet one searches in vain for a single reference to a Jesus movie. In fact, the only 'Bible' movie in Custen's index is Cecil B. DeMille's *The Ten Commandments* (1956).

12 Solomon, *The Ancient World in the Cinema*, p. 3; Stern, R. C., Jefford, C. N. and Guerric DeBona (1999), *Savior on the Silver Screen*. New York: Paulist Press, p. 62.

13 In addition to the popularity of DeMille's film and the exigencies of the Production Code, Tatum suggests that the development of the peplum film, in which Jesus' story is a subplot of a fictional story, may have been a factor. See Tatum, *Jesus at the Movies*, pp. 61–2.

14 This period in American cinematic history is alluded to in Martin Scorsese's 2004 film *The Aviator*, in which director Howard Hughes must defend the size of Jane Russell's 'mammaries' (only her cleavage, in fact) in his film *The Outlaw*.

15 The full text of the Code is available in the Appendix to Leff, L. J., and Simmons, J. L. (1990), *The Dame in the Kimono: Hollywood, Censorship, and the Production Code from the 1920s to the 1960s*. New York: Doubleday, pp. 283–92.

16 Telford, 'Jesus Christ Movie Star: The Depiction of Jesus in the Cinema', 130.

17 Ray's film borrows its title from DeMille's opus, and in some scenes 'quotes' or pays tribute to the earlier film, but in fact it is a completely different film. Originally Ray had planned to call his film *The King of Kings*, as DeMille had done, but revised it slightly in the aftermath of legal problems with the corporation that controlled DeMille's movie. See Tatum, *Jesus at the Movies: A Guide to the First Hundred Years*, p. 77.

18 Tatum, *Jesus at the Movies*, p. 86, citing the unattributed film review in *Time*, October 1961, 27.

19 Cf. Babington, B. and Evans, P. W. (1993), *Biblical Epics: Sacred Narrative in the Hollywood Cinema*, New York, NY, USA: Manchester University Press, pp. 5, 9–10.

20 In 2000 another filmed version, made for television, appeared, directed by Gale Edwards and Nick Morris. Discussion of *Jesus Christ Superstar* in the present study is based on the 1973 Norman Jewison version.

21 Full-stage performances of *Jesus Christ Superstar* took place in Los Angeles, Houston and Toronto, among other North American and European venues in 2004.

22 Gallagher, T. (1998), *The Adventures of Roberto Rossellini: His Life and Films*. New York: Da Capo Press, p. 669.

23 Claymation, short for 'clay animation', is a technique involving the creation of clay or plasticine figures, which are then animated through the use of digital photography. A well-known example is the Wallace and Gromit series.

24 See Tatum's acknowledgements in the second edition of his book, in which he explains how he changed his mind and therefore included a chapter on this film in the second edition of his book. Tatum, *Jesus at the Movies*, p. x.

25 The term 'Palestine' is currently associated with the anticipated homeland of the Palestinians. For scholars of first-century Judaism and Christianity, however, the term denotes the Roman province including Judea. From the conquest of Pompeii until Herod the Great, Palestine was a client kingdom under a local monarch; after Herod's death, it became a Roman province under the authority of a governor.

26 Cf., Medved, M. (1992), *Hollywood Vs. America: Popular Culture and the War on Traditional Values* (1st edn). New York, NY and Grand Rapids, Mich.: HarperCollins; Zondervan, pp. 37–49; Tatum, W. B. (1997), *Jesus at the Movies: A Guide to the First Hundred Years*. Santa Rosa, Calif.: Polebridge Press, pp. 188–92; Babington and Evans, *Biblical Epics: Sacred Narrative in the Hollywood Cinema*, p. 106.

27 This blurring is typical of the Passion Play experience, indicated by the experience of the villagers in Oberammergau, the site of the most well-known Passion Play. James S. Shapiro, *Oberammergau*, passim.

28 *The Passion of the Christ* (2004) was released in a slightly altered form in 2005.

29 Stern et al., *Savior on the Silver Screen*, p. 332.

30 Richard Wightman Fox, R. W. (2004) *Jesus in America: Personal Savior, Cultural Hero, National Obsession* (1st edn). San Francisco: Harper San Francisco, p. 11.

Chapter 20

1 Lists of biblical films are readily available on the internet. The Bible Films Blog webpage run by Matt Page is a very helpful source of information for biblical films, http://biblefilms.blogspot.com/.

2 See Cosandy, R., Gaudreault, A. and Gunning, T. (eds) (1992), *Un Invention Du Diable?*, Sainte-Foy: Les Presses De L'Université Laval. For more discussion of the

early days of biblical films, see Shepherd, D. (2008), 'Prolonging *The Life of Moses*: From spectacle to story in the early cinema', in Shepherd, D. (ed.), *Images of the Word: Hollywood's Bible and Beyond*. Atlanta: Society of Biblical Literature, pp. 11–37.

3 In fact, film was a significant vehicle for mainstreaming Jews. See Gabler, N. (1988), *An Empire of Their Own: How the Jews Invented Hollywood*. New York: Doubleday. On the chauvinistic treatment of women, see Bach, A. (ed.) (1996), 'Biblical glamour and Hollywood glitz', *Semeia* 74, Atlanta: Scholars; and Exum, J. C. (1996), *Plotted, Shot, and Painted: Cultural Representations of Biblical Women*. Sheffield: Sheffield Academic Press.

4 For critique of this passive 'dream cult', see Holloway, R. (1977), *Beyond the Image: Approaches to the Religious Dimension in Cinema*. Geneva: World Council of Churches.

5 See Babbington, B. and Evans, P. W. (1993), *Biblical Epics: Sacred Narrative in the Hollywood Cinema*. Manchester and NY: Manchester University Press.

6 Wood, M. (1989), *America in the Movies* (2nd edn). New York: Columbia University Press, pp. 1–23, 189–96. Wood's work is a major precursor of Bernard Brandon Scott's 1994 *Hollywood Dreams and Biblical Stories*. Minneapolis: Fortress.

7 *Pleasantville* (1998) lampoons such desires.

8 A number of mainstream films at the end of the century also bespoke an increasing sense of metaphysical anxiety. See, for example, *The Matrix* (1999), *The Thirteenth Floor* (1999), *The Truman Show* (1998), and eXistenZ (1999).

9 See Miles, M. (1996), *Seeing and Believing: Religion and Values in the Movies*. Boston: Beacon; and O'Brien, T. (1990), *The Screening of America: Movies and Values from Rocky to Rain Man*. New York: Continuum. In contrast to the mainstreaming of Jews in the spectacle, these films often feature distinctive, Jewish ethnic identity.

10 The oil embargo of the 1970s, the importance of Israel to US foreign policy, the rise of Islamic fundamentalism and terrorism, and recent conflicts with Muslim countries contribute to this negative portrayal, but the fundamental cause may be the cultural identification of the Muslim (or middle-Easterner) as Other to the West. See, for example, the complaints about negative portrayals of the 'Middle Easterners' in *Aladdin* (1992) and in *300* (2006). See also Rubina Ramji's Chapter 16 on 'Muslim Movies' in this volume.

11 For discussion of the tension between science and traditional religion in the spectacles, see Babbington and Evans, *Biblical Epics*; and Forshey, G. E. (1992), *American Religious and Biblical Spectacular*. Westport, CT: Praeger.

12 Reportedly, the film's anti-Semitic elements have made it quite popular in the Muslim world.

13 For current information, see the *Bible Films Blog* webpage.

14 One might extend the comparative context to include most films as films replay video games, prequels or typical cinematic patterns and as thought seems inherently comparative.

15 Babbington and Evans, *Biblical Epics*, is particularly insightful here.

16 Dino De Laurentiis, the producer, intended to film the entire Bible, but the project ended after only one film.

17 The gospel story was shot in fuller form but cut after complaints about its anti-Semitism.

18 Each of these references comes from Reinhartz, A. (2003), *Scripture on the Silver Screen*. Louisville: Westminster John Knox.

19 See Kreitzer, L. J. (1993), *The New Testament in Fiction and Film: On Reversing the Hermeneutical Flow*. Sheffield: Sheffield Academic Press; idem. (1994); *The Old Testament in Fiction and Film: On Reversing the Hermeneutical Flow*. Sheffield: Sheffield Academic Press; idem. (1999); *Pauline Images in Fiction and Film: On Reversing the Hermeneutical Flow*. Sheffield: Sheffield Academic Press); Jewett, R. (1993), *Saint Paul at the Movies:*

The Apostle's Dialogue with American Culture. Louisville: Westminster; idem. (1999); *Saint Paul Returns to the Movies: Triumph over Shame.* Grand Rapids: William B. Eerdmans; and Walsh, R. (2005), *Finding St. Paul in Film.* New York: T & T Clark.

20 For theoretical justification of this approach to film, see Aichele, G. and Walsh, R. (eds), *Screening Scripture: Intertextual Connections Between Scripture and Film.* Harrisburg: Trinity Press International. One might refer to styles one to three as the Bible in film and four to five as the Bible and film. See the organization of Exum, J. C. (ed.) (2006), *The Bible in Film – The Bible and Film.* Leiden: Brill and the selection of essays of both types in Christianson, E. S.; Francis, P., and Telford, W.R. (eds) (2005), *Cinéma Divinité: Religion, Theology and the Bible in Film.* London: SCM; and in Shepherd, *Images of the Word.*

21 See the critique of the biblical spectacle on this point by Schrader, P. (1972), *Transcendental Style in Film: Ozu, Bresson, Dryer.* Berekeley: University of California Press. Babbington and Evans, *Biblical Epics;* and Forshey, *Biblical Spectaculars,* are both helpful analyses of biblical spectacles' connections with culture.

22 See Aichele and Walsh, *Screening Scripture;* and Runions, E. (2003), *How Hysterical: Identification and Resistance in the Bible and Film.* New York: Palgrave Macmillan.

23 Reinhartz, A., *Scripture on the Silver Screen,* is a fine example of the former. Tatum, W. B. (2004), *Jesus at the Movies: A Guide to the First Hundred Years* (rev. edn). Santa Rosa: Polebridge; and Aichele and Walsh, *Screening Scripture,* are examples of the latter.

Chapter 21

1 Doneson, J. E. (2002), *The Holocaust in American Film* (2nd edn). New York: Syracuse University Press, p. 6. There are some films that deal with the aftermath of the Holocaust that might be considered Holocaust films as well, including *Exodus* and *Judgment at Nuremberg* or films that deal with survivorship such as Francine Zuckerman's *Punch Me in the Stomach* or Abraham Ravett's *Half Sister.*

2 Short, K. R. M. and Dolezel, S. (1988), *Hitler's Fall: The Newsreel Witness.* London: Croon Helm.

3 Hirsch, J. (2004), *Afterimage: Film, Trauma, and the Holocaust.* Philadelphia: Temple University Press, pp. 1–3. Since 1974, the film has been housed at Yad Vashem Holocaust Memorial in Israel.

4 Finkelstein, N. G. (2005), *Beyond Chutzpah: On the Misuse of Anti-Semitism and the Abuse of History.* Berkeley and Los Angeles: University of California Press, p. 83.

5 Insdorf, A. (1983), pp. 5–6.

6 Shandler, D. (1999), *While America Watches: Televising the Holocaust.* New York: Oxford University Press.

7 Reimer, R. C. and Reimer, C. J. (1992), *Nazi-Retro Film: How German narrative Cinema Remembers the Past.* New York: Twayne.

8 See the discussion of the story of Job in Chapter 6 by William L. Blizek and Julien Fielding, 'Retelling Religious Stories' in this volume.

9 Hansen, M. B. (2001), *'Schindler's List* is not Shoah', in Zelizer, B. (ed.), *Visual Culture and the Holocaust.* New Brunswick: Rudgers University Press, p. 130.

10 Ibid.

11 Hoberman, J. (1993), 'Spielberg's Oskar', *Village Voice* (21 December), 65.

12 Hansen, M. B. (2001), p. 131.

13 Ginsburg, T. (2007), *Holocaust Film: The Political Aesthetics of Ideology.* Newcastle, U.K.: Cambridge Scholars Publishing, p. 2.

14 Ginsburg, T. (2007), p. 3.

15 Insdorf, A. (1983), p. xi.
16 Avisar, I. (1997), 'Holocaust movies and the politics of collective memory', in Rosenfeld, A. H. (ed.), *Thinking About the Holocaust After Half a Century*. Bloomington: Indiana University Press, p. 53.
17 Baron, L. (2005), *Projecting the Holocaust into the Present: The Changing Focus of Contemporary Holocaust Cinema*. New York: Rowman & Littlefield, p. 4.
18 Toplin, R. B. (2002), *Reel History: In Defense of Hollywood*. Lawrence: University of Kansas Press, p. 58.
19 Landy, M. (2000), 'Cinematic history, melodrama, and the Holocaust', in Signer, M. A. (ed.), *Humanity at the Limit: The Impact of the Holocaust Experience on Jewish and Christians*. Bloomington: Indiana University Press, p. 387.
20 Flanzbaum, H. (2001), 'But Wasn't It Terrific: A Defense of Liking Life Is Beautiful'. *Yale Journal of Criticism*, 14 (1: Spring), 276.
21 Hirsch, J. (2004), *Afterimage: Film, Trauma, and the Holocaust*. Philadelphia: Temple University Press.
22 Rothberg, M. (2000), *Traumatic Realism: The Demands of Holocaust Representation*. Minneapolis: University of Minnesota Press, p. 15.
23 Rothberg, M. (2000), *Traumatic Realism: The Demands of Holocaust Representation*. Minneapolis: University of Minnesota Press, p. 5.
24 Friedlander, S. (1997), *Probing the Limits of Representation: Nazism and the 'Final Solution'*. Cambridge: Harvard University Press, p. 8.
25 Arendt, H. (1994), 'The Image of Hell', in Kohne, J. (ed.), *Essays in Understanding, 1930–1954*. New York: Harcourt, Brace & Co., pp. 197–205, 198.
26 Bathrick, D., Prager, B. and Richardson, M. D. (2008), *Visualizing the Holocaust: Documents, Aesthetics, Memory*. Rochester N.Y.: Camden House, p. 9.
27 Ezrahi, S. D. (2004), 'Questions of Authority', in Hirsch, M. and Kacandes, I. (eds), *Teaching the Representation of the Holocaust*. New York: Modern Language Association, p. 54.
28 For an extensive list of Holocaust films with a brief description of each, see the Holocaust resources at Brandeis University's The National Center for Jewish Film, http://www.brandeis.edu/jewishfilm/Catalogue/filmsaz.htm.

Chapter 22
1 Yao, X. (2000), *An Introduction to Confucianism*. Cambridge: Cambridge University Press, p. 182.
2 Willis, T. M. (1993), 'Redeem', in Metzger, B. M. and Coogan, M. D. (eds), *The Oxford Companion to the Bible*. New York: Oxford University Press, pp. 643–4.
3 See Adele Reinhartz's Chapter 19 on 'Jesus Movies' in this volume.
4 Willis, T. M. (1993), 'Redeem', in Metzger, B. M. and Coogan, M. D. (eds), *The Oxford Companion to the Bible*. New York: Oxford University Press, pp. 643–4.
5 One sometimes hears that characters can 'redeem themselves', which does not really conform to known theological models. Someone should redeem someone else and if no one else is present, then the redeemer would have to be God or another religious figure. Redeeming oneself seems to be a product of modern, Western self-sufficiency. See *Never Die Alone* (2004).
6 In the film's production notes, director David Ayer says of the character: 'Ludlow started out with righteous intentions wanting to save the world but somehow finds himself going very wrong. He's a man with a moral compass, which is why he's so troubled, and senses somehow that his life isn't going the right way'. He continues, explaining that the film deals with the darker aspects of who we are as people, illustrating that there is always an opportunity for redemption. 'The film is

structured like a tragedy and feels like a train wreck, but there is incredible redemption there. There is a message that no matter how far gone you are, there is always a way back'. See http://www.madeinatlantis.com/movies_central/2008/street_kings_production_details.htm.

7 After Dan has taken his wife's brooch, Will asks if he's going to 'hock' it. 'Someday, William . . . you walk in my shoes, you might understand'. Will replies: 'I ain't ever walking in your shoes'.

8 In the DVD audio commentary, James Mangold states that he was hoping for a kind of 'Biblical quality' in the end; a 'kind of washing clean of the earth, both of the tragedy that had been Dan Evans' life and finding something redemptive in it and the misguided venture that had been Ben Wade's and trying to find a new chapter in that as well'.

9 *Angel and the Badman* (1947) centres on Quirt Evans, the film's 'bad man', who after he is wounded is nursed back to health and ultimately redeemed by a Quaker girl and her family. Another film about a 'bad man' redeemed by a woman's love is *Knights of the Range* (1940). *Unforgiven* (1992) turns the tables on the redemption theme. Long before he met his wife, William Munny was a train robber and a cold-hearted killer. But her love and kindness redeemed him; transformed him. Sadly, his wife died, leaving him alone to raise their two children. Times are not good, and he needs money, which is why he accepts a bounty offered by 'wronged' prostitutes. Can he stay a 'redeemed' man or will Munny revert to his old ways?

10 In his book *Cowboy Metaphysics: Ethics and Death in Westerns*, Peter French agrees that the Western positions itself as antithetical to Christianity, at least as it was defined by women. He then demonstrates this by exploring how the men in these films, those who live by Christian values, are shown to be emasculated and left defenceless because of those values. In his afterward, he states that 'the ethics of the Western place very high value on independence, pride, loyalty, friendship or camaraderie, honour, self-reliance, valour and most important, vengeance and moral (righteous) hatred'.

11 Although not a horror film per se, *Chinjeolhan geumjassi* (2005), known in the West as *Sympathy for Lady Vengeance*, is about redemption. The lead character Lee Geum-Ja is blackmailed into serving prison time for a kidnapping that she committed but a murder she did not with the Svengali-like Mr. Baek. When she is released, she vows revenge. In the end, after all of her elaborate planning, she shares her vengeance with the parents of Mr. Baek's other young victims. A 'sinner' seeking absolution, Lee Geum-Ja is redeemed through this selfless act and through the hope offered by her long-lost daughter.

12 As said by Steve Niles, according to the Production Notes for *30 Days of Night*.

13 See other accounts of *The Matrix*.

14 In his essay, 'The Messianic figure in film: Christology beyond the biblical epic', Matthew McEver discusses *One Flew Over the Cuckoo's Nest* in conjunction with *Cool Hand Luke*, *Dead Poet's Society* and *Sling Blade*. In his summary, he states that the first three films indicate that 'humanity is indebted to those who dare to confront, challenge our thinking patterns and willingly suffer for it. *Sling Blade* enlarges our understanding of suffering on behalf of another. Jesus still remains on the silver screen; not as a prophet and teacher from Nazareth, but rather as an unlikely redeemer in a prison, a mental hospital, a class room, or inside the home of an abused child', http://www.unomaha.edu/jrf/McEverMessiah.htm.

15 Emphasis added. From Chen, L. F. (1972), *The Confucian Way: A New and Systematic Study of the Four Books*, translated by Shih Shun Liu, Republic of China: The Commercial Press, p. 303.

16 Harvey, P. (2002), *An Introduction to Buddhism: Teachings, History and Practices*. New York: Cambridge University Press, p. 94.
17 See Matthew McEver's Chapter 25 on 'The Saviour Figure' in this volume.

Chapter 23
1 Schwartz, S. L. (2000), 'I Dream, Therefore I Am: *What Dreams May Come*', *Journal of Religion & Film*, 4 (1). Omaha, NE: University of Nebraska, http://www.unomaha.edu/jrf/IDream.htm.
2 Blizek, W. L. (1999), 'Report from Sundance 1999: Religion in Independent Film', *Journal of Religion & Film*, 3 (1). Omaha, NE: University of Nebraska, http://www.unomaha.edu/jrf/sundance.htm.

Chapter 24
1 Cawkwell, T. (2004), *The Filmgoer's Guide to God*. London: Darton, Longman and Todd Ltd, p. 9.
2 Directed by Gabriel Axel – 1987.
3 Marsh, C. (2001), 'Eating in Community in *Babette's Feast*', in Marsh, C. and Ortiz, G. (eds), *Explorations in Theology and Film*. Chippenham: Blackwell Publishers, p. 214.
4 Also worth considering are the overt Eucharistic parallels.
5 Directed by Martin Brest, this film is itself a pseudo-remake of the 1934 film *Death Takes a Holiday*, directed by Mitchell Leisen.
6 Directed by Bob Fosse – 1979.
7 This character is named only in the credits of the film.
8 This is another film that carries an additional layer of meaning when viewed in light of specifically Christian notions of divinity.
9 . . . probably because these genres are the most likely to deal in archetypal characters.
10 One cannot ignore the parallel to the all-seeing spectacles of Dr. T. J. Eckleburg, from Fitzgerald's *Great Gatsby*.
11 Bergesen & Greeley (2005), pp. 100–101.
12 Directed by Tom Shadyac – 2003.
13 Ibid. – 2007.
14 Directed by John August.
15 This is the only film discussed here where the character of God may be said to be the main character of the plot.
16 Significantly, this is the same character from *The Nines* who says that Gary/Gavin/Gabriel is not technically God. A line of dialog in *The Nines*, as well as explanations given on the commentary track, makes it clear that the God in *God* is Gary/Gavin/Gabriel from *The Nines*.

Chapter 25
1 Taylor, B. (2008), *Entertainment Theology: New Edge Spirituality in a Digital Democracy*. Grand Rapids, MI: Baker Academic, p. 19.
2 Humphries-Brooks, S. (2006), *Cinematic Savior: Hollywood's Making of the American Christ*. Westport, CT: Praeger, p. 4.
3 Ibid.
4 Deacy, C. and Ortiz, G. W. (2008), *Theology and Film: Challenging the Sacred/Secular Divide*. Malden, MA: Blackwell Publishing, p. 28.
5 Baugh, L. (1997), *Imaging the Divine: Jesus and Christ Figures in Film*. Kansas City, MO: Sheed & Ward, p. 157.

6 Deacy and Ortiz, p. 187.
7 Malone, P. (1990), *Movie Christs and Antichrists*. New York, NY: Crossroad Publishing, p. 39. Other westerns you might consider would be *High Plains Drifter* (1971) or *3:10 to Yuma* (2007). For a discussion of *3:10 to Yuma* and redemption, see Julien Fielding's Chapter 22 on 'Redemption and Film' in this volume.
8 Myers, C. (1988), *Binding the Strong Man: A Political Reading of Mark's Story of Jesus*. Maryknoll, NY: Orbis Books, p. 14.
9 Bruce, D. 'The *Matrix*: A Hollywood Jesus review'. *Hollywood Jesus*, http://www.hollywoodjesus.com/matrix.htm. Other science fiction/fantasy movies you might consider include *Planet of the Apes* (2001); *Lord of the Rings* trilogy (2001, 2002, 2003); *I am Legend* (2007) and any of the *Harry Potter* movies.
10 Berrigan, D. (2008), *The Kings and Their Gods: The Pathology of Power*. Grand Rapids, MI: Wm. B. Eerdmans, p. 201.
11 Other movies based on comic book characters you might consider include *Spider-Man* (2002) and *The Incredible Hulk* (2008).
12 Dark, D. (2002), *Everyday Apocalypse*. Grand Rapids, MI: Brazos Press, p. 19.
13 Berrigan, D. (2008), *Exodus: Let My People Go*. Eugene, OR: Cascade Books, p. 39.
14 Deacy and Ortiz, p. 141.
15 Stucky, M. (2005), 'He is the One: *The Matrix Trilogy's* Postmodern Movie Messiah', *Journal of Religion and Film*, 9 (2, October). Omaha, NE: University of Nebraska at Omaha, http://www.unomaha.edu/jrf/Vol9No2/StuckyMatrixMessiah.htm.
16 Ibid.
17 Remark, S., '*Fight Club*: A Hollywood Jesus Movie review', *Hollywood Jesus*, http://www.hollywoodjesus.com/fight_club.html.
18 Taylor, p. 142.
19 Other dramas you might consider include *Sling Blade* (1996), *The Green Mile* (1999) and *Dancer in the Dark* (2001).
20 Pope, R. (2007), *Salvation in Celluloid: Theology, Imagination, and Film*. London: T & T Clark, p. 106.
21 Gleiberman, O. (2008), 'The Dark Knight Movie Review', *Entertainment Weekly*, 1003 (25 July), p. 47.
22 Broadus, M., 'To Job or not to Job: A review of *The Dark Knight*', *Hollywood Jesus*, www.hollywoodjesus.com.
23 Ibid.
24 Pope, p. 92.
25 Taylor, p. 205.
26 Humphries-Brooks, p. 4.

Chapter 26

1 Monier-Williams, M. (1899/1995), *A Sanskrit English Dictionary* (New edn). Delhi: Motilal Banarsidass.
2 The term 'karma' also means the result or product of action. Colloquial use of the word tends to be restricted only to this meaning.
3 BU 4.4.5.
4 Ibid.
5 BU 4.4.3–4.
6 YS 2.13
7 YBh 2.13.
8 Ibid.
9 BU 4.4.6.
10 Ibid.

11 See, for example: 2.47–48; 3.8–9; 9.26–27.

12 A person learns about his or her *dharma* from the scriptures, a teacher, the family and/or the observation of cultured persons.

13 Book 3, Vana Parva, Tīrtha-yatra Parva and CXXXVI.

14 *Devdas* is based on the 1917 novel of the same name by Bengali writer Chattopadhyay, S., as found in Rajadhyaksha, A. and Willemen, P. (1999), *Encyclopaedia of Indian Cinema* (rev. edn). Oxford: Oxford University Press, p. 261.

15 Yet another version of *Devdas* directed by Sudhir Mishra is slated for release in 2009.

16 See, for example, Dwyer, R. and Patel, D. (2002), *Cinema India: The Visual Culture of Hindi Film*. New Jersey: Rutgers University Press, p. 63.

17 This is also a common theme in Indian movies.

18 Miller, B. S. (trans.) (1986), *The Bhagavad-Gita: Krishna's Counsel in Time of War*. New York: Bantam Books, verses 2.62–63.

19 The word '*amma*' means 'mother' in Hindi, but in *Swadeś* Kaveri's role in the family is that of a close, long-term nanny and hence, second mother.

20 This is not to deny that such values did not occur in times before the incursions of Muslims or colonialism.

21 For more on super-hero movies and karma, see below.

22 Monier-Williams.

23 See also Chapter 14 by Desmarais, M. M. and Sindhav, B., 'Hinduism and Film' in this volume.

24 In the *Gītā*, this is devotion and surrender to Kṛṣṇa, who reveals himself to be, and simultaneously transcend, all things.

25 *The Towering Inferno* involves an engineering disaster, *Outbreak* is about the consequences of biological engineering and warfare, and *The Day After Tomorrow* examines global warming.

26 The most popular superhero figures tend to be male.

27 The 2002 movie, directed by Sam Raimi, is, of course, based on the famous *Spider-Man* comic book series written by Stan Lee. The success of the 2002 film has led to two sequels.

28 3.8–9.

29 The 2008 hit movie, directed by Jon Favreau, is based on the comic book series of the same name.

30 Although it is possible that Stark's father did not know about the worst excesses of the company, both his partnership with the antagonist Obadiah Stane (Jeff Bridges) and his choice to profit from the manufacture of ever more destructive weapons could, within the context of karma, be viewed as negative acts leading to negative consequences.

Chapter 27

1 Ostwalt, C. (1998), 'Visions of the End: Secular Apocalypse in Recent Hollywood Film', *Journal of Religion and Film*, 2 (1). Omaha, NE: University of Nebraska, http://www.unomaha.edu/jrf/OstwaltC.htm.

2 Ostwalt, C. (2000) '*Armageddon* at the Millennial Dawn', *Journal of Religion and Film*, 4 (1). Omaha, NE: University of Nebraska, http://www.unomaha.edu/jrf/armagedd.htm.

3 Ostwalt, C. (1995) 'Hollywood and Armageddon: Apocalyptic Themes in Recent Cinematic Presentation', in Martin, J., and Ostwalt, C. (eds), *Screening the Sacred: Religion, Myth, and Ideology in Popular American Film*. Boulder: Westview.

4 Kermode, F. (1967), *The Sense of an Ending: Studies in the Theory of Fiction*. London: Oxford University Press, pp. 44–6; see also pp. 28, 3–5.

5 For example, see Jonas, E. and Fischer, P. (2006), 'Terror Management and Religion: Evidence that Intrinsic Religiousness Mitigates Worldview Defense Following Mortality Salience', *Journal of Personality and Social Psychology*, 91, 566.

6 For example, Berger, P. (1967), *The Sacred Canopy: Elements of a Sociological Theory of Religion*. Garden City, NY: Doubleday.

7 Ostwalt, C. (2003), *Secular Steeples: Popular Culture and the Religious Imagination*. Harrisburg: Trinity Press, pp. 166–7.

8 Ostwalt, C. (1995), 'Hollywood and Armageddon: Apocalyptic Themes in recent cinematic presentation', in Martin, J., and Ostwalt, C. (eds), *Screening the Sacred: Religion, Myth, and Ideology in Popular American Film*. Boulder: Westview, pp. 58–9.

9 Ostwalt, C. (1998), 'Visions of the End: Secular Apocalypse in Recent Hollywood film', *Journal of Religion and Film*, 2 (1). Omaha, NE: University of Nebraska at Omaha, http://www.unomaha.edu/jrf/OstwaltC.htm, and Ostwalt, C. (2000), '*Armageddon* at the Millennial Dawn', *Journal of Religion and Film*, 4 (1), http://www.unomaha.edu/jrf/armagedd.htm.

10 Ibid.

Chapter 28

1 Russell, J. B. (1984), *Lucifer: The Devil in the Middle Ages*. Ithaca, New York: Cornell University Press, p. 63.

2 Ibid., *Lucifer*, p. 225.

3 Link, L. (1995), *The Devil: The Archfiend in Art From the Sixth to the Sixteenth Century*. New York: Harry N. Abrams, p. 51.

4 Davidson, T. (1969), *The Philosophy of Goethe's Faust*. New York: Haskell House Publishers, p. 21.

5 Ibid., p. 38.

6 Ibid., pp. 38–9.

7 Ibid., p. 149.

8 Ibid., p. 143.

9 Russell, J. B. (1986), *Mephistopheles: The Devil in the Modern World*. Ithaca, NY: Cornell University Press, p. 166.

10 Michael W. Cueno, M. W. (2001), *American Exorcism: Expelling Demons in the Land of Plenty*. New York: Doubleday, p. 259.

11 Berger, P. L. (1990), *The Sacred Canopy: A Sociological Theory of Religion*. New York: Anchor Books, p. 29.

12 Cueno, p. 10.

13 Heb. 18–22.

14 This is the only movie in the *Hellraiser* series to present an obvious reference to Satan. In this film, the Devil is more of an abstract concept than a physical being.

15 Christ was a descendent of Rahab. In Matt. 1:5–6, although spelled 'Rachab', Rahab is listed as the great-grandmother of King David. One can infer from this reference that, like Christ, Jericho Cane could be a descendent of Rahab. Cane could also be seen as some incarnation of a Christ-like figure.

16 Marthaler, B. L. et al. (eds) (2003), 'Cenobites', *New Catholic Encyclopedia* (second edn). New York: Gale Group, Vol. 3, p. 334.

17 Russell, L., p. 67.

18 Ibid., p. 211.

19 Nikolas Schreck's book (2000), *The Satanic Screen: An Illustrated Guide to the Devil in Cinema*. London: Creation Books, contains the most up-to-date, comprehensive list of Devil movies.

Chapter 29

1 Portions of this chapter are revised and adapted with permission from Stone, B. (2001), 'The Sanctification of Fear: Images of the Religious in Horror Films', *Journal of Religion and Film*, 5 (2). Omaha, NE: University of Nebraksa, http://www.unomaha.edu/jrf/sanctifi.htm.

2 Cicero, M. T. (1913), *De Officiis*, translated by Miller, W. Cambridge, MA: Harvard University Press, p. 341.

3 Arendt, H. (1963), *Eichmann in Jerusalem: A Report on the Banality of Evil*. London: Penguin.

4 Baudrillard, Jean (2002), *The Transparency of Evil: Essays on Extreme Phenomena*. London: Verso, p. 6.

5 See Bather, N. (2006), *'There is evil there that does not sleep . . .' The Construction of Evil in American Popular Cinema from 1989 to 2002*, Doctoral dissertation, Hamilton and Tauranga, New Zealand: The University of Waikato. Bather argues that 'the spectacular nature of the presentation of evil has caused a loss of moral potency in cinematic narratives of evil. That is, the commodification of cinematic evil de-emphasizes (but does not entirely remove) its ability to engage with notions of social evil', p. 33.

6 Ibid., p. 5.

7 Unless, of course, one blames a divine creator who, if all-powerful, presumably could have created a world without such evil; thus, the so-called 'problem of evil'.

8 Interestingly, so-called 'primitive' religious traditions in Africa, the Caribbean, among Native Americans, or even the early Egyptians are commonly portrayed on film as having a keener respect for the forces of nature, as understanding its power and being careful to pay homage to its deities. The 'black magic' of these traditions is unstable and might be used either for good or for evil and for that reason they are feared but also envied by the 'White man'. See Perez, M. (1972), 'The Puritan Despair', *Focus on the Horror Film*. Englewood Cliffs, NJ: Prentice-Hall, p. 134.

9 Badley, L. (1995). *Film, Horror, and the Body Fantastic*. Westport: Greenwood Press, p. 21.

10 Bather, pp. 11, 37.

11 See Kelly Wyman's essay on 'Satan in the Movies' (Chapter 28) in this volume.

12 Crane, J. L. (1994), *Terror and Everyday Life: Singular Moments in the History of Horror Film*. Thousand Oaks, CA: Sage Publications, p. 21.

13 Badley, p. 9.

14 Alford, C. F. (1997), *What Evil Means to Us*. Ithaca, NY: Cornell University Press, p. 13.

15 Freeland, C. A. (2000), *The Naked and the Undead: Evil and the Appeal of Horror*. Boulder, CO: Westview Press, p. 143.

16 Tudor, A. (1989), *Monsters and Mad Scientists: A Cultural History of the Horror Movie*. Oxford: Blackwell, p. 185.

17 Crane, p. 11.

18 Ingebretsen, E. J. (1998), 'Staking the Monster: A Politics of Remonstrance', *Religion and American Culture*, 8 (1: Winter), 91–116.

19 Badley, *Film, Horror, and the Body Fantastic*, p. 22.

20 Crane, *Terror and Everyday Life*, p. 160.

21 Bather, p. 43.

22 Ibid., p. 100.

23 For a fuller treatment of *Pulp Fiction* in this regard, see Stone, B. P. (2000), 'Theology and Film in Postmodern Culture: A Dialogue with Forrest Gump and Pulp Fiction', *Wesleyan Theological Journal*, 35 (1), 149–64.

24 Leitch, T. M. (1997), 'Know-Nothing Entertainment: What to Say to Your Friends on the Right, and Why it Won't Do Any Good', in *Literature/Film Quarterly*, 25, 3.
25 Kerr, S. (1995), '*Rain Man*', in *The New York Review* (6 April), 42 (6), 23.
26 Travers, P. (1992), 'Tarantino's Twist', in *Rolling Stone*, 692 (4 October), 80.

Index

Names of films or publications starting with 'A' or 'The' will be filed under the first significant word

Made in the USA
Middletown, DE
10 January 2018